Mobile Computing:
Concepts, Methodologies, Tools, and Applications

David Taniar
Monash University, Australia

Volume VI

INFORMATION SCIENCE REFERENCE

Hershey · New York

Director of Editorial Content: Kristin Klinger
Director of Production: Jennifer Neidig
Managing Editor: Jamie Snavely
Assistant Managing Editor: Carole Coulson
Typesetter: Jeff Ash, Michael Brehm, Carole Coulson, Elizabeth Duke, Jennifer Henderson, Chris Hrobak,
                                  Jennifer Neidig, Jamie Snavely, Sean Woznicki
Cover Design: Lisa Tosheff
Printed at: Yurchak Printing Inc.

Published in the United States of America by
        Information Science Reference (an imprint of IGI Global)
        701 E. Chocolate Avenue, Suite 200
        Hershey PA 17033
        Tel: 717-533-8845
        Fax: 717-533-8661
        E-mail: cust@igi-global.com
        Web site: http://www.igi-global.com/reference

and in the United Kingdom by
        Information Science Reference (an imprint of IGI Global)
        3 Henrietta Street
        Covent Garden
        London WC2E 8LU
        Tel: 44 20 7240 0856
        Fax: 44 20 7379 0609
        Web site: http://www.eurospanbookstore.com

Library of Congress Cataloging-in-Publication Data

Mobile computing : concepts, methodologies, tools, and applications / David Taniar, editor.
       v. cm.
    Includes bibliographical references and index.
    Summary: "This multiple-volume publication advances the emergent field of mobile computing offering research on approaches, observa-
tions and models pertaining to mobile devices and wireless communications from over 400 leading researchers"--Provided by publisher.
    ISBN 978-1-60566-054-7 (hardcover) -- ISBN 978-1-60566-055-4 (ebook)
    1. Mobile computing. 2. Wireless communication systems. I. Taniar, David.
    QA76.59.M636 2009
    004.165--dc22
                              2008037391

British Cataloguing in Publication Data
A Cataloguing in Publication record for this book is available from the British Library.

All work contributed to this book set is original material. The views expressed in this book are those of the authors, but not necessarily of
the publisher.

Additional Research Collections found in the "Contemporary Research in Information Science and Technology" Book Series

Data Mining and Warehousing: Concepts, Methodologies, Tools, and Applications
John Wang, Montclair University, USA • 6-volume set • ISBN 978-1-60566-056-1

Electronic Business: Concepts, Methodologies, Tools, and Applications
In Lee, Western Illinois University • 4-volume set • ISBN 978-1-59904-943-4

Electronic Commerce: Concepts, Methodologies, Tools, and Applications
S. Ann Becker, Florida Institute of Technology, USA • 4-volume set • ISBN 978-1-59904-943-4

Electronic Government: Concepts, Methodologies, Tools, and Applications
Ari-Veikko Anttiroiko, University of Tampere, Finland • 6-volume set • ISBN 978-1-59904-947-2

Knowledge Management: Concepts, Methodologies, Tools, and Applications
Murray E. Jennex, San Diego State University, USA • 6-volume set • ISBN 978-1-59904-933-5

Information Communication Technologies: Concepts, Methodologies, Tools, and Applications
Craig Van Slyke, University of Central Florida, USA • 6-volume set • ISBN 978-1-59904-949-6

Intelligent Information Technologies: Concepts, Methodologies, Tools, and Applications
Vijayan Sugumaran, Oakland University, USA • 4-volume set • ISBN 978-1-59904-941-0

Information Security and Ethics: Concepts, Methodologies, Tools, and Applications
Hamid Nemati, The University of North Carolina at Greensboro, USA • 6-volume set • ISBN 978-1-59904-937-3

Medical Informatics: Concepts, Methodologies, Tools, and Applications
Joseph Tan, Wayne State University, USA • 4-volume set • ISBN 978-1-60566-050-9

Mobile Computing: Concepts, Methodologies, Tools, and Applications
David Taniar, Monash University, Australia • 6-volume set • ISBN 978-1-60566-054-7

Multimedia Technologies: Concepts, Methodologies, Tools, and Applications
Syed Mahbubur Rahman, Minnesota State University, Mankato, USA • 3-volume set • ISBN 978-1-60566-054-7

Virtual Technologies: Concepts, Methodologies, Tools, and Applications
Jerzy Kisielnicki, Warsaw University, Poland • 3-volume set • ISBN 978-1-59904-955-7

<u>Free institution-wide online access with the purchase of a print collection!</u>

INFORMATION SCIENCE REFERENCE
Hershey · New York
Order online at www.igi-global.com or call 717-533-8845 ext.100
Mon–Fri 8:30am–5:00 pm (est) or fax 24 hours a day 717-533-7115

List of Contributors

Contents

Volume I

Section I. Fundamental Concepts and Theories

This section serves as the foundation for this exhaustive reference tool by addressing crucial theories essential to the understanding of mobile computing. Chapters found within these pages provide an excellent framework in which to position mobile computing within the field of information science and technology. Individual contributions provide overviews of mobile learning, mobile portals, and mobile government, while also exploring critical stumbling blocks of this field. Within this introductory section, the reader can learn and choose from a compendium of expert research on the elemental theories underscoring the research and application of mobile computing.

Section II. Development and Design Methodologies

This section provides in-depth coverage of conceptual architectures, frameworks and methodologies related to the design and implementation of mobile systems and technologies. Throughout these contributions, research fundamentals in the discipline are presented and discussed. From broad examinations to specific discussions on particular frameworks and infrastructures, the research found within this section spans the discipline while also offering detailed, specific discussions. Basic designs, as well as abstract developments, are explained within these chapters, and frameworks for designing successful mobile applications, interfaces, and agents are discussed.

Volume II

Section III. Tools and Technologies

This section presents extensive coverage of the technology that both derives from and informs mobile computing. These chapters provide an in-depth analysis of the use and development of innumerable devices and tools, while also providing insight into new and upcoming technologies, theories, and instruments that will soon be commonplace. Within these rigorously researched chapters, readers are presented with examples of the tools that facilitate and support mobile computing. In addition, the successful implementation and resulting impact of these various tools and technologies are discussed within this collection of chapters.

Volume III

Section IV. Utilization and Application

This section introduces and discusses the ways in which information technology has been used to shape the realm of mobile computing and proposes new ways in which IT-related innovations can be implemented within organizations and in society as a whole. These particular selections highlight, among other topics, the implementation of mobile technology in healthcare settings, and the evolution of mobile commerce. Contributions included in this section provide excellent coverage of today's mobile environment and insight into how mobile computing impacts the fabric of our present-day global village.

Section V. Organizational and Social Implications

This section includes a wide range of research pertaining to the social and organizational impact of mobile computing around the world. Chapters introducing this section analyze mobile virtual communities and consumer attitudes toward mobile marketing, while later contributions offer an extensive analysis of the accessibility of mobile applications and technologies. The inquiries and methods presented in this section offer insight into the implications of mobile computing at both a personal and organizational level, while also emphasizing potential areas of study within the discipline.

Volume IV

Section VI. Managerial Impact

This section presents contemporary coverage of the managerial implications of mobile computing. Particular contributions address business strategies for mobile marketing, mobile customer services, and mobile service business opportunities. The managerial research provided in this section allows executives, practitioners, and researchers to gain a better sense of how mobile computing can inform their practices and behavior.

Volume V

Section VII. Critical Issues

This section addresses conceptual and theoretical issues related to the field of mobile computing, which include security issues in numerous facets of the discipline including mobile agents, mobile commerce, and mobile networks. Within these chapters, the reader is presented with analysis of the most current and relevant conceptual inquires within this growing field of study. Particular chapters also address quality of service issues in mobile networks, mobile ontologies and mobile web mining for marketing. Overall, contributions within this section ask unique, often theoretical questions related to the study of mobile computing and, more often than not, conclude that solutions are both numerous and contradictory.

Volume VI

Section VIII. Emerging Trends

This section highlights research potential within the field of mobile computing while exploring uncharted areas of study for the advancement of the discipline. Chapters within this section highlight evolutions in mobile services, frameworks, and interfaces. These contributions, which conclude this exhaustive, multi-volume set, provide emerging trends and suggestions for future research within this rapidly expanding discipline.

Preface

In many ways, motion and computing are the two advances that define our modern age. The ability to move previously unimaginable distances and electronically perform complex tasks, both in breathtakingly short amounts of time, has revolutionized and opened up the entire globe. Mobile computing sits in the vibrant junction of these two defining advances. As this modern world demands more mobility and a greater range of computing options, a keen understanding of the issues, theories, strategies and emerging trends associated with this rapidly developing field is becoming more and more important to researchers, professionals and all users alike.

In recent years, the applications and technologies generated through the study of mobile computing have grown in both number and popularity. As a result, researchers, practitioners, and educators have devised a variety of techniques and methodologies to develop, deliver, and, at the same time, evaluate the effectiveness of their use. The explosion of methodologies in the field has created an abundance of new, state-of-the-art literature related to all aspects of this expanding discipline. This body of work allows researchers to learn about the fundamental theories, latest discoveries, and forthcoming trends in the field of medical informatics.

Constant technological and theoretical innovation challenges researchers to remain informed of and continue to develop and deliver methodologies and techniques utilizing the discipline's latest advancements. In order to provide the most comprehensive, in-depth, and current coverage of all related topics and their applications, as well as to offer a single reference source on all conceptual, methodological, technical, and managerial issues in medical informatics, Information Science Reference is pleased to offer a six-volume reference collection on this rapidly growing discipline. This collection aims to empower researchers, practitioners, and students by facilitating their comprehensive understanding of the most critical areas within this field of study.

This collection, entitled **Mobile Computing: Concepts, Methodologies, Tools, and Applications**, is organized into eight distinct sections which are as follows: (1) Fundamental Concepts and Theories, (2) Development and Design Methodologies, (3) Tools and Technologies, (4) Utilization and Application, (5) Organizational and Social Implications, (6) Managerial Impact, (7) Critical Issues, and (8) Emerging Trends. The following paragraphs provide a summary of what is covered in each section of this multi-volume reference collection.

Section One, **Fundamental Concepts and Theories**, serves as a foundation for this exhaustive reference tool by addressing crucial theories essential to understanding mobile computing. Some basic topics impacted by this field are examined in this section through articles such as "A Mobile Computing and Commerce Framework" by Stephanie Teufel, Patrick S. Merten and Martin Steinert. This selection introduces a key topic further developed and discussed through later selections, the intersection of mobile computing and its commercial implications. The selection "Environments for Mobile Learning" by Han-Chieh Chao, Tin-Yu Wu, and Michelle T.C. Kao provides a sampling of how mobility impacts educational trendsetting. Another important basic topic in this section is ushered in by M. Halid Kuscu, Ibrahim Kushchu, and Betty Yu and their contribution entitled "Introducing Mobile Government," which introduces the concept of mobile government and creates a context for discussing various applications, services, and the relevant technologies. "A Taxonomy of Database Operations on Mobile Devices" by Say Ying Lim, David Taniar and Bala Srinivasan informs the vital area of databases while grounding the reader in its possible operations, and "Mobile Portals" by Ofir Turel and Alexander Serenko offers a explanation and exploration of the ability of mobile portals to diffuse and penetrate even remote populations. These are only some of the elemental topics provided by the selections within this comprehensive, foundational section that allow readers to learn from expert research on the elemental theories underscoring mobile computing.

Section Two, **Development and Design Methodologies,** contains in-depth coverage of conceptual architectures and frameworks, providing the reader with a comprehensive understanding of emerging theoretical and conceptual developments within the development and utilization of mobile computing. In opening this section, "Developing Smart Client Mobile Applications" by Jason Gan exemplifies the issues addressed in this section by examining the usability and accessibility of mobile applications and services and suggesting development. The development of mobile applications is also discussed in "Location Area Design Algorithms for Minimizing Signalling Costs in Mobile Networks" by J. Gutierrez, Vilmos Simon and Sándor Imre. Also included in this section is the selection "'It's the Mobility, Stupid': Designing Mobile Government" by Klas Roggenkamp, which lays out the challenges and possibilities of designing for mobile government. Overall, these selections outline design and development concerns and procedures, advancing research in this vital field.

Section Three, **Tools and Technologies**, presents extensive coverage of various tools and technologies and their use in creating and expanding the reaches of mobile computing. The multitude of mobile business applications, their uses and their individual efficiency is explored in such articles as "Evaluation of Mobile Technologies in the Context of Their Applications, Limitations, and Transformation" by Abbass Ghanbary, "Knowledge Representation in Semantic Mobile Applications" by Pankaj Kamthan, and "Mobile Portal Technologies and Business Models" by David Parsons. With a look toward the near future, the selection "A Virtual Community for Mobile Agents" by Sheng-Uei Guan and Fangming Zhu features in-depth discussions of the probable uses and benefits of mobile agents in a variety of fields. The ever-developing culture of mobile multimedia is represented in this section as well, with "Discovering Multimedia Services and Contents in Mobile Environments" by Zhou Wang and Hend Koubaa, "V-Card: Mobile Multimedia for Mobile Marketing" by Holger Nösekabel and Wolfgang Röckelein, and "The Design of Mobile Television in Europe" by Pieter Ballon and Olivier Braet. The rigorously researched chapters contained in this section offer readers countless examples of modern tools and technologies that emerge from or can be applied to mobile computing.

Section Four, **Utilization and Application**, investigates the use and implementation of mobile technologies and informatics in a variety of contexts. One prominent context is mobile phone use, thoroughly analyzed in throughout the world in the articles "Exploring the Use of Mobile Data Services in Europe: The Cases of Denmark and Greece" by Ioanna D. Constantiou and Maria Bina, "The Mobile Phone Telecommunications Service Sector in China" by Michelle W. L. Fong, "United States of America: Renewed Race for Mobile Services" by Mats Samuelsson, Nikhilesh Dholakia and Sanjeev Sardana, and "M-Learning with Mobile Phones" by Simon So. This latter topic, m-learning, is continued by Hans Lehmann, Stefan Berger and Ulrich Remus in "A Mobile Portal for Academe," while Anna Trifonova reaches the root of two vital issues in "Accessing Learning Content in a Mobile System: Does Mobile Mean Always Connected?" Questioning applications and technology is rarely more important than in the health sector, the focus of a number of articles beginning with "Perception of Mobile Technology Provision in Health Service" by Astrid M. Oddershede and Rolando A. Carrasco and ending with "Integrating Mobile-Based Systems with Healthcare Databases" by Yu Jiao, Ali R. Hurson, Thomas E. Potok and Barbara G. Beckerman. This section ends with articles pertaining to commerce, business and government, providing a complete understanding of the successes and limitations of mobile computing.

Section Five, **Organizational and Social Implications**, includes a wide range of research pertaining to the organizational and cultural implications of mobile computing. The section begins with "Mobile Virtual Communities" by Glauber Ferreira, Hyggo Almeida, Angelo Perkusich, and Evandro Costa, a selection explores virtual communities, describing the main issues that have culminated in the creation of this research area, also the topic of "Mobile Virtual Communities of Commuters" by Jalal Kawash, Christo El Morr, Hamza Taha, and Wissam Charaf, "Wireless Local Communities in Mobile Commerce" by Jun Sun, and "From Communities to Mobile Communities of Values" by Patricia McManus and Craig Standing. Akin the idea of community is the topic of trust, the subject of "Consumer Perceptions and Attitudes Towards Mobile Marketing" by Amy Carroll, Stuart J. Barnes and Eusebio Scornavacca. Lastly, "Mobile Networked Text Communication: The Case of SMS and Its Influence on Social Interaction" by Louise Barkhuus provides insight into how certain functions of mobile technology affect social interaction – an important consideration to end this section detailing how mobile computing shapes and is shaped by human culture and logic.

Section Six, **Managerial Impact**, presents contemporary coverage of the managerial applications and implications of mobile computing. Core concepts covered include the impact of mobile computing on business practices, customer and business interaction, and business communication, policies and strategies. "Comprehensive Impact of Mobile Technology on Business" by Khimji Vaghjiani and Jenny Teoh begins the section with an insightful introduction. Also included are the articles "Consumers' Preferences and Attitudes Toward Mobile Office Use: A Technology Trade-Off Research Agenda" by Xin Luo and Merrill Warkentin, "Customer Relationship Management on Internet and Mobile Channels: An Analytical Framework and Research Directions" by Susy S. Chan and Jean Lam, and "Exploring Mobile Service Business Opportunities from a Customer-Centric Perspective" by Minna Pura and Kristina Heinonen, which expound on the concerns surrounding customer relationships with mobile technologies. This section concludes with a insights on topics including telecommunications, the media and gaming industries, knowledge management and mobile enterprising—a few of the subjects necessary to understand managing and mobile computing.

Section Seven, **Critical Issues**, presents readers with an in-depth analysis of the more theoretical and conceptual issues within this growing field of study by addressing topics such as the quality and security of mobile computing. "Mobile Code and Security Issues" by E. S. Samundeeswari and F. Mary Magdalene Jane, "Security of Mobile Code" by Zbigniew Kotulski, and "Security in Mobile Agent Systems" by Chua Fang Fang and G. Radhamani, address necessary security considerations. The article "Privacy and Anonymity in Mobile Ad Hoc Networks" by Christer Andersson, Leonardo A. Martucci and Simone Fischer-Hübner raises similar concerns. The quality of mobile computing services is pondered in articles such as "Quality of Service in Mobile Ad Hoc Networks" by Winston K. G. Seah and Hwee-Xian Tan, "Quality of Service Issues in Mobile Multimedia Transmission" by Nalin Sharda, and "A Study on the Performance of IPv6-Based Mobility Protocols: Mobile IPv6 vs. Hierarchical Mobile IPv6" by Ki-Sik Kong, Sung-Ju Roh and Chong-Sun Hwang. Further discussion of critical issues includes obstacles surrounding ad hoc networking, database querying and management, data dissemination, broadcasting and processing. In all, the theoretical and abstract issues presented and analyzed within this collection form the backbone of revolutionary research in and evaluation of mobile computing.

The concluding section of this authoritative reference tool, **Emerging Trends**, highlights research potential within the field of mobile computing while exploring uncharted areas of study for the advancement of the discipline. The development and deployment of new forms of mobile computing is explored in selections entitled "Bridging Together Mobile and Service-Oriented Computing" by Loreno Oliveira, Emerson Loureiro, Hyggo Almeida and Angelo Perkusich, "Context-Awareness and Mobile Devices" by Anind K. Dey and Jonna Häkkilä, "Component Agent Systems: Building a Mobile Agent Architecture That You Can Reuse" by Paulo Marques and Luís Silva, and "Voice Driven Emotion Recognizer Mobile Phone: Proposal and Evaluations" by Aishah Abdul Razak, Mohamad Izani Zainal Abidin, and Ryoichi Komiya. Other new trends, such as developments concerning RFID, time-critical decisions, collaboration between mobile devices and new concepts supporting user collaboration are included in and stretch our concept of what mobile computing can be. This final section demonstrates that mobile computing, with its propensity for constant change and evolution, will continue to both shape and define the modern face of business, health, culture and human interaction.

Although the contents of this multi-volume book are organized within the preceding eight sections which offer a progression of coverage of important concepts, methodologies, technologies, applications, social issues, and emerging trends, the reader can also identify specific contents by utilizing the extensive indexing system listed at the end of each volume. Furthermore, to ensure that the scholar, researcher, and educator have access to the entire contents of this multi-volume set, as well as additional coverage that could not be included in the print version of this publication, the publisher will provide unlimited, multi-user electronic access to the online aggregated database of this collection for the life of the edition free of charge when a library purchases a print copy. In addition to providing content not included within the print version, this aggregated database is also continually updated to ensure that the most current research is available to those interested in mobile computing.

As mobile computing continues to expand, both in variety and usefulness, this exciting and revolutionary field will prove even more necessary to everyday life. Intrinsic to our ever-modernizing, ever-expanding, global economy is mobility and technology, the two aspects that define the contents of these articles. Continued progress and innovation, driven by a mobile, demanding consumer base, will only further establish how necessary and vital a sure understanding of mobile computing and the changes and challenges influencing today's modern, dynamic world.

The diverse and comprehensive coverage of mobile computing in this six-volume, authoritative publication will contribute to a better understanding of all topics, research, and discoveries in this developing, significant field of study. Furthermore, the contributions included in this multi-volume collection series will be instrumental in the expansion of the body of knowledge in this enormous field, resulting in a greater understanding of the fundamentals while also fueling the research initiatives in emerging fields. We at Information Science Reference, along with the editor of this collection, hope that this multi-volume collection will become instrumental in the expansion of the discipline and will promote the continued growth of mobile computing.

Chapter 7.33
Mobile Caching for Location-Based Services

Jianliang Xu
Hong Kong Baptist University, Hong Kong

INTRODUCTION

Location-based services (LBS) are services that answer queries based on the locations with which the queries are associate; normally the locations where the queries are issued. With a variety of promising applications, such as local information access (e.g., traffic reports, news, and navigation maps) and nearest neighbor queries (e.g., finding the nearest restaurants) (Barbara, 1999; Ren & Dunham, 2000; D. L. Lee, Lee, Xu, & Zheng, 2002; W. C. Lee, Xu, & Zheng, 2004), LBS is emerging as an integral part of daily life.

The greatest potential of LBS is met in a mobile computing environment, where users enjoy unrestricted mobility and ubiquitous information access. For example, a traveler could issue a query like "Find the nearest hotel with a room rate below $100" from a wireless portable device in the middle of a journey. To answer such a query, however, three major challenges have to be overcome:

- **Constrained Mobile Environments:** Users in a mobile environment suffer from various constraints, such as scarce bandwidth, low-quality communication, frequent network disconnections, and limited local resources. These constraints pose a great challenge for the provision of LBS to mobile users.
- **Spatial Data:** In LBS, the answers to a query associated with different locations may be different. That is, query results are dependent on spatial properties of queries. For a query bound with a certain query location, the query result should be relevant to the query as well as valid for the bound location. This requirement adds additional complexity to traditional data management techniques such as data placement, indexing, and query processing (D. L. Lee, 2002).
- **User Movement:** The fact that a mobile user may change its location makes some tasks in LBS, such as query scheduling and cache management, particularly tough. For example, suppose that a mobile user issues a query "Find the nearest restaurant" at loca-

tion *A*. If the query is not scheduled timely enough on the server, the user has moved to location *B* when he or she gets the answer *R*. However, *R* is no longer the nearest restaurant at location *B*.

Caching has been a commonly used technique for improving data access performance in a mobile computing environment (Acharya, Alonso, Franklin, & Zdonik, 1995). There are several advantages for caching data on mobile clients:

- It improves data access latency since a portion of queries, if not all, can be satisfied locally.
- It helps save energy since wireless communication is required only for cache-miss queries.
- It reduces contention on the narrow-bandwidth wireless channel and off-loads workload from the server; as such, the system throughput is improved.
- It improves data availability in circumstances where clients are disconnected or weakly connected because cached data can be used to answer queries.

However, as discussed above, the *constrains* of mobile computing environments, the *spatial* property of location-dependent data, and the *mobility* of mobile users have opened up many new research problems in client caching for LBS. This chapter discusses the research issues arising from caching of location-dependent data in a mobile environment and briefly describes several state-of-the-art solutions.

BACKGROUND

Location Model

Location plays a central role in LBS. A location needs to be specified explicitly or implicitly for any information access. The available mechanisms for identifying locations of mobile users are based on two models:

- **Geometric Model:** A location is specified as an *n*-dimensional coordinate (typically, $n = 2$ or 3); for example , the latitude/longitude pair returned by the global positioning system (GPS). The main advantage of the geometric model is its compatibility across heterogeneous systems. However, providing such fine-grained location information may involve considerable cost and complexity.
- **Symbolic Model:** The location space is divided into disjointed zones, each of which is identified by a unique name. Examples are the Cricket system (Priyantha, Chakraborty, & Balakrishnan, 2000) and the cellular infrastructure. The symbolic model is in general cheaper to deploy than the geometric model because of the lower cost of employing a coarser location granularity. Also, being discrete and well-structured, location information based on the symbolic model is easier to manage.

For ease of illustration, two notions are defined: *valid scope* and *valid scope distribution*. A dataset is a collection of data instances. The *valid scope* of a data instance is defined as the area within which this instance is the only answer with respect to a location-dependent query. With the symbolic location model, a valid scope is represented by a set of logical zone ids. With the geometric location model, a valid scope often takes the shape of a polygon in a two-dimensional space. Since a query may return different instances at different locations, it is associated with a set of valid scopes, which collectively is called the *scope distribution* of the query. To illustrate, consider a four-cell system with a wireless-cell-based location model. Suppose that the nearby restaurant for cell 1 and cell 2 is instance *X*, and the nearby restaurant for cell 3 and cell 4 is instance *Y*. Then, the valid scope of X is {1, 2}, the valid scope of Y is {3, 4}, and the scope distribution of the nearby restaurant query is {{1, 2}, {3, 4}}.

Client Caching Model

There is a cache management module in the client. Whenever an application issues a query, the local cache manager first checks whether the desired data item is in the cache. If it is a cache hit, the cache manager still needs to validate the consistency of the cached item with the master copy at the server. This process is called *cache validation*. In general, data inconsistency is incurred by data updates at the server (called *temporal-dependent invalidation*). For location-dependent information in a mobile environment, cache inconsistency can also be caused by location change of a client (called *location-dependent invalidation*). If it is a cache hit but the cached content is obsolete or invalid, or it is a cache miss, the cache manager requests the data from the server via on-demand access. When the requested data item arrives, the cache manager returns it to the user and retains a copy in the cache. The issue of *cache replacement* arises when the free cache space is not enough to accommodate a data item to be cached. It determines the victim data item(s) to be dropped from the cache in order to allocate sufficient cache space for the incoming data item.

Survey of Related Work

This section reviews the existing studies on cache invalidation and replacement strategies for mobile clients. Most of them were designed for general data services and only a few addressed the caching issues for location-dependent data. Temporal-dependent invalidation has been studied for many years (Barbara & Imielinski, 1994; Cao, 2000; Wu, Yu, & Chen, 1996). To carry out temporal-dependent invalidation, the server keeps track of the update history (for a reasonable length of time)

and sends it, in the form of an invalidation report (IR), to the clients, either by periodic/aperiodic broadcasting or upon individual requests from the clients. In the basic IR approach, the server broadcasts a list of IDs for the items that have been changed within a history window. The mobile client, if active, listens to the IRs and updates its cache accordingly. Most existing temporal-dependent invalidation schemes are variations of the basic IR approach. They differ from one another mainly in the organization of IR contents and the mechanism of uplink checking. A good survey can be found in Tan et al. (2001).

Semantic data caching has been suggested for managing location-dependent query results (Dar, Franklin, Jonsson, Srivatava, & Tan, 1996; Lee, Leong, & Si, 1999), where a cached result is described with the location associated with the query. Unfortunately, the possibility was not explored that a cached data value may be valid for queries issued from locations different from that associated with the original query. As demonstrated in Zheng, Xu, and Lee (2002), the exploration of this possibility can significantly enhance the performance of location-dependent data caching. As a matter of fact, the invalidation information in the proposed methods (to be discussed later in this chapter) can be considered a kind of semantic description, which could improve cache hit rates.

Cache replacement policies for wireless environments were first studied in the *broadcast disk* project (Acharya et al., 1995; Acharya, Franklin, & Zdonik, 1996). In Acharya et al. (1995), the PIX policy takes into consideration both data access probability and broadcast frequency during replacement. In Khanna and Liberatore (2000), the Gray scheme makes replacement decisions based on both data access history and retrieval delay. Motivated by a realistic broadcast environment, an optimal cache replacement policy, called Min-SAUD, was investigated in Xu, Hu, Lee, and Lee (2004). The Min-SAUD policy incorporates various factors that affect cache performance, that is, access probability, retrieval delay, item size, update frequency, and cache validation delay.

In the studies on location-dependent data caching, data-distance based cache replacement policies, Manhattan distance (Dar et al., 1996) and FAR (Ren & Dunham, 2000), have been proposed. Under these two policies, the data that is farthest away from the client's current location is removed during replacement. However, data distance was considered alone and not integrated with other factors such as access probability. Moreover, they did not consider the factor of valid scope area.

CACHING FOR LOCATION-BASED SERVICES

Location-Dependent Cache Invalidation

When the client moves around, location-dependent data cached at a mobile client may become invalid with respect to the new location. The procedure of verifying the validity of location-dependent data with respect to the current location is referred to as *location-dependent cache invalidation*. To perform location-dependent invalidation efficiently, the idea is to make use of validity information of data instances. Specifically, the server delivers the valid scope along with a data instance to a mobile client and the client caches the data as well as its valid scope for later validity checking. The strategy involves two issues, namely validity checking time and validity information organization. Since a query result depends on the location specified with the query only, it is suggested to perform validity checking for a cached data instance until it is queried. For validity information organization, a number of schemes have been proposed (Zheng et al., 2002; Xu, Tang, & Lee, 2003). The proposed schemes can be classified into two categories according to the underlying location model employed. This section introduces two methods, that is, implicit scope information (ISI) and caching-efficiency-based method (CEB), for a symbolic and geometric location model respectively.

Implicit Scope Information (ISI)

Assume a wireless-cell-ID-based symbolic location model. Under the ISI scheme, the server enumerates the scope distributions of all items and numbers them sequentially. The valid scopes within a scope distribution are also numbered sequentially. For any instance of data item i, its valid scope is specified by a 2-tuple (SDN_i, SN_i), where SDN_i is the scope distribution number and SN_i denotes the scope number within this distribution. The 2-tuple is attached to a data instance as its valid scope. For example, suppose there are three different scope distributions (see Table 1) and data item 4 follows distribution 3. If item 4 is cached from cell 6 (i.e., CID = 6), then $SDN_4 =$ 3 and $SN_4 = 3$. This implies that item 4's instance is valid in cells 6 and 7 only.

It can be observed that the size of the validity information for a data instance is small and independent of the actual number of cells in which the instance is valid. Another observation is that a set of data items may share the same scope distribution. As such, the number of scope distributions could be much smaller than the number of items in the database.

At the server-side, a *location-dependent IR* is periodically broadcast in each cell. It consists of the ordered valid scope numbers (SN) for each scope distribution in the cell. For example, in cell 8, the server broadcasts {8, 3, 4} to mobile clients, where the three numbers are the SN values in cell 8 for scope distributions 1, 2, and 3, respectively (see Table 1).

The validity checking algorithm for item i works as follows. After retrieving a location-dependent IR, the client compares the cached SN_i with the SDN_i-th SN in the location-dependent IR received. If they are the same, the cached data

Table 1. An example of data items with different distributions

Cell ID	1	2	3	4	5	6	7	8	9	10	11	12
Scope Distribution (SDN) #1	1	2	3	4	5	6	7	8	9	10	11	12
Scope Distribution (SDN) #2	1			2			3			4		
Scope Distribution (SDN) #3	1			2		3			4		5	

instance is valid. Otherwise, the data instance is invalid. For example, in cell 8, the client checks for the cached instance of data item 4 whose $SDN_4 = 3$ and $SN_4 = 3$. In the broadcast report, the SDN_4-th (i.e., third) SN equals to 4. Therefore, the client knows that the cached instance is invalid. The performance analysis conducted in Xu et al. (2003) shows that the ISI method performs close to an optimal strategy which assumes perfect location information is available on mobile clients.

Caching-Efficiency-Based Method (CEB)

This section discusses location-dependent cache invalidation strategies for a geometric location model. Under this model, there are two basic schemes for representing valid scopes, that is, *polygonal endpoints* and *approximate circle* (Zheng et al., 2002). However, these two schemes perform poorly due to either high overhead or imprecision of the invalidation information. To enhance performance, a generic *caching-efficiency-based* (CEB) method for balancing the overhead and the knowledge of valid scopes was proposed in Zheng et al. (2002).

In the CEB method, a new metric *caching efficiency* was introduced. Suppose that the valid scope of a data instance is v, and v_i' is a subregion contained in v (see Figure 1). Let s be the data size, $A(v_i')$ the area of any scope of v_i', and $O(v_i')$ the storage overhead needed to record the scope v_i'. The caching efficiency of the data instance with respect to a scope v_i' is defined as follows:

Figure 1. An example of possible candidate valid scopes ($v = p(e_1,e_2,...,e_7)$)

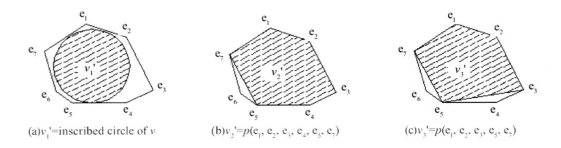

(a)v_1'=inscribed circle of v (b)v_2'=$p(e_1, e_2, e_3, e_4, e_5, e_7)$ (c)v_3'=$p(e_1, e_2, e_3, e_5, e_7)$

$$E(v_i') = \frac{A(v_i')/A(v)}{(s+O(v_i'))/s} = \frac{A(v_i')s}{A(v)(s+O(v_i'))} \quad (1)$$

Let v_i' be the approximated scope information stored in the client cache. Assuming that the cache size is infinite and the probabilities of a client issuing queries at different locations are uniform, $A(v_i')/A(v)$ is the data instance's cache hit ratio when the client issues the query within the valid scope v. In contrast, $(s+O(v_i'))/s$ is the normalized overhead for achieving such a hit ratio. The rationale behind this definition is as follows. When none of the invalidation information is cached, $E(v_i')$ is 0 because the cached data is completely useless; $E(v_i')$ increases with more invalidation information attached. However, if too much overhead is therefore introduced, $E(v_i')$ would decrease again. Thus, a generic method for balancing the overhead and the precision of invalidation information works as follows:

- For a data instance with a valid scope of v, given a candidate valid scope set $V' = \{v_1', v_2',..., v_k'\}$, $v_i' \subseteq v$, $1 \le i \le k$, the CEB method chooses the scope v_i' that maximizes caching efficiency $E(v_i')$ as the valid scope to be attached to the instance.

Figure 1 illustrates an example where the valid scope of the data instance is $v = p(e_1,e_2,...,e_7)$, and v_1', v_2', v_3' are three different subregions of v, $A(v_1')/A(v) = 0.788$, $A(v_2')/A(v) = 0.970$, and $A(v_3')/A(v) = 0.910$. Assume that the data size s is 128 bytes, 8 bytes are needed to represent an endpoint, and 4 bytes for the radius of an inscribed circle; hence $O(v) = 56$, $O(v_1') = 12$, $O(v_2') = 48$, and $O(v_3')= 40$. Thus, $E(v) = 0.696$, $E(v_1') = 0.721$, $E(v_2') = 0.706$, and $E(v_3')= 0.694$. As a result, v_1' is chosen as the valid scope to be attached to the data instance. The simulation based evaluation demonstrates that the CEB method is very effective and outperforms other invalidation methods (Zheng et al., 2002).

Cache Replacement Policies

Because a mobile client has only limited cache space, cache replacement is another important issue to be tackled in client cache management. In traditional cache replacement policies, access probability is considered the most important factor that affects cache performance. A probability-based policy is to replace the data with the least access probability. However, in LBS, besides access probability, there are two other factors, namely *data distance* and *valid scope area*, which have to be considered in cache replacement strategies.

Generally, a promising cache replacement policy should choose as its victim the data item with a low access probability, a small valid scope area, and a long distance if data distance is also an influential factor. This section presents two cost-based cache replacement policies, PA and PAID, which integrate the three factors that are supposed to affect cache performance. The discussions are based on a geometric location model.

- **Probability Area (PA):** As the name suggests, the cost of a data instance under this policy is defined as the product of the access probability of the data item and the area of the attached valid scope. That is, the cost function for data instance j of item i is as follows:

$$c_{i,j} = p_i \cdot A(v'_{i,j}), \quad (2)$$

where p_i is the access probability of item i and $A(v'_{i,j})$ is the area of the attached valid scope $v'_{i,j}$ for data instance j. The PA policy chooses the data with the least cost as its victim for cache replacement.

- **Probability Area Inverse Distance (PAID):** Compared with PA, this scheme further integrates the data distance factor. For the PAID policy, the cost function for data instance j of item i is defined as follows:

$$c_{i,j} = \frac{p_i \cdot A(v'_{i,j})}{D(v'_{i,j})} , \qquad (3)$$

where p_i and $A(v'_{i,j})$ are defined the same as above, and $D(v'_{i,j})$ is the distance between the current location and the valid scope $v'_{i,j}$. Similar to PA, PAID ejects the data with the least cost during each replacement.

Zheng et al. (2002) have evaluated the performance of PA and PAID and demonstrated that PA and PAID substantially outperform the existing policies including LRU and FAR. In particular, consideration of the valid scope area improves performance in all settings, and consideration of the moving direction in calculating data distance is effective only for short query intervals and short moving intervals.

FUTURE TRENDS

Caching of location-dependent data opens up a new dimension of research in mobile computing. As for future work, per user based adaptive techniques can be developed since mobile clients may have different movement patterns. Besides cache invalidation and replacement schemes, it is interesting to investigate *cache prefetching* which preloads data onto the mobile client cache by taking advantage of user mobility. Furthermore, how to incorporate location-dependent data invalidation schemes and semantic caching would be an interesting topic. In addition, battery power is a scarce resource in a mobile computing environment; it is believed that power-aware cache management deserves further in-depth study.

CONCLUSION

LBS has been emerging as the result of technological advances in high-speed wireless networks, personal portable devices, and location positioning techniques. This chapter discussed client cache management issues for LBS. Two location-dependent cache invalidation methods, that is, ISI and CEB, are introduced. The cache replacement issue for location-dependent data was also investigated. Two cache replacement policies, that is, PA and PAID that consider the factors of valid scope area (for both methods) and data distance (for PAID only) and combine these factors with access probability, were presented. With an increasing popularity of LBS, caching of location-dependent data remains a fertile research area that aims to overcome inherent constraints (including power, bandwidth, storage, etc.) in a mobile environment.

REFERENCES

Acharya, S., Alonso, R., Franklin, M., & Zdonik, S. (1995). Broadcast disks: Data management for asymmetric communications environments. *Proceedings of ACM SIGMOD Conference on Management of Data* (pp. 199-210).

Acharya, S., Franklin, M., & Zdonik, S. (1996). Prefetching from a broadcast disk. *Proceedings of the 12th International Conference on Data Engineering* (pp. 276-285).

Barbara, D. (1999). Mobile computing and databases—A survey. *IEEE Transactions on Knowledge and Data Engineering, 11*(1), 108-117.

Barbara, D., & Imielinski, T. (1994). Sleepers and workaholics: Caching strategies for mobile environments. *Proceedings of ACM SIGMOD Conference on Management of Data* (pp. 1-12).

Cao, G.. (2000). A scalable low-latency cache invalidation strategy for mobile environments. *Proceedings of the Sixth ACM International Conference on Mobile Computing and Networking* (pp. 200-209).

Dar, S., Franklin, M. J., Jonsson, B. T., Srivatava, D., & Tan, M. (1996). Semantic data caching and replacement. *Proceedings of the 22nd International Conference on Very Large Data Bases* (pp. 330-341).

Khanna, S., & Liberatore, V. (2000). On broadcast disk paging. *SIAM Journal on Computing, 29*(5), 1683-1702.

Lee, D. L., Lee, W.-C., Xu, J., & Zheng, B. (2002). Data management in location-dependent information services. *IEEE Pervasive Computing, 1*(3), 65-72.

Lee, K. C. K., Leong, H. V., & Si, A. (1999). Semantic Query caching in a mobile environment. *Mobile Computing and Communication Review, 3*(2), 28-36.

Lee, W. C., Xu, J., & Zheng, B. (2004). Data management in location-dependent information services. *Tutorial at the 20th IEEE International Conference on Data Engineering* (pp. 871).

Priyantha, N. B., Chakraborty, A., & Balakrishnan, H. (2000). The cricket location-support system. *Proceedings of the Sixth ACM International Conference on Mobile Computing and Networking* (pp. 32-43).

Ren, Q., & Dunham, M. H. (2000). Using semantic caching to manage location dependent data in mobile computing. *Proceedings of the Sixth ACM International Conference on Mobile Computing and Networking* (pp. 210-221).

Tan, K. L., Cai, J., & Ooi, B. C. (2001). An evaluation of cache invalidation strategies in wireless environments. *IEEE Transactions on Parallel and Distributed Systems (TPDS), 12*(8), 789-807.

Wu, K.-L., Yu, P. S., & Chen, M.-S. (1996). Energy-efficient caching for wireless mobile computing. *Proceedings of the 12th International Conference on Data Engineering* (pp. 336-343).

Xu, J., Hu, Q., Lee, W.-C., & Lee, D. L. (2004). Performance evaluation of an optimal cache replacement policy for wireless data dissemination. *IEEE Transactions on Knowledge and Data Engineering, 16*(1), 125-139.

Xu, J., Tang, X., & Lee, D. L. (2003). Performance analysis of location-dependent cache invalidation schemes for mobile environments. *IEEE Transactions on Knowledge and Data Engineering, 15*(2), 474-488.

Zheng, B., Xu, J., & Lee, D. L. (2002). Cache invalidation and replacement policies for location-dependent data in mobile environments. *IEEE Transactions on Computers (TC), 51*(10), 1141-1153.

KEY TERMS

Cache Invalidation: The procedure of validating whether the cached data is consistent with the master copy at the server.

Cache Replacement: The procedure of finding the victim data item(s) to be dropped from the cache in order to allocate sufficient cache space for an incoming data item.

Location-Based Services (LBS): The services that answer queries based on the locations with which the queries are associate.

Location-Dependent Cache Invalidation: The procedure of verifying the validity of cached location-dependent data with respect to the current location.

Mobile Client: A portable device that is augmented with a wireless communication interface.

Valid Scope: The area within which the data instance is the only answer with respect to a location-dependent query.

Valid Scope Distribution: The collective set of valid scopes for a data item.

Wireless Cell: The radio coverage area in which a mobile client can communicate with the wireless infrastructure.

This work was previously published in Encyclopedia of E-Commerce, E-Government, and Mobile Commerce, edited by M. Khosrow-Pour, pp. 760-765, copyright 2006 by Information Science Reference, formerly known as Idea Group Reference (an imprint of IGI Global).

Chapter 7.34
Location–Aware Query Resolution for Location–Based Mobile Commerce:
Performance Evaluation and Optimization

James E. Wyse
Memorial University of Newfoundland, Canada

ABSTRACT

Location-based mobile commerce incorporates location-aware technologies, wire-free connectivity, and locationalized Web-based services to support the processing of location-referent transactions. In order to provide usable transaction processing services to mobile consumers, location-referent transactions require timely resolution of queries bearing transaction-related locational criteria. This research evaluates Wyse's location-aware method of resolving these queries. Results obtained in simulated mobile commerce circumstances (1) reveal the query resolution behavior of the location-aware method, (2) confirm the method's potential to improve the timeliness of transactional support provided to mobile consumers, and (3) identify the method-related adjustments required to maintain optimal levels of query resolution performance. The article also proposes and provides a preliminary evaluation of a heuristic that may be used in efficiently determining the method-related adjustments needed in order to maximize query resolution performance.

INTRODUCTION

Recent years have witnessed the emergence of transaction-supporting devices directed toward the mobile consumer. Devices range from simple handsets in mobile/cellular phone systems to those involving the convergence of palm-top computing, location-determining technology, and wireless Internet connectivity. Minimally, devices utilized by mobile consumers must incorporate wireless communication capabilities that permit a significant degree of mobility (Leung & Atypas, 2001; Santami, Leow, Lim, & Goh, 2003). Yuan and Zhang (2003) assert that mobile devices with capabilities extending beyond wireless communication to include those that support location awareness add a "much emphasised … new dimension for value creation" (p. 41) to mobile commerce. Location awareness refers to the capability of a device to obtain data about geographical position and then to use the data to retrieve, select, and report information with respect to that position (Butz, Bauss, & Kruger, 2000). Figure 1 illustrates a location-aware mobile commerce (mcommerce) context in which location-aware applications operating on mobile, GPS-enabled, handheld computing devices avail of wireless connectivity to access a variety of

Internet-based servers providing information and functionality to support the transactional activities of mobile consumers.

An essential component in large-scale, location-aware, mobility-supporting applications is a specialized database of transaction-supporting information (Location-Qualified Data Repository, Figure 1). Locational content from the repository is required for the resolution of queries arising from location-referent transactions, transactions in which the relative geographical locations of the prospective transactional parties is a material transactional concern. Siau, Lim, and Shen (2001) and, later, Siau and Shen (2003) call for research on improving the processing of transactional queries in circumstances "where users are constantly on the move and few [end user device] computing resources are available" (p. 13). The research reported here responds to this call; it is

Figure 1. Illustrative configuration of m-commerce components

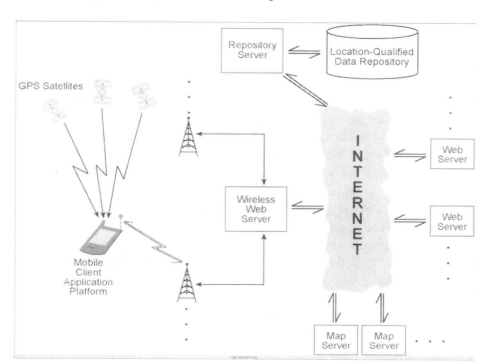

concerned with the timely processing of queries initiated by location-variant (on-the-move) consumers operating resource-limited devices that must rely on centralized repositories of location-qualified information.

The emergence of m-commerce has spawned several streams of research in areas related to the components shown in Figure 1. Some recent studies with respect to these components have been conducted in such areas as mobile user location determination (McGuire, Plataniotis, & Venetsanopoulos, 2005; Quintero, 2005; Samaan & Karmouch, 2005), mobile device interface design (Lee & Benbasat, 2004), mobile business application design (Gebauer & Shaw, 2004; Khungar & Reikki, 2005), and mobility-related wireless connectivity (Chao, Tseng, & Wang, 2005; Chou & Shin, 2005; Cinque, Cotroneo, & Russo, 2005; Lin, Juang, & Lin, 2005; Xu, Shen, & Mark, 2005; Yeung & Kwok, 2005). Research in areas related to mobile commerce has also addressed in various ways the issue of query resolution in mobile computing environments. Kottkamp and Zukunft (1998) developed and evaluated a mobility aware cost model for location-aware query optimization in the context of mobile user location management; Choy, Kwan, and Hong (2000) proposed a distributed database system architecture to support query processing in mobile geographical applications; Lee and Ke (2001) conducted a cost analysis of strategies for query processing in a mobile commerce environment; Lee, Xu, Zheng, and Lee (2002) and Huang, Lin, and Deng (2005) dealt with the validity of query results and the efficiency of query processing through improved mobile device cache management; while Wyse (2003) proposed a location-aware method of locations repository management to support m-commerce transactions. It is the latter area that is addressed here; specifically, this article examines the extent to which query resolution time is affected by implementing Wyse's (2003) location-aware method (LAM) of managing a server-based locational repository.

A synopsis of LAM is provided in Appendix A. The method employs the linkcell construct as a means of transforming locational coordinates in geographical space to spatially-oriented table names in relational space. A specialized search method operates on the transformation to resolve location-referent queries. Results from Wyse's (2003) work suggest that the method significantly improves query resolution performance over that realized from the use of naïve enumerative methods. However, the work notes that the location-aware method's performance was evaluated in limited circumstances (small repository sizes, fixed geographical coverage, limited business categorization) and also points out that the effect of variations in linkcell size on resolution performance remains unexamined. Wyse (2003) also contemplated the existence of a linkcell size that would optimize query resolution performance but offered no approach that would result in its determination.

These contemplations and limitations give rise to four questions to be addressed by the research reported here: (1) Will the location-aware method yield resolution performance profiles consistent with those previously observed when greater repository sizes, larger variations in geographical coverage, and differing business category sets are used? (2) How is linkcell size related to query resolution performance? (3) Is there a specific linkcell size that will optimize resolution performance? and (4) How might an optimal linkcell size be determined? Before providing results that address these questions, some discussion is warranted on the nature of the problem for which the location-aware method is proposed as a solution.

THE REPOSITORY MANAGEMENT PROBLEM

Mobile consumers frequently require information presented in some consumer-centric proximity pattern on the locations of businesses offering products and services in a specified business category. Consumer-centric information may be requested in relation to questions such as *Where is the nearest health food outlet? How far away am I from a golf course? Where am I situated in relation to a medical facility?* The queries arising from such questions must incorporate both a product/service criterion (e.g., medical facility) and a consumer-centric, distance-related criterion (e.g., nearest). Two distinctions between product/service-related criteria and consumer-centric, distance-related criteria have implications for the management of locational repositories. First, product/service-related criteria are invariant with respect to a mobile consumer's location, while consumer-centric, distance-related criteria are not. Nievergelt and Widmayer (1997) recognize the distinction between the two types of criteria and point out its efficiency-related implication: "Spatial data differs from all other types of data in important respects. Objects are embedded in an Euclidean space … and most queries involve proximity rather than intrinsic properties of the objects to be retrieved. Thus, data structures developed for conventional database systems are unlikely to be efficient" (p. 186). The issue of efficiency is readily seen in the second distinction: product-service attribute values are patently resident in a repository, while consumer-centric, distance-related attribute values must be derived from the locational attributes of both the consumer and the business location offering a consumer-targeted product or service. Thus, each change in a consumer's geographical position in general will necessitate a redetermination of values for an appropriate consumer-centric, distance-related attribute.

The requirement to continually requery a repository and redetermine a consumer-centric proximity pattern places an extensive burden on server-side repository functionality. For a given level of computational capability, continual requerying and redetermination eventually results

in service time degradation as repository sizes increase and/or as the number of consumers increases and/or as consumers more frequently change geographic positions. Increased repository size (i.e., a richer set of locations from which the mobile consumer may obtain information on targeted products or services) would likely attract greater numbers of mobile consumers. In turn, greater numbers of consumers would likely motivate the construction of larger, more richly populated repositories, which then would attract even more consumers (Lee, Zhu, & Hu, 2005). Thus, a cycle is created wherein repository sizes will increase and, in the absence of mitigating investments in computational capability, result in a degradation of the service times experienced by consumers accessing the repository. Thus, an important challenge facing those who are tasked with managing large-scale locational repositories is one of minimizing the increase (i.e., degradation) in the service times realized by mobile consumers while at same time enriching (i.e., enlarging) the location-qualified data repository available to mobile consumers.

SOLUTION APPROACHES

The nature of queries initiated by mobile consumers (e.g., Where's the nearest health food outlet?) suggests that the problem of query resolution is conceptually similar to the nearest neighbor (NN) problem, a problem that has received considerable attention in computational geometry. Formally, solutions to the NN problem incorporate constructs and procedures that, when given a set P of n points and a query point q, result in $p \in P$ such that for all $p' \in P$ we have $d(p, q) \leq d(p', q)$ where $d(p', q)$ is the distance between p' and q (Cary, 2001). Several works have developed NN solution algorithms. Arnon, Efrat, Indyk, and Samet (1999), Lee (1999), and Cary (2001) propose solutions from computational geometry, while Kuznetsov (2000) proposes a solution based on the space-filling curves developed by Sierpinski (1912) and Hilbert (Butz, 1969, 1971). These algorithms yield solution times that improve upon those realized from naïve enumerative methods; however, the solution time derived for each algorithm's execution is positively related to n, the number of points in the set P.

A mapping of the terms of the NN problem to aspects of the problem of managing location-qualified data repositories gives n as the repository size, P as the repository, q as the mobile consumer's location, p as the nearest location, and $d(p', q)$ as the distance-related attribute needed to resolve the consumer's query. This mapping formalizes the dependency of this attribute on both the consumer's location (q) and the locational attributes contained in the repository for each location, p'. Furthermore, the condition that $d(p, q) \leq d(p', q)$, for all $p' \in P$, implies that new distance-re-

lated attribute values are required for all records whenever there is any change in the consumer's location (q). This condition in combination with algorithm solution times that are related positively to repository size (n) corroborates the assessment reached in the previous section that the service times associated with mobile consumer access to location-qualified data repositories will degrade as repository size is increased.

An important aspect of mitigating service time degradation is the use of a retrieval algorithm that does not require a determination of $d(p', q)$, for all $p' \in P$. In other words, new distance-related attribute values need not be calculated for all locations in the repository whenever a new q is encountered (i.e., whenever the mobile consumer changes location). The solution algorithms developed in computational geometry generally take this approach; however, these algorithms have

Figure 2. Resultset completion times for enumerative and location-aware methods by repository size

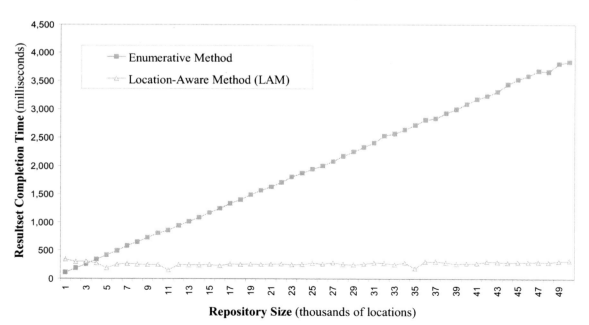

Source: Wyse (2003), p. 135. Reproduced with the permission of Inderscience Publishers.

solution times that increase, albeit in varying ways, as the size of the set P increases. In this report, the location-aware solution approach to be examined also does not require a determination of $d(p', q)$, for all $p' \in P$. As shown by the LAM curve in Figure 2, the method appears capable of producing resultset completion times (RCTs) that, for practical purposes, are invariant with respect to repository size.[1] Thus, LAM implementations would appear to be useful in mitigating the service time degradation attributable to increases in repository size that otherwise would be realized from implementing an enumerative method of query resolution. The Enumerative Method curve shown in Figure 2 illustrates the degradation that otherwise would occur.[2]

Although the goal of the location-aware method's solution algorithm essentially is the same as that for the NN solution algorithms of computational geometry, the method does not draw upon that discipline's constructs and procedures. Instead, as seen in Appendix A, the method relies upon relational database constructs and functionality combined with the structure of a commonly used convention for designating geographical position (latitude and longitude) to construct and manipulate specialized relational tables (linkcells). Previous work used a simulation-based methodology to demonstrate that the location-aware method is a potential solution (illustrated by the LAM curve in Figure 2) to an important problem (illustrated by the Enumerative curve in Figure 2) associated with managing locational repositories. In what follows, the location-aware method is evaluated in simulated circumstances that extend beyond those of previous work. Also, in contrast to previous work, an important task here is determining the existence of a specific (optimal) linkcell construction that would maximize the resolution performance of queries associated with location-referent transactions.

OPTIMAL LINKCELL SIZE DETERMINATION: METHODS AND MEASURES

Appendix A discusses the formulation of the linkcell construct and defines linkcell size. The appendix also notes that changes in linkcell size result in redistributions of repository locations among linkcells and that these redistributions may have a substantial impact on query resolution performance. Wyse's (2003) work on simulated locational repositories used a single linkcell size of 1.0 for all of the various analyses that were conducted, and beyond noting that other linkcell sizes could be used, the work provided little guidance on searching for an optimal linkcell size. Thus, a brute force search strategy was employed in preliminary work here wherein linkcell size (arbitrarily) took an initial value of 0.2 and then was incremented successively (also arbitrarily) by 0.2. This sequence of linkcell sizes was imposed on a series of simulated repository scenarios, each of which consisted of a selected number of randomly generated locations, a selected area of geographical coverage, and a selected number of product-service categories. Resultset completion times (RCTs) were determined at each linkcell size based on queries initiated from 100 randomly chosen locations within the selected geographical area. As previously noted, RCT values indicate the time taken to extract a set of repository locations that represent a resolution of a consumer-initiated query.

Figures 3 and 4 show results from two of the many scenarios on which a brute force search was carried out. All scenarios revealed what appeared to be an optimal linkcell size; however, the optimal value was not generally the same across the scenarios. An optimal linkcell size of 1.0 was revealed for the scenario in Figure 3, while an optimal linkcell size of 0.8 was revealed for the scenario in Figure 4. In its comparison of RCT performance profiles for the Enumerative and LAM methods, Figure 4 illustrates that a poorly chosen linkcell size (e.g., 5.0) could result not just in RCTs that are far removed from optimal values but also in the complete loss of any query resolution performance advantage attributable to LAM. Table 1 provides the results of an analysis of the scenario whose RCT profile appears in Figure 3.

Figure 3. LAM resultset completion times (RCT$_L$) by linkcell size (Repository: 100,000 locations, 100 product-service categories, area N30° to N50° and W070° to W130°)

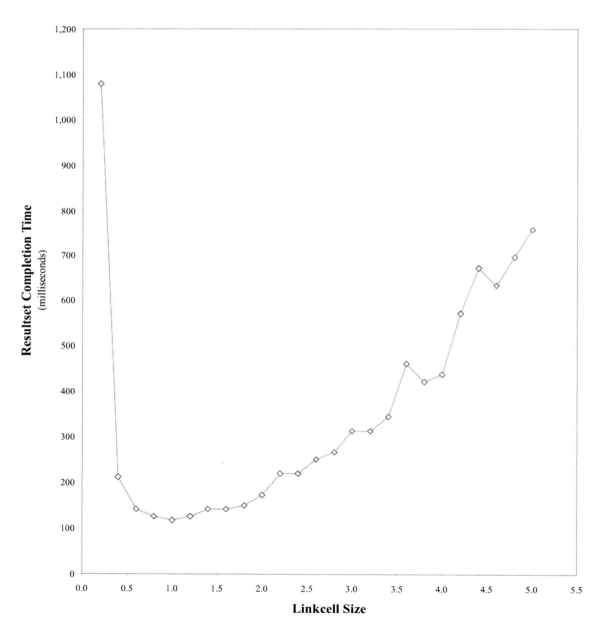

The following discussion of the table's content will provide more detail on the simulation-based methodology used to (1) obtain resultset completion times, (2) explain the mechanism underlying the existence of an optimal linkcell size, and (3) illustrate the trade-offs in repository space consumption required to realize LAM-related gains in query resolution performance.

The methodology used to generate the RCT curves in Figures 3 and 4 is similar to the simula-

Figure 4. Resultset completion times for location-aware and enumerative methods by linkcell size (Repository: 100,000 locations, 200 product-service categories, area N35° to N45° and W080° to W110°)

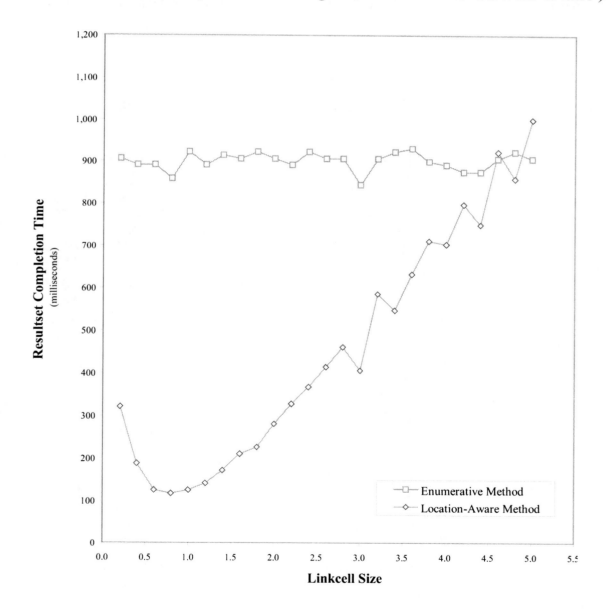

tion-based approach used in Wyse's (2003) evaluative work on the location-aware method. Software called the Linkcell Performance Analyzer (LPA) was developed that (1) generates locational repositories with varying numbers of locations ranging over various geographical areas and referencing different product-service category lists; (2) creates linkcell sets based on repository locations with respect to a specified linkcell size; (3) assembles and processes simulated queries bearing randomly assigned product-service criteria for randomly located consumers; (4) resolves the location-referent queries using both enumerative (E) and location-aware (L) methods; and (5) determines resultset completion times (RCT_E and RCT_L) for each method. Table 1 provides LPA-generated results associated with the RCT_L values plotted in Figure 3. The first column shows the series of linkcell sizes (from 0.2 to 5.0) for the plot's horizontal axis. Columns 6 through 10 report RCT_L statistics derived from simulated queries originating from 100 randomly chosen mobile consumer locations. All five statistics reveal their lowest resultset completion time values at a linkcell size

Table 1. Selected repository scenario (100,000 locations, 100 product-service categories, area N30° to N50° and W070° to W130°)

(1) Selected Linkcell Size	(2) Maximum Number of Linkcells	(3) Linkcells Actually Generated	(4) Mean Linkcell Entries	(5) Probability of Linkcell with Targeted Category	RCT$_L$ (6) Mean	(7) Min	(8) Max	(9) 50th	(10) 90th	(11) Compacted Disk Space (MB)	(12) Repository xLinkcells Multiple
0.2	30,000	28,923	3.5	0.03	1,580	63	8,094	1,079	3,453	358.0	46.6
0.4	7,500	7,500	13.3	0.13	268	16	984	211	516	98.7	12.9
0.6	3,434	3,434	29.1	0.25	182	16	1,047	141	344	49.5	6.4
0.8	1,976	1,976	50.6	0.40	176	16	969	125	328	31.7	4.1
1.0	1,200	1,200	83.3	0.57	144	16	391	117	281	22.4	2.9
1.2	867	867	115.3	0.69	185	16	922	125	373	18.4	2.4
1.4	645	645	155.0	0.79	164	31	531	141	313	17.6	2.3
1.6	546	546	183.2	0.84	165	16	496	141	313	16.2	2.1
1.8	420	420	238.1	0.91	167	16	750	149	281	14.6	1.9
2.0	300	300	333.3	0.96	202	31	969	172	391	13.7	1.8
2.2	290	290	344.8	0.97	231	31	875	219	406	13.4	1.7
2.4	234	234	427.4	0.99	236	31	906	219	422	12.9	1.7
2.6	216	216	463.0	0.99	267	31	656	250	453	12.6	1.6
2.8	176	176	568.2	1.00	296	31	750	266	547	12.2	1.6
3.0	147	147	680.3	1.00	331	31	1,172	313	641	12.1	1.6
3.2	140	140	714.3	1.00	337	31	734	313	594	12.0	1.6
3.4	133	133	751.9	1.00	367	31	1,328	344	578	11.9	1.5
3.6	108	108	925.9	1.00	461	63	1,500	461	797	11.6	1.5
3.8	119	119	840.3	1.00	476	78	1,375	422	895	11.7	1.5
4.0	96	96	1,041.7	1.00	473	31	1,984	438	813	11.5	1.5
4.2	75	75	1,333.3	1.00	585	47	1,703	571	100	11.3	1.5
4.4	90	90	1,111.1	1.00	653	47	2,000	672	1,156	11.5	1.5
4.6	70	70	1,428.6	1.00	696	109	2,500	633	1,156	11.3	1.5
4.8	70	70	1,428.6	1.00	751	78	2,281	696	1,281	11.3	1.5
5.0	48	48	2,083.3	1.00	758	141	1,859	758	1,344	11.0	1.4

of 1.0, a result reflected in the plot of RCT_L's 50th percentile values, as shown in Figure 3.[3]

The results shown in Columns 2, 3, and 4 of Table 1 help to explain why an optimal linkcell size can be expected to exist. Column 2 indicates the maximum number of linkcells that may be created for each linkcell size, a quantity that varies from 30,000 linkcells for a linkcell size of 0.2 down to 48 linkcells for a linkcell size of 5.0. The numbers in Column 2 are the result of allocating the linkcell size along the (arbitrarily chosen) horizontal and vertical extents that encompass a repository's locations. For a linkcell size of 0.2, the chosen extents potentially result in 30,000 relational tables (linkcells), a number that is the product of 300 linkcell size intervals along the repository's horizontal extent (W070° to W130°) and 100 linkcell size intervals along its vertical extent (N30° to N50°).[4] Not all of the maximum number of relational tables may be actually created. Appendix A's discussion on linkcell creation indicates that a relational table corresponding to a linkcell only comes into existence when its name is derived from a repository location. Thus, the number of linkcells actually generated from a repository's locations may be less than the maximum potential number of linkcells. Such an outcome is seen in Column 3 of Table 1, where, for a linkcell size of 0.2, only 28,923 of the 30,000 possible linkcells actually were created.

Column 4 of Table 1 reports the mean number of linkcell entries for each linkcell size and is obtained by dividing the total number of repository locations (100,000, in this case) by the number of linkcells (Column 3) created from those locations. Comparing Columns 3 and 4 will help to reveal why an optimal linkcell size exists. Note that small linkcell sizes result in the generation of large numbers of small relational tables, while large linkcell sizes result in the generation of small numbers of large relational tables. Consequently, as linkcells initially increase in size, query resolution times will improve, because fewer relational tables have to be examined in order to find a location in the targeted product-service category; however, with each increase in linkcell size, query resolution times also will degrade, because more relational table entries have to be examined in order to find a location in the targeted product-service category. The optimal linkcell size corresponds to the size at which the RCT gains from processing fewer linkcells begin to be overwhelmed by the RCT losses incurred from processing linkcells with greater numbers of linkcell entries. The RCT statistics in Columns 6 through 10 of Table 1 indicate that such gains and losses combine to reveal an optimal linkcell size of 1.0.

The generation of a relational table for each linkcell results in the database containing a location-qualified data repository that is larger than the database for the same repository without linkcells. Column 11 of Table 1 shows the disk space consumed by the location-qualified repository for each linkcell size. A linkcell size of 0.2 results in the generation of 28,923 linkcells and requires disk storage of approximately 358 MB, an amount of storage that is almost 47 times the 7.7 MB storage amount consumed by the repository without linkcells (referred to as Repository x-Linkcells in Column 12 of Table 1). At the other end of the linkcell range, a linkcell size of 5.0 results in the generation of 48 linkcells and requires 11.0 MB of storage, or 1.4 times as much storage as the repository x-linkcells. At the observed optimal linkcell size of 1.0, the repository requires 2.9 times the storage required by the repository x-linkcells. In general, disk storage consumption (manifested here by repository xlinkcell multiples) varies across the scenarios investigated. With respect to the results shown in Figure 4, the optimal linkcell size requires a repository that is 2.0 times the repository x-linkcells. Thus, service-level performance gains from using the location-aware method come at a repository space cost that may be several multiples of that required when using the enumerative method.

The fifth column of Table 1 reports the probability $P_{TC}(S)$ that a linkcell of size S contains an entry for a location in the product-service category that is targeted by the mobile consumer. For example, if a mobile consumer initiates a query about the nearest medical facility, which has been assigned, for instance, a product-service code of *C016*, then the targeted category TC is *C016*, and with reference to the results in Table 1 for a linkcell size of 0.2, we see that $P_{C016}(0.2)$ is 0.03. Note that *C016* is one of the 100 product-service categories used to qualify the 100,000 locations in Table 1's repository scenario. As will be explained next, values for $P_{TC}(S)$ were generated to facilitate the search for optimal linkcell sizes in a way that is more computationally efficient and managerially usable than searches using brute force methods.

Formally, the probability that a linkcell contains a location in the targeted product-service category TC is given by:

$$P_{TC}(S) = 1 - (1 - n_{TC}/N)^{N/CS} \qquad (I)$$

where n_{TC} is the number of locations in the repository with product-service code TC,

N is the total number of locations contained in the repository,

C_S is the number of linkcells of size S created from the repository's N locations, and

N/C_S is the mean number of entries per linkcell.

Equation (I) was formulated on the following basis:

(1) As noted in Appendix A, the manner in which linkcells are created, populated, and destroyed results in one and only one linkcell entry for each repository location. Thus, the probability that any linkcell entry bears the targeted product-service code is the ratio of the number of locations in the repository in the targeted product-service category to the total number of locations in the repository in all product-service categories, or n_{TC}/N.

(2) As also noted in Appendix A during its discussions on repository structure, each location in the repository is qualified by one and only one product-service code. Thus, each linkcell entry either bears the targeted product-service code or it does not. Consequently, if the probability that a linkcell entry bears TC is n_{TC}/N, then the probability that a linkcell entry does not bear TC is $(1 - n_{TC}/N)$.

(3) The probability that none of a linkcell's entries bears the targeted code is given by the product of the probabilities that each linkcell entry does not bear the targeted code, or in other terms, $(1 - n_{TC}/N) \times (1 - n_{TC}/N) \times \ldots \times (1 - n_{TC}/N)$, which may be estimated by $(1 - n_{TC}/N)^{N/CS}$.

(4) Hence, the probability that at least one of the linkcell entries bears the targeted code is $(1 - (1 - n_{TC}/N)^{N/CS})$, which is the right-hand side of Equation (I).

An important assumption underlining Equation (I) is the independence of the probabilities of occurrence of repository entries in the same product-service category with respect to geographical location. Since the repositories used here are generated based on a uniform distribution of locations within specified geographical boundaries, the assumption of independent probabilities in this respect is not an unreasonable one, given the simulated circumstances employed here. However, as discussed later in this article, this assumed distribution of locations may not hold in many practical mcommerce circumstances.

An examination of various repository scenarios indicated the potential usefulness of Equation (I) in identifying optimal linkcell sizes more efficiently and conveniently than doing so using a brute force identification approach. Instead of starting the search for an optimal linkcell size at some arbitrary point, the search was started at the linkcell size S that results in a value of $P_{TC}(S)$ that is close to 0.5.[5] Letting $S_{0.5}$ denote the linkcell size such that $P_{TC}(S_{0.5}) \cong 0.5$, then for smaller linkcell sizes ($S < S_{0.5}$), a linkcell examined during a LAM search probably does not contain a location in the consumer-targeted category; however, for larger linkcell sizes ($S > S_{0.5}$), an examined linkcell probably does contain a consumer-targeted location. Thus, somewhere in the vicinity of $S_{0.5}$, it starts to become likely that a linkcell contains a consumer-targeted location, and consequently, searches for RCT minima that begin at $S_{0.5}$ are likely to more quickly identify an optimal linkcell size than would brute search methods.

An analysis of selected repository scenarios suggested that searches initiated at a linkcell size of $S_{0.5}$ were effective in quickly identifying optimal linkcell sizes. In the case of the repository scenario associated with Table 1 and Figure 3, Equation (I) yields $S_{0.5} \cong 0.9$ as the starting linkcell size. The optimal linkcell size revealed by brute force is close by at 1.0. With respect to repository scenario associated with Figure 4, Equation (I) yields $S_{0.5} \cong 0.7$, a linkcell size that is close to the 0.8 linkcell size revealed by brute force. Application of Equation (I) in the context of these two and various other repository scenarios indicated its usefulness in improving the efficiency of optimal linkcell size identification. However, the repository scenarios were chosen arbitrarily, and the results of their analysis provide only a rough indication of both the existence of linkcell size optima and Equation (I)'s managerial usefulness in optima identification.

In the following sections, more comprehensive and rigorous assessments of the existence of linkcell size optima are reported with respect to (1) changes in repository size, (2) variations in a repository's geographical coverage, and (3) differences in the product-service code sets used to qualify a repository's locations. A simulation-based methodology is used wherein RCT curves like those seen in Figures 3 and 4 are constructed. The methodology is similar to that used previously but with three differences: (1) RCT curves

are based on finer linkcell size increments (0.1 vs. 0.2); (2) RCT values are obtained using a greater number of randomized consumer-initiated queries (200 vs. 100); and (3) the $S_{0.5}$-method is used to initiate a brute force search for linkcell size optima.

LINKCELL SIZE OPTIMA AND REPOSITORY SIZE VARIABILITY

Figure 5 plots resultset completion times (RCTs) for repositories that range in size from 20,000 to 500,000 locations. Each point is the 50th percentile of RCTs for 200 queries issued by mobile consumers from randomly selected geographical locations. Table 2 presents linkcell sizes, P_{TC} values, and RCTs for the repositories associated with Figure 5. The geographical coverage area and the number of product-service categories remained fixed for all repository sizes. Three RCT curves are shown in Figure 5(a): (1) the RCT_E values plotted in the topmost curve (and shown in Column 5 of Table 2) are the result of using enumerative query resolution; (2) the RCT_L values plotted in the bottom curve (and shown in Column 6 of Table 2) are the result of using location-aware query resolution and doing so at each repository's observed optimal linkcell size (seen in Column 3 of Table 2); and, (3) the RCT_L values plotted in the middle curve are the result of using location-aware query resolution, but here, the linkcell size is the same for all repository sizes and is set to the observed optimal linkcell size (3.3) for a repository size of 20,000 locations (note the first linkcell size shown in Column 3 of Table 2).

Managerially, the middle curve in Figure 5 reflects a circumstance in which linkcell size is set to its optimal value with respect to some initial repository size and then remains unchanged (unmanaged) as repository growth occurs. The results indicate that an unmanaged linkcell size results in query resolution time deterioration as a repository grows in size. As seen from the point

Figure 5. Resultset completion times by repository size

(a) RCT_E, "Unmanaged" RCT_L, and "Managed" RCT_L

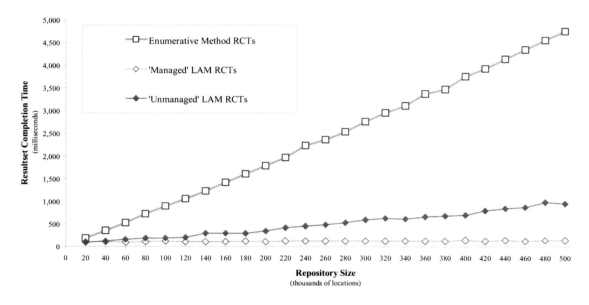

(b) RCT_E and RCT_L at Mean $P_{TC}(S_{OPT})$

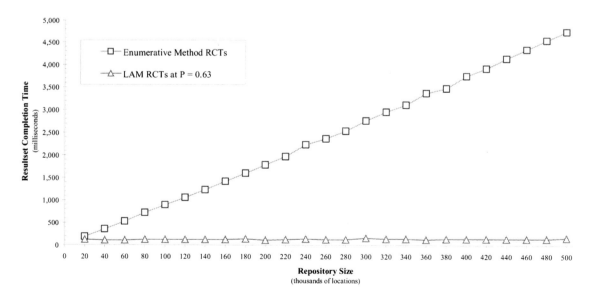

Table 2. Linkcell sizes and resultset completion times by repository size (200 product-service categories, area N30° to N50° and W070° to W130°)

(1) Repository Size (Locations)	(2) $S_{0.5}$ Linkcell Size	(3) Observed S_{OPT} Linkcell Size	(4) $P_{TC}(S_{OPT})$ Prob. linkcell has Targeted Category	(5) RCT_E 50th Percentile	(6) RCT_L 50th Percentile	(7) Linkcell Size at $P_{TC}(S_{OPT})$'s Mean Value	(8) RCT_L for Mean $P_{TC}(S_{OPT})$ Linkcell Size
20,000	3.1	3.3	0.53	187	94	3.9	125
40,000	2.2	2.5	0.65	358	109	2.5	109
60,000	1.7	2.4	0.72	531	94	2.0	109
80,000	1.5	1.4	0.46	723	109	1.9	125
100,000	1.3	1.4	0.54	897	117	1.7	125
120,000	1.3	1.7	0.72	1057	109	1.5	125
140,000	1.1	1.2	0.55	1232	109	1.3	125
160,000	1.1	1.4	0.71	1420	109	1.3	125
180,000	1.0	1.3	0.70	1605	117	1.2	141
200,000	0.9	1.1	0.61	1788	109	1.1	109
220,000	0.9	1.0	0.60	1970	125	1.1	125
240,000	0.9	0.9	0.54	2234	125	1.0	141
260,000	0.8	1.0	0.66	2365	125	1.0	125
280,000	0.8	0.9	0.59	2537	125	0.9	125
300,000	0.8	1.1	0.76	2760	125	0.9	156
320,000	0.7	1.0	0.74	2954	125	0.9	141
340,000	0.7	0.8	0.58	3107	125	0.9	141
360,000	0.7	0.8	0.60	3366	125	0.8	125
380,000	0.7	0.9	0.70	3469	125	0.8	141
400,000	0.7	0.7	0.54	3747	141	0.8	141
420,000	0.6	1.0	0.83	3917	125	0.8	141
440,000	0.6	0.6	0.47	4132	141	0.8	141
460,000	0.6	0.8	0.69	4337	125	0.7	141
480,000	0.6	0.6	0.50	4543	141	0.7	141
500,000	0.6	0.9	0.80	4741	141	0.7	156

on the curve for a 500,000-location repository, RCT_L eventually reaches 953 ms when linkcell size remains unmanaged (i.e., unoptimized), a query resolution time that is almost seven times the RCT_L of 141 ms for a managed (i.e., optimized) linkcell size. This outcome suggests that in order to continually realize optimal query resolution performance, linkcell size must be adjusted as repository size changes.

The observed optimal linkcell size S_{OPT} was identified for each repository size as the linkcell size corresponding to the minimum observed RCT. The search for S_{OPT} began at a linkcell size of $S_{0.5}$ (determined from Equation (I)) and then was expanded above and below $S_{0.5}$ in increments of 0.1 until an RCT minimum was discernable. Table 2 shows $S_{0.5}$ (Column 2) and the observed optimal linkcell size S_{OPT} (Column 3) for each repository size. Comparisons of the values of $S_{0.5}$ and S_{OPT} provide an indication of the usefulness of $S_{0.5}$ in the identification of S_{OPT}. Of the 25 repository sizes, $S_{0.5}$ is within 0.3 for 22 of them and never exceeds 0.7 for any of them. Furthermore, for 24 of the 25 repository sizes, $S_{OPT} >=$

$S_{0.5}$, a result consistent with the previously noted implication of Equation (I) that when $S > S_{0.5}$, a linkcell examined in the course of a location-aware search probably contains a location in the consumer-targeted category. Column 4 of Table 2 shows values for $P_{TC}(S_{OPT})$, the probability that a linkcell contains a consumer-targeted location at the observed optimal linkcell size. These probability figures are consistent with the expectation that optimal linkcell sizes would be rarely observed at a $P_{TC}(S_{OPT})$ value that is substantially below 0.50.

A comparison of the RCT curves in Figure 5(a) indicates that the methodology used to identify S_{OPT} yields linkcell sizes that result in query resolution performance that is not only superior to the conventional enumerative methodology but also substantively independent of repository size. Although these two outcomes are managerially important, the methodology by which they are realized is likely to be regarded as cumbersome and inconvenient by those tasked with repository management. Thus, a simpler method was sought that would be more readily applicable in practical circumstances. In the course of the investigation, it was observed that the use of linkcell sizes derived from Equation (I) with $P_{TC}(S)$ set to the mean value of $P_{TC}(S_{OPT})$ results in RCT values that, for practical purposes, very closely approximate the minimal RCT values associated with optimal linkcell sizes. With respect to the probability values in Column 4 of Table 2, the mean value of $P_{TC}(S_{OPT})$ is 0.63. Column 7 of Table 2 shows the linkcell sizes that result from setting Equation (I) = 0.63 and solving for S. Column 8 presents the RCT values that result from using the linkcell sizes in Column 7. The bottom curve in Figure 5(b) is a plot of Column 8's RCT values. A comparison of Columns 8 and 6 in Table 2 or, equivalently, a comparison of the bottom curves in Figures 5(a) and 5(b) reveals minimal differences in query resolution performance across the examined range of repository sizes.

The outcomes associated with $P_{TC}(S) = 0.63$ suggest that it may be the basis for a practical method of directly identifying performance-optimizing linkcell sizes and one with considerable potential to simplify the repository manager's task of linkcell size determination. Furthermore, the method is structured to an extent that it may be captured in a software module in a straightforward manner. Although this method of linkcell size identification is more convenient and considerably less cumbersome than both the brute force method and the $S_{0.5}$ method, its applicability relies heavily on the validity of setting $P_{TC}(S) =$ mean value of $P_{TC}(S_{OPT})$ as a basis for estimating optimal linkcell sizes. The next two sections provide further assessments of validity in this respect through examinations of circumstances in which (1) geographical area is varied and (2) different product-service code sets are used to qualify the repository's locations. Consistent with the methodological approach used previously, optimal linkcell sizes are identified in both cases, first by the method of constructing RCT curves at successive incremental linkcell sizes in the region of $S_{0.5}$ (i.e., the $S_{0.5}$ method) and, second, by the method of determining linkcell sizes with reference to the mean value of $P_{TC}(S_{OPT})$.

LINKCELL SIZE OPTIMA AND AREA VARIABILITY

Figure 6 plots resultset completion times for a 100,000-location repository whose area of geographical coverage varies over a sequence of 24 areas of increasing size beginning (arbitrarily) with an area bounded by N35° to N40° and W095° to W105° (or 5 degrees of latitude by 10 degrees of longitude) and ending (arbitrarily) with area bounded by N30° to N50° and W070° to W130° (or 20 degrees of latitude by 60 degrees of longitude). For convenience, the areas of increasing size are shown in Figure 6 by the product of their latitu-

Figure 6. Resultset completion times by geographical area

(a) RCT_E, "Unmanaged" RCT_L, and "Managed" RCT_L

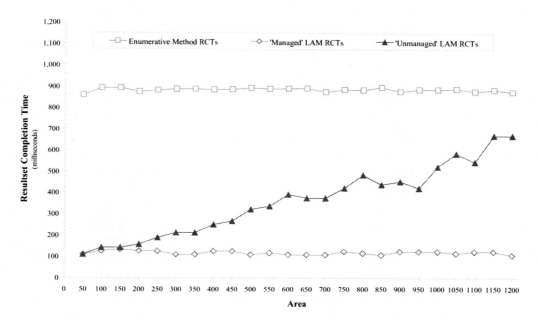

(b) RCT_E and RCT_L at Mean $P_{TC}(S_{OPT})$

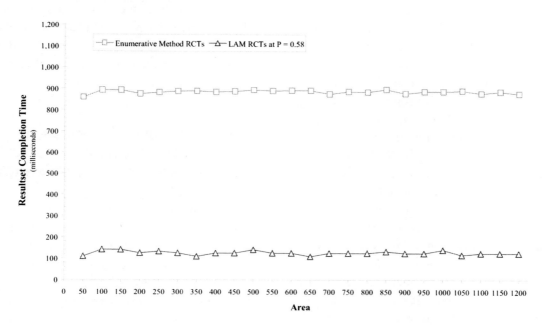

dinal and longitudinal extents (50, 100, 150, ..., 1200). Note that in contrast to the results seen in Figure 5, RCT_E values in this case are essentially invariant with respect to geographical area. A consideration of the enumerative method's procedural details will reveal that although changes in either the number of locations or the number of product-service codes will affect query resolution time, changes in geographical area will not. Changes in geographical area affect the range of values over which the coordinates of locations will vary; however, there is no additional computational burden placed on the enumerative method when different coordinate values are assigned to the same repository locations. Thus, RCT_E values are substantively invariant with respect to geographical area.

Three curves are shown in Figure 6(a): (1) the topmost curve is the result of using the enumerative method; (2) the bottom curve is the result of using the location-aware method and doing so for each area's observed optimal linkcell size; and (3) the middle curve is the result of using the location-aware method with the linkcell size unchanged for all areas from the optimal linkcell size (0.3) for the smallest area. The third curve reflects a circumstance in which linkcell size is set at its optimal value with respect to some arbitrary area and then remains unchanged (unmanaged) as the repository's area of geographical coverage is enlarged. Here, as before, unmanaged linkcell sizes result in query resolution time degradation. As seen from the point on the RCT curve for the largest area, RCT_L eventually reaches 672 ms when linkcell sizes remain unoptimized, a query resolution time that is more than six times the RCT_L of 109 ms for an optimized linkcell size.

The results presented in Figure 6 (a) indicate that in the observed range of geographical coverage, the location-aware method yields query resolution performance that is superior to the enumerative method. However, the results also indicate that linkcell size must be adjusted appropriately in order to maintain this performance

as the area of geographical coverage changes. As previously discussed with respect to repository size, this leads to a consideration of how the burden associated with determining linkcell size optima may be lightened by using the method of assigning sizes with reference to the mean value of $P_{TC}(S_{OPT})$. For the 24 areas associated with the results shown in Figure 6, the mean of $P_{TC}(S_{OPT})$ is 0.58. The bottom curve in Figure 6(b) shows the RCT_L values that result for each of the 24 areas when a linkcell size S is determined by setting Equation (I) =0.58. The curve suggests that as was seen previously for repository size, the application of this method results in linkcell sizes giving query resolution performance that is approximately the same as the performance realized when linkcell sizes are determined by the more cumbersome method of constructing RCT curves at successive incremental linkcell sizes in the region of $S_{0.5}$. Thus, the method of assigning linkcell sizes with reference to the mean value of $P_{TC}(S_{OPT})$ appears to be as useful in the context of variations in geographical area as it is for variations in repository size. Next, the method is assessed with respect to variations in the rate of occurrence of a specific product-service code or, in other words, with respect to using different product-service category sets to qualify repository locations.

LINKCELL SIZE OPTIMA AND TARGETED CATEGORY OCCURRENCE RATE VARIABILITY

Figure 7 plots RCTs for variations in targeted category occurrence rate (TCOR) for a 100,000-location repository whose locations are distributed over a fixed geographical area (the largest of those in Figure 6). TCOR refers to the portion of a repository's locations falling into the product-service category that is targeted by a mobile consumer's query. The results seen previously in Figures 5 and 6 are based on repositories in which

Figure 7. Resultset completion times by targeted category occurrence rate

(a) RCT_E, "Unmanaged" RCT_L, and "Managed" RCT_L

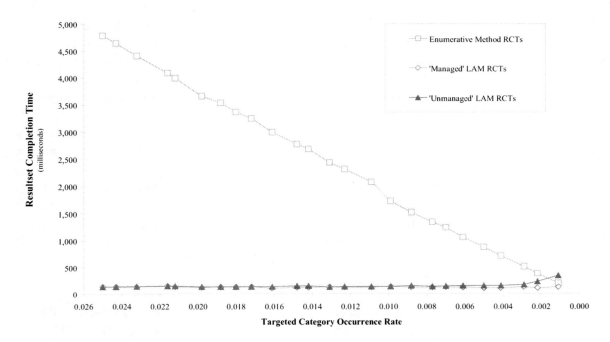

(b) RCT_E and RCT_L at Mean $P_{TC}(S_{OPT})$

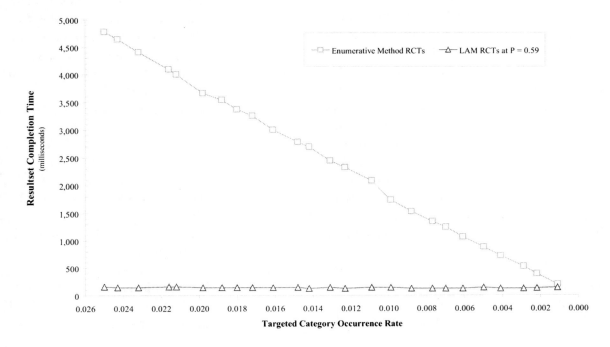

the product-service category attribute for each location was assigned randomly from a set of 200 product-service category codes {C001, C002, ..., C200}. This, in effect, resulted in the rate with which each product-service code occurs across a repository's locations of 1/200 or, equivalently, a fixed TCOR of 0.005. The RCT values shown in Figure 7 correspond to TCOR rates that vary from 0.0250 to 0.0011. The first TCOR value indicates that 0.250 of a repository's locations bear a product-service category code matching a specific consumer-targeted category and corresponds to using a set of 40 product-service codes wherein each code occurs with equal frequency across the repository's locations. The latter TCOR value indicates that 0.0011 of a repository's locations bear a product-service category code matching a specific consumer-targeted category and corresponds to using a set of 909 equally occurring product-service codes.[6]

Figure 7(a) presents the usual three curves: (1) the topmost curve shows enumerative results; (2) the bottom curve shows optimized LAM results; and (3) the middle curve shows unmanaged LAM results. As before, the third curve reflects a circumstance in which linkcell size is set to an optimal value with respect to some initial TCOR value (0.0250, in this case) and then remains unadjusted as TCOR is changed. It is readily seen that in this case, unmanaged linkcell sizes have little appreciable effect on query resolution performance except at the smallest TCOR levels. Not until TCOR reaches 0.002 (500 product-service categories) is there a substantive separation of the two curves. The separation attains a managerially significant level in the vicinity of 0.001 (1,000 product-service categories), in which RCT_L eventually reaches 352 ms, a query resolution time that not only exceeds RCT_E but is also 2.5 times the optimized RCT_L value of 141ms.

As with the analyses respecting repository size and geographical area, TCOR-related analysis also leads to a consideration of how the repository manager's burden associated with determining

linkcell size optima may be lightened by using the method of assigning sizes with reference to the mean value of $P_{TC}(S_{OPT})$. For the 24 TCOR values associated with the results shown in Figure 7, the mean of $P_{TC}(S_{OPT})$ is 0.59. The bottom curve in Figure 7(b) shows the RCT_L values that result for each of the 24 TCOR values when a linkcell size S is derived from Equation (I) = 0.59. The curve suggests, as was seen previously for repository size and geographical area, that the application of this method produces linkcell sizes resulting in query resolution performance that is approximately the same as the performance realized when linkcell sizes are determined by the $S_{0.5}$-method. Thus, the method of assigning linkcell sizes with reference to the mean value of $P_{TC}(S_{OPT})$ appears to be as valid in the TCOR context as it is in the previous two contexts.

LINKCELL SIZE DETERMINATION IN PRACTICAL M-COMMERCE OPERATIONAL CIRCUMSTANCES

The results obtained from the mean value approach to estimating optimal linkcell size in all three contexts, along with the observation that the three mean values (0.63, 0.58, and 0.59) are close to their average value of 0.60, suggest that reasonably valid estimates for optimal linkcell sizes may be obtained for practical purposes in a wide range of circumstances on the basis that:

$$P_{TC}(S) = 1 - (1 - n_{TC}/N)^{N/CS} = 0.6 \qquad (II)$$

The validity of Equation (II)'s use in linkcell size determination was assessed further by revisiting the RCT_L curves with linkcell sizes determined using Equation (II). Doing so yields query resolution performance profiles that are essentially the same as those shown in Figures 5(b), 6(b), and 7(b). Although the linkcell sizes identified through Equation (II) generally differed from those identified by the $S_{0.5}$-method, differences were minimal, and the resulting values for S always fell in a range of linkcell sizes associated with a region of minimal RCT values. Regions in this respect may be discerned in Figures 3 and 4; minimal RCT values are seen in the region in Figure 3 where linkcells vary in size from about 0.8 to 1.2 and in Figure 4 for sizes from about 0.5 to 1.0. These results, along with those seen previously, form the basis for proposing that Equation (II) represents, to this point, a heuristic with some potential to assist repository managers in realizing close-to-optimal query resolution performance and, ultimately, improved support to the location-referent transactions initiated by mobile consumers.

FURTHER WORK

Although the query resolution optimization methods used here appear to be potentially useful in realizing m-commerce service-level improvements, further work is needed in several respects. Preliminary results obtained when the location-aware method is implemented on a different computing platform reveal essentially the same RCT-linkcell size relationships that are reported here but with different RCT values. Such differences are expected and are largely attributable to differences in computational speed; however, further work is needed in order to confirm the validity of the results obtained across a greater variety of computing platforms and operational environments.

Although the major dimensions (repository size, geographical area, product-service category) associated with a location-qualified data repository in an m-commerce operational setting were addressed here, LAM's performance and the methods by which it may be optimized should be assessed in a wider variety of dimensional circumstances. For example, preliminary results from situations in which mobile consumers initiate location-referent queries from locations

that are well beyond a repository's geographical boundaries suggest that values greater than 0.6 should be used to identify optimal linkcell sizes. However, these results also suggest that $P_{TC}(S) \rightarrow 0.6$ as a consumer's geographical position approaches the repository's boundaries. Further work in this respect will validate the method's applicability and assess its performance when repositories with highly localized information are used to support the location-referent queries of remotely located consumers.

Finally, the robustness of $P_{TC}(S)$'s application in circumstances that relax the assumption of a uniform distribution of locations in the same product-service category requires further examination. Product and service providers of similar type often choose locations in a non-independent, proximal fashion (e.g., law firms in legal districts, fast-food services in shopping mall food courts, retail petroleum outlets at highway intersections, etc.). Consequently, pending the outcome of further research in this respect, the use of uniform distributions of locations should be considered an important limitation on the applicability of this study's results in practical mcommerce operational settings.

CONCLUSION

Although any application of the research reported here must be done with an appreciation of its limitations and/or await the outcome of further work, the results obtained address to varying extents the four questions posed at the beginning of this article. With respect to question (1), the query resolution performance profiles observed in previous work for an invariant linkcell size are not inconsistent with those observed here. However, the present study's variant linkcell size combined with its examination of larger repository sizes, variability in geographical area, and differing product-service code sets permitted the observation of appreciable performance degradation in unmanaged circumstances. With respect to question (2), the relationship of query resolution time to linkcell size reflects the varying dominance of two types of retrieval tasks: (1) the processing of relatively large numbers of generally smaller relational tables when linkcell sizes are small and (2) the processing of relatively small numbers of generally larger relational tables when linkcell sizes are large. The interplay of the two retrieval task types consistently produces U-shaped performance curves similar to those presented earlier in this article.

With respect to question (3), the U-shaped relationship between query resolution time and linkcell size always revealed a distinct minima or narrow region of minima indicative of the existence of a specific linkcell size that could be associated with maximum query resolution performance. Finally, with respect to question (4), the optimal linkcell size may be determined in three ways: (1) by brute force, (2) by the $S_{0.5}$-method, and (3) by solving for S such that $P_{TC}(S)$ = 0.6. While the first two linkcell size determination methods were effective in revealing optimal linkcell sizes, the logistics associated with their application limits the feasibility of their deployment in practical mcommerce settings. The third method is considerably less burdensome to deploy, and results suggest that it is a useful linkcell size determination heuristic; however, further work is needed in order to assess its robustness in the face of departures from underlying assumptions and its predictive ability in a wider range of mcommerce circumstances.

REFERENCES

Arnon, A., Efrat, A., Indyk, P., & Samet, H. (1999, October 17-19). Efficient regular data structures and algorithms for location and proximity problems. *Proceedings of the 40th Annual Symposium on Foundations of Computer Science*, New York (pp. 160-170).

Butz, A.R. (1969, May). Convergence with Hilbert's space-filling curve. *Journal of Computer and System Sciences, 3,* 128-146.

Butz, A.R. (1971, April). Alternative algorithm for Hilbert's space-filling curve. *IEEE Transactions on Computers, C-20,* 424-426.

Butz, A., Bauss, J., & Kruger, A. (2000). *Different views on location awareness.* Retrieved September 16, 2005, from http://www.coli.uni-sb.de/sfb378/1999-2001/publications/butzetal2000d-de.html

Cary, M. (2001). Towards optimal ε-approximate nearest neighbor algorithms. *Journal of Algorithms, 41*(2), 417-428.

Chao, C.-M., Tseng, Y.-C., & Wang, L.-C. (2005). Dynamic bandwidth allocation for multimedia traffic with rate guarantee and fair access in WCDMA systems. *IEEE Transactions on Mobile Computing, 4*(5), 420-429.

Chou, C.-T., & Shin, K. (2005). An enhanced inter-access point protocol for uniform intra and intersubnet handoffs. *IEEE Transactions on Mobile Computing, 4*(4), 321-334.

Choy, M., Kwan, M.-P., & Hong, V. (2000). Distributed database design for mobile geographical applications. *Journal of Database Management, 11*(1), 3-15.

Cinque, M., Cotroneo, D., & Russo, S. (2005). Achieving all the time, everywhere access in next-generation mobile networks. *ACM SIGMOBILE Mobile Computing and Communications Review, 9*(2), 29-39.

Gebauer, J., & Shaw, M. (2004). Success factors and impacts of mobile business applications: Results from a mobile e-procurement study. *International Journal of Electronic Commerce, 8*(3), 19-41.

Huang, S.-M., Lin, B., & Deng, Q.-S. (2005). Intelligent cache management for mobile data warehouse systems. *Journal of Database Management, 16*(2), 46-65.

Khungar, S., & Reikki, J. (2005). A context based storage system for mobile computing applications. *ACM SIGMOBILE Mobile Computing and Communications Review, 9*(1), 64-68.

Kottkamp, H.-E., & Zukunft, O. (1998, February 27-March 1). Location-aware query processing in mobile database systems. *Proceedings of the 1998 ACM Symposium on Applied Computing*, Atlanta, Georgia (pp. 416-423).

Kuznetsov, V.E. (2000). Method for storing map data in a database using space filling curves and a method of searching the database to find objects in a given area and to find objects nearest to a location. United States Patent Number 6,021,406, issued February 1, 2000.

Lee, C., & Ke, C.-H. (2001). A prediction-based query processing strategy in mobile commerce systems. *Journal of Database Management, 12*(3), 14-26.

Lee, D. (1999). Computational geometry II. In M. Atallah (Ed.), *Algorithms and theory of computation handbook* (pp. 20-1–20-31). Boca Raton, FL: CRC Press.

Lee, D., Xu, J., Zheng, B., & Lee, W.-C. (2002, July-September). Data management in location-dependent information services. *IEEE Pervasive Computing, 1*(3), 65-72.

Lee, D., Zhu, M., & Hu, H. (2005). When location-based services meet databases. *Mobile Information Systems, 1*(2), 81-90.

Lee, E., & Benbasat, I. (2004). A framework for the study of customer interface design for mobile commerce. *International Journal of Electronic Commerce, 8*(3), 79-102.

Leung, K., & Atypas, J. (2001). Improving returns on m-commerce investments. *The Journal of Business Strategy, 22*(5), 12-13.

Lin, H.-P., Juang, R.-T., & Lin, D.-B. (2005). Validation of an improved location-based handover algorithm using GSM measurement data. *IEEE Transactions on Mobile Computing, 4*(5), 530-536.

McGuire, M., Plataniotis, K., & Venetsanopoulos, A. (2005). Data fusion of power and time measurements for mobile terminal location. *IEEE Transactions on Mobile Computing, 4*(2), 142-153.

Nievergelt, J., & Widmayer, P. (1997). Spatial data structures: Concepts and design choices. In M. van Kreveld, J. Nievergelt, T. Roos, & P. Widmayer (Eds.), *Algorithmic foundations of geographic information systems* (pp. 153-197). Berlin: Springer Verlag.

Quintero, A. (2005). A user pattern learning strategy for managing users' mobility in UMTS networks. *IEEE Transactions on Mobile Computing, 4*(6), 552-566.

Samaan, N., & Karmouch, A. (2005). A mobility prediction architecture based on contextual knowledge and spatial conceptual maps. *IEEE Transactions on Mobile Computing, 4*(6), 537-551.

Santami, A., Leow, T., Lim, H., & Goh, P. (2003). Overcoming barriers to the successful adoption of mobile commerce in Singapore. *International Journal of Mobile Communications, 1*(1/2), 194-231.

Siau, K., Lim, E., & Shen, Z. (2001). Mobile commerce: Promises, challenges, and research agenda. *Journal of Database Management, 12*(3), 4-13.

Siau, K., & Shen, Z. (2003). Mobile communications and mobile services. *International Journal of Mobile Communications, 1*(1/2), 3-14.

Sierpinski, W. (1912). Sur une novelle courbe continue qui remplit tout une aire plaine. *Bulletin International De L'Academie Des Sciences de Cracovie, A*, 462-478.

Wyse, J. (2003). Supporting m-commerce transactions incorporating locational attributes: An evaluation of the comparative performance of a location-aware method of locations repository management. *International Journal of Mobile Communications, 1*(1/2), 119-147.

Xu, L., Shen, X., & Mark, J. (2005). Fair resource allocation with guaranteed statistical QoS for multimedia traffic in a wideband CDMA cellular network. *IEEE Transactions on Mobile Computing, 4*(2), 166-177.

Yeung, M., & Kwok, Y.-K. (2005). Wireless cache invalidation schemes with link adaptation and downlink traffic. *IEEE Transactions on Mobile Computing, 4*(1), 68-83.

Yuan, Y., & Zhang, J. (2003). Towards an appropriate business model for m-commerce. *International Journal of Mobile Communications, 1*(1/2), 35-56.

ENDNOTES

[1]   Resultset Completion (RCT) is the time required to extract a set of repository locations that represents a resolution of a consumer-initiated query.

[2]   The Enumerative Method of query resolution used both in Wyse's (2003) work and in the work here is a method that (1) selects repository locations in the consumer-targeted, product-service category, (2) calculates consumer-relative distances for each of the selected locations, (3) orders the selected locations in ascending order by consumer-relative distance, and (4) presents the first N ordered locations as the resultset that resolves the consumer's query about the nearest N locations (N = 3, in the case of Figure 2).

[3]   Wyse (2003) used mean RCT values as the primary statistic to measure query resolution performance. The work here has chosen to use 50th percentile RCT values as the primary performance measurement statistic, a choice that (1) minimizes the disproportionate impact of the infrequent occurrence of very large query resolution times and (2) is consistent with widely used approaches to measuring and monitoring the response time performance for computer-based transaction processing.

[4]   Formally, the number of linkcells C_S for linkcell size S is given by:

$$C_S = ([UVL/S] - [LVL/S] + 1) \, ([LHL/S] - [RHL/S] + 1)$$

where UVL and LVL represent the upper and lower limits, respectively, of the vertical extent of the geographical area covered by the repository's locations, and LHL and RHL represent the left and right limits, respectively, of the area's horizontal extent. Note that [ ] denotes the greatest integer function.

[5]   The phrase *close to* is used deliberately, since the integrally valued components of $P_{TC}(S)$, primarily C_S, result in values for $P_{TC}(S)$ that rarely will equal 0.5.

[6]   Two observations with respect to Figure 7 are worthy of note: (1) query resolution times are measured at unequal TCOR intervals, and (2) RCT_E values decline as TCORs become smaller (or, equivalently, product-service code sets become larger). With respect to the first observation, the TCOR value of 0.0011 (or 909 equally occurring product-service codes) resulted when LPA was supplied with a TCOR of 0.0010 (or 1,000 equally occurring product-service codes) and then asked to generate a repository in which locations are randomly assigned a product-service code. This randomized assignment results in realized (or output) TCORs that are close to, but generally different from,

supplied (or input) TCORs. Thus, unlike the RCT values seen in Figures 5 and 6, those in Figure 7 generally do not occur at equal intervals. With respect to the second observation, note that increases in the number of product-service codes for a given repository size will result in fewer repository locations in each product-service category, including the category matching the category criteria on a consumer's query. A consideration of

the enumerative method's procedural details will reveal that this circumstance results in fewer instances in which consumer-relative distances must be determined as well as in smaller resultsets that must be sorted. Thus, as TCORs become smaller, the enumerative method completes its work faster, an outcome reflected in the downward sloping curve for RCT_E.

APPENDIX A: THE LOCATION-AWARE METHOD (LAM)

A synopsis of LAM's fundamental components is given in the following with respect to (1) the requisite structure of a location-qualified data repository, (2) a formulation of the linkcell construct, (3) the general tasks of linkcell management (creation, modification, and destruction), and (4) the method's linkcell-based retrieval process. Although LAM's essentials are disclosed here, many of the method's details are not presented. A more comprehensive description may be found in Wyse (2003).

Repository Structure: The solution approach assumes that the location-qualified data repository is a relational database table containing a tuple for each repository location minimally consisting of four attributes: (1) a unique identifier for the location; (2) a horizontal coordinate (e.g., the location's longitude); (3) a vertical coordinate (e.g., the location's latitude); and (4) a code that qualifies each location in terms of its product or service offering. Table A1 provides a sample repository segment.

The Linkcell Construct: LAM relies on a set of auxiliary relational tables referred to as linkcells, which contain subsets of repository content and take relational table names derived from the coordinates of repository locations. Figure A1 illustrates the relationship between a repository's locations and its linkcells. Linkcells are generated based on the existence of repository locations within the area covered by the linkcell. A linkcell's name is derived from the coordinates of any location situated within the linkcell. In order to illustrate how this is accomplished, note L_i's coordinates in Figure A1. Truncating the fractional part of each coordinate yields the linkcell name. Thus, the name for the linkcell containing location L_i is H07V02. The same linkcell name also would be derived from the other two locations contained in the linkcell with L_i.

Formally, a linkcell with the relational table name $H_{NN}V_{MM}$ will contain all repository locations with horizontal coordinate values $H_{NN}.0$ through $H_{NN}.999\cdots$ and vertical coordinate values $V_{MM}.0$ through $V_{MM}.999\cdots$. Each linkcell in its relational table form contains a tuple for each of the repository locations encompassed by the linkcell's

Table A1. Repository segment

Location Identifier	Horizontal Coordinate	Vertical Coordinate	Category Code
•	•	•	•
•	•	•	•
•	•	•	•
L0340	W112.91761	N40.71098	C001
L0341	W089.45995	N49.70451	C007
L0342	W097.81718	N47.78187	C014
L0343	W076.55539	N45.00473	C013
•	•	•	•
•	•	•	•

Figure A1. Locations and linkcells

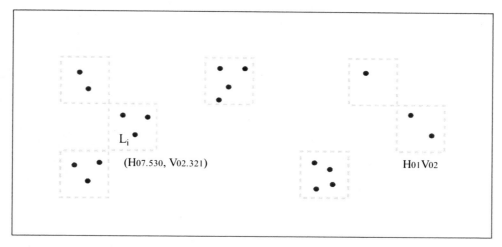

Source: Wyse (2003), p. 125. Reproduced with the permission of Inderscience Publishers.

boundaries. Linkcells, manifested as relational tables, could appear as shown in Table A2 (with longitudes treated as horizontal coordinates and latitudes treated as vertical coordinates).

Linkcells may be varied in size through co-ordinate scaling. For example, if L_i's positional coordinates are scaled by 10, for example, from (H07.530, V02.321) to (H075.30, V023.21), then L_i's linkcell name becomes H075V023, and the linkcell now relates to a smaller geographical area. The smaller area in this instance consists of vertical and horizontal extents that are 1/10th of the respective extents of the original linkcell. (It also should be noted that the coordinate scaling factor for a linkcell's horizontal component may differ from the factor used for its vertical component.) The use of a different linkcell size does not affect the relative positions of a repository's locations; however, using a different linkcell size results in a redistribution of a repository's locations among the linkcells. As seen in the results reported here, redistributions attributable to changes in linkcell

size often have a substantial impact on query resolution performance.

Linkcell Creation, Modification, and Destruction: Whenever a location is added to the repository, a linkcell name is derived from the location's horizontal and vertical coordinates. The derived name is used in order to query the repository about the existence of a corresponding linkcell (relational table). If the linkcell exists, the location's identifier and category code are placed in the linkcell. If the linkcell does not exist, it is created using the name derived from the location's coordinates, and then, the location's identifier and category code are placed in the newly created linkcell. Whenever a location is removed from the repository, a linkcell name is derived from the location's coordinates. Since the location had been previously added to the repository, it is assumed that a linkcell with the derived name already exists. If the location to be removed is the only remaining location in the linkcell, then the linkcell is destroyed. If the linkcell contains

Table A2. Linkcells as relational tables

Linkcell: W112N40	
Location Id	Category Code
L0340	C001
L0736	C016
L2043	C010
L2063	C010

Linkcell: W089N49	
Location Id	Category Code
L0341	C007
L4028	C011

Linkcell: W097N47	
Location Id	Category Code
L0342	C014
L0856	C006
L1021	C001
L1326	C004
L1593	C006
L2148	C016

other location identifiers, then only the attribute tuple for the location to be removed is deleted, and the linkcell is not destroyed. Thus, linkcells (manifested as relational tables) are created, destroyed, and modified dynamically, based on repository changes.

Retrieval Procedure: The procedure relies on two types of linkcells: (1) the Core Linkcell and (2) the Cursor Linkcell. The Core Linkcell obtains its name using the method described previously but not from the coordinates of any repository location; instead, from the coordinates of the

Figure A2. LAM retrieval procedure — Cursor linkcell's naming sequence

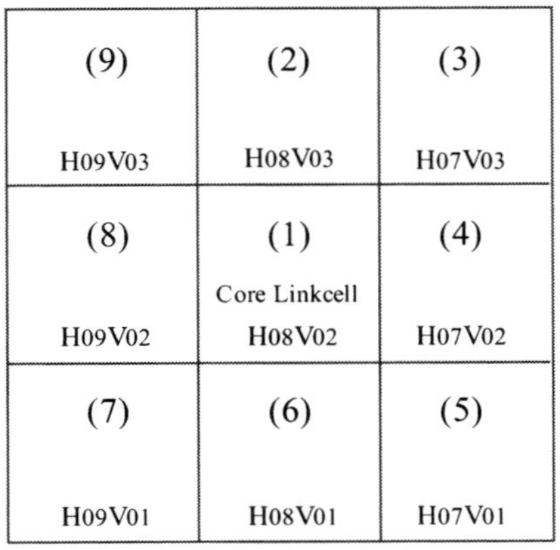

(9)	(2)	(3)
H09V03	H08V03	H07V03
(8)	(1) Core Linkcell	(4)
H09V02	H08V02	H07V02
(7)	(6)	(5)
H09V01	H08V01	H07V01

Source: Wyse (2003), p. 128. Reproduced with the permission of Inderscience Publishers.

consumer's location. The structure of the linkcell construct and its manifestation as a relational table implies that once the Core Linkcell's name is obtained, the search procedure is immediately aware of the existence or non-existence of any repository locations in the immediate vicinity of the consumer. Once derived, the Core Linkcell name remains unchanged; however, the Cursor Linkcell takes on a sequence of linkcell names that effectively moves it in search of other locations in the vicinity of the consumer.

The procedure begins by setting the Cursor Linkcell name to the Core Linkcell name and then checking for the existence of a linkcell with the same name as the Cursor Linkcell. If the linkcell exists, its contents are examined for locations with a category code equal to that sought by the query. When a sought-after location is found, its attributes are placed in the query's resultset. The procedure then expands the search area by generating a sequence of Cursor Linkcell names.

This is done by systematically changing the numeric sections of the Cursor Linkcell's name using a sequence that "moves" the Cursor Linkcell around the Core Linkcell in a clockwise pattern. Whenever the Cursor Linkcell is assigned a new name, it checks for the existence of a linkcell with its currently assigned name. If the linkcell exists, then its contents are examined, and the actions outlined previously are performed, resulting in further locations being accumulated in the query resultset. The numbers in parenthesis in Figure A2 indicate the sequence in which relational table names are generated and examined in the course of a clockwise movement of the Cursor Linkcell. The search area may be expanded further by moving the Cursor Linkcell through a layer of linkcells on the outer periphery of the linkcells previously examined. This outward-spiraling, clockwise-moving process continues until the sought-after number of locations is found.

This work was previously published in the Journal of Database Management, edited by K. Siau, Volume 17, Issue 3, pp. 41-65, copyright 2006 by IGI Publishing, formerly known as Idea Group Publishing (an imprint of IGI Global).

Chapter 7.35
Data Dissemination in Mobile Environments

Panayotis Fouliras
University of Macedonia, Greece

ABSTRACT

Data dissemination today represents one of the cornerstones of network-based services and even more so for mobile environments. This becomes more important for large volumes of multimedia data such as video, which have the additional constraints of speedy, accurate, and isochronous delivery often to thousands of clients. In this chapter, we focus on video streaming with emphasis on the mobile environment, first outlining the related issues and then the most important of the existing proposals employing a simple but concise classification. New trends are included such as overlay and p2p network-based methods. The advantages and disadvantages for each proposal are also presented so that the reader can better appreciate their relative value.

INTRODUCTION

A well-established fact throughout history is that many social endeavors require dissemination of information to a large audience in a fast, reliable, and cost-effective way. For example, mass education could not have been possible without paper and typography. Therefore, the main factors for the success of any data dissemination effort are supporting technology and low cost.

The rapid evolution of computers and networks has allowed the creation of the Internet with a myriad of services, all based on rapid and low cost data dissemination. During recent years, we have witnessed a similar revolution in mobile devices, both in relation to their processing power as well as their respective network infrastructure. Typical representatives of such networks are the 802.11x for LANs and GSM for WANs.

In this context, it is not surprising that the main effort has been focusing on the dissemination of multimedia content–especially audio and video, since the popularity of such services is high, with RTP the de-facto protocol for multimedia data transfer on the Internet. Although both audio and video have strict requirements in terms of packet jitter (the variability of packet delays within the same packet stream), video additionally requires significant amount of bandwidth due to its data size. Moreover, a typical user requires multimedia to be played in real-time, (i.e., shortly after his request, instead of waiting for the complete file to be downloaded; this is commonly referred to as *multimedia streaming*.

In most cases, it is assumed that the item in demand is already stored at some server(s) from where the clients may request it. Nevertheless, if the item is popular and the client population very large, additional methods must be devised in order to avoid a possible drain of available resources. Simple additional services such as fast forward (FF) and rewind (RW) are difficult to support, let alone interactive video. Moreover, the case of asymmetric links (different upstream and downstream bandwidth) can introduce more problems. Also, if the item on demand is not previously stored but represents an ongoing event, many of the proposed techniques are not feasible.

In the case of mobile networks, the situation is further aggravated, since the probability of packet loss is higher and the variation in device capabilities is larger than in the case of desktop computers. Furthermore, ad-hoc networks are introduced, where it is straightforward to follow the bazaar model, under which a client may enter a wall mart and receive or even exchange videos in real time from other clients, such as specially targeted promotions, based on its profile. Such a model complicates the problem even further.

In this chapter, we are focusing on video streaming, since video is the most popular and demanding multimedia data type (Sripanidkul-chai, Ganjam, Maggs, & Zhang, 2004). In the following sections, we are identifying the key issues, present metrics to measure the efficiency of some of the most important proposals and perform a comparative evaluation in order to provide an adequate guide to the appropriate solutions.

ISSUES

As stated earlier, streaming popular multimedia content with large size such as video has been a challenging problem, since a large client population demands the same item to be delivered and played out within a short period of time. This period should be smaller that the time t_w a client would be willing to wait after it made its request. Typically there are on average a constant number of requests over a long time period, which suggests that a single broadcast should suffice for each batch of requests. However, the capabilities of all entities involved (server, clients, and network) are finite and often of varying degree (e.g., effective available network and client bandwidth). Hence the issues and challenges involved can be summarized as follows:

- What should the broadcasting schedule of the server be so that the maximum number of clients' requests is satisfied without having them wait more than t_w?
- How can overall network bandwidth be minimized?
- How can the network infrastructure be minimally affected?
- How can the clients assist if at all?
- What are the security considerations?

In the case of mobile networks, the mobile devices are the clients; the rest of the network typically is static, leading to a mixed, hybrid result. Nevertheless, there are exceptions to this rule, such as the ad hoc networks. Hence, for mobile clients there are some additional issues:

- Mobile clients may leave or appear to leave a session due to higher probability of packet loss. How does such a system recover from this situation?

- How can redirection (or *handoff*) take place without any disruption in play out quality?
- How can the bazaar model be accommodated?

BACKGROUND

In general, without prior knowledge on how the data is provided by the server, a client has to send a request to the server. The server then either directly delivers the data (on demand service) or replies with the broadcast channel access information (e.g., channel identifier, estimated access time, etc.). In the latter case, if the mobile client decides so, it monitors the broadcast channels (Hu, Lee, & Lee, 1998). In both cases, there have been many proposals, many of which are also suitable for mobile clients. Nevertheless, many proposals regarding mobile networks are not suitable for the multimedia dissemination. For example, Coda is a file replication system, Bayou a database replication system and Roam a slightly more scalable general file replication system (Ratner, Reiher, & Popek, 2004), all of which do not assume strict temporal requirements.

The basic elements which comprise a dissemination system are the server(s), the clients, and the intermittent network. Depending on which of these is the focus, the various proposals can be classified into two broad categories: Proposals regarding the server organization and its broadcast schedule, and those regarding modifications in the intermittent network or client model of computation and communication.

Proposals According to Server Organization and Broadcasting Schedule

Let us first examine the various proposals in terms of the server(s) organization and broadcasting schedule. These can be classified in two broad classes, namely *push*-based scheduling (or *proactive*) and *pull*-based scheduling (or *reactive*). Under the first class, the clients continuously monitor the broadcast process from the server and retrieve the required data without explicit requests, whereas under the second class the clients make explicit requests which are used by the server to make a schedule which satisfies them. Typically, a hybrid combination of the two is employed with push-based scheduling for popular and pull-based scheduling for less popular items (Guo, Das, & Pinotti, 2001).

Proposals for Popular Videos

For the case of pushed-based scheduling broadcasting schedules of the so-called *periodic broadcasting* type are usually employed: The server organizes each item in segments of appropriate size, which it broadcasts periodically. Interested clients simply start downloading from the beginning of the first segment and play it out immediately. The clients must be able to preload some segments of the item and be capable of downlink bandwidth higher than that for a single video stream. Obviously this scheme works for popular videos, assuming there is adequate bandwidth at the server in relation to the amount and size of items broadcasted.

Pyramid broadcasting (PB) (Viswanathan & Imielinski, 1995) has been the first proposal in this category. Here, each client is capable of downloading from up to two channels simultaneously. The video is segmented in s segments of increasing size, so that $s_{i+1}=\alpha \cdot s_i$, where $\alpha = \frac{B}{MK}$ and B is the total server bandwidth expressed in terms of the minimum bandwidth b_{min} required to play out a single item, M the total number of videos and K the total number of virtual server channels. Each channel broadcasts a separate segment of the same video periodically, at a speed higher than b_{min}. Thus, with $M=4$, $K=4$ and $B=32$, we have $\alpha=2$, which means that each successive segment is twice the size of the previous one. Each segment is broadcasted continuously from a dedicated channel as depicted in Figure 1. In our example, each server channel has bandwidth $B'=B/K=8 \cdot b_{min}$, which means that the clients must have a download bandwidth of $16 \cdot b_{min}$.

If D is the duration of the video, then the waiting time of a client is at most $M \cdot s_1/B'$. With $D = 120$ and $K = M = 4$, we have $M \cdot s_1/B' = 4 \cdot 8/8 = 4$ time units. Each segment from the first channel requires 1 time unit to be downloaded, but has a play out time of 8 units. Consider the case that a client requests video 1 at the time indicated by the thick vertical arrow. Here the first three segments to be downloaded are indicated by small grey rectangles. By the time the client has played out half of the first segment from channel 1 it will start downloading the second segment from channel 2 and so on. The obvious drawback of this scheme is that it requires a very large download

bandwidth at the client as well as a large buffer to store the preloaded segments (as high as 70% of the video).

In order to address these problems, other methods have been proposed, such as *permutation-based pyramid broadcasting* (PPB) (Aggarwal, Wolf, & Yu, 1996) and *skyscraper broadcasting* (SB) (Hua & Sheu, 1997). Under PPB each of the K channels is multiplexed into P subchannels with P times lower rate, where the client may alternate the selection of subchannel during download. However, the buffer requirements are still high (about 50% of the video) and synchronization is difficult. Under SB, two channels are used for downloading, but with a rate equal to the playing rate B_{min}. Relative segment sizes are 1, 2, 2, 5, 5, 12, 12, 25, 25,...W, where W the width of the skyscraper. This leads to much lower demand on the client, but is inefficient in terms of server bandwidth. The latter goal is achieved by *fast broadcasting* (FB) (Juhn & Tseng, 1998) which

Figure 1. Example of pyramid broadcasting with 4 videos and 4 channels

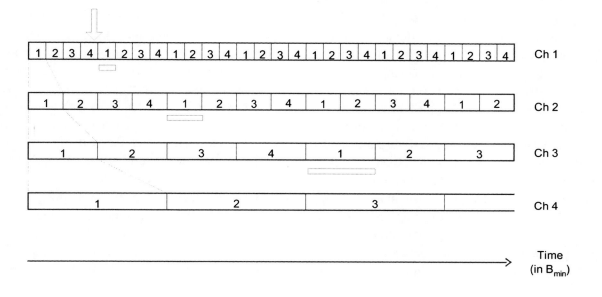

divides the video into segments of geometric series, with K channels of B_{min} bandwidth, but where the clients download from *all K* channels.

Yet another important variation is *harmonic broadcasting* (HB) (Juhn & Tseng, 1997) which divides the video in segments of equal size and broadcasts them on K successive channels of bandwidth B_{min}/i, where $i = 1, \ldots K$. The client downloads from all channels as soon as the first segment has started downloading. The client download bandwidth is thus equal to the server's and the buffer requirements low (about 37% of the total video). However, the timing requirements may not be met, which is a serious drawback. Other variations exist that solve this problem with the same requirements (Paris, Carter, & Long, 1998) or are hybrid versions of the schemes discussed so far, with approximately the same cost in resources as well as efficiency.

Proposals for Less Popular Videos or Varying Request Pattern

In the case of less popular videos or of a varying request pattern pulled-based or reactive methods are more appropriate. More specifically, the server gathers clients' requests within a specific time interval $t_{in} < t_w$. In the simplest case all requests are for the beginning of the same video, although they may be for different videos or for different parts of the same video (e.g., after a FF or RW). For each group (*batch*) of similar requests a new broadcast is scheduled by reserving a separate server channel, (*batching*). With a video duration t_D a maximum of $\lceil t_D/t_{in} \rceil$ server channels are required for a single video assuming multicast.

The most important proposals for *static* multicast batching are: *first-come-first-served* (FCFS) where the oldest batch is served first, *maximum-queue-length-first* (MQLF) where the batch containing the largest amount of requests is served first, reducing average system throughput by being unfair and *maximum-factor-queue-length* (MFQL) where the batch containing the largest

amount of requests for some video weighted by the factor $1/\sqrt{f_i}$ is selected, where f_i is the access frequency of the particular video. In this way the popular videos are not always favored (Hua, Tantaoui, & Tavanapong, 2004).

A common drawback of the proposals above is that client requests which miss a particular video broadcasting schedule cannot hope for a reasonably quick service time, in a relatively busy server. Hence, *dynamic* multicast proposals have emerged, which allow the existing multicast tree for the same video to be extended in order to include late requests. The most notable proposals are *patching, bandwidth skimming,* and *chaining*.

Patching (Hua, Cai, & Sheu, 1998) and its variations allow a late client to join an existing multicast stream and buffer it, while simultaneously the missing portion is delivered by the server via a separate patching stream. The latter is of short duration, thus quickly releasing the bandwidth used by the server. Should the clients arrive towards the end of the normal stream broadcast, a new normal broadcast is scheduled instead of a patch one. In more recent variations it is also possible to have double patching, where a patching stream is created on top of a previous patching stream, but requires more bandwidth on both the client(s) and the server and synchronization is more difficult to achieve.

The main idea in Bandwidth Skimming (Eager, Vernon, & Zahorjan, 2000) is for clients to download a multicast stream, while reserving a small portion of their download bandwidth (*skim*) in order to listen to the closest active stream other than theirs. In this way, hierarchical merging of the various streams is possible to achieve. It has been shown that it is better than patching in terms of server bandwidth utilization, though more complex to implement.

Chaining (Sheu, Hua, & Tavanapong, 1997) on the other hand is essentially a pipeline of clients, operating in a peer-to-peer scheme, where the server is at the root of the pipeline. New clients are added at the bottom of the tree, receiving the first portion of the requested video. If an appropriate pipeline does not exist, a new one is created by having the server feed the new clients directly. This scheme reduces the server bandwidth and is scalable, but it requires a collaborative environment and implementation is a challenge, especially for clients who are in the middle of a pipeline and suddenly lose network connection or simply decide to withdraw. It also requires substantial upload bandwidth to exist at the clients, so it is not generally suitable for asymmetric connections.

Proposals According to Network and Client Organization

Proxies and Content Distribution Networks

Proxies have been used for decades for delivering all sorts of data and especially on the Web, with considerable success. Hence there have been proposals for their use for multimedia dissemination. Actually, some of the p2p proposals discussed later represent a form of proxies, since they cache part of the data they receive for use by their peers. A more general form of this approach, however, involves dedicated proxies strategically placed so that they are more effective.

Wang, Sen, Adler, and Towsley, (2004) base their proposal on the principle of prefix proxy cache allocation in order to reduce the aggregate network bandwidth cost and startup delays at the clients. Although they report substantial savings in transmission cost, this is based on the assumption that all clients request a video from its beginning.

A more comprehensive study based on Akamai's streaming network appears in (Sripanidkulchai, Ganjam, Maggs, & Zhang, 2004). The latter is a static overlay composed of edge nodes located close to the clients and intermediate nodes that take streams from the original content publisher and split and replicate them to the edge nodes. This scheme effectively constitutes a content distribution network (CDN), used not only for multimedia, but other traffic as well. It is reported that under several techniques and assumptions tested, application end-point architectures have enough resources, inherent stability and can support large-scale groups. Hence, such proposals (including p2p) are promising for real-world applications. Client buffers and uplink bandwidth can contribute significantly if it is possible to use them.

Multicast Overlay Networks

Most of the proposals so far work for multicast broadcasts. This suggests that the network infrastructure supports IP multicasting completely. Unfortunately, most routers in the Internet do not support multicast routing. As the experience from MBone (multicast backbone) (Kurose, & Ross, 2004) shows, an overlay virtual network interconnecting "islands" of multicasting-capable routers must be established over the existing Internet using the rest of the routers as end-points of "tunnels." Nevertheless, since IP multicasting is still a best effort service and therefore unsuitable for multimedia streaming, appropriate reservation of resources at the participating routers is necessary. The signaling protocol of choice is RSVP under which potential receivers signal their intention to join the multicast tree. This is a de-facto part of the Intserv mechanism proposed by IETF. However, this solution does not scale well. A similar proposal but with better scaling is DiffServ which has still to be deployed in numbers (Kurose, & Ross, 2004).

A more recent trend is to create an overlay multicast network at the application layer, using unicast transmissions. Although worse than pure multicast in theory, it has been an active area of research due to its relative simplicity, scalability and the complete absence of necessity for modifications at the network level. Thus, the complexity is now placed at the end points, (i.e., the participating clients and server(s)) and the popular point-to-point (p2p) computation model can be employed in most cases. Asymmetric connections must still include uplink connections of adequate bandwidth in order to support the p2p principle.

Variations include P2Cast (Guo, Suh, Kurose, & Towsley, 2003) which essentially is patching in the p2p environment: Late clients receive the patch stream(s) from old clients, by having two download streams, namely the normal and the patch stream. Any failure of the parent involves the source (the initial server), which makes the whole mechanism vulnerable and prone to bottlenecks.

ZigZag (Tran, Hua, & Do, 2003) creates a logical hierarchy of clusters of peers, with each member at a bounded distance from each other and one of them the cluster leader. The name of this technique emanates from the fact that the leader of each cluster forwards data only to peers in different clusters from its own. An example is shown in Figure 2, where there are 16 peers, organized in clusters of four at level 0. One peer from each cluster is the cluster leader or *head* (additionally depicted for clarity) at level 1. The main advantages of ZigZag are the small height of the multicast tree and the amount of data and control

traffic at the server. However, leader failures can cause significant disruption, since both data and control traffic pass through a leader.

LEMP (Fouliras, Xanthos, Tsantalis., & Manitsaris, 2004) is a another variation which forms a simple overlay multicast tree with an upper bound on the number of peers receiving data from their parent. However, each level of the multicast tree forms a virtual cluster where one peer is the local representative (LR) and another peer is its backup, both initially selected by the server. Most of the control traffic remains at the same level between the LR and the rest of the peers. Should the LR fail, the backup takes its place, selecting a new backup. All new clients are assigned by the server to an additional level under the most recent or form a new level under the server with a separate broadcast. Furthermore, special care has been made for the case of frequent disconnections and re-connections, typical for mobile environments; peers require a single downlink channel at play rate and varying, but bounded uplink channels. This scheme has better response to failures and shorter trees than ZigZag, but for very populous levels there can be some bottleneck for the light control traffic at the LR.

Figure 2. ZigZag: Example multicast tree of peers (3 layers, 4 peers per cluster)

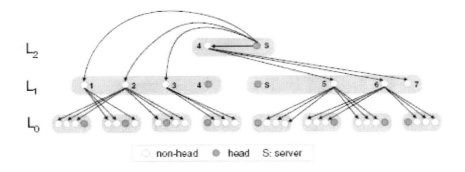

Other Proposals

Most of the existing proposals have been designed without taking into consideration the issues specific to mobile networks. Therefore, there has recently been considerable interest for research in this area. Most of the proposed solutions, however, are simple variations of the proposals presented already. This is natural, since the network infrastructure is typically static and only clients are mobile. The main exception to this rule comes from ad hoc networks.

Add hoc networks are more likely to show packet loss, due to the unpredictable behavior of all or most of the participant nodes. For this reason there has been considerable research effort to address this particular problem, mostly by resorting to multipath routing, since connectivity is less likely to be broken along multiple paths. For example, (Zhu, Han, & Girod, 2004) elaborate on this scheme, by proposing a suitable objective function which determines the appropriate rate allocation among multiple routes. In this way congestion is also avoided considerably, providing better results at the receiver. Also (Wei, & Zakhor, 2004) propose a multipath extension to an existing on-demand source routing protocol (DSR), where the packet carries the end-to-end information in its header and a route discovery process is initiated in case of problems and (Wu, & Huang, 2004) for the case of heterogeneous wireless networks.

All these schemes work reasonably well for small networks, but their scalability is questionable, since they have been tested for small size networks.

COMPARATIVE EVALUATION

We assume that the play out duration t_D of the item on demand is in general longer than at least an order of magnitude compared to t_w. Furthermore, we assume that the arrival of client requests is a Poisson distribution and that the popularity of items stored at the server follows the Zipf distribution. These assumptions are in line with those appearing in most of the proposals.

In order to evaluate the various proposals we need to define appropriate metrics. More specifically:

- Item access time: this should be smaller than t_w as detailed previously
- The bandwidth required at the server as a function of client requests
- The download and upload bandwidth required at a client expressed in units of the minimum bandwidth b_{min} for playing out a single item
- The minimum buffer size required at a client
- The maximum delay during redirection, if at all; obviously this should not exceed the remainder in the client's buffer
- The overall network bandwidth requirements
- Network infrastructure modification; obviously minimal modification is preferable
- Interactive capabilities

Examining the proposals for popular videos presented earlier, we note that they are unsuitable for mobile environments, either because they require a large client buffer, large bandwidth for downloads or very strict and complex synchronization. Furthermore, they were designed for popular videos with a static request pattern, where clients always request videos from their beginning.

On the other hand, patching, bandwidth skimming are better equipped to address these problems, but unless multicasting is supported, may overwhelm the server. Chaining was designed for multicasting, but uses the p2p computation model, lowering server load and bandwidth.

Nevertheless, unicast-based schemes are better in practice for both wired and mobile networks as stated earlier. Although several proposals exist, Zigzag and LEMP are better suited for mobile environments, since they have the advantages of chaining, but are designed having taken into consideration the existence of a significant probability of peer failures, as well as the case of ad hoc networks and are scalable. Their main disadvantage is that they require a collaborative environment and considerable client upload bandwidth capability, which is not always the case for asymmetric mobile networks. Furthermore, they reduce server bandwidth load, but not the load of the overall network.

The remaining proposals either assume a radical reorganization of the network infrastructure (CDN) or are not proven to be scalable.

CONCLUSION AND FUTURE TRENDS

The research conducted by IETF for quality of service (QoS) in IP-based mobile networks and QoS policy control is of particular importance. Such research is directly applicable to the dissemination of multimedia data, since the temporal requirement may lead to an early decision for packet control, providing better network bandwidth utilization. The new requirements of policy control in mobile networks are set by the user's home network operator, depending upon a profile created for the user. Thus, certain sessions may not be allowed to be initiated under certain circumstances (Zheng, & Greis, 2004).

In this sense, most mobile networks will continue being hybrid in nature for the foreseeable future, since this scheme offers better control for administrative and charging reasons, as well as higher effective throughput and connectivity to the Internet. Therefore, proposals based on some form of CDN are better suited for commercial providers. Nevertheless, from a purely technical point of view, the p2p computation model is better suited for the mobile environment, with low server

bandwidth requirements, providing failure tolerance and, most important, inherently supporting ad hoc networks and interactive multimedia.

REFERENCES

Aggarwal, C., Wolf, J., & Yu, P. (1996). A permutation based pyramid broadcasting scheme for video on-demand systems. *IEEE International Conference on Multimedia Computing and Systems (ICMCS '96),* (pp. 118-126), Hiroshima, Japan.

Eager, D., Vernon, M., & Zahorjan, J. (2000). Bandwidth skimming: A technique for cost-effective video-on-demand. *Proceedings of IS&T/SPIE Conference on Multimedia Computing and Networking (MMCN 2000)* (pp. 206-215).

Fouliras, P., Xanthos, S., Tsantalis, N., & Manitsaris, A. (2004). LEMP: Lightweight efficient multicast protocol for video on demand. *ACM Symposium on Applied Computing (SAC'04)* (pp. 1226-1231), Nicosia, Cyprus.

Guo, Y., Das, S., & Pinotti, M. (2001). A new hybrid broadcast scheduling algorithm for asymmetric communication systems: Push and pull data based on optimal cut-off point. *Mobile Computing and Communications Review (MC2R),* 5(3), 39-54. ACM.

Guo, Y., Suh, K., Kurose, J., & Towsley, D. (2003). A peer-to-peer on-demand streaming service and its performance evaluation. *IEEE International Conference on Multimedia Expo (ICME '03)* (pp. 649-652).

Hu, Q., Lee, D., & Lee, W. (1998). Optimal channel allocation for data dissemination in mobile computing environments. *International Conference on Distributed Computing Systems* (pp. 480-487).

Hua, K., Tantaoui, M., & Tavanapong, W. (2004). Video delivery technologies for large-scale deployment of multimedia applications. *Proceedings of the IEEE*, *92*(9), 1439-1451.

Hua, K., & Sheu, S. (1997). Skyscraper broadcasting: A new broadcasting scheme for metropolitan video-on-demand systems. *ACM Special Interest Group on Data Communication (SIGCOMM '97)* (pp. 89-100), Sophia, Antipolis, France.

Hua, K., Cai, Y. & Sheu, S. (1998). Patching: A multicast technique for true video-on-demand services. *ACM Multimedia '98* (pp. 191-200), Bristol, UK.

Juhn, L., & Tseng, L. (1997). Harmonic broadcasting for video-on-demand service. *IEEE Transactions on Broadcasting*, *43*(3), 268-271.

Juhn, L., & Tseng, L. (1998). Fast data broadcasting and receiving scheme for popular video service. *IEEE Transactions on Broadcasting*, *44*(1), 100-105.

Kurose, J., & Ross, K. (2004). *Computer networking: A top-down approach featuring the Internet* (3rd ed.). Salford, UK: Addison Wesley; Pearson Education.

Paris, J., Carter, S., & Long, D. (1998). A low bandwidth broadcasting protocol for video on demand. *IEEE International Conference on Computer Communications and Networks (IC3N'98)* (pp. 690-697).

Ratner, D., Reiher, P., & Popek, G. (2004). Roam: A scalable replication system for mobility. *Mobile Networks and Applications, 9,* 537-544). Kluwer Academic Publishers.

Sheu, S., Hua, K., & Tavanapong, W. (1997). Chaining: A generalized batching technique for video-on-demand systems. *Proceedings of the IEEE ICMCS'97* (pp. 110-117).

Sripanidkulchai, K., Ganjam, A., Maggs, B., & Zhang, H. (2004). The feasibility of supporting large-scale live streaming applications with dynamic application end-points. *ACM Special Interest Group on Data Communication (SIGCOMM'04)* (pp. 107-120), Portland, OR.

Tran, D., Hua, K., & Do, T. (2003). Zigzag: An efficient peer-to-peer scheme for media streaming. *Proceedings of IEEE Infocom* (pp. 1283-1293).

Viswanathan, S., & Imielinski, T. (1995). Pyramid broadcasting for video-on-demand service. *Proceedings of the SPIE Multimedia Computing and Networking Conference* (pp. 66-77).

Wang, B., Sen, S., Adler, M., & Towsley, D. (2004). Optimal proxy cache allocation for efficient streaming media distribution. *IEEE Transaction on Multimedia*, *6*(2), 366-374.

Wei, W., & Zakhor, A. (2004). Robust multipath source routing protocol (RMPSR) for video communication over wireless ad hoc networks. *International Conference on Multimedia and Expo (ICME)* (pp. 27-30).

Wu, E., & Huang, Y. (2004). Dynamic adaptive routing for a heterogeneous wireless network. *Mobile Networks and Applications*, *9*, 219-233.

Zheng, H., & Greis, M. (2004). Ongoing research on QoS policy control schemes in mobile networks. *Mobile Networks and Applications*, *9*, 235-241. Kluwer Academic Publishers.

Zhu, X., Han, S., & Girod, B. (2004). Congestion-aware rate allocation for multipath video streaming over ad hoc wireless networks. *IEEE International Conference on Image Processing (ICIP-04)*.

KEY TERMS

CDN: Content distribution network is a network where the ISP has placed proxies in strategically selected points, so that the bandwidth used and response time to clients' requests is minimized.

Overlay Network: A virtual network built over a physical network, where the participants communicate with a special protocol, transparent to the non-participants.

QoS: A notion stating that transmission quality and service availability can be measured, improved, and, to some extent, guaranteed in advance. QoS is of particular concern for the continuous transmission of multimedia information and declares the ability of a network to deliver traffic with minimum delay and maximum availability.

Streaming: The scheme under which clients start playing out the multimedia immediately or shortly after they have received the first portion without waiting for the transmission to be completed.

This work was previously published in Handbook of Research on Mobile Multimedia, edited by I. Ibrahim, pp. 38-48, copyright 2006 by Information Science Reference, formerly known as Idea Group Reference (an imprint of IGI Global).

Chapter 7.36
Data Broadcasting in a Mobile Environment

A. R. Hurson
The Pennsylvania State University, USA

Y. Jiao
The Pennsylvania State University, USA

ABSTRACT

The advances in mobile devices and wireless communication techniques have enabled anywhere, anytime data access. Data being accessed can be categorized into three classes: private data, shared data, and public data. Private and shared data are usually accessed through on-demand-based approaches, while public data can be most effectively disseminated using broadcasting. In the mobile computing environment, the characteristics of mobile devices and limitations of wireless communication technology pose challenges on broadcasting strategy as well as data-retrieval method designs. Major research issues include indexing scheme, broadcasting over single and parallel channels, data distribution and replication strategy, conflict resolution, and data retrieval method. In this chapter, we investigate solutions proposed for these issues. High performance and low power consumption are the two main objectives of the proposed schemes. Comprehensive simulation results are used to demonstrate the effectiveness of each solution and compare different approaches.

INTRODUCTION

The increasing development and spread of wireless networks and the need for information sharing has created a considerable demand for cooperation among existing, distributed, heterogeneous, and autonomous information sources. The growing diversity in the range of information that is accessible to a user and rapidly expanding technology have changed the traditional notion of timely and reliable access to global information in a distributed system. Remote access to data refers to both mobile nodes and fixed nodes accessing data within a platform characterized by the following:

- low bandwidth,
- frequent disconnection,
- high error rates,
- limited processing resources, and
- limited power sources.

Regardless of the hardware device, connection medium, and type of data accessed, users require timely and reliable access to various types of data that are classified as follows:

- Private data, that is, personal daily schedules, phone numbers, and so forth. The reader of this type of data is the sole owner or user of the data.
- Public data, that is, news, weather information, traffic information, flight information, and so forth. This type of data is maintained by one source and shared by many—a user mainly queries the information source(s).
- Shared data, that is, traditional, replicated, or fragmented databases. Users usually send transactions as well as queries to the information source(s).

Access requests to these data sources can be on-demand-based or broadcast-based.

On-Demand-Based Requests

In this case users normally obtain information through a dialogue (two-way communication) with the database server—the request is pushed to the system, data sources are accessed, operations are performed, partial results are collected and integrated, and the final result is communicated back to the user. This access scenario requires a solution that addresses the following issues.

- **Security and access control.** Methods that guarantee authorized access to the resources.
- **Isolation.** Means that support operations off-line if an intentional or unintentional disconnection has occurred.

- **Semantic heterogeneity.** Methods that can handle differences in data representation, format, structure, and meaning among information sources and hence establish interoperability.
- **Local autonomy.** Methods that allow different information sources to join and depart the global information-sharing environment at will.
- **Query processing and query optimization.** Methods that can efficiently partition global queries into subqueries and perform optimization techniques.
- **Transaction processing and concurrency control.** Methods that allow simultaneous execution of independent transactions and interleave interrelated transactions in the face of both global and local conflicts.
- **Data integration.** Methods that fuse partial results to draw a global result.
- **Browsing.** Methods that allow the user to search and view the available information without any information processing overhead.
- **Distribution transparency.** Methods to hide the network topology and the placement of the data while maximizing the performance for the overall system.
- **Location transparency.** Methods that allow heterogeneous remote access (HRA) to data sources. Higher degrees of mobility argue for higher degrees of heterogeneous data access.
- **Limited resources.** Methods that accommodate computing devices with limited capabilities.

The literature is abounded with solutions to these issues (Badrinath, 1996; Bright, Hurson, & Pakzad, 1992, 1994; Joseph, Tauber, & Kaashoek, 1997; Satyanarayanan, 1996). Moreover, there are existing mobile applications that address the limited bandwidth issues involved in mobility (Demers, Pertersen, Spreitzer, Terry, Theier,

& Welch, 1994; Fox, Gribble, Brewer, & Amir, 1996; Honeyman, Huston, Rees, & Bachmann, 1992; Joseph et al., 1997; Kaashoek, Pinckney, & Tauber, 1995; Lai, Zaslavsky, Martin, & Yeo, 1995; Le, Burghardt, Seshan, & Rabaey, 1995; Satyanarayanan, 1994, 1996).

Broadcast-Based Requests

Public information applications can be characterized by (a) massive numbers of users and (b) the similarity and simplicity in the requests solicited by the users. The reduced bandwidth attributed to the wireless environment places limitations on the rate of the requests. Broadcasting (one-way communication) has been suggested as a possible solution to this limitation. In broadcasting, information is provided to all users of the air channels. Mobile users are capable of searching the air channels and pulling the desired data. The main advantage of broadcasting is that it scales up as the number of users increases and, thus, eliminates the need to multiplex the bandwidth among users accessing the air channel. Furthermore, broadcasting can be considered as an additional storage available over the air for mobile clients. Within the scope of broadcasting one needs to address three issues:

- effective data organization on the broadcast channel,
- efficient data retrieval from the broadcast channel, and
- data selection.

The goal is to achieve high performance (response time) while minimizing energy consumption. Note that the response time is a major source of power consumption at the mobile unit (Imielinski & Badrinath, 1994; Imielinski & Korth, 1996; Imielinski, Viswanathan, & Badrinath, 1997; Weiser, 1993). As a result, the reduction in response time translates into reducing the amount of time a mobile unit spends accessing

the channel(s) and thus has its main influence on conserving energy at the mobile unit.

Chapter Organization

In this chapter, we first introduce the necessary background material. Technological limitations are outlined and their effects on the global information-sharing environment are discussed. Issues such as tree-based indexing, signature-based indexing, data replication, broadcasting over single and parallel channels, data distribution, conflict, and data access are enumerated and analyzed next. Then we present solutions to these issues with respect to the network latency, access latency, and power management. Finally, we conclude the chapter and point out some future research directions.

MOBILE COMPUTING

The mobile computing environment is composed of a number of network servers enhanced with wireless transceivers—mobile support stations (MSSs) and a varying number of mobile hosts (MHs) free to move at will (Figure 1).

The role of the MSS is to provide a link between the wireless network and the wired network. The link between an MSS and the wired network could be either wireless (shown as a dashed line) or wire based. The area covered by the individual transceiver is referred to as a cell. To satisfy a request, an MH accesses the MSS responsible for the cell where the MH is currently located. It is the duty of the MSS to resolve the request and deliver the result back to the client. Once an MH moves across the boundaries of two cells, a handoff process takes place between the MSSs of the corresponding cells. The MH is normally small, lightweight, and portable. It is designed to be compact with limited resources relying on temporary power supplies (such as batteries) as its main power source.

Figure 1. Architecture of the mobile-computing environment

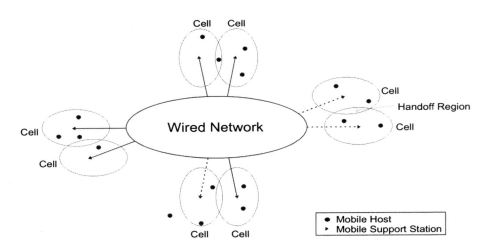

Characteristics of the Mobile Environment

Wireless communication is accomplished via modulating radio waves or pulsing infrared light. Table 1 summarizes a variety of mobile network architectures. Mainly, three characteristics distinguish the mobile computing environment from traditional wired computing platforms, namely, wireless medium, mobility, and portability.

Wireless Medium

The common ground among all wireless systems is the fact that communication is done via the air (and not via cables). This fact changes a major underlying assumption behind the conventional distributed algorithms. The physical layer of the connection is no longer the reliable coaxial or optic cable. Communication over the air is identified by frequent disconnections, low data-rate, high cost, and lack of security (Alonso & Ganguly, 1992; Alonso & Korth, 1993; Chlamtac & Lin, 1997;

Imielinski & Badrinath, 1994; Imielinski & Korth, 1996; Imielinski et al., 1997; Weiser, 1993).

Mobility

Mobility introduces new challenges beyond the scope of the traditional environment. Mobile devices can be used at multiple locations and in transition between these locations. Mobility results in several issues including disconnections due to handoff processes, motion management, location-dependent information, heterogeneous and fragmented networks, security, and privacy.

Portability

There are many variations of portable computer systems with different physical capabilities. However, they share many common characteristics such as limited memory, processing power, and power source. The ideal goal would be to develop a device that is compact, durable, lightweight, and that consumes a minimum amount of power.

Table 1. Mobile network architectures

Architecture	Description
Cellular Networks	• Provides voice and data services to users with handheld phones • Continuous coverage is restricted to metropolitan regions • Movement over a wide area may need user to inform the network of the new location • Low bandwidth for data-intensive applications • Could be based on either analog technology or digital technology
Wireless LANs	• A traditional LAN extended with a wireless interface • Serves small, low-powered, portable terminals capable of wireless access • Connected to a more extensive backbone network, such as a LAN or WAN
Wide Area Wireless Networks	• Special mobile radio networks provided by private service providers (RAM, ARDIS) • Provides nationwide wireless coverage for low-bandwidth data services, including e-mail or access to applications running on a fixed host
Paging Networks	• Receive-only network • No coverage problems • Low bandwidth • Unreliable

Satellite Networks	• Unlike the static, grounded MSSs, satellites are not fixed
	• Normally classified based on their altitudes (from earth) into three classes:
	  • Low Earth Orbit Satellites (LEOS)
	  • Medium Earth Orbit Satellites (MEOS)
	  • Geostationary Satellites (GEOS)

Table 2. Limitations of the mobile environment

Limitations	Concerns/Side Effects
Frequent Disconnections	• Handoff blank out in cellular networks • Long down time of the mobile unit due to limited battery power • Voluntary disconnection by the user • Disconnection due to hostile events (e.g., theft, destruction) • Roaming off outside the geographical coverage area of the window service
Limited Communication Bandwidth	• Quality of service (QoS) and performance guarantees • Throughput and response time and their variances • Efficient battery use during long communication delays
Heterogeneous and Fragmented Wireless Network Infrastructure	• Rapid and large fluctuations in network QoS • Mobility transparent applications perform poorly without mobility middleware or proxy • Poor end-to-end performance of different transport protocols across network of different parameters and transmission characteristics

Table 2 highlights some limitations of the mobile environment.

Broadcasting

The cost of communication is normally asymmetric: Sending information requires 2 to 10 times more energy than receiving the information (Imielinski, Viswanathan, & Badrinath, 1994). In the case of accessing public information, instead of the two-way, on-demand, traditional communication pattern, popular public information can be generated and disseminated over the air channel. The MH requiring the information can tune to the broadcast and access the desired information from the air channel.

In general, data can be broadcast either on one or several channels. Broadcasting has been used extensively in multiple disciplines, that is, management of communication systems (Comer, 1991) and distributed database environments (Bowen, 1992). In this chapter, the term *broadcast* is referred to as the set of all broadcast data elements (the stream of data across all channels). A broadcast is performed in a cyclic manner. The MH can only read from the broadcast, whereas the database server is the only entity that can write to the broadcast.

In the data-broadcasting application domain, power consumption and network latency are proven constraints that limit "timely and reliable" access to information. The necessity of minimizing power consumption and network latency lies in the limitation of current technology. The hardware of the mobile units have been designed to mitigate this limitation by operating in various operational modes such as active, doze, sleep, nap, and so forth to conserve energy. A mobile unit can be in active mode (maximum power consumption) while it is searching or accessing data; otherwise, it can be in doze mode (reduced power consumption) when the unit is not performing any computation. Along with the architectural and hardware enhancements,

efficient power management and energy-aware algorithms can be devised to manage power resources more effectively. In addition, appropriate retrieval protocols can be developed to remedy network latency and hence to allow faster access to the information sources. In general, two issues need to be considered.

- The MH should not waste its energy in continuously monitoring the broadcast to search for information. As a result, the information on the broadcast should be organized based on a disciplined order. Techniques should be developed to (a) instruct the MH of the availability of the data element on the broadcast and (b) if the data element is available, instruct the MH of the location of the data element on the broadcast.
- An attempt should be made to minimize the response time. As will be seen later, this is achieved by shortening the broadcast length and/or reducing the number of passes over the air channel(s).

Data Organization on the Air Channel

Unlike the conventional wired environment, where a disk is assumed to be the underlying storage, data in the mobile environment are stored on air channel(s). A disk and an air channel have major structural and functional differences. The disk has a three-dimensional structure (disks can have a four-dimensional structure if multiple disks are used — redundant arrays of independent disks [RAID]). An air channel, on the other hand, is a one-dimensional structure. The disk has a random-access feature and the air channel is sequential in nature. Finally, the current raw data rate of a disk is generally much higher than that of the air channel.

Zdonik, Alonso, Franklin, and Acharya (1994) and Acharya, Alonso, Franklin, and Zdonik (1995) investigated the mapping of disk pages onto a broadcast channel and the effects of that mapping on the management of cache at the MH. In order to place disk pages onto the data channel, the notion of multiple disks with different sizes spinning at multiple speeds was used. Pages available on faster spinning disks get mapped more frequently than those available on slower disks. In cache management, a nonconventional replacement strategy was suggested. Such a policy assumed that the page to be replaced might not be the least-recently used page in the cache. This is justifiable since the set of pages that are most frequently in demand are also the most frequently broadcast. This work was also extended to study the effect of prefetching from the air channel into the cache of the MH. These efforts assumed the same granularity for the data items on air channel and disk pages: if a data item is to be broadcast more frequently (replicated), the entire page has to be replicated. In addition, due to the plain structural nature of the page-based environment, the research looked at the pages as abstract entities and was not meant to consider the contents of the pages (data and its semantics) as a means to order the pages. In object-oriented systems, semantics among objects greatly influence the method in which objects are retrieved and, thus, have their direct impact on the ordering of these objects or pages. In addition,

the replication should be performed at the data item granularity level.

An index is a mechanism that speeds up associative searching. An index can be formally defined as a function that takes a key value and provides an address referring to the location of the associated data. Its main advantage lies in the fact that it eliminates the need for an exhaustive search through the pages of data on the storage medium. Similarly, within the scope of broadcasting, an index points to the location or possible availability of a data item on the broadcast, hence, allowing the mobile unit to predict the arrival time of the data item requested. The prediction of the arrival time enables the mobile unit to switch its operational mode into an energy-saving mode. As a result, an indexing mechanism facilitates data retrieval from the air channel(s), minimizing response time while reducing power consumption. Table 3 summarizes the advantages and disadvantages of indexing schemes.

The literature has addressed several indexing techniques for a single broadcast channel as well as parallel broadcast channels with special attention to signature-based indexing and tree-based indexing (Boonsiriwattanakul, Hurson, Vijaykrishnan, & Chehadeh, 1999; Chehadeh, Hurson, & Miller, 2000; Chehadeh, Hurson, &

Table 3. Advantages and disadvantages of indexing schemes

Advantages	Disadvantages
Provides auxiliary information that allows mobile users to predict arrival time of objects	Longer broadcast
Enables utilization of different operational modes (active, nap, doze, etc.)	Longer response time
Reduces power consumption (less tune-in time)	Computational overhead due to complexity in retrieval, allocation, and maintenance of the indexes

Tavangarian, 2001; Hu & Lee, 2000, 2001; Imielinski et al., 1997; Juran, Hurson, & Vijaykrishnan, 2004; Lee, 1996).

Signature-Based Indexing

A signature is an abstraction of the information stored in a record or a file. The basic idea behind signatures on a broadcast channel is to add a control part to the contents of an information frame (Hu & Lee, 2000, 2001; Lee, 1996). This is done by applying a hash function to the contents of the information frame, generating a bit vector, and then superimposing it on the data frame. As a result, a signature partially reflects the data content of a frame. Different allocations of signatures on a broadcast channel have been studied; among them, three policies, namely, *single signature*, *integrated signature*, and *multilevel signature*, are studied in Hu and Lee (2000) and Lee (1996).

During the retrieval, a query is resolved by generating a signature based on the user's request. The query signature is then compared against the signatures of the data frames in the broadcast. A successful match indicates a possible hit. Consequently, the content of the corresponding information frame is checked against the query to verify that it corresponds to the user's demands. If the data of the frame corresponds to the user's request, the data is recovered; otherwise, the corresponding information frame is ignored. In general, this scheme reduces the access time and the tune-in time when pulling information from the air channel.

Tree-Based Indexing

Two kinds of frames are broadcast on the air channel: data frames and index frames. The index frame contains auxiliary information representing one or several data attributes pointing to the location of data collection (i.e., information frames) sharing the same common attribute value(s). This information is usually organized as a tree in which the lowest level of the tree points to the location of the information frames on the broadcast channel.

A broadcast channel is a sequential medium and, hence, to reduce the mobile unit's active and tune-in time, and consequently to reduce the power consumption, the index frames are usually replicated and interleaved with the data frames. Two index replication schemes (namely, *distributed indexing* and *(1, m) indexing*) have been studied in Imielinski et al. (1997). In distributed indexing, the index is partitioned and interleaved in the broadcast cycle (Hu & Lee, 2000, 2001; Lee, 1996). Each part of the index in the broadcast is followed by its corresponding data frame(s). In $(1, m)$ indexing, the entire index is interleaved m times during the broadcast cycle (Imielinski et al., 1997; Lee 1996) — the whole index is broadcast before every $1/m$ fraction of the cycle.

Previous work has shown that the tree-based indexing schemes are more suitable for applications where information is accessed from the broadcast channel randomly, and the signature-based indexing schemes are more suitable in retrieving sequentially structured data elements (Hu & Lee, 2000, 2001). In addition, tree-based indexing schemes have shown superiority over the signature-based indexing schemes when the user request is directed towards interrelated objects clustered on the broadcast channel(s). Furthermore, tree-based indexing schemes relative to signature-based indexing schemes are more suitable in reducing the overall power consumption. This is due to the fact that a tree-based indexing provides global information regarding the physical location of the data frames on the broadcast channel. On the other hand, signature-based indexing schemes are more effective in retrieving data frames based on multiple attributes (Hu & Lee, 2000). Table 4 compares and contrasts the signature- and tree-based indexing.

Table 4. Signature-based versus tree-based indexing

Feature	Signature-Based Indexing	Tree-Based Indexing
Less power consumption		✓
Longer length of broadcast	✓	✓
Computational overhead	✓	✓
Longer response time	✓	✓
Shorter tune-in time		✓
Random data access		✓
Sequentially structured data	✓	
Clustered data retrieval		✓
Multi-attribute retrieval	✓	

Data Organization on a Single Channel

An appropriate data placement algorithm should attempt to detect data locality and cluster related data close to one another. An object-clustering algorithm takes advantage of semantic links among objects and attempts to map a complex object into a linear sequence of objects along these semantic links. It has been shown that such clustering can improve the response time by an order of magnitude (Banerjee, Kim, Kim, & Garza, 1988; Chang & Katz, 1989; Chehadeh, Hurson, Miller, Pakzad, & Jamoussi, 1993; Cheng & Hurson, 1991a). In the conventional computing environment, where data items are stored on disk(s), the clustering algorithms are intended to place semantically connected objects physically along the sectors of the disk(s) close to one another (Cheng & Hurson, 1991a). The employment of broadcasting in the mobile computing environment motivates the need to study the proper data organization along the sequential air channel. Figure 2 depicts a weighted directed acyclic graph (DAG) and the resulting clustering sequences achieved when different clustering techniques are applied.

In order to reduce the response time, the organization of data items on an air channel has to meet the following three criteria.

- **Linear ordering.** The one-dimensional sequential access structure of the air channel requires that the object ordering be linear. In a DAG representation of a complex object, an edge between two nodes could signify an access pattern among the two nodes. The *linearity* property is defined as follows: If an edge exists between two objects, o_1 and o_2, and in the direction $o_1 \rightarrow o_2$, then o_1 should be placed prior to o_2.
- **Minimum linear distance between related objects.** In a query, multiple objects might be retrieved following their connection patterns. Intuitively, reducing the distance among these objects along the broadcast reduces the response time and power consumption.

Figure 2. Graph and various clustering methods

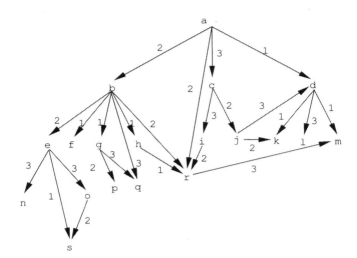

Clustering Method	Resulting Sequence
Depth First	abensofgpqhrmcijdkl
Breadth First	abrcdefgqhijklmnsop
Children-Depth First	abrcdefgqhmnsopijkl
Level Clustering	acibgqprmenosjdlkfh

- **More availability for popular objects.** In a database, not all objects are accessed with the same frequency. Generally, requests for data follow the 20/80 rule — a popular, small set of the data (20%) is accessed the majority of the time (80%). Considering the sequential access pattern of the broadcast channel, providing more availability for popular objects can be achieved by simply replicating such objects.

Figure 3 depicts a directed graph and multiple linear sequences that satisfy the linear ordering property. The middle columns represent the cost of delays between every two objects connected via an edge. For the sake of simplicity and without loss of generality, a data unit is used as a unit of measurement. Furthermore, it is assumed that all data items are of equal size. The cost associated with an edge between a pair of data items is calculated by counting the number of data items that separate these two in the linear sequence. For example, in the abfgchdeij sequence, data items a and d are separated by the sequence bfgch and thus have a cost of 6. The rightmost column represents the total cost associated with each individual linear sequence. An optimal sequence is the linear sequence with the minimum total sum. In a query where multiple related objects are retrieved, a reduced average linear distance

Figure 3. Graph, linear sequences, and costs

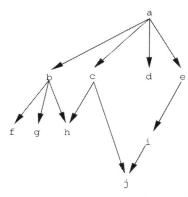

	Linear	Individual Costs										Total
	Sequence	ab	ac	ad	ae	bf	bg	bh	ch	cj	ei	ij	Cost
1	abfgchdeij	1	4	6	7	1	2	4	1	5	1	1	33
2	abfgcheijd	1	4	9	6	1	2	4	1	4	1	1	34
3	abcdefghij	1	2	3	4	4	5	6	5	7	4	1	42
4	abgfeichjd	1	6	9	4	2	1	6	1	2	1	3	36
5	acdeijbhgf	6	1	2	3	3	2	1	6	4	1	1	30
6	adeicjbhgf	6	4	1	2	3	2	1	3	1	1	2	26
7	adecbihgfj	4	3	1	2	4	3	2	3	6	3	4	35
8	adecbhgfij	4	3	1	2	3	2	1	2	6	6	1	31
9	adecijbhgf	6	3	1	2	3	2	1	4	2	2	1	27
10	adbfgcheij	2	5	1	7	1	2	4	1	4	1	1	29
11	adceijbhgf	6	2	1	3	3	2	1	5	3	1	1	28
12	aeidcjbhgf	6	4	3	1	3	2	1	3	1	1	3	28
13	aedcbihgfj	4	3	2	1	4	3	2	3	6	4	4	36
14	aedcijbhgf	6	3	2	1	3	2	1	4	2	3	1	28

translates into smaller average response time. In this example, the best linear sequence achieves a total sum of 26.

Data Organization on Parallel Channels

The broadcast length is a factor that affects the average response time in retrieving data items from the air channel — reducing the broadcast length could also reduce the response time. The broadcast length can be reduced if data items are broadcast along parallel air channels.

Formally, we attempt to assign the objects from a weighted DAG onto multiple channels, while (a) preserving dependency implied by the edges, (b) minimizing the overall broadcast time (load balancing), and (c) clustering related objects close to one another (improving the response time). As one could conclude, there are trade-offs between the second and third requirements: Achieving load balancing does not necessarily reduce the response time in accessing a series of data items.

Assuming that all channels have the same data rate, one can draw many analogies between this problem and static task scheduling in a homogeneous multiprocessor environment — tasks are represented as a directed graph $D \equiv (N, A)$, with nodes (N) and directed edges (A) representing processes and dependence among the processes, respectively. Compared to our environment, channels can be perceived as processors (PEs), objects as tasks, and the size of a data item as the processing cost of a task. There is, however, a major distinction between the two environments. In the multiprocessor environment, information is normally communicated among the PEs, while in the multichannel environment there is no data communication among channels.

The minimum makespan problem, in static scheduling within a multiprocessor environment, attempts to find the minimum time in which n dependent tasks can be completed on m PEs. An optimal solution to such a problem is proven to be NP hard. Techniques such as graph reduction, max-flow min-cut, domain decomposition, and priority list scheduling have been used in search of suboptimal solutions. Similar techniques can be developed to assign interrelated objects closely over parallel channels.

Distribution of data items over the broadcast parallel air channels brings the issue of access conflicts between requested data items that are distributed among different channels. The access conflict is due to two factors:

- the receiver at the mobile host can only tune into one channel at any given time, and
- the time delay to switch from one channel to another.

Access conflicts require the receiver to wait until the next broadcast cycle(s) to retrieve the requested information. Naturally, multiple passes over the broadcast channels will have a significant adverse impact on the response time and power consumption.

Conflicts in Parallel Air Channels

Definition 1. A K-data item request is an application request intended to retrieve K data items from a broadcast.

It is assumed that each channel has the same number of pages (frames) of equal length and, without loss of generality, each data item is residing on only a single page. A single broadcast can be modeled as an N x M grid, where N is the number of pages per broadcast and M is the number of channels. In this grid, K data items ($0 \leq K \leq MN$) are randomly distributed throughout the MN positions of the grid. Based on the common page size and the network speed, the time required to switch from one channel to another is equivalent to the time it takes for one page to pass in the broadcast. Thus, it is impossible for the mobile unit to retrieve both the ith page on Channel A and ($i + 1$)th page on Channel B (where A $\neq$ B). Figure 4 is a grid model that illustrates this issue.

Definition 2. Two data items are defined to be in conflict if it is impossible to retrieve both on the same broadcast.

In response to a user request, the access latency is then directly dependent on the number of passes over the broadcast channels. One method of calculating the number of required passes over the broadcast channels is to analyze the conflicts between data items. For any particular data item, all data items in the same or succeeding page (column) and on a different row (channel) will be in conflict. Thus, for any specific page (data object) in the grid, there are ($2M$ - 2) conflicting pages (data items) in the broadcast (The last column has only M - 1 conflict positions, but it is assumed that N is sufficiently large to make this

Figure 4. Sample broadcast with M = 4, N = 6, and K = 8

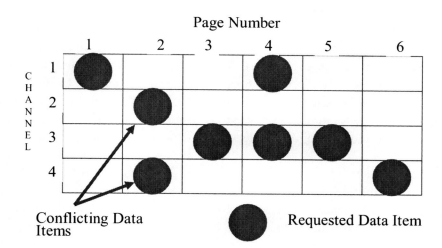

difference insignificant.) These (2*M* - 2) positions are known as the conflict region.

For any particular data item, it is possible to determine the probability of exactly *i* conflicts occurring, or *P(i)*. Because the number of conflicts for any particular data item is bounded by (*M* - 1), the weighted average of these probabilities can be determined by summing a finite series. This weighted average is the number of broadcasts (passes) required to retrieve all *K* data items if all conflicts between data items are independent.

$$B = \sum_{i=0}^{M-1}(i + 1)*P(i) \tag{1}$$

Access Patterns

In order to reduce the impact of conflicts on the access time and power consumption, retrieval procedures should be enhanced by a scheduling protocol that determines data retrieval sequence during each broadcast cycle. The scheduling protocol we proposed is based on the following three prioritized heuristics:

1) Eliminate the number of conflicts
2) Retrieve the maximum number of data items
3) Minimize the number of channel switches

The scheme determines the order of retrieval utilizing a forest - an *access forest*. An access forest is a collection of trees (*access trees*), where each access tree represents a collection of access patterns during a broadcast cycle. Naturally, the structure of the access forest, that is, the number of trees and the number of children that any parent can have, is a function of the number of broadcast channels.

Definition 3. An access tree is composed of two elements: nodes and arcs.

• **Node.** A node represents a requested data item. The nodes are labeled to indicate its conflict status: mnemonically, C_1 represents when the data item is in conflict with another data item(s) in the broadcast and C_0 indicates the lack of conflict.

Each access tree in the access forest has a different node as a root-the root is the first accessible requested data item on a broadcast cycle. This simply implies that an access forest can have at most n trees where n is the number of broadcast channels.

- **Arcs.** The arcs of the trees are weighted arcs. A weight denotes whether or not channel switching is required in order to retrieve the next scheduled data item in the access pattern. A branch in a tree represents a possible access pattern of data items during a broadcast cycle with no conflicts. Starting from the root, the total number of branches

in the tree represents all possible access patterns during a broadcast cycle.

This scheme allows one to generate all possible nonconflicting, weighted access patterns from all channels. The generated access patterns are ranked based on their weights-a weight is set based on the number of channel switches-and then the one(s) that allows the maximum number of data retrievals with minimum number of channel switches is selected. It should be noted that the time needed to build and traverse the access forest is a critical factor that must be taken into account to justify the validity of this approach. The following working example provides a detailed guide to illustrate the generation of the access patterns for each broadcast cycle.

1) **Search.** Based on the user's query, this step determines the offset and the chan-

Figure 5. A parallel broadcast of four channels with eight requested data items

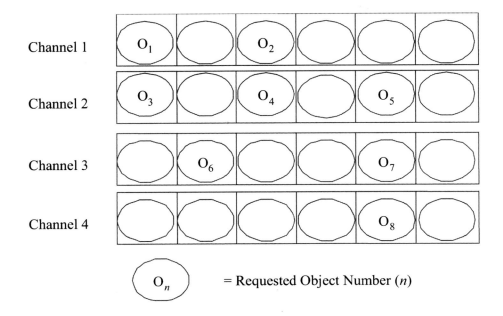

nel number(s) of the requested objects on the broadcast channels. Figure 5 depicts a request for eight data items from a parallel broadcast channel of four channels.

2) **Generation of the access forest.** For each broadcast channel, search for the requested data item with the smallest offset (these objects represent the roots of an access tree). For the example, the data items with the smallest offsets are O_1, O_3, O_6 and O_8. Note that the number of access trees is upper bounded by the number of broadcast channels.

3) **Root assignment.** For each channel with at least one data item requested, generate a tree with root node as determined in Step 2. The roots are temporarily tagged as C_0.

4) **Child assignment.** Once the roots are determined, it is necessary to select the child or children of each rooted access tree: For each root, and relative to its position on the air channel, the algorithm determines the closest nonconflicting data items on each channel. With respect to a data item $O_{i,x}$ at location X on air channel i ($1 \leq i \leq n$), the closest nonconflicting data item is either the data item $O_{i,x+1}$ or the data item $O_{j,x+2}$, $j \neq i$. If the child is in the same broadcast channel as the root, the arc is weighted as 0; otherwise it is weighted as 1. Each added node is temporarily tagged as C_0. Figure 6 shows a snapshot of the example after this step.

5) **Root label update.** Once the whole set of requested data items is analyzed and the access forest is generated, the conflict labels of the nodes of each tree are updated. This

Figure 6. Children of each root

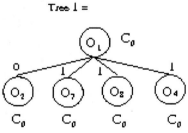

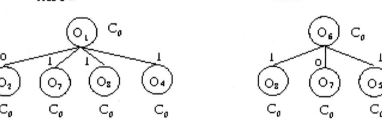

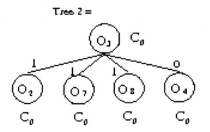

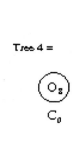

process starts with the root of each tree. If a root is in conflict with any other root(s), a label of C_1 is assigned to all the roots involved in the conflict, otherwise the preset value of C_0 is maintained.

6) **Node label update.** Step 5 will be applied to the nodes in the same level of each access tree in the access forest. As in Step 5, a value of C_1 is assigned to the nodes in conflict. Figure 7 shows the example with the updated labels.

7) **Sequence selection.** The generation of the access forest then allows the selection of the suitable access patterns in an attempt to reduce the network latency and power consumption. A suitable access pattern is equivalent to the selection of a tree branch that:

- has the most conflicts with other branches,
- allows more data items to be pulled off the air channels, and
- requires the least number of channel switches.

The O_3, O_4, and O_5 sequence represents a suitable access pattern for our running example during the first broadcast cycle. Step 7 will be repeated to generate access patterns for different broadcast cycles. The algorithm terminates when all the requested data items are covered in different access patterns. The data item sequence

Figure 7. Final state of the access forest

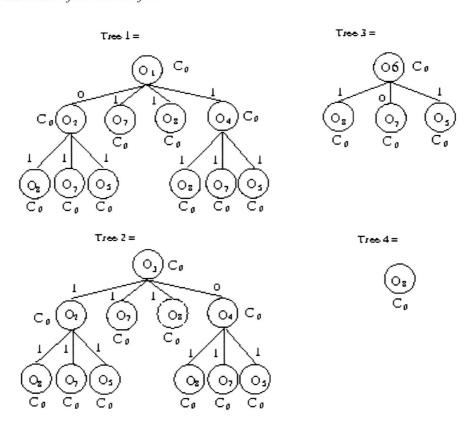

O_1, O_2, and O_7 and data item sequence O_6 and O_8 represent the last two patterns for retrieving all of the data items requested in the example.

DATA ORGANIZATION ON A SINGLE CHANNEL

As noted in the literature, the object-oriented paradigm is a suitable methodology for modeling public data that are by their very nature in multimedia format (Atkinson, Bancilhon, DeWitt, Dittrich, Maier, & Zdonik, 1989; Fong, Kent, Moore, & Thompson, 1991; Hurson, Pakzad, & Cheng, 1993; Kim, 1990). In addition, object-oriented methodology provides a systematic mechanism to model a complex object in terms of its simpler components.

In this section, without loss of generality, we model information units as objects. Object clustering has proven to be an effective means of data allocation that can reduce response times (Banerjee et al., 1988; Chang & Katz 1989; Chehadeh et al., 1993; Cheng & Hurson, 1991b; Lim, Hurson, Miller, & Chehadeh, 1997). In our research, we investigated two heuristic allocation strategies. The first strategy assumes a strict linearity requirement and deals with nonweighted DAGs. The second approach relaxes such restriction in favor of clustering strongly related objects closer to one another and consequently deals with weighted DAGs.

Strict Linearity: ApproximateLinearOrder Algorithm

Definition 4. An independent node is a node that has either one or no parent. A graph containing only independent nodes makes up a forest.

Heuristic Rules
1) Order the children of a node based on their number of descendants in ascending order.

2) Once a node is selected, all of its descendants should be visited and placed on the sequence in a depth-first manner, without any interruptions from breadth siblings.
3) If a node has a nonindependent child, with all of its parents already visited, the nonindependent child should be inserted in the linear sequence before any independent child.

The ApproximateLinearOrder algorithm implements these heuristics and summarizes the sequence of operations required to obtain a linear sequence. The algorithm assumes a greedy strategy and starts by selecting a node with an in-degree of zero and out-degree of at least one.

ApproximateLinearOrder Algorithm

1) traverse DAG using DFS traversal and as each node is traversed
2) append the traversed node N to the sequence
3) remove N from {nodes to be traversed}
4) **if** {nonindependent children of N having all their parents in the sequence} $\neq \varnothing$
5)   *Set* $\leftarrow$ {nonindependent children of N having all their parents in the sequence}
6) **else**
7)   **if** {independent children of N} $\neq \varnothing$
8)   *Set* $\leftarrow$ {independent children of N}
9)   *NextNode* $\leftarrow$ node $\in$ *Set* | node has least # of descendants among the nodes in *Set*

Applying this algorithm to the graph of Figure 3 generates either the 5th or 11th sequence — dependent on whether c or d was chosen first as the child with the least number of independent children. As one can observe, neither of these sequences is the optimal sequence. However, they are reasonably better than other sequences and can practically be obtained in polynomial time. It should be noted that nodes not connected to any other nodes — nodes with in-degree and out-degree of zero — are considered harmful and thus are not handled by the algorithm. Having them in the middle of the sequence introduces delays between objects along the sequence. Therefore, we exclude them from the set of nodes to be traversed and handle them by appending them to the end of the sequence. In addition, when multiple DAGs are to be mapped along the air channel, the mapping should be done with no interleaving between the nodes of the DAGs.

Varying Levels of Connectivity: PartiallyLinearOrder Algorithm

In a complex object, objects are connected through semantic links with different degrees of connectivity. The different access frequency of objects in an object-oriented database reveals that some patterns are more frequently traversed than others (Fong et al., 1991). This observation resulted in the so-called PartiallyLinearOrder algorithm that assumes a weighted DAG as its input and produces a linear sequence. It combines the nodes (single_node) of the graph into multi_nodes in descending order of their connectivity (semantic links). The insertion of single_nodes within a multi_node respects the linear order at the granularity level of the single_nodes. The multi_nodes are merged (with multi_nodes or single_nodes) at the multi_node granularity, without interfering with internal ordering sequences of a multi_node. Figure 8 shows the application of the Partially-LinearOrder algorithm.

PartiallyLinearOrder Algorithm

1) **for** every weight w_s in descending order
2) **for** every two nodes N_1 & N_2 connected by w_s
3) merge N_i & N_j into one multi_node
4) **for** every multi_node MN
5) $w_m = w_s - 1$
6) **for** every weight w_m in descending order
7) **while** $\exists$ adjacent_node AN connected to MN

8) **if** $\exists$ an edge in both directions between MN & AN
9) compute $WeightedLinearDistance_{MN\_AN}$ & $WeightedLinearDistance_{AN\_MN}$
10) merge MN & AN into one multi_node, based on the appropriate direction

Performance Evaluation

Parameters

A simulator was developed to study the behavior of the proposed mapping algorithms based on a

Figure 8. Process of PartiallyLinearOrder

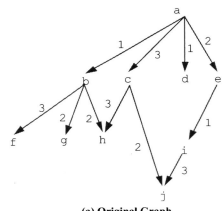

(a) Original Graph

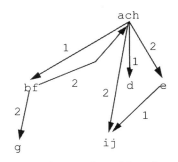

(b) First and Second Iterations

bfgacheijd
(c) Third Iteration

Table 5. Description of parameters

Parameter	Description
Input Parameters	
Number of Nodes	Number of objects within the graph (excluding replication)
Object Size	Sizes of objects (small/medium/large)
Object-Size Distribution	Distribution of the sizes of objects within the database
Next-Node Ratio	Connectivity to next node (random or connection)
Out-Degree Distribution	Distribution of the type of nodes based on their out-degrees
Level Distribution	Semantic connectivity of two objects (weak/normal/strong)
Percentage of Popular Objects	Percentage of objects requested more often than others
Replication Frequency	The number of times a popular object is to be replicated
Output Parameter	
Average Access Delay	In a single query, the average delay between accessing two objects

set of rich statistical parameters. Our test bed was an object-oriented financial database. The OO7 benchmark was chosen to generate the access pattern graphs. We used the NASDAQ exchange (NASDAQ, 2002) as our base model, where data is in both textual and multimedia (graphics — i.e., graphs and tables) formats. Table 5 shows a brief description of the input and output parameters. The simulator is designed to measure the average access delay for the various input parameters. Table 6 provides a listing of the input parameters along with their default values and possible ranges.

Table 6. Input parameter values

Parameter	Default Value	Ranges
Number of Nodes	5,000	400-8,000
Object Size (in Bytes)		
• Small	$2 \leq o < 20$	2-20
• Medium	$20 \leq o < 7K$	20-7K
• Large	$7K \leq o < 50K$	7K-50K
Object-Size Distribution [S:M:L]	1:1:1	0-6:0-6:0-6
Next-Node Ratio [C:R]	8:2	0-10:10-0
Out-Degree Distribution [0:1:2:3]	3:3:2:1	1-6:1-6:1-6:1-6
Level Distribution [W:N:S]	1:1:1	1-4:1-4:1-4
Percentage of Popular Objects	20%	10-50%
Replication Frequency	2	1-10

The default values are set as the value of the parameter when other parameters are varied during the course of the simulation. The ranges are used when the parameter itself is varied.

Results

The simulator operates in two stages.

- Structuring the access-pattern object graph, based on certain statistical parameters, and mapping it along the air channel using various mapping algorithms. To get a wide spectrum of possible graphs, parameters such as (a) the percentage of nonfree nodes, (b) the depths of the trees within the graph, and (c) the amount of sharing that exists between trees through nonfree nodes that were varied. Varying these statistical parameters,

we generated 500 access graphs that were used as part of our test bed. In addition, we simulated three mapping algorithms: a nonlinear, children-depth-first clustering algorithm (Banerjee et al., 1988), and the PartiallyLinearOrder and ApproximateLinearOrder algorithms.

- Generating queries and accessing the requested objects from the air channel. During each run, each query on average accesses 20 objects either through their semantic links or randomly (following the [C:R] value of the next-node ratio). The simulator measured the average access delay. Each point in the curves (Figure 9) is the average result of running the simulator 100,000 times. Finally, we assumed a broadcast data rate of 1Mbit/sec and showed the results in terms of seconds.

Figure 9. Average access delay versus connectivity

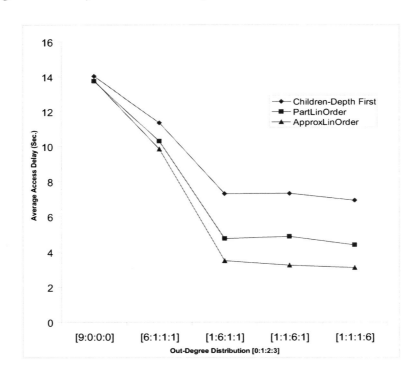

Impact of Number of Objects. ApproximateLinearOrder and PartiallyLinearOrder schemes performed better than the conventional children-depth first by taking the linearity issue into consideration. As expected in all three cases, the average access delay increased as the total number of objects increased. The mapping of additional nodes on the broadcast introduced extra delays between the retrievals of two consecutive objects. Taking a closer look at this effect, we observed that this extra delay is mainly due to an increase in the distance for objects that are retrieved randomly (not based on their semantic links) since the goal of both algorithms is to cluster semantically related objects close to one another. The ApproximateLinearOrder algorithm outperformed the PartiallyLinearOrder algorithm since the latter attempts to cluster strongly connected objects closer to one another than loosely connected ones and, hence, compromises the linearity property for the loosely connected objects. This compromise overshadows the benefit and is amplified as the number of objects increased. To get a better insight on how our proposed schemes compare with the optimal case, two graphs with 10 nodes were constructed and the optimal sequences exhaustively generated. Using the same set of input values, the average access delay for both proposed schemes were simulated and compared against the average access delay for the optimal sequence. The results of ApproximateLinearOrder and PartiallyLinearOrder were 79% and 76%, respectively, of the access delay of the optimal case.

Size Distribution. In this experiment, we observed that the smallest average access delay took place when the air channel contained smaller data items. However, as the population of data items shifted toward the larger ones, the average access delay increased.

Next-Node Ratio. During the course of a query, objects are either accessed along the semantic links or in a random fashion. At one extreme, when all objects were accessed along the semantic links, the average access delay was minimal. The delay, however, increased for randomly accessed objects. Finally, where all the accesses are on a random basis, clustering (and linearity) does not improve the performance, and all mapping algorithms perform equally.

Out-Degree Distribution. This parameter indicates the number of children of a node within the graph — an out-degree of 0 indicates a sink node. Figure 9 shows the effect of varying the out-degree distribution within the graph structure. The point [9:0:0:0] indicates that all the nodes within the graph have an out-degree of 0, with no semantic link among the objects. This is similar to stating that any access to any object within the graph is done on a random basis. In general, the average access delay is reduced as more connectivity is injected in the access graph. It is interesting to note that it would be more desirable to deal with more, but simpler, objects than with few complex objects on the air channel.

In separate simulation runs, the simulator was also used to measure the effect of varying the percentage of popular objects and the replication frequency. These two parameters have the same effect on the total number of objects on the air channel, however, from the access pattern perspective, the semantic of the accesses are different. In both cases, the average access delay increased as either parameter increased. We also observed and measured the average access delay for different degrees of connectivity among objects. The average access delay for objects connected through strong connections is about 4.3 seconds, whereas it is 7.3 and 7.6 seconds for normally and weakly connected objects, respectively. As would be expected, these results show that the improvement is considerable for the objects connected by a strong connection, but for a normal connection, the performance was close to that of the weak-connection case since the algorithm performs its best optimization for strongly connected objects.

Section Conclusion

In this section, two heuristically based mapping algorithms were discussed, simulated, and analyzed. Performing the mapping in polynomial time was one of the major issues of concern while satisfying linearity, locality, and replication of popular objects. The ApproximateLinearOrder algorithm is a greedy-based approximation algorithm that guarantees the linearity property and provides a solution in polynomial time. The PartiallyLinearOrder algorithm guarantees the linearity property for the strongest related objects and relaxes the linearity requirement for objects connected through looser links. Finally, it was shown that the proposed algorithms offer higher performance than the traditional children-depth-first algorithm.

DATA ORGANIZATION ON PARALLEL CHANNELS

Reducing the broadcast length is one way to satisfy timely access to the information. This could be achieved by broadcasting data items along parallel air channels. This problem can be stated formally as follows: Assign the data items from a weighted DAG onto multiple channels while (a) preserving dependency implied by the edges, (b) minimizing the overall broadcast time (load balancing), and (c) clustering related data items close to one another (improving the response time). Realizing the similarities between these objectives and the task-scheduling problem in a multiprocessor environment, we proposed two heuristic–based, static scheduling algorithms, namely the largest object first (LOF) algorithm and the clustering critical-path (CCP) algorithm.

The Largest Object First Algorithm

This algorithm relies on a simple and localized heuristic by giving priority to larger data items.

The algorithm follows the following procedure: For each collection of data items, recursively, a "proper" node with in-degree of 0 is chosen and assigned to a "proper" channel; a "proper" channel is the one with the smallest overall size and a "proper" node is the largest node with in-degree of 0. The assigned node along with all of its out-edges are eliminated from the object DAG. This results in a set of nodes with in-degree of 0. These nodes are added to the list of free nodes and then are selected based on their sizes. This process is repeated until all the nodes of the DAG are assigned.

Definition 5. A free node is a node that either has an in-degree of 0 (no parent) or has all of its parents allocated on a channel. A free node is a candidate node available for allocation.

Assuming that there are n nodes in the graph, the algorithm requires the traversal of all the nodes and thus requires n steps. At each step, the algorithm searches for the largest available node whose parents have been fully allocated. This would require at most $O(n^2)$. Therefore, the overall running time of the algorithm is $O(n^3)$. The LOF algorithm respects the dependency among the nodes, if any, and achieves a better load balancing by choosing the largest object first. This algorithm, however, does not allocate objects based on the degree of connectivity and/or the total size of the descendent objects that could play a significant role in balancing the loads on the channels. In addition, this algorithm does not necessarily cluster related object on the parallel air channels.

LOF Algorithm

1) **repeat (2-4)** until all nodes are assigned
2)   assign a free node with the largest weight whose parents are fully allocated to the least-loaded channel
3)   remove all out-edges of the assigned node from the DAG

4)   insert resulting free nodes into the list of free nodes

The Clustering Critical-Path Algorithm

A critical path is defined as the longest sequence of dependent objects that are accessed serially. A critical path is determined based on the weights assigned to each node. A weight is defined based on several parameters such as the size of the data item, the maximum weight of the descendents, the total weight, and the number of descendents.

Definition 6. A critical node is a node that has a child with an in-degree greater than 1.

Load Balancing

Critical Node effect. Allocate a critical node with the highest number of children with in-degrees greater than 1 first.

Number of children with in-degrees of 1. Allocate nodes with the highest number of children with in-degrees of 1 first. This could free up more nodes to be allocated in parallel channels.

Clustering Related Objects

The weight of a node should be made a function of the weights of the incoming and outgoing edges. The weight of each node is calculated based on Equation 2. It should be noted that:

- There is a trade-off between load balancing and clustering related objects: The allocation strategy for the purpose of load balancing could upset the clustering of related objects and vice versa. Therefore, we propose a factor to balance the two requirements. This factor takes a constant value $\in [0,1]$ and can be assigned to favor either requirement over the other.

- The size of a data item is a multiple of a constant value.

- The weight of an edge is a multiple of a constant value.

$$W = MWC + F\left[S + NCID1 + \sum_{i=1}^{NCIDM} SPC_i - NCIDM(S)\right] + (1-F)\left[(NMIW)MIW + \frac{1}{(NMOW)MOW}\right]$$

(2)

where

W weight of a node

MWC maximum weight among the node's children

F factor of optimizing for load balancing versus clustering related objects

S size of a node (object)

$NCID1$ number of children with in-degrees of 1

$NCIDM$ number of children with in-degrees greater than 1

SPC size of all parent objects

MIW maximum weight of incoming edges

$NMIW$ number of maximum-weighted incoming edges

MOW maximum weight of outgoing edges

$NMOW$ number of maximum-weighted outgoing edges

The algorithm required to assign the weight of every node in the graph with time complexity of $O(n^2)$ (n is the number of nodes in the DAG) is as follows.

ASSIGNWEIGHTS(DAG) Algorithm

1) for every node i (Starting at the leaf nodes and traversing the DAG in a breadth-first manner)
2) Calculate SPC_i
3) Calculate W_i

The CCP algorithm takes a DAG as its input and calls the AssignWeights Algorithm. The running time of the CCP algorithm is equal to the running time of AssignWeights plus the running time of the *repeat* loop. The loop has to be repeated n times and Line 4 can be done in $O(n)$.

Therefore, the overall running time of the CCP algorithm is $O(n^2)$.

CCP(DAG) Algorithm

1) AssignWeights(DAG)
2) **repeat** until all the nodes have been processed
3) Select the free node N with the largest weight
4) **if** all parents of N are fully allocated on the channels
5) place it on the currently least-loaded channel
6) **else**
7) Fill up the least-loaded channel(s) with nulls up to the end of the last allocated parent of N then place N on it.

Performance Evaluation

To evaluate the performance of the proposed algorithms, our simulator was extended to measure the average response time per data item retrieval. To measure the effectiveness of the algorithms across a more unbiased test bed, the degree of connectivity among the data items in the DAG was randomly varied, and 100 different DAGs were generated. In every DAG, the out-degrees of the nodes were determined within the range of 0 and 3. To limit the experimentation running time, a decision was made to limit the number of nodes of each DAG to 60. The weights connecting the nodes, similar to the experiment reported in previously, were categorized as strong, normal, and weak, and were uniformly distributed along the edges of a DAG.

The simulation is accomplished in two steps: In the first step, every DAG is mapped onto the air channels using the LOF and CCP algorithms. In the second step, the simulator simulates the process of accessing the air channels in order to retrieve the data items requested in a query. Among the requested data items, 80% were selected based on their semantic relationship within the DAG and

20% were selected randomly. Finally, the average response time was calculated for 100,000 runs.

1) **Number of Air Channels.** As anticipated, increasing the number of channels resulted in a better response time for both the LOF and CCP. However, this improvement tapered off as the number of channels increased above a certain threshold value, since, additional parallelism provided by the number of channels did not match the number of free nodes available to be allocated, simultaneously. In addition, as expected, the CCP method outperformed the LOF method—the CCP heuristics attempt to smooth the distribution of the objects among the air channels while clustering the related objects.

2) **Out-Degree Distribution.** In general, the CCP method outperformed the LOF method. When the out-degree distribution is biased to include nodes with larger out-degrees (i.e., making the DAG denser), the LOF performance degrades at a much faster rate than the CCP method. This is due to the fact that such bias introduces more critical nodes and a larger number of children per node. The CCP method is implicitly capable of handling such cases.

3) **Factor of Load Balancing versus Clustering Related Objects.** To get a better insight on the operations of the CCP method, we analyzed its behavior by varying the load balancing and degree of clustering (F; Equation 2). In this experiment, 80% of the data items requested by each query were related through certain semantic links and the rest were selected randomly. As can be seen (Figure 10), biasing in favor of clustering degrades the average response time for randomly selected data items. Optimization based on clustering increases the overall length of the broadcast, thus, contributing to larger response time for randomly accessed objects. For semantically related data

Figure 10. Load balancing versus clustering

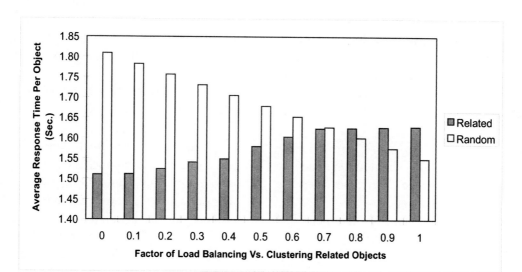

items, however, decreasing F influenced the broadcast to favor the allocation of related data items closer to one another, thus improving the average response time. Such rate of improvement, however, declined as F reached a certain threshold value (0.2 in this case). At this point the behavior of the system reaches a steady state (the objects cannot be brought closer to one another). In different simulation runs, the ratio of randomly selected and semantically related data items varied in the ranges between 30/70% and 70/30% and the same behavior was observed. This figure can be productive in tuning the performance of the CCP method. Assuming a feedback channel is to be used to collect the statistics of the users' access pattern, F can be adjusted adaptively to match the access pattern. As an example, if the frequency of accessing data items based on their connection is equivalent to

that of accessing data items randomly, then a factor value of 0.7 would generate the best overall response time.

Section Conclusion

This section concentrated on the proper mapping of data items on multiple parallel air channels. The goal was to find the most appropriate allocation scheme that would (a) preserve the connectivity among the data items, (b) provide the minimum overall broadcast time (load balancing), and (c) cluster related data items close to one another (improving the response time). Applying the LOF heuristic showed an improvement in load balancing. However, it proved short in solving the third aforementioned requirement. The CCP algorithm was presented to compensate this shortcoming. Relying on the critical path paradigm, the algorithm assumed several heuristics and showed better performance.

ENERGY-EFFICIENT INDEXING

In this section, we investigate and analyze the usage of indexing and indexed-based retrieval techniques for data items along the single and parallel broadcast channel(s) from an energy-efficient point of view. In general, index-based channel access protocols involve the following steps.

1) **Initial probe.** The client tunes into the broadcast channel to determine when the next index is broadcast.
2) **Search.** The client accesses the index and determines the offset for the requested data items.
3) **Retrieve.** The client tunes into the channel and pulls all the required data items.

In the initial probe, the mobile unit must be in active, operational mode. As soon as the mobile unit retrieves the offset of the next index, its operational mode could change to doze mode. To perform the *Search* step, the mobile unit must be in active mode, and when the unit gets the offset of the required data items, it could switch to doze mode. Finally, when the requested data items are being broadcast (*Retrieve* step), the mobile unit changes its operational mode to active mode and tunes into the channel to download the requested data. When the data is retrieved, the unit changes to doze mode again.

Object-Oriented Indexing

Object-oriented indexing is normally implemented as a multilevel tree. We can classify the possible implementation techniques into two general schemes: single-class indexing and hierarchical indexing. In the single-class scheme, multiple multilevel trees are constructed, each representing one class. In this case, the leaf nodes of each tree point to data items belonging only to the class indexed by that tree. A query requesting all objects with a certain ID has to navigate all these trees. On the other hand, the hierarchical scheme constructs one multilevel tree representing an index for all classes. The same query has to only navigate the common tree.

Data Indexing on a Single Air Channel

We assume an *air-channel page* as the storage granule on the air channel. Due to the sequential nature of the air channel, the allocation of the nodes of a multilevel tree has to follow the navigational path used to traverse the tree, starting at the root. Therefore, an ordering scheme is used to sequentially map the nodes on the air channel. Similarly, data items are allocated onto air channel pages following their index.

Storage Requirement

The overall storage requirement is the sum of the storage required by the inner and leaf nodes. For both schemes, the structure of the inner node is the same (Figure 11). An inner node is a collection of records, where each record is composed of a [*Key, pointer*] pair. Assume the order of the tree is o and the fan-out of every node is f ($o \leq f \leq 2o$, except for the root where $2 \leq f \leq 2o$). The leaf node structures of both schemes are shown in Figure 12. As can be seen, the main difference between the two schemes is that the hierarchical scheme requires a list of classes that have data items indexed by the index.

For the sake of simplicity, and without loss of generality, we assume that there are no overflow pages, furthermore assuming the following notations.

P size of air-channel page
K average number of distinct keys for an attribute
S average size of a leaf-node index record in a single-class index

Figure 11. Inner-node structure of single-class and hierarchical schemes

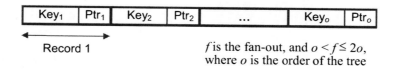

f is the fan-out, and $o < f \leq 2o$, where o is the order of the tree

Figure 12. Leaf-node structure of single-class and hierarchical schemes

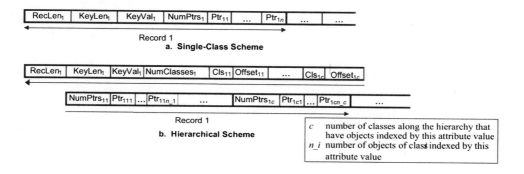

c number of classes along the hierarchy that have objects indexed by this attribute value

n_i number of objects of class indexed by this attribute value

H average size of a leaf-node index record in a hierarchical index

L number of leaf-node pages

IN number of inner-node pages for either scheme

$$L_{Single-Class} = \left\lceil K / \left\lfloor P / S \right\rfloor \right\rceil \tag{3}$$

$$L_{Hierarchical} = \left\lceil K / \left\lfloor P / H \right\rfloor \right\rceil \tag{4}$$

$$IN = 1 + \left\lfloor L / f \right\rfloor + \left\lfloor \left\lfloor L / f \right\rfloor / f \right\rfloor + \ldots \tag{5}$$

It should be noted that in the case of a single-class scheme, Equations 3 and 5 should be calculated for all the classes.

Timing Analysis

To perform the timing analysis, one has to consider the domain of a query. The cardinality of the domain of a query is the number of classes to be accessed by the query along the hierarchy. Our timing analysis evaluates the *response* and *active* time as the performance metrics. The response time is defined as the time elapsed between the first user access to the air channel and when the required information is retrieved. The active time is defined as the time during which the mobile unit has to be active accessing the channel. In the timing analysis, we use the number of pages as our unit of measurement. Finally, to support our protocols, we assume that every air-channel page contains control information indicating the location of the first page of the next index. This can simply be implemented as an offset (2 or 4 bytes).

a) **Hierarchical Method.** In this scheme, whether the domain of the query covers one class or all classes along the hierarchy, the same index structure has to be traversed. The protocol is shown below.

Hierarchical Protocol

1) Probe onto channel and get offset to the next index *active*
2) Reach the index *doze*
3) Retrieve the required index pages *active*
4) Reach the required data pages *doze*
5) Retrieve required data pages *active*

- **Response Time.** Assume I_H and D denote the size of the index and data, respectively. On average, it takes half the broadcast (the size of the broadcast is $I + D$) to locate the index from the initial probe. Once the index is reached, it has to be completely traversed before data pages appear on the broadcast. On average, it takes half the size of the data to locate and retrieve the required data items. Thus, the response time is proportional to:

$$\frac{I_H + D}{2} + I_H + \frac{D}{2} = \frac{3I_H}{2} + D = Broadcast + \frac{I_H}{2}$$

(6)

- **Active Time.** The mobile unit's modules have to be active to retrieve a page. Once the index is reached, a number of inner-node pages have to be accessed in order to get and retrieve a leaf-node page. The number of pages to be retrieved at the index is equal to the height of the index tree ($\log_f(D)$). Finally, the amount of the data pages to be read is equal to the number of data items

to be retrieved that reside on distinct pages (NODP). Therefore, the active time is:

$$1 + \log_f(D) + NODP$$

(7)

b) **Single-Class Method.** In this scheme, we assume that the first page of every index contains information indicating the location of each index class. This structure can be implemented by including a vector of pairs [class_id, offset]. Assuming that the size of the offset and the class_id is 4 bytes each, the size of this structure would be 8c, where c is the number of class indexes on the broadcast.

Single-Class Protocol

1) Probe onto channel and get offset to the next index *active*
2) Reach the index *doze*
3) Retrieve offsets to the indexes of required classes *active*
4) for every required class
5) Reach the index *doze*
6) Retrieve the required index pages *active*
7) Reach the required data *doze*
8) Retrieve required data pages *active*

- **Response Time.** The size of a single index and its associated data are labeled as I_i and D_i, respectively. Since the total number of objects to be indexed is the same in single-class and hierarchical indexes, the sum of all D_i for all classes is equal to D. Assume a query references a set of classes where x and y stand for the first and last classes to be accessed. The average distance to be covered to get to x is half the distance covering the indexes and data between the beginning of y and the beginning of x. Once the index x is located, then all the indexes and data of all the classes between x and y (including those of x) have to be traversed. Once y is reached, its index and half of its data (on average) have to be traversed. Thus, the response time is proportional to:

$$\frac{\sum_{i=y}^{x-1}(I_i + D_i)}{2} + \sum_{i=x}^{y}(I_i + D_i) - \frac{D_y}{2} \qquad (8)$$

Equation 8 provides a general means for calculating the average response time. However, the results are dependent on the location of the probe and the distance between x and y. It has been shown that the response time is lower bounded by half the size of the broadcast and upper bounded by slightly above the size of the broadcast. Further discussion on this issue is beyond the scope of this chapter and the interested reader is referred to Chehadeh, Hurson, and Kavehrad (1999).

- **Active Time.** Similar to the hierarchical case, the active time is dependent on the number of index pages and data pages to be retrieved. Therefore, the active time is the sum of the height of the trees for all the indexes of classes to be retrieved plus the number of the corresponding data pages. This is shown in the Equation 9. The 2 in the front accounts for the initial probe plus the additional page containing the index of classes (Line 3 in the protocol).

$$2 + \sum_{i=x}^{y}\left[\log_f(D_i) + NODP_i\right] \qquad (9)$$

Performance Evaluation

Our simulator was extended to study both the response time and energy consumption with respect to the two allocation schemes. The overall structure of the schema graph determines the navigational paths among the classes within the graph. The relationships of the navigational paths within the graph influence the number and structure of indexes to be used.

- **Inheritance Relationship.** Within an inheritance hierarchy, classes at the lower level of the hierarchy inherit attributes of the classes at the upper level. Therefore, data items belonging to the lower-level classes tend to be larger than those within the upper levels. The distribution of the number of data items is application dependent. In our analysis, and without loss of generality, we assumed the data items to be equally distributed among the classes of the hierarchy.

- **Aggregation Relationship.** In an aggregation hierarchy, data items belonging to lower classes are considered "part of" data items and those at the higher ends are the "collection" of such parts. Therefore, data items belonging to higher classes are generally larger than those belonging to the lower ones. In addition, the cardinality of a class at the upper end is smaller than a class at the lower end.

As a result, the organization of classes within the schema graph has its influence on the distribution of both the number and size of data items among the classes of the database. We assumed an average of eight classes for each hierarchy and categorize the sizes of data items as small, medium, large, and very large. Furthermore, 60% of the data items have distinct keys and the value of any attribute is uniformly distributed among the data items containing such attribute. Table 7 shows a list of all the input parameters assumed for this case.

The information along the broadcast channel is organized in four different fashions: the hierarchical and single-class methods for the inheritance and aggregation relationships. Table 8 shows the data and index page sizes for these organizations. Note that it is the number of data items (not data

Table 7. Input parameters

Parameter	Value (Default/Range)
Number of Data Items on Broadcast	5,120
Average Number of Classes Along Hierarchy	8
Percentage Distribution of Number of Data Items in Inheritance Hierarchy	25,25,25,25%
Percentage Distribution of Number of Data Items in Aggregation Hierarchy	40,30,20,10%
Distribution of Data Size [S,M,L,VL]	16,512,3K,6K bytes
Distribution of the Data Sizes in Inheritance Hierarchy	VL,L,M,S
Distribution of the Data Sizes in Aggregation Hierarchy	S,M,L,VL
Percentage of Classes to be Retrieved (Default/Range)	70% / [10-100%]
Average Number of Data Items to Retrieve per Class	2
Fan-Out in Index Tree	5
Average Number of Data Items with Distinct Key Attribute per Class	60% of data items per class
Size of Air-Channel Page	512 bytes
Broadcast Data Rate	1 M bits/sec
Power Consumption Active Mode	130 mW
Power Consumption Doze Mode	6.6 mW

Table 8. Number of index and data pages

	Aggregation/ Hierarchical	Aggregation/ Single [Eight Classes]	Inheritance/ Hierarchical	Inheritance/ Single [Eight Classes]
I n d e x Pages	2,343	67,63,49,39,36,32,18,16	2,343	40,40,40,40,40,40,40,40
D a t a Pages	13,562	73,75,652,769,2504,28140,3206,3502	34,015	12517,11520,5253,4252,637,440,25,20

Table 9. Response time degradation factor relative to the no-index scheme

Aggregation/ Hierarchical	Aggregation/ Single	Inheritance/ Hierarchical	Inheritance/ Single
1.17	1.05	1.1	1.02

pages) that controls the number of index blocks. Within each indexing scheme, for each query, the simulator simulates the process of probing the air channel, getting the required index pages, and retrieving the required data pages. In each query, on average, two data items from each class are retrieved. The simulation measures the response time and amount of energy consumed.

a)   **Response Time.** Placing an index along the air channel contributes to extra storage overhead and thus longer response time. Hence, the best response time is achieved when no index is placed, and the entire broadcast is searched. Table 9 shows the degradation factor in the average response time due to the inclusion of an index in the broadcast. The factor is proportional to the ratio of the size of the index blocks to that of the entire broadcast.

Figure 13 shows the response time for all four different broadcast organizations. From the figure, one could conclude that for both the inheritance and aggregation cases, the

response time of the hierarchical organization remained almost constant (with a slight increase, as the number of classes to retrieve increases). This is due to the fact that regardless of the number of classes and the location of the initial probe, all accesses have to be directed to the beginning of the index (at the beginning of the broadcast). The slight increase is attributed to the increase in the total number of objects to be retrieved — assuming that the objects to be retrieved are distributed uniformly along the broadcast. It should be noted, however, that such an increase is only minor since the response time is mainly influenced by the initial procedure.

Two observations can be made: (a) the single-class method offers a better response time than the hierarchical case and (b) the response time for the single-class method increases as the number of retrieved classes increase. The first observation is due to the fact that in the single-class method, accesses do not have to be directed to the beginning

Figure 13. Response time versus number of retrieved classes

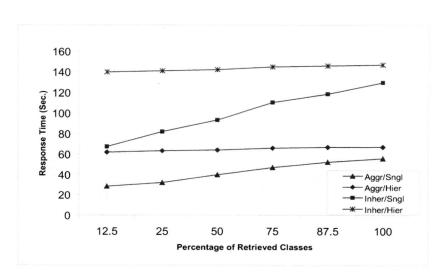

of the broadcast. The second observation is due to the fact that an increase in the number of classes to be retrieved directly increases the number of index and data pages to be accessed.

Indexing based on the aggregation relationship offers lower response time than indexing based on the inheritance relationship since the distribution of the number of objects in the inheritance relationship is more concentrated on the larger objects. Having larger objects results in a longer broadcast, and, hence, it takes longer to retrieve the objects.

b)   **Energy.** For each query, the amount of energy consumed is the sum of the energy consumed while the unit is in both active and doze modes. In the case where no index is provided, the mobile unit is in active mode during the entire probe. However, in the case where an index is provided, the active time is proportional to the number of index and data pages to be retrieved. As expected, the active time increases as the number of

retrieved classes increases. The hierarchical method searches only one large index tree, whereas the single-class method searches through multiple smaller index trees. The number of pages to retrieve per index tree is proportional to the height of the tree. For a query spanning a single class, the single-class method produces a better active time than the hierarchical method. As the number of classes to be retrieved increases, the hierarchical tree is still traversed only once. However, more single-class trees have to be traversed, and, hence, results in an increase in the active time.

In both the single-class and the hierarchical methods, the aggregation case requires lower active time than the inheritance case since the inheritance case has larger objects, thus requiring the retrieval of more pages. For the sake of practicality, we utilized the power consumption data of the Hitachi SH7032 processor: 130 mW when active and 6.6 mW when in doze. Since power is the amount of energy consumed per unit

Figure 14. Detailed energy consumption

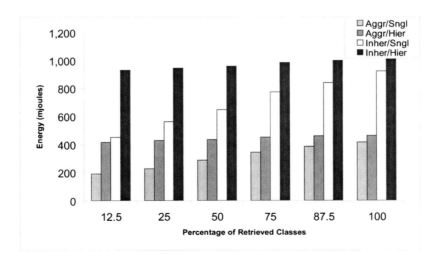

of time, the total energy can be calculated directly using Equation 10:

$$Energy = (ResponseTime - ActiveTime)DozeModePower + (ActiveTime)ActiveModePower$$

$$(10)$$

Figure 14 details the energy consumed during the entire query operation in mjoules. The power consumption of the mobile unit is much higher while the unit is in active mode, with a ratio of 19.7. However, our experiments showed that, in general, the duration of the active-mode operations was much smaller than doze-mode operations. As a result, the energy consumed during doze time was the dominating factor. As can be seen from Figure 14, the single-class method is superior to the hierarchical method. This is very similar to the results obtained for the response time, and similarly, the power consumption of the single-class method is lower than that of the hierarchical method.

Data Indexing on Parallel Air Channels

Allocation of Object-Oriented Indexing on Parallel Air Channels

Figure 15 shows the allocation of the single-class and hierarchical-based schemes on the two parallel air channels. For the single-class indexing scheme (Figure 15a), the index and data of each class are distributed and placed along the channels. The hierarchical indexing scheme (Figure 15b) places the index on one channel, and divides and distributes the data among the channels. The most popular data items can be put in the free space. Note that in both cases, similar to the single air channel, it is possible to interleave and distribute the index pages and associated data pages using a variety of methods.

Figure 15. Allocation of single-class and hierarchical indexes on two parallel air channels

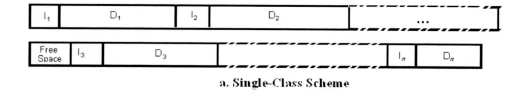

a. Single-Class Scheme

b. Hierarchical Scheme

I$_i$	Index of single class i
D$_i$	Data of single class i
I_H	Hierarchical index
D/c	Data on each channel

Storage Requirement

In the case of broadcasting along parallel air channels, the storage requirement is the same as that for a single air channel.

Timing Analysis

In the case of parallel air channels, one has to account for switching between channels when analyzing access time and power consumption. During the switching time, the pages that are being broadcast on different channels cannot be accessed by the mobile unit. In addition, the mobile unit at each moment of time can tune into one channel—*overlapped page range*. By considering the average page size (512 bytes), communication bandwidth (1Mbit/sec), and switching time (the range of microseconds), we assume that the overlapped page range equals two pages. Finally, we assumed that the power consumption for switching between two channels is 10% of the power consumed in active mode. Equation 11 calculates the power consumption.

a) **Hierarchical Method.** The following protocol shows the sequence of operations.

Hierarchical Protocol

1) Probe onto channel and retrieve offset to the next index *active*
2) Do {Reach the next index *doze*
3) Retrieve the required index pages *active*
4) Do {Reach the next possible required data page *doze*
5) Retrieve the next possible required data page *active*
6) }while every possible required data page is retrieved from the current broadcast
7) } while there are unaccessed data items becuse of overlapped page range

$EnergyConsumption = (ResponseTime - ActiveTime) * DozeModePower$
$+ (ActiveTime) * ActiveModePower + TheNumberOfSwitching * 10\% * ActiveModePower$

$$(11)$$

- **Response Time.** I_H and D are used to denote the size of the hierarchy index and data, respectively. For the c-channel environment, the average size of data on each channel is D/c. To locate the index from the initial probe, it takes half the broadcast of one channel (the size of the broadcast is $I_H + D/c$). Once the index is reached, it has to be completely traversed before data pages appear on the broadcast and, on average, it takes half the size of the data to locate and retrieve the required data items. Thus, the response time from the initial probe to the first complete broadcast is proportional to

$$(I_H + D/c)/2 + I_H + (D/c)/2 = 3 I_H/2 + D/c \qquad (12)$$

Because of the overlapped page range, the mobile units may not be able to get all of the required data during one complete broadcast (e.g., because of conflicts). Therefore, it has to scan the next broadcast. Let P be the probability of the data that are in the same overlapped page range. The distance from the last location to the next index is also half the size of the data of one channel. Once the index is reached, the same process will occur. Thus, the response time from the last location of the previous broadcast until the mobile unit can acquire all of the required data is proportional to

$$P * (D/2c + I_H + D/2c) = P * (I_H + D/c) \qquad (13)$$

As a result, on average, the response time is proportional to

$$(1.5 + P) I_H + (1 + P) D/c \qquad (14)$$

- **Active Time.** The mobile unit has to be active during the first probe (to retrieve a page). Once the index is reached, a number of nonleaf node pages have to be accessed in order to get and retrieve a leaf-node page. The number of pages to be retrieved at the index is equal to the height of the index tree ($\log_f(D)$). The amount of the data pages to be read is equal to the *NODP*. Again, because of the overlapped page range among parallel air channels, the probability of accessing the index of the next broadcast has to be included. Therefore, the active time is proportional to

$$1 + \log_f(D) + NODP + P * \log_f(D) \qquad (15)$$

b) **Single-Class Indexing Scheme**

Single-Class Protocol

1) Probe onto channel and retrieve offset to the next index *active*
2) Do {Reach the next index *doze*
3) Retrieve offsets to the indexes of required classes *active*
4) Reach the next possible index *doze*
5) Retrieve the next possible required index page *active*
6) Do {Reach the next possible index or data page *doze*
7) Retrieve the next possible index or data page *active*
8) } while not (all indexes and data of required classes are scanned)
9) } while there are some data pages which are not retrieved because of overlapped page range

- **Response Time.** As before, the size of a single index and its associated data are labeled as I_i and D_i, respectively. The response time is simply driven by dividing Equation 8 by the number of the air channels (Equation 16):

$$\frac{\sum_{i=y}^{x-1}(I_i + D_i)}{2c} + \frac{\sum_{i=x}^{y}(I_i + D_i)}{c} - \frac{D_y}{2c} \qquad (16)$$

Let *P* be the probability of the data that are in the same overlapped page range. Thus, the response time for getting the remaining required data items on the second broadast probe is proportional to

$$P * \left(\frac{\sum_{i=y}^{x-1}(I_i + D_i)}{2c} + \frac{\sum_{i=x}^{y}(I_i + D_i)}{c} - \frac{D_y}{2c} \right) \qquad (17)$$

As a result, the response time is proportional to

$$(1 + P) * \left(\frac{\sum_{i=y}^{x-1}(I_i + D_i)}{2c} + \frac{\sum_{i=x}^{y}(I_i + D_i)}{c} - \frac{D_y}{2c} \right) \qquad (18)$$

- **Active Time.** Similar to the hierarchical case, the active time is the sum of the height of the trees for all the indexes of the classes to be retrieved plus the number of the corresponding data pages. This is shown in Equation 19. The *2* at the beginning of the equation accounts for the initial probe plus the additional page containing the index of classes. Because of the overlapped page range among parallel air channels, the probability of accessing the index of the next broadcast has to be included. Therefore, the active time is proportional to

$$2 + \sum_{i=x}^{y} \left[\log_f(D_i) + NODP_i \right] + \frac{P}{2} \sum_{i=x}^{y} \log_f(D_i) \qquad (19)$$

Performance Evaluation

Once again, our simulator was extended to study the response time and energy consumption of the single-class and hierarchical indexing schemes in parallel air channels based on the input parameters presented in Table 7.

a) **Response Time.** In the case of no indexing, the response time was constant and independent of the number of channels. This is due to the fact that without any indexing mechanism in place, the mobile unit has to scan every data page in sequence until all required data pages are acquired. Moreover, when indexing schemes are in force, the response time lessens as the number of channels increases.

For the inheritance and aggregation cases, the response time decreases as the number of channels increases. This is due to the fact that, as the number of channels increases, the length of the broadcast becomes shorter. However, the higher the number of channels, the higher the probability of conflicts in accessing data residing on different channels in the overlapped page range. As a result, doubling the number of channels will not decrease the response time by half.

For both the inheritance and aggregation indexing schemes, the single-class method offers a better response time than the hierarchical method. The single-class method accesses do not have to be started at the beginning of the broadcast. For the hierarchical method, on the other hand, any access has to be started from the beginning of the broadcast, which makes the response time of the hierarchical method longer. Indexing based on the aggregation relationship offers a lower response time than that of the inheritance relationship because the distribution of data items in the inheritance relationship is more concentrated on the larger data items.

b) **Energy.** The active time is proportional to the number of index and data pages to be retrieved. For broadcast data without an index, the active time is the same as the response time. In addition, for all four indexing schemes, the active time remains almost constant and independent of the number of air channels. This is because the active time is proportional to the number of index and data pages to be retrieved.

In general, the hierarchical method requires less active time than the single-class method. The hierarchical method searches only one large index tree, whereas the single-class method searches through multiple smaller index trees, and the number of pages to be retrieved per index tree is proportional to the height of the tree. In both the single-class and the hierarchical methods, the indexing based on an aggregation relationship requires lower active time than the inheritance method. This is simply due to the fact that the inheritance relationship resulted in larger data items, thus requiring the retrieval of more pages.

In a separate simulation run we observed the total energy consumption. It was concluded that the total energy consumption of broadcasting without any indexing schemes is much higher than that of broadcasting supported by indexing, and the energy consumption of the single-class method is lower than that of the hierarchical method. This is very similar to the results obtained for the response time. When indexing was supported, energy consumption, on average, decreased about 15 to 17 times in the case of the aggregation relationship and the inheritance relationship, respectively.

Figure 16 shows the detail of energy consumption for the aggregation relationship. As the number of channels increases, the energy

Figure 16. Detailed energy consumption

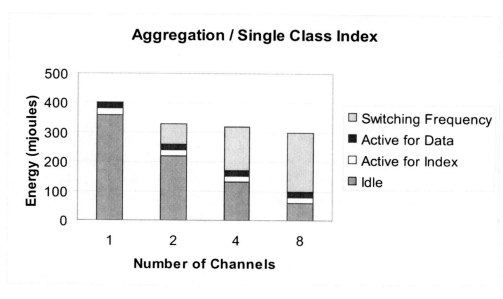

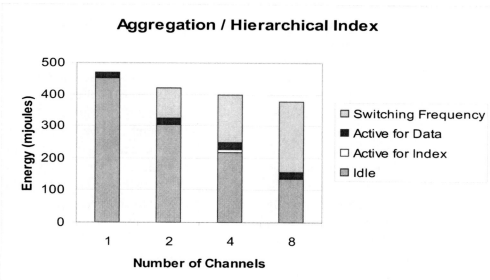

consumption during idle time decreases. The energy consumption for retrieving indexes increases because the probability of the data being in the same overlapped page range increases. The higher this probability, the more the mobile unit has to get the index from the next broadcast. Finally, the energy consumption for switching between two different channels increases because the required data are distributed among the channels. The larger the number of channels, the more distributed is the data among the channels, and, consequently, the more frequent switching between channels.

Section Conclusion

This section investigated an energy-efficient solution by the means of applying indexing schemes to object-oriented data broadcast over single and parallel air channels. Two methods, namely, the hierarchical and single-class methods, were explored. Timing analysis and simulation were conducted to compare and contrast the performance of different indexing schemes against each other. It was shown that including an index degrades the response time moderately, however, such degradation is greatly offset by the improvement in energy consumption. For a single air channel, broadcasting with supported indexing schemes increased the response time when compared with broadcasting without indexing support. However, the response time is reduced by broadcasting data with an index along parallel air channels. Moreover, the response time decreased as the number of air channels is increased. Relative to nonindexed broadcasting, the mobile unit's energy consumption decreased rather sharply when indexing is supported. For a set of queries retrieving data items along the air channel(s), the single-class indexing method resulted in a faster response time and lower energy consumption than the hierarchical method.

CONFLICTS AND GENERATION OF ACCESS PATTERNS

One of the problems associated with broadcasting information on parallel air channels is the possibility for conflicts between accessing data items on different channels. Because the mobile

unit can tune into only one channel at a time, some data items may have to be retrieved on subsequent broadcasts. In addition, during the channel switch time, the mobile unit is unable to retrieve any data from the broadcast. Conflicts will directly influence the access latency and, hence, the overall execution time. This section is intended to provide a mathematical foundation to calculate the expected number of passes required to retrieve a set of data items requested by an application from parallel air channels by formulating this problem as an *asymmetric traveling salesman problem* (TSP). In addition, in an attempt to reduce the access time and power consumption, we propose heuristic policies that can reduce the number of passes over parallel air channels. Analysis of the effectiveness of such policies is also the subject of this section.

Enumerating Conflicts

Equation 1 showed the number of broadcasts (passes) required to retrieve K data items from M parallel channels if conflicts between data items are independent. To calculate $P(i)$, it is necessary to count the number of ways the data items can be distributed while having exactly i conflicts, then divide it by the total number of ways the K data items can be distributed over the parallel channels. In order to enumerate possible conflicting cases, we classify the conflicts as single or double conflicts as defined below.

Definition 7. A single conflict is defined as a data item in the conflict region that does not have another data item in the conflict region in the same row. A double conflict is a data item that is in the conflict region and does have another data item in the conflict region in the same row.

The number of data items that cause a double conflict, d, can range from 0 (all single conflicts) up to the number of conflicts, i, or the number of remaining data items, $(K-i-1)$. When counting combinations, each possible value of d must be considered separately. The number of possible combinations for each value of d is summed to determine the total number of combinations for the specified value of i. When counting the number of ways to have i conflicts and d double conflicts, four factors must be considered.

- Whether each of the $(i - d)$ data items representing a single conflict is in the left or right column in the conflict region. Because each data item has two possible positions, the number of variations due to this factor is $2^{(i-d)}$.
- Which of the $(M - 1)$ rows in the conflict region are occupied by the $(i - d)$ single conflicts. The number of variations due to this factor is $\binom{M-1}{i-d}$.
- Which of the $(M-1)-(i-d)$ remaining rows in the conflict region are occupied by the d double conflicts; $(i-d)$ is subtracted because a double conflict cannot occupy the same row as a single conflict. The number of variations due to this factor is $\binom{(M-1)-(i-d)}{d}$
- Which of the $(MN - 2M + 1)$ positions not in the conflict region are occupied by the $(K - i - d - 1)$ remaining data items. The number of variations due to this factor is $\binom{MN-2M+1}{K-i-d-1}$.

Note that these sources of variation are independen from each other and, hence:

$$P(i) = \frac{\sum_{d=0}^{d \leq MIN(i,K-i-1)} 2^{(i-d)} \binom{M-1}{i-d}\binom{(M-1)-(i-d)}{d}\binom{MN-2M+1}{K-i-d-1}}{\binom{MN-1}{K-1}}$$

(20)

If the conflicts produced by one data item are independent from the conflicts produced by all other data items, then Equation 20 will give the number of passes required to retrieve all K requested data items. However, if the conflicts produced by one data item are not independent of the conflicts produced by other data items,

additional conflicts will occur which are not accounted for in our analysis. Equation 20 will thus underestimate the number of broadcasts required to retrieve all K data items.

Retrieving Data from Parallel Broadcast Air Channels in the Presence of Conflicts

The problem of determining the proper order to retrieve the requested data items from the parallel channels can be modeled as a TSP. Making the transformation from a broadcast to the TSP requires the creation of a complete directed graph G with K nodes, where each node represents a requested object. The weight w of each edge (i, j) indicates the number of broadcasts that must pass in order to retrieve data item j immediately after retrieving data item i. Since any particular data item can be retrieved in either the current broadcast or the next broadcast, the weight of each edge will be either 0 or 1. A weight of 0 indicates that the data item j is after data item i in the broadcast with no conflict. A weight of 1 indicates that data item j is either before or in conflict with data item i.

Simulation Model

The simulation models a mobile unit retrieving data items from a broadcast. A broadcast is represented as an N x M two-dimensional array, where N represents the number of data items in each channel of a broadcast and M represents the number of parallel channels. For each value of K, where K represents the number of requested data items $(1 \leq K \leq M)$, the simulation randomly generates 1,000 patterns representing the uniform distribution of K data items among the broadcast channels. The K data items from each randomly generated pattern are retrieved using various retrieval algorithms. The number of passes is recorded and compared. To prevent the randomness of the broadcasts from affecting the comparison of the algorithms, the same broadcast is used for each algorithm in a particular trial and the mean value is reported for each value of *K*. Finally, several algorithms for ordering the retrieval from the broadcast, both TSP related and non-TSP related, were analyzed.

Data Retrieval Algorithms

Both exact and approximate TSP solution finders and two heuristic based methods were used to retrieve the data items from the broadcast.

a) **TSP Methods.** An exact TSP solution algorithm was used to provide a basis for comparison with the other algorithms. These algorithms are simply too slow and too resource intensive. While a better implementation of the algorithm may somewhat reduce the cost, it cannot change the fact that finding the exact solution will require exponential time for some inputs. Knowing the exact solution to a given TSP does, however, allow us to evaluate the quality of a heuristic approach. A TSP heuristic based on the assignment problem relaxation requires far less CPU time and memory than the optimal tour finders, so it is suitable for use on a mobile unit. A publicly available TSP solving package named TspSolve (Hurwitz & Craig, 1996) was used for all TSP algorithm implementations.

b) **Next Data Item Access.** The strategy used by this heuristic is simply to always retrieve the next available data item in a broadcast. This can be considered as a greedy approach. It is also similar to the nearest neighbor approach to solving TSP problems.

c) **Row Scan.** A simple *row scan* heuristic was also used. This algorithm simply reads all the data items from one channel in each pass. If a channel does not have any requested data in it, it is skipped. This algorithm will always require as many passes as there are

channels with requested data items in them. The benefit of this algorithm is that it does not require any time to decide on an ordering. It can thus begin retrieving data items from a broadcast immediately. This is especially important when a large percentage of the data items in a broadcast are requested.

Results

As expected, the TSP methods provide much better results than both the two heuristic-based algorithms. Our simulations showed that the TSP heuristic performed almost exactly as well as the optimal TSP algorithm. This is a very interesting observation because it means that one can use a fast heuristic to schedule retrievals of data items from the broadcast without any performance degradation.

In Figure 17, the TSP methods show that the number of broadcasts required to retrieve all *K* requested data items from a broadcast is much greater than the number of broadcasts predicted by Equation 20 — Equation 20 was based on the assumption that the conflicts among the requested data items are independent. Figure 17 used five parallel channels and 20 pages per channel. It is also interesting to note that the straightforward row scan nearly matches the performance of the TSP-based algorithms when more than about 45% of the total number of data items is requested. In this case, there are so many conflicts that it is virtually impossible to avoid having to make as many passes as there are parallel channels. When this occurs, it is better to do the straightforward row scan than to spend time and resources running a TSP heuristic.

Optimal Number of Broadcast Channels

More channels mean that a given amount of information can be made available in a shorter period of time at the expense of more conflicts.

Figure 17. Comparison of several algorithms for retrieving objects from parallel channels

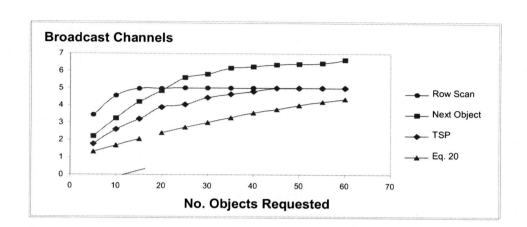

The simulation results showed that it is always advantageous to use more broadcast channels. While there will be more conflicts between data items, this does not quite counteract the shorter broadcast length of the many-channel broadcasts. This was especially evident when only a few data items in a broadcast were being accessed.

Ordered Access List

The scope of the general access protocol for indexed parallel-channel configuration in the presence of conflicts was extended in order to use heuristics that can generate the ordered access list of requested data items that reduces

- the number of passes over the air channels and
- the number of channel switches.

During the *Search* step, the index is accessed to determine the offset and the channel of the requested data items. Then, a sequence of access patterns is generated. Finally, the *Retrieval* step is performed following the generated access patterns.

Extended Retrieval Protocol

1) Probe the channel and retrieve the offset to the next index
2) Access the next index
3) Do {Search the index for the requested object
4) Calculate the offset of the object
5) Get the channel on which the object will be broadcast
6) } while there is an unprocessed requested object
7) Generate access patterns for the requested objects (using retrieval scheme)
8) Do {Wait for the next broadcast cycle
9) Do {Reach the first object as indicated by the access pattern
10) Retrieve the object
11) } while there is an unretrieved object in the access pattern

12) } while there is an unprocessed access pattern

Performance Evaluation

We extended the simulator to emulate the process of accessing data from a hierarchical indexing scheme in parallel air channels. Moreover, the simulator also analyzes the effect of conflicts on the average access time and power consumption.

Our retrieval scheme, based on the user request, generates a retrieval forest representing all possible retrieval sequences. However, as expected, the generated retrieval forest grows exponentially with the number of requested data items. The key observation needed to reduce the size of the tree is to recognize that each requested data item has a unique list of children, and the number of children for a particular data item is limited to the number of channels. The simulator takes advantage of these observations to reduce the size of the retrieval tree and the calculation time without sacrificing accuracy.

The generation of the user requests was performed randomly, representing a distribution of K data items in the broadcast. In various simulations runs, the value of K was varied from one to $N \times M$—in a typical user query of public data, K is much less than $N \times M$. Finally, to take into account future technological advances, parameters such as transmission rate and power consumption in different modes of operation were fed to the simulator as variable entities.

The simulator calculates the average active time, the average idle time, the average query response time, the average number of broadcast passes, the number of channel switches, and the energy consumption of the retrieval process. As a final note, the size of the index was 13.52% of the size of the broadcast (not including the index) and the number of channels varied from 1 to 16 (2 to 17 when an independent channel was used for transmitting the index).

Simulation Model

For each simulation run, a set of input parameters, including the number of parallel air channels, the broadcast transmission rate, and the power consumption in different operational modes, was passed to the simulator. The simulator was run 1,000 times and the average of the designated performance metrics was calculated. The results of the simulations where an indexing scheme was employed were compared against a broadcast without any indexing mechanism. Two indexing scenarios were simulated.

- **Case 1.** The index was transmitted with the data in the first channel (index with data broadcast).
- **Case 2.** The index was transmitted over a dedicated channel in a cyclic manner.

Results

A comparison between the extended retrieval protocol against the row scan algorithm was performed. The index transmission was performed in a cyclic manner on an independent channel, and the number of requested data items was varied between 5 and 50 out of 5,464 securities within the NASDAQ exchange database. The simulation results showed that, regardless of the number of parallel air channels, the proposed algorithm reduces both the number of passes and the response time compared to the row scan algorithm. Moreover, the energy consumption was also reduced, but only when the number of data items retrieved was approximately 15 or less (Table 10).

Relative to the row scan algorithm, one should also consider the expected overhead of the proposed algorithm. The simulation results showed that in the worst case, the overhead of the proposed algorithm was slightly less than the time required to transmit one data page.

Table 10. Improvement of proposed algorithm versus row scan (10 data items requested)

# of Channels	# of Passes	Response Time	Energy
2	48.0%	28.0%	2.7%
4	68.0%	43.6%	3.1%
8	72.3%	46.5%	3.3%
16	71.8%	40.8%	3.4%

a) **Response Time.** Figures 18 to 20 show the response times in terms of the number of data items requested and the number of broadcast channels. Three cases were examined.

- **Case 1. Data and index are intermixed on broadcast channel(s).** Figure 18 shows the response times for different numbers of broadcast channels when retrieving the full range of existing data items from the broadcast. It can be concluded that when a few data items are requested, the response time decreases as the number of channels increases.

After a certain threshold point, the response time increases as the number of channels increases. This is due to an increase in the number of conflicts and hence an increase in the number of passes over the broadcast channels to retrieve the requested data.

- **Case 2. Index is broadcast over a dedicated channel in cyclic fashion.** Similar to Case 1, Figure 19 depicts the simulation results when retrieving the full range of existing data from the broadcast. Again, as expected, the

Figure 18. Response time (Case 1)

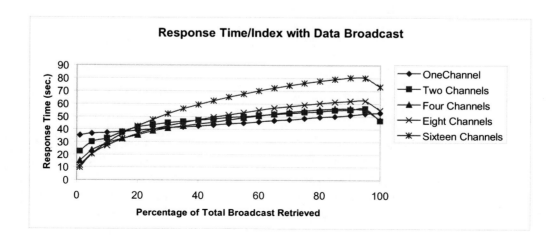

Figure 19. Response time (Case 2)

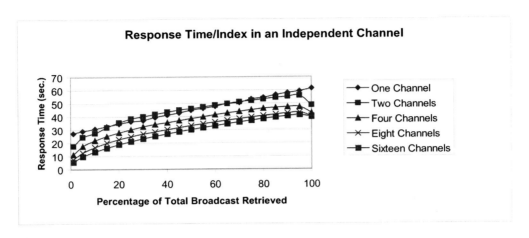

Figure 20. Response time (Case 3)

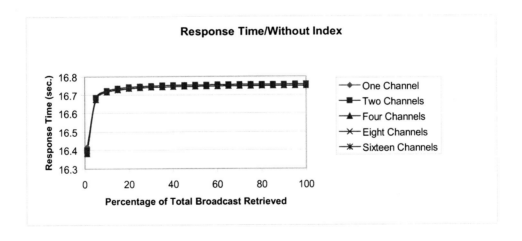

response time decreases as the number of channels increases. Comparing the results for one-channel and two-channel configuration, we can conclude that in some instances the two-channel configuration is not as effective — there is the possibility of conflicts, many of which unavoidably cause an increase in the number of passes and hence longer response time.

- **Case 3. No indexing is employed.** From Figure 20 one can conclude that the response time remains relatively constant regardless of the number of channels used. In this organization, the user must scan the same amount of data regardless of the user query and number of parallel channels.

In general, employment of an indexing scheme reduces the response time when retrieving a relatively small number of data items. As the percentage of data items requested increases, the number of conflicts increases as well. The proposed retrieval protocol tries primarily to reduce the conflicts in each pass of the broadcast; however, when the number of potential conflicts increases considerably, some conflicts become unavoidable, causing an increase in the number of passes and hence an increase in the response time. When the percentage of requested data approaches 100%, the response time reduces. This proves the validity of the proposed scheduling algorithm since it generates the same retrieval sequence as the row scan method.

b) **Switching Frequency.** Again, three cases were examined.
- **Case 1 & Case 2. Employment of indexing schemes.** Figure 21 shows the switching frequency for Case 1 and Case 2—the switching pattern is not affected by the indexing policy employed. From this figure one can conclude that the switching frequency increases as the number of channels and number of data items retrieved increase. This can be explained by an increase in the number of conflicts; as the proposed method tries to reduce the number of conflicts, the switching frequency will increase. Also, as stated previously, an increase in the number of channels increases the number of conflicts as well. One can notice that when the percentage of data items requested exceeds 50%, the switching frequency begins to decrease. This is due to the fact that the proposed method does not attempt to switch channels as often to avoid the conflicts as the number of conflicts increases substantially.

Figure 21. Switching frequency (Case 1 and Case 2)

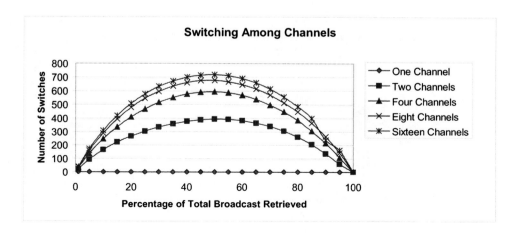

- **Case 3. No indexing is employed.** When no indexing technique is utilized, the row scan method is employed, producing a constant switching frequency independent of the number of data items requested. The switching frequency is, at the most, equal to the number of total channels employed in the simulation.

c) **Energy Consumption.** Figures 22 and 23 depict detailed energy consumption when 1% of data items on the broadcast are requested. It can be observed that the energy consumption is almost the same; however, Case 1 consumes more energy than Case 2 in doze mode.

Figure 22. Energy consumption (Case 1)

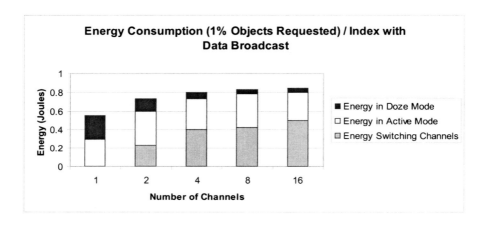

Figure 23. Energy consumption (Case 2)

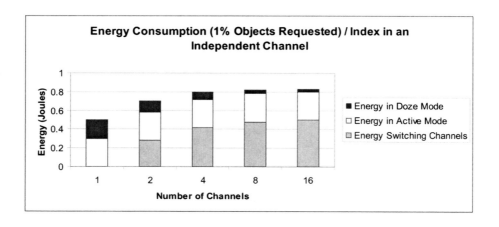

- **Case 1 & Case 2. Employment of indexing schemes.** In general, due to the increase in the number of channel-switching frequency, the energy consumption increases as the number of channels increases. In addition, we noted that the energy consumption increases when up to 50% of the broadcast data items are requested, then it decreases as the number of requested data items increases. This is directly related to the channel-switching frequency. In Case 1, in many instances, the mobile unit must wait in doze mode while the index is retransmitted.
- **Case 3. No indexing is employed.** When no indexing technique is used (Figure 24), the energy consumption varies only minimally due to the nature of the row scan algorithm employed.

From these figures we can observe that both Case 1 and Case 2 consume less power than Case 3 when a small percentage of data items is retrieved (around 1%). When the percentage of data items requested increases, the number of conflicts, the switching frequency, and, consequently, the energy consumption increase.

d) **Number of Passes.** As a note, the number of passes is independent of the index allocation scheme. Therefore, the number of passes for Cases 1 and 2 is the same.
- **Case 1 & Case 2. Employment of indexing schemes.** The increase in the number of passes is directly related to the increase in the number of channels and increase in the number of data items requested (Figure 25). An increase in the number of channels implies an increase in the number of conflicts, and, hence, the higher possibility of unavoidable conflicts, resulting in an increase in the number of passes. It can be noticed that when the number of data items requested is large, the number of passes exceeds the number of channels available. This is due to the priority order of the heuristics used in the proposed retrieval algorithm. In general, it is improbable that a query for public data requests a lot of data

Figure 24. Energy consumption (Case 3)

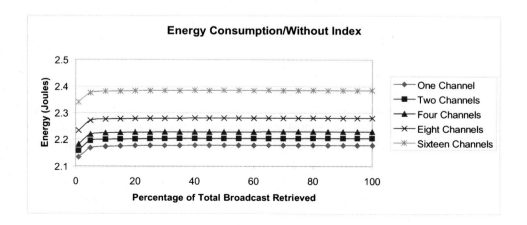

Figure 25. Number of passes over the parallel channels

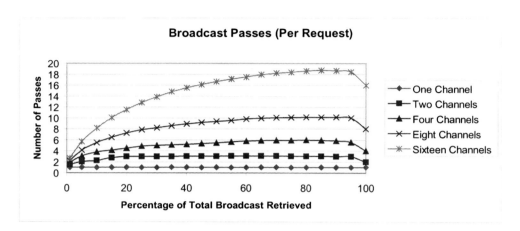

items from the broadcast channels. Our experience showed that for a query requesting up to 50 data items, the proposed method reduces the number of passes compared to Case 3.

- **Case 3. No indexing is employed.** In contrast, when no indexing technique is employed, the number of passes required is a function of the number of air channels. In the worst case we need N passes where N is the number of broadcast channels.

Section Conclusion

Conflicts directly influence the access latency and, hence, the overall execution time. This section provided a mathematical foundation to calculate the expected number of passes required to retrieve a set of data items requested by an application from parallel air channels. In addition, in an attempt to reduce the access time and power consumption, heuristics were used to develop access policies

that reduce the number of passes over the parallel air channels. Analysis of the effectiveness of such policies was also the subject of this section.

CONCLUSION AND FUTURE RESEARCH DIRECTIONS

This chapter aims to address the applicability and effectiveness of data broadcasting from two viewpoints: energy and response time. Within the scope of data broadcasting, we discussed different data allocation schemes, indexing approaches, and data retrieval methods for both single and parallel air channels. Comparisons of different algorithms were demonstrated through simulation results.

The scope of this research can be extended in many directions. For instance, we assumed that the resolution of queries happens on an individual basis at the mobile unit. It may be possible to reduce computation by utilizing a buffer and bundling several queries together, processing them as a whole. Our proposed scheduling scheme was based on three prioritized heuristics. It is interesting to investigate a new set of heuristics that can reduce the switching frequency while retrieving a large percentage of data items from the broadcast.

ACKNOWLEDGMENT

This work would have not been possible without the sincere effort of many students who participated in the development of conceptual issues as well as simulation results. We would like to thank them. In addition, this work in part has been supported by the Office of Naval Research and the National Science Foundation under the contracts N00014-02-1-0282 and IIS-0324835, respectively.

REFERENCES

Acharya, S., Alonso, R., Franklin, M., & Zdonik, S. (1995). Broadcast disks: Data management for asymmetric communication environments. *Proceedings of ACM SIGMOD International Conference on the Management of Data*, (pp. 199-210).

Alonso, R., & Ganguly, S. (1992). Energy efficient query optimization. *Technical Report MITL-TR-33-92*, Princeton, NJ: Matsushita Information Technology Laboratory.

Alonso, R., & Korth, H. F. (1993). Database system issues in nomadic computing. *Proceedings of ACM SIGMOD Conference on Management of Data*, (pp. 388-392).

Atkinson, M., Bancilhon, F., DeWitt, D., Dittrich, K., Maier, D., & Zdonik, S. (1989). The object-oriented database system manifesto. *Proceedings of Conference on Deductive and Object-Oriented Databases*, (pp. 40-57).

Badrinath, B. R. (1996). Designing distributed algorithms for mobile computing networks. *Computer Communications, 19*(4), 309-320.

Banerjee, J., Kim, W., Kim, S.-J., & Garza, J. F. (1988). Clustering a DAG for CAD databases. *IEEE Transactions on Software Engineering, 14*(11), 1684-1699.

Boonsiriwattanakul, S., Hurson, A. R., Vijaykrishnan, N., & Chehadeh, C. (1999). Energy-efficient indexing on parallel air channels in a mobile database access system. *Proceedings of the Third World Multiconference on Systemics, Cybernetics, and Informatics, and Fifth International Conference on Information Systems Analysis and Synthesis, IV,* (pp. 30-38).

Bowen, T. F. (1992). The DATACYCLE architecture. *Communication of ACM, 35*(12), 71-81.

Bright, M. W., Hurson, A. R., & Pakzad, S. (1992). A taxonomy and current issues in multidatabase systems. *IEEE Computer, 25*(3), 50-60.

Bright, M. W., Hurson, A. R., & Pakzad, S. (1994). Automated resolution of semantic heterogeneity in multidatabases. *ACM Transactions on Database Systems, 19*(2), 212-253.

Chang, E. E., & Katz, R. H. (1989). Exploiting inheritance and structure semantics for effective clustering and buffering in an object-oriented DBMS. *Proceedings of ACM SIGMOD Conference on Management of Data*, (pp. 348-357).

Chehadeh, Y. C., Hurson, A. R., & Tavangarian, D. (2001). Object organization on single and parallel broadcast channel. *Proceedings of High Performance Computing*, (pp. 163-169).

Chehadeh, Y. C., Hurson, A. R., & Kavehrad, M. (1999). Object organization on a single broadcast channel in the mobile computing environment [Special issue]. *Multimedia Tools and Applications Journal, 9*, 69-94.

Chehadeh, Y. C., Hurson, A. R., & Miller L. L. (2000). Energy-efficient indexing on a broadcast channel in a mobile database access system. *Proceedings of IEEE Conference on Information Technology*, (pp. 368-374).

Chehadeh, Y. C., Hurson, A. R., Miller, L. L., Pakzad, S., & Jamoussi, B. N. (1993). Application of parallel disks for efficient handling of object-oriented databases. *Proceedings of the Fifth IEEE Symposium on Parallel and Distributed Processing*, (pp. 184-191).

Cheng, J.-B. R., & Hurson, A. R. (1991a). Effective clustering of complex objects in object-oriented databases. *Proceedings of ACM SIGMOD Conference on Management of Data*, (pp. 22-27).

Cheng, J.-B. R., & Hurson, A. R. (1991b). On the Performance issues of object-based buffering. *Proceedings of International Conference on Parallel and Distributed Information Systems*, (pp. 30-37).

Chlamtac, I., & Lin, Y.-B. (1997). Mobile computing: When mobility meets computation. *IEEE Transactions on Computers, 46*(3), 257-259.

Comer, D. C. (1991). *Internetworking with TCP/IP Volume I: Principles, Protocols, and Architecture* (2nd ed.). Englewood Cliffs, NJ: Prentice Hall.

Demers, A., Pertersen, K., Spreitzer, M., Terry, D., Theier, M., & Welch, B. (1994). The bayou architecture: Support for data sharing among mobile users. *Proceedings of IEEE Workshop on Mobile Computing Systems and Applications*, (pp. 2-7).

Fong, E., Kent, W., Moore, K., & Thompson, C. (1991). *X3/SPARC/DBSSG/OODBTG Final Report*. Available from NIST.

Fox, A., Gribble, S. D., Brewer, E. A., & Amir, E. (1996). Adapting to network and client variability via on-demand dynamic distillation. *Proceedings of ASPLOS-VII*, Boston, Massachusetts, (pp. 160-170).

Honeyman, P., Huston, L., Rees, J., & Bachmann, D. (1992). The LITTLE WORK project. *Proceedings of the Third IEEE Workshop on Workstation Operating Systems*, (pp. 11-14).

Hu, Q.L., & Lee, D. L. (2000). Power conservative multi-attribute queries on data broadcast. *Proceedings of IEEE International Conference on Data Engineering (ICDE 2000)*, (pp. 157-166).

Hu, Q. L., & Lee, D. L. (2001). A hybrid index technique for power efficient data broadcast. *Distributed and Parallel Databases Journal, 9*(2), 151-177.

Hurson, A. R., Chehadeh, Y. C., & Hannan, J. (2000). Object organization on parallel broadcast channels in a global information sharing environment. *Proceedings of IEEE Conference on Performance, Computing, and Communications*, (pp. 347-353).

Hurson, A. R., Pakzad, S., & Cheng, J.-B. R. (1993). Object-oriented database management systems. *IEEE Computer, 26*(2), 48-60.

Hurwitz, C. & Craig, R. J. (1996). *Software Package Tsp_Solve 1.3.6*. Available from http://www.cs.sunysb.edu/~algorithm/implement/tsp/implement.shtml.

Imielinski, T., & Badrinath, B. R. (1994). Mobile wireless computing: Challenges in data management. *Communications of the ACM, 37*(10), 18-28.

Imielinski, T., & Korth, H. F. (1996). Introduction to mobile computing. In T. Imielinski and H. F. Korth (Eds.), *Mobile computing* (pp. 1-43). Boston: Kluwer Academic.

Imielinski, T., Viswanathan, S., & Badrinath, B. R. (1994). Energy efficient indexing on air. *Proceedings of ACM SIGMOD Conference on Management of Data*, (pp. 25-36).

Imielinski, T., Viswanathan, S., & Badrinath, B. R. (1997). Data on air: Organization and access.

IEEE Transactions on Computer, 9(3), 353-372.

Joseph, A. D., Tauber, J. A., & Kaashoek, M. F. (1997). Mobile computing with the rover toolkit [Special issue]. *IEEE Transactions on Computers, 46*(3), 337-352.

Juran, J., Hurson, A. R., & Vijaykrishnan, N. (2004). Data organization and retrieval on parallel air channels: Performance and energy issues. *ACM Journal of WINET, 10*(2), 183-195.

Kaashoek, M. F., Pinckney, T., & Tauber, J. A. (1994). Dynamic documents: Mobile wireless access to the WWW. *IEEE Workshop on Mobile Computing Systems and Applications*, 179-184.

Kim, W. (1990). *Introduction to object-oriented databases.* Cambridge, MA: MIT Press.

Lai, S. J., Zaslavsky, A. Z., Martin, G. P., & Yeo, L. H. (1995). Cost efficient adaptive protocol with buffering for advanced mobile database applications. *Proceedings of the Fourth International Conference on Database Systems for Advanced Applications.*

Lee, D. L. (1996). Using signatures techniques for information filtering in wireless and mobile environments [Special issue]. *Distributed and Parallel Databases, 4*(3), 205-227.

Lee, M. T., Burghardt, F., Seshan, S., & Rabaey, J. (1995). InfoNet: The networking infrastructure of InfoPad. *Proceedings of Compcon*, (pp. 779-784).

Lim, J.B., & Hurson, A. R. (2002). Transaction processing in mobile, heterogeneous database systems. *IEEE Transactions on Knowledge and Data Engineering, 14*(6), 1330-1346.

Lim, J. B., Hurson, A. R., Miller, L. L., & Chehadeh, Y. C. (1997). A dynamic clustering scheme for distributed object-oriented databases. *Mathematical Modeling and Scientific Computing, 8*, 126-135.

Munoz-Avila, A., & Hurson, A. R. (2003a). Energy-aware retrieval from indexed broadcast parallel channels. *Proceedings of Advanced Simulation Technology Conference (High Performance Computing)*, (pp. 3-8).

Munoz-Avila, A., & Hurson, A. R. (2003b). Energy-efficient objects retrieval on indexed broadcast parallel channels. *Proceedings of International Conference on Information Resource Management*, (pp. 190-194).

NASDAQ World Wide Web Home Page. (2002). Retrieved May 11, 2004, from http://www.nasdaq.com

Satyanarayanan, M. (1996). Fundamental challenges in mobile computing. *Proceedings* of *15th ACM Symposium on Principles of Distributed Computing*, (pp. 1-7).

Satyanarayanan, M., Noble, B., Kumar, P., & Price, M. (1994). Application-aware adaptation for mobile computing. *Proceedings of the Sixth ACM SIGOPS European Workshop*, (pp. 1-4).

Weiser, M. (1993). Some computer science issues in ubiquitous computing. *Communications of the ACM, 36*(7), 75-84.

Zdonik, S., Alonso, R., Franklin, M., & Acharya, S. (1994). Are disks in the air just pie in the sky? *Proceedings of Workshop on Mobile Computing Systems and Applications*, (pp. 1-8).

This work was previously published in Wireless Information Highways, edited by D. Katsaros, A. Nanopoulos, and Y. Manalopoulos, pp. 96-154, copyright 2005 by IRM Press (an imprint of IGI Global).

Chapter 7.37
Multimedia over Wireless Mobile Data Networks

Surendra Kumar Sivagurunathan
University of Oklahoma, USA

Mohammed Atiquzzaman
University of Oklahoma, USA

ABSTRACT

With the proliferation of wireless data networks, there is an increasing interest in carrying multimedia over wireless networks using portable devices such as laptops and personal digital assistants. Mobility gives rise to the need for handoff schemes between wireless access points. In this chapter, we demonstrate the effectiveness of transport layer handoff schemes for multimedia transmission, and compare with Mobile IP, the network layer-based industry standard handoff scheme.

I. INTRODUCTION

Mobile computers such as personal digital assistants (PDA) and laptop computers with multiple network interfaces are becoming very common. Many of the applications that run on a mobile computer involve multimedia, such as video conferencing, audio conferencing, watching live movies, sports, and so forth. This chapter deals with multimedia communication in mobile wireless devices, and, in particular, concentrates on the effect of mobility on streaming multimedia in wireless networks.

Streaming multimedia over wireless networks is a challenging task. Extensive research has been carried out to ensure a smooth and uninterrupted multimedia transmission to a mobile host (MH) over wireless media. The current research thrust is to ensure an uninterrupted multimedia transmission when the MH moves between networks or subnets. Ensuring uninterrupted multimedia transmission during handoff is challenging because the MH is already receiving multimedia from the network to which it is connected; when it moves into another network, it needs to break the connection with the old network and establish a connection with the new network. Figure 1 shows an MH connected to Wireless Network

1; when it moves, it has to make a connection with the new network, say Wireless Network 2. The re-establishment of a new connection takes a considerable amount of time, resulting in the possibility of interruption and resulting loss of multimedia.

The current TCP/IP network infrastructure was not designed for mobility. It does not sup- port handoff between IP networks. For example, a device running a real-time application, such as video conference, cannot play smoothly when the user hands off from one wireless IP network to another, resulting in unsatisfactory performance to the user.

Mobile IP (MIP) (Perkins, 1996), from the In- ternet Engineering Task Force (IETF), addresses

Figure 1. Illustration of handoff with mobile node connected to Wireless Network 1

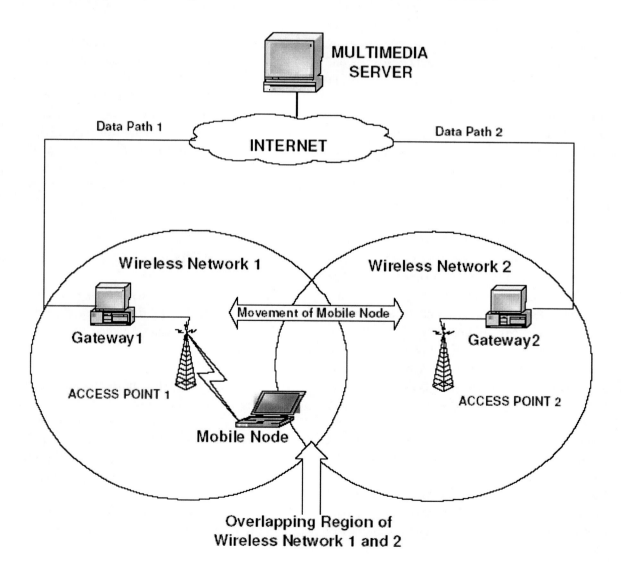

the mobility problem. MIP extends the existing IP protocol to support host mobility, including handoff, by introducing two network entities: home agent (HA) and foreign agent (FA). The HA and FA work together to achieve host mobility. The correspondent node (CN) always communicates with the mobile node (MN) via its home network address, even though MH may not dwell in the home network. For CN to have seamless access to MN, the MH has to be able to handoff in a timely manner between networks.

Handoff latency is one of the most important indicators of handoff performance. Large handoff latency degrades performance of real-time applications. For example, large handoff latency will introduce interruption in a video conference due to breaks in both audio and video data transmission. In addition to high handoff latency, MIP suffers from a number of other problems including triangle routing, high signaling traffic with the HA, and so forth. A number of approaches to reduce the MIP handoff latency are given next.

Mobile IP uses only one IP; a certain amount of latency in data transmission appears to be unavoidable when the MH performs a handoff. This is because of MN's inability to communicate with the CN through either the old path (because it has changed its wireless link to a new wireless network) or the new path (because HA has not yet granted its registration request). Thus, MH cannot send or receive data to or from the CN while the MH is performing registration, resulting in interruption of data communication during this time interval. This interruption is unacceptable in a real-world scenario, and may hinder the widespread deployment of real-time multimedia applications on wireless mobile networks. Seamless IP-diversity based generalized mobility architecture (SIGMA) overcomes the issue of discontinuity by exploiting multi-homing (Stewart, 2005) to keep the old data path alive until the new data path is ready to take over the data transfer, thus achieving lower latency and lower

loss during handoff between adjacent subnets than Mobile IP.

The *objective* of this chapter is to demonstrate the effectiveness of SIGMA in reducing handoff latency, packet loss, and so forth, for multimedia transmission, and compare with that achieved by Mobile IP. The *contribution* of this chapter is to describe the implementation of a real-time streaming server and client in SIGMA to achieve seamless multimedia streaming during handoff. SIGMA *differs* from previous work in the sense that all previous attempts modified the hardware, infrastructure of the network, server, or client to achieve seamless multimedia transmission during handoff.

The rest of this chapter is organized as follows. Previous work on multimedia over wireless networks is described in the next section. The architecture of SIGMA is described in the third section, followed by the testbed on which video transmission has been tested for both MIP and SIGMA in the fourth section. Results of video over MIP and SIGMA and presented and compared in the fifth section, followed by conclusions in the last section.

BACKGROUND

A large amount of work has been carried out to improve the quality of multimedia over wireless networks. They can be categorized into two types:

- Studies related to improving multimedia (e.g., video or audio) over wireless networks. They do not consider the mobility of the MN, but attempt to provide a high quality multimedia transmission within the same wireless network for stationary servers and clients.
- Studies related to achieving seamless multimedia transmission during handoffs. They

consider mobility of the MH and try to provide a seamless and high quality multimedia transmission when the MH (client) moves from one network to another.

Although our interest in this chapter is seamless multimedia transmission during handoffs, we describe previous work on both categories in the following sections.

Multimedia over Wireless Networks

Ahmed, Mehaoua, and Buridant (2001) worked on improving the quality of MPEG-4 transmission on wireless using differentiated services (Diffserv). They investigated QoS provisioning between MPEG-4 video application and Diffserv networks. To achieve the best possible QoS, all the components involved in the transmission process must collaborate. For example, the server must use stream properties to describe the QoS requirement for each stream to the network. They propose a solution by distinguishing the video data into important video data and less important video data (such as complementary raw data). Packets which are marked as less important are dropped in the first case if there is any congestion, so that the receiver can regenerate the video with the received important information.

Budagavi and Gibson (2001) improved the performance of video over wireless channels by multiframe video coding. The multiframe coder uses the redundancy that exists across multiple frames in a typical video conferencing sequence so that additional compression can be achieved using their multiframe-block motion compensation (MF-BMC) approach. They modeled the error propagation using the Markov chain, and concluded that use of multiple frames in motion increases the robustness. Their proposed MF-BMC scheme has been shown to be more robust on wireless networks when compared to the base-level H.263 codec which uses single frame-block motion compensation (SF-BMC).

There are a number of studies, such as Stedman, Gharavi, Hanzo, and Steele (1993), Illgner and Lappe (1995), Khansari, Jalai, Dubois, and Mermelstein (1996), and Hanzo and Streit (1995), which concentrate on improving quality of multimedia over wireless networks. Since we are only interested in studies that focus on achieving seamless multimedia transmission during handoff, we do not go into details of studies related to multimedia over wireless networks. Interested readers can use the references given earlier in this paragraph.

Seamless Multimedia over Mobile Networks

Lee, Lee, and Kim (2004) achieved seamless MPEG-4 streaming over a wireless LAN using Mobile IP. They achieved this by implementing packet forwarding with buffering mechanisms in the foreign agent (FA) and performed pre-buffering adjustment in a streaming client. Insufficient pre-buffered data, which is not enough to overcome the discontinuity of data transmission during the handoff period, will result in disruption in playback. Moreover, too much of pre-buffered data wastes memory and delays the starting time of playback. Find the optimal pre-buffering time is, therefore, an important issue in this approach.

Patanapongpibul and Mapp (2003) enable the MH to select the best point of attachment by having all the reachable router advertisements (RA) in a RA cache. RA cache will have the entire router's link whose advertisements are heard by the mobile node. These RAs are arranged in the cache according to a certain priority. The priority is based on two criteria: (1) the link signal strength, that is, signal quality and SNR level, and (2) the time since the RA entry was last updated. So the RAs with highest router priority are forwarded to the IP packet handler for processing. The disadvantage of this method includes extra memory for the RA cache.

Pan, Lee, Kim, and Suda (2004) insert four components in the transport layer of the video server and the client. These four components are: (1) a path management module, (2) a multipath distributor module at the sender, (3) a pair of rate control modules, and (4) a multipath collector module at the receiver. They achieve a seamless video by transferring the video over multiple paths to the destination during handoffs. The overhead of the proposed scheme is two-fold: reduction in transmission efficiency due to transmission of duplicated video packets and transmission of control packets associated with the proposed scheme, and processing of the proposed scheme at the sender and receiver.

Boukerche, Hong, and Jacob (2003) propose a two-phase handoff scheme to support synchronization of multimedia units (MMU) for wireless clients and distributed multimedia systems. This scheme is proposed for managing MMUs to deliver them to mobile hosts on time. The two-phase scheme consists of: setup handoff and end handoff. In the first phase, setup handoff procedure has two major tasks: updating new arrival BSs and maintaining the synchronization for newly arrived mobile hosts (MHs). If an MH can reach another BS, then MH reports "new BS arrived" to its primary BS. End handoff procedure deals with the ordering of MMUs and with the flow of MMUs for a new MH. Any base station can be a new primary base station. The algorithm notifies MHs, BSs, and servers, and then chooses the closest common node from the current primary base station and new base stations. This method suffers from the disadvantage of additional overhead of updating the base station (BS) with newly arrived BSs and ordering of MMUs.

SIGMA FOR SEAMLESS MULTIMEDIA IN MOBILE NETWORKS

Limitations of previously proposed schemes in achieving seamless multimedia transmission during handoff in a wireless environment have been discussed in the previous section. In this section, we will discuss our proposed handoff scheme, called SIGMA, which has been designed for seamless multimedia transmission during handoffs, followed by its advantages over previous schemes.

Introduction to SIGMA

To aid the reader in getting a better understanding of SIGMA, in this section, we describe the various steps involved in a SIGMA handoff. A detailed description of SIGMA can be found in Fu, Ma, Atiquzzaman, and Lee (2005). We will use the stream control transmission protocol (Stewart, 2005), a new emerging transport layer protocol from IETF, to illustrate SIGMA.

Stream control transmission protocol's (SCTP) multi-homing (see Figure 2) allows an association between two endpoints to span across multiple IP addresses or network interface cards. One of the addresses is designated as the primary while the other can be used as a backup, in the case of failure of the primary address, or when the upper layer application explicitly requests the use of the backup. Retransmission of lost packets can also be done over the secondary address. The built-in support for multi-homed endpoints by SCTP is especially useful in environments that require high-availability of the applications, such as Signaling System 7 (SS7) transport. A multi-homed SCTP association can speedup recovery from link failure situations without interrupting any ongoing data transfer. Figure 2 presents an example of SCTP multi-homing where two nodes,

Figure 2. An SCTP association featuring multi-homing

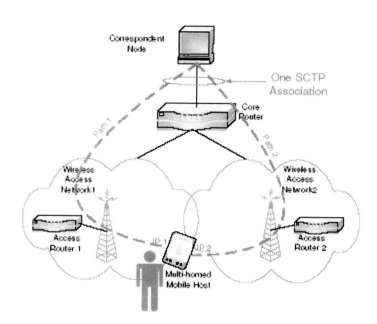

CN and MH, are connected through two wireless networks, with MH being multi-homed. One of MN's IP addresses is assigned as the primary address for use by CN for transmitting data packets; the other IP address can be used as a backup in case of primary address failure.

STEP 1: Obtain New IP Address

Referring to Figure 2, the handoff preparation procedure begins when the MH moves into the overlapping radio coverage area of two adjacent subnets. Once the MH receives the router advertisement from the new access router (AR2), it should initiate the procedure of obtaining a new IP address (IP2 in Figure 2). This can be accomplished through several methods: DHCP, DHCPv6, or

IPv6 Stateless Address Autoconfiguration (SAA) (Thomson & Narten, 1998). The main difference between these methods lies in whether the IP address is generated by a server (DHCP/DHCPv6) or by the MH itself (IPv6 SAA). For cases where the MH is not concerned about its IP address but only requires the address to be unique and routable, IPv6 SAA is a preferred method for SIGMA to obtain a new address since it significantly reduces the required signaling time.

STEP 2: Add IP Addresses to Association

When the SCTP association is initially setup, only the CN's IP address and the MH's first IP address (IP1) are exchanged between CN and

MH. After the MH obtains another IP address (IP2 in STEP 1), MH should bind IP2 into the association (in addition to IP1) and notify CN about the availability of the new IP address (Fu, Ma, Atiquzzaman, & Lee, 2005).

SCTP provides a graceful method to modify an existing association when the MH wishes to notify the CN that a new IP address will be added to the association and the old IP addresses will probably be taken out of the association. The IETF Transport Area Working Group (TSVWG) is working on the "SCTP Address Dynamic Reconfiguration" Internet draft (Stewart, 2005), which defines two new chunk types (ASCONF and ASCONF-ACK) and several parameter types (Add IP Address, Delete IP address, Set Primary Address, etc.). This option will be very useful in mobile environments for supporting service reconfiguration without interrupting on-going data transfers.

In SIGMA, MH notifies CN that IP2 is available for data transmission by sending an ASCONF chunk to CN. On receipt of this chunk, CN will add IP2 to its local control block for the association and reply to MH with an ASCONF-ACK chunk indicating the success of the IP addition. At this time, IP1 and IP2 are both ready for receiving data transmitted from CN to MH.

STEP 3: Redirect Data Packets to New IP Address

When MH moves further into the coverage area of wireless access network2, data path2 becomes increasingly more reliable than data path1. CN can then redirect data traffic to the new IP address (IP2) to increase the possibility of data being delivered successfully to the MH. This task can be accomplished by the MH sending an ASCONF chunk with the Set-Primary-Address parameter, which results in CN setting its primary destination address to MH as IP2.

STEP 4: Updating the Location Manager

SIGMA supports location management by employing a location manager that maintains a database which records the correspondence between MH's identity and current primary IP address (Reaz, Atiquzzaman, & Fu, 2005). MH can use any unique information as its identity, such as the home address (as in MIP), domain name, or a public key defined in the public key infrastructure (PKI).

Following our example, once the Set-Primary-Address action is completed successfully, MH should update the location manager's relevant entry with the new IP address (IP2). The purpose of this procedure is to ensure that after MH moves from the wireless access network1 into network2, further association setup requests can be routed to MH's new IP address IP2. This update has no impact on existing active associations.

We can observe an important difference between SIGMA and MIP: the location management and data traffic forwarding functions are coupled together in MIP, whereas they are *decoupled in SIGMA to speedup handoff and make the deployment more flexible*.

STEP 5: Delete or Deactivate Obsolete IP Address

When MH moves out of the coverage of wireless access network1, no *new* or *retransmitted* data packets should be directed to address IP1. In SIGMA, MH can notify CN that IP1 is out of service for data transmission by sending an ASCONF chunk to CN (Delete IP Address). Once received, CN will delete IP1 from its local association control block and reply to MH with an ASCONF-ACK chunk indicating the success of the IP deletion.

A less aggressive way to prevent CN from sending data to IP1 is for the MH to advertise a zero receiver window (corresponding to IP1) to CN (Goff, Moronski, Phatak, & Gupta, 2000). This will give CN an impression that the interface (on which IP1 is bound) buffer is full and cannot receive any more data. By deactivating instead of deleting the IP address, SIGMA can adapt more gracefully to MH's zigzag (often referred to as ping pong) movement patterns and reuse the previously obtained IP address (IP1), as long as the lifetime of IP1 has not expired. This will reduce the latency and signaling traffic that would

have otherwise been caused by obtaining a new IP address.

Timing Diagram of SIGMA

Figure 3 summarizes the signaling sequences involved in SIGMA. Here we assume IPv6 SAA and MH initiated Set-Primary-Address. Timing diagrams for other scenarios can be drawn similarly, but are not shown here because of space limitations. In this figure, the numbers before

Figure 3. Timeline of signaling in SIGMA

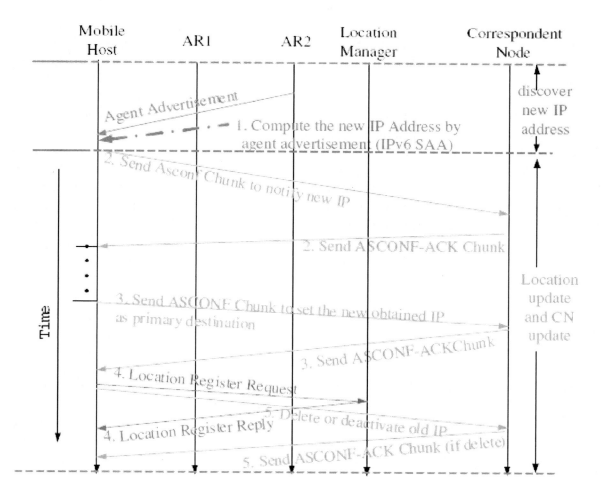

the events correspond to the step numbers in the previous sub-sections, respectively.

Advantages of SIGMA over the Previous Works

A number of previous work have considered seamless multimedia transmission during handoff, as mentioned in the second section, which have their own disadvantages. Here, we discuss the advantages of SIGMA over previous work. Lee et al. (2004) performed pre-buffering adjustment in client. Playback disruption may occur if the pre-buffered data is not enough to overcome the discontinuity of data transmission that occurs during handoff. Moreover, excessive pre-buffered data wastes memory usage and delays the starting time of playback. Find the optimal pre-buffering time is an important issue in this approach. Since SIGMA does not pre-buffer any data in the client, such optimization issues are not present in SIGMA.

Patanapongpibul et al. (2003) use the router advertisement (RA) cache. The disadvantage of this method is that it needs extra memory for RA cache; SIGMA does not involve any caching and hence does not suffer from such memory problems. Pan et al. (2004) use multipath (as discussed earlier), which suffers from (1) reduction in bandwidth efficiency due to transmission of duplicated video packets and transmission of control packets associated with the proposed scheme, and (2) processing overhead at the sender and receiver. Absence of multipaths or duplicate video packets in SIGMA results in higher link bandwidth efficiency.

Boukerche et al. (2003) proposed a two-phase handoff scheme which has additional overhead of updating the base station (BS) with newly arrived BSs, and also ordering of multimedia units (MMUs). In SIGMA, there is no feedback from MH to any of the base stations, and hence does not require ordering of multimedia units or packets.

EXPERIMENTAL TESTBED

Having reviewed the advantages of SIGMA over other schemes for multimedia transmission in the previous section, in this section, we present experimental results for SIGMA as obtained from an experimental setup we have developed at the University of Oklahoma. We compare the results of handoff performance during multimedia transmission over both SIGMA and Mobile IP. To make a fair comparison, we have used the same test bed for both MIP and SIGMA. Figure 4 (to be described later) shows the topology of our test bed, which has been used by a number of researchers—Seol, Kim, Yu, and Lee (2002), Wu, Banerjee, Basu, and Das (2003), Onoe, Atsumi, Sato, and Mizuno (2001)—for measurement of handoff performance. The difference in data communication between the CN and the MH for MIP and SIGMA lies in the lower layer sockets: the file sender for MIP is based on the regular TCP socket, while that for SIGMA is based on SCTP socket. We did not use the traditional *ftp* program for file transfer because it was not available for the SCTP protocol. To obtain access to the SCTP socket, we used Linux 2.6.2 kernel with Linux Kernel SCTP (LKSCTP) version 2.6.2-0.9.0 on both CN and MN. A number of MIP implementations, such as HUT Dynamics (HUT), Stanford Mosquito (MNET), and NUS Mobile IP (MIP), are publicly available. We chose HUT Dynamics for testing MIP in our test bed due to the following reasons: (1) Unlike Stanford Mosquito, which integrates the FA and MN, HUT Dynamics implements HA, FA, and MH daemons separately. This architecture is similar to SIGMA where the two access points and MH are separate entities. (2) HUT Dynamics implements hierarchical FAs, which will allow future comparison between SIGMA and hierarchical Mobile IP. Our MIP testbed consists four nodes: correspondent node (CN), foreign agent (FA), home agent (HA), and mobile node (MN). All the nodes run corresponding agents developed by HUT Dynamics.

The hardware and software configuration of the nodes are given in Table 1.

The CN and the machines running the HA and FA are connected to the Computer Science (CS) network of the University of Oklahoma, while the MH and access points are connected to two separate private networks. The various IP addresses are shown in Table 2. IEEE 802.11b is used to connect the MH to the access points.

The network topology of SIGMA is similar to the one of Mobile IP except that there is no HA or FA in SIGMA. As shown in Figure 4, the machines which run the HA and FA in the case of MIP act as gateways in the case of SIGMA. Table 1 shows the hardware and software configuration for the SIGMA experiment. The various IP addresses are shown in Table 2. The experimental procedure of Mobile IP and SIGMA is given next:

1. Start with the MH in Domain 1.
2. **For Mobile IP:** Run HUT Dynamics daemons for HA, FA, and MN. **For SIGMA:** Run the SIGMA handoff program, which has two functions: (1) monitoring the link

Table I. Mobile IP and SIGMA testbed configurations

Node	Hardware	Software	Operating System
Home Agent(MIP) Gateway1 (SIGMA)	Desktop, two NICs	HUT Dynamics 0.8.1 Home Agent Daemon (MIP)	Redhat Linux 9 kernel 2.4.20
Foreign Agent (MIP) Gateway2 (SIGMA)	Desktop, two NICs	HUT Dynamics 0.8.1 Foreign Agent Daemon (MIP)	Redhat Linux 9 kernel 2.4.20
Mobile Node	Dell Inspiron- 1100 Laptop, one Avaya 802.11b wireless card	HUT Dynamics 0.8.1 Mobile Node Daemon (MIP), File receiver	Redhat Linux 9 kernel 2.4.20
Correspondent Node	Desktop, one NIC	File sender	Redhat Linux 9 2.6.20

Table 2. Mobile IP and SIGMA network configurations

Node	Network Configuration
Home Agent (MIP) Gateway1 (SIGMA)	eth0: 129.15.78.171, gateway 129.15.78.172; eth1:10.1.8.1
Foreign Agent (MIP) Gateway2 (SIGMA)	eth0: 129.15.78.172 gateway 129.15.78.171; eth1: 10.1.6.1
Mobile Node	Mobile IP's Home Address: 10.1.8.5 SIGMA's IP1: 10.1.8.100 SIGMA's IP2 : 10.1.6.100
Correspondent Node	129.15.78.150

Figure 4. SIGMA and Mobile IP testbed

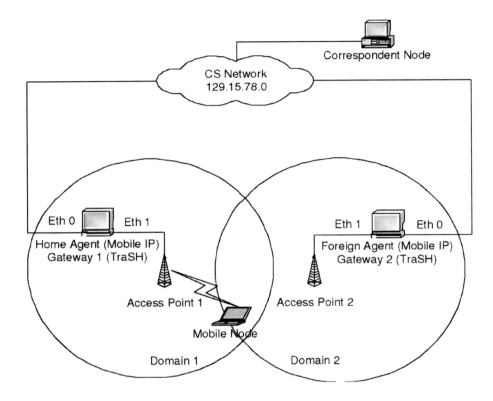

layer signal strength to determine the time to handoff, and (2) carrying out the signaling shown in Figure 4.

3. Run file sender/video server and file receiver/ video client (using TCP sockets for Mobile IP, using SCTP sockets for SIGMA) on CN and MN, respectively.

4. Run Ethereal (ETHEREAL) on the CN and MH to capture packets.

5. Move MH from Domain 1 to Domain 2 to perform handoff by Mobile IP and SIGMA. Capture all packets sent from CN and received at MN.

RESULTS

Various results were collected on the experimental setup and procedure described earlier. In this section, we present two kinds of results: file transfer and multimedia transmission. The reason for showing the results of file transfer is to prove that SIGMA achieves seamless handoff not only for multimedia but also for file transfers.

Results for File Transfer

In this section, we present and compare the results of handoffs using MIP and SIGMA for file transfer. For comparison, we use throughput, RTT, and handoff latency as the performance measures. *Throughput* is measured by the rate at which packets are received at the MN. *RTT* is the time required for a data packet to travel from the source to the destination and back. We define *handoff latency* as the time interval between the MH receiving the last packet from Domain 1 (previous network) and the first packet from Domain 2 (the new network). The experimental results are described next.

Results from Mobile IP Handoff

Figure 5 shows the throughput during Mobile IP handoff between Domain 1 and Domain 2. The variations in throughput within HA (from 20 second to 30 second) and within FA (from 37 second to 60 second) are due to network conges-tion arising from cross traffic in the production CS network.

The average throughput before, during and after handoff are 2.436 Mbps, 0 Mbps and 2.390 Mbps, respectively. Figure 6 shows the packet trace during MIP handoff. The actual handoff latency for MIP can be clearly calculated by having a zoomed-in view of the packet trace graph. Figure 7 shows a zoomed-in view of the packet trace, where the calculated handoff latency is eight seconds for Mobile IP. Figure 8 shows the RTT for the MIP handoff. As we can see, the RTT is high for eight seconds (the handoff latency time), during the handoff.

The registration time (or registration latency) is also a part of the handoff latency. Registration latency, the time taken by the MH to register with the agent (HA or FA), is calculated as follows. Ethereal capture showed that the MH sent a

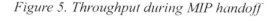

Figure 5. Throughput during MIP handoff

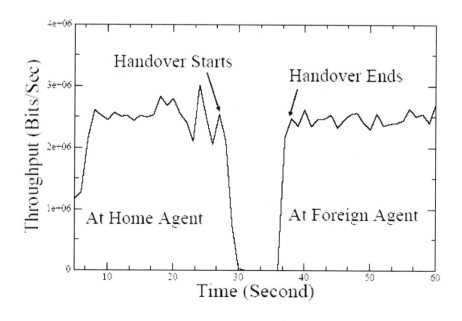

Figure 6. Packet trace during MIP handoff

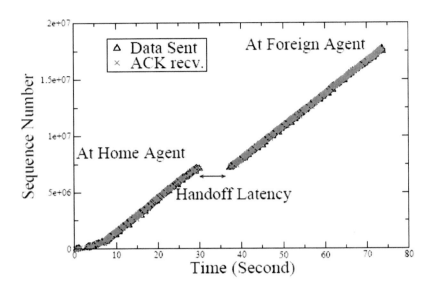

Figure 7. Zoomed in view during MIP handoff instant

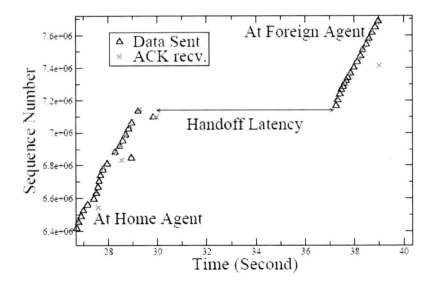

Figure 8. RTT during MIP handoff

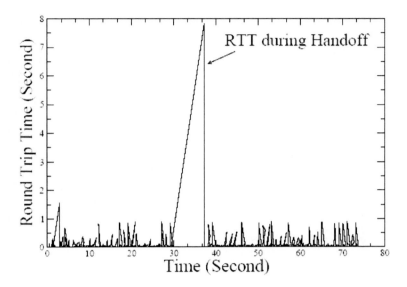

registration request to the HA at time t = 14.5123 second and received a reply from the HA at t = 14.5180 second. Hence, the calculated registration time for registering with HA is 5.7 milliseconds. Similarly, during MIP handoff, Ethereal capture showed that the MH sent a registration request to FA at time t =7.1190 second and received a reply from the FA at t =7.2374, resulting in a registration time of 38.3 milliseconds. This is due to the fact that after the MH registers with the HA, it can directly register with the HA. On the other hand, if it registers with the FA, the MH registers each new care-of-address with its HA possibly through FA. The registration latency is, therefore, higher when the MH is in the FA.

Results from SIGMA Handoff

Figure 9 shows the throughput during SIGMA handoff where it can observed that the throughput does not go to zero. The variation in throughput is due to network congestion arising from cross traffic in the production CS network. Although we cannot see the handoff due to it being very small, it should be emphasized that the ethereal capture showed the handoff starting and ending at t = 60.755 and t = 60.761 seconds, respectively, that is, a handoff latency of six milliseconds.

Figure 10 shows the packet trace during SIGMA handoff. It can be seen that packets arrive at the MH without any gap or disruption; this is also a powerful proof of SIGMA's smoother handoff as compared to handoff in Mobile IP. This experimentally demonstrates that *a seamless handoff can be realized with SIGMA*. Figure 11 shows a zoomed-in view of the packet trace during the SIGMA handoff period; a handoff latency of six milliseconds can be seen between the packets arriving at the old and new paths.

Figure 9. Throughput during SIGMA handoff

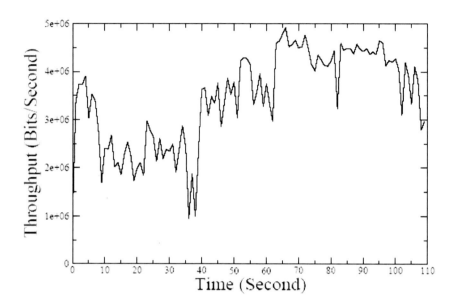

Figure 10. Packet trace during SIGMA handoff

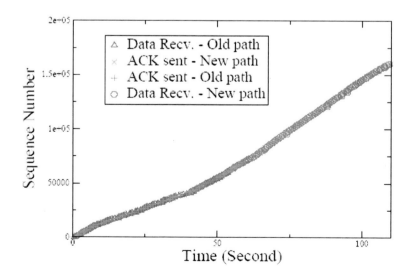

Figure 11. Zoomed in view during SIGMA handoff

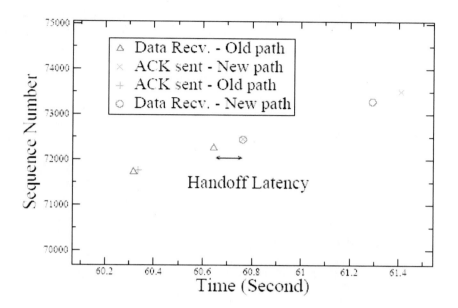

Figure 12. RTT during SIGMA handoff

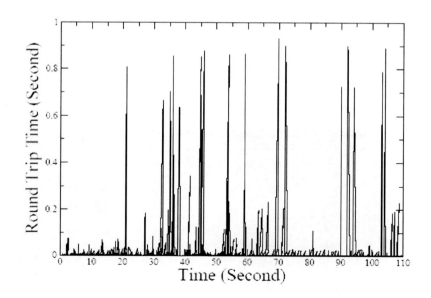

Figure 12 shows the RTT during SIGMA handoff. A seamless handoff is evident from the absence of any sudden RTT increase during handoff.

Result of Multimedia Data Transfer

To test the handoff performance for multimedia over SIGMA, we used a streaming video

Figure 13. Throughput of video during SIGMA handoff

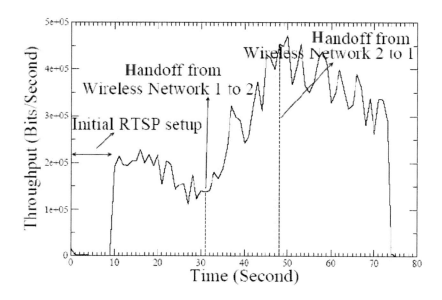

Figure 14. Screen shot of MPEG4-IP player

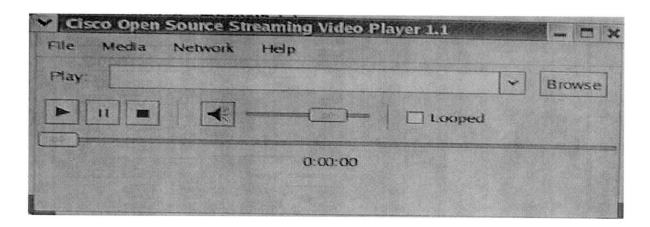

client and a streaming server at the MH and CN, respectively (details in the fourth section). Apple's Darwin Streaming Server (DARWIN) and CISCO's MPEG4IP player (MPEG) were modified to stream data over SCTP. A seamless handoff, with no interruption in the video stream, was achieved with SIGMA.

Figure 13 shows the throughput of multimedia (video) data, when the MH moves between subnets. The connection request and setup between the client and server is carried out during the first 10 seconds. It can be seen that the throughput does not drop during handoff at time = 31 second when MH moves from wireless network 1 to 2. A second handoff takes place when the MH moves from network 2 to network 1 at time = 48. It is seen that seamless handoff is achieved by SIGMA for both the handoffs.

Figure 14 shows a screen capture of the MPEG4IP player used in our experiment. Figure 15 shows the video playing in the player during handoff, where "rtsp://129.15.78.139/fta.sdp" represents the server's IP address and the streaming format (SDP).

Comparison of SIGMA and MIP Handoffs

We observed previously that the registration time of MIP was only 0.1 second, and the handoff latencies of MIP and SIGMA were eight seconds and six milliseconds, respectively. We describe the reasons for the MIP handoff latency being much longer than its registration time in the following:

Figure 15. Screen-shot of MPEG4-IP player playing streaming video

1. In HUT Dynamics, the MIP implementation used in this study, the MH obtains a registration lifetime after every successful registration. It originates another registration on expiry of this lifetime. So it is possible for the MH to postpone registration even after it has completed a link layer handoff and received FA advertisements. This may introduce some delay which can be up to the duration of a life time.

2. As mentioned in the previous section, the registration of MH also costs some time, measured as 38.3 milliseconds in our test-bed.

The handoff latency in MIP comes from three factors: (1) remaining home registration lifetime after link layer handoff which can be from zero to a lifetime, (2) FA advertisement interval plus the time span of last time advertisement which is not listened by MN, and (3) registration latency. During these three times, the CN cannot communicate through either the previous path because it has completed link layer handoff, or the new path because MH has not yet completed the registration. As a result, the throughput was zero during this time. Obviously, such shortcoming has been eliminated in SIGMA through multi-homing and decoupling of registration and data transfer. Consequently, data continue to flow between the CN and MH during the handoff process.

CONCLUSION AND FUTURE TRENDS

We have shown that SIGMA achieves seamless multimedia transmission during handoff between wireless networks. As future work, video streaming can be tested over SIGMA during vertical handoffs, that is, between wireless LANs, cellular, and satellite networks.

ACKNOWLEDGMENT

The work reported in this chapter was funded by National Aeronautics and Space Administration (NASA) grant no. NAG3-2922.

REFERENCES

Ahmed, T., Mehaoua, A., & Buridant, G. (2001). Implementing MPEG-4 video on demand over IP differentiated services. *Global Telecommunications Conference, GLOBECOM*, San Antonio, TX, November 25-29 (pp. 2489-2493). Piscataway, NJ: IEEE.

Boukerche, A., Hong, S., & Jacob, T., (2003). A two-phase handoff management scheme for synchronizing multimedia units over wireless networks. *Proc. Eighth IEEE International Symposium on Computers and Communication*, Antalya, Turkey, June-July (pp. 1078-1084). Los Alamitos, CA: IEEE Computer Society.

Budagavi, M., & Gibson, J. D. (2001, February). Multiframe video coding for improved performance over wireless channels. *IEEE Transactions on Image Processing, 10*(2), 252-265.

DARWIN. Retrieved June 23, 2005, from http://developer.apple.com/darwin/projects/streaming/

ETHEREAL. Retrieved June 30, 2005, from www.ethereal.com

Fu, S., Atiquzzaman, M., Ma, L., & Lee, Y. (2005, November). Signaling cost and performance of SIGMA: A seamless handover scheme for data networks. *Journal of Wireless Communications and Mobile Computing, 5*(7), 825-845.

Fu, S., Ma, L., Atiquzzaman, M., & Lee, Y. (2005). Architecture and performance of SIGMA: A seamless mobility architecture for data networks. *40th IEEE International Conference on Com-*

munications (ICC), Seoul, Korea, May 16-20 (pp. 3249-3253). Institute of Electrical and Electronics Engineers Inc.

Goff, T., Moronski, J., Phatak, D. S., & Gupta, V. (2000). Freeze-TCP: A true end-to-end TCP enhancement mechanism for mobile environments. *IEEE INFOCOM*, Tel Aviv, Israel, March 26-30 (pp. 1537-1545). NY: IEEE.

Hanzo, L., & Streit, J. (1995, August). Adaptive low-rate wireless videophone schemes. *IEEE Trans. Circuits Syst. Video Technol., 5*(4), 305-318.

HUT. Retrieved June 1, 2005, from http://www.cs.hut.fi/research/dynamics/

Illgner, R., & Lappe, D. (1995). Mobile multimedia communications in a universal telecommunications network. *Proc. SPIE Conf. Visual Communication Image Processing*, Taipei, Taiwan, May 23-26 (pp. 1034-1043). USA: SPIE.

Khansari, M., Jalai, A., Dubois, E., & Mermelstein, P. (1996, February). Low bit-rate video transmission over fading channels for wireless microcellular system. *IEEE Trans. Circuits Syst. Video Technol., 6*(1), 1-11.

Lee, C. H., Lee, D., & Kim, J. W. (2004). Seamless MPEG-4 video streaming over Mobile-IP enabled wireless LAN. *Proceedings of SPIE, Multimedia Systems and Applications*, Philadelphia, Pennsylvania, October (pp. 111-119). USA: SPIE.

LKSCTP. Retrieved June 1, 2005, from http://lksctp.sourceforge.net

MIP. Retrieved June 1, 2005, from opensource.nus.edu.sg/projects/mobileip/mip.html

MNET. Retrieved June 1, 2005, from http://mosquitonet.stanford.edu/

MPEG. Retrieved June 1, 2005, from http://mpeg4ip.sourceforge.net/faq/index.php

Onoe, Y., Atsumi, Y., Sato, F., & Mizuno, T. (2001). A dynamic delayed ack control scheme on Mobile IP networks. *International Conference on Computer Networks and Mobile Computing*, Los Alamitos, CA, October 16-19 (pp. 35-40). Los Alamitos, CA: IEEE Computer Society.

Pan, Y., Lee, M., Kim, J. B., & Suda, T. (2004, May). An end-to-end multipath smooth handoff scheme for streaming media. *IEEE Journal on Selected Areas in Communications, 22*(4), 653-663.

Patanapongpibul, L., & Mapp, G. (2003). A client-based handoff mechanism for Mobile IPv6 wireless networks. *Proc. Eighth IEEE International Symposium on Computers and Communications*, Antalya, Turkey, June-July (pp. 563-568). Los Alamitos, CA: IEEE Computer Society.

Perkins, C. (1996). IP mobility support. *IETF RFC 2002*, October.

Reaz, A. S., Atiquzzaman, M., & Fu, S. (2005). Performance of DNS as location manager. *IEEE Globecom*, St. Louis, MO, November 28-December 2 (pp. 359-363). USA: IEEE Computer Society.

Seol, S., Kim, M., Yu, C., & Lee., J. H. (2002). Experiments and analysis of voice over MobileIP. *13th IEEE International Symposium on Personal, Indoor and Mobile Radio Communications (PIMRC)*, Lisboa, Portugal, September 15-18 (pp. 977-981). Piscataway, NJ: IEEE.

Stedman, R., Gharavi, H., Hanzo, L., & Steele, R. (1993, February). Transmission of subband-coded images via mobile channels. *IEEE Trans. Circuit Syst. Video Technol., 3*, 15-27.

Stewart, R. (2005, June). *Stream control transmission protocol (SCTP) dynamic address configuration*. IETF DRAFT, draft-ietf-tsvwgaddip-sctp-12.txt.

Thomson, S., & Narten, T. (1998, December). *IPv6 stateless address autoconfiguration.* IETF RFC 2462.

Wu, W., Banerjee, N., Basu, K., & Das, S. K. (2003). Network assisted IP mobility support in wireless LANs. *Second IEEE International Symposium on Network Computing and Applications, NCA'03*, Cambridge, MA, April 16-18 (pp. 257-264). Los Alamitos, CA: IEEE Computer Society.

Chapter 7.38
High Performance Scheduling Mechanism for Mobile Computing Based on Self-Ranking Algorithm

Hesham A. Ali
Mansoura University, Egypt

Tamer Ahmed Farrag
Mansoura University, Egypt

ABSTRACT

Due to the rapidly increasing number of mobile devices connected to the Internet, a lot of research is being conducted to maximize the benefit of such integration. The main objective of this article is to enhance the performance of the scheduling mechanism of the mobile computing environment by distributing some of the responsibilities of the access point among the available attached mobile devices. To this aim, we investigate a scheduling mechanism framework that comprises an algorithm that provides the mobile device with the authority to evaluate itself as a resource. The proposed mechanism is based on the "self ranking algorithm" (SRA), which provides a lifetime opportunity to reach a proper solution. This mechanism depends on an event-based programming approach to start its execution in a pervasive computing environment. Using such a mechanism will simplify the scheduling process by grouping mobile devices according to their self-ranking value and assigning tasks to these groups. Moreover, it will maximize the benefit of the mobile devices incorporated with the already existing Grid systems by using their computational power as a subordinate value to the overall power of the system. Furthermore, we evaluate the performance of the investigated algorithm extensively, to show how it overcomes the connection stability problem of the mobile devices. Experimental results emphasized that the proposed SRA has a great impact in reducing the total error and link utilization compared with the traditional mechanism.

INTRODUCTION

Mobile computing and commerce are spreading rapidly, replacing or supplementing wired computing. Moreover, the wireless infrastructure upon which mobile computing is built may reshape the entire information technology (IT) field. Therefore, it is fair to say that nowadays, mobile devices have a remarkable high profile in the most common communication devices. Individuals and organizations around the world are deeply interested in using wireless communication, because of its flexibility and its unexpected and fast development. The first solution to the need for mobile computing was to make computers small enough so they could be easily carried. First, the laptop computer was invented; later, smaller and smaller computers, such as 3G, personal digital assistants (PDAs) and other handhelds, appeared. Portable computers, from laptops to PDAs and others, are called mobile devices. In recent years, a great development took place on the Internet and with mobile technologies. Consequently, the next step will be merging these two technologies, leading to the Wireless Internet. The Wireless Internet will be much more than just Internet access from mobile devices; the Wireless Internet will be almost invisible, as people will use mobile services and applications directly. On the other hand, these services and applications will be acting as our agents, conducting searches and communicating with other services and applications to satisfy our needs. Not only will the integration of mobile technology and the Internet paradigm reinforce the development of the new context-aware applications, but it also will sustain traditional features, such as user preferences, device characteristics, properties of connectivity and the state of service and usage history. Furthermore, the context includes features strictly related to user mobility, such as a user's current geospatial location (time and/or space). As direct use of existing Internet applications in a mobile environment is usually unsatisfactory, services and applications need to take into account the specific characteristics of mobile environments. The next section will provide an overview of mobile devices as well as the present relation model between mobile devices and the Grid.

Mobile Devices' Development

The number of individuals and organizations relying on wireless devices is continually increasing. Table 1 represents a statistical study of current and future increase in the sales of wireless equipment and the considerable growth in the sales of mobile phones.

Table 1 shows the rapid growth in sales rates of wireless equipment, and they serve the purpose of being a good metric of the flourishing future of mobile computing. From 2001 to 2005, investments on mobile devices are expected to increase by 41% and reach $31 billion. In 2004, the laptops on the market reached 39.7 million. On the other hand, not only did the number of mobile devices and wireless equipment increase, but also the computational power and memory storage. As a result, mobile computing and wireless Internet became a very important research area. This article will approach it from the computational Grid viewpoint.

Mobile Devices and the Computational Grid

The interaction between mobile devices and the computational Grid, such as depicted in Figure 1, can be classified into two models:

1. **Mobile as a user of Grid resources:** The development in the computational power of mobile devices, such as smart phones,

Table 1. Worldwide wireless LAN equipment shipments (1000s of units) (Navrati Saxena, 2005)

Product Segment	2001	2002	2003	2004	2005	2006
Adapters	6890	12599	21333	30764	41417	50415
Access Points	1437	1965	3157	3919	4851	5837
Broadband Gateways	552	850	1906	3365	5550	7941
Other WLAN Equipment	47	59	82	105	132	158
Total	8926	15473	26478	38153	51950	64351

PDAs, and so forth, will be limited due to its size, battery life, bandwidth and storage of data. However, when this integration occurs, all of the huge computational power and stored data of the Grid will be available to the mobile client. The mobile clients send their requests to the access point (AP), which can be considered as the Grid gateway; the scheduler is responsible for finding a suitable resource to perform the incoming request (Sanver, 2004).

2. **Mobile as a Grid resource:** When one mobile device is considered a resource, it will be a very inferior and low-ranking resource compared with a personal computer (PC). Meanwhile, because of the large number of mobile devices that can be used, it can be a worthwhile computational power. Also, because of its large geographical distribution, it can be considered a very excellent data collector, which can be used in many applications, such as geographical information systems, weather news, and so forth. Relatively, there are two approaches to integrate the mobile device into the existing Grid; *the first* is that all the information of every mobile device is recorded in the scheduler, so every device is considered to be one Grid resource. *The second approach* is one in which the information of the mobile devices is hidden from the scheduler; it considers all the devices connected to an access point as one Grid resource, and the access point responsible for scheduling tasks on the mobile devices is also connected to it.

This article introduces SRA, which will be used to build a mobile computing scheduling mechanism. Before introducing the proposed algorithm, an overview about related work in the scheduling mechanism in the Grid is given,

Figure 1. An overview of integration of mobile devices with computational grid

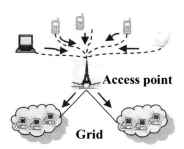

followed by a detailed description of the targeted problem at hand and a proposed framework. Moreover, the proposed SRA will be introduced, along with the simulation used to state the proposed algorithm and, finally, the results of that simulation will be analyzed.

RELATED WORK

Before elaborating on the problem, five of the most recent systems, especially on scheduling algorithms, are studied (He, 2003; Buyya, 2003; Somasundara, 2004; Berman & Casanova, 2005). Although the researchers have very different parameters and concepts, all of them have two main objectives. The first is to increase the utilization of the system, while the second is to find a suitable resource (as the economic cost, quality of services [QoS], deadline, etc.).

Table 2 shows a comparison between the most recent systems. Undoubtedly, one of the common problems that face any system when dealing with a large number of resources is "Load Balancing." Due to the fact that the ranking value of the resources is different, each of these systems

Table 2. Comparison between referenced systems

Project Features	Condor (Arun A. Somasundara, 2004)	Sphinx (Jang-uk In , 2004)	DBC (Rajkumar Buyya, 2003)	Disconnected operation service (Sang-Min Park, 2003)	QoS Guided Scheduling (Xiaoshan He ,2003)
Mobility	----	----	----	Job Proxy	----
Load Balancing	Backfilling	Resource usage Accounts and Users Quotas	Improved by considering Time deadline addition to Cost	----	QoS Guided improve but not direct solution
Long Beginning Time	Backfilling	Resource usage Accounts (Quotas)	Improved by considering Time deadline and Cost	----	----
Resource Ranking Parameters	By The User	Percent of resource usage account used	Cost	disconnection rate and the reconnection rate	Availability of required QoS
Multi Scheduler	supported	----	----	supported	----
Resource Reservation	Future work	supported	Future work	----	----
QoS support	----	supported	Future work	----	supported
Scheduling Constrains	FIFO, user priorities	user priorities	Budget, deadline	----	QoS (one dimensional)

endeavors to solve the problem, as illustrated in Table 2. Another problem is how the system will deal with the mobility of clients and resources. Noticeable is the limitation of research that takes into account the mobility of the resources (Nurmi, 2004; Park, 2003). The study of these five systems shows that they are based on different parameters to rank the resource, but the most popular are QoS and the economic cost (He, 2003; Buyya, 2003). The expressions used in Table 2 are explained here:

- **Backfilling:** A technique that tries to fill the gaps in the scheduling operation by executing the low-priority functions in the low-ranking resources that have not been used for a long time. This increases the system's overall utilization and makes a kind of load balancing between the resources (Somasundara, 2004).
- **Resource usage accounts (quotas):** Each resource must be assigned to certain functions according to its usage account. Preventing the resource from not being used can be caused by the presence of high QoS resources. This approach gives the scheduler force more functions to be assigned to a certain resource by maximizing its quota (In, 2004).
- **Job proxy:** Created when the mobile user submits a job, it is responsible for the interaction between the mobile device and the system. It can also simulate mobile action in case of mobile disconnecting. It does this until the mobile is connected again. If the mission is accomplished and the mobile is still disconnected, it stores the result for a certain time-out duration (Park, 2003).
- **QoS guided:** The QoS Guided scheduler has a kind of intelligence as not to consume the high QoS resource in performing the jobs that need low QoS. It does this to save its power to the other tasks that need this high QoS (He, 2003).

SCHEDULING AND THE CONNECTION STABILITY PROBLEM

The new approach in the computing area is *Internet computing*. It uses the already existing infrastructure of the Internet and builds its own Grid using devices interconnected to the Internet (Frontier, 2004). This is a very economical approach, because there is no need to build a special infrastructure. On the other hand, a lot of questions and issues raise, such as: "Do we need to build a new infrastructure of a grid to integrate the mobile devices as a grid user or as a grid resource?" and "What about the already existing grid projects?" (Gradwell, 2003; Dail, 2002; Frey, 2001; Berman, 2005). Figure 2 shows how the already existing infrastructure can be ordered and organized to create an infrastructure that helps to integrate the mobile devices with existing Grid systems like Condor, GriPhyN and Grid2003. This infrastructure aims at using huge computational power due to the large number of Internet users. It also aims at using the different services and resources available in the already existing Grid projects. Above all, the main objective is to use the Internet network to connect the mobile devices to the other parts of this infrastructure and to put all these services and computational power available to the mobile device. Finally, it aims at increasing the computational power and number of services of the system by integrating the large number of mobile devices distributed around the world (Saxena, 2005).

The most important problem that can face any Grid system is to develop a scheduling mechanism to manage such integration. The previous scheduling mechanisms depended on QoS (He, 2003), cost (Buyya, 2002; Barmouta, 2003) or a hybrid between other parameters (In, 2004; Takefusa, 2001) to select the best scheduling decision. Due to this integration and the mobility of the device, a new parameter appeared. This parameter represents the stability of the connection established between the devices and the access

Figure 2. The system infrastructure organization

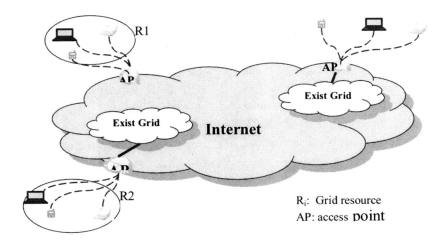

point; in other words, the rate of disconnecting and the rate of reconnecting. All of the already existing systems make the scheduler monitor and evaluate the performance and availability of its attached resources. This was acceptable with PCs, but because of the huge number of mobile devices expected to attach to the scheduler, a very high overload on the scheduler can happen. So, the scheduler slows down more and more as the number of the attached resources increases.

Plan of Solution

To overcome the overhead resulted from collecting the data at the access point scheduler and storing the historical ones of the mobile device performance, an SRA will be investigated. This algorithm has two key points: The *first* is to provide the mobile device with the authority to evaluate and rank itself and remove this task from the central point (scheduler). *Second* is considering the mobility of the resource as important metrics in such an environment. Therefore, the main

aim of this algorithm is to calculate a ranking value for each attached mobile device that may be considered as a metric of the mobile performance. Moreover, it will be used to classify the mobile devices into groups to make the process of scheduling simpler and faster.

PROPOSED FRAMEWORK

Figure 3 depicts the framework and system components relationship for the given organization in Figure 2. The following design guidelines must be adhered to: (1) Use opportunistic schedulers introduced in the Condor (Somasundara, 2004), because it is an excellent idea to make a good load balance between high-ranking resources and low-ranking ones (e.g., mobile devices); (2) Use the mobile proxy introduced in Park (2003), but we changed its name from job proxy to our proposed name "mobile proxy" which will be the interface between the mobile client and the other components of the system; and (3) Use

Figure 3. Mobile device scheduling framework and components relationship

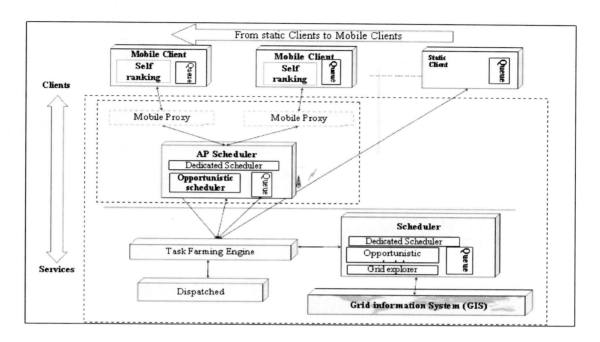

multi-schedulers because of the distribution of the considered infrastructure.

Proposed Framework Entities

In the following, the entities participating in the given framework are defined and their functions explained, as well as how they interact with each other.

- **The Task Farming Engine (TFE):** Responsible for partitioning the requested job into small tasks that will be assigned to resources to perform them using the scheduler and dispatcher.
- **The Scheduler**: Responsible for resource discovery, resource trading, resource selection and tasks assignment.

- **The Dispatcher:** Responsible for the actual assigning of tasks to the resources decided by the scheduler, monitoring execution of the tasks and controlling the process of collecting the different partitions of the job. Finally, it sends the overall result to the job requester.
- **Grid Information System (GIS):** Can be considered as the resources characteristics database used by the scheduler to find a suitable resource to perform the requested tasks using the resource QoS, cost, rank.
- **Dedicated Scheduler:** Each resource is assigned to one dedicated scheduler who has all rights to use the resource at any time except if the resource owner needs his resource. This monopoly may lead to non-functioning of some resources because

they are in the resources' list of certain Dedicated Schedulers, besides other high-ranked resources. So, these high-ranked resources will be preferred to the scheduler. This problem may be resolved by the temporary claiming of the resource to another type of scheduler named "opportunistic scheduler." This problem causes holes in the scheduling operation.

- **Opportunistic scheduler:** When the dedicated scheduler claims some of its resources because they were idle for a long time or they had a low-ranking value, which made them useless for a long time. The opportunistic scheduler tries to use this resource to

execute some small tasks that may end before the dedicated scheduler needs the resource again. This operation is named "Backfilling." Note that this method will maximize utilization of the overall system.

If a mobile client is connected to an access point, the first step is to create a mobile proxy object, which will be considered as a simulation of the mobile device. So, it may store the hardware specification of the mobile and its current location, and it may also monitor the movement of the mobile from one access point to another. This mobile proxy information will be the base knowledge on which the scheduler builds its work.

Figure 4. Request processing flow

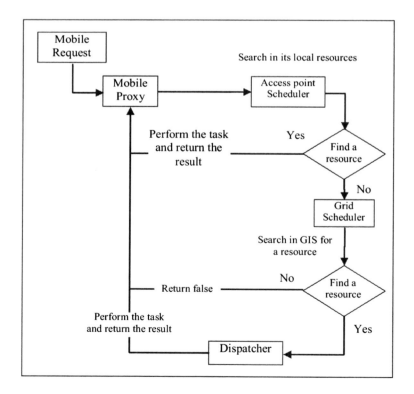

Figure 4 depicts a request-processing scenario. If the mobile client makes a request, this request will be stored in the mobile proxy. Then, it goes to a scheduler using the scheduling mechanism, trying to find a suitable resource to perform this request from its local connected resources. If the access point scheduler does not find a suitable resource, it forwards this request to a higher-level scheduler, which usually has static PCs with more computational power. This scheduler uses the GIS to find a suitable resource. When the resource is located, the dispatch assigns the requested task to this resource. When the task is performed, the outcome returns to the mobile proxy, which is responsible for sending the result to the mobile client in its current location.

PROPOSED SRA

The idea of the SRA is to reduce the dependability on the access point scheduler and distribute this overhead among the attached mobile devices. This can be done by making every mobile able to evaluate itself. Then, the access point can use this ranking value in the process of scheduling.

The trigger to start this algorithm execution depends on the event-based programming approach. The events that were taken into account are: (1) the event of disconnecting the mobile device and its scheduler, because this event means the end of the last connected period; (2) the event of reconnecting the mobile device to its scheduler, because this event means the end of the last disconnected period; and (3) the event of finishing a task, because this event changes the value of the mobile utilization. The self ranking value (R) has two parts: First is the Connectivity metric (M_{CD}), which can be considered as a metric of performance and connectivity of the mobile device, as well. The second part is the utilization metric (U), which can be considered as a metric of the success of the mobile device in performing the assigned task. When the mobile client has a new ranking value, this value must be sent to the mobile proxy to be entered as a parameter in the scheduling process.

Figure 5. Rank metric map

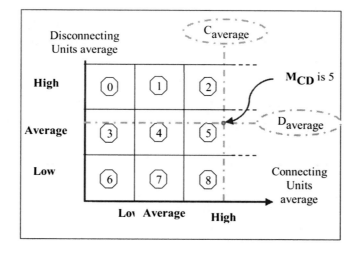

Figure 6. SRA for determining mobile device ranking value

0   Imports the prestored values :

t_s : the start of the last reconnection event. t_e: the end of the connection period .

T_u :Time unit defined by the scheduler N_c : number of reconnecting event occurring.

N_D: number of disconnecting event occurring.

$C_{average}$: The average number of time units to being connecting continually

$D_{average}$: the average number of time units being disconnecting continually

N_s : the number of successfully performed tasks   N : total number of tasks assigned to the device.

1   Wait for incoming event and check it.

2   *if the event is Disconnecting Event at time (t) then :*

2.1 Replace the prestored value t_e with the new value t   : $t_e = t$

2.2 Calculate the Connection Period P_c by using the stored value of t_s and t_e: $P_c = t_e - t_s$

2.3 Calculate number of time units X_c of the connection period P_c by using T_u provided by the Scheduler :

2.4 Calculate the new value of $C_{average}$ by using the prestored value of $C_{average}$ and the prestored N_c:

$$C_{average(new)} = C_{average\ (old)} * N_c + X_c/N_c + 1$$

2.5 $N_c = N_c + 1.$

2.6 Calculate the connectivity metric M_{CD} by using the new calculated $C_{average}$ and the prestored $D_{average}$ as coordinates of a point in the "rank metric map".

3   *if the event is reconnecting Event at time (t) then :*

3.1 Replace the prestored value t_s with the new value t   :$t_s = t$

3.2 Calculate the disconnection Period P_D by using the stored value of t_s and t_e: $P_D = t_s - t_e$

3.3 Calculate number of time units X_D of the disconnection period P_D by using T_u provided by the Scheduler :

$$X_D = P_D / T_u$$

3.4 Calculate the new value of $D_{average}$ by using the prestored value of $D_{average}$ and the prestored N_D:

$$D_{average(new)} = D_{average\ (old)} * N_D + X_D/N_D + 1$$

3.5 $N_D = N_D + 1.$

3.6 Calculate the connectivity metric M_{CD} by using the new calculated $D_{average}$ and the prestored $C_{average}$ as coordinates of a point in the "rank metric map".

4   *if the event is Task finish notification Event at time (t) then :*

4.1 if this is a success notification then : $N_s = N_s + 1.$

4.2 N=N+1.

4.3 Calculate the Utilization metric U using the stored values of N_s and N : $U = (N_s / N) * 2$

5   Finally Using the M_{CD} and U values to calculate the Rank Value R as the following:

$$R = M_{CD} + U$$

The considered parameters to be used in the SRA are: the average number of time units being connected continually ($C_{average}$), the average number of time units being disconnected continually ($D_{average}$) and the previous utilization history metric (U). The calculated values of $C_{average}$ and $D_{average}$ will be used as a key to the proposed ranking map, which is used to calculate *the first* part of the rank value that measures the mobile performance and connectivity. The overall ranking value is assumed to be between 1 and 10. This part represents 80% of this value; this percentage can be changed according to the schedulers' administrators. Figure 5 shows the rank metric map, which is based on two roles, first as the $C_{average}$ value increases, the rank must increase also. Second, as $D_{average}$ value increases, the rank must decrease. The $C_{average}$ and $D_{average}$ is used to calculate values. It works as a coordinator of the connectivity metric (MCD) on the rank metric map. The second part of the ranking value is the metric of the utilization of the mobile devices. So, it is calculated by the ratio between the number of the successful tasks and the number of all tasks. Summation of the two parts will generate the overall ranking value of the mobile device. Figure 6 shows the proposed algorithm.

SIMULATION MODEL

Validation of the proposed algorithm is done via simulation. The investigated simulation program is composed of three modules. The first is responsible for generating a random movement path for the mobile devices, while the second is responsible for tracking the generated path, and this will be done through the access point. Finally, the third is responsible for tuning critical parameters values and collecting outputs parameters, which are required to calculate $C_{average}$ and $D_{average}$.

Mobile Device Movement Mechanism

The mobile device movement path that will be generated is based on a mechanism that guarantees a random path as follows:

1. Generate random black-and-white areas as shown in Figure 7a. White areas imply that there is an available connection between the mobile device and the scheduler access point; black areas depict disconnection.
2. Divide the whole area into small rectangular areas, as shown in Figure 7b.
3. Generate a point within each rectangle at a random position, as shown in Figure 7c.

Figure 7. Steps of random movement path generation

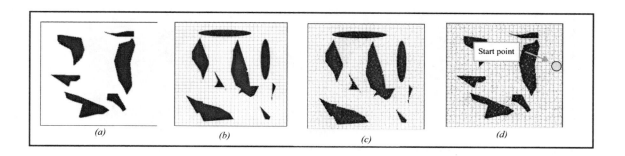

4.   Save the position of the generated points in an array.

5.   Select one point from the previous array in random fashion to be the starting point of the movement path, as shown in Figure 7d.

6.   Select one of the possible eight directions shown in Figure 8 for the next hop.

7.   Continue the movement towards the previous selected direction for a random number of hops.

8.   Repeat steps 6 and 7 until the required length of movement path is acquired.

9.   Store all the selected points in steps 6, 7 and 8 to represent a path for mobile device movement.

10.   Repeat steps 2-9 to generate another mobile movement path.

Figure 9 illustrates some examples of the generated random mobile movement paths based on the previous mechanism.

AP and Monitoring the Mobile Device

This module simulates the AP monitoring of the mobile device movement process. In such a process, the AP sends an "Are you alive?" message. If there is an available connection, the mobile device responses with an "I'm alive" message. The time between sending and receiving is called the response time T_r; this time can

Figure 8. Choose a random direction from eight possible

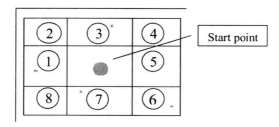

Figure 9. Examples of the random mobile movement paths

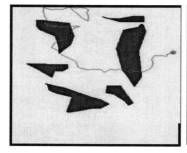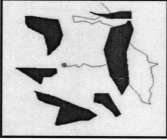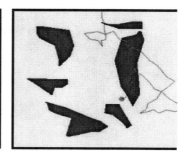

Figure 10. AP monitoring of the mobile device movement process

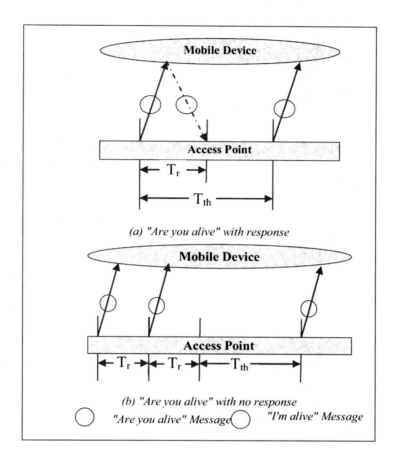

be determined experimentally. The AP waits for another threshold time T_{th} before sending the next monitoring message. On the other hand, if there is no response for T_r, the access point will send a message again. According to the response of the previous simulation, the AP reports the mobile device status. Figure 10 shows this process.

At this point, we have to notice that reducing T_{th} will lead to more accurate results, but on the other hand, the number of messages will increase. This means high-link usage, which is considered from the application point of view to be a bad usage.

Parameters Setting, Collecting, and Calculating

The different parameters, which are required for comparing the self-ranking against the traditional AP ranking from a network utilization and accuracy point of view, are calculated in this module.

First, the speed of the mobile device movement and T_{th} and T_r is tuned. Some parameters from the first and second modules are collected and stored, including: the length of the generated path, the number of connections and disconnections during the movement on the path, the total number of "Are you alive?" messages, and the number of messages with and without response. So, $C_{average}$ and $D_{average}$ can be calculated.

PERFORMANCE ANALYSIS AND DISCUSSION

Based on the previous discussion, on the change of the number of mobile devices used during the experiment (50, 75 and 100 mobiles) or on the change of the value of T_{th} (2, 4 and 6 seconds), various experiments are performed. Two factors were constant: the length of the movement path, which was selected to be relatively long (10000 hop); and T_r, which was selected to be relatively small (0.5 second). Each of these experiments will be repeated for different movement speeds, from low mobility (with average movement speed of 2 m/s) to high mobility (with average movement speed of 30 m/s).

The average error in calculating the $C_{average}$ and $D_{average}$ has been calculated for each experiment at each used speed, and their summation represents the total error in the experiment. Also, the number of network messages exchanged between AP and the mobile device, in both the AP monitoring and self monitoring, has been counted.

Figures 11, 12, and 13 show that the percentage of the total error increases rapidly as the movement speed of mobile device increases. This result is expected, because as movement speed increases, the ability of AP to sense the change in the mobile connectivity will be more and more limited. Also, the figures show that when the value of T_{th} increases, the percentage of the total error increases also, while the number of exchanged network messages decreases. This result is expected, because T_{th} represents the time between two monitoring messages; as this time increases, that means reduction in the ability of AP to sense the change in mobile connectivity. The figures show the comparison between the number of exchanged messages between AP and mobile devices in the case of self monitoring and case of AP monitoring. Note that, in the case of AP monitoring, the number approximately

Figure 11. Total error and link utilization at number of mobiles = 50

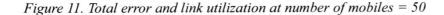

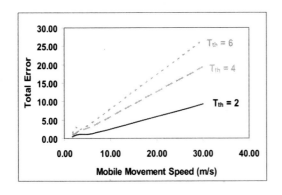
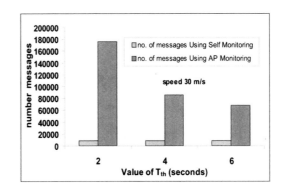

Figure 12. Total error and link utilization at number of mobiles = 75

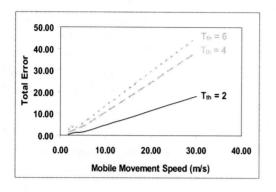
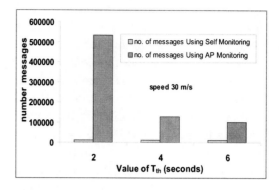

Figure 13. Total error and link utilization at no of mobiles = 100

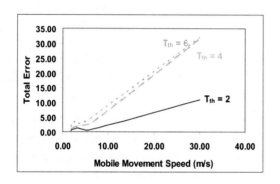
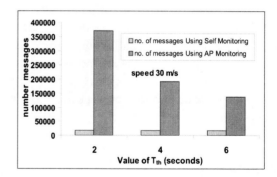

doubled more than 70 times compared to the case of self-monitoring.

CONCLUSION

This article points out an overview of the issues of mobile devices integration with the existing Grid. It shows that when some authorization is impeded within the mobile client, every mobile can evaluate its own performance. The traditional method makes an overhead on the scheduler to perform a historical evaluation to the mobile performance, which makes it busy in a secondary task and leaves its main task of scheduling. So, the SRA will be the base of a scheduling mechanism that will schedule the tasks on the mobile devices. The originality of the proposed mechanism concentrates on mobile cooperating with services at the AP. Using such a mechanism will lead to *minimizing* the calculation time consumed in mobile ranking and evaluating before starting the scheduling process. Moreover, it will lead also to *minimizing* the amount of stored data at the scheduler and *simplifying* the scheduling process by grouping the mobile devices according to their self-ranking value and assigning tasks to these groups. Finally, it will result in *maximizing* the profit of the mobile devices integrated with the already existing Grid systems by using their computational power as an addition to the system's overall power. In brief, the outcome will be *maximizing* system utilization and making the system more flexible to integrate any new devices without any need to increase the system complexity.

In this article, we present the newly emerging technical issues for realizing this mobile Grid system, and particularly focus on the job scheduling algorithm to achieve more reliable performance. However, there are still challenging problems, such as limited energy, device heterogeneity, security and so on. We will tackle these issues in future works and develop a prototype of a mobile Grid system.

REFERENCES

Barmouta, A., & Buyya, R. (2003, April 22-26). GridBank: A Grid Accounting Services Architecture (GASA) for distributed systems sharing and integration. In *Proceedings of the Parallel and Distributed Processing Symposium (IPDPS 2003)*, Nice, France (p. 245). IEEE Computer Society.

Berman, F., & Casanova, H. (2005). New Grid scheduling and rescheduling methods in the GrADS project. *International Journal of Parallel Programming, 32*(2-3), 209-229.

Buyya, R., Abramson, D., & Giddy, J. (2002). Economic models for resource management and scheduling in Grid computing. *Concurrency and Computation: Practice and Experience (CCPE) Journal, 14*(13-15), 1507-1542.

Buyya, R., & Murshed, M. (2002). GridSim: A toolkit for the modeling and simulation of distributed resource management and scheduling for Grid computing. *Concurrency and Computation: Practice and Experience (CCPE) Journal, 14*(13-15), 1175-1220.

Buyya, R., Murshed, M., & Abramson, D. (2003, June 24-27). A deadline and budget constrained cost-time optimization algorithm for scheduling task farming applications on global Grids. In *Proceedings of the International Conference on Parallel and Distributed Processing Techniques and Applications (PDPTA'02)*, Las Vegas, NV.

Dail, H., Casanova, H., & Berman, F. (2002). A decoupled scheduling approach for the GrADS program development environment. In *Proceedings of the 2002 ACM/IEEE Conference on Supercomputing. Conference on High Performance Networking and Computing*, Baltimore, MD (pp. 1-14).

Frey, J. (2001, August 7-9). Condor-G: A computation management agent for multi-institutional Grids. In *Proceedings of the Tenth IEEE Symposium on High Performance Distributed Computing (HPDC10)*, San Francisco, CA..

Frontier. (2004). *The premier Internet computing platform* (White Paper). Retrieved from http://www.parabon.com/clients/clientWhitePapers.jsp

Gradwell, P. (2003). *Overview of Grid scheduling systems*. Retrieved from http://www.peter.me.uk/phd/writings/computing-economy-review.pdf

He, X. (2003). A QoS guided scheduling algorithm for Grid computing [Spcial issue Grid computing]. *Journal of Computer Science and Technology (JCS&T), 18*(4).

In, J.-u., & Avery, P. (2004, April). Policy based scheduling for simple quality of service in Grid computing. In *Proceedings of the 18th International Parallel and Distributed Processing Symposium (IPDPS 2004)*, Santa Fe, NM.

Nurmi, D., Wolski, R., & Brevik, J. (2004). *Model based checkpoint scheduling for volatile resource environments* (Technical Report). Santa Barbara: University of California Santa Barbara, Department of Computer Science.

Park, S.-M., Ko, Y.-B., & Kim, J.-H. (2003, December 15-18). Disconnected operation service in mobile Grid computing. In *Proceedings of Service-Oriented Computing — ICSOC 2003: First International Conference*, Trento, Italy.

Sanver, M., Durairaju, S.P., & Gupta, A. (2004). Should one incorporate mobile-ware in parallel and distributed computation? In *Proceedings of the 10th International Conference on High Performance Computing (HiPC 2003)*, Hyderabad, India.

Saxena, N. (2005, April 3-7). New hybrid scheduling framework for asymmetric wireless rnvironments with request repetition. In *Proceedings of the Third International Symposium on Modeling and Optimization in Mobile, Ad Hoc, and Wireless Networks (WiOpt'05)*, Riva del Garda, Trentino, Italy (pp. 368-376).

Saxena, N., Basu, K., Das, S.K., & Pinotti, C.M. (2005, April). A dynamic hybrid scheduling algo-rithm with clients' departure for impatient clients in heterogeneous environments. In *Proceedings of the 19th IEEE International Parallel and Distributed Processing Symposium (IPDPS'05)*, Rhodes Island, Greece.

Somasundara, A.A., Ramamoorthy, A., & Srivastava, M.B. (2004, December 5-8). Mobile element scheduling for efficient data collection in wireless sensor networks with dynamic deadlines. In *Proceedings of the 25th IEEE International Real-Time Systems Symposium (RTSS'04)*, Lisbon, Portugal (pp. 296-305).

Sulistio, A., Yeo, C.S., & Buyya, R. (2003, June). Visual modeler for Grid Modeling and Simulation (GridSim) toolkit. In *Proceedings of the International Conference on Computational Science (ICCS 2003), Part III*, Melbourne, Australia (pp. 1123-1132).

Takefusa, A. (2001, August). A study of deadline scheduling for client-server systems on the computational Grid. In *Proceedings of the 10th IEEE Symposium on High Performance and Distributed Computing (HPDC'01)*, San Francisco, CA (p. 406).

Yu, D. (2003, November 13-15). Divisible load scheduling for Grid computing. In *Proceedings of the 16th International Conference on Parallel and Distributed Computing Systems (PDCS 2003)*, Marina del Rey, CA.

This work was previously published in the International Journal of Information Technology and Web Engineering, edited by D. Rine and G. Alkhatib, Volume 1, Issue 2, pp. 43-59, copyright 2006 by IGI Publishing, formerly known as Idea Group Publishing (an imprint of IGI Global).

Chapter 7.39
Multilayered Approach to Evaluate Mobile User Interfaces

Maria de Fátima Queiroz Vieira Turnell
Universidade Federal de Campina Grande (UFCG), Brazil

José Eustáquio Rangel de Queiroz
Universidade Federal de Campina Grande (UFCG), Brazil

Danilo de Sousa Ferreira
Universidade Federal de Campina Grande (UFCG), Brazil

ABSTRACT

This chapter presents a method for the evaluation of user interfaces for mobile applications. The method is based upon an approach that combines user opinion, standard conformity assessment, and user performance measurement. It focuses on the evaluation settings and techniques employed in the evaluation process, while offering a comparison between the laboratory evaluation and field evaluation approaches. The method's presentation and the evaluation comparison will be supported by a discussion of the results obtained from the method's application to a case study involving a Personal Digital Assistant (PDA). This chapter argues that the experience gained from evaluating conventional user interfaces can be applied to the world of mobile technology.

INTRODUCTION

As proposals for new techniques and methods emerge for the evaluation of mobile device usability, it becomes more difficult for practitioners to choose among them. To be able to evaluate the efficacy of these techniques and methods, as well as to reproduce their steps, they have to be described in a level of detail not often found in the literature. Claims are often made without solid statistical results and are usually based on superficial descriptions. This makes it difficult, if not impossible, to compare alternative choices. Given the features of these new devices (such as mobility, restrictive resources for information input and output, and dynamic contexts of use), HCI specialists may question the efficacy of the methods, techniques, and settings already known to them from previous experiences. Thus, the major question that is addressed is whether it is possible to adapt the methods, techniques, and settings from previous evaluation experiences to this new class of devices, given their distinctive features.

The most frequent question raised in the vast majority of studies presented in the literature is whether to adopt a field approach or a laboratory approach. However, little is discussed in terms of which techniques are best suited for the specific evaluation target and its context of use. While this polemic subject may represent to the HCI specialist an import concern, it is equally important to consider the efficacy of the method, which accompanies this choice of approach (efficacy meaning the quality of the answers to the questions formulated as the basis of the evaluation). This is because the efforts employed in the evaluation may not pay off if a method is not well chosen or well employed.

This chapter presents a method for evaluating mobile devices based upon a set of techniques already known to the HCI specialist community. Each technique evaluates the problem from different perspectives: the user perspective (expressed as views on the product obtained through a questionnaire), the specialist's perspective (expressed when analyzing the user performance during the usability evaluation), and the usability community perspective (expressed in the form of standards conformity assessment). Each of these perspectives identifies evaluation problems and, when overlaid, they lead to a more reliable and complete product appraisal.

The remainder of this chapter is structured as follows. The second section gives a brief overview of the evaluation approaches currently in use for mobile devices, according to the literature review. The third section outlines the multi-layered approach. The fourth section illustrates the application of the multi-layered approach by means of a case study involving a Personal Digital Assistant (PDA). The fifth section discusses the results

of the case study and their implications for the questions posed in this chapter. Finally, the sixth section concludes with the discussion of future trends in evaluation methods and how to apply the existing experience to the evaluation of this new class of products.

USER INTERFACE EVALUATION FOR MOBILE DEVICES

In the context of user-centered design processes, a significant portion of usability work involves the coordinated acquisition of valid and reliable data by a team of professionals. These specialists have varied backgrounds and skills and employ a number of evaluation methods. The expected result is an improved system design. This is achieved by the successful identification of a system's usability problems that might impact the interaction quality for a range of users.

Usability data consists of any information that can be used to measure or identify factors affecting the usability of a system being evaluated (Hilbert & Redmiles, 2000). These data are crucial for designing successful systems intended for human use. Such data are gathered by usability evaluation methods and techniques that can assign values to usability dimensions (Rosson & Carroll, 2002) and/or indicate usability deficiencies in a system (Hartson, Andre, & Williges, 2003). According to the International Organization for Standardization (ISO, 1998), usability dimensions are commonly taken to include user efficiency, effectiveness, and subjective satisfaction with a system in performing a specified task in a specified context.

Usability data are gathered via either analytic or empirical methods (Nielsen, 1993; Mayhew, 1999; Rosson & Carroll, 2002). Analytic methods, in which a system is evaluated based on its interface design attributes, are usually conducted by HCI specialists and do not involve human participants performing tasks. This means that these methods often rely on the specialists' judgment. Empirical methods, in which the system is evaluated based on observed performance in actual use, involve data collection of human usage.

Other classifications include direct methods (recording actual usage) and indirect methods (recording accounts of usage) (Holzinger, 2005). There are also formative and summative methods (Wixon & Wilson, 1997). The direct methods are used to generate new ideas and gather data during the development of a system in order to guide iterative design (Hix & Hartson, 1993). The indirect methods are used to evaluate existing systems and gather data to evaluate a completed system in use (Scriven, 1967). Discovery methods (also called qualitative methods) are used to discover how users work, behave, and think, and what problems they have. Decision methods (also called quantitative methods) are used in selecting a design among several alternatives or in picking elements of interface designs (Wixon & Wilson, 1997).

In essence, usability data have been classed in a number of other models and frameworks, often focusing on (1) the approach employed for gathering the data (including the resources expended and the degree of formality) (Danielson, 2006); (2) the context of use (including lighting, noise level, network connectivity, communication costs, communication bandwidth, and the social situation) (ISO, 1998; ISO, 1999; Jones & Marsden, 2006); (3) the nature and fidelity of the artifact being evaluated (EATMP, 2000); and (iv) the goal of the acquisition process (Kan, 2002).

It is a fact that usability evaluation for stationary computer systems has grown in the last two decades. In spite of debates still taking place within the HCI area, they are often based on a tacit understanding of basic concepts. One example of this understanding is in relation to the distinction between field and laboratory evaluation approaches and their importance to the area. Classical extensive guidelines were written that describe how usability evaluation in controlled

environments should be conducted (e.g., Dumas & Reddish, 1999; Mayhew, 1999; Nielsen, 1993). Additionally, experimental evaluations of the relative strengths and weaknesses of different techniques are available that can be applied in a usability evaluation (e.g., Molich et al., 1998).

In the last decade, methodologies and approaches in HCI have been challenged by the increasing focus on systems for wearable, handheld, and mobile computing devices. One such move beyond office, home, and other stationary-use settings has pointed to the need for new approaches in designing and evaluating these systems (Kjeldskov, 2003). While the primarily task-centered evaluation approaches may be applicable to the desktop computing paradigm (often structured with relatively predictable tasks), they may not be directly applicable to the often-unpredictable continuous interaction possibilities and relatively unstable mobile settings. Additionally, it is not easy for evaluation methods to integrate completely or even adequately in real world or simulated settings contexts during the evaluation process. Authors argue that mobile computing demands not only real users but also a real or simulated context with device interaction tasks. It also demands real tasks or realistic task simulations.

There are a number of studies that discuss the question of whether the evaluation should be carried out in a laboratory or field context (e.g., Goodman et al., 2004; Kjeldskov & Stage, 2004; Kjeldskov et al., 2005; Po et al., 2004). All of these papers have a common theme, in that they apply a multi-method approach to performance measurement and discuss solutions for efficient data analysis. Nonetheless, it is important to note that the approach to usability evaluation depends on the relevance of the results presented as well as on the quality of the data analysis process. In general, the reports only present the results of the data analysis, omitting the details of the analysis process itself. While the data gathering method is critical for data quality, a more rigorous analysis on user comments and problem reports could help specialists better assess their choices.

There is a lot of current human-computer interaction research on alternatives for data collection methods and techniques. However, adequate data analysis and validation are only presented in few cases (e.g., Nielsen, 1994; Dumas & Redish, 1999; Po et al., 2004). In general, this aspect of the HCI research is poorly described in the literature, there being only vague conclusions and little guidance for attempts at successfully replicating the findings in other evaluation contexts. Many methods and techniques have been employed in the analysis of empirical data gathered during usability evaluations. Examples are for field testing analysis, video data analysis (Sanderson & Fisher, 1994), expert analysis (Molich et al., 1998), and head-mounted video and cued recall (Omodei et al., 2002). Its time-consuming character and its poor applicability for industrial purposes can explain the absence of an in-depth usage data analysis when under resource constraints (Baillie & Schatz, 2005). Nonetheless, it is strongly recommended for research purposes as a means to support new findings. For the same reason, it is equally important to provide sufficient detail to allow for replication and a substantiated choice of methods with similar levels of description.

THE MULTILAYERED EVALUATION APPROACH

The method described here was originally proposed for evaluating desktop interfaces. It was then adapted to evaluate the usability of mobile devices. It is based upon a multi-layered approach that combines standard conformity assessment, user performance measurement, and user satisfaction measurement. Each one of these evaluation techniques detects problems from a specific point of view. The multilayered approach is based on the premise that the combination of techniques

(triangulation) will produce complementary and more robust results.

Standard Conformity Assessment

According to the International Organization for Standardization (ISO), conformity assessment means checking whether products, services, materials, processes, systems, and personnel measure up to the requirements of standards (ISO, 2006).

In its original version, this evaluation method adopts the standard ISO 9241 (*Ergonomic Requirements for Office Work with Visual Display Terminals*).

In the PDA case study it was found that only some parts of this standard can be applied to this mobile device: Parts 11 (ISO 9241-11, 1998), 14 (ISO 9241-14, 1997), 16 (ISO 9241-16, 1999), and 17 (ISO 9241-17, 1998). There are also some other standards that apply to this kind of device such as the ISO/IEC 14754 (*Pen-based Interfaces—Common gestures for text editing with pen-based systems*) (ISO/IEC 14754, 1999) and others that, although applicable to mobile devices, do not apply in this specific case. Examples are the ISO/IEC 18021 (*User interfaces for mobile tools for management of database communications in a client-server model*), since it is for devices capable of performing data interchange with servers (ISO/IEC 18021, 2002); and ITU-T E.161 (*Arrangement of digits, letters, and symbols on telephones and other devices that can be used for gaining access to a telephone network*, also known as ANSI T1.703-1995/1999, and ISO/IEC 9995-8:1994) (ITU, 2001).

User Satisfaction Measurement

User satisfaction has received considerable attention from researchers since the 1980s as an important surrogate measure of information systems success (Aladwani & Palvia, 2002; Goodhue &

Thompson, 1995; Bailey & Pearson, 1983). While most user satisfaction measuring instruments were not Web-based at the time of development, others have been successfully validated in a Web-based environment (e.g., De Oliveira et al., 2005).

The user satisfaction diagnosis provides an insight into the level of user satisfaction with the product, highlighting the importance of the problems found and their impact on the product acceptance.

User Performance Measurement

The user performance measurement aims in general to provide data on the effectiveness and efficiency of a user's interaction with a product. It enables comparisons with similar products, or with previous versions of the same product along its development. Additionally, it can highlight areas where a product can be enhanced to improve usability. When used with the other methods, the evaluator can build a complete picture of the usability of a system.

The most significant user interface problems can be found by conducting experiments (usability tests) with representative users to observe how quickly, easily, and safely they can operate a product. The major change introduced in the original method concerns the introduction of field tests as a complement to the original laboratory tests.

The Experiment: Comparing Field and Laboratory Use of a PDA

The main objective of this study is to investigate the need for adapting the original evaluation method to the context of mobile devices, based on the analysis of the influence of the context (field versus laboratory and mobility versus stationary interaction) on the evaluation of mobile devices and applications.

The mobile device chosen as the target for this study was a PDA, the *Nokia 770 Internet*

Tablet and some of its native applications. Tests were performed in a controlled environment (the usability laboratory) and also in the field. Twenty-four users took part in the experiment, divided into two groups of twelve.

Experiment Design

The study was designed to investigate the influence of the context (field and laboratory) and associated aspects such as mobility, settings, and so forth, and the user experience on the evaluation results. The independent variables are those that are not influenced by the context, by the test facilitator, or by external factors such as noise and lighting. An experiment plan was drawn from the study's objectives. The independent variables were chosen as follows:

- **Task context** comprises factors that may affect the users' behavior and their performance during the experiment (usability test). These factors may be internal or external to the user. The external factors originate in the field environment, examples being noise level and light intensity. The internal factors, on the other hand, are stress or other health conditions that may affect the user's mental and physical abilities.
- **User mobility** refers to the conditions under which the task is being performed. An example is if the user is required to work while being mobile, that is, moving between places or wandering while working.
- **User experience level** refers to the user's knowledge regarding mobile devices in particular and desktop computers systems in general.

The dependent variables are all dependant on the user's experience level:

- **Task time** represents the time taken by a device's user to perform a task.

- **Number of incorrect choices** measures how many times the user has made incorrect choices while selecting options in the interface through a menu dialogue.
- **Number of incorrect actions** measures how many times the same error (excluding the number of incorrect choices) was committed by the user while performing a task.
- **Number of accesses to the online help** and **number of accesses to the printed help** measure how many times the user accessed the online and printed help while performing a task.
- **Perceived usefulness** represents the user's opinion about the usefulness of the mobile application for the prescribed task.

- **Perceived ease of use** represents the user subjective satisfaction when using the mobile device.

Table 1 summarizes the experiment plan, which states the independent and dependent variables to be observed during the experiment and used as indicators to answer the research questions.

Test Environment

A software tool was used in the field environment to remotely capture the device's screen through a wireless connection to the lab. The user inputs (through keypad and stylus) were registered by a micro-camera coupled to the device and also

Table 1. Plan for the experiment with the device Nokia 770

EXPERIMENT PLAN	
Target-Problems	1. With the shape/dimensions of the product 2. With the mechanisms for information input/output 3. With the processing power 4. With the navigation between functions 5. With information legibility
Test Objectives	1. Investigating the target problems 2. Detecting other problems
Objective Indicators	1. Task execution time 2. Number of incorrect actions 3. Number of incorrect choices 4. Number of repeated errors 5. Number of accesses to the online help 6. Number of off-line help (printed manuals) accesses
Subjective Indicators	1. Product ease of use 2. Task completion easiness 3. Input mechanism ease of use 4. Text input modes ease of use 5. Understandability of terms and labels 6. Understandability of messages 7. Help mechanism efficiency

remotely connected to the laboratory through a wireless connection. The interaction was registered in the controlled environment using two video cameras installed in the laboratory. One was focused on the users´ facial expressions and the other registered the device screen. As in the field environment, software was used to remotely capture the device's screen. Since the field setting required a wireless network, the field experiment was performed in the area surrounding the university's computer department. In both cases, the test facilitator was a human interface specialist who remained within reach in case the user required any explanation on the test procedure.

Participants

Users participating in the PDA experiment were selected on the basis of having previous experience with mobile devices (such as mobile phones), computers, and the Internet. They were also required to have some familiarity with the English language, since this is the language adopted in the device's user interface and in its documentation. The user sample was then classed according to the users' experience level into the categories shown in Table 2.

The recruited users were divided into two groups of 12 to participate in the field and laboratory tests. Based on user experience level, both groups were then subdivided into three subgroups of four beginners, four intermediates and four experts.

Materials

Laboratory Test Materials

- **Hardware:** The Nokia 770 Internet Tablet; PC based Workstation (2); Video cameras (3); Microphones (2).
- **Software:** VNC (Virtual Network Computing) software to capture the screens during the interaction with the device; the WebQuest tool with the questionnaires pre-test (to gather the user profile) and post-test (to collect and process the user satisfaction level).
- **Miscellaneous:** The Nokia 770 Internet Tablet Manual; chronometer (1); CDs for video backup; participant registration form; test conditions acceptance forms on which the users declared their acceptance of the experiment conditions; task script that consists of a written task description to guide the user during the session (versions for the user and for the evaluator); Form for event log.

Table 2. User sample categorization

CHARACTERISTIC \ CATEGORY	Beginner	Intermediate	Expert
Previous Computer Knowledge	Basic/ Intermediate	Intermediate/ Advanced	Intermediate/ Advanced
Previous Experience with *Nokia*	No	No	Yes

Field Test Materials

- **Hardware:** The Nokia 770 Internet Tablet; PC-based Portable (laptop) Workstation (1); wireless video micro-camera (1); apparatus to support the video micro-camera (1); television set (1); VCR equipment (1).
- **Software:** VNC (Virtual Network Computing) software to capture the screens during the interaction with the device; WebQuest tool with the questionnaires pre-test (to gather the user profile) and post-test (to collect and process the user satisfaction level).
- **Miscellaneous:** Chronometer (1); CDs and VHS tapes for video backup; participant registration form; test conditions acceptance forms on which the users declared to accept the experiment conditions; task script that consists of a written task description to guide the user during the session (versions for the user and for the evaluator); form for event log.

Camera Apparatus

The apparatus shown in Figure 1 was built to couple a video micro-camera to the mobile device. This allowed the recording of user interaction through a remote link with the laboratory computer.

The WebQuest Tool

A Web tool named *WebQuest* supports the method application (De Oliveira et al., 2005). This tool was developed to support the specialist during data collection, to provide automatic score computation, to perform statistical analysis, and to generate graphical results. *WebQuest* also enables the specialist to reach a more diverse and geographically widespread sample of users through the Internet. One of its features is a flexible questionnaire structure, which enables specific

context adaptation and, by means of an estimation model, ensures a higher degree of confidence on the indicators of user satisfaction. Currently *WebQuest* supports two questionnaires: (i) a pre-test questionnaire, the *USer* (*User Sketcher*), conceived to raise the profile of the system users; and (ii) a post-test questionnaire, the *USE* (*User Satisfaction Enquirer*), conceived to raise the user degree of satisfaction with the system. The pre-test questionnaire incorporates a model to estimate the user's subjective satisfaction and can be answered directly on the Web. The questions are related to the users´ physical characteristics, knowledge, and skills. Both questions and answers are configurable.

As for the *USE* (*User Satisfaction Enquirer*), it allows gathering quantifiable variables on the user acceptance of the device. Three of its aspects are of special interest. Firstly, it incorporates a model to estimate user subjective satisfaction. Secondly, the questionnaires can be answered directly on the Web. Thirdly, the items are partially or totally configurable. The adoption of an estimation model by *USE* allowed us to establish

Figure 1. Apparatus to support video camera during experiment

a subjective satisfaction coefficient directly from the inspection of the respondents' samples. The *WebQuest* tool allows the specialist to easily edit the questionnaire's items. These items are organized into groups: (1) *fixed*, which are applicable to various evaluation contexts and thus are not allowed to be altered; (2) *semi configurable*, which allow for changes in the answer options; and (3) *configurable*, which can be fully configured (both the question and respective options of answers). *USE* supports the specialist from the data collection through to automatic score computation, performing statistical analysis, and generating graphics with the results.

Experiment Procedure

The techniques employed in the experiment procedure were the observation and subsequent video analysis for accumulating quantitative data (such as time spent and error rate). An automated video capturing tool recorded the interactions of the subjects during the field tests to ensure a non-intrusive observation method. During task execution, the users were asked for their consent before being filmed. The conditions of test-subject participation included a written commitment not to disclose any product information. The users were also asked to give consent so that their images and/or sound recordings made during the experiment could be used for research purposes or in a multimedia product evaluation report. On the other hand, the users were given assurances from the evaluation team that no personal information or individual performance results would be disclosed.

The first step in following the method consisted in defining the evaluation scope for the product as well as a scenario for the test. Table 3 illustrates the sequence of tasks performed during the experiment.

The decision was based on a heuristic evaluation performed by the evaluation team. This initial step also supports the definition of a general profile for the user sample and a classification into categories. Following, the method the evaluation objectives were defined. These became the basis for choosing the product evaluation scenario (product context of use and laboratory settings) and the corresponding tasks to be performed by the users during the experiment. Having planned the evaluation, a pilot test was conducted to verify the adequacy of the proposed experiment procedural, materials, and environment. Through this fine tuning procedure it was found, in the PDA case study, that the time to perform the tasks had been underestimated. This resulted in re-dimensioning the test scenario to six tasks, with a review of the tasks themselves to fit the established session time of sixty minutes to prevent user tiredness.

All subjects were submitted to the same procedure prescribed in the experiment protocol. The study was conducted first in a laboratory setting and then in the field environment. During the field tests the participants were taken outdoors, and the tasks were conducted in an environment that was as close to real-use conditions as possible.

The experiment conducted in the usability laboratory had the audio and video of each session recorded. In the field experiment, only the

Table 3. Test scenario and sequence of tasks to be performed during experiment

TASKS IN SCRIPT	
T01	Initializing the device
T02	Searching for books in an online store
T03	Visualizing a PDF file
T04	Entering textual information
T05	Using the electronic mail
T06	Using the audio player

video of the sessions was recorded, supplemented by comments written by the specialist. As described in the experiment protocol, each session consisted of the following steps: (1) introducing the user to the test environment by explaining the test purpose, the procedure to be followed and the ethics involved in terms of the conditions of participation; (2) applying the pre-test questionnaire; (3) performing the task script; (4) applying the post-test questionnaire; and (5) performing a non-structured interview.

At the time of the experiment, the *Nokia 770 Internet Tablet* device was not yet widely known in the Brazilian market. The users who claimed to have had no previous contact with it were given a quick introduction. This introduction consisted of an instructional material given to the recruited users and also a quick explanation about the device's input and output modes and its main resources.

Results

The results obtained from the experiment in which the multi-layered method was applied support the original assumption that, in spite of the distinctive features of this class of devices, it is possible to adapt from the evaluation experience with conventional devices. This conclusion is supported by the evidence that the evaluation context did not significantly influence the user performance or the opinion about the device's usability, given through the analysis of the objective and subjective indicators associated with the experiment.

Standard Conformity Assessment Results

The results of the conformity assessment to the standards ISO 9241 Parts 14 and 16 and ISO 14754 are illustrated in Table 4. According to ISO, conformity assessment results can be summarized by computing an *adherence rate* (AR). This is the percentage of the applicable recommendations (Ar) that were successfully adhered to (Sar).

In spite of the device's characteristics that limit the number of applicable recommendations, these results corroborate the idea that the standards inspection is still applicable in the evaluation process. The efficacy of this technique can be considerably improved if it is based upon standards conceived specifically for mobile devices, which could evidence more usability problems.

Table 4. Nokia 770 conformity assessment with standards

Standard	#Sar	#Ar	AR (%)
ISO 9241 Part 14	45,0	53,0	84,9
ISO 9241 Part 16	26,0	33,0	78,8
ISO 14754	4,0	11,0	36,4

Sar—Successfully adhered recommendations
Ar—Applicable recommendations
AR—Adherence Rate

$$AR = \frac{Sar}{Ar} x100\%$$

User Satisfaction Measurement Results

For the PDA case study context, both questions and answers of the *USE* questionnaire were configured. The questionnaire was applied soon after the usability test and answered using the mobile device itself. As mentioned before, its purpose was to collect information on the user's degree of satisfaction with the device and on aspects such as interface navigation, documentation, and overall impressions.

The *USE* was composed of three sections. The first section is relative to "the product Use and Navigation." It is composed of 17 items and focuses on aspects such as menu items, navigation between functions, understandability of the messages, ease of use of the basic functionalities, and of the device's input and output mechanisms. The second section consists of six questions related to the online and off-line (printed manuals) documentation. The last section ("You and the product") consists of 15 items and aims to get the user's impressions and product acceptance level. The first 23 items use a 5-point semantic scale (1: *very easy*; 2: *easy*; 3: *not easy nor difficult*; 4: *difficult*; and 5: *very difficult*). The last 15 items use another 5-point semantic scale (1: completely agree; 2: agree; 3: do not agree nor disagree; 4: disagree; and 5: completely disagree). The users were asked to answer the questions and to assign an importance level to each one of them, on a scale from 0 to 10.

For the post-test questionnaire, *USE* adopts the model proposed by Bailey and Pearson (Bailey & Pearson, 1983) for measuring the overall user's sense of satisfaction. The following adaptations to the dimensions were considered: (1) the association of only one (1) semantic differential scale to the items, instead of the four (4) semantic differential scales, as proposed in the original model; (2) the adoption of a 5-point Likert scale, delimited by the ends -2 and 2 (instead of the 7-point scales delimited by the ends -3 and 3 as originally proposed); and (3) the incorporation of a

11-point importance scale (0 corresponding to *non applicable*), varying from 0.0 to 1.0 in intervals of 0.1 (instead of the original 7-point scales, which varied from 0.1 to 1.0 in intervals of 0.15).

The user's subjective satisfaction indicators for the PDA case study were 0.330 for the laboratory experiment and 0.237 for the field experiment. The normalized value ranges of the user satisfaction concerning a product are 0.67 to 1.00 (*Extremely Satisfied*), 0.33 to 0.66 (*Very satisfied*), 0.01 to 0.32 (*Fairly satisfied*), 0.00 (*Neither satisfied nor unsatisfied*), 0.01 to 0.32 (*Fairly dissatisfied*), 0.33 to 0.66 (*Very dissatisfied*), and 0.67 to 1.00 (*Extremely dissatisfied*). This is in accordance with the Bailey and Pearson model (Bailey & Pearson, 1983). The results obtained correspond respectively to *Very satisfied* and *Fairly satisfied*.

Performance Measurement Results

The User Sample Profile

The user sample profile was drawn with the support of the questionnaire *USer*. It was composed of 13 male and 11 female users, of which eight were *undergraduate students*, 12 *post-graduate students*, two *graduate level*, and two *post-graduate level*. The ages varied between *18* and *29* years. They were mainly *right handed* and mostly used some sort of reading aid (either *glasses* or *contact lenses)*. All of them had at least one year of *previous experience of computer systems* and were currently using computers on a *daily* basis.

User Performance Data Analysis

After having analyzed the data gathered during the experiment on the user performance and having analyzed the list of problems found with this technique, it was possible to evaluate their impact and class them as: minor (50%), medium (50%), major (0%), consistency (35.7%), recurrent (64.3%), and general (0%).

The data analysis consisted of a statistical processing and had two main purposes: (1) to investigate the influence of the context on the results of the evaluation method (through the comparison of the results obtained from both environments); and (2) to investigate the influence of the user experience with the mobile device on the test results within each context. For the latter purpose, the three categories illustrated in Table 2 were used.

The statistic analysis performed consisted of: (1) building a report with univariance statistics; (2) generating the covariance matrices for the objective and subjective indicators that were previously defined; (3) applying the one-way F ANOVA test (Tabachnick & Fidell, 2006) to the data obtained from the previous step in order to investigate possible differences; and (4) applying the Tukey-Kramer process (Tabachnick & Fidell, 2006) to the one-way F ANOVA results aiming to investigate if the found differences were statistically significant to support inferences from the selected sample. The result of this technique was the identification of 13 problems, of which 92.3% were found in the laboratory and 61.5% in the field as: Laboratory (38.5%); Field (7.7%); and Laboratory & Field (53.8%).

Overlaying Results

Since the multi-layered evaluation is based upon a triangulation of results, Table 5 summarizes the usability problem categories identified by the three techniques.

The numbers correspond to the identification of each problem from a list of problems found through each technique. As can be seen from Table 5, some of the usability problem categories were more related to the performance measurement (e.g., hardware aspects, help mechanisms, processing capacity) whereas others (e.g., menu navigation, presentation of menu options) were identified by the conformity assessment. It was possible to identify 66.7% of the problems found

by other methods when combining the results from the post-test questionnaire with the user comments made during the experiment and the informal interview at the end of the experiment. This confirms the importance of combining techniques to obtain a more complete result when performing usability evaluation. It must be pointed out that 29.62% of the problems based on the user opinion about the product were in disagreement with the results of the other two evaluation dimensions (specialist and the community points of view). This discrepancy can originate from the users' perception of product quality and the perception of their own skills to perform the task, accepting full responsibility over the difficulties that might arise during the interaction. When overlaying the problems in Table 5, in the category *Menu navigation*, the same problem was found by the techniques Standards Inspection and Performance Measurement.

DISCUSSION

From this study's data analysis it became evident that certain problem categories are better found by specific techniques, as shown in Table 5. For instance, problems associated to the device's physical characteristics are better found by means of conformity assessment, whereas the user performance located problems associated to the device's applications.

The analysis of the pre-test and post-test questionnaires and the informal interviews showed that domain knowledge and computer literacy have significant influence on user performance with mobile devices. This was true both under laboratory conditions and in the field, in relation to the incidence of errors. The univariate analyses of variance of the performance variables: *Time*, *Errors*, and *Accesses to help, are* presented in Table 6.

From this table, it can be seen that the user experience level had a more significant effect on

Table 5. Overlay of results obtained with the three evaluation techniques

PROBLEM CATEGORY	SI	PM	SM
Location and sequence of menu options	✓ (05)		✗ (05)
Menu navigation	✓ (02)	✓ (01)	
Presentation of menu options	✓ (02)		
Information feedback	✓ (01)		
Object manipulation	✓ (05)		
Symbols and icons	✓ (02)		✗ (02)
Text entry via stylus (Writing recognition)	✓ (07)	✓ (01)	✓ (08)
Text entry via virtual keyboard		✓ (01)	✓ (01)
Processing power		✓ (02)	✓ (02)
Hardware issues		✓ (03)	✓ (03)
Fluent tasks execution		✓ (05)	✓ (05)
Online and offline help		✓ (01)	✓ (01)

Legend:

SI—Standards Inspection   ✗ - Contradictory findings
PM—Performance Measurement   ✓ - Consistent findings

Table 6. Influence of the user experience on the performance indicators: Time, Number of errors, and accesses to help

Independent variable	Dependent variable	p-Value (Lab)	p-Value (Field)	Significance ($\alpha=0.05$)
Experience	Task Time	0.081	0.081	Not significant
Experience	Errors	0.011	0.002	Significant
Experience	Help Accesses	0.427	-	Not significant

the number of errors in the field experiment than in laboratory experiment.

The studies in the literature fit basically into two categories: (1) user mobility, which means moving while using the device (inside of a laboratory or outdoors) and (2) user attention division. However, this study considers both aspects as part of the task context. In this experiment, the field test subjects were free to choose between moving or remaining still as they performed the task with the mobile device. During the informal interview the users stated that in a real context they would not perform the experiment tasks on the move, since they demanded too much attention. The specialist encouraged users to wander around the environment, although they could choose to enter a room in the building, sit down, or even lay the device on a table (which they did in most cases, under the argument that this setting was more comfortable). The movement registered was limited to situations in which the user waited for some device processing. (e.g., Web page downloads). There was a clear interference of the environment on the user attention during the field tests while moving.

The device's physical characteristics affected the user performance and the data gathering during the experiment. Outdoors, in ambient light, the device's legibility was reduced and aggravated by the reflections on the screen. According to the user's opinion stated during the informal interview, the camera apparatus did not interfere with the task execution, but the majority decided to lay the device down during task execution.

As for the entry of text information, the users showed a preference for the virtual keyboard instead of hand written character recognition. Based on their comments, as well as on the informal interview, it was concluded that writing long messages is very cumbersome both using the virtual keyboard and using the handwriting recognition application. Confirming previous findings, the experiment demonstrated that applications that require a lot of interaction and user attention are inappropriate for performing while walking due to attention division. This conclusion reinforces that, for the device targeted in this study, in spite of its mobility, the evaluation settings did not need to differ substantially from the one employed in the evaluation of stationary devices since the users tend not to wander while performing tasks that demand their attention or consisted of text input.

Until recently, studies have been published which deal with new paradigms and evaluation techniques for mobile devices. Few of the proposed new techniques are really innovative if compared to the ones traditionally employed. On the other hand, the main argument for proposing new techniques concerns the user and device mobility and the influence of this mobility on user performance. In contrast, this study evaluated the effect of mobility not only from the user performance perspective but also from user opinion point of view and the user level of satisfaction. From the application of the multi-layered approach, the data gathered and analyzed support the initial assumption that minor adaptations in the traditional evaluation techniques and respective settings are adequate to accommodate the evaluation of the category of mobile devices targeted by this study.

The conclusions corroborate with the views of the authors and that of Po (Po, 2003) that the laboratory and field evaluations do not diverge but are complimentary. As shown in this study, they both add to the evaluation process, producing data that is significant to the process and reinforcing the relevance of a multi-layered approach for the usability evaluation of mobile devices.

FUTURE TRENDS

Mobile devices impose challenges to the usability evaluation that are unique in respect to the observation strategies and the conception of test scenarios. With the continuous technological advances, a wider variety of new devices is being released into the market, challenging users with the complexity of the interaction. In this scenario, the importance of the product usability is undisputable as is also the correct choice of evaluation methods, techniques, and tools.

One emerging trend in the mobile devices evaluation field is the possibility of gathering data in an unobtrusive way, using tools for remote, and automatic data capture that are transparent to the user. Developing those tools is a challenging activity given the inherent restrictions presented by the mobile devices (such as their limited processing power and limited storage capacity). But, in spite of the current limitations, it was shown in this study that the tools are becoming available to provide a great contribution to the evaluation setup and that these tools would benefit from further development.

REFERENCES

Aladwani, A., & Palvia, P. (2002). Developing and validating an instrument for measuring user-perceived Web quality. *Information & Management, 39*, 467-476.

Bailey, James E., & Pearson, S. W. (1983). Development of a tool for measuring and analyzing computer user satisfaction. *Management Science, 29*(5), 530-545.

Baillie, L., & Schatz, R. (2005). Exploring multimodality in the laboratory and the field. In *Proceedings of the 7th International Conference on Multimodal Interfaces* (pp. 100–107).

Danielson, D. R. (2006). Usability data quality. In C. Ghaoui (Ed.), *Encyclopedia of human-computer interaction* (pp. 661-667). Hershey, PA: Idea Group Reference.

De Oliveira, R. C. L., De Queiroz, J. E. R., Vieira Turnell, M. F. Q. (2005). WebQuest: A configurable Web tool to prospect the user profile and user subjective satisfaction. In G. Salvendy (Ed.), *Proceedings of the 2005 Human-Computer Interaction Conference. (The management of information: E-business, the Web, and mobile computing)* (Vol. 2) Nevada: Lawrence Erlbaum Associates (U.S. CD-ROM Multi Platform).

Dumas, J. S., & Redish, J. C. (1999). A practical guide to usability testing (revised ed.). Exeter, UK: Intellect.

EATMP. (2000). *Human factors integration in future ATM systems—Methods and tools* (Tech. Rep. HRS/HSP-003-REP-03). European Organization for the Safety of Air Navigation—European Air Traffic Management Programme. Retrieved August 13, 2006, from http://www.eurocontrol.int/humanfactors/gallery/content/public/docs.

Goodhue, D. L., & Thompson, R. L. (1995). Task-technology fit and individual performance. *MIS Quarterly, 19*(2), 213-236.

Goodman, J., Brewster, S., & Gray, P. (2004). Using field experiments to evaluate mobile guides. In *Proceedings of 3rd Annual Workshop on HCI in Mobile Guides* (pp. 1533-1536).

Hartson, H. R., Andre, T. S., & Williges, R. C. (2003). Criteria for evaluating usability evaluation methods. *International Journal of Human-Computer Interaction, 15*(1), 145-181.

Hilbert, D. M., & Redmiles, D. F. (2000). Extracting usability information from user interface events. *ACM Computing Surveys, 32*(4), 384-421.

Hix, D., & Hartson, H. R. (1993). *Developing user interfaces: Ensuring usability through product & process.* New York: John Wiley and Sons, Inc.

Holzinger, A. (2005). Usability engineering methods (UEMs) for software developers. *Communications of the ACM, 48*(1), 71-74.

ISO 9241-11. (1998). *Ergonomic requirements for office work with visual display terminals*

(VDTs)—Part 11: Guidance on usability. International Organization for Standardization, Geneva, Switzerland.

ISO 9241-14. (1997). *Ergonomic requirements for office work with visual display terminals (VDTs)—Part 14: Menu dialogues.* International Organization for Standardization, Geneva, Switzerland.

ISO9241-16. (1999). *Ergonomic requirements for office work with visual display terminals (VDTs)—Part 16: Direct manipulation dialogues.* International Organization for Standardization, Geneva, Switzerland.

ISO9241-17. (1998). *Ergonomic requirements for office work with visual display terminals (VDTs)—Part 17: Form filling dialogues.* International Organization for Standardization, Geneva, Switzerland.

ISO 13407. (1999). *Human-centered design processes for interactive systems.* International Organization for Standardization, Switzerland.

ISO. (2006). *ISO and conformity assessment.* Retrieved September 23, 2006, from http://www.iso.org/iso/en/prods-services/otherpubs/pdf/casco_2005-en.pdf.

ISO/IEC 14754. (1999). Information technology—pen-based interfaces—common gestures for text editing with pen-based systems. International Organization for Standardization, Geneva, Switzerland.

ISO/IEC 18021. (2002). *Information technology—user interfaces for mobile tools for management of database communications in a client-server model.* International Organization for Standardization, Geneva, Switzerland.

ITU-T E.161. (2001). *Arrangement of digits, letters and symbols on telephones and other devices that can be used for gaining access to a telephone net-work.* International Telecommunications Union-telecommunications, Geneva, Switzerland.

Jones, M., Marsden, G. (2006). *Mobile interaction design.* Chichester, West Sussex: John Wiley and Sons, Inc.

Kan, S. H. (2002). *Metrics and models in software quality engineering* (2nd ed.). Reading, MA: Addison-Wesley Professional.

Kjeldskov, J., Graham, C., Pedell, S., Vetere, F., Howard, S., Balbo, S., & Davies, J. (2005). Evaluating the usability of a mobile guide: The influence of location, participants and resources. *Behavior and Information Technology, 24*(1), 51–65.

Kjeldskov, J., & Stage, J. (2004). New techniques for usability evaluation of mobile systems. *International Journal on Human and Computer Studies, 60*(5-6), 599–620.

Mayhew, D. J. (1999). *The usability engineering lifecycle.* San Francisco: Morgan Kaufmann Publishers Inc.

Molich, R., Bevan, N., Curson, I., Butler, S., Kindlund, E., Miller, D., et al. (1998). Comparative evaluation of usability tests. In *Proceedings of the Usability Professionals Association Conference* (pp. 189-200).

Nielsen, J. (1993). *Usability engineering.* Boston: Academic Press.

Omodei, M. A., Wearing, J., & McLennan, J. P. (2002). Head-mounted video and cued recall: A minimally reactive methodology for understanding, detecting and preventing error in the control of complex systems. In *Proceedings of the 21st European Annual Conference of Human Decision Making and Control.*

Po, S., Howard, S., Vetere, F., & Skov, M. B. (2004). Heuristic evaluation and mobile usability: Bridging the realism gap. In *Proceedings of the Mobile HCI* (pp. 49–60).

Rosson, M. B., & Carroll, J. M. (2002). *Usability engineering: Scenario-based development of human-computer interaction.* San Diego, CA: Academic Press.

Sanderson, P., & Fisher, C. (1994). Usability testing of mobile applications: A comparison between laboratory and field testing. *Human-Computer Interaction, 9,* 251–317.

Scriven, M. (1967). The methodology of evaluation. In R. W. Tyler, R. M. Gagne, & M. Scriven (Eds.), *Perspectives in curriculum evaluation* (pp. 39- 83). Skokie, IL: Rand McNally.

Tabachnick, B. G., & Fidell, L. S. (2006). *Experimental designs using ANOVA* (1st ed.). Duxbury Applied Series. Pacific Grove, CA: Duxbury Press.

Wixon, D., & Wilson, C. (1997). The usability engineering framework for product design and evaluation. In M. Helander, T. K. Landauer, & P. Prabhu (Eds.), *Handbook of human-computer interaction* (2nd ed.) (pp. 653-688). New York: John Wiley and Sons, Inc.

KEY TERMS

Conformity Assessment: A collective term used for a number of techniques used to determine if a product, system, or process (including design) meets a defined specification.

Device Mobility during a Usability Evaluation: The ability to interact with the user and continue to perform its functions while being transported.

Efficacy of an Evaluation Method or Technique: Translated into the number of problems found, gravity of those problems versus the time, and cost of performing the experiments.

Likert Scale: An attitude scale in which respondents indicate their degree of agreement/disagreement with a given proposition concerning some object, aspect, person, or situation.

Multi-Layered Evaluation Approach: A product or prototype usability evaluation method that combines techniques for data gathering and analysis based on multiple perspectives (the user's, the specialist's, and the usability community). The results are overlaid in order to find discrepancies and offer more robust results.

User Mobility during the Usability Evaluation: The ability to move while performing a task with a product.

User Performance Measurement: The process of gathering actual data from users as they work with a system and its documentation. Usually, the user is given a set of tasks to complete and the evaluator measures the relevant parameters such as the percentage of tasks or subtasks successfully completed, time required to perform each task or subtask, frequency and type of errors, duration of pauses, indications of user frustration, and the ways in which the user seeks assistance.

User Satisfaction Measurement: The process of obtaining qualitative and quantitative information which indicates the extent to which user expectations concerning some object, process, product, or situation are being met. Such information can be obtained in a variety of ways, both formally and informally.

Virtual Network Computing (*VNC*): A desktop sharing system that uses the RFB (Remote Frame Buffer) protocol to remotely control another computer. It transmits the keyboard presses and mouse clicks from one computer to another over a network, relaying the screen updates back in the other direction.

This work was previously published in Handbook of Research on User Interface Design and Evaluation for Mobile Technology, edited by J. Lumsden, pp. 847-862, copyright 2008 by Information Science Reference, formerly known as Idea Group Reference (an imprint of IGI Global).

Chapter 7.40
Mobile Information Processing Involving Multiple Non-Collaborative Sources

Say Ying Lim
Monash University, Australia

David Taniar
Monash University, Australia

Bala Srinivasan
Monash University, Australia

ABSTRACT

As more and more servers appearing in the wireless environment provide accesses to mobile users, more and more demand and expectation is required by mobile users toward the available services. Mobile users are no longer satisfied with obtaining data only from one server, but require data from multiple servers either at the same or different locations. This eventually leads to the need for information gathering that spans across several non-collaborative servers. This article describes some of our researches in information gathering from multiple non-collaborative servers that may involve servers that not only accept direct queries from mobile users but also servers that broadcast data. We also look at how location dependent data plays an important role to mobile information gathering.

INTRODUCTION

The direction of the mobile technology industry is beginning to emerge and advance at a rapid pace as more mobile users have evolved (Myers & Beigl, 2003). Interests in mobile technology have grown exponentially over the last few years and are greatly influenced especially by the dramatic reduction in the cost of hardware and protocol standardization (Hurson & Jiao, 2005; Kapp, 2002). The increase in progression and advancement of mobile technology has created a new paradigm of computing called mobile computing in which people are allowed to be connected wirelessly to access data anytime, anywhere without having to worry about the distance barrier (Lee, Zhu, & Hu, 2005; Lee et al., 2002; Madria, Bhargava, Pitoura, & Kumar, 2000). Users have also become more productive with the achievement of mobility since they are able to access a full range of resources regardless of where they are located and where they are able to get hold of real time information.

The emerging growth of the use of intelligent mobile devices (e.g., mobile phones and PDAs) opens up a whole new world of possibilities, which includes delivering information to mobile devices that are customized and tailored according to their current location (Gutting et al., 2000; Tsalgatidou, Veijalainen, Markkula, Katasonov, & Hadjiefthymiades, 2003; Xu et al., 2003). Mobile queries are requests for certain information that are initiated by mobile users to the appropriate servers from their mobile devices. Query processing in a mobile environment may involve join processing from either single or several different servers with the mobile devices (Liberatore, 2002; Lo, Mamoulis, Cheung, Ho, & Kalnis, 2003). In addition, mobile queries can be performed regardless of where the users are located and the results obtained are influenced by the location of the user. Data that are downloaded from different locations would be different and there is a need to bring together these data according to a user who may want to synchronize the data that are downloaded from different location to be consolidated into a single output. Thus, the intention is to take into account location dependent factors, which allow mobile users to query data without facing location problems (Song, Kang, & Park, 2005; Tse, Lam, Ng, & Chan, 2005; Xu, Tang, & Lee, 2003). This concept is associated with location dependent query.

One of the main objectives of this article is to demonstrate the importance of allowing mobile users who believe that obtaining data from a single server is not enough and may need further processing with data that are obtained from other servers. Furthermore, the user may get data from several servers that are from the same or different providers. In other words, there are times when the user has the desire to gather data from several non-collaborative servers into their mobile devices (Lo, et al, 2003; Malladi & Davis, 2002). Mobile devices have made it capable for mobile users to process and retrieve data from multiple remote databases by sending queries to the servers and then process the multiple data gathered from these sources locally on the mobile devices (Mamoulis, Kalnis, Bakiras, & Li, 2003; Ozakar, Morvan, & Hameurlain, 2005). By processing the data locally, mobile users would have more control over what they actually want as the final result of the query. They can therefore choose to query data from different servers and process them locally according to their requirements. Also, by being able to obtain specific data over several different sites, it would help bring optimum results to mobile user queries. Furthermore, by driving away the computation on the client device, the bandwidth computation may also be reduced.

Example 1: *A mobile user may want to know where the available vegetarian restaurants are in the city he or she is currently visiting. There are two major servers (e.g., tourist office and the vegetarian community) that may give information about the available vegetarian restaurants. First, using his or her wireless PDA, he or she would download information broadcast from the tourist office. Then, he or she would download the information provided by the vegetarian community. After obtaining the lists from the two information providers, he or she may perform an operation on his or her mobile device that joins the contents from the two relations obtained earlier from the two non-collaborative organizations. This illustrates the importance of assembling information obtained from multiple non-collaborative sources* *in a mobile device in order to obtain more comprehensive information.*

This article investigates the need for information gathering spanning several non-collaborative servers that may bring to mobile users. Furthermore, due to the various nature of how a server may disseminate their data (e.g., through ad-hoc queries or data broadcasting), this article also evaluates the query processing methods involving the previously mentioned strategies.

In this article, we first present an insight of the background of mobile environment, non-collaborative servers, and prospective applications for information gathering from multiple sources. By formulating the taxonomy, it helps to give understanding of the possible database operations that can be performed on the mobile devices. We will also describe the process of information gathering that results from multiple servers that involves location dependent data, which are then followed by a system prototype. Finally, the last section concludes the article. Note that in this article we use the term mobile client, mobile user, and users interchangeably.

BACKGROUND AND PRELIMINARIES

Before discussing more details, the process of information gathering, and its rationale, this section would first introduce some background and preliminaries related to mobile query processing in a typical mobile environment, which involves multiple non-collaborative servers. Firstly, this section provides some introductory knowledge on the wireless environment covering what constitutes the architecture of a typical mobile computing environment, followed by the usefulness of obtaining information from multiple sources and lastly the prospective application of this study.

Mobile Computing Environment: A Background

Mobile computing has provided mobile users the ability to access information anytime, anywhere. It enables mobile users to query databases from their mobile devices over the wireless communication channels (Imielinski & Badrinath, 1994). In general, mobile users with their mobile devices and servers that store data are involved in a typical mobile environment (Lee et al., 2005; Madria et al., 2000; Wolfson, 2002). Each of these mobile users communicates with a single server or multiple servers that may or may not be collaborative with one another. This server is also known as mobile base station (MBS), which the mobile users communicate to in order to carry out any activities such as transaction and information retrieval. The servers supply its services to a wide range of users who are within the active region through a wireless interface. Thus, mobile users have to be within a specific region to be able to receive a signal in order to connect to the servers.

Figure 1 depicts a mobile environment architecture where two servers are involved, *S1* and *S2*, in location *A* and location *B* respectively. Mobile users move freely within the different region to obtain different data by accessing the different servers via sending a query and receiving the results back to the mobile device upon completion of processing.

Example 2: *A property investor, while driving his or her car, downloads a list of nearby apartments for sale from a real-estate agent. As he or she moves, he or she downloads the requested information again from the same real-estate agent. Because his or her position has changed since he or she first inquires, the two lists of apartments for sale would be different due to the relative location when this investor was inquiring the information. Based on these two lists, the investor would prob-*

Figure 1. Mobile environment architecture

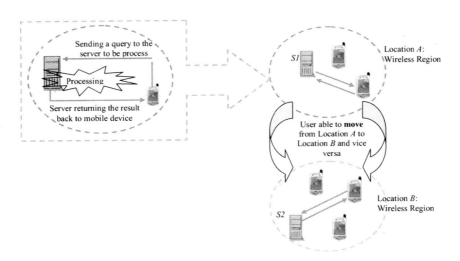

ably like to perform an operation on his or her mobile device to show only those apartments that exist in the latest list, and not in the first list.

Hence, in a typical mobile environment, it is unacceptable to meet with situations where a mobile user is currently obtaining data from a current active region and is still not feeling satisfied with the result. This leads to the need of further processing with other data that can only be obtained from other servers that may or may not be collaborative to each other.

Overview of Non-Collaborative Servers

The term collaborative usually relates to the traditional distributed databases whereby the desire to integrate the data of a particular enterprise and to provide centralized and controlled access to that data (Bell & Grimson, 1992; Ceri & Pelagatti, 1984; Özsu & Valduriez, 1999). The technology of distributed database may not be appropriate for

use in the mobile environment, which involves not only the nomadic clients, which move around, but also non-collaborative servers, which are basically servers that are maintained by different organizations (Lo et al., 2003).

Therefore, non-collaborative servers would refer to servers that do not know each other and do not have any relation between one another. There are basically just individual server providers, which disseminate data to the users and they do not communicate with one another. Since each server can just be an independent service provider, often these independent servers are specialized within the domain of the information they are providing.

An example of such a server that disseminates information on restaurants normally just focuses on the restaurants information and limited supporting information, which can sometimes be included (e.g., how to get there--the transportation is just supporting information since it does not exactly show the route on how to get there from a particular location the user is currently at). Therefore, there is still a need to obtain full information from multiple servers, which in this case are the restaurant and transportation servers separately.

In addition, not all service providers are supported by the usage of a mediator (Lo et al., 2003). Therefore, information obtained from other independent non-related service providers needs to be processed individually. It is not a fair assumption that all service providers are linked through a mediator. Hence, in our research, we focus on independent service providers, which refers to non-collaborative servers. Thus, it is vital to consider gathering information from non-collaborative servers because it is often not enough to just get data from a single server.

Prospective Applications

Information gathering in the context of mobile environment is a source where collecting various data together regardless of whether it is related or not related as long as it is useful for the mobile users. There exists several significant influences of information gathering from multiple sources that lies on personal applications. Next, we show summarized lists of some promising applications that bring great impacts to mobile users.

- **Entertainment applications:** Shopping appears to be a popular trend and hobby. Often shoppers would prefer to go to shops that give the lowest price for the item they are interested in buying. Many shops in the same shopping complex may sell the same item, but they are different companies and they are not related with one another. Thus, with the ability of getting the information, especially the pricing for the desired item, separately from the various shops could aid users in deciding which shops to go to that offers a better price.

Example 3: *A mobile user who is currently in a shopping complex is interested in a buying a tennis racquet. There are two different sports shops in the complex, sports shop A and sports shop B, that sell the tennis racquet that the user wants to buy. So first, by sending a query to shop A, he or she obtains a list of the prices for the tennis racquet. Then he or she sends a query to shop B, which again he or she will get a list of prices for the tennis racquet. So with these two lists, the mobile user can do a local processing, which compares the matching racquets and displays the shop that gives a lower price for the respective racquets that are being matched.*

- **Tourism applications:** Tourism brings value added in terms of economical growth to not only the country, but also the physical relationship between the visitor and the producer of a good or service. Tourism is an important element to boost the country's reputation and economy. Thus, it is important to give both local and international travelers the best and most convenient. Giving the ability of information gathering from multiple sources tends to emerge as valuable services to the mobile travelers regardless of where their current geographical coordinates.

Example 4: *An international tourist, while traveling to a foreign country, does not know the where abouts of the tourist attraction spots. He or she looks for famous tourist spots recommended by both the transport office and tourism office. First, using his or her wireless PDA, he or she would download information broadcast from the tourism office to get a list of the famous tourist spots. Then, he or she would download the information provided by the transport office to get information on the available transportation. Once he or she obtains the lists from the two information providers, he or she may perform an operation on his* or her mobile device that joins the contents to match the tourist spots together with transport information on how to get there.

- **Emergency responses applications:** There are times especially when someone on the highway is having trouble with their car and needs to find the nearest possible petrol station that offers car services as soon as possible. In this circumstance, the person on the highway can use his or her mobile device to make a query as he or she travels along the highway to look for a petrol station that offer car services. This comes into the category of emergency cases, as it is rare and is not needed all the time.

Example 5: *A traveler currently in location A wants to know where the nearest gas station is (petrol kiosk) and using the mobile device, they downloaded a list of available petrol kiosk nearby to his or her current surrounding location. As they travel further until they arrive in location B, he or she makes another query to get another list of petrol kiosk, but this time the list is somewhat different since he or she has been driving and the location has moved from A to B. Therefore, based on these two lists, the traveler wants to display only those petrol kiosks that provide car service regardless of whether it is in A or B.*

- **Double checking applications:** Data that are stored in the servers that are to be disseminate to the public can sometimes be outdated due to the company that manages the data being closed down or other undesired catastrophes. If the users are still able to query for the data, part of the data may not be accurate anymore since it has not been maintained and updated well. This will make the data worthless if the users download it. Therefore, a certain degree that allows the users to see the data that is downloaded are obtained from a reliable source or not may be

useful if the ability of processing data that are obtained from one server together with another list of data obtained from another server as a double checking precaution.

Example 6: *This example requires an assumption of one property that can be handled by several estate agents. A user obtains a list of properties in the city that are ready for sale from real-estate agent A. Without knowing, real-estate agent A has just been declared bankrupt and the lists that are currently in the server have not been updated since. Thus, some of the properties that the user has downloaded have actually been sold. Without knowing all this, since the user is able to obtain another list of properties in the city from another agent, which is agent B, this list would have been able to be used as a reference list to the previous list that was obtained from agent A. Since one property can be handled by several agents, the properties for sale in the city between list A and list B should be the same. The only difference may be the price on whether the agent is selling it cheaper or more expensive than the other. Thus, by seeing the difference in the availability of the properties between the two lists, this information can appear to the mobile user that one or the other is not correct since we have to assume one property is to be handled by several agents.*

In summary, we can see from the previous sample application domain that obtaining from a single place is not sufficient enough to provide the desired results to the mobile users. The mobile users often require several data that are non-related with one another to be gathered and processed together so that a higher level and meaningful information can be obtained. By giving more flexibility to the mobile users to "mix-and-match" non-related data from several servers proves to return a more comprehensive result that is able to satisfy the needs of the users. Therefore, information gathering from multiple non-collaborative servers brings benefits and gives a good prospect for users to achieve a higher quality and productive information.

MOBILE USER QUERIES

The context of mobile user queries in this article is that the mobile queries contain operations that are being carried out when multiple lists of data are obtained from multiple servers (Lim, Taniar, & Srinivasan, 2006). In this section, we will present a taxonomy of the mobile user queries in two elements namely (i) *non-location-based on-mobile queries* and (ii) *location-based on-mobile queries*.

- In non-location-based on-mobile queries, the need to obtain constructive information often requires mobile users to download lists from multiple sources to be integrated and processed together. In a mobile environment, joins are used to bring together information from two or more different information sources. It joins multiple data from different servers into a single output to be displayed on the mobile device. The idea of this is basically to ensure mobile users have the ability to reduce the query results with maximum return of satisfaction because with the additional post-processing, the output results can be greatly reduced based on the user's requirements and needs before the final display on the device.

Consider Example 1 presented earlier where it shows how a join operation is needed to be performed on a mobile device as the mobile user downloads information from two different sources, which are the tourist office and the vegetarian community. In this case, two pieces of information might be joined on the restaurant IDs from the two different lists. This therefore, illustrates a simple on-mobile join case, where it

is basically a process of combining data from one relation to another.

- Location-based on-mobile queries have become a growing trend due to the constant behaviour of mobile users who move around. Location-dependent processing is of interest in a number of applications, especially those that involve geographical information systems (Cai & Hua, 2002; Cheverst, Davies, & Mitchell, 2000; Jung, You, Lee, & Kim, 2002; Tsalgatidou et al., 2003). An example query might be "to find the nearest petrol kiosk" or "find the three nearest vegetarian restaurants." As the mobile users move around, the query results may change and would therefore depend on the location of the issuer. This means that if a user sends a query and then changes his or her location, the answer of that query has to be based on the location of the user issuing the query (Seydim, Dunham, & Kumar, 2001; Waluyo, Srinivasan, & Taniar, 2005). Location dependent processing involves the circumstances when mobile users are in the situation where they download a list when in a certain location and then they move around and download another list in their new current location. Or another circumstance might be a mobile user might already have a list in his or mobile device but moves and needs to download the same list again but from a different location. In any case, there is a need to synchronize these lists that have been downloaded from a different location.

Consider Example 2 presented earlier. It shows an example of how location dependent queries processes are being carried out. With the two different lists on hand that the investor currently had based on the properties in the two different locations, the investor would probably like to perform some kind of database operation on his or her mobile device. The difference in the list is due to the moving location from one point to another point by the investor.

MODELS OF INFORMATION PROCESSING

There are times when a user may need to query several non-collaborative servers in order to obtain a more comprehensive list of data. The user may need to perform some database operations locally on the mobile device based on the list of data that has been downloaded from the remote databases.

Figure 2 models the various strategies that the server can adopt. *Server strategy* involves mobile users sending queries to the server for processing (Seydim et al., 2001). It relates to processing to be taken by the server to process and return the results based on the mobile user queries. *On-air strategy* is similar to traditional broadcasting

Figure 2. Query processing strategies

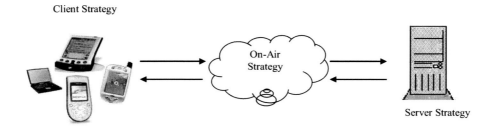

Figure 3. Example of assembling information from two different servers

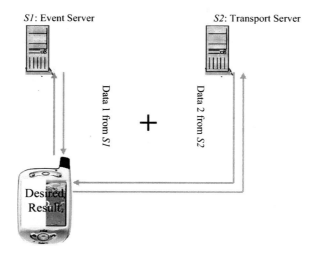

techniques whereby the sets of database items are broadcasted through the air to a large number of mobile users over a single channel or multiple channel (Tran, Hua, & Jiang, 2001; Triantafillou, Harpantidou, & Paterakis, 2001). With the set of data on the air, mobile users can tune into one or more channel to get the data. *Client strategy* relates to maintaining cached data in the local storage and being able to have the ability to do local processing if queries results are being sent back to the mobile device and stored in the cache memory. Thus, efficient cache management is critical in mobile query processing (Cao, 2003; Elmargamid, Jing, Helal, & Lee, 2003; Xu, Hu, Lee, & Lee, 2004; Zheng, Xu, & Lee, 2002).

Lists of information can be obtained from servers that distribute their respective data using various strategies such as server strategy, on-air strategy, and client strategy. Each of the available servers has their associated query processing strategies and they can be processed together regardless of whether part of the servers use a different strategy.

Example 7: *Suppose a mobile user wants to know the timetable for the transportation services to a particular event. Each of the transportation timetables, as well as the event, is stored in different servers and maintained by two different organizations. Transport servers would deal with transportation data while an event server would deal with current events that are happening. Therefore, in order to know the transportation timetable for a particular event, the user has to gather data from the two different servers, which is first sending a query to obtain the event list into the mobile device, and then sending another query to the transport server to obtain the list of transportations. Now these two lists are in the mobile device and are ready to be processed locally to match the transportation timetable onto the respective events. This exemplifies the importance of assembling information from multiple servers*

into a single information, which is the desired result as the outcome on the PDA.

Assuming that both transport and event servers are individual servers that accept direct query from the users, Figure 3 models an illustration of how two different lists are obtained from two different sources to be processed locally. This achieves the object of processing information obtained from multiple non-collaborative servers.

In the following sub section, we will uncover several case studies and explain how multiple non-collaborative servers that use the different strategies integrate its results into useful information for the mobile users. Just for illustration and simplicity purposes, we only illustrate situations where there are only two servers that are in use.

Case Study 1: Both Servers use Server Strategy

Without acknowledging the current standing location of the user, we would like to allow the user to be able to carry out simple database operations locally on the mobile device such as simple join between the different lists of data that are downloaded into the mobile device from the remote databases. We would first examine cases where the two different servers that the users need to obtain its information from to be integrated together are both using server strategies as being modeled in Figure 4.

Server strategy has limited functionalities since it provides dedicated point-to-point connections in accepting the mobile users request directly. This is due to the limited bandwidth that is available. Therefore, if suddenly there are many users wishing to send a request to the same server, the server may be congested. Thus, server strategy may cause an increase in exceeding usage of bandwidth especially when too many data requests are being sent out by the mobile users.

Figure 4. Example of on mobile query processing

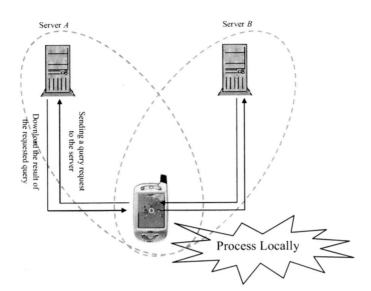

The overwhelming mobile users requests may affect the query performance. This can easily cause a scalability bottleneck with a large mobile user population.

As far as the cost remains a major concern to a wide majority of mobile users, obtaining data via server strategy may be expensive or cost effective. This is because mobile users are establishing a direct communication to the server, which is how server strategy provides exclusive point-to-point communications between the user and server, which in this case the server processes the query that is being sent by the mobile users and returns the results back to the mobile users (Sun, Shi, & Shi, 2003).

In addition to the previous issues that users may face when obtaining data from servers that accept direct requests, there are several other additional complexities such as deciding which servers to download first in order to reduce memory consumptions and minimize transfer costs as

well worthless or unnecessary data transfers. The techniques obtained from servers indicate there is a need to download in advance at least a list of data from one side of the server to the mobile device. Due the limitation of memory, it would be wise to use a technique that is able to utilize the minimum memory. Both response and access time are also a major concern because they may slow down the results from the query especially when the number of requesting queries is increasing.

Case Study 2: Server Strategy and On-Air Strategy

There are situations when certain data are broadcast on a public wireless channel, which requires the user to tune into the broadcast channel to filter out the relevant data. Users have no control in issuing queries directly to the servers. Therefore, we are concerned with how users can efficiently obtain their specific request without being able to send a query to the servers that use the broadcasting system. In this system, by broadcasting it actually lets an arbitrary number of users access the data simultaneously. Therefore, this may be acquainted with issued of over population in accessing a particular data that may slow down the access. In other words, when encountering a multiple non-collaborative servers setting, some servers may not able to accept queries that are directly issued by the mobile users but rather provide data broadcasting.

Figure 5 illustrates an example of a server that supports data broadcast in conjunction with another server that supports direct query. Example, in order to gather data from the two non-collaborative servers, whereby one server supports data broadcast and another server supports direct query, the mobile users would need to tune into the wireless channel to obtain the desired data from the server that supports data broadcast and issue a query to the other server, which accept direct query.

When determining the on-air strategy to be used over server strategy or client strategy,

one important issue is to determine an optimal broadcast sequence for the data items that are to be distributed to the mobile users. This refers to data broadcast scheduling, which one must look at in order to have minimal access time and minimal tuning time in receiving the required data items. By prioritizing the data items and using a good selection mechanism can reduce the broadcast cycle length, which eventually is able to reduce the query response time (Chung et al., 2001; Lee, Lo, & Chen, 2002). The data items can be characterized as both "hot" and "cold" and this can be the determinant of which data item should be given a higher priority over the others (Zhang & Gruenwalk, 2002).

Another alternative to the selection mechanism, in taking into account of reducing response time, is to have more than one broadcast channel whereby the broadcast data can be distributed to more than one broadcast channel. In most cases, data items are broadcast over a single channel as it avoids additional issue of the organization of data and allocation while having more than one channel (Imielinski, Viswanathan, & Badrinath, 1997). Furthermore, the use of a single chan-

Figure 5. Example of on mobile querying broadcasted data

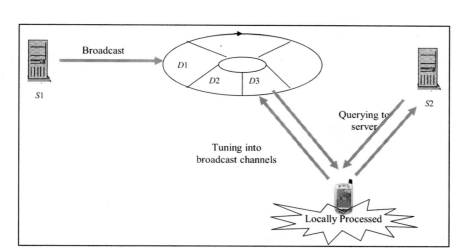

nel appears to be more problematic especially when there are a large number of data items to be broadcast, thus, with the adoption of multiple channels to broadcast data, the chance of reducing long delays before obtaining the desired data items can be achieved.

The next factor that could help reduce response time would be concerning the organization of the data items especially when retrieving multiple data items is required. An illustration of such a situation can be a mobile client wants to send a query to retrieve multiple stock prices concurrently. This is an example of multiple data items retrieval and in order to retrieve such query in a more efficient way, the need to consider the semantic relationship between the data items is required (Chung et al., 2001; Ren & Dunham, 2000). However, in order to predict which data item that the mobile client would be interested in next is difficult because there is not much knowledge of any future query that is available. Existing related work has investigated the use of access graphs to represent the dependency of the data items (Lee et al., 2002). Other existing algorithms that have been investigated to identify the most effective organization of the data items includes heuristics algorithm (Hurson et al., 2005) and randomized algorithm (Bar-Noy, Naor, & Schieber, 2000).

The last possible deciding factor for query response time can be determined by incorporating broadcast indexing scheme. Indexing scheme can reduce tuning time for the mobile client to access their required data item (Lee, Leong, & Si, 2002). By applying this scheme, mobile clients can conserve their battery life and thus, results in energy saving because the clients can switch to "doze" mode and back to "active" mode only when he or she knows the desired data item is about to arrive.

Although the on-air strategy appears to be more scalable in comparison to the server strategy, there are still limitations that it brings to the users because most users would find it easier to send a direct request to a specific server. In addition,

since the data that are being broadcast are usually open to the public, there are privacy issues that may arise. Thus, if the mobile user wants to obtain private data, they would have to rely on the server strategy rather than the on-air strategy. Therefore, by being able to incorporate strategies that are able to accommodate the request of the users to bring it more flexibility like how server strategy does for the users maybe beneficial.

Case Study 3: Server Strategy and Client Strategy

Caching frequently accessed data in a client's local storage becomes prominent in improving the performance and data availability of data access queries (Chan, Si, & Leong, 1998). This is made available by caching the frequently accessed data items in the local mobile device storage as well as when frequent disconnection occurs, the query can still be partially processed from caches and at least some of the results from the previous queries can be returned to the users (Lee et al., 2002). This is because the mobile device is able to keep the existing data and if the user needs the same exact data, the downloading can be minimized if the mobile device recognizes that the data has been previously loaded into the device. Caching at the mobile client helps in relieving the low bandwidth constraints imposed in the mobile environment (Kara & Edwards, 2003). Issues that characterize the caching mechanism would include cache granularity, cache coherence, and cache replacement.

Figure 6 shows whenever a user issues a query, it first searches its cache and if a valid copy is found in the cache, it will return the results immediately. Otherwise it can also search the client's other local cache for the required results or it can be obtained either through the server or broadcast (on-air) strategy. Thus, it is often important to have cache management because often a user may download similar data repeatedly from the same source.

Figure 6. Example of on mobile querying with cache data

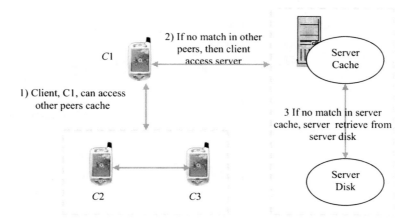

In general, the main limitation that limits the ability of having to cache everything on the mobile device mainly lies on the limited memory capacity. Therefore, one of the challenges that concerns the local cache memory is to exploit algorithms that can maximize the cache capacity to reduce the repeated transfer cost as much as possible and increase the respond time to the user's queries request. As we are concerned, the existing works on caching for mobile devices are still not sufficient for the new nomadic types of queries. A vast range of existing has been greatly being done on the issue of cache replacement and cache granularity and employing them into several possible cases in the real mobile environment situations. Index caching has been popular to save memory caching to improve query response time as well as managing space more efficiently, which is significant for location dependent queries. A few related works to this have also been done (Xu et al., 2003; Xu et al., 2004; Zheng et al., 2002). We also need to identify which mobile device has the request cache data that the other

mobile users can access, as well as to make sure the cache data is still up to date before allowing the other interested users to access it (Elmargamid et al., 2003).

LOCATION DEPENDENT QUERY PROCESSING

Whenever a user moves from one location to another, the objects being queried can turn out to be different according to their geographical coordinates. Hence, location dependent plays an important role (Saltenis & Jensen, 2002; Sistla, Wolfson, Chamberlain, & Dao, 1997; Waluyo et al., 2005). It is important to show the mobile user, who is moving from one location to another location frequently, that the queries he or she sends, depends on the location that he or she is querying from.

Figure 7 shows that when a user is in location *A,* the query results are P1,P2, P3, P4, and P5, but as he or she moves toward location *B* and send the

Figure 7. Example of on mobile location dependent query processing

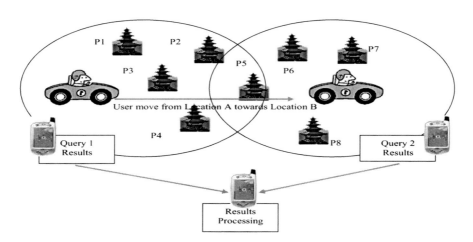

query again, the results now are P5, P6, P7, and P8. This shows that the change of user's query results are reflected by the change of the user's location. Basically with this, two query results that are obtained from Query 1 and Query 2 respectively, the user would like to process them together on the mobile device to obtain the just the desired data.

The main problem in this location dependent are the consistency problems that may arise, especially when the database is updated in the midst of processing a query. Furthermore, in order to ensure the shortest path, whereby we will first go for the server that stored the desired results, which can be obtained faster and easier or that can be obtained nearest to our current geographical coordinate compared to obtaining from another server. So, it is crucial to ensure the mobile users are able to obtain the shortest path to the desired destination. Some other issues would involve information processing when the results of the queries are obtained from different locations. We also need to learn how we are able to select the server to perform the query that is available

from different locations so that we can answer the query more efficiently and correctly.

One important issue can be illustrated as follows. For instance, there are two locations, *A* and *B*. The user has a query in mind and based on the optimization in regards to the shorter path theory, the user will need to download information from location *B* and then send to location *A* for processing. But at the moment, the user is in location *A* and is going to location *B* soon. So, if following the optimization theory, this will require the user to first go to location *B* to download the desired data, and then move back to location *A* even though the current location of the user is now in *A*. In this method, there may arise a risk; maybe by the time the user goes to location *B*, the desired item is no longer available or there may have been network congestion and so on. If this occurs, the user would waste their time going to location *B* to get the desired data. Thus, we may need a different processing method where the user can start downloading from location *A* or just the partial key until the cache is full, and then when going to location *B*, send the request to *B* to download the remaining items based on the key that is already in the cache.

For example, in Case Study 1, which involves querying to different servers that are utilizing the server strategy, it is obvious that in order to minimize the cost, we need to first download the list that has fewer records and then send it to the other server for matching. But if the location aspect is there, it might not be possible to choose which server to access first because it is dictated by the relative location. So this arises one important issue that needs to be looked at to what are the other aspect besides selecting servers that contain fewer records to be downloaded first.

Another example, based on Case Study 2, where we involve two servers in different locations, where the server in location *A* does not accept queries but the server in location *B* accepts queries. The issue may occur if the user is required to get the data from location *B* first, which accepts queries and then send to the server in location *A* that does not accept queries. This may create a problem because once we obtain the desired results from location *B* through sending a query to request the desired data, the results will then be sent to our mobile device. However, with this data, we are required to send to the server in location *A,* maybe to perform some comparison but that server does not accept queries, but only broadcasts data out to the mobile user. So our problem would be how can we then select another better technique that can reverse the situation so that we can get tune into the broadcast channel to get the data first and then only send the obtained data to the server to be process for the final results.

The last example based on Case Study 3 where caching is involved, a mobile user is currently in location *A* and wants to obtain data from location *A* before moving to location *B*. It might be a good idea while in location *A*, that the user requests the desired data from peer mobile users whether they have data from location *B* (maybe just partial), so that the user can "borrow" this data before having to personally go to location *B* to get those data. Or

if they can only obtain location *B* data partially from the peer mobile user during their visit in location *A*, they can still benefit from less downloads transfer when they go to location *B* to obtain the desired data since they already have partial key, they can just request the exact information that is needed based on the partial key.

Existing related work has been done on computing the shortest path search by using compact exit hierarchy (CEH) and applying semantic location model (Lee et al., 2005), thus the issue is whether the method can be integrated into the situation when the need of combining the results with the other list of information are needed. Other previous work relates to investigating techniques in decreasing the access time and to also have the organizing time shorter especially when there are a number of updates at once and quick enough to respond to the users. Also being done in past research work about improving the consistency of data and response time for the mobile users in retrieving the required data. Since location dependent query deals with geographical coordinates of the mobile users, it is important to also look at minimizing movements of users. This refers to helping reduce the mobile user having to go back to the previous location to obtain additional data if he or she forgets when he or she was there before.

IMPLEMENTATION AND SYSTEM PROTOTYPE

We have implemented our proposed methods on a mobile environment whereby the server and mobile device architecture consists of two desktop computers, which act as servers of two different locations, and a PDA as a mobile device, which wirelessly connects to both servers. Initially the PDA is connected to one server and requests the data from that server. When the PDA is moved, it requests data from the second server. In this environment, we have simulated location-based query processing. The database in the servers uses MS SQL server, and both servers provides the mobile device with an access to the database. We use C# programming language within the .NET framework to program our proposed methods. Initially, the development is purely done at a desktop, and without involving the PDA. The testing was done using the Pocket PC emulator, which comes with the Visual Studio .Net. Once the testing is complete, the deployment is done by transferring down the executable from PC Emulator to the real PDA through the MS Active Sync, in which it copies not only the executable program, but also the visual .Net run time

In this section, we describe a query-processing prototype that involves multiple non-collaborative servers. This prototype is built on the idea from Example 1. Basically the prototype shows a sample interface design on how the final product would appear on the mobile user's PDA. Recalling Example 1, the mobile user is interested to know all vegetarian restaurants that are available

in the country he or she is currently located. The mobile user is interested in obtaining recommendations from both servers, the tourist office and the vegetarian community servers. In this prototype design, we do not incorporate any location dependent processing and we assume that the current country (location) is Australia. Figure 8a models the final display on the PDA for the mobile user and Figure 8b models a sample screen shot of informing user the next page is being processing.

From this prototype, we can see that it only shows the basic features, which are the results in tabular format that is simple and straightforward. This can be a limitation especially when in today's world, multimedia has emerged as an important component in human interaction. A lot of people are demanding multimedia features now due to the vast benefits on what multimedia information can bring to the mobile users. Not only does the incorporation of multimedia elements enhance the appearance and make the information more

Figure 8. Final output of prototype design

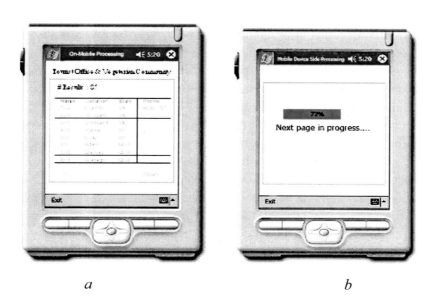

a   *b*

interesting, but it also gives a better interaction between the user and the device. For instance, a person who is blind may not read what is displayed on the PDA screen, but with the ability to incorporate multimedia feature, the results can be translated into "voice" talk instead of just displaying the results. This shows one importance on what multimedia information can bring around to the mobile users.

CONCLUSION AND FUTURE DIRECTION

In this article, we have presented possible applications that will be beneficial for information gathering from multiple non-collaborative sources. A brief taxonomy of the possible database operations involving multiple sources is also presented. We have also demonstrated not every server that is available in the wireless environment accepts direct queries from the users. There are some situations when the servers do not have the ability to accept direct queries and we need to process that data together with data that are obtained based on direct queries. As the wireless and mobile communication of mobile users has increased, location has become a very important constraint. A list of data obtained from different locations brings in different contents, and hence, there is a need to efficiently make these different lists of data into a single valuable piece of information for mobile users. All the issues and limitations have been outlined accordingly to where the lists of data are obtained via server, on-air, or client strategies. A sample prototype is being designed to demonstrate where the project may be applied in real life application.

Our future work is to further investigate the gathering processing techniques to further optimize the response and the data processing that is obtained from the non-collaborative servers. Since there are several issues that arise regardless of whether the lists are obtained from the server, on-air, or client strategy, they are difficult and very challenging to overcome. Thus, further investigation on choosing the right technique for each strategy according to situations should be done individually before processing several lists that are obtained from various strategies together. In addition, individually evaluating the best technique to obtain certain lists of data from each strategy should also be done to obtain the suitable technique. It is also beneficial to explore on the issues of scalability in terms of the servers that are needed to process together maintain the same efficiency or improve efficiency even though *n* servers are involved.

REFERENCES

Bell, D., & Grimson, J. (1992). *Distributed database systems*. Addison-Wesley.

Cai, Y., & Hua, K. A. (2002). An adaptive query management technique for real-time monitoring of spatial regions in mobile database systems. In *Proceedings of 21st IEEE International Conference on Performance, Computing, and Communications* (pp. 259-266).

Ceri, S., & Pelagatti, G. (1984). *Distributed databases: Principles and systems*. New York: McGraw-Hill.

Chan, B. Y., Si, A., & Leong, H. V. (1998). Cache management for mobile databases: Design and evaluation. In *Proceedings of the International Conference on Data Engineering (ICDE)* (pp. 54-53).

Cheverst, K., Davies, N., Mitchell, K., & A., F. (2000). Experiences of developing and deploying a context-aware tourist guide. In *Proceedings of the 6th Annual International Conference on Mobile Computing and Networking* (pp. 20-31).

Elmargamid, A., Jing, J., Helal, A., & Lee, C. (2003). Scalable cache invalidation algorithms for mobile data access. *IEEE Transactions on Knowledge and Data Engineering, 15*(6), 1498-1511.

Gutting, R. H., Bohlen, M. H., Erwig, M., Jensen, C. S., Lorentzos, N. A., Schneider, M., & Vazierginiannis, M. (2000). A foundation for representing and querying moving objects. *ACM Transactions on Database Systems Journal, 25*(1), 1-42.

Hurson, A. R., & Jiao, Y. (2005). Data broadcasting in mobile environment. In D. Katsaros, A. Nanopoulos, & Y. Manolopoulos (Eds.), *Wireless information highways.* London: IRM Press Publisher.

Jung, II, D., You, Y. H., Lee, J. J., & Kim, K. (2002). Broadcasting and caching policies for location-dependent queries in urban areas. In *Proceedings of the of the 2nd International Workshop on Mobile Commerce* (pp. 54-59).

Kapp, S. (2002). 802.11: Leaving the wire behind. *IEEE Internet Computing, 6.*

Lee, D. K., Xu, J., Zheng, B., & Lee, W. C. (2002). Data management in location-dependent information services. *IEEE Pervasive Computing, 2*(3), 65-72, July-Sept.

Lee, D. K., Zhu, M., & Hu, H. (2005). When location-based services meet databases. *Mobile Information Systems, 1*(2), 2005.

Lee, K. C. K., Leong, H. V., & Si, A. (2002). Semantic data access in an asymmetric mobile environment. In *Proceedings of the 3rd Mobile Data Management* (pp. 94-101).

Liberatore, V. (2002). Multicast scheduling for list requests". In *Proceedings of IEEE INFOCOM Conference* (pp. 1129-1137).

Lim, S. Y., Taniar, D., & Srinivasan, B. (2006). A taxonomy of database operations on mobile devices. *Handbook of Research on Mobile Multimedia,* accepted for publication, 2006.

Lo, E., Mamoulis, N., Cheung, D. W., Ho, W. S., & Kalnis, P. (2003). In *Processing ad-hoc joins on mobile devices.* Technical report, The University of Hong Kong (2003). Retrieved from http://www.csis.hku.hk/~dbgroup/techreport

Madria, S. K., Bhargava, B., Pitoura, E., & Kumar, V. (2000). Data organisation for location-dependent queries in mobile computing. In *Proceedings of ADBIS-DASFAA* (pp. 142-156).

Malladi, R., & Davis, K. C. (2002). Applying multiple query optimization in mobile databases. In *Proceedings of the 36th Hawaii International Conference on System Sciences* (pp. 294-303).

Mamoulis, N., Kalnis, P., Bakiras, S., & Li, X. (2003). Optimization of spatial joins on mobile devices. In *Proceedings of the SSTD.*

Myers, B. A., & Beigl M. (2003). Handheld computing. *IEEE Computer Magazine, 36*(9), 27-29.

Özsu, M. T., & Valduriez, P. (1999). Principles of distributed database systems (2nd ed.). Prentice Hall.

Ozakar, B., Morvan, F., & Hameurlain, A. (2005). Mobile join operators for restricted sources. *Mobile Information Systems, 1*(3).

Ren, Q., & Dunham, M. H. (2000). Using semantic caching to manage location-dependent data in mobile computing. In *Proceedings of the 6th International Conference on Mobile Computing and Networking* (pp. 210-221).

Seydim, A.Y., Dunham, M. H., & Kumar, V. (2001). Location-dependent query processing. In *Proceedings of the 2nd International Workshop on Data Engineering on Mobile and Wireless Access (MobiDE'01)* (pp. 47-53).

Si, A., & Leong, H. V. (1999). Query optimization for broadcast database. *Data and Knowledge Engineering, 29*(3), 351-380.

Sistla, A. P., Wolfson, O., Chamberlain, S., & Dao, S. (1997). Modeling and querying moving objects. In *Proceedings of the 13th International Conference on Data Engineering* (pp. 422-432).

Saltenis, S., & Jensen, C. S. (2002). Indexing of moving objects for location-based services. *Proceedings of ICDE* (pp. 463-472).

Song, M., Kang, S. W., & Park, K. (2005). On the design of energy-efficient location tracking mechanism in location-aware computing. *Mobile Information Systems, 1*(2), 109-127.

Tran, D. A., Hua, K. A., & Jiang, N. (2001). A generalized design for broadcasting on multiple physical-channel air-cache. In *Proceedings of the ACM SIGAPP Symposium on Applied Computing (SAC'01)* (pp. 387-392).

Triantafillou, P., Harpantidou, R., & Paterakis, M. (2001). High performance data broadcasting: A comprehensive systems "perspective." In *Proceedings of the 2nd International Conference on Mobile Data Management (MDM 2001)* (pp. 79-90).

Tsalgatidou, A., Veijalainen, J., Markkula, J., Katasonov, A., & Hadjiefthymiades, S. (2003). Mobile e-commerce and location-based services: Technology and requirements. In *Proceedings of the 9th Scandinavian Research Conference on Geographical Information Services* (pp. 1-14).

Tse ,P. K. C., Lam, W. K., Ng, K. W., & Chan, C. (2005). An implementation of location-aware multimedia information download to mobile system. *Journal of Mobile Multimedia, 1*(1), 33-46.

Waluyo, A. B., Srinivasan, B., & Taniar, D. (2005). Research on location-dependent queries in mobile databases. *International Journal of Computer Systems Science & Engineering, 20*(3), 77-93, March.

Wolfson, O. (2002). Moving objects information management: The database challenge. In *Proceedings of the 5th Workshop on Next Generation Information Technology and Systems (NGITS)* (pp. 75-89).

Xu, J., Hu, Q., Lee, W. C., & Lee, D. L. (2004). Performance evaluation of an optimal cache replacement policy for wireless data dissemination. *IEEE Transaction on Knowledge and Data Engineering (TKDE), 16*(1), 125-139.

Xu, J., Tang, X., & Lee, D. L. (2003). Performance analysis of location-dependent cache invalidation schemes for mobile environments. *IEEE Transactions on Knowledge and Data Engineering (TKDE), 15*(2), 474-488.

Xu, J., Zheng, B., Lee, W. C., & Lee, D. L. (2003). Energy efficient index for querying location-dependent data in mobile broadcast environments. *Proceedings of the 19th IEEE International Conference on Data Engineering (ICDE '03)* (pp. 239-250).

Zheng, B., Xu, J., Lee, D. L. (2002). Cache invalidation and replacement strategies for location-dependent data in mobile environments. *IEEE Transactions on Computers, 51*(10), 1141-1153.

This work was previously published in the International Journal of Business Data Communications and Networking, edited by J. Gutierrez, Volume 3, Issue 2, pp. 72-93, copyright 2007 by IGI Publishing, formerly known as Idea Group Publishing (an imprint of IGI Global).

Chapter 7.41
A Bio-Inspired Approach for the Next Generation of Cellular Systems

Mostafa El-Said
Grand Valley State University, USA

INTRODUCTION

In the current 3G systems and the upcoming 4G wireless systems, *missing neighbor pilot* refers to the condition of receiving a high-level pilot signal from a Base Station (BS) that is not listed in the mobile receiver's neighbor list (LCC International, 2004; Agilent Technologies, 2005). This pilot signal interferes with the existing ongoing call, causing the call to be possibly dropped and

Figure 1. Missing pilot scenario

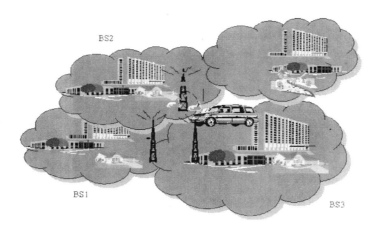

increasing the handoff call dropping probability. Figure 1 describes the missing pilot scenario where BS1 provides the highest pilot signal compared to BS1 and BS2's signals. Unfortunately, this pilot is not listed in the mobile user's active list.

The horizontal and vertical handoff algorithms are based on continuous measurements made by the user equipment (UE) on the Primary Scrambling Code of the Common Pilot Channel (CPICH). In *3G systems,* UE attempts to measure the quality of all received CPICH pilots using the Ec/Io and picks a dominant one from a cellular system (Chiung & Wu, 2001; El-Said, Kumar, & Elmaghraby, 2003). The UE interacts with any of the available radio access networks based on its memorization to the neighboring BSs. As the UE moves throughout the network, the serving BS must constantly update it with neighbor lists, which tell the UE which CPICH pilots it should be measuring for handoff purposes. In *4G systems*, CPICH pilots would be generated from any wireless system including the 3G systems (Bhashyam, Sayeed, & Aazhang, 2000). Due to the complex heterogeneity of the 4G radio access network environment, the UE is expected to suffer

from various carrier interoperability problems. Among these problems, the missing neighbor pilot is considered to be the most dangerous one that faces the 4G industry.

The wireless industry responded to this problem by using an inefficient traditional solution relying on using antenna downtilt such as given in Figure 2. This solution requires shifting the antenna's radiation pattern using a mechanical adjustment, which is very expensive for the cellular carrier. In addition, this solution is permanent and is not adaptive to the cellular network status (Agilent Technologies, 2005; Metawave, 2005).

Therefore, a self-managing solution approach is necessary to solve this critical problem. Whisnant, Kalbarczyk, and Iyer (2003) introduced a system model for dynamically reconfiguring application software. Their model relies on considering the application's static structure and run-time behaviors to construct a workable version of reconfiguration software application. Self-managing applications are hard to test and validate because they increase systems complexity (Clancy, 2002). The ability to reconfigure a software application requires the ability to deploy

Figure 2. Missing pilot solution: Antenna downtilt

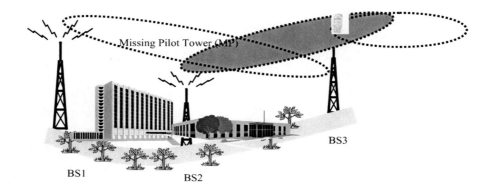

a dynamically hardware infrastructure in systems in general and in cellular systems in particular (Jann, Browning, & Burugula, 2003).

Konstantinou, Florissi, and Yemini (2002) presented an architecture called NESTOR to replace the current network management systems with another automated and software-controlled approach. The proposed system is inherently a rule-based management system that controls change propagation across model objects. Vincent and May (2005) presented a decentralized service discovery approach in mobile ad hoc networks. The proposed mechanism relies on distributing information about available services to the network neighborhood nodes using the analogy of an electrostatic field. Service requests are issued by any neighbor node and routed to the neighbor with the highest potential.

The autonomic computing system is a concept focused on adaptation to different situations caused by multiple systems or devices. The IBM Corporation recently initiated a public trail of its Autonomic Toolkit, which consists of multiple tools that can be used to create the framework of an autonomic management system. In this article, an autonomic engine system setting at the cellular base station nodes is developed to detect the missing neighbor (Ganek & Corbi, 2003; Haas, Droz, & Stiller, 2003; Melcher & Mitchell, 2004). The autonomic engine receives continuous feedback and performs adjustments to the cell system's neighboring set by requiring the UE to provide signal measurements to the serving BS tower (Long, 2001).

In this article, I decided to use this toolkit to build an autonomic rule-based solution to detect the existence of any missing pilot. The major advantage of using the IBM autonomic toolkit is providing a common system infrastructure for processing and classifying the RF data from multiple sources regardless of its original sources. This is a significant step towards creating a transparent autonomic high-speed physical layer in 4G systems.

PROPOSED SOLUTION

The proposed AMS relies on designing an autonomic high-speed physical layer in the smart UE and the BS node. *At the UE side,* continuous CPICH pilot measurements will be recorded and forwarded to the serving BS node via its radio interface. *At the BS node,* a scalable self-managing autonomic engine is developed using IBM's autonomic computing toolkit to facilitate the mobile handset's vertical/horizontal handover such as shown in Figure 3. The proposed engine is cable of interfacing the UE handset with different wireless technologies and detects the missing pilot if it is existed.

The autonomic engine relies on a generic log adapter (GLA), which is used to handle any raw measurements log file data and covert it into a standard format that can be understood by the autonomic manager. Without GLA, separate log adapters would have be coded for any system that the autonomic manager interfaced with. The BS node will then lump all of the raw data logs together and forward them to the Generic Log Adapter for data classification and restructuring to the common base event format. Once the GLA has parsed a record in real time to common base event format, the autonomic manager will see the record and process it and take any action necessary by notifying the BS node to make adjustments to avoid the missing pilot and enhance the UE devices' quality of service.

PERFORMANCE MEASUREMENTS AND KEY FINDINGS

To test the applicability of the proposed solution, we decided to use the system's response time, AS's service rate for callers experiencing missing pilot problem, and the performance gain as performance metrics. Also, we developed a Java class to simulate the output of a UE in a heterogeneous RF access network. Table 1 summarizes

Figure 3. Autonomic base station architecture

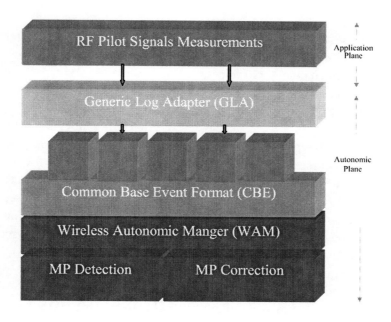

Table 1. Summary of the system performance analysis

	Log File Size in (# Records)	System Response Time in (Sec)	Processing Rate by the Base Station in (Records/Sec)
Trial Experiment 1	985	145	6.793103448
Trial Experiment 2	338	95	3.557894737
Trial Experiment 3	281	67	4.194029851
Trial Experiment 4	149	33	4.515151515
Average Processing Rate by the Base Station in (Records/Sec)	4.765044888		
Base Station Service Rate For callers experiencing missing pilot problem (Records/Sec)	5.3		
Performance Gain	1.112266542		

the simulation results for four simulation experiments with different log files size.

The results shown in Table 1 comply with the design requirements for the current 3G system. This is illustrated in the following simple example.

DESIGN REQUIREMENTS FOR 3G SYSTEMS

- The 3G cell tower's coverage area is divided into three sectors, with each sector having (8 traffic channel * 40 call/channel = 320 voice traffic per sector) and (2 control channels * 40 callers/channels = 80 control traffic per sector).

- The overlapped area between towers (hand-off zone) occupies 1/3 of the sector size and serves (1/3 of 320 = 106 callers (new callers and/or exciting ones)). If we consider having the UE report its status to the tower every 5 seconds, we could potentially generate 21.2 records in 1 second.

- It is practical to assume that 25% of the 21.2 reports/second accounts for those callers that may suffer from the missing pilot problem—that is, the tower's service rate for missing neighbor pilot callers is 21.2/4 = 5.3 records/second. This is the threshold level used by the tower to accommodate those callers suffering from the missing pilot problem.

ANALYSIS OF THE RESULTS

- Response time is the time taken by the BS to process, parse the incoming log file and detect the missing neighbor pilot. It is equal to (145, 95, 67, and 33) for the four experiment trials. All values are in seconds.

- Processing rate by the base station is defined as the total number of incoming records divided by the response time in (records/second). It is equal to (6.7, 3.5, 4.1, and 4.5) for the four experiment trials.

- The UE reports a missing pilot problem with an average rate of 4.7 records/second.

- The base station's service rate for callers experiencing the missing pilot problem = 5.3 records/second.

- The performance gain is defined as:

$$\frac{\text{Base Station Service Rate For callers experiencing missing pilot problem in (Records/Sec)}}{\text{Average Processing Rate by the Base Station in (Records/Sec)}}$$

$$= 5.3/4.7 = 1.1$$

- Here it is obvious that the service rate (5.3 records/second) is greater than the UE's reporting rate to the base station node (4.7 records/second). Therefore, the above results prove that the proposed solution does not overload the processing capabilities of the BS nodes and can be scaled up to handle a large volume of data.

FUTURE TRENDS

An effective solution for the interoperability issues in 4G wireless systems must rely on an adaptive and self-managing network infrastructure. Therefore, the proposed approach in this article can be scaled to maintain continuous user connectivity, better quality of service, improved robustness, and higher cost-effectiveness for network deployment.

CONCLUSION

In this article, we have developed an autonomic engine system setting at the cellular base station (BS) nodes to detect the missing neighbor. The autonomic engine receives continuous feedback and performs adjustments to the cell system's neighboring set by requiring the user equipment (UE) to provide signal measurements to the serving BS tower. The obtained results show that the proposed solution is able to detect the missing pilot problem in any heterogeneous RF environment.

REFERENCES

Agilent Technologies. (2005). Retrieved October 2, 2005, from http://we.home.agilent.com

Bhashyam, S., Sayeed, A., & Aazhang, B. (2000). Time-selective signaling and reception for communication over multipath fading channels. *IEEE Transaction on Communications, 48*(1), 83-94.

Chiung, J., & Wu, S. (2001). Intelligent handoff for mobile wireless Internet. *Journal of Mobile Networks and Applications, 6,* 67-79.

Clancy, D. (2002). *NASA challenges in autonomic computing. Almaden Institute 2002, IBM Almaden Research Center,* San Jose, CA.

El-Said, M., Kumar, A., & Elmaghraby, A. (2003). Pilot pollution interference cancellation in CDMA systems. *Special Issue of Wiley Journal: Wireless Communication and Mobile Computing on Ultra Broadband Wireless Communications for the Future, 3*(6), 743-757.

Ganek, A., & Corbi, T. (2003). The dawning of the autonomic computing era. *IBM Systems Journal, l42*(1), 5-19.

Haas, R., Droz, P., & Stiller, B. (2003). Autonomic service deployment in networks. *IBM Systems Journal, 42*(1), 150-164.

Jann, L., Browning, A., & Burugula, R. (2003). Dynamic reconfiguration: Basic building blocks for autonomic computing on IBM pSeries servers. *IBM Systems Journal, 42*(1), 29-37.

Konstantinou, A., Florissi, D., & Yemini, Y. (2002). Towards self-configuring networks. *Proceedings of the DARPA Active Networks Conference and Exposition* (pp. 143-156).

LCC International. (2004). Retrieved December 10, 2004, from http://www.hitech-news.com/30112001-MoeLLC.htm

Lenders, V., May, M., & Plattner, B. (2005). Service discovery in mobile ad hoc networks: A field theoretic approach. *Special Issue of Pervasive and Mobile Computing, 1,* 343-370.

Long, C. (2001). *IP network design.* New York: McGraw-Hill Osborne Media.

Melcher, B., & Mitchell, B. (2004). Towards an autonomic framework: Self-configuring network services and developing autonomic applications. *Intel Technology Journal, 8*(4), 279-290.

Metawave. (2005). Retrieved November 10, 2005, from http://www.metawave.com

Whisnant, Z., Kalbarczyk, T., & Iyer, R. (2003). A system model for dynamically reconfigurable software. *IBM Systems Journal, 42*(1), 45-59.

KEY TERMS

Adaptive Algorithm: Can "learn" and change its behavior by comparing the results of its actions with the goals that it is designed to achieve.

Autonomic Computing: An approach to self-managed computing systems with a minimum of human interference. The term derives from the body's autonomic nervous system, which controls key functions without conscious awareness or involvement.

Candidate Set: Depicts those base stations that are in transition into or out of the active set, depending on their power level compared to the threshold level.

Missing Neighbor Pilot: The condition of receiving a high-level pilot signal from a base station (BS) that is not listed in the mobile receiver's neighbor list.

Neighbor Set: Represents the nearby serving base stations to a mobile receiver. The mobile receiver downloads an updated neighbor list from the current serving base station. Each base station or base station sector has a unique neighbor list.

Policy-Based Management: A method of managing system behavior or resources by setting "policies" (often in the form of "if-then" rules) that the system interprets.

Virtual Active Set: Includes those base stations (BSs) that are engaged in a live communication link with the mobile user; they generally do not exceed three base stations at a time.

This work was previously published in Encyclopedia of Mobile Computing and Commerce, edited by D. Taniar, pp. 63-67, copyright 2007 by Information Science Reference, formerly known as Idea Group Reference (an imprint of IGI Global).

Section VIII
Emerging Trends

This section highlights research potential within the field of mobile computing while exploring uncharted areas of study for the advancement of the discipline. Chapters within this section highlight evolutions in mobile services, frameworks, and interfaces. These contributions, which conclude this exhaustive, multi-volume set, provide emerging trends and suggestions for future research within this rapidly expanding discipline.

Chapter 8.1
Bridging Together Mobile and Service-Oriented Computing

Loreno Oliveira
Federal University of Campina Grande, Brazil

Emerson Loureiro
Federal University of Campina Grande, Brazil

Hyggo Almeida
Federal University of Campina Grande, Brazil

Angelo Perkusich
Federal University of Campina Grande, Brazil

INTRODUCTION

The growing popularity of powerful *mobile devices,* such as modern cellular phones, smart phones, and PDAs, is enabling *pervasive computing* (Weiser, 1991) as the new paradigm for creating and interacting with computational systems. Pervasive computing is characterized by the interaction of mobile devices with embedded devices dispersed across *smart spaces,* and with other mobile devices on behalf of users. The interaction between user devices and smart spaces occurs primarily through services advertised on those environments. For instance, airports may offer a notification service, where

the system registers the user flight at the check-in and keeps the user informed, for example, by means of messages, about flight schedule or any other relevant information.

In the context of smart spaces, *service-oriented computing* (Papazoglou & Georgakopoulos, 2003), in short SOC, stands out as the effective choice for advertising services to mobile devices (Zhu, Mutka, & Ni, 2005; Bellur & Narendra, 2005). SOC is a computing paradigm that has in services the essential elements for building applications. SOC is designed and deployed through *service-oriented architectures* (SOAs) and their applications. SOAs address the flexibility for dynamic binding of services, which applications need to locate and execute a given operation in a pervasive computing environment. This feature is especially important due to the dynamics of smart spaces, where resources may exist anywhere and applications running on mobile clients must be able to find out and use them at runtime.

In this article, we discuss several issues on bridging mobile devices and service-oriented computing in the context of smart spaces. Since smart spaces make extensive use of services for interacting with personal mobile devices, they become the ideal scenario for discussing the issues for this integration. A brief introduction on SOC and SOA is also presented, as well as the main architectural approaches for creating SOC environments aimed at the use of resource-constrained mobile devices.

BACKGROUND

SOC is a distributed computing paradigm whose building blocks are distributed services. Services are self-contained software modules performing only pre-defined sets of tasks. SOC is implemented through the deployment of any software infrastructure that obeys its key features. Such features include loose coupling, implementation neutrality, and granularity, among others (Huhns & Singh, 2005). In this context, SOAs are software architectures complying with SOC features.

According to the basic model of SOA, service providers advertise service interfaces. Through such interfaces, providers hide from service clients the complexity behind using different and complex kinds of resources, such as databanks, specialized hardware (e.g., sensor networks), or even combinations of other services. Service providers announce their services in service registries. Clients can then query these registries about needed services. If the registry knows some provider of the required service, a reference for that provider is returned to the client, which uses this reference

for contacting the service provider. Therefore, services must be described and published using some machine-understandable notation.

Different technologies may be used for conceiving SOAs such as grid services, Web services, and Jini, which follow the SOC concepts. Each SOA technology defines its own standard machineries for (1) service description, (2) message format, (3) message exchange protocol, and (4) service location.

In the context of pervasive computing, services are the essential elements of smart spaces. Services are used for interacting with mobile devices and therefore delivering personalized services for people. Owning to the great benefits that arise with the SOC paradigm, such as interoperability, dynamic service discovery, and reusability, there is a strong and increasing interest in making mobile devices capable of providing and consuming services over wireless networks (Chen, Zhang, & Zhou, 2005; Kalasapur, Kumar, & Shirazi, 2006; Kilanioti, Sotiropoulou, & Hadjiefthymiades, 2005). The dynamic discovery and invocation of services are essential to mobile applications, where the user context may change dynamically, making different kinds of services, or service implementations, adequate at different moments and places.

However, bridging mobile devices and SOAs requires analysis of some design issues, along with the fixing of diverse problems related to using resources and protocols primarily aimed at wired use, as discussed in the next sections.

INTEGRATING MOBILE DEVICES AND SOAS

Devices may assume three different roles in a SOA: service provider, service consumer, or service registry. In what follows, we examine the most representative high-level scenarios of how mobile devices work in each situation.

Consuming Services

The idea is to make available, in a wired infrastructure, a set of services that can be discovered and used by mobile devices. In this context, different designs can be adopted for bridging mobile devices and service providers. Two major architectural configurations can be derived and adapted to different contexts (Duda, Aleksy, & Butter, 2005): direct communication and proxy aided communication. In Figure 1 we illustrate the use of direct communication.

In this approach, applications running at the devices directly contact service registries and service providers. This approach assumes the usage of fat clients with considerable processing, storage, and networking capabilities. This is necessary because mobile clients need to run applications coupled with SOA-defined protocols, which may not be suited for usage by resource-constrained devices.

However, most portable devices are rather resource-constrained devices. Thus, considering running on mobile devices applications with significant requirements of processing and memory footprint reduces the range of possible client devices. This issue leads us to the next approach, proxy-aided communication, illustrated in Figure 2.

In this architectural variation, a proxy is introduced between the mobile device and the SOA infrastructure, playing the role of mobile device proxy in the wired network. This proxy interacts via SOA-defined protocols with registries and service providers, and may perform a series of content adaptations, returning to mobile devices results using lightweight protocols and data formats.

This approach has several advantages over the previous one. The proxy may act as a cache, storing data of previous service invocations as well as any client relevant information, such as bookmarks and profiles. Proxies may also help client devices by transforming complex data into lightweight formats that could be rapidly delivered through wireless channels and processed by resource-constrained devices.

Advertising Services

In a general way, mobile devices have two choices for advertising services (Loureiro et al., 2006): the push-based approach and the pull-based approach. In the first one, illustrated in Figure 3, service providers periodically send the descriptions of the services to be advertised directly to potential clients, even if they are not interested in such services (1). Clients update local registries with information about available services (2), and if some service is needed, clients query their own registries about available providers (3).

Figure 1. Direct communication between mobile client and SOA infrastructure

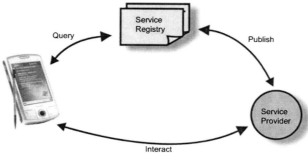
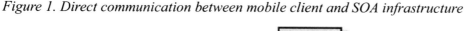

Figure 2. Proxy intermediating communication between mobile client and SOA

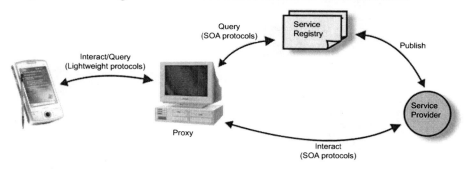

Figure 3. Push-based approach

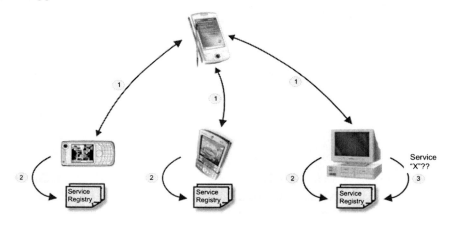

Figure 4. Pull-based approach with centralized registry

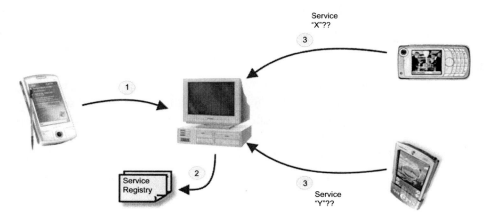

Figure 5. Pull-based approach with distributed registries

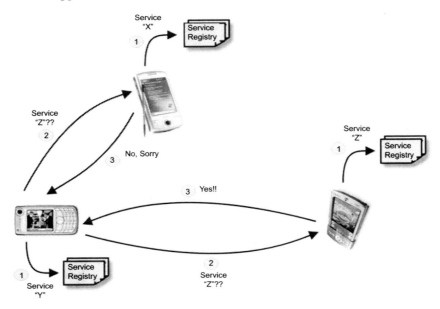

In the pull-based approach, clients only receive the description of services when they require a service discovery. This process can be performed in two ways, either through centralized or distributed registries. In the former, illustrated in Figure 4, service descriptions are published in central servers (1), which maintain entries about available services (2). Clients then query this centralized registry in order to discover the services they need (3).

In the distributed registry approach, illustrated in Figure 5, the advertisement is performed in a registry contained in each provider (1). Therefore, once a client needs to discover a service, it will have to query all the available hosts in the environment (2) until discovering some service provider for the needed service (3).

ISSUES ON INTEGRATING MOBILE DEVICES AND SOAs

Regardless of using mobile devices for either consuming or advertising services in SOAs, both *mobility* and the *limitations* of these devices are raised as the major issues for this integration. Designing and deploying effective services aimed at mobile devices requires careful analysis of diverse issues related to this kind of service provisioning.

Next, we depict several issues that arise when dealing with mobile devices in SOAs. This list is not exhaustive, but rather representative of the dimension of parameters that should be balanced when designing services for mobile use.

Suitability of Protocols and Data Formats

SOAs are primarily targeted at wired infrastructures. Conversely, small mobile devices are known by their well-documented limitations. Thus, protocols and formats used in conventional SOAs may be inadequate for use with resource-constrained wireless devices (Pilioura, Tsalgatidou, & Hadjiefthymiades, 2002; Kilanioti et al., 2005).

For instance, UDDI and SOAP are, respectively, standard protocols for service discovery and messaging in Web services-based SOAs. When using UDDI for service discovery, multiple costly network round trips are needed. In the same manner, SOAP messages are too large and require considerable memory footprint and CPU power for being parsed. Hence, these two protocols impact directly in the autonomy of battery-enabled devices.

Disconnected and Connected Services

In the scope of smart spaces, where disconnections are the norm rather than the exception, we can identify two kinds of services (Chen et at., 2005): disconnected and connected services. The first ones execute by caching the inputs of users in the local device. Once network connectivity is detected, the service performs some sort of synchronization. Services for messaging (e.g., e-mail and instant messages) and field research (e.g., gathering of data related to the selling of a specific product in different supermarkets) are some examples of services that can be implemented as disconnected ones.

Connected services, on the other hand, are those that can only execute when network connectivity is available in the device. Some examples of connected services include price checking, ordering, and shipment tracking. Note, however, that these services could certainly be implemented as disconnected services, although their users will

generally need the information when demanded, neither before nor later. Therefore, there is no precise categorization of what kind of services would be connected or disconnected, as this decision is made by the system designer.

User Interface

User interfaces of small portable devices are rather limited in terms of screen size/resolution and input devices, normally touch screens or small built-in keyboards. This characteristic favors services that require low interaction to complete transactions (Pilioura et al., 2002). Services requiring many steps of data input, such as long forms, tend to: stress users, due to the use of non-comfortable input devices; reduce device autonomy, due to the extra time for typing data; and increase the cost of data transfer, due to larger amounts of data being transferred.

A possible alternative for reducing data typing by clients is the use of context-aware services (Patterson, Muntz, & Pancake, 2003). Context-aware services may reduce data input operations of mobile devices by inferring, or gathering through sensors, information about a user's current state and needs.

Frequent Temporary Disconnections

Temporary disconnections between mobile device and service provider are common due to user mobility. Thus, both client applications and service implementations must consider the design of mechanisms for dealing with frequent disconnections.

Different kinds of services require distinct solutions for dealing with disconnections. For instance, e-business applications need machineries for controlling state of transactions and data synchronization between mobile devices and service providers (Sairamesh, Goh, Stanoi, Padmanabhan, & Li, 2004). Conversely, streaming service requires seamless reestablishment and transference of sessions between access points as the user moves (Cui, Nahrstedt, & Xu, 2004).

Security and Privacy

Normally, mobile devices are not shared among different users. Enterprises may benefit from this characteristic for authenticating employees, for instance. That is, the system knows the user and his/her access and execution rights based on profiles stored in his/her mobile devices. However, in commercial applications targeted at a large number of unknown users, this generates a need of anonymity and privacy of consumers. This authentication process could cause problems, for example in case of device thefts, because the device is authenticated and not the user (Tatli, Stegemann, & Lucks, 2005).

Security also has special relevance when coping with wireless networks (Grosche & Knospe, 2002). When using wireless interfaces for information exchange, mobile devices allow any device in range, equipped with the same wireless technology, to receive the transferred data. At application layer, service providers must protect themselves from opening the system to untrusted clients, while clients must protect themselves from exchanging personal information with service providers that can use user data for purposes different than the ones implicit in the service definition.

Device Heterogeneity and Content Adaptation

Modern mobile devices are quite different in terms of display sizes, resolutions, and color capabilities. This requires services to offer data suitable for the display of different sorts of devices. Mobile devices also differ in terms of processing capabilities and wireless technologies, which makes harder the task of releasing adequate data and helper applications to quite different devices.

Therefore, platform-neutral data formats stand out as the ideal choice for serving heterogeneous sets of client devices. Another possible approach consists of using on-demand data adaptation. Service providers may store only one kind of best-suited data format and transform the data, for example, using a computational grid (Hingne, Joshi, Finin, Kargupta, & Houstis, 2003), when necessary to transfer the data to client devices. Moreover, dynamic changes of conditions may also require dynamic content adaptation in order to maintain pre-defined QoS threshold values. For instance, users watching streamed video may prefer to dynamically reduce video quality due to temporary network congestion, therefore adapting video data, and to maintain a continuous playback instead of maintaining quality and experiencing constant playback freezing (Cui et al., 2004).

Consuming Services

As discussed before, system architects can choose between two major approaches for accessing services of SOAs from mobile devices: direct communication and proxy-aided communication. The two approaches have some features and limitations that should be addressed in order to deploy functional services. Direct communication suffers from the limitations of mobile devices and relates to other discussions presented in this article, such as adequacy of protocols and data formats for mobile devices and user interface.

If, on the one hand, proxy-aided communication seems to be the solution for problems of the previous approach, on the other hand it also brings its own issues. Probably the most noted is that proxies are single points of failures.

Furthermore, some challenges related to wired SOAs are also applicable to both approaches discussed. Service discovery and execution need to be automated to bring transparency and pervasiveness to the service usage. Moreover, especially in the context of smart spaces, services need to be personalized according to the current user profile, needs, and context. Achieving this goal may require describing the semantics of services, as well as modeling and capturing the context of the user (Chen, Finin, & Joshi, 2003).

Advertising Services

A number of issues and technical challenges are associated with this scenario. The push-based approach tends to consume a lot of bandwidth of wireless links according to the number of devices in range, which implies a bigger burden over mobile devices.

Using centralized registries creates a single point of failure. If the registry becomes unreachable, it will not be possible to advertise and discover services. In the same manner, the discovery process is the main problem with the approach of distributed registries, as it needs to be well designed in order to allow clients to query all the hosts in the environment.

Regardless of using centralized or distributed registries, another issue rises with mobility of service providers. When service providers move between access points, a new address is obtained. This changing of address makes service providers inaccessible by clients that query the registry where it published its services. Mechanisms for updating the registry references must be provided in order for services to continue to be offered to their requestors.

FUTURE TRENDS

The broad list of issues presented in this article gives suggestions about future directions for integrating SOC and mobile devices. Each item depicted in the previous section is already an area of intensive research. Despite this, both SOC and mobile computing still lack really functional and mature solutions for the problems presented.

In particular, the fields of context-aware services and security stand out as present and future hot research fields. Besides, the evolution itself of mobile devices towards instruments with improved processing and networking power, as well as better user interfaces, will reduce the complexity of diverse challenges presented in this article.

CONCLUSION

In this article we have discussed several issues related to the integration of mobile devices and SOC. We have presented the most representative architectural designs for integrating mobile devices to SOAs, both as service providers and service consumers.

While providing means for effective integration of mobile devices and service providers, SOC has been leveraging fields such as mobile commerce and pervasive computing. Nonetheless, several issues remain open, requiring extra efforts for designing and deploying truly functional services.

REFERENCES

Bellur, U., & Narendra, N. C. (2005). Towards service orientation in pervasive computing systems. *Proceedings of the International Conference on Information Technology: Coding and Computing (ITCC'05)* (Vol. II, pp. 289-295).

Chen, H., Finin, T., & Joshi, A. (2003). An ontology for context-aware pervasive computing environments. *The Knowledge Engineering Review, 18*(3), 197-207.

Chen, M., Zhang, D., & Zhou, L. (2005). Providing Web services to mobile users: The architecture design of an m-service portal. *International Journal of Mobile Communications, 3*(1), 1-18.

Cui, Y., Nahrstedt, K., & Xu, D. (2004). Seamless user-level handoff in ubiquitous multimedia service delivery. *Multimedia Tools Applications, 22*(2), 137-170.

Duda, I., Aleksy, M., & Butter, T. (2005). Architectures for mobile device integration into service-oriented architectures. *Proceedings of the 4ᵗʰ International Conference on Mobile Business (ICBM'05)* (pp. 193-198).

Grosche, S.S., & Knospe, H. (2002). Secure mobile commerce. *Electronics & Communication Engineering Journal, 14*(5), 228-238.

Hingne, V., Joshi, A., Finin, T., Kargupta, H., & Houstis, E. (2003). Towards a pervasive grid. *Proceedings of the 17ᵗʰ International Parallel and Distributed Processing Symposium (IPDPS'03)* (p. 207.2).

Huhns, M.N., & Singh, M.P. (2005). Service-oriented computing: Key concepts and principles. *IEEE Internet Computing, 9*(1), 75-81.

Kalasapur, S., Kumar, M., & Shirazi, B. (2006). Evaluating service oriented architectures (SOA) in pervasive computing. *Proceedings of the 4ᵗʰ IEEE International Conference on Pervasive Computing and Communications (PERCOMP'06)* (pp. 276-285).

Kilanioti, I., Sotiropoulou, G., & Hadjiefthymiades, S. (2005). A client/intercept based system for optimized wireless access to Web services. *Proceedings of the 16ᵗʰ International Workshop on Database and Expert Systems Applications (DEXA'05)* (pp. 101-105).

Loureiro, E., Bublitz, F., Oliveira, L., Barbosa, N., Perkusich, A., Almeida, H., & Ferreira, G. (2007). Service provision for pervasive computing environments. In D. Taniar (Ed.), *Encyclopedia of mobile computing and commerce.* Hershey, PA: Idea Group Reference.

Papazoglou, M. P., & Georgakopoulos, D. (2003). Service-oriented computing: Introduction. *Communications of the ACM, 46*(10), 24-28.

Patterson, C. A., Muntz, R. R., & Pancake, C. M. (2003). Challenges in location-aware computing. *IEEE Pervasive Computing, 2*(2), 80-89.

Pilioura, T., Tsalgatidou, A., & Hadjiefthymiades, S. (2002). Scenarios of using Web services in m-commerce. *ACM SIGecom Exchanges, 3*(4), 28-36.

Sairamesh, J., Goh, S., Stanoi, I., Padmanabhan, S., & Li, C. S. (2004). Disconnected processes, mechanisms and architecture for mobile e-business. *Mobile Networks and Applications, 9*(6), 651-662.

Tatli, E. I., Stegemann, D., & Lucks, S. (2005). Security challenges of location-aware mobile business. *Proceedings of the 2ⁿᵈ IEEE International Workshop on Mobile Commerce and Services (WMCS'05)* (pp. 84-95).

Weiser, M. (1991). The computer for the 21ˢᵗ century. *Scientific American, 265*(3), 66-75.

Zhu, F., Mutka, M. W., & Ni, L. M. (2005). Service discovery in pervasive computing environments. *IEEE Pervasive Computing, 4*(4), 81-90.

KEY TERMS

Grid Service: A kind of Web service. Grid services extend the notion of Web services through the adding of concepts such as statefull services.

Jini: Java-based technology for implementing SOAs. Jini provides an infrastructure for delivering services in a network

Mobile Device: Any low-sized portable device used to interact with other mobile devices and resources from smart spaces. Examples of mobile devices are cellular phones, smart phones, PDAs, notebooks, and tablet PCs.

Proxy: A network entity that acts on behalf of another entity. A proxy's role varies since data relays to the provision of value-added services, such as on-demand data adaptation.

Streaming Service: One of a number of services that transmit some sort of real-time data flow. Examples of streaming services include audio streaming or digital video broadcast (DVB).

Web Service: Popular technology for implementing SOAs built over Web technologies, such as XML, SOAP, and HTTP.

This work was previously published in Encyclopedia of Mobile Computing and Commerce, edited by D. Taniar, pp. 71-77, copyright 2007 by Information Science Publishing (an imprint of IGI Global).

Chapter 8.2
Context–Awareness and Mobile Devices

Anind K. Dey
Carnegie Mellon University, USA

Jonna Häkkilä
Nokia Research Center, Finland

ABSTRACT

Context-awareness is a maturing area within the field of ubiquitous computing. It is particularly relevant to the growing sub-field of mobile computing as a user's context changes more rapidly when a user is mobile, and interacts with more devices and people in a greater number of locations. In this chapter, we present a definition of context and context-awareness and describe its importance to human-computer interaction and mobile computing. We describe some of the difficulties in building context-aware applications and the solutions that have arisen to address these. Despite these solutions, users have difficulties in using and adopting mobile context-aware applications. We discuss these difficulties and present a set of eight design guidelines that can aid application designers in producing more usable and useful mobile context-aware applications.

INTRODUCTION

Over the past decade, there has been a widespread adoption of mobile phones and personal digital assistants (PDAs) all over the world. Economies of scale both for the devices and the supporting infrastructure have enabled billions of mobile devices to become affordable and accessible to large groups of users. Mobile computing is a fully realized phenomenon of everyday life and is the first computing platform that is truly ubiquitous. Technical enhancements in mobile computing, such as component miniaturization, enhanced computing power, and improvements in supporting infrastructure have enabled the creation of more versatile, powerful, and sophisticated mobile devices. Both industrial organizations and academic researchers, recognizing the powerful combination of a vast user population and a sophisticated computing platform, have focused tremendous effort on improving and enhancing the experience of using a mobile device.

Since its introducion in the mid-1980s, the sophistication of mobile devices in terms of the numbers and types of services they can provide has increased many times over. However, at the same time, the support for accepting input from users and presenting output to users has remained relatively impoverished. This has resulted in slow interaction, with elongated navigation paths and key press sequences to input information. The use of predictive typing allowed for more fluid interaction, but mobile devices were still limited to using information provided by the user and the device's service provider. Over the past few years, improvements to mobile devices and back-end infrastructure has allowed for additional information to be used as input to mobile devices and services. In particular, context, or information about the user, the user's environment and the device's context of use, can be leveraged to expand the level of input to mobile devices and support more efficient interaction with a mobile device. More and more, researchers are looking to make devices and services *context-aware*, or adaptable in response to a user's changing context.

In this chapter, we will define context-awareness and describe its importance to human-computer interaction and mobile devices. We will describe some of the difficulties that researchers have had in building context-aware applications and solutions that have arisen to address these. We will also discuss some of the difficulties users have in using context-aware applications and will present a set of design guidelines that indicate how mobile context-aware applications can be designed to address or avoid these difficulties.

What is Context-Awareness

The concept of context-aware computing was introduced in Mark Weiser's seminal paper 'The Computer for the 21st Century' (Weiser, 1991). He describes ubiquitous computing as a phenomenon *'that takes into account the natural human environment and allows the computers themselves to vanish into the background.'* He also shapes the fundamental concepts of context-aware computing, with computers that are able to capture and retrieve context-based information and offer seamless interaction to support the user's current tasks, and with each computer being able to *'adapt its behavior in significant ways'* to the captured context.

Schilit and Theimer (1994a) first introduce the term *context-aware computing* in 1994 and define it as software that "adapts according to its location of use, the collection of nearby people and objects, as well as changes to those objects over time." We prefer a more general definition of context and context-awareness:

Context is any information that can be used to characterize the situation of an entity. An entity is a person, place or object that is considered relevant to the interaction between a user and an application, including the user and applications themselves, and by extension, the environment the user and applications are embedded in. A system is context-aware if it uses context to provide relevant information and/or services to the user, where relevancy depends on the user's task. (Dey, 2001)

Context-aware features include using context to:

- Present information and services to a user
- Automatically execute a service for a user and
- Tag information to support later retrieval

In supporting these features, context-aware applications can utilize numerous different kinds of information sources. Often, this information comes from sensors, whether they are software sensors detecting information about the networked, or virtual, world, or hardware sensors detecting information about the physical world. Sensor data can be used to recognize the usage situation for instance from illumination, temperature, noise level, and device movements (Gellersen, Schmidt & Beigl, 2002; Mäntyjärvi &

Seppänen, 2002). Typically, sensors are attached to a device and an application on the device locally performs the data analysis, context-recognition, and context-aware service.

Location is the most commonly used piece of context information, and several different location detection techniques have been utilized in context-awareness research. Global positioning system (GPS) is a commonly used technology when outdoors, utilized, for example, in car navigation systems. Network cellular ID can be used to determine location with mobile phones. Measuring the relative signal strengths of Bluetooth and WLAN hotspots and using the hotspots as beacons are frequently used techniques for outdoors and indoors positioning (Aalto, Göthlin,Korhonen et al., 2004; Burrell & Gay, 2002; Persson et al., 2003). Other methods used indoors include ultrasonic or infrared-based location detection (Abowd et al., 1997; Borriello et al., 2005).

Other commonly used forms of context are time of day, day of week, identity of the user, proximity to other devices and people, and actions of the user (Dey, Salber & Abowd, 2001; Osbakk & Rydgren, 2005). Context-aware device behavior may not rely purely on the physical environment. While sensors have been used to directly provide this physical context information, sensor data often needs to be interpreted to aid in the understanding of the user's goals. Information about a user's goals, preferences, and social context can be used for determining context-aware device behavior as well. Knowledge about a user's goals helps prioritize the device actions and select the most relevant information sources. A user's personal preferences can offer useful information for profiling or personalizing services or refining information retrieval. The user may also have preferences about quality of service issues such as cost-efficiency, data connection speed, and reliability, which relate closely to mobile connectivity issues dealing with handovers and alternative data transfer mediums. Finally, social context forms an important type of context as mobile devices are commonly used to support communication between two people and used in the presence of other people.

Relevance to HCI

When people speak and interact with each other, they naturally leverage their knowledge about the context around them to improve and streamline the interaction. But, when people interact with computers, the computing devices are usually quite ignorant of the user's context of use. As the use of context essentially expands the conversational bandwidth between the user and her application, context is extremely relevant to human-computer interaction (HCI). Context is useful for making interaction more efficient by not forcing users to explicitly enter information about their context. It is useful for improving interactions as context-aware applications and devices can offer more customized and more appropriate services than those that do not use context. While there have been no studies of context-aware applications to validate that they have this ability, anecdotally, it is clear that having more information about users, their environments, what they have done and what they want to do, is valuable to applications. This is true in network file systems that cache most recently used files to speed up later retrieval of those files, as well as in tour guides that provide additional information about a place of interest the user is next to.

Relevance to Mobile HCI

Context is particularly relevant in mobile computing. When users are mobile, their context of use changes much more rapidly than when they are stationary and tied to a desktop computing platform. For example, as people move, their location changes, the devices and people they interact with changes more frequently, and their goals and needs change. Mobility provides additional opportunities for leveraging context but also requires additional context to try and understand how the user's goals are changing. This places extra burden on the mobile computing platform, as it needs to sense potentially rapidly changing context, synthesize it and act upon it. In the next section, we will discuss the difficulties that application builders have had with building context-aware applications and solutions that have arisen to address these difficulties.

BUILDING MOBILE CONTEXT-AWARE APPLICATIONS

The first context-aware applications were centered on mobility. The Active Badge location system used infrared-based badges and sensors to determine the location of workers in an indoor location (Want et al., 1992). A receptionist could use this information to route a phone call to the location of the person being called, rather than forwarding the phone call to an empty office. Similarly, individuals could locate others to arrange impromptu meetings. Schilit, Adams and Want,(1994b) also use an infrared-based cellular network to location people and devices, the PARCTAB, and describe 4 different types of applications built with it (Schilit et al., 1994b). This includes:

- **Proximate selection:** Nearby objects like printers are emphasized to be easier to select than other similar objects that are further away from the user;
- **Contextual information and commands:** Information presented to a user or commands parameterized and executed for a user depend on the user's context;
- **Automatic contextual reconfiguration:** Software is automatically reconfigured to support a user's context; and
- **Context-triggered actions:** If-then rules are used to specify what actions to take based on a user's context.

Since these initial context-aware applications, a number of common mobile context-aware applications have been built: tour guides (Abowd et al., 1997; Cheverst et al. 2000; Cheverst, Mitchell & Davies, 2001), reminder systems (Dey & Abowd, 2000; Lamming & Flynn, 1994) and environmental controllers (Elrod et al., 1993; Mozer et al., 1995). Despite the number of people building (and re-building) these applications, the design and implementation of a new context-aware ap-

plication required significant effort, as there was no reusable support for building context-aware applications. In particular, the problems that developers faced are:

- Context often comes from non-traditional devices that developers have little experience with, unlike the mouse and keyboard.
- Raw sensor data is often not directly useful to an application, so the data must be abstracted to turn it into useful context.
- Context comes from multiple distributed and heterogeneous sources, and this context often needs to be combined (or fused) to be useful. This process often results in uncertainty that needs to be handled by the application.
- Context is, by its very nature, dynamic, and changes to it must be detected in real time and applications must adjust to these constant changes in order to provide a positive user experience to users.

These problems resulted in developers building every new application from scratch, with little reuse of code or design ideas between applications.

Over the past five years or so, there has been a large number of research projects aimed at addressing these issues, most often trying to produce a reusable toolkit or infrastructure that makes the design of context-aware applications easier and more efficient. Our work, the Context Toolkit, used a number of abstractions to ease the building of applications. One abstraction, the context widget is similar to a graphical user interface widget in that it abstracts the source of an input and only deals with the information the source produces. For example, a location widget could receive input from someone manually entering information, a GPS device, or an infrared positioning system, but an application using a location widget does not have to deal with the details of the underlying sensing technology, only with the information the sensor produces: identity of the object being located, its location and the time when the object was located. Context interpreters support the interpretation, inference and fusion of context. Context aggregators collect all context-related to a specific location, object or person for easy access. With these three abstractions, along with a discovery system to locate and use the abstractions, an application developer no longer needs to deal with common difficulties in acquiring context and making it useful for an application, and instead can focus on how the particular application she is building can leverage the available context. Other similar architectures include JCAF (Bardram, 2005), SOCAM (Gu, Pung & Zhang, 2004), and CoBRA (Chen et al., 2004).

While these architectures make mobile context-aware applications easier to build, they do not address all problems. Outstanding problems needing support in generalized toolkits include representing and querying context using a common ontology, algorithms for fusing heterogeneous context together, dealing with uncertainty, and inference techniques for deriving higher level forms of context such as human intent. Despite these issues, these toolkits have supported and continue to support the development of a great number of context-aware applications. So, now that we can more easily build context-aware applications, we still need to address how to design and build *usable* mobile context-aware applications. We discuss this issue in the following section.

USABILITY OF MOBILE CONTEXT-AWARE APPLICATIONS

With context information being provided as implicit input to applications and with those applications using this context to infer human intent, there are greater usability concerns than with standard applications that are not context-aware. Bellotti and Edwards discuss the need for context-aware applications to be *intelligible*, where the inferences made and actions being taken are made available to end-users (Bellotti & Edwards, 2001). Without this intelligibility, users of context-aware applications would not be able to decide what actions or responses to take themselves (Dourish, 1997).

To ground our understanding of these abstract concerns, we studied the usability and usefulness of a variety of context-aware applications (Barkhuus & Dey, 2003a; 2003b). We described a number of real and hypothetical context-aware applications and asked subjects to provide daily reports on how they would have used each application each day, whether they thought the applications would be useful, and what reservations they had about using each application. All users were given the same set of applications, but users were split into three groups with each group being given applications with a different level of proactivity. One group was given applications that they would personalize to determine what the application should do for them. Another group was provided with information about how their context was changing, and the users themselves decided how to change the application behavior. The final group was evaluating applications that autonomously changed their behavior based on changing context. Additional information was also gathered from exit interviews conducted with subjects.

Users indicated that they would use and prefer applications that had higher degrees of proactivity. However, as the level of proactivity increased, users had increasing feelings that they were losing control. While these findings might seem contradictory, it should be considered that owning a mobile phone constitutes some lack of control as the user can be contacted anywhere and at anytime; the user may have less control but is willing to bear this cost in exchange for a more interactive and smoother everyday experience. Beyond this issue of control, users had other concerns with regards to the usability of context-aware applications. They were concerned by the lack of feedback, or intelligibility, that the applications provided. Particularly for the more proactive versions of applications, users were unclear how they would know that the application was performing some action for them, what action was being performed, and why this action was being performed. A third concern was privacy. Users were quite concerned that the context data that was being used on mobile platforms could be used by service providers and other entities to track their location and behaviors. A final concern that users had was related to them evaluating multiple context-aware applications. With potentially multiple applications vying for a user's attention, users had concerns about information overload. Particularly when mobile and focusing on some other task, it could be quite annoying to have multiple applications on the mobile device interrupting and requesting the user's attention simultaneously or even serially.

In the remainder of this chapter, we will discuss issues for designing context-aware applications that address usability concerns such as these.

Support for Interaction Design

Despite all of the active research in the field of context-aware computing, much work needs to be done to make context-awareness applications an integral part of everyday life. As context-awareness is still a very young field, it does not have established design practices that take into account its special characteristics. The development of applications has so far been done primarily in research groups that focus more on proof-of-concept and short-term use rather than deployable, long-term systems. For most of these applications, the interaction design has rarely been refined to a level that is required for usable and deployable applications. Particularly for applications aimed at consumers and the marketplace, robustness, reliability and usability must be treated more critically than they are currently, as these factors will have a significant impact on their success.

Currently, the lack of existing high-quality, commercial, and publicly available applications limits our ability to assess and refine the best practices in interaction design of context-aware mobile applications. As there is very little experience with real-life use of these applications, the ability of developers to compare and iterate on different design solutions is very restricted. As user groups for a particular application mostly do not exist yet, much of the current research is based on hypothesized or simulated systems rather that actualized use situations. Knowledge

of what device features people fancy and which they just tolerate, and when application features become insignificant or annoying, are issues that are hard to anticipate without studies of long-term real-life usage.

As with any other novel technology, bringing it to the marketplace will bring new challenges. Bringing context-awareness to mobile devices as an additional feature may lead to situations where the interaction design is performed by people with little experience in context-aware computing. Using well-established commercial platforms such as mobile phones or PDAs often means that user interface designers only have experience with conventional mobile user interfaces. On the other hand, the technical specifications of an application are often provided by people who have no expertise in human-computer interaction issues. When entering a field that involves interdisciplinary elements, such as mobile context-awareness, providing tools and appropriate background information for designers helps them to recognize the risks and special requirements of the technology.

Hence, there are several factors which make examining context-awareness from the usability and interaction design perspective relevant. Failures in these may lead not only to unprofitable products, but may result in an overall negative effect—they may slow down or prevent the underlying technology from penetrating into mass markets.

Usability Risks for Mobile Context-Aware Applications

A system and its functionality are often described with mental models that people form from using the system. According to Norman (1990), one can distinguish between the designer's mental model and the user's mental model. The designer's model represents the designer's understanding and idea of the artefact being constructed, whereas the user's model is the user's conceptual model of the same artefact, its features and functionality, which has developed through her interaction with the system. In order to respond to the user's needs, efficiently fulfil the user's goals and satisfy the user's expectations, the designer's and user's understanding of the device or application should be consistent with each other, in other words, the user's model and designer's model should be the same (Norman, 1990).

To ensure the best possible result, the mental models of different stakeholders in application development and use have to meet each other. First, the mental models of the application's technical designer and user interface designer should be consistent. This means that the user interface designer should have a basic understanding of the special characteristics of context-aware technology. Second, the designer's and user's mental models of the application should be the same. People's perception of context may differ significantly from each other, and both attributes and the measures used to describe context may vary greatly (Hiltunen, Häkkilä & Tuomela, 2005; Mäntyjärvi et al., 2003). The relationship between the designer's and the user's mental models should be checked with user tests several times during the design process. Without this careful design, there are two significant usability risks that may result: users will be unable to explain the behavior of the context-aware application, nor predict how the system will respond given some

user action. While this is true of all interactive systems, it is especially important to consider for context-aware systems as the input to such systems is often implicit.

Context-awareness has several characteristics that can be problematic in interaction design. Figure 1 summarizes potential usability risks with context-aware applications.

A fundamental cause of potential usability risks is *uncertainty in context recognition*, which can be due to different reasons, such as detection accuracy, information fusion, or inferring logic. This is a key issue for designing the user interface for a mobile context-aware application, as it affects the selected features, their functionality and accuracy. In practice, features such as the proactivity level may be designed differently if the confidence level in context recognition can be estimated correctly. Uncertainty is a part of the nature of context-aware applications. Thus, it is important that the application and UI designers share a common understanding of the matter and take it into account when designing both the application and its user interface.

Application complexity has a tendency to grow when functions are added and it forms a potential risk for context-aware applications, as they use a greater number of information sources than

Figure 1. Sources of usability risks and their potential consequences related to context-aware mobile applications. Consequences that are unique to context-aware mobile applications are in the smaller rectangle on the right.

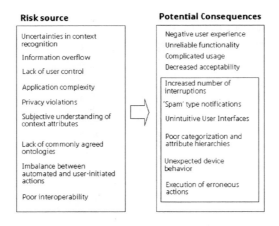

traditional mobile applications. Hiding the complex nature of the technology while maintaining a sufficient level of feedback and transparency so that the user can still make sense of the actions the device is performing (i.e., intelligibility) is a challenging issue. Here, the involvement of user-centric design principles is emphasized. Usability testing and user studies performed in an authentic environment combined with iterative design are key elements to producing well-performing user interface solutions.

Poor interoperability of services and applications relates to the absence of standardization in this maturing field and it limits the application design, available services, and seamless interaction desired across a wide selection of devices and users. Interoperability issues have gained much attention with the current trend of mobile convergence, where different mobile devices resemble each other more and more, yet providing services for them must be performed on a case-by-case basis.

Subjective understanding of context attributes creates a problem for user interface design, as the measures, such as the light intensity or noise level in everyday life are not commonly understood by end-users in terms of luxes or decibels but in relative terms such as 'dark,' 'bright,' 'silent' or 'loud.' This issue is connected to the *lack of commonly agreed ontologies,* which would guide the development of context-aware applications. The difficulties in categorizing context attributes and modeling context is evident from the literature (Hiltunen, Häkkilä & Tuomela, 2005; Mäntyjärvi et al., 2003).

As indicated earlier, *privacy violations* are possible with mobile context-aware systems collecting, sharing and using a tremendous amount of personal information about a user. When such information is shared with a number of different services, each of which will be contacting the user, *information overflow* often results. One can imagine a potential flow of incoming advertisements when entering a busy shopping street, if every shop within a radius of one hundred meters was to send an advertisement to the device. Information overflow is particularly a problem for the small screens that are typical with handheld devices.

As our earlier studies illustrated, the *lack of user control* can easily occur with mobile device automation, when context-triggered actions are executed proactively. However, the promise of context-awareness is that it provides "ease of use" by taking over actions that the user does not want to do or did not think to do for themselves. Any solution for correcting the *imbalance between the set of automated actions and user-initiated actions*, must take user control into account.

The consequences resulting from these usability risks are numerous. The general outcome can be a negative user experience. This may result from an increased number of interruptions, spam, and the execution of erroneous or otherwise unintuitive device behavior. Unreliable device functionality, and unintelligible user interfaces can lead to reduced acceptability of context-aware applications in the marketplace.

Design Guidelines for Mobile Context-Aware Applications

Context-awareness typically contains more risks than conventional, non-context-aware technology. At the same time, context-awareness can offer much added value to the user. In order to provide this value to end-users and avoid these negative design consequences and minimize usability risks, we have sought to provide a set of design guidelines that can offer practical help for designers who are involved in developing context-aware mobile applications (Häkkilä & Mäntyjärvi, 2006). These general guidelines have been validated in a series of user studies (Häkkilä & Mäntyjärvi, 2006) and should be taken into account when selecting the features of the application and during the overall design process.

GL1. Select appropriate level of automation. A fundamental factor with context-awareness is that it incorporates uncertainty. Uncertainty in context-recognition is caused by several different sources, such as detection accuracy, information fusion, or inferring logic. This is a key issue in designing user interfaces, as it affects the selected

Figure 2. How uncertainty in context-recognition should affect the selected level of automation/proactivity

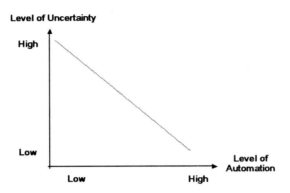

features, their functionality and accuracy. In practice, features such as the automation level or level of proactivity may be designed differently if the confidence level of context recognition can be estimated correctly. The relationship between uncertainty and selected application automation level is illustrated in Figure 2. As shown in Figure 1, *uncertainties in context recognition* create significant usability risks, however, by selecting an appropriate level of automation, an application designer can acknowledge this fact and address it appropriately. The greater the uncertainty is in the context-recognition, the more important it is not to automate actions. The automation level has also a direct relationship with user control, and its selection has a large impact on the number of expected interruptions the system creates for the user. The level of automation must be considered in relation to the overall application design, as it affects numerous issues in the user interface design.

GL 2. Ensure user control. The user has to maintain the feeling that he is in the control over the device. The user, who normally has full control over his mobile device, has voluntarily given some of it back to the device in order to increase the ease of use of the device. To address this *lack of user control*, an important usability risk, the user must be able to take control of the device and context-aware application at any time. The desire to take control can happen in two basic

circumstances—either the device is performing erroneous actions and the user wants to take a correcting action, or the user just wishes to feel in control (a feeling that users often have). The user has to have enough knowledge of the context-aware application and the device functionality in order to recognize malfunctioning behavior, at least in the case where context-recognition errors lead to critical and potentially unexpected actions. The perception of user control is diminished if the device behaves in unexpected manner or if the user has a feeling that the device is performing actions without him knowing it. User control can be implemented, for example, with confirmation dialogues however, this must be balanced with the need to minimize unnecessary interruptions, our next guideline.

GL3. Avoid unnecessary interruptions. Every time the user is interrupted, she is distracted from the currently active task, impacting her performance and satisfaction with the system. In most cases, the interruption leads to negative consequences, however if the system thinks that the interruption will provide high value or benefit to the user, allowing the interruption is often seen as positive. Examples of this are reminders and alarm clocks. The user's interruptibility depends on her context and the user's threshold for putting up with intrusion varies with each individual and her situation. Some context-aware functionality is so important that the user may want the application to override all other ongoing tasks. This leads to a tension between avoiding unnecessary interruptions and supporting user control (GL2).

GL4. Avoid information overflow. The throughput of the information channel to each user is limited, and users can fully focus only on a small number of tasks at one time. In order to address the usability risk of *information overflow* where several different tasks or events compete for this channel, a priority ordering needs to be defined. Also, the threshold for determining the incoming event's relevancy in the context must be considered in order to avoid unnecessary interruptions (GL3). Systems should not present too much information at once, and should implement filtering techniques for to avoid messages that may appear to be spam to users. Also, information should be arranged in a meaningful manner to maintain and maximize the understandability of the system.

GL 5. Appropriate visibility level of system status. The visibility level of what the system is doing has to be sufficient for the user to be aware of the application's actions. While this guideline has been co-opted from Nielsen and Molich's user interface heuristics (1990), it has special meaning in context-aware computing. The implicit nature of context-awareness and natural *complexity of these types of applications* means that users may not be aware of changes in context, system reasoning or system action. When uncertainty in context-awareness is involved, there must be greater visibility of system state in order to allow the user to recognize the risk level and possible malfunctions. Important actions or changes in context should also be made visible and easily understandable for the user, despite the fact that users may have *subjective understandings of context attributes* and that there may be *no established ontology*. System status need not be overwhelming and interrupting to the user but can be provided in an ambient or peripheral fashion, where information is dynamically made more visible as the importance value grows, and may eventually lead to an interruption event to the user if its value is high enough.

GL 6. Personalization for individual needs. Context-awareness should allow a device or application to respond better to the individual user's personal needs. For instance, an application can implement filtering of interruptions according to the user's personal preferences. Personalization may also be used to improve the subjective understanding of context attributes. Allowing the user to name or change context attributes, such as location names or temperature limits, may contribute to better user satisfaction and ease of use. User preferences may change over time, and their representation in the application can be adjusted, for example implicitly with learning techniques or explicitly with user input settings.

GL 7. Secure user's privacy. *Privacy* is a central theme with personal devices, especially with devices focused on supporting personal communication, and impacts, for example trust, frequency of use, and application acceptability. Special care should be taken with applications that employ context sharing. Privacy requirements often vary between who is requesting the information, the perceived value of the information being requested and what information is being requested, so different levels of privacy should be supported. If necessary, users should have the ability to easily specify that they wish to remain anonymous with no context shared with other entities.

GL 8. Take into account the impact of social context. The social impact of a context-aware application taking an action must be part of the consideration in deciding whether to take the action or not. The application and its behavior reflects on users themselves. In some social contexts, certain device or user behavior may be considered awkward or even unacceptable. In such situations, there must be an appropriate *balance of user-initiated and system-initiated actions*. Social context has also has an effect on interruptibility. For example, an audible alert may be considered as inappropriate device behavior in some social contexts.

Once an application has been designed with these guidelines, the application must still be evaluated to ensure that the usability risks that have been identified for mobile context-aware systems have been addressed. This evaluation can take place in the lab, but is much more useful when conducted under real, *in situ*, conditions.

SUMMARY

Context-aware mobile applications, applications that can detect their users' situations and adapt their behavior in appropriate ways, are an important new form of mobile computing. Context-awareness has been used to overcome the deficit of the traditional problems of small screen sizes and limited input functionalities of mobile devices, to offer shortcuts to situationally-relevant device functions, and to provide location sensitive device actions and personalized mobile services.

Context-awareness as a research field has grown rapidly during recent years, concentrating on topics such as context-recognition, location-awareness, and novel application concepts. Several toolkits for enabling building context-aware research systems have been introduced. Despite their existence, there exist very few commercial or publicly available applications utilizing context-awareness. However, the multitude of research activities in mobile context-awareness allow us to make reasonable assumptions about tomorrow's potential applications. For example, navigation aids, tour guides, location-sensitive and context-sensitive notifications and reminders, automated annotation and sharing of photographs, use of metadata for file annotation, sharing or search are topics which frequently appear in the research literature and will likely be relevant in the future. In addition, using context-awareness to address the needs of special user groups, for example in the area of healthcare also appears to be a rich area to explore.

Despite the active research in context-awareness, there is much that remains to be addressed in interaction design and usability issues for context-aware mobile applications. Due the novelty of the field and lack of existing commercial applica-

tions, design practices for producing usable and useful user interfaces have not yet evolved, and end-users' experiences with the technology are not always positive. We have presented a set of 8 design guidelines which have been validated and evaluated in a series of user studies, which point to areas where user interface designers must focus efforts in order to address the usability issues that are commonly found with mobile context-aware applications.

While context-aware applications certainly have more usability risks than traditional mobile applications, the potential benefits they offer to end-users are great. It is important that application designers and user interface designers understand each other's perspectives and the unique opportunities and pitfalls that context-aware systems have to offer. With context-aware applications, careful application and interface design must be emphasized. The consequences resulting from usability risks include an overall negative user experience. Unsuccessful application design may result in diminished user control, increased number of interruptions, spam, and the execution of erroneous device actions or otherwise unintuitive behaviour. Unreliable device functionality and an unintuitive user interface can lead to decreased acceptability of the context-aware features in the marketplace.

In this chapter we have discussed the notion of context-awareness and its relevance to both mobile computing and interaction design in mobile computing. We have described technical issues involved in building context-aware applications and the toolkits that have been built to address these issues. Despite the existence of these toolkits in making context-aware applications easier to build, there are several additional issues that must be addressed in order to make mobile context-aware applications usable and acceptable to end-users. We have presented a number of design guidelines that can aid the designers of mobile context-aware applications in producing applications with both novel and useful functionality for these end-users.

REFERENCES

Aalto, L, Göthlin, N., Korhonen, J., & Ojala T. (2004). Bluetooth and WAP Push based location-aware mobile advertising system. In *Proceedings of the 2ⁿᵈ International Conference on Mobile Systems, Applications and Services* (pp. 49-58).

Abowd, G. D., Atkeson, C. G., Hong, J., Long, S., Kooper, R.. & Pinkerton, M. (1997). Cyberguide: a mobile context-aware tour guide. *ACM Wireless Networks, 3*, 421-433.

Bardram, J. (2005). The java context awareness framework (JCAF)—A service infrastructure and programming framework for context-aware applications. In *Proceedings of Pervasive 2005* (pp. 98-115).

Barkhuus, L., & Dey, A.K. (2003a). Is context-aware computing taking control away from the user? Three levels of interactivity examined. In *Proceedings of UBICOMP 2003* (pp. 149-156).

Barkhuus, L., & Dey, A.K. (2003b). Location-based services for mobile telephony: A study of users' privacy concerns. In *Proceedings of INTERACT 2003* (pp. 709-712).

Bellotti, V., & Edwards, K. (2001). Intelligibility and accountability: Human considerations in context-aware systems. *HCI Journal, 16*, 193-212.

Borriello, G., Liu, A., Offer, T., Palistrant, C., & Sharp, R. (2005). WALRUS: Wireless, Acoustic, Location with Room-Level Resolution using Ultrasound. In *Proceedings of the 3ʳᵈ International Conference on Mobile systems, application and services (MobiSys'05)*, (pp. 191-203).

Burrell, J., & Gay, G. K. (2002). E-graffiti: Evaluating real-world use of a context-aware system. *Interacting with Computers, 14*, 301-312.

Chen, H., Finin, T. and Joshi, A. Chen, H., Finin, T., & Joshi, A. (2004). Semantic Web in the Context Broker Architecture. (2004). In *Proceedings of the Second IEEE international Conference on Pervasive Computing and Communications (Percom'04)*, (pp. 277-286).

Cheverst, K., Davies, N., Mitchell, K., & Friday, A. (2000). Experiences of developing and deploying a context-aware tourist guide: The GUIDE project. In *Proceedings of the 6ᵗʰ annual international conference on Mobile computing and networking (MobiCom)*, (pp. 20-31).

Cheverst, K., Mitchell, K., & Davies, N. (2001). Investigating Context-Aware Information Push vs. Information Pull to Tourists. In *Proceedings of MobileHCI'01*,

Dey, A.K., & Abowd, G.D. (2000). CybreMinder: A context-aware system for supporting reminders. In *Proceedings of the International Symposium on Handheld and Ubiquitous Computing* (pp. 172-186).

Dey, A.K., Salber, D., & Abowd, G.D. (2001). A conceptual framework and a toolkit for supporting the rapid prototyping of context-aware applications. *Human-Computer Interaction Journal 16*(2-4), (pp. 97-166).

Dourish, P. (1997). Accounting for system behaviour: Representation, reflection and resourceful action. In Kyng and Mathiassen (Eds.), *Computers and design in context* (pp. 145-170). Cambridge, MA: MIT Press.

Elrod, S., Hall, G., Costanza, R., Dixon, M., & des Rivieres, J. Responsive office environments. *Communications of the ACM 36*(7), 84-85.

Gellersen, H.W., Schmidt, A., & Beigl, M. (2002). Multi-sensor sontext-awareness in mobile devices and smart artefacts. *Mobile Networks and Applications, 7*, 341-351.

Gu, T., Pung, H.K., & Zhang, D.Q. (2004). A middleware for building context-aware mobile services. In *Proceedings of IEEE Vehicular Technology Conference* (pp. 2656-2660).

Häkkilä, J., & Mäntyjärvi, J. (2006). Developing design guidelines for context-aware mobile applications. In *Proceedings of the IEE International*

Conference on Mobile Technology, Applications and Systems.

Hiltunen, K.-M., Häkkilä, J., & Tuomela, U. (2005). Subjective understanding of context attributes – a case study. In *Proceedings of Australasian Conference of Computer Human Interaction (OZCHI) 2005*, (pp. 1-4).

Lamming, M., & Flynn. M. (1994). Forget-me-note: Intimate computing in support of human memory. In *Proceedings of Friend21: International Symposium on Next Generation Human Interface* (pp. 125-128).

Mäntyjärvi, J., & Seppänen, T. (2002). Adapting applications in mobile terminals using fuzzy context information. In *Proceedings of Mobile HCI 2002* (pp. 95-107).

Mäntyjärvi, J., Tuomela, U., Känsälä, I., & Häkkilä, J. (2003). Context Studio—Tool for Personalizing Context-Aware Application in Mobile Terminals. In *Proceedings of Australasian Conference of Computer Human Interaction (OZCHI) 2003* (pp. 64-73).

Mozer, M.C., Dodier, R.H., Anderson, M., Vidmar, L., Cruickshank III, R.F., & Miller, D. The Neural Network House: An Overview. In L. Niklasson & M. Boden (Eds.), *Current trends in connectionism*, (pp. 371-380). Hillsdale, NJ: Erlbaum.

Nielsen, J., & Molich, R. (1990). Heuristic evaluation of user interfaces. In *Proceedings of CHI 1990* (pp. 249-256).

Norman, D. A. (1990). *The design of everyday things*. New York, NY: Doubleday.

Osbakk, P., & Rydgren, E. (2005). Ubiquitous computing for the public. In *Proceedings of Pervasive 2005 Workshop on Pervasive Mobile Interaction Devices (PERMID 2005)*, (pp. 56-59).

Persson, P., Espinoza, F., Fagerberg, P., Sandin, A., & Cöster, R. (2003). GeoNotes: A Location-based information System for Public Spaces. In K. Hook, D. Benyon & A. Munro (Eds.), *Readings*

in Social Navigation of Information Space (pp. 151-173). London, UK: Springer-Verlag.

Schilit, B., & Theimer, M. (1994a). Disseminating active map information to mobile hosts. *IEEE Computer 8*(5), 22-32.

Schilit, B., Adams, N., & Want, R. (1994b). Context-aware computing applications. In *Proceedings of the IEEE Workshop on Mobile Computing Systems and Applications* (pp. 85-90).

Want, R., Hopper, A., Falcao, V., & Gibbons, J. (1992). The Active Badge Location System. *ACM Transactions on Information Systems, 10*(1), 91-102.

Weiser, M. (1991). The computer for 21st century. *Scientific American,* 265(3), 94-104.

KEY TERMS

Context: Any information that can be used to characterize the situation of an entity. An entity is a person, place or object that is considered relevant to the interaction between a user and an application, including the user and applications themselves, and by extension, the environment the user and applications are embedded in.

Context-Awareness: A system is context-aware if it uses context to provide relevant information and/or services to the user, where relevancy depends on the user's task.

Design Guidelines: Guidelines or principles that, when followed, can improve the design and usability of a system.

Interaction Design: The design of the user interface and other mechanism that support the user's interaction with a system, including providing input and receiving output.

Mobile Context-Awareness: Context-awareness for systems or situations where the user and her devices are mobile. Mobility is particularly relevant for context-awareness as the user's context changes more rapidly when mobile.

Usability Risks: Risks that result from the use of a particular technology (in this case, context-awareness) that impact the usability of a system.

This work was previously published in Handbook of Research on User Interface Design and Evaluation for Mobile Technology, edited by J. Lumsden, pp. 205-217, copyright 2008 by Information Science Publishing (an imprint of IGI Global).

Chapter 8.3
Policy–Based Mobile Computing

S. Rajeev
PSG College of Technology, India

S. N. Sivanadam
PSG College of Technology, India

K. V. Sreenaath
Arizona State University, USA

ABSTRACT

Mobile computing is associated with mobility of hardware, data and software in computer applications. With growing mobile users, dynamicity in catering of mobile services becomes and important issue. Polices define the overall behavior of the system. Policy based approaches are very dynamic in nature because the events are triggered dynamically through policies, thereby suiting mobile applications. Much of the existing architectures fail to address important issues such as dynamicity in providing service, Service Level provisioning, policy based QoS and security aspects in mobile systems. In this chapter we propose policy based architectures and test results catering to different needs of mobile computing

INTRODUCTION

Policies are rules that govern the overall functioning of the system. *Policy computing* is used in a variety of areas. *Mobile computing,* with its ever-expanding networks and ever-growing number of users, needs to effectively implement a policy-based approach to enhance data communication. This can result in increasing customer satisfaction as well as efficient mobile network management.

POLICY COMPUTING AND NEED FOR POLICY-BASED MOBILE COMPUTING

Policies in society and organizations are often captured and enforced as laws, rules, procedures, contracts, agreements, and memorandums. Policies are rules that govern the choices of system behavior. A policy is defined as "a definite goal, course or method of action to guide and determine present and future decisions." Security policies define what actions are permitted or not permitted, for what or for whom, and under what conditions. Management policies define what actions need to be carried out when specific events occur within a system or what resources must be allocated under specific conditions. They are widely used for the mobile user whose requirements are dynamic.

Policy-based computing is the art of using policy-based approaches for effective and efficient computing; it is widely used because of its dynamicity. Hence in areas such as mobile computing, policy computing can be effectively used.

Much of the existing network systems' are configured statically (Fankhauser, Schweikert, & Plattner, 1999). In the present-day scenario, the number of mobile/wireless network users increases day by day. With the static systems being deployed, it is very difficult to achieve the needed dynamicity for mobile computing resulting from changing user base. In order to achieve efficient communication for fluctuating user base, policy-based systems need to be implemented in different areas of the existing wireless mobile network infrastructure.

POLICY IN MOBILE COMPUTING

Mobile computing is conducted by intermittently connected users who access network resources that need to escalate with increasing computing needs. Mobile computing has expanded the role of broadcast radio in data communication, and with increasing users, providing quality service becomes a challenging issue. The mobile users must be provided with the best possible service so that the service provider can stay in competition with peer service providers. In order for the best possible service to be provided to the mobile

users, there are certain criteria that should be met. They are:

- The quality of service should be guaranteed.
- There should be effective service-level agreement (SLA) between the mobile user and the service provider.
- Security should be foolproof.

With the existing system (without a policy-based approach), it becomes very difficult to achieve the mentioned criteria. It is very difficult to provide a guaranteed quality of service (QoS), which is also dynamic (not statically configured). Moreover SLA is a very static procedure. Because of the mobility and dynamicity of mobile networks, SLAs also must be made very dynamic. Similarly, security should also be made very dynamic and efficient. To overcome all these shortcomings of the existing system, *a policy-based approach should be used in mobile networks.*

Policy computing can be effectively implemented in mobile networks using policy compilers. Policies can be written in different ways. There are different languages for writing policies that are used for different purposes of specifying policies. In order that the "security policies" be specified, languages such as Trust Policy Language (TPL), LaSCO, and so forth are used. In a similar way, for specifying management-related policies, languages such as Ponder, Policy Maker, and so forth are used. Thus for different scopes of application of policies, specific languages are used.

Policy validation checks a solution's conformance to the policy file. The actual process of policy validation has three primary stages. First, a node or hierarchy change event in Solution Explorer (such as add, drag, or delete event) begins the validation process. Then the validation process maps items discovered in the solution (such as files, references, classes, or interface definitions) to a corresponding Template Description Language (TDL) policy ELEMENT node. Finally, for recognized ELEMENT nodes, the validation process checks the parent ELEMENT for policy compatibility with the child ELEMENT. When the policies are compatible, the validation process applies any ELEMENT-specific policy.

APPLICATIONS OF POLICY COMPUTING

Policy-based management is an over-arching technology for an automated management of networks (Lewis, 1996). Policy-based management is being adopted widely for different domains like quality of service, wireless networks, service-level agreement, virtual private networks (VPNs), network security, and IP address allocation. Therefore policy-based networking configures and controls the various operational characteristics of a network as a whole, providing the network operator with a simplified, logically centralized, and automated control over the entire network. In a wireless/mobile network, events are user and time based. These events are very dynamic in nature in order to provide the best service to the mobile users and also to maximize the profit of the service provider. But most of the existing systems are very static in nature. With the static systems being deployed, it is very difficult to achieve the needed dynamicity for mobile computing. In order to achieve this, policy-based systems need to be implemented in different areas of the existing wireless mobile network infrastructure such as QoS in wireless networks (especially differentiated networks), security, and SLAs.

Policy-Based Architecture for Security

Some of the key issues involved in providing services for wireless networks are (Sivanandam, Santosh Rao, Pradeep, & Rajeev, 2003):

1. **Bandwidth Cost:** Depending upon the number of users connected, the location (e.g., urban or remote), and the type of service (e.g., video, audio, etc.) being offered, dynamic allocation of bandwidth plays an important role.
2. **Limited Memory:** Today's wireless device places constraints on the amount of data that it can hold. Moreover, this limit depends upon the device being used and hence causes greater concern with low memory devices.
3. **Access Cost:** Optimizing the cost (Boertien, Janssen, & Middelkoop, 2001) of accessing and transferring data is more complex in wireless networks than in wired networks. If the number of servers used by a service or the number of services provided by an enterprise increases, then maintaining service consistency would turn out to be a cost factor in itself.
4. **Scalability Requirements:** These requirements force the service provider to think in terms of developing a solution that would support increasing and decreasing the number of services offered by the enterprise.

These constraints adversely affect the process of implementation of wireless/mobile services over the existing architecture. To overcome this, an identity management architecture for a wireless differentiated service schema that could be implemented using LDAP (lightweight directory access protocol) (Hodges & Morgan, 2002), directory structures are constructed.

Policy Warehouse

The concept of differentiated services entitles the maintenance of a large amount of information pertaining to the user (e.g., user names, passwords, services registered, premium amount, etc.) and an efficient quick access mechanism to retrieve the relevant details. This overhead increases when it comes to wireless services. Here, the policy warehouse acts as the information backbone of the service provisioning system. The service provisioning engine contacts the policy warehouse whenever the service provider forwards to it a request from the user, after the right user has been authenticated.

1. **Id-Synch and P-Synch:** The synchronization of user identities and passwords pertaining to a single user is highly crucial in providing a hassle-free connection to services that require subscription to external back-end service providers. This architecture uses Id-Synch and P-Synch mechanisms for identity synchronization and password synchronization respectively.

2. **Meta Directories:** In general, service providers need to maintain a global user profile to uniquely identify a user over the various services provided to him. This information, which mainly comprises a collection of information pertaining to the user sign-on details of various services, is stored in meta directories. This profile makes it easy for the service provisions engine to authenticate the user. The architecture has a provision of compiling as well as retrieving meta directory information.

3. **LDAP Access Engine and Directory Structures:** Information pertaining to the user is stored in lightweight directory structures that can be retrieved using the LDAP. Directory structures are used to store user information because they provide a systematic mechanism for organizing data under a common head like user profiles, user services, user privileges, and so forth that are organized in a hierarchical manner on multiple workstations that are distributed over a network. This not only makes data retrieval fast, querying complexity less, and volume of data storage minimum, but it also makes easy implementation of poli-

cies that depend on the enterprise using the system.

The LDAP engine acts as an interface between the various servers like Id-Synch and P-Synch, and directories like meta directories and the underlying LDAP directory structures. They process the request for data from the higher layers and hand over the appropriate data to the requested application in the required format.

The LDAP directory services are part of the directory-enabled network services (DEN) that provide standard APIs for the access of network objects.

Service Provisioning Mechanism

The service provisioning system can be generally viewed in the following stages:

- **User Login:** In this stage, the user sends his details like User Name, Password, and Chip Index Number to the service provider for authentication.

- **Service Provider:** The Service Provider has to perform the following two actions on a service request:

  1. **Authentication:** The authentication is accomplished using the DSAP (distributed substring authentication protocol) (Sivanandam et al., 2003). This is done by fragmenting the user details into sub-strings and distributing them over a network which is monitored by a central authentication system. When the user is required to authenticate, the protocol fetches the appropriate sub-strings from the network and compares them to the user input. A match signifies a valid user. After this stage, the appropriate user policy is fetched from the policy warehouse using the service provisioning engine.

Figure 1. Policy-based provisioning

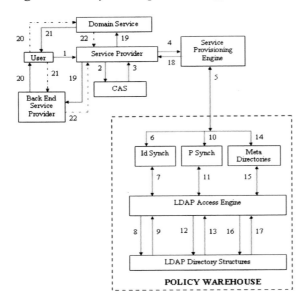

Policy Based Architecture for QoS

The interface to the network device and the information models required for specifying policies are either standardized or being standardized in IETF and DMTF. An architecture for a policy-based QoS management system for Diffserv-based wireless networks, which are based on COPS for interfacing with the network device and on LDAP for interfacing with a directory server for storing policies, is constructed. The Diffserv policies are installed based on role combination assigned to the network device interfaces. The directory access could become a bottleneck in scaling the performance of the policy server, and it can be improved substantially by employing appropriate policy caching mechanisms. The framework considers various QoS parameters in the wireless network and proposes the policy-based architecture for QoS management in wireless networks.

Wireless Network QoS Parameters

The wireless/mobile network is affected by the following QoS parameters:

- **High Loss Rate:** Wireless/mobile networks are characterized by more frequent packet losses because of fading effects. The scheduler may think that a certain DSCP is being satisfied with the required number of packets scheduled, but the receiver is not receiving the packets at the required rate. It will be useful to have feedback from the receiver so that some compensation techniques can be employed. The base station (BS) can better handle compensation of lost bandwidth using this information.

- **Battery Power Constraints:** Current mobile battery technology does not allow more than a few hours of continuous mobile operation. Two of the major consumers of power in a mobile network are the network interface (14%) and the CPU/memory (21%). There-

2. **Providing the Service:** This is the last step of the service provisioning. In this stage, the actual service that the user has requested is granted. The service could be from a back-end service provider or from the main service provider. This detail is an abstraction to the user who undertakes all transactions with the main service provider only. When the user disconnects from the service, intimation is sent to both the back-end service provider and to the main service provider. This has two implications: firstly, the main service provider's load is shared by the back-end service provider, and secondly, the intimation during the connection termination ensures that the main service provider gets the appropriate usage details. This can act as verification of the details that the back-end service provider will submit later.

fore, network protocols should be designed to be more energy efficient (Agrawal, Chen, & Sivalingam, 1999). The mobile device can use the signaling mechanism to periodically send messages about its power level to the BS. The BS can then use this information to dynamically decide packet scheduling, packet dropping, and so forth.

- **Classification of Packets within a Flow:** Present Diffserv (Chan, Sahita, Hahn, & Mc-Cloghrie, 2003) mechanisms treat all packets within a flow identically. Even though a distinction can be made between packets as in-profile or out-of-profile, all in-profile packets are treated the same way. In many situations (e.g., while using layered video), it may be necessary to distinguish packets within a flow. This is because some packets from a flow level could be more important than the others, and a local condition like power level may lead to different treatments of these packets. Thus, the packets within a flow must be made distinguishable, and bits in the TOS field may be used for this purpose. To summarize, the various possible factors needed to make the Diffserv architecture suitable for wireless networks were discussed in this section.

- **Low Bandwidth:** Wireless networks available today are mostly low bandwidth systems. Most of the current LANs operate at 2 Mbps with migration up to 11 Mbps available. However, the available wireless LAN bandwidth is still an order of magnitude less than the typical wired LAN bandwidth of 100 Mbps. This leads to two decisions. First, the signaling protocol should be very simple and highly scalable. It is also better to modify an existing protocol for compatibility with other existing network protocols. Second, the mobile should not be swamped with too much data from a wired sender with higher network bandwidth. This can be handled to a large extent by transport

protocol control, but the problem can be alleviated by handling it partially at the base station. Therefore, mechanisms may be used at the BS to send data to the mobile devices based on current conditions such as channel condition, bandwidth available, and so forth.

Policy-Based QoS

The IETF Resource Allocation Protocol (RAP) working group has defined, among other standards, the policy-based admission control framework, and the common open policy service (COPS) protocol and its extension—COPS for provisioning (COPS-PR). COPS is a simple query protocol that facilitates communication between the policy clients and remote policy server(s). Two policy control models have been defined: outsourcing and provisioning. While COPS supports the outsourcing model, its extension COPS-PR integrates both the outsourcing and provisioning models. The outsourcing model is tailored to signaling protocols such as the resource *reservation protocol* (RSVP) (Braden, Zhang, Berson, Herzog, & Jamin, 1997), which requires traffic management on a per-flow basis. On the other hand, the provisioning or configuration model is used to control aggregate traffic-handling mechanisms such as the Differentiated Services (Diffserv) architecture. In the outsourcing model, when the PEP receives an event (e.g., RSVP reservation request) that requires a new policy decision, it sends a request (REQ) message to the remote policy decision point (PDP). The PDP then makes a decision and sends a decision (DEC) message (e.g., accept or reject) back to the PEP. The outsourcing model is thus PEP driven and involves a direct 1:1 relation between PEP events and PDP decisions. On the other hand, the provisioning or configurations model (Chan et al., 2001) makes no assumptions of such direct one-to-one correlation between PEP events and PDP decisions. The PDP may proactively provision the PEP reacting to external

Figure 2. Policy-based management system architecture

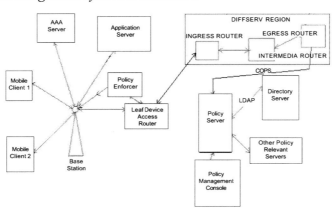

events, PEP events, and any combination thereof (N: M correlation). Provisioning thus tends to be PDP driven and may be performed in bulk (e.g., entire router QoS configuration) or in portions (e.g., updating a Diffserv marking filter).

Architecture of a Policy-Based Management System for a Diffserv-Based Wireless Network

Figure 2 illustrates the architecture of the policy-based management system for Diffserv-based wireless networks. The policy server is responsible for interpreting higher-level policies and translating them into device-specific commands for realizing those policies. For allocating resources on inter-domain links and for implementing SLAs, the policy server (especially the bandwidth broker component) has to communicate with the policy server in the provider.

The policy server is mainly responsible for the following:

*   retrieving relevant policies created by the network administrator through the policy console after resolving any conflicts with existing policies;

*   translating the policies relevant for each PEP into the corresponding policy information base (PIB) commands;
*   arriving at policy decisions from relevant policies for policy decision requests, and maintaining those decision states; and
*   taking appropriate actions such as deletion of existing decision states or modification of installed traffic control parameters in the PEP for any modifications to currently installed policies.

All the policies are stored in the LDAP server. The policy editor (PE) is the entity responsible for creating, modifying, or deleting policy rules or entries in the LDAP server. LDAP protocol provides access to directories supporting the X.500 models, while not incurring the resource requirements of the X.500 directory access protocol (DAP). It is specifically targeted at management applications and browser applications that provide read/write interactive access to directories. It does not have the mechanism to notify policy consumers of changes in the LDAP server. Therefore, it is the responsibility of the policy editor to indicate the changes in the LDAP server, as and when required, using an internal event messaging service. The policy server, in addition to querying the LDAP server, queries other policy-relevant servers such as Certificate server, Time server, and so on.

The policy management client—also referred to as the policy editor—provides a high-level user interface, for operator input translates this input into the proper schema for storage in the directory server and pushes it out to the directory for storage. The authentication, authorization, and accounting (AAA) server is responsible for authentication, authorization, and accounting of the user after the relevant policies have been picked and enforced in the policy enforcers (routers). This AAA server is used by the base station to check if the user is authenticated and authorized for the resource he requests, and to check if he is accounted. The policy enforcer nearer to the base station enforces the policy decisions taken from the policy server. The base station then requests the nearest application server (after policies are enforced) and waits for the response from the application server.

The base station first sends the request to the leaf access router, which then sends it to the ingress router in the region. The ingress router then passes on the requests to the intermediate router. The request passes through the other intermediate routers and reaches the egress router, which sends the request to the policy server through COPS.

Policy-Based Architecture for SLA

Mobile ad hoc networks (MANETs) are autonomous networks operating either in isolation or as "stub networks" connecting to a fixed infrastructure. Depending on the nodes' geographical positions, transceiver coverage patterns, transmission power levels, and co-channel interference levels, a network can be formed and unformed on the fly. Ad hoc networks have found a growing number of applications: wearable computing, disaster management/relief and other emergency operations, rapidly deployable military battle-site networks, and sensor fields, to name a few. The main characteristics of ad hoc networks are:

- **Dynamic Topological Changes:** Nodes are free to move about arbitrarily. Thus, the network topology may change randomly and rapidly over unpredictable times.
- **Bandwidth Constraints:** Wireless links have significantly lower capacity than wired links. Due to the effects such as multiple accesses, multi-path fading, noise, and signal interference, the capacity of a wireless link can be degraded over time and the effective throughput may be less than the radio's maximum transmission capacity.
- **Multi-Hop Communications:** Due to signal propagation characteristics of wireless transceivers, ad hoc networks require the support of multi-hop communications; that is, mobile nodes that cannot reach the destination node directly will need to relay their messages through other nodes.
- **Limited Security:** Mobile wireless networks are generally more vulnerable to security threats than wired networks. The increased possibility of eavesdropping, spoofing, and denial-of-service (DoS) attacks should be carefully considered when an ad hoc wireless network system is designed.
- **Energy Constrained Nodes:** Mobile nodes rely on batteries for proper operation. As an ad hoc network consists of several nodes, depletion of batteries in these nodes will have a great influence on overall network performance. Therefore, one of the most important protocol design factors is related to device energy conservation.

To support mobile computing in ad hoc wireless networks, a mobile host must be able to communicate with other mobile hosts that may not lie within its radio transmission range. Therefore in order for one mobile host in the ad hoc network to communicate with the other not lying in its transmission range, some other hosts in its transmission range should route the packets from the source to the destination host. The conventional routing protocols used in wired networks cannot be effectively used in ad hoc networks. Hence new routing mechanisms are suggested which may be used for routing in ad hoc networks. Routing issues in ad hoc networks are beyond the scope of this chapter and are not considered here.

Since many mobile hosts may be within transmission range of each other, there may be multiple routes for a packet to reach a destination. Therefore the source host should decide which route to use to send the packets to reach its destination. Obviously, the sending host has to decide on the best optimal route before sending its packets towards the destination. Thus, there should be a service level agreement between the source mobile host and the host which routes the packets to the destination host. Moreover there are certain constraints based on the characteristics of the ad hoc network which play a major role in deciding which route is optimal, given there are more routes to reach the destination.

Architectural Framework of the Policy-Based Mobile Ad Hoc Network

MANET is a collection of mobile hosts forming a temporary network without the aid of any centralized administration or standard support services. The architecture for the policy-based SLAs in ad hoc networks is given below. The architecture is designed where at least one host has connectivity with the wired network. In the architecture shown in Figure 3, the policy server is placed in the wired network. Polices are stored in the directory server. The ad hoc 'host1' is within the vicinity of both 'host2' and 'host3'. 'Host4' is not within the transmission region of 'host1'. So when 'host1' wants to send a packet to 'host4', intermediatory hosts, 'host2' and 'host3', help 'host1' with connection establishment.

Assuming that both the host services satisfy the constraints of 'host1', 'host1' must choose a service level agreement among the two. In this case since 'host1' is connected to a base station, which in turn is connected to the wired network having the policy server, 'host1' can query the policy server through the base station and then the leaf access router and edge router. For simplicity we have shown the policy server being connected to the base station through only a few hops. But in practice it may be many hops away from it. Once the request reaches the policy server, it takes appropriate policies from the directory server through the LDAP.

The policy server also communicates with other relevant policy servers such as Time Servers, Certificate Servers, and AAA servers, and validates the host providing service by means of certificates and AAA. The policy server makes the decision on whether the host providing the service is an authenticated one, and his services are authorized with accountability and certificates. Then the policy server based on the higher level polices stored in the directory server chooses an agreement among the available agreements. The decision to choose an agreement from among the available ones may be done giving more weight to those performance metrics which affect the overall performance the most. Over a period of time, the history of the hosts providing the service will be stored; solutions based on a neural network model may be used for finding an optimal solution. Once the policy server chooses an agreement, it sends its reply back to 'host1', which agrees for the service with the appropriate host.

Policy Based E-Supply Chain Management Architecture

Internet-based e-purchases and e-supply chain management are now being widely used. This however has a major disadvantage of very limited mobility and the absence of a dynamic policy that will efficiently manage the entire supply chain.

Figure 3. Architecture of policy-based MANET

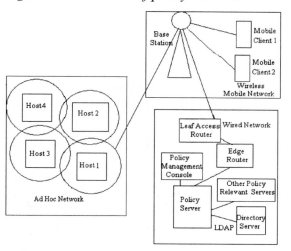

The activities that are required to provision mobile users comprise a surprisingly large number of steps that cross an entire enterprise. Policy setting and implementation, approval workflows, physical resource setup/teardown (provisioning), account maintenance, reconciliation of actual resource assignments with approved user lists, audit, and overall service management are some examples. They are together called policy-based provisioning. An extension to e-purchases through mobile phones using policy-based e-supply chain management is constructed.

Architecture of Policy-Based E-Supply Chain Management

The architectural framework of the e-purchase through policy based e-supply chain management is shown in Figure 4. Mobile customer, policy server, nodes (1-4), and suppliers (1 and 2) form the key elements of the proposed architecture. The mobile consumer requests the policy server of the service provider through the base station. The mobile user's authentication, authorization, and accounting rights are then verified by the AAA server. If the mobile user is found to be an authenticated one and his request for service is

an authorized one, then the policy server fetches the corresponding policies for the user from the directory server through LDAP. The policy server of the service provider is connected to other nodes (Node 1 to Node 4) in the Internet. The nodes of the suppliers such as 'supplier1' and 'supplier2' are also connected to the nodes through the public network (Internet). When the relevant policies are fetched from the directory server, the user's request is sent to an efficient supplier who will supply the product to the mobile customer. The supply chain is made electronic as discussed earlier and is policy based. Once the user's request is sent to an efficient supplier relatively nearby to the customer, the ordered products will be delivered to the mobile customer through the shipping department. The billing of the products purchased is taken into the credit account of the mobile user and is charged along with the mobile phone bill, simplifying user billing and payment. The customer at the end of the month would pay the bill through the electronic account facility available with his existing bank account. Thus the whole process of placing the purchase order, delivering the product through the supply chain, and paying for the product is made electronically, thereby facilitating the customers, who are mostly travelers and tourists.

CASE STUDY

A simulation for the policy-based MANET shown in Figure 3 was performed using the QualNet Network Simulator, using the simplex method to solve the linear program model given below, and using the Ponder Toolkit. The mathematical model is given in the following section.

Mathematical Model

A mathematical model considered for policy-based MANET uses Linear Programming and Simplex Method to solve it. The following perfor-

Figure 4. Framework of e-purchase through policy-based e-supply chain management

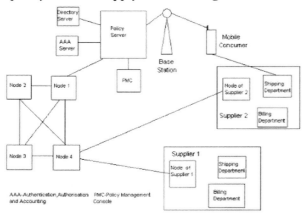

mance metrics that are crucial for effective SLA trading and choice of route are considered in our model: (a) Bandwidth, (b) Delay, (c) Demand, (d) Packet Loss, (e) Congestion, (f) Queuing Delay, (g) Throughput, (h) Buffer Capacity, (i) Battery Consumption, and (j) Mobility. Let,

> T_{ij} = Total (maximum) Bandwidth (channel capacity) available from host i to host j.
> U_{ij} = Bandwidth being used for traffic flow between host i to host j at instant 't'.
> R_{ij} = Reserved bandwidth from host i to host j.

Hence the bandwidth that can be leased to other hosts G_{ij} is given by $G_{ij} = T_{ij} - U_{ij} - R_{ij}$.

Let the required bandwidth—that is, the bandwidth consumed by the host k to reach host j through host i—be RB_{ij}.

And,

> D_{ij} = Delay from host i to host j.
> C_{ij} = Cost of reaching host j through host i.
> F_{ij} = Fraction of bandwidth bought from host i to reach host j.

The objective here is to minimize the cost of reaching host j through other hosts.

$$Minimise \sum_{i,j} F_{ij}C_{ij} \qquad (1)$$

As stated earlier, in the above equation represents the cost hostcharges to reach host through host.

Constraints

There are a set of constraints that define the model. The first constraint is the demand for bandwidth to reach host j through host i; De_{ij} should be less than or equal to the amount of bandwidth host i is ready to offer for cost to reach host j, G_{ij}.

$$DE_{ij} \leq \sum_{i,j} G_{ij} \qquad (2)$$

The following constraints check if the service performance metrics in the service offered by the host i to reach host j fall within the predetermined and pre-calculated boundaries as expected by host k which needs the service. These boundary constants for the performance metrics can also be set dynamically and SLA negotiated accordingly.

Buffer Capacity B_{ij} should not be less than a bearable value given by the constant N=Number of packets that can be buffered.

$$B_{ij} \geq N \qquad (3)$$

The time delay D should be set to a limit expressed by a constant '$p1$'as expected by the 'ISP k' which needs the service. The constant '$p1$' is arrived as derived as follows:

'$p1$' = Propagation Time + Transmission Time + Queuing Delay (+ Setup Time)
Propagation Time: Time for signal to travel length of network
= Distance/Speed of light
Transmission Time = Size/Bandwidth

Therefore, we have

$$D_{ij} \leq p1 \tag{4}$$

Queuing Delay Q_{ij} should not exceed an allowable limit 'p2' expressed as

$$p2 = \frac{D}{2} \times (N-1)$$

where, D = the time delay, N is the Buffer Capacity

$$Q_{ij} \leq p2 \tag{5}$$

The Packet Loss P_{ij} for the service provided should not exceed a maximum limit set as constant 'p3', and Congestion in the channel offered for service Co_{ij} should also be within the acceptable limits represented by the constant 'p4', both of which are arrived at as shown as follows:

T_{min} = Minimum Inter-Arrival Time observed by the receiver.
P_0 = Out of order packet.
P_i = Last in-sequence packet received before P_0.
T_g = Time between arrival of packets P_0 and P_i.
n = Packets missing between P_i and P_0.

If $(n+1)T_{min} \leq T_g < (n+2)T_{min}$, then n missing packets are lost due to transmission errors and hence 'p3'='n'and

$$P_{ij} \leq p3 \tag{6}$$

Else n missing packets are assumed to be lost due to congestion and hence 'p4'='n' and

$$Co_{ij} \leq p4 \tag{7}$$

Throughput TH_{ij} should be greater than or equal to 'p5', which is given by

$$p5 = \{MSS / RTT\} \times C / (\sqrt{p})$$

where,

MSS = Maximum Segment size in bytes, typically 1460 bytes.
RTT = Round Trip Time in seconds, measured by TCP.
p = Packet loss.
C = Constant assumed to be 1.

$$TH_{ij} \geq p5 \tag{8}$$

The jitter J_{ij} should be within the acceptable limit 'p6' given by

$$p6 = p6 + (|D(i-1,i)| - p6)/16$$

given

$$D(i,j) = (R_j - S_j) - (R_i - S_i)$$

where, S_i, S_j are sender timestamps for packets i, j and R_i, R_j are receiver timestamps for packets i, j.

Therefore

$$J_{ij} \leq p6 \tag{9}$$

The Battery Consumption BC_{ij} for the offered service should be within the boundary constant 'p7',

$$BC_{ij} \leq p7 \tag{10}$$

The Mobility Factor M_{ij} which gives the idea of how long the host j will be in the transmission range of host for which packets need to be routed should not be smaller than a particular constant represented by 'p8',

$$M_{ij} \geq p8 \tag{11}$$

This mobility factor M_{ij} plays a crucial role in ad hoc networks because the hosts are all mobile. It may be minutes or in any preferred time unit as the case may be. We generally assume that a mobile which has joined the ad hoc has more probability of staying in the network than the ones which came earlier than that. But the exact nature of the mobility of a host can be predicted only based on past performances of the mobile.

Non-Negativity Constraints

The following are the non-negativity constraints applied in the model:

Cost C_{ij} should always be positive,

$$C_{ij} \geq 0 \qquad (12)$$

Table 1. Performance metrics and other parameters of the hosts

Performance Metrics	Host 1	Host 2	Host 3
Total Bandwidth Allocated (MBps)	3	6	5
Bandwidth Used at Instant (MBps)	2	2	1
Reserve Bandwidth (MBps)	0	1	1
Remaining Bandwidth G_{ij} (MBps)	1	3	3
Demand for Bandwidth to Reach 'host4' (MBps)	1	0	0
Delay (x 10-3/sec)	7	8	10
Packet Loss Factor	7	5	6
Congestion Factor	30 2	0	25
Queuing Delay (x 10-4sec)	8	7	10
Throughput (x 103 Bits/sec)	100	100	90
Buffer Capacity (No. of Packets)	9	10 8	
Battery Consumption (mWh)	-	8	9
Mobility Factor? Minutes	-	25 1	8

Fraction of bandwidth bought from host *i* to reach host *j*, F_{ij} should also be positive,

$$F_{ij} \geq 0 \qquad (13)$$

The bandwidth that can be offered for cost to other hosts by host *i* should be positive,

$$G_{ij} \geq 0 \qquad (14)$$

Given the objective, for example, to minimize the agreement cost along with the performance metrics constraints, the proposed linear programming model solved using simplex method suffices for arriving at a suitable agreement for service with other hosts. There are always cases that the above model will fetch more than one solution if other solutions exist. Hence in such cases the decision of choosing the most appropriate of the available solutions should be taken which is described in the next section.

Table 2. Performance metrics and other parameters of 'host2' and 'host3'

Performance Metrics	Host 2	Host 3
Delay (x 10-3/sec)	2.9	3.1
Packet Loss Factor	0.2	0.3
Congestion Factor	0.3	0.3
Queuing Delay (x 10-4sec)	0.2	0.2
Throughput (x 103 Bits/sec)	4.2	4.2
Buffer Capacity (No. of Packets)	20 1	5
Battery Consumption (mWh)	8	9
Mobility Factor (minutes)	25 1	8
Jitter (x 10-4sec)	3.9	4.1
Fraction of Bandwidth that Can Be Given F_{ij} (MBps)	1	1
Cost C_{ij} ($)	2	6

The test environment has four ad hoc hosts from 'host1' to 'host4', as shown in Figure 3. The total bandwidth, used bandwidth, reserve bandwidth, battery consumption, mobility factor, and other performance metrics of the hosts are tabulated below.

In the simulation test environment, 'host1' needs to communicate with 'host4', which is not in its transmission range. So both 'host2' and 'host3' offer the service to 'host1'. Using the mathematical model proposed, 'host1' decides upon the suitable service among the offers using the SLA trading algorithm (Rajeev, Sivanandam, Sreenaath, & Bharathi Manivannan, 2005) and the mathematical model given previously. Since only the service offered by 'host2' adheres to the performance metric constraints, 'host1' chooses the service offered by 'host2'. All the simulation is done with respect to the packet flow from 'host1' to 'host4'.

The trade for the service is decided by using the simplex method to solve the linear programming model and SLA trading algorithm, by which a feasible solution is obtained. The performance constraints and other parameters of the hosts are given in Tables 1 and 2. According to the constraints given by 'host1' for the required service, the simplex method and SLA trading algorithm are used, and the best bid among the bids offered by the two hosts ('host2' and 'host3') is selected. Since only the bid for the service offered by

'host2' satisfies the constraints of 'host 1', SLA between 'host1' and 'host 2' takes place. The LP model is solved by using the simplex method. As only the trade provided by 'host2' satisfies all the constraints with the objective of minimum cost, the Service offered by 'host2' is agreed upon for trade.

From the performance metrics and the constraints on performance metrics, the objective of minimizing cost is arrived at (see Figure 5 and Table 3). Thus an effective SLA is traded between 'host1' and 'host2', satisfying the constraints on the performance metrics which affect the service.

CONCLUSION AND FUTURE DIRECTIONS

Policy computing can be effectively used in mobile computing in various arenas such as QoS, security, SLA, and e-purchase. The architectural framework demonstrated in the case study gives insight as to how QoS, SLA, and security can be implemented in mobile networks. Policy-based architectures for billing in mobile networks are currently being constructed which could bring transparency in mobile billing with added dynamicity.

Table 3. Original and final value of the objective

Objective	Original Value	Final Value
$\sum_{i,j} F_{ij} G_{ij} C_{ij}$ of 'host2' ($)	12 6	
Cost of 'host2' ($)	4 2	

Figure 5. Objective

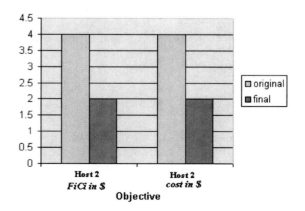

REFERENCES

Agrawal, P., Chen, J. C., & Sivalingam, K. M. (1999). *Energy efficient protocols for wireless networks*. Norwell, MA: Kluwer Academic Publishers.

Braden, R., Zhang, L., Berson, S., Herzog, S., & Jamin, S. (1997). *Resource ReSerVation Protocol (RSVP)—version 1 functional specification*. IETF RFC 2205.

Chan, K. et al. (2001). *COPS usage for policy provisioning (COPS-PR)*. IETF RFC 3084.

Chan, K., Sahita, R., Hahn, S., & McCloghrie, K. (2003). *Differentiated Services quality of service policy information base*. IETF RFC 3317.

Fankhauser, G., Schweikert, D., & Plattner, B. (1999). *Service level agreement trading for the Differentiated Services architecture*. Technical Report No. 59, Computer Engineering and Networks Lab, Swiss Federal Institute of Technology, Switzerland.

Hodges, J., & Morgan, R. (2002). *Lightweight Directory Access Protocol (v3): Technical specification*. IETF RFC 3377.

Lewis, L. (1996). Implementing policy in enterprise networks. *IEEE Communications Magazine, 34*(1), 50-55.

Rajeev, S., Sivanandam, S. N., Sreenaath, K. V., & Bharathi Manivannan, A. S. (2005). Policy-based SLA for wireless ad hoc networks. In *Proceedings of the International Conference on Services Management,* India.

Sivanandam, S. N., Santosh Rao, G., Pradeep, P., & Rajeev, S. (2003). Policy-based architecture for authentication in wireless Differentiated Services using Distributed Substring Authentication Protocol (DSAP). In *Proceedings of the International Conference on Advanced Computing,* India.

This work was previously published in Handbook of Research in Mobile Business, edited by B. Unhelkar, pp. 613-629, copyright 2006 by Information Science Reference, formerly known as Idea Group Reference (an imprint of IGI Global).

Chapter 8.4
Field Evaluation of Collaborative Mobile Applications

Adrian Stoica
University of Patras, Greece

Georgios Fiotakis
University of Patras, Greece

Dimitrios Raptis
University of Patras, Greece

Ioanna Papadimitriou
University of Patras, Greece

Vassilis Komis
University of Patras, Greece

Nikolaos Avouris
University of Patras, Greece

ABSTRACT

This chapter presents a usability evaluation method for context aware mobile applications deployed in semi-public spaces that involve collaboration among groups of users. After reviewing the prominent techniques for collecting data and evaluating mobile applications, a methodology that includes a set of combined techniques for data collection and analysis, suitable for this kind of applications is proposed. To demonstrate its applicability, a case study is described where this methodology has been used. It is argued that the method presented here can be of great help both for researchers that study issues of mobile interaction as well as for practitioners and developers of mobile technology and applications.

INTRODUCTION

Mobile devices are part of many peoples' everyday life, enhancing communication, collaboration, and information access potential. Their vital characteristics of mobility and anywhere connectivity can create new forms of interaction in particular contexts, new applications that cover new needs that emerge, and change the affordances of existing tools/applications.

A case of use of such devices, with particular interest, concerns *public places rich in information* for their visitors, in which mobile technology can provide new services. Examples of such places, are *museums* and other sites of culture (Raptis, Tselios, & Avouris, 2005), *public libraries* (Aittola, Parhi, Vieruaho, & Ojala, 2004; Aittola, Ryhänen, & Ojala, 2003), and *exhibition halls* and *trade fairs* (Fouskas, Pateli, Spinellis, & Virola, 2002). In these places, mobile devices can be used for information collection and exchange, for ad hoc communication with fellow visitors, and for supporting face-to-face interaction.

Usability evaluation of mobile applications is of high importance in order to discover, early enough, the main problems that users may encounter while they are immersed in these environments. Traditional usability evaluation methods used for desktop software cannot be directly applied in these cases since many new aspects need to be taken in consideration, related to mobility and group interaction. Therefore, there is a need either to adapt the existing methods in order to achieve effective usability evaluation of mobile applications or to create new ones. An important issue, that is discussed here, is the *process* and *media* used for recording user behaviour.

Data collection during usability studies is a particularly important issue as many different sources of data may be used. Among them, *video and audio* recordings are invaluable sources for capturing the context of the activity including the users' communication and interaction. It has been reported that in cases of studies that audio and video recordings were lacking, it was not possible to explain why certain behaviour was observed (Jambon, 2006). Recording user behaviour is a delicate process. Video and audio recording must be as unobtrusive as possible in order not to influence the behaviour of the subjects while, on the other hand, the consent of the users for their recording should be always obtained. In addition, questions related to the frame of the recorded scene, viewing angle, and movement of the camera are significant. It must be stressed that there is a trade off between capturing the interaction with a specific device and capturing the overall scene of the activity. For example, often, crucial details may be missing from a video if recording the scene from a distance. Therefore, this video has to be complemented by other sources of related information, like screen captures of the devices used.

In order to conduct a successful usability evaluation, apart from collecting activity data, techniques and tools are needed for analysis of the collected information. In the last years, new usability evaluation techniques have emerged, suitable for mobile applications. Many of these methods focus mainly on user interaction with the mobile device, missing interaction between users, and user interaction with the surrounding environment.

Taking into consideration these aspects, the aim of this chapter is to discuss techniques and tools used first, for collecting data during usability evaluation studies of mobile devices, and then for the analysis of these data. In the process, a combination of a screen capturing technique and some tools that can be used for analysis of data of usability studies are presented.

BACKGROUND

The usability of a product has been traditionally related with the ease of use and learn to use, as well as with supporting users during their interaction with the product (Dix, Finley, Abowd, & Beale, 2003; Schneiderman & Plaisant, 2004). There have been many attempts to decompose further the term and render it operational through attributes and apt metrics. According to ISO 9241-

11 standard, usability is defined as the "*extend to which a product can be used with effectiveness, efficiency and satisfaction in a specified context of use*" (ISO 9241). According to this view, a product's usability is directly related to the *user*, the *task*, and the *environment*. Consequently, usability cannot be studied without taking into consideration the goals and the characteristics of typical users, the tasks that can be accomplished by using the product, and the context in which it is going to be used. Making a step further on defining usability, the same standard suggests three potential ways in which the usability of a software product can be measured:

a. By analysis of the *features of the product* required for a particular context of use. Since ISO 9241 gives only partial guidance on the analysis process, in a specific problem there can be many potential design solutions, some more usable than others.

b. By analysis of the *process of interaction*. Usability can be measured by modeling the interaction with a product for typical tasks. However, current analytic approaches do not produce accurate estimates of usability since interaction is a dynamic process which is directly related to human behaviour that cannot be accurately predicted.

c. By analyzing the *effectiveness and efficiency*, which results from use of the product in a particular context, that is, measuring performance as well as the satisfaction of the users regarding the product.

Having in mind the three perspectives, there is a need for combining methods that capture the specific situation of use in a specific domain. Usability evaluation methods can be grouped in four categories (Nielsen, 1993): *Inspection, user testing, exploratory, and analytic methods.* Many techniques have been devised along these lines and have been extensively used in usability

evaluation of desktop applications. Therefore the first approach in evaluating mobile applications was to apply these existing techniques. Such an approach can be found in Zhang. and Adipat's (2005) survey of usability attributes in mobile applications which identified nine attributes that are most often evaluated: learnability, efficiency, memorability, user errors, user satisfaction, effectiveness, simplicity, comprehensibility, and learning performance. Such an approach is, however, limited, given the special characteristics of mobile devices with respect to desktop environments (Kjeldskov & Graham, 2003).

The mobile applications introduce new aspects to evaluate. The evaluation cannot be limited only to the device (typical scenario in desktop applications) but it must be extended to include aspects of context. The context in which the application is used is highly relevant to usability issues and often bears dynamic and complex characteristics. There is the possibility that a single device is used in more than a single context, in different situations, serving different goals and tasks of a single or a group of users. Also, group interaction, a common characteristic in mobile settings, gives a more dynamic character to the interaction flow of a system and increases the complexity of the required analysis as well as the necessity of observational data.

Along these lines, a new breed of methods for usability evaluation has been proposed (Hagen, Robertson, Kan, & Sadler, 2005; Kjeldskov & Graham, 2003; Kjeldskov & Stage, 2004). The process of selecting appropriate usability attributes to evaluate a mobile application depends on the nature of the mobile application and the objective of the study. A variety of specific measures (e.g., task execution time, speed, number of button clicks, group interactions, seeking support, etc.) have been proposed to be used for evaluation of different usability attributes of specific mobile applications. In the next section problems of data collection during mobile usability studies will be discussed.

Data Collection Techniques

A significant step during a usability evaluation study is to collect appropriate observational data to be analyzed. Hagen, Robertson, Kan, and Sadler (2005) classify the data collection techniques for mobile human-computer interaction in three categories: (a) *Mediated data collection (MDC)*, access to data through participant and technology, *do it*—the user makes himself the data collection; *use it*—data is collected automatically through logs; *wear it*—user wears recording devices that collect the data. (b) *Simulations and enactments (SE)* where some form of pretending of actual use is involved and (c) *combinations* of the above techniques. A review of different techniques of data collection, according to Hagen, Robertson, & Kan (2005) is shown in Table 1.

The data that are collected by these techniques come either directly from the user (through interviews, questionnaires, focus groups, diaries, etc.), by the evaluator (i.e., notes gathered during the experiment, observation of videos, etc.) or by raw data (log files, etc). All types of data need to be analyzed in order to become meaningful. Such data, in most cases, are in the following forms:

- *Log files* which contain click streams of user actions. These data can be derived by the application itself or by an external tool that hooks into the operating system message handler list. The latter case for mobile devices requires many system resources and therefore is not technologically feasible today, even in the most powerful mobile devices, like PDAs.

- *Audio/video recordings* of the users made through various means, like wearable mini cameras and/or audio recorders, static video cameras, operator or remote controlled cameras, from close or a far distance.

- *Screen recordings* by video cameras or by direct screen capturing through software (running on the device) the interaction

Table 1. Existing techniques for data collection used in studies of mobile technology. Adapted from Hagen, Robertson, and Kan (2005). F=Field, L=Laboratory, MDC=Mediated Data Collection, SE=Simulation and Enactments

Method	Description	Site*	Category
Artefacts (e.g. documents)	The use of objects or documents as sources for data collection. They may be objects (or photos of objects) from daily life or documents that users have created with devices being tested.	F	MDC
User Diaries	Users document information about their actions or thoughts, or impressions, often daily, for a period of time. Entries can be open and interpretive, or highly structured depending on the study.	F	MDC
Emulators	Emulators on desktop computers are used to simulate the interface of a potential mobile application.	L	SE
Focus Groups	Small groups of people are facilitated in unstructured discussion about an issue.	F, L	SE
Heuristics	Heuristics, often usability guidelines or design principles are applied by expert users to predict usability problems.	F, L	SE
Interviews	Interviews capture subject data from talking directly to participants. They can be open or structured and conducted in the field (including contextual interviews), online, over the phone and in labs.	F, L	SE
Log File analysis	Use logs are generated automatically (such as internet log files) or from systems specifically developed to capture content data and meta data.	F	MDC
NASA Task Load Analysis	Used in usability testing to determine work load.	F, L	SE
Observation/ Shadowing	Observation is used in field studies to capture use in context and can include, covert observation, participant observation, observing a place, or following a person. Data collection can include note taking, photography, and video.	F	MDC
Online data	Researchers gain access to information about the lives of users, and use practices from websites, forums and mailing lists.	F	MDC
Questionnaires	Quantitative or qualitative questionnaires are used to collect user opinions, feedback in evaluation, create user profiles or collect data about existing use practices. They can be done in person, or via phone or web.	F	SE
Role playing	Users and researchers play out different roles, or act out tasks or scenarios to explore existing and future use concepts	F, L	SE
Scenarios	Scenarios provide information about use situations giving examples of how technologies are used in practice.	F, L	SE
Think-Aloud	Participants describe out loud what they are thinking while they complete tasks using a device or prototype.	F, L	SE

Figure 1. A) Shadowing technique (see also Kjeldskov & Stage, 2004); B) Recording screen with wireless camera (see also Betiol & de Abreu Cybis, 2005)

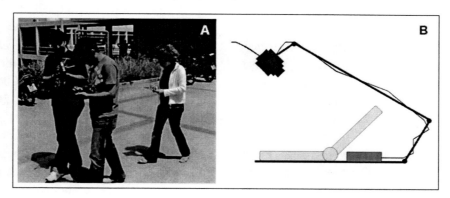

flow in form of screen snapshots. This is a sequence of image representations of the user interface at certain instances that are usually taken at varying frequencies, usually a few snapshots per second. The screen snapshots can be stored either locally on the device (since it is feasible to store a large amount of data in memory cards) or on a central server over a wireless network connection

Screen recordings of mobile devices are invaluable resources that can greatly help evaluators identify usability problems. Various techniques can be used for capturing the screen of a mobile device: One is the recording of the screen by using a mini wireless camera (Figure 1B). It can be very helpful in cases of individual users but it is not suitable in the case of an application that involves beaming actions (e.g., Bluetooth, infrared) and/or interaction with the physical space because it can influence negatively the use of the device and can create obstacles in the infrared beams, sensors, or readers attached to the device (i.e., to an RFID reader). The main advantage of this technique is that the camera records, besides the screen, the movements of the users fingers or stylus, capturing valuable data identifying potential interaction problems (for example, the user hesitates to click something because the interface or the dialogs are confusing).

An alternative technique is the shadowing technique which can effectively work for individual users (Figure 1A). Again, this technique is not suitable for group activities, where the subjects often form groups and move continuously. Even in cases that it is considered possible to record properly, there could be many events missing because of the frequent movements of the subjects or the shielding of the screen by their body and hands.

The direct observation technique has also certain limitations (Cabrera et al., 2005; Stoica et al., 2005) because the observer must distribute his attention to many subjects. In case there are observers available for each user they will restrict the mobility of the users and they will distract their attention when being in so close range. Consequently, all these techniques impose the presence of the observer to the users, thus affecting their behavior.

Another significant issue that directly affects the usability evaluation is related to the location in which the study is conducted. There are many arguments in favour of *field usability studies* (Nardi, 1996; Kjeldskov, Skov, Als, & Hoegh, 2004; Zhang & Adipat, 2005; Kaikkonen, Kallio, Kekalaien, Kankainen, & Cankar, 2005). Comparative studies between laboratory and field evaluation studies have drawn, however, contradictory conclusions. In a recent survey of evaluation studies of mobile technology (Kjeld-skov & Graham, 2003), 71% of the studies were performed in the laboratory, which revealed a tendency towards building systems based on trial and error and evaluating systems in controlled environments at the expense of studying real use of them. So the question of what is useful and what is perceived problematic from a user perspective often is not adequately addressed.

In summary, in order to conduct a usability evaluation of a mobile application/system, there is a need to take into consideration the attributes that are going to be measured, the data collected for these measurements, the location in which the evaluation will take place, and finally, the appropriate tools to analyze them, having always in mind the user and the context of interaction.

Data Analysis

Usability evaluation of mobile applications is more complex than desktop software evaluation since new characteristics such as group activity and the interaction with the surrounding environment need to be taken into consideration. In order to acquire an understanding of group activity and performance, huge amounts of structured and unstructured data of the forms discussed in the previous section need to be collected. These data should capture the activity of subjects, including their movements, facial expressions, gestures, dialogues, interaction with the devices, and objects in the environment. Analysis of these data require special attention on details as well as the context of use, thus it can be a tedious process which can be facilitated by a suitable analysis tool (Benford et al., 2005).

Various tools have been developed to support usability evaluation studies and, in general, to record and annotate human activity. These tools often handle video and audio recordings and synchronize them with text files, containing hand-taken notes. This combination creates a dataset that is rich in information which is then annotated through an adequate annotation scheme, which creates quantitative and qualitative measures of the observed user-device interaction. Typical examples of such tools are: the *Observer XT* (Noldus, 2006), *HyperResearch* (Hesse-Biber, Dupuis, & Kinder, 1991; ResearchWare, 2006), *Transana* (Transana, 2006), *NVivo* (QSR, 2006; Rich & Patashnick, 2002; Welsh, 2002), and *Replayer* (Tennent & Chalmers, 2005). From them, only *Replayer* and *Observer XT* have special provisions for mobile settings. The extra characteristics in evaluation of mobile applications (group activity and interaction with the surrounding space) demand the extended use of multimedia files that thoroughly capture the activity. Thus, there is a need for a tool that combines and interrelates all of the observational data in a compact dataset and gives to the usability expert the ability to easily navigate them from multiple points of view (access in user—device interaction, access in user—space interaction).

All of the tools utilize video sources at a different extend, with the exception of *NVivo* that focuses more in textual sources. *NVivo* allows linking of evaluator's notes with video extracts, without permitting more fine grained handling of video content. On the other hand, *HyperResearch* and *Transana* do support flexible handling of video sources but they do not allow the integration and synchronous presentation of multiple video sources in the same study. Thus, *NVivo*, *HyperResearch*, and *Transana* cannot successfully respond to the extra characteristics of mobile applications. On the other hand, *Replayer* is a distributed, cross platform toolkit that allows the integration of multiple video sources and presents analysis data in various forms such as histograms and time series graphs. Although *Replayer* efficiently supports usability analysis of mobile applications, its failure to handle and to compare data that come from various studies makes it not suitable for cases of multiple studies

Table 2. Characteristics of usability evaluation tools

	Multiple multimedia sources	Aggregated results from multiple studies
Observer XT	☑	☑
HyperResearch		☑
Transana		
NVivo		☑
Replayer	☑	
ActivityLens	☑	☑

in which there is need to aggregate and generalise the findings. On the contrary, *Observer XT* is a powerful commercial tool, widely used in observation studies, that enables the synchronous presentation of multiple video files and also the derivation of overall results about the activity of multiple subjects. Although *Observer XT* meets the requirements of new characteristics of mobile applications, its use requires a prior lengthy training period.

A tool that has been especially adapted for analysis of data from mobile applications' evaluation studies is the *ActivityLens* which attempts to tackle some of the limitations of existing tools. Its main advantage is its ability to integrate multiple heterogeneous qualitative but also quantitative data. It allows the usability expert to directly access the collected data, thus to simultaneously focus on users' movements on the surrounding environment and user-device interaction. To sum up, *ActivityLens* supports analysis of collected data and produces results that cover the overall activity concerning all the participants.

Weitzman and Miles (as cited in Berkowitz, 1997) suggest that a criterion for the selection of an adequate analysis tool is related to the amount, types, and sources of data to be analyzed and the types of analyses that will be performed. In Table 2 a description is provided about how the tools support the extra characteristics of usability evaluation studies of mobile applications.

Data Analysis through ActivityLens

ActivityLens is a tool that embodies features especially designed for usability evaluation of mobile applications. *ActivityLens* is an evolution of the earlier Collaboration Analysis Tool (ColAT) (Avouris, Komis, Margaritis, & Fiotakis, 2004; Avouris, Komis, Fiotakis, Margaritis, & Voyiatzaki, 2005), originally designed for video analysis of collaborative learning activities. It was found particularly suitable for the proposed approach which involves multiple perspectives of the activity, based on different multimedia data.

In *ActivityLens*, all the collected data are organized into *Studies*. An example of a *Study* is the usability evaluation that was conducted in a Historical Cultural museum, described in the next sections. The tool allows *Projects* that belong to a specific *Study* to be defined. A *Project* is defined by the evaluator and can have different perspectives depending on the situation. For example, a *Project* can be defined as the set of data gathered from various groups over a set period of time, or it can be defined as a set of data of a specific group of users.

These data can be video and audio files, log files, images, and text files, including hand-taken notes of the observers. *ActivityLens* supports almost all the common video and audio file formats including file types that are produced by mobile devices such as .mp4 and .3gp. The

Figure 2. The usability evaluation tool—ActivityLens

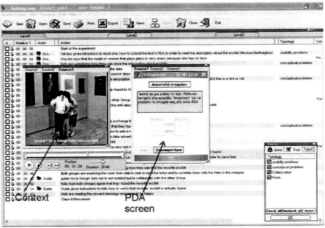

Figure 3. Event filtering tool through ActivityLens

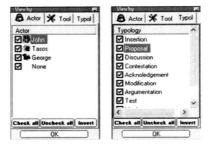

observed activity is reported in an XML log file. This file describes the activity as a set of events, reported in sequential order, following this typical structure:

<event id>, <time-stamp>, <actor>, <tool>, <event-description>, <type of event>, <comments of evaluator>

The log file events are presented via a simple spreadsheet view in order to be easily accessible for inspection and annotation. In addition, *ActivityLens* permits integration and synchronization of the collected multimedia files.

All the data can be reproduced and annotated on-the-fly in order to highlight interesting events.

An example is shown in Figure 2, in which an overview video and a PDA screen are synchronized and annotated. The annotation of the observed events is based on a classification scheme defined by the evaluator. For example, an evaluator is analyzing videos that describe the activity of a group of students that try to solve a problem. During the activity some students propose ways to solve the problem and argue about it. Thus, one representative type of event could be defined as "Proposal." For usability studies, an evaluator can define typologies based on usability attributes, concerning for instance, user errors, comments expressing subjective view, and events marking successful completion of tasks.

Figure 4. Sources of observational data

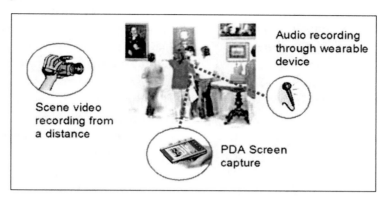

ActivityLens provides the evaluator with the ability to reduce the huge amount of collected data through an event filtering mechanism. This feature is of high importance because it helps the evaluator to focus on interesting sequences of events and makes them emerge from the "noise." The evaluator is allowed to define criteria for specific Actors, tools used, and types of events or any combination between them. For example, the evaluator can choose to view all occurrences of "Proposals" made by "George" or "John." The criteria selection tool is shown in Figure 3.

PROPOSED METHODOLOGY

Based on the outlined data and analysis requirements, in this section a methodology suitable for usability evaluation of mobile applications is proposed. This method is proposed for applications deployed in places like museums, libraries, and so forth, in which groups of users interact among themselves and with the environment, in various ways. These semi-public spaces represent 'living organisms' that project, in a visible and tangible form, the various facets of information. For example, in a museum such applications assist the visitors in discovering and acquiring knowledge. A museum can be characterized as an ecology (Gay & Hebrooke, 2004) that is

constituted by two main entities, the exhibits and the visitors, populating the same space. Items of the collection are exhibited to visitors, who react by discovering them in a way that is, at a large extent, influenced by the surrounding space. Also, visitors usually interact with each other, for example, because they comment the exhibits independently from the use of technology. This methodology involves, initially, the preparing study phase, the recording activity phase, and then the analysis of the activity.

Preparing the Study

Usually, activities that are expected to take place in semi-public spaces are desirable to be conducted in the field. For example, visitors inside a museum enjoy an experience that cannot be fully reproduced inside a laboratory. Therefore, the evaluator needs to conduct a study in a representative place, which should be adapted accordingly without disturbing its normal operation. Issues to be tackled are related with technological restrictions (e.g., wireless network infrastructure), recruitment of an adequate number of typical users, the extent of the study, and so forth. Consequently, it is evident that the preparation phase of the evaluation is a very important one, as it builds the foundation for a subsequently successful study.

Recording Activity Phase

A prerequisite in such environments is the low level of activity interference by the observers in order to minimize the behavioral change caused to the participants by the uncomfortable feeling of being observed and thus "disorienting the balance" in the ecology. The proposed recording activity includes an innovative combination of existing data gathering techniques in order to achieve the considered goal. The sources of data (Figure 4) include: (a) screen recordings of the mobile devices, (b) audio recordings using wearable recorders, (c) video recordings from the distance, where the camera is operated by an operator or preferably by remote control, and as complementary source (d) interviews and questionnaires to the users. A brief discussion of the process of collecting these data is included next.

(a) Screen Grabbing on the Mobile Device

In order to tackle problems related to the application nature (collaboration, interaction with the environment) it is proposed that the mobile device also be used as a screen recording device. The collected information can be in the form of screen-shots or aggregated in a low frame-rate video. The main requirement for a mobile device to become a screen recording device is that it must run a multitasking operating system in order to allow a background process to run in parallel with the main application. At the current technological status, this is the case for most mobile devices (PDAs and smart phones), as the main operating systems are multitasking: Symbian OS, Windows Mobile, Palm OS (version 6.0 onwards), Java OS, and so forth. Also, the needs of the market drove the mobile devices to handle large amounts of data that have to be consulted, edited, and updated by the user while speaking, browsing, watching TV, and so forth. As a result, mobile devices evolved from a single process, sequential to multitasking,

and obtained increased storage capacities which permit the users to store a lot of information on them. Therefore, a mobile device can capture, by a parallel process, the screen and either save the pictures on their memory or send them directly to a server via a wireless connection.

A prototype application that is suitable for the Pocket PC/Windows Mobile environment has been developed and runs in parallel with the application which has to be evaluated. It captures screen snapshots and stores them on the device at a predefined time interval. In the tests, a compressed quarter VGA (240x320) screen shot was at most 32 KB that at a rate of 4 per second lead to a needed storage of about 450 MB/hour. It must be stressed that far better compression rates can be achieved by using video encoders.

The decision to grab the screen with a steady frequency and not per number of events, that would make sense in order to stop recording when the device is not used, was imposed by the technical current limitation: the scarce support for global system hooks on the Windows Mobile operating system. The lack of support is due to the fact that such hooks can critically affect the performance of the device.

(b) Audio Recording with Wearable Devices

Audio can capture dialogs between users that express difficulty in interacting with the application and the environment, or disagreement. Audio recordings can often reveal problems that users do not report during interviews or questionnaires.

The audio recordings from the inbuilt microphone of the video camera are sometimes not very useful due to the noise and to the fact that usually the dialogues are in a low voice. Also, the distance between the subject and the camera does not allow recording of good quality sound. The ideal solution would be that the mobile device itself could record both the screen and the audio. Unfortunately, this is not feasible because of several reasons:

- The performance of the device degrades significantly by having two background processes running simultaneously, the one related to screen grabbing, discussed in (a) and the one to audio recording.
- The sounds that are produced by the device itself, in most cases, cover any other sound in the surrounding environment (i.e., a narration played back covers the dialogue.
- The storage might be a problem. Depending on the audio quality and compression used, 1 hour of recorded sound can take from 50 MB to 700 MB.

For these reasons, it seems that the most suitable solution is to use a wearable audio recorder that can store several hours of sound. These devices are very light; they weight less than 50 grams, including the battery. The user can wear it with the help of a neck strap or put it in a pocket and adjust a clip microphone. The wearable audio recorders guarantee that rich information concerning the dialogs between the subjects will not be lost, collaborating and interacting with the application and the environment.

(c) Discrete/Unobtrusive Video Recording

To complement the dialogs and the screen recordings, it is necessary to capture, in video, the ensemble. From this video, recording the context of the events, the social interactions between the group members (peers) and/or between groups can be depicted. In order to decrease as much as possible the level of obtrusion, the camera must be preferably maneuvered through remote control (allowing zoom and angle changes) or at least by a cameraman that will keep a large enough distance from the activity in order not to disturb the users. Often, many video recordings may need to be

Figure 5. Recording and analysis phases of proposed methodology: Interesting incidents are observed in the media files and are cross-checked for better understanding. These incidents are analyzed in terms of device and activity usability issues.

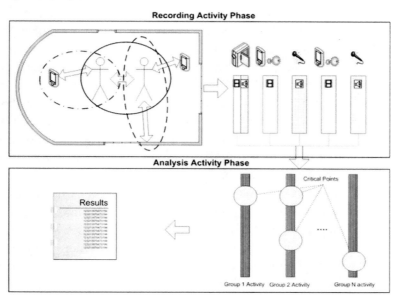

made from various angles, distance, or focusing in different aspects. These may be mixed in a single video stream if adequate equipment is used, or, more often, may be kept as separate sources of information. By studying these video recordings the evaluator can obtain a clear idea about the place in which the activity took place.

(d) Interviews and Questionnaires

Considering that the sources constitute the objective information, the users' subjective view through interviews and questionnaires also need to be obtained. Through these sources, which vary depending on the situation, someone can formulate results regarding *user's satisfaction, learning performance,* and so forth; attributes sometimes difficult to obtain simply through observation.

Analysing Activity Phase

The purpose of the analysis is to identify instances of use of the devices and the infrastructure, which identify usability problems of the technology used. Analysis of recorded activity of groups in semi-public spaces is not a simple process. Researchers have not only to focus just on the devices but to take into account more complicated issues concerning the interaction between groups, the interaction between peers in a certain group, and the interaction with the surrounding space. This analysis has to be meticulously performed in order to cover the above issues. During analysis all the collected sources that describe the group activity have to be combined and iteratively inspected. Initially, a quick inspection of recorded activity helps usability experts to isolate the segments that need thorough analysis. Then, detailed inspection of these segments is required to interpret the observed interaction and depict the usability problems. This process can help usability experts to detect certain critical points of interaction that can be further examined in order to measure their

frequency and dispersion between groups and to be clear how they affect the use of mobile applications. The proposed methodology concerning the recording and analysis process can be seen in Figure 5.

EVALUATING USABILITY OF A COLLABORATIVE CONTEXT AWARE EDUCATIONAL GAME

An example of a study in which the proposed technique was applied was a usability evaluation of a collaborative mobile learning application supported by PDAs in a cultural-historical museum (Tselios et al., 2006). The study involved 17 students of the 5th-grade of an elementary school (11 years old) who were invited to visit the museum and use the prototype of an educational application that was temporarily installed there. All the students were familiar with the use of mobile phones but they had no former experience with PDAs. Furthermore, most of them described themselves in a pre-study questionnaire, as users of desktop computer systems on a daily basis.

The study took place in two of the museums' halls in which portraits and personal objects of important people of the local community were exhibited. First, a short introduction to the activity was provided by a member of the research team who undertook the role of the guide. The educational activity was designed in a way that students were motivated to read information about these important people and collaboratively search in order to locate a specific exhibit according to the activity scenario. The children were divided in two groups and each group consisted of two teams of 4 or 5 children each. Each group participated in a different session for approximately 1 hour.

In order to achieve the scenario's goal, each team was provided with a PDA equipped with a RFID tag reader. They used this equipment to locate hints that were hidden inside textual descriptions of the exhibits. These were obtained by scanning the exhibit RFID tags. The students could store the hints it in a notepad of the PDA. After collecting all or most of the hints the teams were encouraged to share their hints, through beaming, to each other.

Then the students, using the found information, had to locate a specific-favorite exhibit which matched the description provided by the hints. When two teams agreed that they had found the favorite exhibit, they checked the correctness of their choice by scanning with both PDA's the RFID tag. A correct choice was indicated by the system with a verification message while a wrong one suggested a new search. When the study was over each student was requested to answer a set of questions related to the group activity in the museum.

Preparation of the Evaluation Study

During the preparation of the study the museum was contacted and the permission to run the evaluation study was obtained. The space of the museum was examined well in advance (e.g., for determining wireless network setup options) and afterwards a small scale pilot was run in a simulated environment in order to check the suitability of the technological infrastructure. In order to ensure the participation of subjects, a school in the vicinity of the museum was contacted and participation of a school party was requested for the study.

Collecting Data

In order not to miss important contextual information, three video cameras were used in this study. Two of them were steadily placed in positions overlooking the halls while the third one was handled by an operator who tenderly followed the students from a convenient distance. One student per team wore a small audio recorder in order to capture the dialogues between them, while interacting with the application and the environment. Furthermore, snapshots of the PDA screens were captured during the collaborative activity and stored in the PDA's memory. After the completion of the study, the guide, who was a member of the evaluator team, had an interview with the students, asking them to provide their opinion and experiences from the activity in the museum; while back at school a week later, their teacher asked them to write an essay describing their experience.

Figure 6. A) Instance of user—RFID tag interaction problem. B) and C) Photos from the collaboration activity inside the museum

Analysing Data with ActivityLens

In order to analyse all the collected data according to the proposed methodology, ActivityLens, that has already been effectively used in similar studies was used (Cabrera et al., 2005; Stoica et al., 2005).

The main reasons that ActivityLens was used among the discussed tools was its capacity of organizing observations into Studies (collection of projects) and its ability to present multiple perspectives of the whole activity (by integrating multiple media sources). Although Observer XT provides even more capabilities than ActivityLens, the choice of ActivityLens seemed to fit better the specific use case since its use did not require a long training time. In addition, ActivityLens permits easy access to the activities of the subjects recorded in different data sources.

Three usability experts, with different levels of experience, analysed the collected data in order to increase the reliability of the findings. Initially, a new *ActivityLens Study* including four projects (each project concerns the observations of a team) was created. The integrated multimedia files were extensively studied and the most interesting situations were annotated. It must be clarified that it was not wanted for the behaviour of each individual team member to be studied but wished that the performance of the whole team be evaluated. The performed analysis through ActivityLens revealed several problems related to the children's interaction with the device and the overall setting, given the surrounding physical space and groups.

Several problems were identified when the students interacted with the handheld devices.

The analysis indicated that almost all the groups could not successfully scan the Exhibits tags in their initial attempts and get information about the exhibits. The RFID tags were located underneath each exhibits label. Since the users had no clear indication of where to place the tag scanner, some of them experienced difficulties

interacting with them. Also, there was an unexpected delay in the scanning process between tag and PDA (the PDA needed about 2 seconds to scan the tag). While from the scene, video recording, it seemed that the user was repeatedly scanning the same label, combining this with the PDA screen recording gave the real reason of this behavior—repeated unsuccessful tries to scan the tag. The users learned after a few frustrating attempts that they should target the center of the tags and hold the device for a couple of seconds.

A problem that troubled a specific group was the use of a scrollbar in the textual description of the exhibits. The users were not familiar with the procedure of scrolling on a PDA and they repeatedly discussed it amongst themselves. This problem was identified through the combined use of the audio and screen recording and was not visible from the scene video.

An unexpected problem was related to the content of some exhibits descriptions. They contained the word "hints" which confused the children and they were not sure if this was or was not a hint that they could add to the notepad. This was spotted from the complementary use of the overview video with the dialogue audio recordings. The problem was overcome by asking the help of the guide.

With the use of ActivityLens many problems that were related to the interaction with the physical space were managed to be detected. The most important one was that some of the exhibits tags were placed on the walls in such positions that they were not accessible by short students. In Figure 6 an instance of this problem is shown.

Another interesting element that was made clear through the students' dialogues and the videos was that in a certain area of the room an exhibit inspired fear to some of the children (e.g., a faceless piano player). Particularly, one student was clearly afraid to get near the puppet and said to the other members: "I am not going near her. She is very scary!!! Look at her, she has no face!" This situation made the team avoid that area, which contained exhibits with useful information for the activity.

The children that participated in the study often expressed their concern about being delayed in their play due to the presence of other museum visitors (at a certain point an independent school party crowded the hall). Through the audio it was obvious that the kids expressed their frustration because they were delayed in playing the game and the visitors, because they were disturbed by the kids. These problems escape from the traditional usability analysis that focuses only on the device, because they contain the interaction between the user and the surrounding physical space.

The third dimension of the evaluation concerned investigation of the collaborative nature of the activity and the learning performance. An interesting observation was that by having two teams searching for hints at the same time, and the fact that one of the teams was more successful than the other, constituted a powerful motivation for the second team to search for hints. This was observed from the complementary scene video (pinpointing the event) and the dialog recordings (exclamations, etc.). Also, that some kids were too excited in using the PDAs and did not allow anyone else to use them was observed. Thus, disputes over use of the device influenced negatively the team spirit. From the audio streams, the disappointment of the kids that were not allowed to use the device were managed to be spotted.

Regarding the learning performance through the audio files and the PDA's screen it was found that one team was not reading the descriptions to locate the hints but they were searching for the parentheses that indicated the existence of a hint. It must be said that the solution with the parentheses and not colored text was adopted because it was wanted that those specific situations be avoided, but this did not actually work in all teams. In the future version, the hints will be visible only when the users click on them inside the description of the exhibits.

The results are also based on a study of questionnaires, independently of the ActivityLens analysis. In this point, the limitation of ActivityLens in analyzing user questionnaires has to be underlined. This weakness is a matter of further development and research.

In order to have a general view about the educational value of the activity when the children returned to their classrooms, they wrote an essay in which they reported on the museum experience. The teacher's view after going through these texts was that almost all the kids that participated in the activity learned something meaningful in a funny and enjoyable way. However, a more systematic study on these issues should involve a more quantitative experimental approach through a pre and post-test questionnaire and a control group.

CONCLUSION

This chapter has presented a brief overview of usability evaluation techniques for mobile applications, including collection of multiple observational data and their analysis. Due to the growing use of mobile devices, it is evident that there is a need for established techniques that support the collection and analysis of data while conducting usability evaluations. Since there are considerable differences between desktop and mobile environments, researchers are obliged to develop and fine tune these new techniques. Through this chapter a methodology for evaluating mobile applications focusing on collection and use of observational data was proposed. The proposed methodology was demonstrated through a usability study of an educational game in a Historical Museum.

The proposed recording activity technique can be characterized as unobtrusive regarding the users and allows evaluators to study the activity in conditions as close as possible to the typical conditions of use of the application, through various perspectives. The ActivityLens tool was used for analysis of the collected data which facilitates interrelation and synchronization of various data sources and was found particularly useful since the collected data were of particularly high volume and often a finding was based on a combination of data sources. The methodology revealed usability problems of the application as well as issues about collaboration and interaction with the environment that would not be easy to discover in the laboratory and without the combined use of the multiple media data.

Studies that take place in semi-public spaces and involve groups of people have to tackle various problems. In most cases the willingness of people but also the availability of spaces is difficult to be guaranteed for the long periods of time. Researchers that conduct such studies have to be as unobtrusive as possible to the users and pay special attention in order to minimize interference with the environment.

A limitation of the proposed approach is that it requires the users to carry light equipment (audio recorders) and also that a screen capturing software had to be installed in the mobile devices. However, these limitations did not inhibit the users to act naturally and recreate a realistic but controlled context of use. The typical studies of the proposed approach lasted a short time and thus, it is difficult to measure long term usability aspects like memorability and long term learning attitudes. It is still under investigation how to extend this technique to long term mobile usability studies involving different contexts of use.

What is however, missing from the story is an analysis scheme that can describe user interaction with the surrounding physical and information space and metrics that map usability attributes. Such a scheme would describe usability as a set of attributes that refer to interaction with the device, interaction with the space, and group interactions. This scheme could be supported by a tool like ActivityLens which facilitates easy navigation of the collected media data, allowing creation of pointers to incidents in the data, justifying the calculated

values of the usability attributes. Definition of such a scheme should however, be the result of a wider research community process.

REFERENCES

Aittola, M., Parhi, P., Vieruaho, M., & Ojala, T. (2004). Comparison of mobile and fixed use of SmartLibrary. In S. Brewster & M. Dunlop (Eds.), *Proceedings of 6th International Symposium on Mobile Human-Computer Interaction (Mobile HCI 2004)* (pp 383-387). Berlin: Springer.

Aittola, M., Ryhänen, T., & Ojala, T. (2003). SmartLibrary—Location-aware mobile library service. In L. Chittaro (Ed.), *5th International Symposium on Human-Computer Interaction with Mobile Devices and Services (Mobile HCI 2003)* (pp. 411-416). Berlin: Springer.

Avouris, N., Komis, V., Fiotakis, G., Margaritis, M., & Voyiatzaki, E. (2005). Logging of fingertip actions is not enough for analysis of learning activities. In *Proceedings of AIEDs Workshop on Usage Analysis in learning systems*. Retrieved February 27, 2007, from http://lium-dpuls.iut-laval.univ-lemans.fr/aied-ws/.

Avouris, N., Komis, V., Margaritis, M., & Fiotakis, G. (2004). An environment for studying collaborative learning activities. *Journal of International Forum of Educational Technology & Society, 7*(2), 34-41.

Benford, S., Rowland, D., Flintham, M., Drozd, A., Hull, R., Reid, J., Morrison, J., & Facer, K. (2005). Life on the edge: supporting collaboration in location-based experiences. *Proceedings of the SIGCHI conference on Human Factors in computing systems CHI 2005* (pp. 721-730). New York: ACM Press.

Berkowitz, S. (1997). Analyzing qualitative data. In J. Frechtling & L. Sharp Westat (Eds.), *User-friendly handbook for mixed method evaluations*.

Retrieved February 27, 2007, from http://www.ehr. nsf.gov/EHR/REC/pubs/NSF97-153/start.htm

Betiol, H. A., & de Abreu Cybis, W. (2005). Usability testing of mobile devices: A comparison of three approaches. In M. F. Costabile & F. Paterno (Eds.), *Proceedings of IFIP TC13 International Conference on Human-Computer Interaction (INTERACT 2005)* (pp. 470-481). Berlin: Springer.

Cabrera, J. S., Frutos, H. M., Stoica, A. G., Avouris, N., Dimitriadis, Y., Fiotakis, G., & Demeti, K. (2005). Mystery in the museum: Collaborative learning activities using handheld devices. In M. Tscheligi, R. Bernhaupt, & K. Mihalic (Eds.), *Proceedings of the 7th International Conference on Human Computer Interaction with Mobile Devices & Services (Mobile HCI 2005)* (pp. 315-318). New York: ACM Press.

Dey, A. (2001). Understanding and using context. *Personal and Ubiquitous Computing Journal, 5*(1), 4-7.

Dix, A., Finley, J., Abowd, G., & Beale, R. (2003). *Human-computer interaction* (3rd ed.). Hertfordshire: Prentice Hall.

Fouskas, K., Pateli, A., Spinellis, D., & Virola, H. (2002). *Applying contextual inquiry for capturing end-users behaviour requirements for mobile exhibition services*. Paper presented at the 1st International Conference on Mobile Business. Athens, Greece.

Gay, G., & Hebrooke, H. (2004). *Activity-centered design. An ecological approach to designing smart tools and usable systems*. Cambridge, Massachusetts: MIT Press.

Hagen, P., Robertson, T. & Kan, M. (2005). *Methods for understanding use of mobile technologies*. Technical Report. Retrieved September 20, 2006, from http://research.it.uts.edu.au

Hagen, P., Robertson, T., Kan, M., & Sadler, K. (2005). Emerging research methods for understanding mobile technology use. In *Proceedings of the 19th Conference of the Computer-Human Interaction Special Interest Group (CHISIG) of Australia on Computer-human interaction: Citizens online: Considerations for today and the future OzCHI 2005* (pp. 1-10). New York: ACM Press.

Hesse-Biber, S., Dupuis, P., & Kinder, T. S. (1991). HyperRESEARCH, a computer program for the analysis of qualitative data with an emphasis on hypothesis testing and multimedia analysis. *Qualitative Sociology, 14,* 289-306.

Jambon, F. (2006). Reality testing of mobile devices: How to ensure analysis validity? In *Proceedings of CHI 2006 Workshop on Reality Testing: HCI Challenges in Non-Traditional Environments*. Retrieved February 27, 2007, from http://www.cs.indiana.edu/surg/CHI2006/WorkshopSchedule.html

Kaikkonen, A., Kallio, T., Kekalaien, A., Kankainen, A. & Cankar M. (2005). Usability testing of mobile applications: A comparison between laboratory and field testing. *Journal of Usability Studies, 1*(1), 4-16.

Kjeldskov, J., & Graham, C. (2003). A review of Mobile HCI research methods. In L. Chittaro (Ed.), *5th International Symposium on Human-Computer Interaction with Mobile Devices and Services (Mobile HCI 2003)* (pp. 317-335). Berlin: Springer.

Kjeldskov, J., & Stage, J. (2004). New techniques for usability evaluation of mobile systems. *International Journal of Human-Computer Studies, 60,* 599-620.

Kjeldskov, J., Skov, M. B., Als, B. S., & Hoegh, R. T. (2004). Is it worth the hassle? Exploring the added value of evaluating the usability of context-aware mobile systems in the field. In S. Brewster & M. Dunlop (Eds), *6th International Symposium on Mobile Human-Computer Interaction (Mobile HCI 2004)* (pp 61-73). Berlin: Springer.

Nardi, B. (1996). Studying context: a comparison of activity theory, situated action models, and distributed cognition. In B. Nardi (Ed.), *Context and consciousness: Activity theory and human-computer interaction* (pp. 69-102). Cambridge, Massachusetts: MIT Press.

Nielsen, J. (1993). *Usability engineering.* London: Academic Press.

Raptis, D., Tselios, N., & Avouris, N. (2005). Context-based design of mobile applications for museums: a survey of existing practices. In M. Tscheligi, R. Bernhaupt, & K. Mihalic (Eds.), *Proceedings of the 7th international Conference on Human Computer interaction with Mobile Devices & Services (Mobile HCI 2005)* (pp. 153-160). New York: ACM Press.

Rich, M., & Patashnick, J. (2002). Narrative research with audiovisual data: Video intervention/prevention assessment (VIA) and NVivo. *Int. Journal of Social Research Methodology* 5(3), 245-261.

Schneiderman, B., & Plaisant, K. (2004). *Designing the user interface: Strategies for effective human-computer interaction* (4th ed.). Boston: Addison Wesley.

Stoica, A., Fiotakis, G., Cabrera, J. S., Frutos, H. M., Avouris, N. & Dimitriadis, Y. (2005, November). *Usability evaluation of handheld devices: A case study for a museum application.* Paper presented at the 10th Panhellenic Conference on Informatics (PCI2005), Volos, Greece.

Tennent, P., & Chalmers, M. (2005). Recording and understanding mobile people and mobile technology. In *Proceedings of the 1st International Conference on E-social science.* Retrieved February 27, 2007, from http://www.ncess.ac.uk/conference_05.htm/papers/

Tselios, N., Papadimitriou, I., Raptis, D., Yiannoutsou, N., Komis, V., & Avouris, N. (2006). *Design for mobile learning in museums.* To appear in J.

Lumsden (Ed.), *Handbook of User interface design and evaluation for mobile technology.* Hershey, PA: IGI Global.

Welsh, E. (2002). Dealing with data: Using NVivo in the qualitative data analysis process. *Forum Qualitative Social Research Journal,* 3(2). Retrieved February 27, 2007, from http://www.qualitative-research.net/fqs-texte/2-02/2-02welsh-e.htm

Zhang, D., & Adipat, B. (2005). Challenges, methodologies, and issues in the usability testing of mobile applications. *International Journal of Human-Computer Interaction, 18*(3), 293-308.

KEY TERMS

ActivityLens: A usability analysis tool used to support usability studies for mobile and collaborative applications analyzing multiple media data.

Context: Any information that can be used to characterize the situation of an entity. An entity should be treated as anything relevant to the interaction between a user and an application, such as a person, a place, or an object, including the user and the application themselves. (Dey, 2001).

Context Aware: A device, a system, or an application that has the ability to sense aspects of context and change its behaviour accordingly.

Data analysis tool: A software package that supports extracting meaningful information and conclusions from collected data.

Data Collection: The process of gathering raw or primary specific data from a single source or from multiple sources.

Screen Recording: The operation of capturing the output of a devices' screen.

Semi-Public Space: A place which is public to people and imposes a set of common, and universally acceptable rules regarding their behaviour i.e. a museum, library, theatre.

Usability Evaluation: The process of assessing the usability of a given system or product.

This work was previously published in Handbook of Research on User Interface Design and Evaluation for Mobile Technology, edited by J. Lumsden, pp. 997-1013, copyright 2008 by Information Science Publishing (an imprint of IGI Global).

Chapter 8.5
Mobile Design for Older Adults

Katie A. Siek
University of Colorado at Boulder, USA

ABSTRACT

The global population of older people is steadily growing and challenging researchers in the human computer interaction community to design technologies to help them remain independent and preserve their quality of life. Researchers are addressing this challenge by creating assistive technology solutions using information appliances, such as personal digital assistants and mobile phones. Some have questioned whether older people can use information appliances because of age related problems. This chapter discusses work related to designing, implementing, and evaluating mobile applications for the aging. A discussion about what researchers should consider during the design process for information appliances shows the unique challenges posed by this population.

INTRODUCTION

Our world population is aging. The United States National Institute of Health estimates that the global older adult[1] population grows by 795,000 each month. They project that by 2030, the global older population will grow by 847,000 per month (Kinsella & Velkoff, 2001). In response to this increase, researchers in human computer interaction, social sciences, and ubiquitous computing communities are developing applications to help older people live independent and productive lives. Researchers use *information appliances* (Norman, 1999), such as personal digital assistants (PDAs) (Carmien, DePaula, Gorman, & Kintsch, 2004; Coroama & Rothenbacher, 2003) and mobile phones (Helal, Giraldo, Kaddoura, & Lee, 2003), to create *assistive technologies* for older people.

We contend that older adults can use information appliances if the physical and virtual interfaces are designed to meet their varying needs. Some may argue that older adults do not use information appliances and thus, researchers do not have to adjust designs for this population. However, a recent report in the United Kingdom revealed that 49% of older adults own a mobile phone and of that group, 82% make one or more calls per week (Office of Communications [OfCom], 2006). Thus, older adults are using information appliances, but they do encounter numerous problems, such as font and icon readability and interface complexity issues, discussed in greater detail in the background section.

Other people argue that since younger adults use information appliances now, they will not have a problem using similar technology in the future. Indeed, 82% of all United Kingdom residents own a mobile phone, whereas only 36% of people over 75 years old own a mobile phone (Office of Communications [OfCom], 2006). However, we know that (1) as people age their physical and cognitive abilities do not remain constant and (2) the *digital divide* is still present; factors such as age, socioeconomic status, and disabilities affect individuals' access to technology. Although *walk-up-and-use* systems are becoming more prevalent in our everyday lives, we cannot assume that by giving older people new technology, they will be able to easily interact with the device and application. We must work together now to create a set of guidelines to help inform the design and development of future technologies for older people to avoid problems associated with *technology determinism* (Warschauer, 2003).

In this chapter, we discuss issues that must be addressed when designing information appliance interfaces for older adults. We begin by highlighting design related work with older people and technology - traditional computers and information appliances. We then discuss best practices for conducting user studies with older populations and design issues to consider when developing applications and devices. We conclude the chapter with ideas for future work and challenges to the design, interaction, and technical communities.

BACKGROUND

We discuss how older people interact with traditional computers and information appliances in this section. The related work delves into design and interaction studies because interactions, physical and cognitive, have a major influence on design. Researchers have looked at how older populations interact with traditional desktop computers. Researchers are just beginning to look at how older populations interact with information appliances.

There has been a proliferation of information appliances designed for the general public, including PDAs, mobile phones, remote controls, digital cameras, digital music players, and game playing devices. The interfaces to these vary considerably, suggesting there may be variable age-related performance effects. Hence, when creating applications for older populations, designers must consider age-related abilities such as vision, dexterity, coordination, and cognition. Researchers have discovered that within older populations, there are noticeable differences in abilities, and that different design methodologies, such as universal design (Abascal & Civit, 2001) and user sensitive inclusive design (Newell & Gregor, 2001) should be used. Here we discuss some of the research that has been done to better understand older populations' interaction with technology.

Older People and Traditional Computers

Bernard, Liao, and Mills (2001) found that older people could read faster with a larger, more legible 14-point san serif font on websites. Researchers at

Georgia Tech studied how multimodal feedback (sound, touch, visual effect) could assist participants with varying vision problems perform basic mouse tasks (drag and drop). They found that all groups performed better when sound was added; however, groups performed the best when all three modal feedbacks were used (Jacko, Scott, Sainfort, Barnard, Edwards, Emery, et al., 2003).

A number of recent studies focused on the ability of older populations to use PC input devices (Chaparro, Bohan, Fernandez, & Choi, 1999; Charness, Bosman, & Elliott, 1995; Laursen, Jensen, & Ratkevicius, 2001; Smith, Sharit, & Czaja, 1999). The studies showed that older people completed tasks slower than younger groups. Charness et al. (1995) evaluated control key, mouse, and light-pen input devices and found older people preferred the light pen, followed by the mouse and control keys.

Smith et al. (1999) and Laursen et al. (2001) found older people made more mistakes than younger people and had difficulty with fine motor control tasks such as double clicking. Chaparro et al. (1999) found older people performed "point and click" and "click and drag" tasks slower than younger people, but with the same amount of accuracy. The researchers believed the reason that older people were slower was because of reduced fine motor control, muscle strength, and pincher strength associated with older age.

Older People and Information Appliances

Most of the human computer interaction studies on older adults and technology focus on the usability of traditional desktop computers. The usability of information appliances will be scrutinized more carefully as pervasive computing technology applications become more widespread. Researchers are already assessing the needs of older people with respect to mobile phones.

Maguire and Osman (2003) found that older people primarily considered mobile phones as a way to assist in emergencies, whereas younger people saw mobile phones as a way to interact socially. Older people were interested in small phones with large buttons and location aware systems. More specifically, older women were interested in finding the nearest retail shop that met their needs with location aware systems, whereas older men wanted to know how to get places with various forms of transportation. Abascal and Civit (2001) looked at the pros and cons of older adults using mobile phones. They found that older adults liked the safety and increased autonomy mobile phones gave them. But, they were primarily concerned about social isolation and loss of privacy by using a mobile phone. Sri Hastuti Kurniawan (2006) found that older women felt safer with a mobile phone. Unlike younger counterparts, older women wanted brightly colored, bulkier phones with an antenna so it would be easily identifiable in a cluttered purse.

Ziefle and Bay (2005) looked at the cognitive complexity of older adults using mobile phones. They found that older adults performed just as well as younger adults on less cognitively complex mobile phones. They also reported that as the mobile phone interaction became more complex, older participants' performance suffered. Irie, Matsunaga, and Nagano (2005) created a mobile phone for elders by relying heavily on speech input technologies to help decrease complexity and input methods.

Most of the findings in these studies for mobile phones can apply to PDAs as well; however, the needs assessments differ because PDAs have larger physical interfaces and different input mechanisms. The lack of research in the area of PDA technology use by the older adults prompted Darroch, Goodman, Brewster, and Gray (2005) to evaluate a suitable font size for older people who needed to read text on a PDA screen. They found older people preferred reading 12-point font on PDAs, but could read fonts as small as 10 points. The authors pointed out that the lower resolution of their PDA screen could account for the smaller font size preferred by participants than what Bernard and colleagues had previously reported. We looked at how older adults physically interacted with PDAs. We found that older adults had no problem pushing buttons, identifying icons, voice recording, or barcode scanning. Similar to the Darroch study, we found that although older participants preferred to read icons 25-mm large, they could read icons less than 15-mm large (Siek, Rogers, & Connelly, 2005).

Researchers must take into consideration what drives older adults to adopt new technologies for assistive applications to help the target population. Melenhorst, Rogers, and Caylor (2001) found that older adults must understand the benefits of information appliances and alternative communication mediums before they will consider the necessary training to use new technology. In addition, researchers found that for older adults to adopt a new technology, they must feel the technology is useful, convenient, safe, and simple to use, especially in older adults with varying cognitive and physiological abilities (Smither & Braun, 1994).

The findings from this body of research suggest that older people can use information appliances; however, designers and researchers must look at these findings to help inform their designs. More specifically, researchers must look at the physical device capabilities, interface design, and interaction techniques.

MAIN FOCUS OF THE CHAPTER

In this chapter, we broadly define older adults as people over 65 years old. It is difficult to define an ideal older adult because of the variability in older populations' abilities affected by age, illness, and cognitive or physiological decline. Thus, when designing for older populations, it is important to carefully define the target population, recruit older adults who meet the defined criteria, conduct meaningful requirements gathering and user

studies, and design *prototypes* with older adults in mind. Here we discuss each of these items in more detail from our experiences in developing assistive applications for older adults.

Recruiting Older Target Populations

The first thing designers and researchers must figure out is what type of older population they would like to target. Will the application or device be for older people with cognitive impairments? Will it be for older people with physical disabilities? Or will the design be for *all* older people? Eisma and colleagues (Eisma, Dickinson, Goodman, Mival, Syme, & Tiwari, 2003) recommend bringing in older people early on in the design process to assist with requirements gathering and prototype development. They found that the different backgrounds of older people and designers mutually inspired the group to create realistic aims for the project. Older people on the design team can help answer questions specific about the abilities of the targeted population. Researchers must keep in mind that if the design is for all older people, the target population will have to be large enough to test people with varying physical, mental, and social abilities.

Researchers typically post fliers, e-mail calls for participations on mailing lists, and recruit participants from their work or university. This may not be the best way to find a pool of older adult participants. Older participants may not have the same *social networks* as the researchers. Thus, researchers should branch out and connect with community centers, religious groups, veteran meetings, assisted living centers, disability support groups, alumni associations, or adult communities to recruit an older diverse population. Typically, researchers can set up a meeting with the activities coordinator, technology group, or outreach liaison to meet older adults.

I would have no need for one of these, so I don't have to touch it. [PDA handed to audience mem-

ber] But, what if I break it? [Grabs PDA more confidently after researcher says she does not have to worry about breaking it. Pushes a few buttons on the screen.] Well look at that – I could show pictures to my friends.

– Audience member speaking to presenter after recruiting presentation

Similar to any participant population, older adults want to know what is expected of them and what the researcher will do with the data. When recruiting older participants, it is easiest to volunteer to give a presentation about the intended study that includes why the research is being done, what type of person you are looking for (e.g., user profile data), what the participant will have to do, and how the data will be used. The researchers can field questions from the audience to assuage future participants' concerns. Presentations are also the perfect time to hand out preliminary questionnaires to audience members and schedule future meetings for *focus groups, interviews,* or user studies. If participants are expected to use technology that may be unfamiliar to them, bring along the information appliance and let audience members play with the technology after the presentation. Emphasize that you are not testing the participants, but the device or application, and that the device or application cannot be broken with simple interactions. Guided hands-on interactions can change a person's view of the technology as shown in the audience member quoted previously.

Meeting with Older Adults

Designers and researchers will inevitably have to meet with the older adults in their target population during requirements gathering and user studies. There has been quite a bit of research (Eisma et al., 2003; Kurniawan, 2006; Zajicek, 2004) that looks into the best way to meet with older adults. Focus groups and semistructured interview ses-

sions are the most popular meeting methods for requirements gathering and user studies. In this section, we briefly summarize the pros and cons of each method and give tips for best practices.

I have my walking group at 9, craft group at 10:30, doctors at 11:30, lunch at 1 ...

– Participant and facilitator attempting to schedule another meeting time

A common misconception is that older adults have plenty of time to meet with designers and researchers because they may be retired or work fewer hours. However, researchers may quickly find that some older adults have equally busy schedules. Taking notes about what each person is interested in based on the person's schedule can give insight into how the information appliance would fit into the person's everyday life. The quote about scheduling a meeting shows the participant's varied activities. Would the information appliance always be with her/him during the study? If so, how would she/he carry it when attending each meeting? If not, how can we remind her/him to bring the information appliance to only certain activities? We found that older adults with lower social-economic status have busy schedules too because they were more likely to have chronic illness or responsible for caring for family members.

Participant 1: I do not understand what you are saying. I have to see your lips!

Participant 2: I cannot see the screen because of glare.

– Participants' comments during a focus group

Focus groups typically allow researchers to get peoples' opinions, test ideas for specifications, evaluate prototypes, and learn more from the group by spontaneous discussions. Researchers are divided on how beneficial focus groups are when working with older adults. Zajicek (2004) found that focus groups with over three older people are challenging because of hearing impairments, visual impairments, cognitive abilities, and the ability to follow a conversation. Kurniawan (2006) reported no problems and found that focus groups with over three older people tended to work together and help with *cooperative learning* exercises.

For prototypes that run on information appliances, we found focus groups challenging because of screen glare problems and complex interactions. Information appliances are small; thus, when trying to show a feature or explain an interaction, it is difficult to show it to all participants at once. We have issued each participant an information appliance in focus groups, with multiple researchers on hand to help the facilitator explain concepts, interface components, and interactions. This method allows the participants to see the proposed application and associated small interface components. It also gives the participants the chance to interact with the device and see how input methods are different for information appliances than with traditional desktop computers. Participants typically talked with the facilitator or to the people next to them to compare what they saw and discuss what they thought. Unfortunately, this type of focus group requires more time, preparation, and coaching by researchers. In addition, time must be set-aside for the group to discuss their ideas about the information appliance or application.

Alternatively, we have projected the interface or device onto a larger viewing surface so everyone sees the screen and can discuss the issue at hand. Participants were more likely to talk openly and start new discussions about interface components. The latter method allowed us to guide the discussion more efficiently, but it did not give the participants' the same realistic feel for the interface with smaller buttons and less-controlled

interactions as the former method. Designers will have to take into consideration the focus group interaction method to receive appropriate feedback from participants.

Interviews allow the facilitator to work one-on-one with a participant and ask more in-depth questions, or evaluate applications and devices more carefully. We found that we get the most detailed information about interface usability during semistructured interviews with accompanying task-centered user studies. The interview typically is quieter and has fewer distractions for the older user. In addition, the older user has a chance to interact with the device without worrying what others may think of him for not knowing how to do something on the information appliance.

My daughter thinks I am not smart because I cannot use a computer. But you know what—my daughter is not as smart as she thinks she is. One time when she was twelve, she came home from school and...

– Participant comment during interview

Our main problem with interviews, and sometimes with focus groups, is keeping on schedule. Older participants are more likely to share stories with the facilitator about their feelings towards technology when interacting in a one-on-one session. This rich data is useful, but there is a fine balance between keeping the conversation going and making sure the conversation does not diverge too much from the subject at hand, as shown in the previous quote. Another problem we encountered is that older people are more determined to finish each task than their younger counterparts, and will spend extra time to complete the tasks. We found that one-on-one interviews typically lasted one third longer than when working with younger participants.

Figure 1. Example of icon sizes older adults can view (preferred size and smallest viewable size) on a PDA

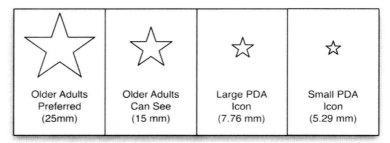

Physical Interfaces

In this section, we discuss some basic guidelines for the physical design of information appliances based on related work and our experiences. We found that older populations are interested in somewhat larger, more colorful physical devices and input components, although designers must find a balance between size and the perception of size.

When researchers conduct ethnographic studies or conduct studies where technology is discussed, but may not be necessarily used for data analysis, we find a persistent theme; most older adult populations want larger information appliances and input components (e.g., buttons, track wheels, etc.). A larger, bulky information appliance is easier to find, identify, and hold in one hand. Larger input components allow for quicker input. Indeed, a study found that older populations would prefer less overall functionality in exchange for larger buttons (Kurniawan, 2006). In terms of output, older adults would prefer to see a screen with more colors or contrast rather than have a larger screen.

In contrast, when studies have participants interact with the information appliance, they find that bigger is not always better. For example, participants in our studies were worried that their large fingers would press more than one button on an information appliance. The participants soon found that their perception of size was unfounded; they were able to interact with the smaller interface components (Siek et al., 2005). Another study found that older populations with specific physical ailments, such as paralysis, preferred smaller information appliances so they could be tucked into pockets easier (Eisma et al., 2003).

Since older populations are so diverse in abilities, it is difficult to create a strict guideline that specifies criteria of older adults who can use the information appliance. Instead, we have adopted an informal method of bringing information appliances to recruitment meetings and watching how older people interact with the devices. When we give an individual an information appliance, we collect her/his preliminary questionnaire and record comments about how she/he interacted with the device. After the recruitment meeting, the design team meets to discuss the interactions and questionnaire data to make correlations. Occasionally, we invite a clinician or an older adult to help us make conclusions about criteria needed to use the information appliance.

Virtual Interfaces

Similar to physical information appliance design, older adults are interested in the size of interface components and text. In addition, they prefer more common terminology to assist with interactions. Something that has not been studied with information appliances is cognitive interactions and interactions with small widgets and interface components. In this section, we briefly discuss virtual interface guidelines that should be considered when designing information appliance applications for older people.

Older populations typically prefer larger fonts (e.g., 12-point font) (Darroch et al, 2005; Kurniawan, 2006) and icon sizes (e.g., 25mm) (Siek et al., 2005), as shown in Figure 1, but can read much smaller fonts (e.g., 10-point font) and icon sizes (e.g., 15mm). Design teams should take this information into consideration if they prefer to display interface information with text and icons. An application can be more appealing to older adults by using their font and icon size preferences; however, excess scrolling could make the application too complex. Indeed, we have found older populations have difficulty understanding the concept of scrolling on traditional computer Web browsers.

Besides the size of icons, older populations prefer realistic, picture-quality renderings to portray information in icons (Siek et al., 2005). Older participants prefer more detailed icons because the details helped them identify the function of the icon more efficiently.

Audience member 1: Why do I have to press Start to turn off my computer?

Audience member 2: Why do I have to press an apple to turn off my computer?

– Audience members' questions after recruiting presentation

Terminology used in virtual interfaces and user guides are often confusing to the general public. We found older users are more likely to voice their concerns and confusion about terminology. As the previous quote shows, audience members asked simple questions about the Windows and Apple desktop interfaces. At first it stumped the

researcher; the reason why we press start and an apple symbol is because we always have. But just because we always have does not mean it is correct. If you would like to turn off your computer and in affect *end* all programs, why would one press start? These questions quickly prompted others to voice their concerns about e-mail and cell phone terminology. Researchers have documented older adults confusion about three-letter acronyms (e.g., SMS, MMS, etc.) and mobile phone terminology (e.g., What is a cell? What is roaming if I am always moving with a mobile phone?).

In this section, we described best practices that helped us and our fellow researchers develop successful information appliance applications for older adults. Since the older adults could use the applications and adopted them in their everyday lives, we assume these practices will help other researchers. We discuss in the next section future research directions for interface input components and interactions with these components. Research in this area will provide practitioners with guidelines to make consistently successful design decisions for information appliances.

FUTURE TRENDS

Information appliances are relatively new technologies, and mobile applications geared strictly towards older adult populations are only beginning to emerge. Researchers will continue to develop assistive applications for elders because of increases in the global older adult population. We must continue to address the issues proposed in this section to help further develop a guideline for information appliance development for older populations.

Researchers know how large common text and icons should be. We must look at how older populations use standard interface component widgets. Can they use standard size widgets with decreased fine motor skills? How large should the widget be?

I can only text people on my mobile phone if they text me first. I just push the reply button. I do not understand how to use the address book or how to enter people's names.

– Participant during interview

Cognitive interactions and interface complexity have been studied with traditional computers and Web sites. Currently, researchers have not delved into these issues for information appliances. Since information appliances have smaller screens and limited input capabilities, there will naturally be more interface screens and with it, increased complexity. As the participant noted in the quote, text messaging on mobile phones requires the user to input data from multiple sources (e.g., address book or alphanumeric key strokes) and send the message. However, once someone has sent a text message, it is easier to push one button and reply to the message. This interaction pattern could be a motivator for future research. How can we use this idea of one button interaction or precached contact data to increase communication mediums for older adults?

Interactions between the physical device and interface components are another area that must be researched for older adults to effectively use information appliances. For example, Charness and colleagues found that older adults had difficulties with traditional computer mouse and directional keyboard input because of varying fine motor control skills and the mapping between lateral movements with the mouse and the coordinate system on the screen. They found that light pens were optimal for older adults (Charness et al., 1995). In terms of information appliances, PDA screen input is similar to a light pen for optimal input. Despite this connection, designers must take into consideration that older adults may not have the fine motor control needed to select the standard, tiny interface components on PDA screens. In addition, current mobile phones pose an even bigger challenge, given the directional key presses needed to scroll and input information. It would be interesting to study if having these interactions close to the screen and on the same coordinate plane, such as in information appliances, will affect older peoples' perception of ease with information appliance input.

Along with standard interface development, researchers must strive to diversify the pool of older participants in their studies. Most studies summarized in this chapter worked with educated older populations. Indeed, recruitment from private assisted-living communities is fairly easy because the older adults who live in the community are educated and curious about technology. But a pessimistic view of the future may be that with such a large, ever growing population of older adults, the people who cannot afford private care will be monitored remotely by information appliances and *context aware* systems. If we create design guidelines and information appliance systems tested by people who are comfortable with technology, then we are leaving out the population who may need to use this technology one day. Researchers and designers must try to diversify their user pools by looking at education and socioeconomic status of their participants.

CONCLUSION

In this chapter, we looked at current research conducted with older adult populations using traditional desktop computers and information appliances. Research in the area of interface design for older adults is deficient because information appliances are relatively new, and design of assistive applications for older adults is just beginning to mature. We discussed issues and best practices that must be addressed when designing for information appliances. More specifically, we looked at the diversity of older adults, recruiting target populations, meeting with older adults in focus groups and interviews, and physical and virtual interface design considerations. We feel these best practices are useful for researchers and the general practitioner because of our success with developing applications for older adults. Researchers and designers must strive to diversify their older adult target populations and consider people with different physical, cognitive, and emotional abilities. In addition, people from varying socioeconomic groups must be considered for the study to see how computing experience affects performance with information appliances.

REFERENCES

Abascal, J., & Civit, A. (2001). Universal access to mobile telephony as a way to enhance the autonomy of elderly people. In *Proceedings of the 2001 EC/NSF Workshop on Universal Accessibility of Ubiquitous Computing: Providing for the Elderly* (pp. 93-99). New York, NY: ACM Press.

Bernard, M., Liao, C. H., & Mills, M. (2001). The effects of font type and size on the legibility and reading time of online text by older adults. In *CHI '01 Extended Abstracts on Human Factors in Computing Systems* (pp. 175-176). New York, NY: ACM Press.

Carmien, S., DePaula, R., Gorman, A., & Kintsch, A. (2004). Increasing workplace independence for people with cognitive disabilities by leveraging distributed cognition among caregivers and clients. *Computer Supported Cooperative Work, 13*(5-6), 443-470.

Chaparro, A., Bohan, M., Fernandez, J., & Choi, S. (1999). The impact of age on computer input device - Psychophysical and psychological measures. *International Journal of Industrial Ergonomics, 24*(5), 503-513.

Charness, N., Bosman, E. A., & Elliott, R. G. (1995). *Senior-friendly input devices: Is the pen mightier than the mouse?* Paper presented at the 103rd Annual Convention of the American Psychological Association Meeting, New York.

Coroama, V., & Rothenbacher, F. (2003). The chatty environment - Providing everyday independence to the visually impaired. In *UbiHealth 2003*.

Darroch, I., Goodman, J., Brewster, S. A., & Gray, P. D. (2005). The effect of age and font size on reading text on handheld computers. In *Lecture Notes in Computer Science: Human-Computer Interaction - Interact 2005* (pp. 253-266). Berlin/Heidelberg, Germany: Springer.

Eisma, R., Dickinson, A., Goodman, J., Mival, O., Syme, A., & Tiwari, L. (2003). Mutual inspiration in the development of new technology for older people. In *Proceedings of INCLUDE 2003* (pp. 7:252-7:259). London, United Kingdom.

Helal, S., Giraldo, C., Kaddoura, Y., & Lee, C. (2003, October). Smart phone based cognitive assistant. In *UbiHealth 2003*.

Irie, T., Matsunaga, K., & Nagano, Y. (2005). University design activities for mobile phone: Raku Raku PHONE. *Fujitsu Sci. Tech. J., 41*(1), 78-85.

Jacko, J. A., Scott, I. U., Sainfort, F., Barnard, L., Edwards, P. J., Emery, V. K., et al. (2003). Older adults and visual impairment: What do exposure times and accuracy tell us about performance gains associated with multimodal feedback? In *Proceedings of the SIGCHI Conference on Human Factors in Computing Systems* (pp. 33-40). New York, NY: ACM Press.

Kinsella, K., & Velkoff, V. A. (2001). *An aging world: 2001* (U.S. Census Bureau, Series P95/01-1). Washington, DC: U.S. Government Printing Office.

Kurniawan, S. (2006). An exploratory study of how older women use mobile phones. In *Proceedings of UbiComp 2006: Ubiquitous Computing* (pp. 105-122). New York, NY: ACM Press.

Laursen, B., Jensen, B. R., & Ratkevicius, A. (2001). Performance and muscle activity during computer mouse tasks in young and elderly adults. *European Journal of Applied Physiology, 25*, 167-183.

Maguire, M., & Osman, Z. (2003). Designing for older inexperienced mobile phone users. In *Proceedings of HCI International 2003* (pp. 22-27), Mahwah, New Jersey: Lawrence Erlbaum Associates.

Melenhorst, A.-S., Rogers, W. A., & Caylor, E. C. (2001). The use of communication technologies by older adults: Exploring the benefits from the user's perspective. In *Proceedings of the Human Factors and Ergonomics Society 45ᵗʰ Annual Meeting* (pp. 221-225).

Newell, A. F., & Gregor, P. (2001). Accessibility and interfaces for older people - A unique, but many faceted problem. In EC/NSF *Workshop on Universal Accessibility of Ubiquitous Computing: Providing for the Elderly*.

Norman, D. (1999). *The invisible computer: Why good products can fail, the personal computer is so complex, and information appliances are the solution.* Boston: MIT Press.

Office of Communications. (2006). *Media literacy audit: Report on media literacy amongst older people.* London, United Kingdom: OfCom.

Siek, K. A., Rogers, Y., & Connelly, K. H. (2005). Fat finger worries: How older and younger users physically interact with PDAs. In *Lecture Notes in Computer Science: Human-Computer Interaction - Interact 2005* (pp. 267-280). Berlin/Heidelberg, Germany: Springer.

Smith, M. W., Sharit, J., & Czaja, S. J. (1999). Age, motor control, and the performance of computer mouse tasks. *Human Factors, 41*(3), 389-396.

Smither, J. A., & Braun, C. C. (1994). Technology and older adults: Factors affecting adoption of automatic teller machines. *The Journal of General Psychology, 121*(4), 381-389.

Warschauer, M. (2003). Demystifying the digital divide. *Scientific American*, 42-47.

Zajicek, M. (2004). Successful and available: Interface design exemplars for older users. *Interacting with Computers, 16*, 411-430.

Ziefle, M., & Bay, S. (2005). How older adults meet complexity: Aging effects on the usability of different mobile users. *Behaviour and Information Technology, 24*(5), 375-389.

KEY TERMS

Assistive Technologies: Applications and devices that pair human computer interaction techniques and technology to enhance the quality of life for people with various special needs.

Context Aware Systems: Technology embedded into our environments that communicates location, action, and other variables to help monitor the environment or individual.

Cooperative Learning: A method that allows individuals with different abilities to work together to improve their understanding of a subject.

Digital Divide: The gap between groups of people who do and do not have access to information technology.

Information Appliances: Electronic devices that allow people to send and receive various types of media (e.g., PDAs, mobile phones).

Focus Groups: A small group of selected participants who are asked questions about what they think about a specific topic or product (e.g., prototype); participants are free to discuss and build on what other participants say.

Interview: A participant is asked a series of questions by a facilitator to learn the participant's personal thoughts about a topic or product (e.g., prototype). Facilitators ask more open-ended questions in semistructured interviews and adapt future questions based on participants' feedback.

Prototype: A software or paper-based system that has a subset of the final application functionality; integral part of software development that allows researchers to get feedback from users before developing a fully functional system

Social Network: Connections between individuals with personal and professional relationships. Often the strength of the connections and influences of relationships are taken into account.

Technology Determinism: Idea that by introducing technology, people will understand and be able to use it.

Walk-Up-and-Use: Technologies that allow people to use the device or application without previous training or instruction (e.g., bank machines, self check-out kiosks at stores).

ENDNOTE

[1]   Older people are defined here as 65 years old and over.

This work was previously published in Handbook of Research on User Interface Design and Evaluation for Mobile Technology, edited by J. Lumsden, pp. 624-634, copyright 2008 by Information Science Publishing (an imprint of IGI Global).

Chapter 8.6
Design for Mobile Learning in Museums

Nikolaos Tselios
University of Patras, Greece

Ioanna Papadimitriou
University of Patras, Greece

Dimitrios Raptis
University of Patras, Greece

Nikoletta Yiannoutsou
University of Patras, Greece

Vassilis Komis
University of Patras, Greece

Nikolaos Avouris
University of Patras, Greece

ABSTRACT

This chapter discusses the design challenges of mobile museum learning applications. Museums are undoubtedly rich in learning opportunities to be further enhanced with effective use of mobile technology. A visit supported and mediated by mobile devices can trigger the visitors' motivation by stimulating their imagination and engagement, giving opportunities to reorganize and conceptualise historical, cultural and technological facts in a constructive and meaningful way. In particular, context of use, social and constructivist aspects of learning and novel pedagogical approaches are important factors to be taken in consideration during the design process. A thorough study of existing systems is presented in the chapter in order to offer a background for extracting useful design approaches and guidelines. The chapter closes with a discussion on our experience in designing a collaborative learning activity for a cultural history museum.

INTRODUCTION

Use of mobile devices spreads in everyday human activities. These devices offer portability, wireless communication and connectivity to information resources and are primarily used as mobile digital assistants and communication mediators. Thus, it is no surprise that various attempts to use mobile appliances for learning purposes have been reported either inside or outside school (Roschelle, 2003). The term *mobile learning* or *m-learning* has been coined and concerns the use of wireless technologies, portable appliances and applications in the learning process without location or time restrictions. Practitioners' reports (Perry, 2003; Vahey & Crawford, 2002) and scientific findings (Norris & Soloway, 2004; Roschelle, 2003; Zurita & Nussbaum, 2004) communicate promising results in using these applications in various educational activities. The related bibliography proposes various uses of mobile appliances for learning. These Activities might concern access and management of information and communication and collaboration between users, under the frame of various learning situations.

A particular domain related to collaborative learning is defined as the support provided towards the educational goals through a coordinated and shared activity (Dillenbourg, 1999). In such cases, peer interactions involved as a result of the effort to build and support collaborative problem solving, are thought to be conducive to learning. On the other hand, traditional groupware environments are known to have various technological constraints which inflict on the learning process (Myers et al., 1998). Therefore, mobile collaborative learning systems (mCSCL) are recognized as a potential solution, as they support a more natural cooperative environment due to their wireless connectivity and portability (Danesh, Inkpen, Lau et al., 2001). While the mobility in physical space is of primary importance for establishing social interaction, this ability is reduced when interacting through a desktop system. It is evident that, by retaining the ability to move around it is easier to establish a social dialogue and two discrete communication channels may be simultaneously established through devices: one physical and one digital. Additionally, a mobile device can be treated as an information collector in a lab or in an information rich space (Rieger & Gay, 1997), as a book, as an organizing medium during transportation or even as a mediation of rich and stimulating interaction with the environment (i.e., in a museum). Effective usage of mobile appliances has been reported in language learning, mathematics, natural and social sciences (Luchini et al., 2002).

Furthermore, various technological constraints need to be taken in consideration during the design of activities which involve mobile devices. Such an example is the small screen, which cannot present all the information of interest while the lack of a full keyboard creates constraints in relation to data entry (Hayhoe, 2001). There is a need to provide the user with the possibility to 'go large' by getting information from both the virtual and physical world, while simultaneously 'going small,' by retrieving the useful and complementary information and getting involved into meaningful and easy to accomplish tasks (Luchini et al., 2002). In addition, despite the fact that technological solutions are proliferating and maturing, we still have a partial understanding of how users take effectively advantage of mobile devices. Specifically, in relation to communication and interaction, we need to investigate how mobile technology can be used for development of social networks and how it can provide richer ways for people to communicate and engage with others. In public spaces, like museums, a crucial question is if the serendipitous exchanges and interactions that often occur should be supported through mobile technology, how and where the interaction between people takes place and how is affected by this novel technology. Clearly, a better understanding of social activities and social interactions in public spaces should emerge to answer these questions.

A number of the aforementioned issues are discussed next in the context of a museum visit. First, we analyse how the context can affect any activity and application design. Then, we outline the most promising mobile learning applications and finally, we present our experiences of introducing collaborative learning activities using a novel approach based on the best practices surveyed previously, in a large scale project for a cultural history museum.

INTERACTION DESIGN FOR MOBILE APPLICATIONS

Interaction design is one of the main challenges of mobile applications design. Direct transfer of knowledge and practices from the user-desktop interaction metaphor, without taking in consideration the challenges of the new interaction paradigm is not effective. A new conceptualization of interaction is needed for ubiquitous computing. The traditional definition (Norman, 1986) of the user interface as a "means by which people and computers communicate with each other," becomes in ubiquitous computing, the means by which the people and the environment communicate with each other *facilitated* by mobile devices. As a result, interaction design is fundamentally different. In the traditional case, the user interacts with the computer with the intention to carry out a task. The reaction of the computer to user actions modifies its state and results in a dialogue between the human and the machine.

On the other hand, the user interaction with mobile devices is triadic, as the interaction is equally affected not only by the action of the user and the system's response, but by the context of use itself. The level of transparency of the environment, taking into account the presence of the mobile device and the degree of support to 'environmental' tasks meaningful to the user, are new issues to be considered. Consequently, new interaction design and evaluation criteria are required, since the design should not only focus on the user experience but pay also attention to the presence of other devices or objects of interest, including the level of awareness of the environment. By building the virtual information space into the real, the real is enhanced, but conversely, by drawing upon the physical, there is the opportunity to make the virtual space more tangible and intuitive and lower the overall cognitive load associated with each task.

To summarize, a number of design principles are proposed for mobile applications design:

a. Effective and efficient *context awareness* methods and models, with respect to the concept of context as defined by Dey (2001): 'Context is any information that can be used to characterize the situation of an entity. An entity is a person, place, or object that is considered relevant to the interaction between a user and an application, including the user and applications themselves.'

b. Presentation of useful information to the user *complementary* to the information communicated by the environment.

c. *Accurate and timely update* of environmental data that affect the quality of interaction.

d. Contextualized and personalized information according to *personal needs*.

e. Information should be *presented to the user* rather than having the user searching for it.

Failure to look into these design issues can lead to erroneous interaction. For example, delays of the network, lack of synchronization between two artifacts of the environment or slight repositioning of the device can lead to misconceptions and illegal interaction states. In addition, information flow models should be aligned according to the information push requirement and relevant user modeling and adaptation techniques to support this flow of information should be defined. Finally, new usability evaluation techniques, concerning mobile applications should emerge to shape a novel interaction paradigm.

Dix et al. (2000) present a framework to systematically address the discussed design issues and successive context awareness elements are inserted in the design process: (a) the *infrastructure* level (i.e., available network bandwidth, displays' resolution), (b) the *system* level (type and pace of feedback and feed through), (c) the *domain* level (the degree of adaptability that a system must provide to different users) and (d) the *physical* level (physical attributes of the device, location method and the environment). All these elements should be tackled independently and as a whole in order to study the effect of every design decision to each other.

We formulate the interaction design aspects discussed through the problem of designing a mobile learning application for a museum. During the visit a user has only a partial understanding of the available exhibits. This situation can be supported by complementary information included in the physical environment, for example alternative representations, concerning the historical role of the people or the artifacts presented the artistic value of a painting (Evans & Sterry, 1999), and so forth. This cognitive process of immersion into the cultural context, represented by the museum exhibits, could be supported by drawing upon the stimuli produced during the visit using context aware mobile devices. Therefore, these devices should be viewed as tools to enhance the involvement of a user in the cultural discovery process, tools that challenge the user to imagine the social, historical and cultural context, aligning her to a meaningful and worthy experience.

It is not argued here that the infusion of mobile technologies in museums will necessarily result to meaningful learning processes. Our analysis involves the potential use of the technology when integrated in educational activities (Hall & Bannon, 2006), which will offer a structured

learning activity according to the characteristics of museums' content and the functionalities of the technologies used. To better illustrate this point (a) we briefly present a set of selected exemplary cases which demonstrate different ways of integrating mobile educational applications in museums and (b) we provide a more detailed account of such an application that we designed for a museum in Greece.

In the next section a number of approaches supporting such a visit are reviewed and examined using the design aspects as guiding paradigm and point of reference. Since the goal of the visitor is to see and learn more and not to explicitly use technology, a deep understanding of visitors' needs is important during the design phase, to avoid disturbances that can destruct her from her objective. Therefore, decisions made for the technology used and the styles of interaction, with the involved devices, have to deal with user's patterns of visit. Having the above requirements in hand, we use the framework proposed by Dix et al. (2000) to organize a coherent characteristics inspection of some representative examples of mobile museum guides.

MOBILE DEVICES AS MUSEUM GUIDES

In this section, some representative design approaches for mobile museum applications are discussed. An extended survey is included in Raptis, Tselios and Avouris (2005). The first system named "Electronic Guidebook," deployed in the Exploratorium science museum (Fleck et al., 2002), tries to involve the visitors to directly manipulate the exhibits and provides instructions as well as additional science explanations about the natural phenomena people are watching. The system of the Marble Museum of Carrara (Ciavarella & Paterno, 2004) stores the information locally in the PDA's memory, uses a map to guide the visitors around the museum and presents content of different abstraction levels (i.e., room, section and exhibit). The "ImogI" system uses Bluetooth to establish communication between the PDAs and exhibits and presents the closest exhibits to the user, (Luyten & Coninx, 2004). The "Sotto Voce" system gives details about everyday things located in an old house (Grinter et al., 2002) by having pictures of the walls on the PDA's screen and asking from the user to select the exhibit she is interested in, by pressing it. The "Points of Departure" system (www.sfmoma.org) gives details in video and audio form by having 'thumbnails' of exhibits on the PDA's screen. It also uses 'Smart Tables' in order to enrich the interaction. A system, in the Lasar Segall Museum, Sao Paolo, Brazil (Dyan, 2004), automatically delivers information to the PDA, about more

than 3,000 paintings. In the Tokyo University Digital Museum a system uses three different approaches to deliver content. The PDMA, in which the user holds the device above the exhibit she is interested in, the Point-it, in which the visitor uses laser-pointer to select specific exhibits and finally the Museum AR in which visitors wear glasses in order to get details about the exhibits (Koshizuka & Sakamura, 2000).

The system developed in the C-Map project, (Mase, Sumi, & Kadobayashi, 2000), uses active badges to simulate the location of the visitor, allowing tour planning and a VR system, controlled by the gestures of the visitor. In a Tour guide (Chou, Lee, Lee et al., 2004), the information about the exhibits is automatically presented and there is no variation in the form of the visit, but subjec-

Table 1. Design decisions affecting system context

	Location technology	Storage of information	Flow of information	Additional functions
"Antwerp project"	IrDA	In Server	Active	Cameras
C-Map	IrDA	In Server	Active, exhibit recommendations	Active Badges, Screens
Hippie	IrDA	In Server	Active, info presented based on the history of visit	
ImogI	Bluetooth	Info stored in Bluetooth transmitters	Active, proximity manager	
Lasar Segal Museum	IrDA	In Server	Passive	
Marble Museum	IrDA	Locally stored info, abstraction levels	Active, history of the visit	
PDMA, Point it, Museum AR	IrDA	In Server	Active	laser pointer, glasses
PEACH project	IrDA	In Server	Passive, task migration	Screens
Points of departure		Locally stored info	Active	Screens
Rememberer	RFID	In Server	Passive	Cameras
Sotto Voce		Locally stored info	Active	
Tour Guide System (Taiwan)	IrDA	In Server	Passive, subjective tour guides	

tive tour guides are used. A different approach is the one adopted in the Museum of Fine Arts in Antwerp (Van Gool, Tuytelaars, & Pollefeys, 1999), in which the user is equipped with a camera and selects exhibits, or details of an exhibit by taking pictures. A tour guide in the PEACH project, (Rocchi, Stock, Zancanaro et al., 2004), which migrates the interaction from the PDA to screens and uses a TV-like metaphor, using 'newscasters' to deliver content. Finally, a nomadic information system, the Hippie, developed in the framework of the HIPS project, (Oppermann & Specht, 1999), allows the user to access a personal virtual space during or after the visit. In the latter system, an electronic compass is used to identify the direction of a visitor.

The *infrastructure* context concerns the connections between the devices that comprise the system and influence the validity of the information that is provided through them to the users and needs not only to be addressed in problematic situations. It is also related with the validity and timely updates of available information. This can be clearly seen in collaboration activities where the user constantly needs to know the location of other users, the virtual space, the shared objects, and so forth. In the specific museum domain the results may not be so critical but can lead the user to various misunderstandings.

The mentioned systems use an indirect way of informing the user that her requests have been carried out: the user sees and hears the reflection of her requests on the PDA. There is no clear notification that the user's demands are executed successfully or not. Some of the systems use external factors, as signs of success, such as a led light ("Rememberer") and audio signals ("Marble Museum"). But in general terms, the user is on his or her own when problems occur and the systems leave it up to her to find it out, by observing that, there is no progress. We have to point that it could be very distracting and even annoying to have feedback messages in every state of interaction, but it is important for designers,

to include a non-intrusive approach to inform that there is a problem and provide constructive feedback to overcome it.

Regarding the *system* context we can distinguish four different approaches as a means of awareness technology. In the first approach (Table 1), the PDA is the whole system. There are no other devices or awareness mechanisms involved and the information presented to the user is stored locally in the PDA. The second approach uses RFID tags to establish communication between the PDAs and the exhibits and the third which uses Bluetooth to establish communication with the exhibits and deliver content. The forth and most common approach uses IrDA technology to estimate the position of the visitor in space. Usually, IrDA tags are placed near every exhibit or in the entrance of each exhibition room and Wi-Fi derives the information to the PDA from a server Also, many different additional devices are built and integrated into these systems like screens (as a standalone devices or as interacting devices with the PDAs, where the user has the opportunity to transmit sequentially her interaction with the system from the PDA to a Screen). Regarding the *location*, all the studied systems use a topological approach to identify the position of a PDA, which informs approximately the system about the user's location. However, in the case of a museum with densely place exhibits, a more precise Cartesian approach can yield accurate user localization.

Domain context concerns aspects related to the situated interaction that takes place in the specific domain. Often in museum applications there is a lack of information about user profiles and characteristics. It is however important to consider that each visitor in a museum has different expectations, and is interested in different aspects regarding the exhibits. In the studied systems only in those that allow interaction of the users with servers there is a possibility for personalized interaction. Most of the systems require from the user to login, answer some specific questions, in order to build a model of the user and present the information in her PDA according to her language, her expertise level and her physical needs (i.e., bigger fonts for those with sight impediments). When domain context is absent from the design process the system operates as a tool suited for the needs of a single hypothetical 'ideal' user. In such an environment this 'ideal' user will likely represent the needs and expectations of a small fraction of real visitors.

The system may push information to the user or it may wait until the user decides to pull it from the system. In the first case, special consideration should be taken to the user's specific activity and objective. Questions related to situated domain context are the following: Does the system propose any relevant information based on the history of users interaction? Does it adapt to actions repeatedly made by the user? Does it present content in different ways? For example, the "ImogI" system rearranges the order of the icons putting in front the mostly used ones. Also, in PEACH and in 'Points of Departure' the user can change the interaction medium from PDAs to Screens, in order to see more detailed information.

The *physical* context lays in the relation of the system with the physical environment and in problems concerning the physical nature of the devices. However, in the studied systems there is not a single mechanism of identifying the physical conditions. For example, in a room full with people, where a lot of noise exists, it would be appropriate if the system could automatically switch from an audio to a text presentation.

From the survey of the mobile guides applications presented here it seems that efficient design approaches could be achieved by augmenting physical space with information exchanges, by allowing collaboration and communication, by enhancing interactivity with the museum exhibits and by seamlessly integrating instantly available information delivered in various forms. However, the synergy between technology and pedagogy is not straightforward especially if we take into account the need to tackle issues such as efficient context integration, transparent usage of the PDA, and novel pedagogical approaches to exploit the capabilities of mobile devices. As a result, after discussing in detail usages of a mobile device as a mean of museum guidance, in the following, we attempt to discuss explicit educational activities mediated by mobile devices and a specific example of a new Mobile Learning environment.

DESIGNING MUSEUM MOBILE EDUCATIONAL ACTIVITIES

The level of exploitation of mobile devices in a museum setting is increasing and part of this use may have educational value. In this section we will focus on the added value of integrating educational mobile applications in museums. We will start our analysis by posing two questions that we consider central to this issue: (a) what is changing in the learning process taking place in a museum when mediated by mobile technology and (b) why these changes might be of educational or pedagogical interest? We will attempt to address these questions by focusing on three aspects related not only to the characteristics of mobile technology but also to the results of its integration in a museum. Specifically we will discuss: (a) the types of interaction between the visitor and the learning environment (e.g., the museum), (b) the learning activities that these interactions can support and (c) the role of context and motion in learning.

One facet of the learning process when mediated by mobile technology in museum visits involves the tangibility of museum artifacts: distant museum exhibits that were out there for the visitors allowing them just to observe now can be virtually touched, opened, turned and decomposed. In this case, technology provides to the user the key to open up the exhibit, explore it and construct an experience out of it. The traditional reading of information and observation of the exhibit is considered as one-dimensional "information flow" from the exhibit to the user. Mobile technology facilitates the transformation of the one dimensional relationship to a dialectic relationship between the user and the exhibit. Furthermore, this relationship can now include another important component (apart of the exhibits) of the museum environment: the other visitors. By providing a record of user–exhibit interaction for other visitors to see, reflect upon and transform technology can support social activities of communication, co-construction, and so forth between the visitors. To sum up, mobile technology mediates three types of interaction between the learner and the learning environment of a museum: (a) "exhibit–user" interaction (b) "user –exhibit" interaction and (c) "between the users" interaction about "a" and "b."

The enrichment of interaction between the learner and the museum might result in more or different learning opportunities (Cobb, 2002) the characteristics of which are outlined here. Specifically, the dialectic relationship between the user and the museum artifacts, mediated by mobile devices, might offer chances for analysis of the exhibit, experimentation with it, hypothesis formulation and testing, construction of interpretation, information processing and organization, reflection and many more, according to the educational activity designed. Collaboration and communication about the exhibits and information processing about them makes possible socio-constructive learning activities. By comparing these elements of the learning process to the reading or hearing of information about the exhibits (which is a the starting point for a non technology mediated museum visit) we realize that mobile technology has the potential to offer an active role to the learner: she can choose the information she wants to see, open up and de-construct an exhibit if she is interested in it, see how other visitors have interacted with a certain exhibit, discuss about it with them, exchange information,

store information for further processing and use and so on.

Up until now, we described the role of mobile technology in learning with respect to two characteristics of the museum as learning environment: the exhibits and the other visitors. Another characteristic of the museum, which differentiates it from other learning environments (e.g., classroom) is that learning in a museum takes place while the learner moves. Learning while moving, quite often takes place very effectively without the support of technology. However there are cases that further processing with appropriate equipment is needed or some structuring of this "mobile learning experience" is proved to be useful. Mobile technologies can find in museums an important area of implementation not only because museum visits are structured around motion but because we have to support visitors *during* and not just after or before the visit (Patten, Arnedillo Sanchez et al., 2006). But why is it important to support learning during the visit? The answer here comes from the theory of situated learning (Lave & Wenger, 1991) which underlines the role of context in learning. Specifically, context facilitates knowledge construction by offering the practices, the tools, and the relevant background along with the objectives towards which learning is directed and has a specific meaning or a special function (knowledge is used for something). Finally, the use of mobile devices provides a new and very attractive way of interacting with the museum content especially for young children (Hall & Bannon, 2006).

As mentioned previously a large number of mobile applications have been developed during previous years for use in the museums (Raptis et al., 2005). All these mobile applications can add educational value to a museum visit in various ways. A survey of mobile educational applications for use inside the museum, led us to a categorization according to the educational approach followed in every occasion. The first category includes applications that mainly deliver information to the visitor and concerns the vast majority of applications created for museums. Mobile devices take the place of the museums' docents and offer predetermined guided tours based upon certain thematic criteria. The aforementioned applications offer the museum visitor an enhanced experience which can support the learning process through a behaviorist approach. Enhancement is succeeded by supplying multimedia and context-related content.

The second category of applications, suitable for educational use in museums, consists of applications which provide tools that can support the learning process in a more profound way. Compared to the first category, they provide information about the exhibits of a museum but furthermore they include a series of functions that increase the interactivity with the user. Such an example is the Sotto Voce System (Grinter et al., 2002), which includes an electronic guide with audio content and the ability of synchronized sharing of this content between visitors. Thus, the users can either use individually the guide or "eavesdrop" to the information that another visitor listens.

Another example is the applications developed for the Exploratorium, a science museum in San Francisco (Fleck et al., 2002). In this museum, the visitor has the possibility to manipulate and experiment with the exhibits. Also, an electronic guidance was designed to provide information about the exhibits and the phenomena related with them, posing relative questions to provide deeper visitors' engagement. These applications are closer to social-cultural learning theories as they provide the user with tools to organize and control the provided information.

The third category of educational applications presents a specific educational scenario. Usually, game-based activities where the users, mostly children aged 5-15, are challenged to act a role and complete carefully designed pedagogical tasks. Such an example is the MUSEX application (Yatani, Sugimot & Kusunoki, 2004), deployed in

the National Museum of Emerging Science and Innovation in Japan. MUSEX is a typical drill and practice educational system in which children work in pairs and are challenged to answer a number of questions. Children select an exhibit with their RFID reader equipped PDA and a question is presented in the screen with four possible answers. The activity is completed when each pair collects twelve correct answers. Children may collaborate and communicate either physically or via transceivers and monitor each group progress through a shared screen. After the completion of the activity the participators have the possibility to visit a Website and track their path inside the museum. The users can deeply interact with the exhibits, review the progress of her partner or ask for help (Yatani et al., 2004).

DinoHunter project includes several applications for the transmission of knowledge through game-based and mixed reality activities in the Senckenberg museum, Frankfurt, Germany. Three of these applications, namely DinoExplorer, DinoPick and DinoQuiz, are being supported by mobile technologies (Feix, Gobel, & Zumack, 2004). DinoExplorer delivers information to the users as an electronic guide, DinoPick allows the users to pick one part of the body of a dinosaur and get more multimedia information about this specific part and DinoQuiz provides a set of questions for further exploration of the exhibits of the museum.

Mystery at the Museum is another mobile, game-based, educational activity created for the Boston Museum of Science. It engages visitors in exploring and thinking in depth about the exhibits, thus making connections across them and encourages collaboration (Klopfer, Perry, Squire et al., 2005). High School students and their parents are called to solve a crime mystery where a band of thieves has stolen one of the exhibits. The users try to locate the criminals by using a PDA and a walkie-talkie. The participants must select upon the role of a technologist, a biologist or a detective. Depending on the chosen role they can interview virtual characters, pick up and examine virtual objects by using virtual equipment (e.g., microscope), collect virtual samples via infrared tags or exchange objects and interviews through the walkie-talkies. A study confirmed deep engagement of the participants and extensive collaboration due to the roles set.

Another similar approach is presented through the Scavenger Hunt Game activity used in the Chicago Historical Society Museum (Kwak, 2004). In this case, the children are challenged to answer a series of questions related to the exhibits and the local history. They undertake the role of a historical researcher and they are called to answer 10 multiple choice questions while examining the exhibits. Each user is individually engaged into the activity and her progress is evaluated in a way similar to electronic games. The Cicero Project implemented in the Marble Museum of Carrara introduces a variety of games to the visitors (Laurillau & Paternò, 2004). The games vary from finding the missing parts of a puzzle to answering questions about the exhibits. Its main characteristic is the support it provides to the visitors to socially interact and collaboratively participate in activities concerning the exhibits of the museum, through peer-awareness mechanisms.

A series of mobile educational activities was also carried out in the frame of the Handscape Project in the Johnson Museum (Thom-Santelli, Toma, Boehner et al., 2005). The "Museum Detective" engage students in role-playing activities. Children working in pairs are called to locate an object described by one clue and learn as much as possible for it. A series of multiple-choice questions is presented for further exploration of the exhibit. Four types of interactive element are also provided for the exhibits: a painting, a drawing activity and a building activity and a multimedia narrative. The multiple-choice questions and the building activity were drill and practice activities and the rest were activities allowing children to make their own creations.

The systems of the latter category present coherent learning experiences comprised of planned and organized pedagogic activities, where an intervention has been purposefully designed to result a positive impact on children's cognitive and affective development. With respect to the contextual and interaction issues presented in the previous sections, we attempt to present in the next section an integrated application that involves children as role-playing characters by exploring the museum using a PDA.

AN EXAMPLE OF MOBILE ACTIVITY DESIGN FOR INDOOR MUSEUM VISIT

The "Inheritance" activity discussed here, is designed to support learning in the context of a cultural/historical museum visit. The application involves role-playing, information retrieval, data collecting and collaboration educational activities, suitable for children aged 10 or above working in teams of two or three members each. The activity scenario describes an imaginary story where the students are asked to help the Museum in finding the will of a deceased historian, worked for years in it. This will is hidden behind the historians' favorite exhibit. Clues to locate the document are scattered among the descriptions of some exhibits. If the children manage to find the will, all of the property of the historian will be inherited by the museum and not by his "greedy relatives." The scenario urges the students to read the description of the exhibits, find the clues and collaboratively locate the specific one.

During the design process of the activity we had to study the *museum context*, the *mobile technology* used and the *learning approach* to be followed in order to achieve the desired pedagogical outcome. The survey discussed in the previous section led us to adopt the following interaction design decisions. A PDA with wireless network capability is used and an RFID reader is attached to it to 'scan' the RFID tags used to identify the exhibits. Wi-Fi infrastructure is being used to deliver data and establish communication between the visitors. When an exhibit is scanned, the PDA sends a request for information to the server which delivers the appropriate content presented in the form requested by the user. Data exchange between two users is accomplished through alignment of their devices while pointing one to the other, which mimics the exhibit scanning procedure. We also opted for small chunks of text since reading at low resolution screens reduces reading comprehension significantly.

The educational design of the activity was inspired by the social and cultural perspective of constructivism. It was structured around a set of learning objectives relevant to the thematic focus of the museum, to the exhibits' information, to the age and previous knowledge of the students, and to the fact that involves a school visit (as opposed to individual museum visits). The basic elements which shaped the activity were:

a. **Engagement of interest:** Engagement and interest hold an important role in the learning process. Student interest in a museum should not be taken for granted, especially because a visit arranged by the school is not usually based on the fact that some students might be interested to the theme of the museum. In the inheritance activity we considered to trigger student interest by engaging them in a game. The setting, the rules and the goal of the game were presented in the context of a story.

b. **Building on previous knowledge:** The focus of the activity was selected with respect to the history courses that students were taught in school. They had a general idea about the specific period of the Greek history and the activity offered complementary information about certain issues of this period. Building on previous knowledge was expected to support students in problem solving and hypothesis formulation and testing.

c. **Selecting–processing–combining pieces of information:** The scenario is structured around the idea that students read the offered information, select what is relevant to their inquiry and combine it with other pieces of information that have selected and stored earlier. Thus the students are expected to visit and re-visit the relevant exhibits, go through the information that involves them as many times as they think necessary and not just retrieve that information but combine it and use it in order to find the favorite exhibit which is the end point of the game

Figure 1. Screenshots of the "Inheritance" application: (a) Dialogue for RFID tags reading (b) information for a selected exhibit (c) clue selection (d) the notepad screen.

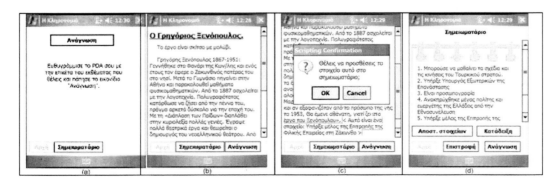

Figure 2. Children engaged in the activity

d. **Hypothesis formulation and testing:** When students have selected enough information from the exhibits around one room of the museum they can attempt to use some of the clues they have selected in order to find the favorite exhibit. If they fail they can go around the room to collect more information and try again.

e. **Communication and collaboration:** The activity is designed to facilitate inter and intra-group collaboration. Specifically, two groups of students are expected to collaborate to determine which exhibit they will interact with, to exchange clues using their PDA and to discuss their ideas about the favorite exhibit.

During the activity, the participating teams are free to explore any exhibit. Each team is provided with a PDA to extract information related to the exhibits by reading the tags attached to each of the exhibits (Figure 1). Only some of the exhibits contain 'clues,' which give information about the favourite exhibit to be found. Children must locate them, store them in the PDAs notepad and after collecting all or most of the clues the teams are able to beam their clues to each other. After collecting all six clues the students are challenged to locate the favorite exhibit. When both teams agree that one exhibit is the favorite one, they can check the correctness of their choice by reading with both PDAs the RFID tag of the chosen exhibit.

After the development of a prototype application, a case study was conducted inside the museum in order to validate the design choices. Seventeen students, aged 11, participated in the study (Figure 2). Data concerning all involving elements were collected to study the activity in depth. The activity was videotaped, PDA screen recording has been used and voice recorders were used to record dialogues among the participants.

The goal of the data analysis was twofold. First, to identify problems children encountered during the process in relation to each of the activity's elements. Then, to identify the nature of the interactions occurred during the procedure. Our analysis is based on the Activity Theory, concerning mainly human practices from the perspective of consciousness and personal development. It takes into account both individual and collaborative activities, the asymmetrical relation between people and things, and the role of artifacts in everyday life. The activity is seen as a system of human processes where a subject works on an object in order to obtain a desired outcome. In order to accomplish a goal, the subject employs tools, either conceptual or embodiments. Activity

Figure 3. Description according to the activity theory model

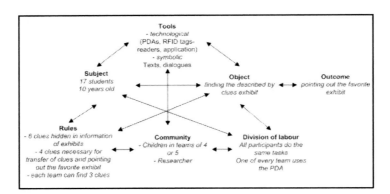

Table 2. An extract of the data analysis presenting action of the 'reading and searching for clues' class

Time	Actor	Tool	Events
00 : 08 : 50	Group1	PDA	Selection of "read"
00 : 08 : 52	Group1	texts	Information D. Stefanou
00 : 09 : 21	Group1	PDA	scrolling
00 : 09 : 33	Group1	PDA	scrolling
00 : 09 : 38	Group1	PDA	scrolling
00 : 09 : 42	Group1	PDA	scrolling
00 : 09 : 45	Group1	PDA	scrolling
00 : 09 : 49	Group1	PDA	scrolling
00 : 09 : 57	Group1	PDA	scrolling
00 : 10 : 02	Group1	PDA	scrolling
00 : 10 : 03	Group1	Dialogue	It doesn't have any (clues) here

is consisted by different components which are (Figure 3): (a) *subject*, (the persons engaged in the activity), (b) *object* (scope of the activity), (c) its *outcome* (c) *tools* used by the subjects (d) *rules-roles* that define the activity process, (e)*community* (context of the activity) and (f)*division of labour* (tasks division among the participants, Kuuti, 1995; Zurita & Nussbaum, 2004).

Activity Theory is of fundamental importance to deeper understand learning with mobile devices while visiting a museum, since in this case knowledge construction is mediated by cultural tools in a social context. The data collected were analyzed with the use of the Collaboration Analysis Tool (ColAT) environment which supports a multilevel description and interpretation of collaborative activities through fusion of multiple data (Avouris, Komis, Fiotakis et al., 2004).

In our analysis, an activity is a procedure during which objects become knowledge through three different levels-steps. Operation is the lower level where routine processes facilitate the completion of goal-oriented actions which in turn constitute the activity. Dialogues, user operations in the application and observations derived from the videos were transcribed in this first level of analysis. The actors, the operations and the mediating tools were noted in this level. Actors were the two participating teams and the researcher. The mediating tools were the dialogue among children and the researcher, texts of information (symbolic) and the application (technological). Some examples of operations in our case are text scrolling, RFID tag reading and transition from one screen to another. Analysis of these user operations led us to the identification of a problem in the use of the application. For example, due to data transfer delay from the server to the PDA, users in some occasions were frustrated and selected repeatedly an action due to lack of timely feedback.

In the second level, the different actions presented among the structural components of the activity are being studied. In order to identify and categorize the actions, a series of typologies were introduced. Typologies were set according to the goal and the mediating tool of each action. For example when children used the PDA to read the text information (mediating tools) their goal was not always the same. Three different typologies were used to describe the situation when the children read carefully the information provided ("Reading of information"), when they were reading the information and searched for clues also ("Reading and searching for clues"), and finally when they were "Searching for clues only." A "Reading and searching for clues" action example is presented in Table 2. Children scroll down the text and one of them states in the end of this action that they were unable to find a clue. When children search only for clues without paying attention to the information we observe rapid scrolling. A clear indication that they have already found all the clues is when children read only the information.

Other actions defined in our study were related to the dialogue between the children and the researcher aimed to overcome difficulties in using the application or understanding the rules-roles of the activity. Typologies where also introduced to describe the interaction between children related to the next step in the procedure (…"*Should we go there? …ok*") and the exchange of thoughts about the solution of the activity (…"*Well, tell me, the first clue is? …He could spy the Turkish army*"…).
In the third level of analysis, patterns identified concerning the evolution of the procedure.

Clearly, the basic goals of the activity as described previously in this section have been fulfilled. Data analysis indicated that children were highly motivated by the activity and collaborated in order to achieve their goal. As derived from the analysis, the teams adopted different strategies to accomplish the task. Collaboration was observed mainly while making the choice of the next exhibit to be examined. After completing the task of finding the clues, the two teams collaborated more closely. They divided the work needed to find the exhibit described by the clues and looked in different parts of the room while collaborating and sharing their thoughts and suppositions. They used the clues as information filters thus eliminating the ones that did not match. Additionally, the learning result of this activity, as derived from subsequent students' essays describing the visit experience, was a deeper understanding of the historical role of the persons represented in the exhibits and their interrelations.

CONCLUSION AND FUTURE WORK

This chapter attempted to present current design approaches for mobile learning applications in the context of a museum visit. In addition, thorough study of similar approaches took place, which lead to useful design patterns and guidelines. As discussed, design of mobile learning systems, is not a straightforward process. In addition to the challenge of integrating the concept of context into the design process and independently from context conceptualization, a comprehension of pedagogical goals, desired learning transfers, user typical needs and objectives should take place. We argue that proper design decisions should take into account a solid theoretical cognitive framework, as well as the special characteristics of the mobile devices used and the challenges of such an informal learning setting. A suitable activity should be properly supported by adequate interaction models, deeper understanding of the tasks involved to carry out the activity as a whole and their expectations while carrying out specific actions. For this reason, further validation of our proposed activity, took place in the actual museum. The activity was enjoyed by the students and enhanced their motivation to learn more about the cultural and historical context represented by the exhibits. The latter challenge has been better illustrated while discussing our experience of designing a collaborative learning activity in a cultural history museum and a case study validating its usefulness.

Clearly, the future of learning technology in museums lies in the blending, not the separation, of the virtual and the real world. That is because learning in a museum context could be conceived as the integration, over time, of personal, socio-cultural, and physical contexts. The physical setting of the museum in which learning takes place mediates the personal and socio-cultural setting. The so called 'interface transparency' should be treated as an effort to seamlessly integrate the computational device to our natural environment. This goal could be achieved by augmenting physical space with information exchanges, allowing collaboration and communication, enhancing interactivity with the museum exhibits and by seamless integrating instantly available information delivered in various forms. However, the synergy between technology and pedagogy is not straightforward, especially if we take into account the need to tackle issues such as efficient context integration, transparent usage of PDA, and novel pedagogical approaches to exploit the capabilities of the mobile devices. Therefore, further research effort should take place to experience established methods and practices.

REFERENCES

Avouris, N., Komis, V., Fiotakis, G., Dimitra-copoulou, A., & Margaritis, M. (2004). Method and Tools for analysis of collaborative problem-solving activities. In *Proceedings of ATIT2004, First International Workshop on Activity Theory Based Practical Methods for IT Design* (pp. 5-16). Retrieved on February 28, 2007 from http://www.daimi.au.dk/publications/PB/574/PB-574.pdf

Chou, L., Lee, C., Lee, M., & Chang, C. (2004). A tour guide system for mobile learning in museums. In J. Roschelle, T.W. Chan, Kinshuk & S. J. H. Yang (Eds.), *Proceedings of 2nd IEEE International Workshop on Wireless and Mobile Technologies in Education—WMTE'04* (pp. 195-196). Washington, DC: IEEE Computer Society.

Ciavarella, C., & Paterno, F. (2004). The design of a handheld, location-aware guide for indoor environments. *Personal Ubiquitous Computing, 8,* 82–91.

Cobb, P. (2002). Reasoning with tools and inscriptions. *The Journal of the Learning Sciences, 11*(2-3), 187-215.

Danesh, A., Inkpen, K.M., Lau, F., Shu, K., & Booth, K.S. (2001). Geney: Designing a collaborative activity for the palm handheld computer. In *Proceedings of the SIGCHI conference on Human Factors in Computing Systems—CHI 2001* (pp. 388-395). New York: ACM Press.

Dey, A. (2001). Understanding and using context. *Personal and Ubiquitous Computing Journal, 5*(1), 4-7.

Dillenbourg, P. (Ed.) (1999). *Collaborative learning: Cognitive and computational approaches.* Oxford, UK: Elsevier Science.

Dix, A., Rodden, T., Davies, N., Trevor, J., Friday, A., & Palfreyman, K. (2000). Exploiting space and location as a design framework for interactive mobile systems. *ACM Transactions on Computer-*

Human Interaction, 7(3), 285–321.

Dyan, M. (2004). *An Introduction to Art, the Wireless Way.* Retrieved on March 25, 2005 from http://www.cooltown.com/cooltown/mpulse/1002-lasarsegall.asp

Evans, J., & Sterry, P. (1999). Portable computers and interactive multimedia: A new paradigm for interpreting museum collections. *Journal Archives and Museum Informatics, 13*, 113-126.

Feix, A., Göbel, S., & Zumack, R. (2004). DinoHunter: Platform for mobile edutainment applications in museums. In S. Göbel, U. Spierling, A. Hoffmann, I. Iurgel, O. Schneider, J. Dechau & A. Feix (Eds.), *Proceedings of the Second International Conference on Technologies for Interactive Digital Storytelling and Entertainment: Conference Proceedings—TIDSE 2004* (pp. 264-269). Berlin: Springer.

Fleck, M., Frid, M., Kindberg, T., Rajani, R., O'Brien-Strain, E., & Spasojevic, M. (2002). From informing to remembering: Deploying a ubiquitous system in an interactive science museum. *Pervasive Computing, 1*(2), 13-21.

Grinter, R. E., Aoki, P. M., Szymanski, M. H., Thornton, J. D., Woodruff, A., & Hurst, A. (2002). Revisiting the visit: understanding how technology can shape the museum visit. In *Proceedings of the 2002 ACM Conference on Computer Supported Cooperative Work—CSCW 2002,* (pp. 146-155). New York: ACM Press.

Hall, T., & Bannon, L. (2006). Designing ubiquitous computing to enhance children's learning in museums. *Journal of Computer Assisted Learning, 22,* 231–243.

Hayhoe, G. F. (2001). From desktop to palmtop: creating usable online documents for wireless and handheld devices. In *Proceedings of the IEEE International Conference on Professional Communication Conference–IPCC 2001* (pp. 1-11).

Klopfer, E., Perry, J., Squire, K., Jan, M., &

Steinkuehler, C. (2005). Mystery at the museum: a collaborative game for museum education. In T. Koschmann, T. W. Chan & D. Suthers (Eds.), *Proceedings of the 2005 conference on Computer support for collaborative learning: the next 10 years!* (pp. 316-320). Mahwah, NJ: Lawrence Erlbaum.

Koshizuka, N., & Sakamura, K. (2000). The Tokyo University Museum. In *Kyoto International Conference on Digital Libraries: Research and Practice* (pp. 85-92).

Kuuti, K. (1995). Activity theory as a potential framework for human-computer interaction research. In B. Nardi (Ed.), *Context and consciousness: Activity theory and human computer interaction* (pp. 17-14). Cambridge: MIT Press.

Kwak, S.Y. (2004). *Designing a handheld interactive scavenger hunt game to enhance museum experience.* Unpublished diploma thesis, Michigan State University, Department of Telecommunication, Information Studies and Media.

Laurillau, Y., & Paternò, F. (2004). Supporting museum co-visits using mobile devices. In S. Brewster & M. Dunlop (Eds), *Proceedings of the 6th International Symposium on Mobile Human-Computer Interaction—Mobile HCI 2004* (pp 451-455). Berlin: Springer.

Lave, J., & Wenger, E. (1991). *Situated learning: Legitimate peripheral participation.* New York: Cambridge University Press.

Luchini, K., Quintana, C., Krajcik, J., Farah, C., Nandihalli, N., Reese, et al. (2002). Scaffolding in the small: Designing educational supports for concept mapping on handheld computers. In *CHI 2002 Extended Abstracts on Human Factors in Computing Systems* (pp. 792-793). New York: ACM Press.

Luyten, K., & Coninx, K. (2004). ImogI: Take control over a context aware electronic mobile guide for museums. *In proceedings of the 3rd*

Workshop on HCI in Mobile Guides. Retrieved on February 24, 2007 from http://research.edm. luc.ac.be/~imogi/

Myers, B. A., Stiel, H., & Gargiulo, R. (1998). Collaboration using multiple PDAs connected to a PC. In *Proceedings of the ACM 1998 Conference on Computer Supported Cooperative Work — CSCW '98* (pp. 285-294). New York: ACM.

Mase, K., Sumi, Y., & Kadobayashi, R. (2000). The weaved reality: What context-aware interface agents bring about. In *Proceedings of the Fourth Asian Conference on Computer Vision - ACCV2000* (pp. 1120-1124).

Norman, D. A. (1986). Cognitive engineering. In D. A. Norman & S. W. Draper (Eds.), *User centered systems design* (pp. 31-61). Mahwah, NJ: Lawrence Erlbaum.

Norris, C., & Soloway, E. (2004). Envisioning the handheld-centric classroom. *Journal of Educational Computing Research, 30*(4), 281-294.

Oppermann, R., Specht, M., & Jaceniak, I. (1999). Hippie: A nomadic information system. In H. W. Gellersen (Ed.), *Proceedings of the First International Symposium Handheld and Ubiquitous Computing - HUC'99* (pp. 330-333). Berlin: Springer.

Patten, B., Arnedillo Sanchez, I., & Tangney, B. (2006). Designing collaborative, constructionist and contextual applications for handheld devices. *Computers and Education, 46,* 294-308.

Perry, D. (2003). *Handheld Computers (PDAs) in Schools.* BECTA ICT Research Report. Retrieved on February 26, 2007 from http://www.becta.org. uk/ page_documents/research/handhelds.pdf

Raptis, D., Tselios, N., & Avouris, N. (2005). Context-based design of mobile applications for museums: a survey of existing practices. In M. Tscheligi, R Bernhaupt & K. Mihalic (Eds.), *Proceedings of the 7th international Conference on Human Computer interaction with Mobile*

Devices & Services- Mobile HCI 2005 (pp. 153-160). New York: ACM Press.

Rieger, R., & Gay, G. (1997). Using mobile computing to enhance field study. In R.P. Hall, N. Miyake & N. Enyedy (Eds.), *Proceedings of Computer Support for Collaborative Learning –CSCL 1997* (pp. 215–223). Mahwah, NJ: Lawrence Erlbaum.

Rocchi, C., Stock, O., Zancanaro, M., Kruppa, M., & Krüger, A. (2004). The museum visit: Generating seamless personalized presentations on multiple devices. In J. Vanderdonckt, N. J. Nunes & C. Rich (Eds.), *Proceedings of the Intelligent User Interfaces - IUI 2004* (pp. 316-318). New York: ACM.

Roschelle, J. (2003). Unlocking the learning value of wireless mobile devices. *Journal of Computer Assisted Learning, 19*(3), 260-272.

Thom-Santelli, J., Toma, C., Boehner, K., & Gay, G. (2005). Beyond just the facts: Museum detective guides. In *Proceedings from the International Workshop on Re-Thinking Technology in Museums: Towards a New Understanding of People's Experience in Museums* (pp. 99-107). Retrieved on February 25, 2007 from http://www. idc.ul.ie/museumworkshop/programme.html

Vahey, P., & Crawford, V. (2002). *Palm education pioneers program final evaluation report.* Menlo Park, CA: SRI International.

Van Gool, L., Tuytelaars, T., & Pollefeys, M. (1999). Adventurous tourism for couch potatoes. (Invited). In F. Solina & A. Leonardis (Eds.), *Proceedings of the 8th International Conference on Computer Analysis of Images and Patterns – CAIP 1999* (pp. 98-107). Berlin: Springer.

Yatani, K., Sugimoto, M., & Kusunoki, F. (2004). Musex: A System for Supporting Children's Collaborative Learning in a Museum with PDAs. In J. Roschelle, T.W. Chan, Kinshuk & S. J. H. Yang (Eds.), *Proceedings of 2nd IEEE International*

Workshop on Wireless and Mobile Technologies in Education – WMTE'04 (pp 109-113). Washington, DC: IEEE Computer Society.

Zurita, G., & Nussbaum, M. (2004). Computer supported collaborative learning using wirelessly interconnected handheld computers. *Computers and Education, 42*, 289-314.

KEY TERMS

Activity Theory: Is a psychological framework, with its roots in Vygotsky's cultural-historical psychology. Its goal is to explain the mental capabilities of a single human being. However, it rejects the isolated human being as an adequate unit of analysis, focusing instead on cultural and technical mediation of human activity.

Context: Context is any information that can be used to characterize the situation of an entity. An entity is a person, place, or object that is considered relevant to the interaction between a user and an application, including the user and applications themselves (Dey, 2001).

Context-Aware: The ability to sense context.

Interaction Design: Interaction design is a sub-discipline of the design notion which aims to examine the role of embedded behaviors and intelligence in physical and virtual spaces as well as the convergence of physical and digital products. In particular, interaction design is concerned with a user experience flow through time and is typically informed by user research design with an emphasis on behavior as well as form. Interaction design is evaluated in terms of functionality, usability and emotional factors.

Mobile Device: A device which is typically characterized by mobility, small form factor and communication functionality and focuses on handling a particular type of information and related tasks. Typical devices could be a Smartphone or a PDA. Mobile devices may overlap in definition or are sometimes referred to as information appliances, wireless devices, handhelds or handheld devices.

Mobile Learning: Is the delivery of learning to students who are not keeping a fixed location or through the use of mobile or portable technology.

Museum Learning: A kind of informal learning which is not teacher mediated. It refers to how well a visit inspires and stimulates people into wanting to know more, as well as changing how they see themselves and their world both as an individual and as part of a community. It is a wide concept that can include not only the design and implementation of special events and teaching sessions, but also the planning and production of exhibitions and any other activity of the museum which can play an educational role.

Chapter 8.7
Component Agent Systems:
Building a Mobile Agent Architecture That You Can Reuse

Paulo Marques
University of Coimbra, Portugal

Luís Silva
University of Coimbra, Portugal

ABSTRACT

One central problem preventing widespread adoption of mobile agents as a code structuring primitive is that current mainstream middleware implementations do not convey it simply as such. In fact, they force all the development to be centered on mobile agents, which has serious consequences in terms of software structuring and, in fact, technology adoption. This chapter discusses the main limitations of the traditional platform-based approach, proposing an alternative: component-based mobile agent systems. Two case studies are discussed: the JAMES platform, a traditional mobile agent platform specially tailored for network management, and M&M, a component-based system for agent-enabling applications. Finally, a bird's eye perspective on the last 15 years of mobile agent systems research is presented along with an outlook on the future of the technology. The authors hope that this chapter brings some enlightenment on the pearls and pitfalls surrounding this interesting technology and ways for avoiding them in the future.

INTRODUCTION

A mobile agent (Chess et al., 1994; White, 1996) is a simple, natural and logical extension of the remote distributed object concept. It is an object with an active thread of execution that is capable of migrating between different hosts and applications. By using mobile agents, the programmer is no longer confined to have static objects and perform remote invocations but can program the objects to move directly between applications. In itself, a mobile agent is just a programming abstraction: an active object that can move when needed. It is a structuring primitive, similar to the notion of class, remote object, or thread.

Two possible approaches for the deployment of mobile agents in distributed applications are:

a. To use a middleware platform that provides all the mechanisms and support for the execution of mobile agents. The basic characteristic of platform-based systems is that there is an infrastructure where all agents execute. This infrastructure typically corresponds to a daemon or service on top of which the agents are run. All agents co-exist on the same infrastructure. When the programmer develops an application, he is in fact modeling different mobile agents, which execute on the platform. Typically, this is done by extending a `MobileAgent` class or a similar construct. In fact, some of the mobile agents may not even be mobile but just static service agents interfacing with other functionalities of the system. Examples include, among others, the SOMA platform (Bellavista, Corradi, & Stefanelli, 1999), D'Agents (Kotz et al., 1997), Ajanta (Tripathi et al., 2002), Aglets (Aglets Project Homepage, 2006; Lange & Oshima, 1998), and JAMES (Silva et al., 1999). This is by far the most common approach.

b. An alternative approach is to provide the support for mobile agents as software components that can be more easily integrated in the development of applications. This approach is followed by the M&M project (Marques, 2003), described in this chapter.

In this chapter, we present the results of two major projects that have been conducted in our research group: JAMES and M&M.

The **JAMES** platform was developed in collaboration with SIEMENS and consisted of a traditional mobile agent platform especially optimized for network management applications.

Our industrial partners used this platform to develop some mobile agent-based applications that were integrated into commercial products. These applications used mobile agents to perform management tasks (accounting, performance management, system monitoring, and detailed user profiling) that deal with very large amounts of data distributed over the nodes of GSM networks. With this project, we learned that this technology, when appropriately used, provides significant competitive advantages to distributed management applications.

The main motivation for the second project, M&M, was to facilitate the development process and the integration of mobile objects within ordinary applications. M&M abandoned the classic concept of mobile agent platforms as extensions of the operating system. Instead, this middleware is able to provide for agent mobility within application boundaries, rather than within system boundaries. Its objective was to demonstrate that it is possible to create an infrastructure such that the mobile agent concept can be leveraged into existing object-oriented languages in a simple and transparent way, without interfering in the manner in which the applications are normally structured. In order to achieve this goal, a component-oriented framework was devised and implemented, allowing programmers to use mobile agents as needed. Applications can still be developed using current object-oriented techniques but, by including certain components, they gain the ability to send, receive, and interact with agents. The component palette was implemented using the JavaBeans technology and was, furthermore, integrated with ActiveX (Box, 1997; Denning, 1997), allowing programmers from any programming language that supports COM/ActiveX to take advantage of this paradigm. To validate the soundness of the approach, a large number of applications have been implemented using M&M. Two application domains were of particular interest: agent-enabling web servers (Marques, Fonseca, Simões, Silva,

& Silva, 2002a) and disconnected computing (Marques, Santos, Silva, & Silva, 2002b).

The rest of the chapter is organized as follows:

- In the **Background** section, a general introduction to platform-based systems for mobile agents is presented, followed by a case study: the JAMES platform;
- Then, in the **Component-Based Mobile Agent Systems** section, an alternative model is discussed, based on binary software components. In particular, it addresses some of limitations of the platform-based approach, presenting the M&M case study and its implications;
- The next section gives a **Bird's Eye Perspective** on the state of mobile agent technology;
- Finally, the last section presents the **Conclusion** and an outlook on the future of mobile agent technology.

BACKGROUND

Mobile Agent Platforms

The foundation for most platform-based systems is a server that sits on top of the operating system and where all agents execute. The platform is responsible for housing the agents and for providing every single feature needed by them and their surrounding environment (Delamaro, 2002; Marques, Simões, Silva, Boavida, & Gabriel, 2001). It provides functionalities like migration support, naming, security, inter-agent communication, agent tracking, persistence, external application gateways, platform management, and fault-tolerance. In fact, the agent platform plays the role of the "operating system of agents."

This list of supported features in an agent platform is by no means complete. Many application-specific domains have specific requirements.

This leads to domain-specific implementations, having special features to address domain-specific requirements. Examples include: the JAMES platform (Silva et al., 1999), for telecommunication applications; aZIMAS (Arumugam, Helal, & Nalla, 2002) for supporting mobile agents in web servers; SOMA (Bellavista, 1999) for interoperability and integration with CORBA.

Figure 1 presents the typical architecture of such a system. As said, the operating system sits on the bottom. In the middle, there is the agent platform where all the agents execute. On the top, there are the agents belonging to all applications. This last point is especially important. Since all agents execute on top of the platform, usually all the agents from all applications can see each other. Although agents/applications can be divided into namespaces, as it happens in some platforms, and security permissions can be configured for proper access, in most cases the notion of application is quite weak or even inexistent.

In terms of programming model, in most platforms, the only support provided for application development is around the concept of mobile agent. Everything becomes a mobile agent, even entities that are conceptually services or gateways. Typically, inter-agent communication mechanisms are used to allow interactions between the different parts of the system. Some authors even refer to the concept of "whole application as a mobile agent" as the *fat-agent model* (Simões, Reis, Silva, & Boavida, 1999).

In Figure 2, this concept is illustrated. The developers have implemented two different applications, A and B, which in practice are just a set of mobile agents. True mobile agents are represented as white pawns. Black pawns represent static entities that are programmed as mobile agents due to the lack of proper infrastructure for application development. The interactions are fully based on inter-agent communication mechanisms. The concept of application is largely based on conventions about which agents communicate with what. Interestingly, many times there is even the

Figure 1. The mainstream mobile agent platform architecture

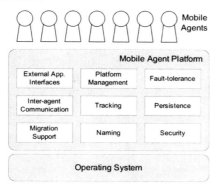

need to set up agents with special interfaces (and permissions) that are able to communicate with external applications via inter process communication (IPC) mechanisms. As strange as it seems, it is not uncommon for the only IPC mechanism available to provide integration with external entities to be a socket connection. It is also common for the agent platform to mediate all the access to operating system resources, especially if support for security is provided by the platform.

Developing distributed applications based on mobile agent systems has important advantages over the traditional client-server type of interactions. Mobile agents allow, among other things (Lange & Oshima, 1999), for: *reduced network traffic, easy software upgrading on-demand, easy introduction of new services in the network, higher robustness for the applications, support for disconnected computing, higher scalability, easy integration of vendor-proprietary systems,* and *higher responsiveness in the interactions with other systems.*

The JAMES Platform

In 1998, realizing the importance and advantages of using mobile agents in distributed systems, a consortium was setup for developing a mobile agent platform oriented for the development of applications in the field of telecommunication and network management. The project was called JAMES, and its partners were the University of Coimbra (Portugal), SIEMENS S.A. (Portugal), and SIEMENS AG (Germany); the being was implemented under the umbrella of a European Eureka Program (Σ!1921).

The JAMES platform provides the running environment for mobile agents. There is a distinc-

Figure 2. Applications on a standard agent platform are implemented as different mobile agents that map all the required functionality

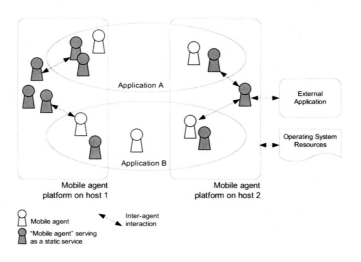

Figure 3. An overview of the JAMES platform

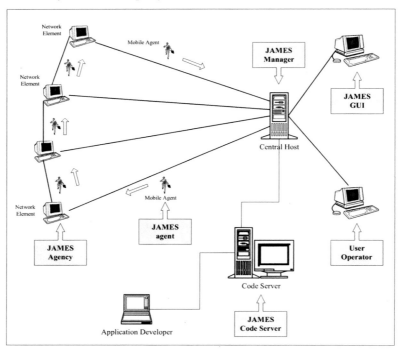

tion between the software environment that runs in the manager host and the software that executes in the network elements (NEs): the central host executes the JAMES manager while the nodes in the network run a JAMES agency. The agents are written by application programmers and execute on top of that platform. The JAMES system provides a programming interface that allows the full manipulation of mobile agents. Figure 3 presents a global snapshot of the system, with a special description of a possible scenario where the mobile agents will be used.

Every NE runs a Java virtual machine and executes a JAMES agency that enables the execution of the mobile agents. The JAMES agents will migrate through these machines of the network to access some data, execute some tasks, and produce reports that will be sent back to the JAMES manager. There is mechanism of authentication in the JAMES agencies to control the execution of agents and to avoid the intrusion of non-official agents. The communication between the different machines is done through stream sockets. A special protocol was developed to transfer the agents across the machines in a robust way and is atomic to the occurrence of failures.

The application developer writes the applications that are based on a set of mobile agents. These applications are written in Java and should use the JAMES API for the control of mobility. After writing an application, the programmer should create a JAR with all the classes that make part of the mobile agent. This JAR file is placed in a JAMES code server. This server can be a different machine or in the same machine where the JAMES manager is executing. In both cases, it maintains a code directory with all the JAR files available and the mapping to the corresponding mobile agents.

The host machine that runs the JAMES manager is responsible for the whole management of the mobile agent system. It provides the interface to the end-user, together with a graphical user for the remote control and monitoring of agents, places, and applications. The JAMES GUI is the main tool for management and administration of the platform. With this interface, the user can manage all the agents and agencies in the system.

For lack of space we will not describe the inner details of the JAMES platform. However, in the following list we present the key features of our mobile agent system:

- Portability of the applications, through the use of the Java language;
- High-performance in mobility through the use of caching and prefetching techniques;
- Security mechanisms for code authentication;
- Resource control service to manage the use of underlying resources;
- An overview of the JAMES Platform (CPU, memory, disk and operating system resources);
- System monitoring;
- Fault-tolerance through the use of checkpointing and reconfiguration;
- Easy-to-use programming interface;
- Scalable execution of mobile agents, through the use of decentralized protocols;
- Easy customization of the software;
- "On-the-fly" software upgrading;
- Interoperation with classical network management protocols, like SNMP;
- Distributed management and easy configuration of the network;

The result of this platform was further exploited by the industrial partners that have developed some applications for performance management in telecommunications networks using mobile-agent technology and the JAMES platform.

COMPONENT-BASED MOBILE AGENT SYSTEMS

Introduction

Having completed the JAMES project, several important lessons were learned. Possibly the most important was that using a *mobile agent platform* as middleware seriously limits the acceptance of mobile agents as a structuring and programming paradigm. The problem is not the mobile agents by themselves but the use of monolithic platform for developing and deploying them. Platforms force the programmer to adopt a completely different development model from the one in mainstream use (object-oriented programming). When using an agent platform, the programmer is forced to center its development, its programming units, and its whole applications on the concept of agent. Although useful and relatively simple to implement, the use of platforms limit the acceptance of mobile agents as simple programming constructs (Kotz, Gray, & Rus, 2002).

In this section, we start by exploring how traditional mobile agent platforms limit the acceptance of mobile agents as a structuring primitive, and then we present M&M, an agent system specifically for overcoming those limitations.

Limitations of the Platform-Based Model

The reasons why the platform architecture limits the acceptance of the mobile agent paradigm can be seen from three perspectives: the programmer, the end-user, and the software infrastructure itself.

The Programmer

One fundamental aspect of the mobile agent paradigm is that, by itself, it does not provide more functionality than what is attainable with the traditional client/server model. One of the major advantages of the mobile agent paradigm is that *logically* (i.e., without considering its physical implementation), its functionalities as a whole and as a structuring primitive—*an active thread of execution that is able to migrate*—are particularly adapted for distributed computing (Papaioannou, 2000). Mobile agent technology, in itself, has no killer application (Chess et al., 1994; Kotz et al., 2002).

Taking this into consideration, a relevant question is: What strong reason can motivate a programmer to consider using mobile agents to develop its applications? After all, everything that can be attained by using mobile agents can be done using client/server. The most important reason, as discussed before, is that a mobile agent is a logical structuring primitive very adapted for distributed computing. Still, for it to be accepted, the price to be paid by the programmer cannot be too high. With traditional agent platforms, typically it is.

The problems include: the mobile agent concept is not readily available at the language level; the applications have to be centered on the mobile agents; and a complicated interface between the agents and the applications and operating system resources must be written. The programmers want to develop their applications as they currently do, by using object-oriented techniques, and by using mainstream APIs. Agents will typically play a small role on the application structuring. Current platforms force exactly the opposite. Instead of being middleware, agents are the *frontware*.

If one looks at history, it is easy to understand that the RPC success is due to its strong integration with structured programming environments. RPCs did not force programmers to abandon their programming languages, environments, and methodologies. On the contrary, RPCs embraced them. Understandably, if the RPC model had required completely different languages and methodologies, it would have failed. Programmers would have continued to use sockets. After all, everything that can be done using an RPC can be done using a socket, granted that it is so with different degrees of difficulty. The argument also applies to RMI and its integration with object-oriented languages. Remote method invocation did not require different languages or environments but instead blended into existing systems. In both cases, developers started to use the new technologies because: (a) they were readily integrated at the language level and into their programming environments; (b) the applications could continue to be developed using the existing methodologies and only use the new technologies as needed; c) no workarounds were necessary for integrating with existing applications.

The point is that mobile agent technology should not necessarily force complete agent-based software design. It should be a complement to traditional object-oriented software development and easily available to use in ordinary distributed applications, along with other technologies.

The End-User

From the viewpoint of the user, if an application is going to make use of mobile agents, it is first necessary to install an agent platform. The security permissions given to the incoming agents must also be configured, and the proper hooks necessary to allow the communication between the agents and the application must be setup. While some of these tasks can be automated by using installation scripts, this entire setup package is too much of a burden.

Usually, the user is not concerned with mobile agents nor wants to configure and manage mobile agent platforms. The user is much more concerned with the applications than with the middleware they are using in the background. In the currently available mobile agent systems, the agents are central and widely visible. They are not the background middleware but the foreground applications.

Also, the term *mobile code* has very strong negative connotations, which makes the dissemination of mobile agent technology difficult. The user is afraid of installing a platform capable of receiving and executing code without its permission. This happens even though the existence of mobile code is present in technologies like Java, in particular in Applets, RMI, and JINI. The fundamental difference is that in those cases, the user is shielded from the middleware being used. In many cases, using mobile agents does not pose an increased security threat, especially if proper authentication and authorization mechanisms are in place. However, because the current agent platforms do not hide the middleware from the user, the risk associated with the technology is perceived as being higher than it is. This causes users to back away from applications that make use of mobile agents.

The Software Infrastructure

One final limitation of the platform-based approach lies in the architecture itself. Generally speaking, there are very few platforms that provide means for extensibility. Typically, the platform is a monolithic entity with a fixed set of functionalities. If it is necessary to provide new functionality, for instance, a new inter-agent communication mechanism, that functionality is directly coded into the platform. What this means is that if there are new requirements or features to be supported, it is necessary to recompile the whole platform and deploy it in the distributed infrastructure. This lack of support for system extensibility has several important consequences.

The first important consequence is management costs. As the name indicates, the *platform* is a software infrastructure that must be managed and attended at all times. Currently, when

an operator deploys an agent-based application, it does not gain just one new application to administrate. Besides the application, it gains a full-blown agent platform to manage. This type of cost is not negligible. For instance, it is curious to observe how sensitive the network management and telecommunications communities are to management costs, even though they are amongst the ones that can most benefit from the use of this technology (Picco, 1998; Simões, Rodrigues, Silva, & Boavida, 2002).

Another facet of the monolithic structure of the agent platform problem has to do with changing requirements. It is well known in the software industry that the requirements of applications are constantly changing. In fact, this knowledge has motivated a whole series of software methodologies that take this into account, as rapid development (McConnell, 1996) and eXtreme programming (Beck, 1999). In most of the current agent platforms, each time a feature is added or an error corrected, the software is recompiled, originating a new version. Although it is quite simple to upgrade an application based on mobile agents—it may be as simple as to kill the agents and send out new ones—the same does not happen to the agent infrastructure. When there is a new version of the agent infrastructure, it is necessary to manually redeploy it across the distributed environment.

Even though it is easy to devise code-on-demand solutions for the complete upgrade of agent platforms or to use server-initiated upgrades, as in the case of JAMES (Silva et al., 1999), most existing platforms do not provide for it. In many cases, the cost of redeploying the software across the infrastructure may be unacceptable. This is a second type of management cost that must be paid. In terms of deployment, it would be much more appealing to have an infrastructure where parts could be plugged in, plugged out, and reconfigured as necessary. Voyager (Glass, 1997), MOA (Milojicic, Chauhan, & la Forge, 1998), and gypsy (Lugmayr, 1999) provided the first experiments in this area, though, due to the monolithic architecture of most platforms, this type of solution is not readily available for them.

The M&M Agent System

The most distinctive characteristic of M&M is that there are no agent platforms. Instead, the agents arrive and depart directly from the applications they are part of. The agents exist and interact with the applications from the inside, along with the other application objects.

The applications become agent-enabled by incorporating well-defined binary software components into their code. These components give them the capability of sending, receiving, and interacting with mobile agents. The applications themselves are developed using the current best-practice software methods and become agent-enabled by integrating these "mobility components," that is, M&M framework components. We call this approach ACMAS—*application centric mobile agent systems*—since the applications are central and mobile agents are just part of the system playing specific roles.

The key idea is that the different functionality typically found on a monolithic agent platform is factored out as independent pluggable components that can be added or removed from the applications. No underlying agent platform is involved. In Figure 4, the approach is shown. Here, an application is being run on two different hosts. This application was built by using object-oriented programming and by incorporating generic components, like the ones that provide easy database connectivity or graphics toolkits, and mobility-related components, as the ones that provide migration support and agent tracking. Agents are able to migrate between applications by using the mobility-related components.

Comparing this model with the platform-based architecture, it is quite clear that the applications are no longer a set of agents. In this approach, when inside an application, an agent is just another object that has an associated thread of execution. The agents are just like any other objects of the application. Different applications incorporate the specific components necessary for their operation, executing them side-by-side. Another advantage of this approach is that agents can be specific to their applications, not having all the agents from all the applications coexisting together.

Figure 4. The applications become agent-enabled by incorporating well-defined binary components

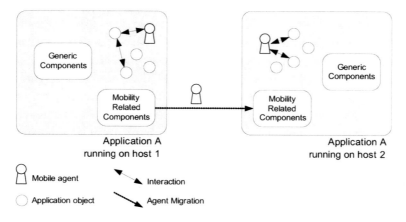

The M&M Component Palette

When developing an application by using the ACMAS approach, three different types of components are involved: generic third-party off-the-shelf components; application-specific components; and mobile agent-related components (see Figure 5):

- **Third-party off-the-shelf components** are components that are commercially available from software makers. Currently, there is a large variety of components available for the most different things, like accessing databases, designing graphical user interfaces, messaging, and others. All these components can be used for building the applications without having to re-implement the required functionalities.
- **Domain-specific components** are modules that must be written in the context of the application domain being considered, providing functionalities not readily available

off-the-shelf. For instance, while implementing a particular application, it may be necessary to write special parsers for extracting information from files or to write supporting services for allowing agents to monitor the hardware of a machine. These modules can be coded as components and incorporated into the application.
- **Mobile agent-related components** provide the basic needs in terms of mobile-agent infrastructure. These components provide the functionalities typically found in agent platforms: mobility support, inter-agent communication mechanisms, agent tracking, security, and others. The M&M component palette fits into this category.

When writing an application, the programmer assembles the necessary components and interconnects them by using programmatic glue. The application logic that mandates the execution of the program can be a separate module or be embedded in the wiring of the components. Typi-

Figure 5. Applications are created by assembling the necessary components

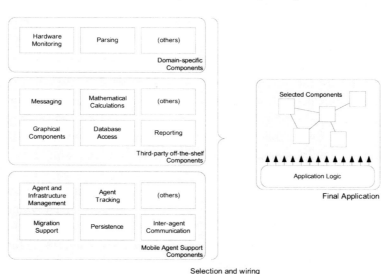

Table 1. Available components in the M&M component palette

Component(s)	Functionality
Mobility component	Provides the basic support for agent mobility, agent control, and monitoring. It incorporates an extensibility mechanism that allows other components to interact with the mobile agents.
Management components	Allows agents and the instantiated components to be monitored and controlled locally and remotely by applications and by administrative agents.
Agent tracking components	Allows the agents, local, and external applications to know the location of each agent in the distributed application.
Security component	Allows agents to safely execute inside the applications and for the applications to safely execute the agents. It is responsible for the provision of authentication and authorization services, and of monitoring and controlling what operations each agent is allowed to perform.
Local communication components	Supports message exchange between agents and applications or other agents, in the context of a single running application, using several paradigms (message passing and publisher-subscriber, both synchronously and asynchronously).
Global communication components	Allows the agents and the applications to exchange messages using several paradigms (message passing and publisher-subscriber, both synchronously and asynchronously), in the global context of a distributed application.
Disconnected computing components	Provides support for disconnected computing, allowing agents to be saved into persistent storage if they are not able to migrate to a disconnected device, and to migrate when the device comes back online. Persistent storage is also implemented as a separate component.
Web publishing components	Allows agents that migrate to a Web server to publish information and act as Web resources.

cal examples of the former are backend database and transaction processing applications; examples of the latter are form-based applications for data entering and querying. The final application is the combination of components, wiring glue, and backend application logic.

When considering a component palette for supporting mobile agents, two different aspects must be considered. On the one hand, there are components that are integrated into the application, giving it special abilities in terms of interacting with mobile agents. One example of this is a component that gives the application the ability to track the agents whenever they migrate.

On the other hand, when programming the mobile agents themselves, there are components that can be used for building them, for instance, a component that when included in a mobile agent gives it the ability to communicate with other mobile agents. Currently, the M&M framework supports both types.

Thus, when discussing the component palette of M&M, presented in Table 1, it is important to realize that there are components for including into the applications and components for including into agents. In fact, some of the components can even be used for both purposes (e.g., the client components of inter-agent communication).

Another important point is that sometimes the components do not implement the full functionality of a service and serve only as access points to certain functionalities. For instance, the client component for agent tracking connects to a network server that holds and updates the location of the agents. It should be noted that the M&M component list is by no means static or fixed. The M&M framework has well-defined interfaces that allow third-party developers to create new components and add them to the system and to upgrade existing components. In fact, M&M somewhat resembles a Lego system where new pieces can be created and fitted into the existing ones.

Figure 6 shows an application being created in a visual development tool and being agent-enabled by using M&M. On the left it is possible to see that the mobility component has been included; on the right, the properties of this component are shown; on the top, the M&M component palette is visible.

A detailed account of the M&M system and its implementation can be found in Marques (2003).

Consequences of Using a Component-Based Approach

Using a component-based approach for developing applications that use mobile agents has several important consequences. Some of these consequences are directly related to the characteristics of component technology, others are a product of the way M&M was designed. Some of the most important aspects are:

- **The users do not see agents or manage agent platforms:** As agents are sent back into the middleware instead of being "front-

ware," what the users ultimately see are applications and their interface. The adoption of a certain application is once again based on its perceived added value, not on the technology that it is using. Also, because users do not have to manage agents nor platforms, applications become conceptually simpler. No middleware infrastructure is explicitly visible to install and maintain. Although there are still distributed applications to install and manage, this is much easier than managing a separate infrastructure shared by a large number of distributed applications with different policies and requirements.

- **Tight integration with the end applications:** Since the agents can migrate from end-applications to end-applications, interacting with them from the inside, development becomes much more straightforward. There is no need to set up service agents, configure their policies, and devise workarounds based on IPCs. Once inside an application, a mobile agent is just a thread of execution that can access all the objects of that application, under proper security concerns. This contributes to better performance and scalability since the interaction with the applications does not have to go through the middlemen—the service agents.

- **Tight integration with existing programming environments:** For supporting mobile agents in an application, all the developer has to do is to include some of the components into the application and interconnect them. The applications can continue to be developed using object-oriented methodologies, having the necessary support for active migrating objects. By using M&M components in the applications, developers do not have to center all the development on the agents. Agents become just "one more" powerful distributed programming construct, as once advocated by Papaioannou (Papaioannou, 2000). What this means is that the development model is well integrated with current software development practices and environments. The path to using mobile agents in the applications becomes as smooth as using, for instance, remote method invocation.

- **Possibility of using visual development tools:** Software components are normally designed so that they can be manipulated visually. Instead of focusing on an API approach, components emphasize on well-defined visual entities with properties and interconnections that the programmer can configure visually. This can result in a large increase in productivity, a smoother learning curve, and a wider acceptance of a technology. By using a component-based approach, M&M takes benefit of all these characteristics.

- **Support for any programming language:** It is possible to use a JavaBeans/ActiveX bridge to encapsulate JavaBeans components as ActiveX ones. Thus, in the Windows platform it is possible to use a JavaBeans component from any programming environment, as long as it supports COM/ActiveX. This was the approach taken in the M&M framework. By using such a bridge, it was possible to have applications written in several languages—Visual Basic, Visual C++, Java, and so forth—sending and receiving agents between them. Even though, from a research point of view, this might not seem so important, from an integration and acceptance point of view it is quite important: It is directly related to whether a technology gets to be used or not.

- **Security can be integrated into the application:** One of the valuable lessons learned when designing the Internet was the importance of the end-to-end argument in system design (Saltzer, Reed, & Clark, 1984). There is a fragile balance between what can be offered generically by an infrastructure and what should be left to the application design on the endpoints. In terms of security, this is especially important. In many cases, it is only at the end applications, and integrated with the application security policies and its enforcement, that it is possible to take sensible security decisions. By using components directly integrated into the applications, the security of the mobile agents of an application becomes integrated with the security policies of the application itself.

- **Only the necessary components are included in each application:** Because the developer is implementing its application and only using the necessary features of mobile code, only the required components that implement such features need to be included. What this means is that it is not necessary to have a gigantic platform that implements every possibly conceivable feature, because in the end many of these features are not used in most applications. By using specific components it is possible to build a software infrastructure that is much more adapted to the needs of each specific application.

- **Extensibility and constant evolution:** In the last section it was discussed how "changing requirements" are an important problem and how monolithic platforms are ill-equipped to deal with new features, new releases, and redeployment. By using a component-based approach, it is possible to continually implement new components, with new features and characteristics, without implying the rebuilding of a new version of "the platform." The component palette can always be augmented.

- **Reusability and robustness:** One of the acclaimed benefits of using components is their tendency to become more robust over time. As a component is more and more reused in different applications, more errors are discovered and corrected, leading to new and more robust versions. Because components are black boxes with well defined interfaces and functionalities, they are also easier to debug and correct. By using a component-based approach to implement a mobile agent framework, it is also possible to benefit from these advantages.

Overall many applications have been implemented using M&M accessing its usefulness, easy of use, and close integration with programming environments and software. In this context, two application domains were of particular interest: agent-enabling web servers and supporting disconnected computing.

- The M&M component framework allows any Web server that supports the *servlet specification* to send, receive, and use mobile agents. M&M provides a clean integration, requiring neither a custom-made Web server nor a special purpose agent platform. A full account of this exploration can be found in Marques et al. (2002a).

- Finally, supporting disconnected computing has allowed us to understand the current limitations of the framework in supporting very low-level operations. This account can be found in Marques et al. (2002b).

A BIRD'S EYE PERSPECTIVE

Over the years, there has been a huge proliferation of mobile agent platforms. In fact, already in 1999 there were 72 known platforms. Nevertheless, the technology is still far from common use by mainstream programmer and, oddly as it seems, there now seems to exist more agent platforms than mobile agent-based applications.

In the previous sections, we have discussed how the agent platform architecture seriously impairs the actual leverage of the mobile agent paradigm into real applications, by real programmers, to real users. The paradigm does not bring a "one order of magnitude" increase in functionality, and at the same time, the agent platform architecture imposes a too-high price

Figure 6. Screen capture of the M&M component palette being used for developing a demonstration application

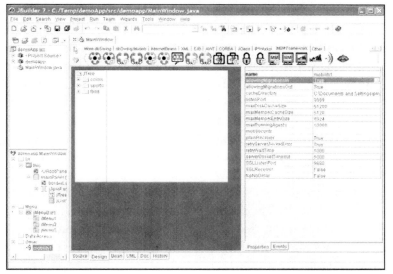

to developers, users, systems administrators, and institutions that could make use of the technology. The road imposed by the platform architecture is not one of integration with existing tools and environments but one of complete conversion to a new architecture. This conversion is asked for without giving anything substantial enough in return, and imposing many limitations on what can be implemented and how.

About the Proliferation of Mobile Agent Platforms

In our view, the huge proliferation of mobile agent platforms is directly connected with two factors: (a) the monolithic nature of agent platforms; (b) the advent of the Java language.

When considering different application fields, each one has its specific requirements. For instance, in the network management area, an important requirement is integration with SNMP. In other domains, there are others. Because in most cases it is not possible to extend a generic agent platform to take into account the needs of a certain application domain, what has happened is that researchers, and in fact the industry, have developed many new agent platforms that try to address specific domains. The Java language made it extremely easy to develop basic infrastructures for object and thread mobility, and thus to experiment in this area. In most cases, these platforms were developed from scratch.

The problems with these platforms are: they are not reusable across domains (many times not even across problems in a single domain); they do not take into account results in research (e.g., how to properly implement agent tracking or fault-tolerance); and, because in many cases they are quite experimental, they lack the robustness needed to be usable in the real world. The result is the current huge number of platforms that are not used by anyone and a large disappointment with the mobile agent paradigm.

The Mobile Agent Community

Another important problem is that the mobile agent community is too biased on the platform architecture, and little concerned with its integration with existing systems and infrastructures. This strong bias is easy to observe in practice. For instance, when looking at standards for mobile agents systems such as MASIF (OMG, 2000), from the Object Management Group, and FIPA (FIPA, 2000; FIPA, 2002), from the Foundation for Intelligent Physical Agents, it can be seen that the standardization effort was done around the concept of "agent platform", the platform on top of which all agents *should* execute. Neither alternative execution models nor any provisioning for integration with existing programming environments were considered.

Curiously, two of the most respected researchers in the area of intelligent agents—Nick Jennings and Michael Wooldridge—have long been arguing about the dangers of trying to leverage agents into the market. In the classic article *Software Engineering with Agents: Pitfalls and Pratfalls* (Wooldridge & Jennings, 1999), they examine what has been happening in the intelligent agent community. But, in fact, the observations also apply to the mobile agent community. Some of the key lessons from their experience are: "*You oversell agents,*" "*You ignore related technology,*" "*You ignore legacy,*" "*You obsess on infrastructure,*" and "*You see agents everywhere*". These are all relevant points if one wants to bring the mobile agent paradigm into real-world programming environments.

This view is somewhat supported by the success of Voyager (Glass, 1997) when compared with other agent infrastructures. Voyager is not a mobile agent platform but an ORB that, among other things, is also able to send and receive agents. Voyager does not force everything to be centered on agents, nor forces the applications to be agents. Applications are developed using ordinary methods and can use Voyager as an ordinary ORB. In practice, what has happened is that programmers who were using Voyager as a commercial ORB understood that they also had support for sending and receiving "active threads." Not having any prejudice, they started using this facility. Users continued to see applications as they always had, and system administrators did not gain complex agent platforms to manage.

Security

Security is traditionally singled out as the biggest problem facing mobile agents, and that prevented their dissemination as a paradigm. The idea of having arbitrary code that can execute on a host can be a scary one. There is the danger of resource stealing, denial-of-service attacks, data spying, and many other problems (Farmer, Guttman, & Swarup, 1996; Greenberg, Byington, & Harper, 1998).

Even so, although there are still some hard problems to be solved in a practical way, like the malicious host problem (Hohl, 1998) and proper resource control, security is probably one of the most active areas of research in mobile agent systems (e.g., Loureiro, 2001, contains an extensive survey on existing research on the topic).

When developing mobile agent applications, two different scenarios have to be considered. The first scenario consists of deploying an application that uses mobile agents in a closed environment. What this means is that it is possible to identify a central authority that controls all the nodes of the network where the agents are deployed. For example, a network operator may deploy an agent platform on its network, for being able to deliver new services in an easy and flexible way. Although different users, with different permissions, may create agents, the key point is that there is a central authority that is able to say who has what permissions and guarantee that nodes do not attack agents.

A completely different scenario is to have agents deployed in an open environment. In this picture, agents migrate to different nodes controlled by different authorities, possibly having very different goals. One classic example of this situation is an e-commerce application on the Internet. Different sites may deploy an agent platform, allowing agents to migrate to their nodes and query about products and prices, and even perform transactions on behalf of their owners. Here the sites will be competing against each other for having the agents making the transactions on their places. There is no central authority, and each site may attack the agents, stealing information from them, or making them do operations that they were not supposed to do.

Although it may appear that deploying applications on closed environments is too restrictive, there is a large number of applications that are worth deploying in such setting. Examples include network management, telecommunication applications, software distribution and upgrading, parallel and distributed processing, and groupware. For such environments, the currently available solutions are well adapted and sufficient. In many cases, it is a matter of proper authentication and authorization mechanisms, associated with a public key infrastructure.

The key argument is that although a lot of research is still necessary for securely deploying agents in open environments, there is a multitude of applications that can be developed securely for existing computing infrastructures in closed environments. On closed environments, besides the psychological effect of having code that is able to migrate between hosts, there is no additional risk when compared with existing technologies. The risks are similar to having *rexec* daemons running on machines, or using code servers in Java RMI.

In our view, the argument that it is security that is preventing the deployment of mobile agent technology is a misguided one. Many applications can be developed securely; and considering distributed systems, there are many technologies that operate without any special security considerations. That lack of security has not prevented them from being developed or having a large user base. A classical example is SNMP.

Agent Languages: Could They Be the Solution?

Over the years, many researchers came up with new languages that express mobile processes and mobile computations directly (e.g., Visual Obliq, Cardelli, 1995; Jocaml Conchon, & Fessant, 1999; Nomadic Pict & Wojciechowski, 1999). Although these languages integrate the mobile agent paradigm at the language level and are interesting in terms of the lessons learned in expressing new abstractions, they present the same generic problem as the platform architecture.

These languages force the programmers to use completely different programming paradigms and software structuring methodologies. At the same time, because using mobile agents does not bring any large increase in productivity nor enables anything important that cannot be achieved by classical means, programmers are not compelled to try out these new languages. In fact, it does not make much sense to ask developers to abandon proven development techniques and environments in favor of new languages that do not allow anything new or powerful, have not proven themselves, and force all the development to be centered on different abstractions.

The mobile agent technology should be available at the language level, but this means that the middleware should allow the creation, management, and integration with mobile entities directly, probably through an API at the same level than other programming libraries. It means that the programmer should be able to continue to use its current programming environments, languages, and development methodologies. When necessary, and only then, it should be able to create an active thread of execution that would be able to migrate and interact with the objects on different applications. This does not mean that all the development should be centered on the agents or that new languages are really necessary.

CONCLUSION

Mobile agent research is now almost 15 years old. Many valuable lessons have been learned in areas so diverse as persistence, resource allocation and control, tracking, state capture, security, communication, coordination, and languages. Nevertheless, no killer application has emerged, and only a few commercial applications have been developed. Two standardization efforts were made and failed.

Although the mobile agent paradigm has not entered the realm of mainstream programming, the fact is that *mobile code* and *mobile state* are now mainstream programming techniques. This has happened not as most researchers would expect it to have, namely as mobile agents, but in many different and more subtle ways. Java RMI code servers are a standard mechanism in use. Java object serialization and .NET's Remoting mechanism, which are for everyday use, offer state mobility and also code mobility in certain circumstances. Remotely upgradeable software, ActiveX-enabled pages, and other forms of code and state mobility are now so common that we do not even think about them. Even mainstream undergraduate books like Coulouris, Dollimore, and Kindberg (2000) and Tanenbaum and Steen (2002) discuss code and state mobility, and even mobile agents, without any prejudice. Books that are not mobile agent-specific but are related to code mobility are available (Nelson, 1999). Mobile code and mobile state have entered the realm of distributed programming.

It is always hard and error prone to make predictions. But, quoting Kotz et. al., it is also our view that "*The future of mobile agents is not specifically as mobile agents*" (Kotz, 2002). We also do not believe that the future of mobile agents is connected to the use of agent platforms as we know them today. That belief arises from our experiences with the JAMES and M&M systems, as presented in this chapter.

In our view, the future of mobile agents will be a progressive integration of mobile agent concepts into existing development environments. This integration will be as readily available at the API level as object serialization and remote method invocation have become. The programmer will be able to derive from a base class and with no effort have an object that is able to move between applications. That class and that object will be ordinary ones among the hundreds or thousands used in any particular application. This evolution will probably occur as the development of object serialization APIs becomes more complete, powerful, and easy to use.

ACKNOWLEDGMENT

We would like to thank to all the students and researchers that over the years worked on the JAMES and M&M systems. Also, this investigation was partially supported by the Portuguese Research Agency – FCT, through the CISUC Research Center (R&D Unit 326/97).

REFERENCES

Aglets Project Homepage (2006). Retrieved April 27, 2006, from http://sourceforge.net/projects/aglets

Arumugam, S., Helal, A., & Nalla, A. (2002). aZIMAs: Web mobile agent system. *Proceedings of 6th International Conference on Mobile Agents (MA'02)* (LNCS 2535). Barcelona, Spain: Springer-Verlag.

Beck, K. (1999). *eXtreme programming explained: Embrace change.* Addison-Wesley.

Bellavista, P., Corradi, A., & Stefanelli, C. (1999). A secure and open mobile agent programming environment. *Proceedings of the 4th International Symposium on Autonomous Decentralized Systems (ISADS'99)*, Tokyo, Japan.

Box, D. (1997). *Essential COM.* Addison-Wesley.

Cardelli, L. (1995). A language with distributed scope. *Computing Systems Journal, 8*(1).

Chess, D., Grossof, B., Harrison, C., Levine, D., Parris, C., & Tsudik, G. (1994). *Mobile Agents: Are they are good idea? (RC19887).* IBM Research.

Conchon S., & Fessant, F. (1999). Jocaml: Mobile agents for objective-caml. *Proceedings of the Joint Symposium on Agent Systems and Applications/Mobile Agents (ASA/MA'99),* Palm Springs, CA.

Coulouris, G., Dollimore, J., & Kindberg, T. (2000). *Distributed systems: Concepts and design* (3rd ed.). Addison-Wesley.

Delamaro, M., & Picco, G. (2002). Mobile code in .NET: A porting experience. *Proceedings of 6th International Conference on Mobile Agents (MA'02)* (LNCS 2535). Barcelona, Spain: Springer-Verlag.

Denning, A. (1997). *ActiveX controls inside out* (2nd ed.). Redmond, WA: Microsoft Press.

FIPA. (2000). *FIPA agent management support for mobility specification.* DC000087C. Geneva, Switzerland: Foundation for Intelligent Physical Agents.

FIPA. (2002). *FIPA abstract architecture specification.* SC00001L. Geneva, Switzerland: Foundation for Intelligent Physical Agents.

Farmer, W., Guttman, J., & Swarup, V. (1996). Security for mobile agents: Issues and requirements. *Proceedings of the 19th National Information Systems Security Conference (NISSC'96),* Baltimore.

Glass, G. (1997). *ObjectSpace voyager core package technical overview*. ObjectSpace.

Greenberg, M., Byington, J., & Harper, D. (1998). Mobile agents and security. *IEEE Communications Magazine, 36*(7).

Gschwind, T., Feridun, M., & Pleisch, S. (1999). ADK: Building mobile agents for network and systems management from reusable components. *Proceedings of the Joint Symposium on Agent Systems and Applications/Mobile Agents (ASA/MA'99)*, Palm Springs, CA.

Hohl, F. (1998). A model of attack of malicious hosts against mobile agents. In *Object-Oriented Technology, ECOOP'98 Workshop Reader / Proceedings of the 4ᵗʰ Workshop on Mobile Object Systems (MOS'98): Secure Internet Mobile Computations* (LNCS 1543). Brussels, Belgium: Springer-Verlag.

Kotz, D., Gray, R., Nog, S., Rus, D., Chawla, S., & Cybenko, G. (1997). AGENT TCL: Targeting the needs of mobile computers. *IEEE Internet Computing, 1*(4).

Kotz, D., Gray, R., & Rus, D. (2002). Future directions for mobile agent research. *IEEE Distributed Systems Online, 3*(8).

Lange, D., & Oshima, M. (1998). Mobile agents with Java: The Aglet API. *World Wide Web Journal,* (3).

Lange, D., & Oshima, M. (1999). Seven good reasons for mobile agents. *Communications of the ACM, 42*(3).

Loureiro, S. (2001). *Mobile code protection*. Unpublished doctoral dissertation, Institut Eurecom, ENST, Paris.

Lugmayr, W. (1999). *Gypsy: A component-oriented mobile agent system*. Unpublished doctoral dissertation, Technical University of Vienna, Austria.

Marques, P. (2003). *Component-based development of mobile agent systems*. Unpublished doctoral dissertation, Faculty of Sciences and Technology of the University of Coimbra, Portugal.

Marques, P., Fonseca, R., Simões, P., Silva, L., & Silva, J. (2002a). A component-based approach for integrating mobile agents into the existing Web infrastructure. In *Proceedings of the 2002 IEEE International Symposium on Applications and the Internet (SAINT'2002)*. Nara, Japan: IEEE Press.

Marques, P., Santos, P., Silva, L., & Silva, J. G. (2002b). Supporting disconnected computing in mobile agent systems. *Proceedings of the 14ᵗʰ International Conference on Parallel and Distributed Computing and Systems (PDCS2002)*. Cambridge, MA.

Marques, P., Simões, P., Silva, L., Boavida, F., & Gabriel, J. (2001). Providing applications with mobile agent technology. *Proceedings of the 4ᵗʰ IEEE International Conference on Open Architectures and Network Programming (OpenArch'01)*, Anchorage, AK.

McConnell, S. (1996). *Rapid development: Taming wild software schedules*. Redmond, WA: Microsoft Press.

Milojicic, D., Chauhan, D., & la Forge, W. (1998). Mobile objects and agents (MOA), design, implementation and lessons learned. *Proceedings of the 4ᵗʰ USENIX Conference on Object-Oriented Technologies (COOTS'98)*, Santa Fe, NM.

Nelson, J. (1999). *Programming mobile objects with Java*. John Wiley & Sons.

OMG. (2000). *Mobile agent facility, version 1.0*. Formal/00-01-02: Object Management Group.

Papaioannou, T. (2000). *On the structuring of distributed systems: The argument for mobility*. Unpublished doctoral dissertation, Loughborough University, Leicestershire, UK.

Picco, G. (1998). *Understanding, evaluating,*

formalizing, and exploiting code mobility. Unpublished doctoral dissertation, Politecnico di Torino, Italy.

Saltzer, J., Reed, D., & Clark, D. (1984). End-to-end arguments in system design. *ACM Transactions in Computer Systems, 2*(4).

Silva, L., Simões, P., Soares, G., Martins, P., Batista, V., Renato, C., et al. (1999). James: A platform of mobile agents for the management of telecommunication networks. *Proceedings of the 3rd International Workshop on Intelligent Agents for Telecommunication Applications (IATA'99)* (LNCS 1699). Stockholm, Sweden: Springer-Verlag .

Simões, P., Reis, R., Silva, L., & Boavida, F. (1999). Enabling mobile agent technology for legacy network management frameworks. *Proceedings of the 1999 International Conference on Software, Telecommunications and Computer Networks (SoftCOM1999),* FESB-Split, Split/Rijeka Croatia, Trieste/Venice, Italy.

Simões, P., Rodrigues, J., Silva, L., & Boavida, F. (2002). Distributed retrieval of management information: Is it about mobility, locality or distribution? *Proceedings of the 2002 IEEE/IFIP Network Operations and Management Symposium (NOMS2002),* Florence, Italy.

Tanenbaum, A., & Steen, M. (2002). *Distributed systems: Principles and paradigms.* Prentice Hall.

Tripathi, A., Karnik, N., Ahmed, T., Singh, R., Prakash, A., Kakani, V., et al. (2002). Design of the Ajanta system for mobile agent programming. *Journal of Systems and Software, 62*(2).

White, J. (1996). Telescript technology: Mobile agents. In J. Bradshaw (Ed.), *Software agents.* AAI/MIT Press.

Wojciechowski, P., & Sewell, P. (1999). Nomadic pict: Language and infrastructure design for mobile agents. *Proceedings of the Joint Symposium on Agent Systems and Applications/Mobile Agents (ASA/MA'99),* Palm Springs, CA.

Wooldridge, M., & Jennings, N. (1999). Software engineering with agents: Pitfalls and pratfalls. *IEEE Internet Computing, 3*(3).

This work was previously published in Architectural Design of Multi-Agent Systems: Technologies and Techniques, edited by H. Lin, pp. 95-114, copyright 2007 by Information Science Reference, formerly known as Idea Group Reference (an imprint of IGI Global).

Chapter 8.8
Building Applications to Establish Location Awareness:
New Approaches to Design, Implementation, and Evaluation of Mobile and Ubiquitous Interfaces

D. Scott McCrickard
Virginia Polytechnic Institute and State University (Virginia Tech), USA

Miten Sampat
Feeva Technology, Inc., USA

Jason Chong Lee
Virginia Polytechnic Institute and State University (Virginia Tech), USA

ABSTRACT

An emerging challenge in the design of interfaces for mobile devices is the appropriate use of information about the location of the user. This chapter considers tradeoffs in privacy, computing power, memory capacity, and wireless signal availability that accompany the obtaining and use of location information and other contextual information in the design of interfaces. The increasing ability to integrate location knowledge in our mobile, ubiquitous applications and their accompanying tradeoffs requires that we consider their impact on the development of user interfaces, leading to an agile usability approach to design borne from agile software development and usability
engineering. The chapter concludes with three development efforts that make use of location knowledge in mobile interfaces.

INTRODUCTION

A key challenge in the emerging field of ubiquitous computing is in understanding the unique user problems that new mobile, wearable, and embedded technology can address. This chapter focuses on problems related to location determination—different ways to determine location at low cost with off-the-shelf devices and emerging computing environments, and novel methods for integrating location knowledge in the design of applications. For example, many Web sites use location knowledge from IP addresses to automatically provide the user with relevant weather and traffic information for the current location. There is significant opportunity in the use of location awareness for human-computer interaction (HCI) researchers to explore information-interaction paradigms for the uncertainty and unpredictability that is inherent to many location detection systems—particularly indoor systems that use Wifi signals which can be blocked by roofs, walls, shelves, and even people!

The prior knowledge of location to make such decisions in the presentation of information affords it to be categorized as *context awareness*, the use information that can be used to identify the situation of an entity to appropriately tailor the presentation of and interaction with information to the current situation (Dey, 2001). While context awareness can include a wide variety of information—including knowledge of who is in your surrounding area, events that are happening, and other people in your vicinity—this chapter focuses on the identification and use of location information, perhaps the most cheaply and readily available type of context information. This chapter considers the tradeoffs in privacy, computing power, memory capacity, and wireless (Wifi) signal availability in building interfaces that help users in their everyday tasks. We discuss our own SeeVT system, which uses Wifi signals in location determination (Sampat, Kumar, Prakash, & McCrickard, 2005). The SeeVT system provides the backbone for supplying location information to mobile devices on a university campus. Numerous interfaces built on SeeVT provide timely and appropriate location information to visitors in key areas of the campus.

The increasing ability to integrate location knowledge in our mobile, ubiquitous applications requires that we consider its impact on the development of user interfaces. This chapter describes the merging of agile software development methods from software engineering with the scenario-based design (SBD) methodology from usability engineering to create a rapid iteration design approach that is heavy in client feedback and significant in its level of reusability. Also presented are three interfaces developed using our Agile Usability methodology, focusing on the benefits found in using the Agile Usability approach and the tradeoffs made in establishing location awareness.

BACKGROUND

From the early days, navigation has been central to progress. Explorers who set sail to explore the oceans relied on measurements with respect to the positions of celestial bodies. Mathematical and astronomical techniques were used to locate oneself with respect to relatively stationery objects. The use of radio signals proved to be fairly robust and more accurate, leading to the development of one of the first modern methods of navigation during World War II, called long range navigation (LORAN). LORAN laid the foundation of what we know as the Global Positioning System or GPS (Pace et al., 1995). Primarily commissioned by the United States Department of Defense for military purposes, GPS relies on 24 satellites that revolve around the Earth to provide precision location information in three dimensions. By relying on signals simultaneously received by four satellites, GPS provides much higher precision than previous techniques. GPS navigation is used in a wide range of applications from in-car navigation, to geographic information system (GIS)-mapping, to GPS-guided bombs.

GPS has become the standard for outdoor location-awareness as it provides feedback in a familiar measurement metric. Information systems like in-car navigators have adopted GPS as the standard for obtaining location, since it requires little or no additional infrastructure deployments and operates worldwide. However, GPS has great difficulty in predicting location in dense urban areas, and indoors, as the signals can be lost when they travel through buildings and other such structures. With an accuracy of about 100 meters (Pace et al., 1995), using GPS for indoor location determination does not carry much value. Along with poor lateral accuracy, GPS cannot make altitude distinctions of three to four meters—the average height of a story in a building—thus making it hard to determine, for example, whether a device is on the first floor or on the second floor. Despite continued progress through technological enhancements, GPS has not yet evolved sufficiently to accommodate the consumer information-technology space. This chapter primarily focuses on technologies making inroads for indoor location determination.

While GPS has clear advantages in outdoor location determination, there have been other efforts focused around the use of sensors and sensing equipment to determine location within buildings and in urban areas. Active Badges was one of the earliest efforts at indoor location determination (Want, Hopper, Falcao, & Gibbons, 1992). Active Badges rely on users carrying badges which actively emit infrared signals that are then picked up by a network of embedded sensors in and around the building. Despite concerns about badge size and sensor deployment costs, this and other early efforts inspired designers to think about the possibilities of information systems that could utilize location-information to infer the context of the user, or simply the context of use. One notable related project is MIT's Cricket location system, which involved easy-to-install motes that acted as beepers instead of as a sensor network (Priyantha, Chakraborty, & Balakrishnan, 2000). The user device would identify location based on the signals received from the motes rather than requiring a broadcast from a personal device. Cricket was meant to be easy to deploy, pervasive, and privacy observant. However, solutions like Cricket require deployment of a dense sensor network—reasonable for some situations, but lacking the ubiquity

necessary to be an inexpensive, widely available, easy-to-implement solution.

To provide a more ubiquitous solution, it is necessary to consider the use of existing signals—many of which were created for other purposes but can be used to determine location and context. For example, mobile phone towers, IEEE 802.11 wireless access points (Wifi), and fixed Bluetooth devices (as well as the previously mentioned GPS) all broadcast signals that have identification information associated with them. By using that information, combined with the same sort of triangulation algorithms used with GPS, the location of a device can be estimated. The accuracy of the estimation is relative to the number and strength of the signals that are detected, and since one would expect that more "interesting" places would have more signals, accuracy would be greatest at these places—hence providing best accuracy at the most important places. Place Lab is perhaps the most widespread solution that embraces the use of pre-existing signals to obtain location information (LaMarca et al., 2005). Using the broadcasted signals discussed previously, Place Lab allows the designer to establish location information indoors or outdoors, with the initiative of allowing the user community to contribute to the overall effort by collecting radio environment signatures from around the world to build a central repository of signal vectors. Any client device using Place Lab can download and share the signal vectors for its relevant geography—requiring little or no infrastructure deployment. Place Lab provides a location awareness accuracy of approximately 20 meters.

Our work focuses specifically on the use of Wifi access networks, seeking to categorize the benefits according to the level of access and the amount of information available in the physical space. We propose three categories of indoor location determination techniques: *sniffing* of signals in the environment, *Web-services access* to obtain information specific to the area, and *smart algorithms* that take advantage of other information available on mobile devices. In the remainder of this chapter, we describe these techniques in more detail, and we discuss how these techniques have been implemented and used in our framework, called SeeVT using our Agile Usability development process.

CATEGORIZING INDOOR LOCATION DETERMINATION TECHNIQUES

When analyzing location awareness, it is clear that the goal is not just to obtain the location itself, but information associated with the location—eventually leading to full context awareness to include people and events in the space, as described in Dey (2001). For example, indoor location awareness attributes such as the name of the building, the floor, surrounding environments, and other specific information attributed with the space are of particular interest to designers. Designers of systems intended to support location awareness benefit not only from location accuracy, but also from the metadata (tailored to the current level of location accuracy) that affords several types of cross-interpretations and interpolations of location and other context as well.

Access to this information can be stored with the program, given sufficient computing power and memory. This approach is reasonable for small areas that change infrequently—a library or a nature walk could be examples. Information about the area can be made accessible within the application with low memory requirements and rapid information lookup. However, changes to the information require updates to the data, a potentially intolerable cost for areas where location-related changes occur frequently. For example, a reconfigurable office building where the purpose and even the structure of cubicles change frequently would not be well served by a standalone application. Instead, some sort of Web-based repository of information would best meet its needs. Taking this model another step, a

mobile system could request and gather information from a wide range of sources, integrating it for the user into a complete picture of the location. As an example, a university campus or networked city would benefit from a smart algorithm that integrated indoor and outdoor signals of various types to communicate a maximally complete picture of the user's location.

Of course, each added layer of access comes with additional costs as well. Simple algorithms may sense known signals from the environment (for example, GPS and wireless signals) to determine location without broadcasting presence. However, other solutions described previously might require requesting or broadcasting of information, revealing the location to a server, information source, or rogue presence—potentially resulting in serious violations of privacy and security. The remainder of this section describes the costs and benefits for three types of indoor location determination approaches: sniffing, Web services, and smart algorithms.

Sniffing

As the name suggests, sniffing algorithms sense multiple points of a broadcast environment, using the points to interpret the location of a device. The radio environment is generally comprised of one or more standard protocols that could be used to interpret location—modern environments include radio signals including Wifi, Bluetooth, microwaves, and a host of other mediums—creating interesting possibilities for location interpolation. Sniffing is also desirable because all location interpolation and calculations are performed on the client device, eliminating the need for a third-party service to perform the analysis and produce results. As mentioned previously, there are some benefits and disadvantages to this approach.

Performing the location determination on the client device eliminates the need for potentially slow information exchange over a network. This approach gives designers the flexibility they need in order to perform quick and responsive changes to the interfaces as well as decision matrices within their applications. For example, a mobile device with a slow processor and limited memory will need a highly efficient implementation to achieve a speedy analysis. A limiting factor for this approach is the caching of previously known radio vectors. Since most analysis algorithms require a large pool of previously recorded radio-signal vectors to interpolate location, it translates into large volumes of data being precached on the client device. A partial solution for this exists already, precaching only for regions that the user is most likely to encounter or visit. Though this is not a complete solution to the resource crunch, it is a reasonable approach for certain situations with periodic updates or fetches when radio-vectors are upgraded or the system encounters an unknown location.

Herecast is an example of a system using the sniffing model (Paciga & Lutfiyya, 2005). It maintains a central database of known radio vectors, which are then published to client devices on a periodic basis. The clients are programmed to cache only a few known locations that the user has encountered, and relies largely on user participation to enter accurate location information when they enter new areas that the system has not encountered before. The accuracy for these systems is generally acceptable, but there is always the worry of not having a cache of an area that the application is about to encounter. The lack of linking to a service also means that other contextual information associated with the location is hard to integrate with this approach due to device caching constraints and metadata volatility.

Web-Services Model

Keeping with the fundamental idea of mobile devices facing a resource crunch, this approach has client devices and applications use a central service for location determination. This means that the client device simply measures or "sees" the radio environment and reports it to the central service. The service then performs the necessary computation to interpolate the user location (potentially including other timely information) and communicates it back to the client. This also allows the client to store a minimal amount of data locally and to perform only the simplest of operations—important for mobile devices that often trade off their small size for minimal resources.

The approach is elegant in many ways, but faces several challenges in its simplistic approach such as the problem of network latency leading to lengthy times to perform the transactions. However, as the speed and pervasiveness of mobile networks is on the rise, as is the capability of silicon integration technologies for mobile platforms, designing large-scale centralized systems based on the Web-services model will be a reasonable approach for many situations. Mobile online applications such as Friend Finders and child tracking services for parents are classic examples of tools that require central services to allow beneficial functionality to the end user.

Our own SeeVT system uses the Web services model by allowing its clients to perform Simple Object Access Protocol (SOAP) Web service calls to a standard Web interface, and submit a radio vector for analysis. It then performs the necessary location determination using a probabilistic algorithm and returns the location to the client. SeeVT provides the interface designer access to functionality on the service end as well. It allows the designers to control sessions and monitor the progress of clients by using a logging feature, and provides handles to integrate other widgets as well. For example, if an application wants to perform a search based on the user's current location, SeeVT allows the designer to add functionality to its modules to perform further server-side computations.

Smart Algorithms

Looking ahead, algorithms that span large and diverse geographic areas will require the integration of many signals, information requests, and additional inputs. Place Lab attempts to address this issue for all radio signals (LaMarca et al., 2005). Currently it can compute location using mobile phone tower signals, Wifi, fixed Bluetooth devices, and GPS. However, we expect that other information will be used for location determination in the near future. For example, the ARDEX project at Virginia Tech seeks to use cameras—quickly becoming commonplace on mobile devices—to create a real-time fiducially-based system for location determination based on augmented reality algorithms (Jacobs, Velez, & Gabbard, 2006). The goal of the system is to integrate it with SeeVT such that anyone at defined hot spots can take a picture of their surrounding area and obtain information about their location. In an interesting twist on this approach, the GumSpots positioning system allows users to take a picture of the gum spots on the ground in urban areas and performs image recognition on them to return user location (Kaufman & Sears, 2006). Other information recording devices could be used in similar ways to help determine or enhance the understanding of our current location.

BUILDING INTERFACES FOR LOCATION-KNOWLEDGEABLE DEVICES

This section begins with a discussion on possible application scenarios that can leverage location knowledge in mobile devices. This section first describes *Agile Usability*, an extension of agile software development methodologies to include key aspects of usability engineering—resulting in an interface building technique that is well suited to ubiquitous and location-knowledgeable computing devices, both from the standpoint of interaction as well as development processes. Next, three case studies illustrate real world applications that have been built using these processes. Each case study describes key aspects of the application, illustrating one of the indoor location determination techniques and highlighting key lessons learned from the use of Agile Usability.

Agile Software Development, Usability Engineering, and Agile Usability

Ubiquitous and pervasive systems are often introduced to augment and support everyday tasks in novel ways using newly developed technology or by using existing technology in different ways. Since end-user needs are often ill-defined for ubiquitous systems, development needs to quickly incorporate stakeholder feedback so the systems can be iteratively improved to address new and changing requirements. This section discusses the use of an agile development methodology to build ubiquitous systems. Based on our own work (Lee et al., 2004; Lee, Chewar, & McCrickard, 2005; Lee & McCrickard, 2007) and on prior investigation of agile development methods (Beck, 1999; Constantine, 2001; Koch, 2004), we present a usability engineering approach for the construction of interfaces for mobile and ubiquitous devices.

Agile software development methodologies have been developed to address continuous requirements and system changes that can occur during the development process. They focus on quick delivery of working software, incremental releases, team communication, collaboration, nd the ability to respond to change (Beck et al., 2001). One stated benefit of agile methods is a flattening of the cost of change curve throughout the development process. This makes agile methods ideally suited to handle the iterative and incremental development process needed to effectively

Figure 1. The agile usability process. The central design record bridges interface design with implementation issues. This enables incremental improvement incorporating feedback from project stakeholders and usability evaluations.

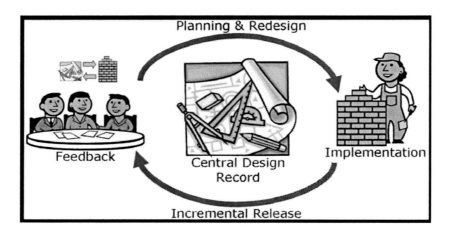

engineer ubiquitous systems. One shortcoming of many agile methods is a lack of consideration for the needs of end users (Constantine, 2001). Current agile development methodologies have on-site clients to help guide the development process and ensure that all required functionality is included. However, many ubiquitous and pervasive systems require continuous usability evaluations involving end-users to ensure that such systems adequately address their needs and explore how they are incorporated in people's daily tasks and affect their behavior. Researchers, including Miller (2005), Constantine (2001), and Beyer, Holtzblatt, and Baker (2004) have developed ways to integrate system and software engineering with usability engineering. We present our approach to agile usability engineering, henceforth referred to as Agile Usability, with the added benefit of usability knowledge capture and reuse.

Our approach combines the software development practices of extreme programming (XP) with the interaction design practices of scenario-based design (SBD) (Beck, 1999; Rosson & Carroll, 2002). The key features of this process are

an incremental development process supported by continual light-weight usability evaluations, close contact with project stakeholders, an agile interface architecture model, known as a central design record (CDR), that bridges interface design and system implementation issues, and proactive knowledge capture and reuse of interface design knowledge (Figure 1).

Running a large-scale requirements analysis process for developing ubiquitous systems is not as beneficial as when designing other types of systems as it can be very difficult to envision how a ubiquitous system will be used in a specific situation or how the introduction of that system will affect how people behave or use it. In this type of development process, portions of the system are developed and evaluated by end users on a continual basis. This helps developers in uncovering new requirements and dealing with changing user needs as development proceeds. This type of development process requires some amount of discipline and rigor in terms of the types of development practices to follow. Specific details of these XP programming practices are detailed

Figure 2. Screenshots from three applications built on SeeVT. From the left, the alumni tour guide, VTAssist, and SeeVT-ART

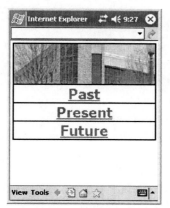  

in Beck's book on the subject (Beck, 1999). Our use of these practices are elaborated in a technical report (Lee, Wahid, McCrickard, Chewar & Congleton, 2007).

An incremental development process necessitates close collaboration with customers and end users to provide guidance on what features are needed and whether the system is usable. Ideally, representatives from these groups will be onsite with the developers working in the same team. Our customers were not strictly on site, although they were in the same general location as the developers. Regularly scheduled meetings and continual contact through e-mail and IM were essential to maintaining project velocity.

The key design representation is the central design record (CDR), which draws on and makes connections between design artifacts from XP and SBD. Stories that describe individual system features are developed and maintained by the customer with the help of the developers. They are prioritized by the customer and developed incrementally in that order. These include all features needed to develop the system including underlying infrastructure such as databases, networking software, or hardware drivers. Scenarios, which are narratives describing the system in use, are used to communicate interface design features and behaviors between project stakeholders. Claims, which describe the positive and negative psychological effects of interface features in a design, are developed from the scenarios to highlight critical interaction design features. Story identification and development may lead to changes to the scenarios and claims. The reverse may also be true. This coupling between interface design and system implementation is critical for ubiquitous systems as developers must deal with both interactional and technological issues when deploying a system to the population.

In addition to acting as a communication point between stakeholders and highlighting connections between interface design and implementation, the CDR is important as a record of design decisions. As developers iterate on their designs, they often need to revisit previous design decisions. The explicit tradeoffs highlighted in the claims can be used by developers and clients to determine how best to resolve design issues that come up. Perhaps most important, Agile Usability drives developers to explore key development techniques in the development of location-based interfaces—the techniques used advance the field and can be reused in other situations.

Agile Usability has been applied in numerous situations, three of which are highlighted in this chapter as case studies. Each case study describes how the user tasks were identified, how stakeholder feedback was included, how our agile methodology was employed, and how appropriate location detection technologies were integrated. The discussion portion of this section will compare and contrast the lessons learned in the different case studies—highlighting specific usability engineering lessons and advancements that can be used by others.

Case Study 1: Alumni Tour Guide

The alumni tour guide application was built for visitors to the Virginia Tech (VT) campus. The system notifies users about points-of-interest in the vicinity as and when they move about the VT campus (Nair et al., 2006). This image-intensive system provides easy-to-understand views of the prior and current layout of buildings in the current area. By focusing on an almost exclusively image-based presentation, users spend little time reading text and more time reflecting on their surroundings and reminiscing about past times in the area. See Figure 2 for a screenshot of the guide.

The earliest prototypes of the tour guide proposed a complex set of operations, but task analyses and client discussions performed in the Agile Usability stages indicated that many alumni—particularly those less familiar with handheld and mobile technology—would be unlikely to want to seek out solutions using the technology. Instead, later prototypes and the final product focused on the presentation and contrast of historical and modern images of the current user location. For example, alumni can use the tour guide to note how an area that once housed some administrative offices in old homes has been rebuilt as a multistory technology center for the campus. This pictorial comparison, available at any time with only a few clicks, was well received by our client as an important step in connecting the campus of the past with the exciting innovations of the present and future.

As the target users are alumni returning to campus, most are without access to the wireless network, and the logistics are significant in providing access to the thousands of people who return for reunions, sporting events, and graduations. As such, the Alumni Tour Guide uses the sniffing location detection method to identify current location. This method fits well with the nature of the tasks of interest to alumni: they care most about the general space usage and the historical perspectives of a location that change little over time.

Case Study 2: VTAssist

Building interfaces is often difficult when the target audience has needs and skills different than those of the developer: for example, users with mobility impairments. It often takes many iterations to focus on the most appropriate solutions—a perfect candidate for Agile Usability. A pair of developers used our methodology to build VTAssist, a location-aware application to enable users with mobility impairments, specifically users in wheelchairs, to navigate a campus environment (Bhatia, Dahn, Lee, Sampat, & McCrickard, 2006). VTAssist helps people in wheelchairs navigate in an environment more conducive to those who are not restricted in movement. Unlike typical handhelds and Tablet PC applications (the two platforms for which VTAssist was created), the VTAssist system must attract the user's attention at times of need or danger, guide them to alternate paths, and provide them with a means to obtain personal assistance when necessary. Perhaps most importantly, VTAssist allows users to quickly and easily supply feedback on issues and difficulties at their current location—both helping future visitors and building a sense of community among those who traverse the campus. See Figure 2 for a screenshot of the VTAssist.

In developing VTAssist using Agile Usability, we found that needs and requirements changed over time requiring that the methodology account for those changes. For example, the original design was intended to help wheelchair users find location accessible resources and locations, but later the need was identified to keep that information constantly updated, resulting in the addition of the collaborative feedback feature. It was this feature that was deemed most important to the system—the feature that would keep the information in VTAssist current, and would enable users to take an active role in maintaining the information, helping others, and helping themselves.

Due to the importance of the feedback feature in maintaining up-to-date information for those in wheelchairs, VTAssist uses the Web services model. Certainly it would be possible to obtain some benefit from the sniffing model, but the client reaction indicated the importance of user feedback in maintaining an accurate database of problems and in providing feedback channels to frustrated users looking for an outlet for their comments. In addition, the server-side computations of location and location information (including comments from users and from facility administrators) results in faster, more up-to-date reports about the facilities.

Case Study 3: Conference Center Guide

The conference center guide, known as SeeVT-ART, addresses the desires of visitors and alumni to our area in coming to, and generally in returning to, our university campus—specifically the campus alumni and conference center (Kelly, Hood, Lee, Sampat, & McCrickard, 2006). SeeVT-ART provides multimodal information through images, text, and audio descriptions of the artwork featured in the center. Users can obtain alerts about interesting regional and university-specific

features within the center and they can be guided to related art by the same artist or on the same topic. The alerts were designed to be minimally intrusive, allowing users to obtain more information if they desired it or to maintain their traversal through the center if preferred. See Figure 2 for a screenshot of SeeVT-ART.

Agile Usability was particularly effective in this situation because of the large amount of input from the client, who generated a lot of ideas that, given unlimited time and resources, would have contributed to the interface. Agile Usability forced the developers to prioritize—addressing the most important changes first while creating placeholders illustrating where additional functionality would be added. Prioritization of changes through Agile Usability also highlighted the technological limitations of the underlying SeeVT system, specifically those related to the low accuracy of location detection, and how that influenced the system design. For example, when a user enters certain areas densely populated with artistically interesting objects, SeeVT-ART requires the user to select from a list of the art pieces, as it is impossible to determine with accurate precision where the user is standing or (with any precision) what direction the user is facing. These limitations suggested the need for smart algorithms that use information about the area and that integrate additional location determination methods.

Smart algorithms that store location data over time and use it to improve location detection can be useful in determining data such as the speed at which a user is walking and the direction a user is facing. SeeVT-ART can use this data to identify the piece of art at which a user most likely is looking. Our ongoing work is looking at integrating not only the widely accessible broadcast signals from GPS, cellular technology, and fixed Bluetooth, but also RFID, vision algorithms, and augmented reality (AR) solutions. Our early investigation into a camera-based AR solution combines information about the current location with image processing by a camera mounted on the handheld to identify the artwork and augment the user's understanding of it with information about the artist, provenance, and so forth. These types of solutions promise a richer and more complete understanding of the importance of a location than any one method could accomplish alone.

CONCLUSION AND FUTURE DIRECTIONS

The three location-knowledgeable SeeVT applications described in this document offer a glimpse into the possibilities for location-knowledgeable mobile devices. The increasing presence of wireless networks, improvements in the power and utility of GPS, and development of other technologies that can be used to determine location portends the ubiquity of location-knowledgeable applications in the not-too-distant future. Delivery of location-appropriate information in a timely and useful manner with minimal unwanted interruption will be the goal of such systems. Our ongoing development efforts seek to meet this goal.

In support of our development efforts, we explore new usability engineering approaches particularly appropriate for location-knowledgeable applications. The use of stories and the knowledge capturing structures of Agile Usability combined with its rapid multiple iterations enable convergence on solutions to the most important issues faced by emerging application areas. We repeatedly found that designers are able to identify issues of importance to the target users, while keeping in perspective the design as a whole. Our ongoing work seeks ways to capture and share the knowledge produced from designing these applications not only within a given design but across designs, leading to the systematic scientific advancement of the field.

In the future, these developing Agile Usability techniques will be supported by specific tools and toolkits for leveraging the location-awareness needs of on-the-go users. An early contribution that can be drawn from this work is the novel methods for supporting location awareness in users—browseable historical images of the current location, rapid feedback methods for reporting problems, new map presentation techniques—all methods that should be captured in a toolkit and reused in other location awareness situations.

REFERENCES

Bahl, P., & Padmanabhan, V. N. (2000). RADAR: An in-building RF-based user location and tracking system. In *Proceedings of IEEE INFOCOM, Tel Aviv, Israel,* (Vol. 2, pp. 775-784).

Beck, K. (1999, October). Embracing change with extreme programming. *IEEE Computer, 32*(10), 70-77.

Beck, K., Beedle, M., van Bennekum, A., Cockburn, A., Cunningham, W., Fowler, M. et al. (2001). *The Agile Manifesto.* Retrieved January 25, 2008, from http://agilemanifesto.org

Beyer, H. R., Holtzblatt, K., & Baker, L. (2004). An agile customer-centered method: Rapid contextual design. In *Proceedings of Extreme Programming and Agile Methods 2004 (XP/Agile Universe),* Calgary, Canada (pp. 50-59).

Bhatia, S., Dahn, C., Lee, J. C., Sampat, M., & McCrickard, D. S. (2006). VTAssist-a location-based feedback notification system for the disabled. In *Proceedings of the ACM Southeast Conference (ACMSE '06),* Melbourne, FL (pp. 512-517).

Constantine, L. L. (2001). Process agility and software usability: Toward lightweight usage-centered design. *Information Age, 8*(2). In L. Constantine (Ed.), *Beyond chaos: The expert edge in managing software development.* Boston: Addison-Wesley.

Dey, A. K. (2001). Understanding and using context. *Personal and Ubiquitous Computing, 5*(1), 4-7.

Jacobs, J., Velez, M, & Gabbard, J. (2006). AR-DEX: An integrated framework for handheld augmented reality. In *Proceedings of the First Annual Virginia Tech Center for Human-Computer Interaction Research Experience for Undergrads Symposium*, Blacksburg, VA (p. 6).

Kaufman, J., & Sears, J. (2006). GSPS: GumSpots positioning system. In *IPT 2006 Spring Show*. Retrieved January 25, 2008, from http://itp.nyu.edu/show/detail.php?project_id=539

Kelly, S., Hood, B., Lee, J. C., Sampat, M., & McCrickard, D. S. (2006). *Enabling opportunistic navigation through location-aware notification systems*. Pending paper submission.

Koch, A. S. (2004). *Agile software development: Evaluating the methods for your organization.* Artech House Publishers.

LaMarca, A., Chawathe, Y., Consolvo, S., Hightower, J., Smith, I., Scott, J., et al. (2005). Place lab: Device positioning using radio beacons in the wild. In *Proceedings of the 3rd International Conference on Pervasive Computing (Pervasive 2005),* Munich, Germany (pp. 134-151).

Lee, J. C., Chewar, C. M., & McCrickard, D. S. (2005). Image is everything: Advancing HCI knowledge and interface design using the system image. In *Proceedings of the ACM Southeast Conference (ACMSE '05),* Kennesaw, GA (pp. 2-376-2-381).

Lee, J. C., Lin, S., Chewar, C. M., McCrickard, D. S., Fabian, A., & Jackson, A. (2004). From chaos to cooperation: Teaching analytic evaluation with LINK-UP. In *Proceedings of the World Conference on E-Learning in Corporate, Government, Healthcare, and Higher Education (E-Learn '04),* Washington, D.C. (pp. 2755-2762).

Lee, J. C., & McCrickard, D. S. (2007). Towards extreme(ly) usable software: Exploring tensions between usability and agile software development. In *Proceedings of the 2007 Conference on Agile Software Development (Agile '07),* Washington DC, (pp. 59-70).

Lee, J. C., Wahid, S., McCrickard, D. S., Chewar, C. M., & Congleton, B. (2007). Understanding Usability: Investigating an Integrated Design Environment and Management System. *International Journal of Information Technology and Smart Education (ITSE), 2*(3), 161-175.

Miller, L. (2005). Case study of customer input for a successful product. In *Proceedings of the Agile 2005 Conference,* Denver, CO (pp. 225-234).

Nair, S., Kumar, A., Sampat, M., Lee, J. C., & McCrickard, D. S. (2006). Alumni campus tour: Capturing the fourth dimension in location based notification systems. In *Proceedings of the ACM Southeast Conference (ACMSE '06),* Melbourne, FL (pp. 500-505).

Pace, S., Frost, G. P., Lachow, I., Frelinger, D., Fossum, D., Wassem, D. et al. (1995). *The global positioning system: Assessing national policies* (Ref. No. MR-614-OSTP). Rand Corporation.

Paciga, M., & Lutfiyya, H. (2005). Herecast: An open infrastructure for location-based services using WiFi. In *Proceedings of Wireless and Mobile Computing, Networking, and Communications (WiMoB 2005),* Montreal, Canada (pp. 21-28).

Priyantha, N. B., Chakraborty, A., & Balakrishnan, H. (2000). The cricket location-support system. In *Proceedings of the Sixth Annual International Conference on Mobile Computing and Networking (MOBICOM 2000),* Boston, MA (32-43).

Rosson, M .B., & Carroll, J. M. (2002). *Usability engineering: Scenario-based development of human-computer interaction.* New York: Morgan Kaufman.

Sampat, M., Kumar, A., Prakash, A., & McCrickard, D. S. (2005). Increasing understanding of a new environment using location-based notification systems. In *Proceedings of 11th Internation-*

alConference on Human-Computer Interaction (HCII '05). Las Vegas, NV.

Sciacchitano, B., Cerwinski, C., Brown, I., Sampat, M., Lee, J. C., & McCrickard, D. S. (2006). Intelligent library navigation using location-aware systems. In *Proceedings of the ACM Southeast Conference (ACMSE '06),* Melbourne, FL (pp. 371-376).

Tom, H. (1994). The geographic information systems (GIS) standards infrastructure. *StandardView, 2*(3), 33-142.

Want, R., Hopper, A., Falcao, V., & Gibbons, J. (1992). The active badge location system. *ACM Transactions on Information Systems, 40*(1), 91-102.

Youssef, M., & Agrawala, A. K. (2004). Handling samples correlation in the Horus system. In *Proceedings of IEEE INFOCOM.* Hong Kong, China.

KEY TERMS

Agile Usability: Design methodologies that incorporate practices from agile software development methods and usability engineering methods to enable the efficient development of usable software.

Extreme Programming: An agile software development methodology centered on the values of simplicity, communication, feedback, courage, and respect.

Location Awareness: Functionality in mobile devices that allows them to calculate their current geographic location.

Mobile Devices: Handheld, portable computing devices such as smart phones and personal digital assistants.

Scenario-Based Design: Usability engineering methodology that uses descriptions of how people accomplish tasks—scenarios—as the primary design representation to drive the development and analysis of systems.

SeeVT: Location aware system that uses Wifi signals to calculate the position of wireless-enabled mobile devices.

Ubiquitous Computing: Technology embedded in the environment that becomes implicit and tightly integrated into peoples' day to day tasks.

Wifi: Wireless local area networking technology and standards developed to improve the interoperatility of wireless communication devices.

Chapter 8.9
From Ethnography to Interface Design

Jeni Paay
Aalborg University, Denmark

Benjamin E. Erlandson
Arizona State University, USA

ABSTRACT

This chapter proposes a way of informing creative design of mobile information systems by acknowledging the value of ethnography in HCI and tackling the challenge of transferring that knowledge to interface design. The proposed approach bridges the gap between ethnography and interface design by introducing the activities of field-data informed design sketching, on a high level of abstraction, followed by iterative development of paper-based mock-ups. The outcomes of these two activities can then be used as a starting point for iterative prototype development—in paper or in code. This is particularly useful in situations where mobile HCI designers are faced with challenges of innovation rather than solving well-defined problems and where design must facilitate future rather than current practice. The use of this approach is illustrated through a design case study of a context-aware mobile information system facilitating people socialising in the city.

INTRODUCTION

This chapter looks at the mobile technology design problem of taking an ethnographic-based approach to gathering field data and making this data available to the design process in a form that is easily assimilated by designers to inform user-centred design of mobile technology. Interface design for mobile technologies presents unique and difficult challenges that sometimes render traditional systems design methods inadequate. Ethnography is particularly well-suited to design for mobile technology. Mobile usability is often highly contextual and ethnographic approaches can facilitate richer understandings of mobile use contexts providing insight into the user's perspective of the world. Exploring the huge potential of mobile devices presents designers with a unique opportunity for creativity. In thinking about mobile technology design for *future*, rather than *current* practice, the challenge becomes even greater.

Before this discussion proceeds further it is worth clarifying the use of the term *ethnography*. Traditionally, ethnographic studies within sociology are conducted from a particular theoretical viewpoint and for the purpose of contributing to theory. However, ethnography, as it is understood in HCI research, generally refers to a collection of techniques used for gathering and organizing field materials from observational studies (Dourish, 2006). By its very definition, ethnography is primarily a form of reportage. It provides both empirical observational data, and makes an analytical contribution in the organization of that data. The virtue of ethnography is that it takes place in real-world settings and provides access to the ways people perceive, understand, and do things (Hughes et al., 1997). Ethnographically-oriented field methods can be used in HCI to provide a deeper understanding of an application domain, a holistic understanding of users, their work, and their context, which can then be drawn into the design process at the earliest stages (Millen, 2000). Ethnographic studies involve detailed observations of activities within their natural setting, providing rich descriptions of people, environments and interactions, and acknowledging the situated character of technology use (Millen, 2000). These observations can provide valuable insights into the processes needed for systems requirements specifications (Sommerville et al., 1993).

In the literature, the terms ethnography and ethnomethodology are both used to refer to field studies using ethnographic methods to understand how people perceive their social worlds. Other terms such as technomethodology (Button & Dourish, 1996), rapid ethnography (Millen, 2000) and design ethnography (Diggins & Tolmie, 2003) are also used to distinguish different aspects of the use of ethnography in the design of technology.

For the sake of simplicity, this chapter uses the term ethnography to encompass these understandings as being important to the discussion of the relationship between their outputs and the inputs they provide to the design process.

For ethnography to make a worthwhile contribution to the design of mobile technologies, we need to find ways for translating ethnographic findings into forms that are suitable for informing design processes. In the following sections, the historical relationship between ethnography and HCI is discussed, including how it has been incorporated into the process of interface design. The theoretical and methodological background for how to gather and interpret ethnographic data and use this for informing design is described. A design case study is then presented in which an ethnographic approach has been applied to mobile technology design in a real world research project through a structured series of activities. The overall process is described, and the two steps of developing *design sketches* and *paper-based mock-ups* are introduced as a way of bridging the gap between ethnography and interface design. Finally, lessons learned from using design sketches and paper-based mock-ups in the development process are outlined.

BACKGROUND

Ethnography and HCI

The issue of bridging the gap between ethnography and interface design has been a topic of discussion in HCI research for over a decade. Ethnography is now regarded as a common approach to HCI research and design (Dourish, 2006). Yet there is still no overall consensus on how best to incorporate the results of ethnographic fieldwork into the design processes (Diggins & Tolmie, 2003). In the early 90s seminal work by sociologists, such as Suchman, Hughes, Harper, Heath and Luff, inspired the use of ethnography for understanding the social aspects of work processes and informing user interface design (Hughes et al., 1995). However, researchers struggled with the challenge of utilizing insights provided by ethnography into the activity of designing. By the mid 90s, ethnography was hailed as a new approach to requirements elicitation for interactive system design, particularly through its application in the development of computer-supported cooperative work (CSCW) systems (Hughes et al., 1995). Even so, some researchers still held reservations about the ability of ethnographic methods to inform design (Hughes et al., 1997) and ethnography was regarded as a relatively untried approach to systems development, despite the fact that it was increasingly being used to inform and critique actual systems (Button & Dourish, 1996). Toward the end of the 90s, researchers were beginning to develop systematic approaches to social analyses for the purpose of influencing design (e.g., Viller & Sommerville, 1999). However, despite many research efforts, bridging the gap between ethnography and design still remains a matter of concern to HCI researchers today (Diggins & Tolmie, 2003).

The turn towards ethnography within HCI was motivated by a growing need to design for complex real world situations. This began with the belief that methods from the social sciences, such as ethnography, could provide means for understanding these contextual issues of technology use better. In the light of today's ubiquitous and mobile networked computing environments, the need to understand contexts of technology use, such as peoples' dynamic work and social practices, is challenging HCI researchers and designers more than ever. Supporting innovation in a world of emerging technologies can be done by submerging designers, who understand emerging technical possibilities, into rich ethnographic field data about potential users' lives and current practices (Holtzblatt, 2005). In this way technology design drives an understanding of the user's situation, which in turn, propels innovation.

Ethnography and Interface Design

The process of transition from field data to prototype design is a difficult one (Cheverst et al., 2005; Ciolfi & Bannon, 2003). A design process involving ethnography generally starts with observations and interviews collected through ethnographic methods. Key findings are then summarized and design ideas are drawn out with a set of features that can be tied back to the findings. The next step involves, "design suggestions" or "design implications," which may evolve into requirements through the development of a low-fidelity prototype. This prototype is then iterated with feedback from users and evolves into the operational system. The data collected by ethnographic methods reflects the richness of the user's situation in a way that is difficult to derive from a limited set of questions or measures as employed in traditional analysis methods (Wixon, 1995). In contrast to traditional systems analysis that looks at data, structures, and processing, ethnography is concerned with participants and interactions (Sommerville et al., 1993). This provides the designer with a rich understanding of the context of use for the artifacts that are being designed (Millen, 2000). In looking at a situation through the user's eyes rather than the designers, ethnography provides a view of the situation that is independent of design preconceptions (Hughes et al., 1997).

Ethnography has much to contribute to interface design—particularly in mobile device design due to the highly contextual nature of mobile usability and use. However, one of the main problems is finding a suitable mechanism for the transference of knowledge between these two fundamentally different disciplines. Ethnographic findings need to be understood and communicated to designers (Hughes et al., 1995). And yet, current mechanisms for incorporating ethnographic findings into the design process still fail to capture the value of these investigations (Dourish, 2006).

Ethnography deals in "the particular," and software design in "the abstract" (Viller & Sommerville, 1999). While willing to listen to each other, both disciplines speak different languages and use different methodologies. Ethnographers deal in text, notes, reports, and transcriptions, and produce detailed results giving a rich and concrete portrayal of the particulars of everyday practical action in context, presented in a discursive form; software designers and engineers deal in the creation and manipulation of more formal graphical abstractions, notations and description techniques to simplify the complexity of the situation and extract critical features. Ethnographers avoid judgements; designers make them. Where ethnographers take an analytic role, including gathering and interpreting data, software designers have a synthesis role, designing from abstract models of situations (Button & Dourish, 1996; Hughes et al., 1995). In addition to the problems of communication there are also problems of timing. Ethnography is generally conducted over a long period of time; in fact, it is difficult to define an end point for gathering understanding. On the other hand, software designers are often under restricted time pressure to deliver a product.

The problem has been in finding a timely method and a suitable form to present field findings that can be assimilated by and are readily usable for designers (Hughes et al., 1995; Viller & Sommerville, 1999). The needs of the software designer have to be aligned with a representation of the essential "real world" practices of users in context. Simply describing the social events being observed is not sufficient, designers need to be able to model and use this understanding in design.

USING ETHNOGRAPHY IN THE DESIGN PROCESS

Gathering Data

From HCI research it can be seen that using ethnography as a data gathering method requires the development of more structured approaches to conducting and reporting from ethnographic studies that better support the development of design requirements.

One approach is to conduct ethnography concurrently with design and bring ethnographic results into the design process in a more systematic way throughout the development process. This can, for example, be achieved through meetings between ethnographers and the design team (Hughes et al., 1995). This approach results in a change in the way that ethnography is conducted. Rather than extended periods in the field, ethnographers working in cooperation with software designers to create a system design, making short and focused field studies, reporting back to designers, and often taking design questions back into the field to focus their observations and questions to users. To structure the process, the communication of fieldwork to designers can be supported by dedicated software packages (Diggins & Tolmie, 2003; Sommerville et al., 1993). In this situation, the ethnographic record becomes a joint resource with ethnographers regularly reporting their findings in an electronic form, and designers using this content to develop structured design requirements. Constructing these records in a connected manner preserves backward and forward traceability between ethnographic findings and evolving system requirements.

Another approach is to lead into the design process through *rapid ethnography* (Millen, 2000). Rapid ethnography provides the field worker with a broad understanding of the situation which can then be used to sensitize designers to the use situation rather than identifying specific design issues. It is aimed at gaining a reasonable understanding of users and their activities in the short time available for this in a software development process. Rapid ethnography provides a more structured approach to ethnographic field studies by limiting the scope of the research focus before entering the field. It focuses time spent in the field by using key informants in the real situation and interactive observation techniques. Rapid ethnography also uses multiple observers in the field to ensure several views of the same events and to create a richer representation and understanding of the situation (Millen, 2000).

Interpreting Data

Ethnography is not simply about the collection of data in the field, it is also about reflection on and interpretation of that field data. Effective communication between ethnography and design is at the heart of the matter of bridging the gap between the two disciplines (Hughes et al., 1997). By recognizing the different natures and input and output requirements of ethnography and interface design, integration between the two disciplines can be achieved through enhancing and structuring the communication between them during the interpretation phase.

One approach to interpreting the data collected is to have a cross-discipline team participating in the fieldwork. In this situation designers go into the field with ethnographers to experience themselves how users work. They also contribute to the representation of the gathered data, shaping it into a form that is easier for designers to use (Diggins & Tolmie, 2003). Representing ethnographic findings through pictorial stories, drawings, data models, analogies and metaphors are ways to communicate field learning to cross-discipline teams (Millen, 2000). Videotapes of field observations and design documentaries play a similar role using a more designer-accessible communication mode than a written report (Raijmakers et al., 2006).

Another approach to interpretation is to have both ethnographers and designers involved in the conceptual design process. In this situation, the ethnographer is an ongoing member of the design team, providing grounded insights and interpretations into the abstracted requirements as they evolve and the design emerges. The ethnographer acts as a substitute user during the design process (Viller & Sommerville, 1999). Through their knowledge of the actual situation, they can participate in discussions with the designers, providing insights and access to instances of specific relevant situations.

A third approach is for the designer to play the part of a pseudo-ethnographer. This involves designers going "into the wild" and being exposed to users by watching real work while it is being done, and hence truly experiencing the richness of work (Wixon, 1995). Structured methods such as rapid ethnography and *contextual design* (Beyer & Holtzblatt, 1998) make this possible. In contextual design, the user and the designer explore the design space together using *contextual interview* or *facilitated enactment* of their practices in context (Holtzblatt, 2005). *Affinity diagramming*, from the contextual design method, provides a synthesis of the data into hierarchical classifications where the meaning contained in the data elements can be reflected on in relation to the design question, facilitating understanding and innovation for designers.

Informing Design

After the ethnographically gathered field data has been interpreted, abstracted findings are used to derive design opportunities and design requirements. The designer uses the outputs from the interpretation of the field data as input into the design process. Sometimes the ethnographers are involved in this design process bringing their intimate knowledge of the users and the situation of use, and their deep relationship to the data, to the team (Cheverst et al., 2005). They participate in the identification of design incentives by drawing attention to general design opportunities, and relevant topics and concerns. Otherwise, the designers must draw understanding entirely from the reports, discussions, diagrams and models, which represent the ethnographic record.

Design is a matter of making, and is used to create and give form to new ideas and new things (Fallman, 2003). A recent approach to informing design and achieving a close connection between the design team and the field data is the use of field observation videos or design documentaries. These videos mediate between ethnographic and design perspectives. As the design team watches them they incorporate interpretation of data into the design process on the fly through discussions drawing design sensitivities and identifying design concerns. Designers become sensitized to relevant issues visible in the real world interactions depicted in the video (e.g., Ciolfi & Bannon, 2003; Raijmakers et al., 2006). This method requires a high level of design experience, and in bridging the gap between ethnography and design, these designers work in an inspirational, ephemeral and creative way. For others this creative leap across the divide is very difficult, and more structured methods are needed to guide the process of envisioning design from ethnographic outputs. In response to new interface design challenges, including mobile technology, HCI researchers are investigating new techniques for guiding designers through this difficult transition – of particular interest to this chapter are the techniques of *design sketching* (Buxton, 2007), *paper-based mock-ups* (Ehn & Kyng, 1991) and *paper prototyping* (Snyder, 2003).

Design sketching is fundamental to the process of design, and can be used by information system designers to bring about the realization of an idea in the way designers think (Fallman, 2003). Sketching is the art of giving form to the unknown; it makes it possible to "see" ideas or envision whole new systems, and is especially critical in the early ideation phase of design

(Buxton, 2007). According to Buxton, sketches should be rapid, timely, inexpensive, disposable, plentiful, clear, un-detailed, light, informal representations that practitioners can produce and interact with to suggest and explore ideas. Sketching is not only a way to visualize existing ideas, but it is about shaping new ideas. In making a sketch of something, the visualization talks back to the designer with a new perspective on that idea, providing a link between vision and realization of new ideas.

Paper-based mock-ups are closely related to the notion of design sketching. In this technique from the participatory design tradition, representational artifacts are constructed from paper, cardboard and materials at hand. Informed by studies of practice, mock-ups can play an important mediating role in connecting use requirements and design possibilities in a form recognizable to multi-disciplinary design teams (Ehn & Kyng, 1991). These mock-ups can be used to incorporate materials from the ethnographic study, embody envisioned new technological possibilities, convey design ideas in relation to existing practices and reveal requirements for new practices (Blomberg & Burrell, 2003).

Paper prototyping is a widely used technique for designing, testing and refining user interfaces (Snyder, 2003). This technique helps with the development of interfaces that are useful, intuitive, and efficient, by initiating testing of the interface at a stage when the design is in its formative stages and therefore still open to the input of new ideas. Paper prototyping can be used to reflect on field study findings while developing and refining the design (Holtzblatt, 2005). A collection of interface designs, drawn from ideas generated through design sketching and paper-based mock-ups are given functional and navigational connections through the process of paper prototyping. A paper prototype is a useful vehicle for giving visual form to identified design requirements. It forms the focus for design refinement discussions and cognitive walkthroughs by the design team, and

Figure 1. The overall process of designing the Just-for-Us mobile information system

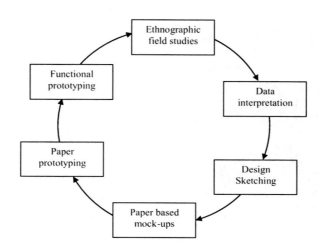

is in itself part of the design specification for implementation of the system.

A DESIGN CASE STUDY

The project used as a design case study in this chapter involved the development of a context-aware mobile information system, *Just-for-Us,* designed to facilitate people socialising in the city by providing information about people, places, and activities in the user's immediate surroundings. The case study location was a specific city precinct covering an entire city block, Federation Square, Melbourne, Australia. This location was chosen because it is a new, award-winning architectural space providing a variety of activities through restaurants, cafes, bars, a museum, art galleries, cinemas, retail shops, and several public forums spanning an entire city block. The design intention for the civic space was to incorporate digital technologies into the building fabric creating a combination of virtual information space and physical building space for people to experience. Thus, this particular place provided a unique

setting for studying people's situated social interactions in a "hybrid" space and for inquiring into the user experience of mobile technology designed to augment such a physical space with a digital layer.

Process

The Just-for-Us mobile information system was designed specifically for Federation Square on the basis of an ethnographic study of people socialising there. The development process involved seven major activities:

- Ethnographic field studies
- Field data interpretation
- Design sketching on a high level of abstraction
- Paper-based mock-up development
- Iterative paper prototyping
- Implementation of a functional prototype
- Field studies of prototype use in-situ

The specific content and outcome of these activities are described in the following subsections.

Figure 2. Ethnographic observations and contextual interviews at Federation Square

Details of the implemented system and findings from the field study of its use are not covered here, but can be found in Kjeldskov and Paay (2006).

As illustrated in Figure 1, data from ethnographic field studies of situated social interactions in public were subjected to data interpretation, using the *grounded theory* approach (Strauss & Corbin, 1990) and affinity diagramming (Beyer & Holtzblatt, 1998). In trying to bridge the gap between our ethnographic data and actual mobile device interface design, outcomes from the interpretation of field data were used to inform a systematic activity of design sketching (Buxton, 2007). The purpose of this activity was to generate design ideas on a high level of abstraction inspired by ethnographic findings but without getting into too much detail about specific look, feel and functionality. On the basis of selected design sketches, we developed a number of paper-based mock-ups (Ehn & Kyng, 2991) of potential design solutions. This forced us to become more specific, but still allowed us to focus on overall functionality and interaction rather than on technical details. After this, we engaged in a number of paper prototyping (Snyder, 2003) iterations with the purpose of developing a detailed set of system requirements and a coherent interface concept prior to writing any program code. Finally, these specifications were implemented in a functional prototype allowing us to introduce new technology into the field and revisit peoples' socialising behavior in the city while using the operational Just-for-Us context-aware mobile information system.

Gathering and Interpreting Data

The aim of our ethnographic field study was to inquire into peoples' social interactions at Federation Square. The field study was guided by a subset of McCullough's typology of everyday situations (McCullough, 2004) for classifying peoples' social activities when out on the town: eating, drinking, talking, gathering, cruising, belonging, shopping, and attending. The study applied a rapid ethnography approach and consisted of a series of contextual interviews (Beyer & Holtzblatt, 1998) and ethnographic field observations (Blomberg & Burrell, 2003) with the designers acting as pseudo-ethnographers and gathering the field data (Figure 2). Three different established social groups participated in the study. Each group consisted of three young urban people, mixed gender, between the ages of 20 and 35, with a shared history of socialising at Federation Square. The groups determined the activities undertaken and the social interactions that they engaged in. Prior to the field visits, each group received a 10-minute introduction to the study followed by a 20-minute interview about their socialising experiences and preferences. This introduction occurred at a place familiar to the group, where they might meet before socialising in the city. This encouraged them to reflect on past social interactions, to relax about the visit, and gave the interviewer insight into the situated interactions that the group typically participated in. One of the members of the group was then taken to Federation Square and asked to arrange to meet up with the other members of the group. The group was then asked to do what they would usually do as a group when socialising out on the town—while "thinking aloud" as they moved around the space, and responding to

Figure 3. Graphical image of inhabited social context at Federation Square

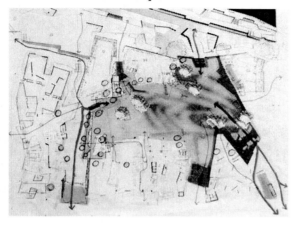

Figure 4. Affinity diagram of situated social interactions at Federation Square

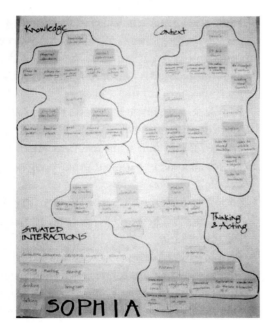

questions from the interviewer. Two researchers were present in the field, providing multiple views on the data collected.

Each field visits lasted approximately three hours and allowed the groups to engage in a number of social activities. The outcome of the ethnographic field studies amounted to eight hours of video and approximately 30 pages of written notes.

In addition to the observational studies of people socialising at Federation Square an architecturally trained observer carried out a single *expert audit* (Lynch, 1960) focusing on the physical space of Federation Square. The expert audit documented architectural elements and their relationships to surrounding context, including the people inhabiting the space through 124 digital photographs and corresponding field notes.

Interpreting data gathered from the ethnographic study involved two phases. Firstly, photographic data and written notes from the expert audit were analyzed using *content analysis* (Millen, 2000) and affinity diagramming (Beyer & Holtzblatt, 1998). Concepts and themes describing the physical space of Federation Square were overlaid onto a map of the precinct to produce a color-coded multi-layered abstraction of the space (Figure 3). This provided an overview of the spatial properties of Federation Square highlighting constraints and enablers for situated social interactions there with traceable links back to specific observations.

Secondly, video data from the contextual interview and observational field study of people socialising at Federation Square was transcribed and then analyzed using open and axial coding adapted from *grounded theory* analysis (Strauss & Corbin, 1990). Identifying key words or events in the transcript, and analyzing the underlying phenomenon created the initial open codes. Analysis of these codes resulted in a collection of categories relating to actions and interactions. After the codes were grouped into categories, higher-level themes were extracted using axial

Figure 5. Design sketching informed by interpreted ethnographic field data. The delineated area corresponds to the paper-based mock-up produced later and highlighted on Figure 6.

coding. Affinity diagramming was then used to draw successively higher levels of abstraction from the data by grouping and sorting the themes until a set of high-level concepts, representing the essence of the data and encompassing all lower level themes, had been formed. The process of affinity diagramming produced a hierarchical conceptual framework containing three overall clusters of themes abstracted from the transcripts (Figure 4). This provided a rich story about how people interact with each other while socialising in public, with traceable links back to specific observations in the field study sessions.

As illustrated in Figures 3 and 4, outcomes from the interpretation of our ethnographic field data were primarily on an abstract level, providing a deeper understanding of peoples' situated social interactions in the physical space of Federation Square. While this is an important part of the foundation for good design, in their current form these outputs did not point towards any particular design ideas. As an example, the analytical outcomes from interpreting the field data included a series of qualitative statements similar to those in the following list (For a detailed account of findings from the ethnographic field studies see Paay and Kjeldskov (2005)).

- Federation Square has four key districts with distinctly different characteristics, each with an associated landmark.
- Federation Square has visible surroundings, general paths, general entrances, focal structures and no clear paths, so people need to use the structures and surrounds in finding their way around the space.
- People socialising at Federation Square like getting an overview of what is happening around them, and want to know about the presence and activities of other people.
- People's past experience with places and people at Federation Square play an important factor in choosing places and activities for socialising.
- People give directions at Federation Square by referring to shared experiences and visible elements, and use their history and physical familiarity with a place to find their way around using familiar paths.

In order to move forward from data interpretation toward an overall design concept as well as actual interface design and system requirements for a context-aware mobile information system for people socialising at Federation Square, the design team engaged in two steps of developing

Figure 6. One of the paper-based mock-ups of possible mobile device screens

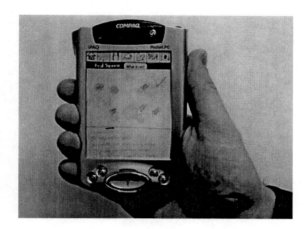

design sketches and paper-based mock-ups (as described earlier). Each of these techniques produced interface design artifacts on different levels of detail and abstraction. These two "bridging" steps between ethnography and interface design are described in the following sections.

Design Sketching

The first step in the design of the Just-for-Us mobile information system was to develop a series of conceptual design ideas based on the insight from our data analysis. For this purpose, the design team spent two days generating, discussing, sketching, and refining design ideas on the basis of the abstract models of the architectural space of Federation Square and the clustering of themes in the affinity diagram from the analysis of people socialising there.

The design sketching activity was done in a dedicated design workspace with sheets of A1 paper lining the walls on which we could sketch and refine design ideas. Each sketch took its origin in a specific finding or observation from the interpreted field data. This field finding would

firstly be discussed in more detail to ensure shared understanding among the design team. Secondly, we would start sketching possible design ideas, for example, how to facilitate an observed practice. Hence, we were, in a sense, using collaborative data analysis, as described in the rapid ethnography method, to drive the generation of design ideas.

During the process of sketching, the conceptual outcomes from the data interpretation phase were continually revisited and, in turn, the sketches were continuously annotated with post-it notes referring to the data. For example, a section of the affinity diagram included the themes of "social experience," encompassing "past experience" and "shared experience." A diagram was then sketched to explore the intersections between past and shared experiences in groups of friends. In this way, we ensured a strong link between data and design, and maintained clear traceability between the two. This activity was about sketching the social concepts that came out of the data models, not about generating solutions. In doing this, we were able to explore the field data findings in a graphical form, and to explore derivations from these concepts by generating multiple understandings of them. Design sketching was used as a mechanism to understand the field outcomes, to generate graphical overviews of the design space, and create graphical representations of design opportunities within that space.

The outcome from the two-day design workshop was a collection of design sketches on A1 paper (Figure 5), each describing conceptually a potential design idea or design opportunity, for parts of the Just-for-Us mobile information system, including envisioned general functionality, general ideas for graphical design and user interaction, with clear references back to the empirical data.

The design sketches provided a new visual abstraction to the ethnographically interpreted field data, translating understanding encapsulated in the abstract findings into design parlance.

Figure 7. Detailed paper prototype screen (left) and the corresponding final functional prototype screen (right), designed from the paper-based mock-up highlighted in Figure 6

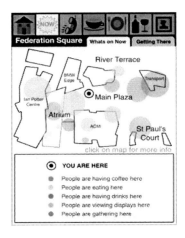

Engaging in the process of design sketching rather than jumping straight to specifying system requirements, enabled us to see the ethnographic findings from a new perspective and to play with design ideas on a high level of abstraction. This allowed us to distance ourselves from the role of "problem solvers" and to explore instead, on a conceptual level, design ideas facilitating potential future practice in technology use.

Paper-Based Mock-Ups

While useful for generating and working with overall design ideas, conceptual design sketches are far too abstract for informing specific system requirements. Hence, moving directly on to detailed prototype design and implementation is likely to commit designers to specific solutions too early and impede their flexibility to try out new ideas. In an attempt to overcome this problem, the next step of our process from ethnography to interface design was to produce a series of paper-based mock-ups of possible specific design solutions (Figure 6).

The production of paper-based mock-ups took place over several days and facilitated a series of long discussions within the design team leading to an overall concept for the Just-for-Us mobile information system providing functionality such as: an augmentation of the user's physical surroundings; chat capability with friends out on the town; content indexed to the user's physical and social context and history of interactions in the city; a graphical representation of places, people and activities within the user's vicinity; and way-finding information based on indexes to landmarks and familiar places. These design ideas were screen-based solutions to design opportunities identified during design sketching.

Working with each of these ideas in more detail, the paper-based mock-ups gave the design team a medium for trying out and modifying specific design ideas for what the system should be able to do and what it should look like—long before any actual coding was done. Consequently, the mock-ups coming out of this activity had already undergone several iterations of redesign and refinements.

Discussions during the mock-up phase took place on different levels of abstraction: from screen design, system functionality, privacy issues, problems designing for small screens, what aspects of the user's context to capture in the system, and how to do this. We also had several discussions about whether or not the implementation of the produced mock-ups would be feasible within current mobile technologies, and if not, which enabling technologies would have to be developed. Through these discussions and continued refinements and redesigns, a set of specific design requirements slowly began to take shape—gradually taking us into the "safer ground" of interface design.

Prototyping

Having completed the paper-based mock-up phase, the final steps of our development process were much more straightforward. On the basis of the mock-ups, more detailed paper prototypes were produced using Adobe Photoshop (Figure 7 left). This forced the design team to work within the graphical limitations of the target device and to use the specific graphical user interface elements available in the target browser, for this web based application. Also, the detailed paper prototypes allowed the designers to discuss some of the more dynamic interaction issues such as navigation structure and handling of pushed information. While most design changes were done in Adobe Photoshop at this time, some of the more serious issues, such as how to fit the Internet chat screen(s) into the limited design space, forced the design team back to working with paper-based mock-ups for a short time. After several cognitive walkthroughs, a full paper prototype with a detailed set of requirements was agreed upon and implemented as an operational mobile web site providing context-aware information to users, with very few modifications (Figure 7 right).

The design specified by the paper prototype was implemented as a functional Web-based system accessible through the Web browser of a PDA (personal digital assistant) providing context-related information, dynamic maps and location specific annotated graphics to the user. It also keeps a history of the user's visits to places around the city. The functional prototype uses WLAN or GPRS for wireless Internet access and resolves the user's location and the presence of friends in vicinity by means of Bluetooth beacons potentially embedded into the environment. The implementation of a functional prototype allowed us to close the circle depicted in Figure 1 by returning to Federation Square to do an ethnographic field study of people socialising there—this time facilitated by the Just-for-Us system. For details on this use study see Kjeldskov and Paay (2006).

FUTURE TRENDS

The future trends for bridging between ethnography and interface design for mobile technologies are many. As a part of a drive toward more user centered innovative design for both current and future practice, new techniques are emerging, which respond to the specific challenges of mobile technology design and use. These include, for example, cultural probes, digital ethnography, video diaries, film documentaries, facilitated enactment, acting-out in context, role-playing and body storming. Through these new techniques, the roles of ethnographers, designers, and future users are becoming more interwoven, facilitating a smoother and more effortless transition from ethnography to interface design. Techniques such as these reflect the fact that mobile technology design is not only about designing for existing work practices but also about designing for future practices in peoples' private and social lives and responding to the challenge of innovating for non-work in as yet non-existing use situations. They also respond to issues raised by many researchers that mobile technologies are often used in dynamic and continually changing contexts, offering information directly related to those contexts, and that it can be very difficult to predict what future user-adaptations of mobile technology might evolve.

The techniques of sketching and mocking-up introduced in this chapter are not new. Both have a long tradition in other design disciplines. However, like many of the above emerging approaches, we have combined existing techniques in a new way that provides designers with a more structured path to follow when making the difficult transition of transferring knowledge from the field into the design process.

CONCLUSION

This chapter addresses the issue of ethnography informing interface design for mobile technologies. It has described how ethnographic studies can be used in HCI design and how such studies can be useful for understanding current practice as well as providing a backdrop for envisioning potential future practice. However, as confirmed in the literature, bridging between ethnography and design is difficult, and techniques are needed that enable designers to better use ethnographic findings in the design process. In response to this, the two steps of conceptual design sketching and creating paper-based mock-ups have been proposed as bridging activities between ethnographic data interpretation and iterative prototype development.

Illustrating how this can be done in practice, this chapter has described a recent project involving the design of a context-aware mobile information system on the basis of a rapid ethnographic field study. In this project, the process of design sketching from analytical data made a useful link between interpretation and design. It provided a means of communicating a conceptual understanding of current practice into the early stages of interface design, and helped "translate" findings from the field data into design parlance. Working with sketches allowed the design team to play with design ideas on a conceptual level

rather than moving straight to specifying system requirements. It also allowed them to distance themselves from the role of "problem solvers" and to explore instead potential future practice of technology use.

The process of creating and refining paper-based mock-ups on the basis of selected design sketches gave the design team a medium for being a bit more specific while still maintaining a high level of flexibility. It allowed for drilling down into some specific design ideas and the exploration and modification of ideas for interface design and functionality before doing any coding. It also allowed the team to engage in discussions about possible screen designs, different functionality, privacy, small screens, etc., and to rapidly implement, evaluate, and refine design ideas. By working with paper-based mock-ups, it was possible to generate a strong set of specific design requirements, which provided a solid foundation for subsequent activities of paper and functional prototyping.

Innovative interface design for mobile technologies is both an art and a science. It requires us to be creative and inspired as well as structured and focused. Facilitating creativity and inspiration provides the art. Grounding interface design in empirically informed understanding of people and current practice provides the science. The challenge we are faced with is not just how to perform the art and science of design better individually, but more so how to support a fruitful interplay between the two. For this purpose, techniques such as conceptual design sketching and creation of paper-based mock-ups are valuable tools for researchers and designers on their journey from ethnography to interface design.

REFERENCES

Beyer, H., & Holtzblatt, K. (1998). *Contextual design—Defining customer centred systems*. San Francisco: Morgan Kaufmann.

Blomberg, J., & Burrell, M. (2003). An ethnographic approach to design. In J. Jacko & A. Sears (Eds.), *Handbook of human-computer interaction* (pp. 964-986). Mahwah, NJ, USA: Lawrence Erlbaum Associates Inc.

Button, G., & Dourish, P. (1996). Technomethodology: Paradoxes and possibilities. In *Proceedings of CHI 96*, (pp. 19-26). Vancouver, Canada: ACM.

Buxton, B. (2007). *Sketching user experiences: Getting the design right and the right design*. San Francisco, Morgan Kaufman Publishers.

Cheverst, K., Gibbs, M., Graham, C., Randall, D., & Rouncefield, M. (2005). Fieldwork and interdisciplinary design. *Notes for tutorial at OZCHI 2005*. Retrieved October 24, 2007, from http://www.comp.lancs.ac.uk/rouncefi/Tutout.html

Ciolfi, L. & Bannon, L. (2003). Learning from museum visits: Shaping design sensitivities. In *Proceedings of HCI International 2003* (pp. 63-67). Crete, Greece: Lawrence Erlbaum.

Diggins, T., & Tolmie, P. (2003). The 'adequate' design of ethnographic outputs for practice: some explorations of the characteristics of design resources. *Personal and Ubiquitous Computing, 7*, 147-158.

Dourish, P. (2006). Implications for Design. In *Proceedings of CHI 2006* (pp. 541-550). Montreal, Canada: ACM.

Ehn, P., & Kyng, M. (1991). Cardboard computers: Mocking-it-up or hands-on the future. In J. Greenbaum & M. Kyng (Eds.), *Design at work: Cooperative design of computer systems* (pp. 167-195). Hillsdale, NJ, USA: Lawrence Erlbaum Associates, Publishers.

Fallman, D. (2003). Design-oriented human-computer interaction. In *Proceedings of CHI 2003* (pp. 225-232). Florida, USA: ACM.

Holtzblatt, K. (2005). Customer-centred design for mobile applications. *Personal and Ubiquitous Computing, 9*, 227-237.

Hughes, J., King, V., Rodden, T., & Andersen, H. (1995). The role of ethnography in interactive systems design. *Interactions, 2*(2), 56-65.

Hughes, J., O'Brien, J., Rodden, T., & Rouncefield, M. (1997). Designing with ethnography: A presentation framework for design. *In Proceedings of DIS '97* (pp. 147-158). Amsterdam, Holland: ACM.

Kjeldskov, J., & Paay, J. (2006). Public pervasive computing in the city: Making the invisible visible. *IEEE Computer, 39*(9), 30-35.

Lynch, K. (1960). *The image of the city*. Cambridge, MA, USA: The MIT Press.

McCullough, M. (2004). *Digital ground—Architecture, pervasive computing and environmental knowing*. Cambridge, MA, USA: The MIT Press.

Millen, D. R. (2000). Rapid ethnography: Time deepening strategies for HCI field research. In *Proceedings of DIS '00* (pp. 280-286). Brooklyn, NY: ACM.

Paay, J., & Kjeldskov, J. (2005). Understanding situated social interactions in public places. In *Proceedings of Interact 2005* (pp. 496-509). Rome, Italy: Springer-Verlag.

Raijmakers, B., Gaver, W., & Bishay, J. (2006). Design documentaries: Inspiring design research through documentary film. In *Proceedings of DIS 2006* (pp. 229-238). Pennsylvania, USA: ACM.

Snyder, C. (2003). *Paper prototyping*. San Francisco: Morgan Kaufmann Publishers.

Sommerville, I., Rodden, T., Sawyer, P., Bentley, R., & Twidale, M. (1993). Integrating ethnography into the requirements engineering process. In *Proceedings of IEEE International Symposium on Requirements Engineering* (pp. 165-181). San Diego, CA, USA: IEEE Computer Society Press.

Strauss, A. L., & Corbin, J. (1990). *Basics of qualitative research*. Newbury Park, CA, USA: Sage Publications.

Viller, S., & Sommerville, I. (1999). Coherence: An approach to representing ethnographic analyses in systems design. *Human-Computer Interaction, 14*, 9-41.

Wixon, D. (1995). Qualitative research methods in design and development. *Interactions, 2*(4), 19-24.

KEY TERMS

Affinity Diagramming: One of the techniques of the contextual design process, used during data interpretation sessions to group related individual points together, creating a hierarchical diagram showing the scope of issues in the work domain being studied.

Content Analysis: A qualitative research technique for gathering and analyzing the content of text, where content can be words, meanings, pictures, symbols, ideas, themes, or any message that can be communicated, to reveal messages in the text that are difficult to see through casual observation.

Contextual Design: A collection of techniques supporting a customer-centered design process, created by Beyer and Holtzblatt (1998), for finding out how people work to guide designers to find the optimal redesign for work practices.

Design Sketch: A graphical representation of a concept or design idea on a high level of abstraction. It should be quick, timely, open, disposable, un-detailed, and informal, and is usually hand-drawn on paper.

Expert Audit: A field reconnaissance done by an architecturally trained observer maping the presence of various elements of the physical environment and making subjective categorizations based on the immediate appearance of these elements in the field and their visible contribution to the image of the city.

Ethnography: A collection of techniques used for gathering and organizing field materials from observational studies, involving detailed observations of activities within their natural setting, to providing rich descriptions of people, environments and interactions.

Grounded Theory: A theory based analytical approach, which takes a set of data collected using ethnographic methods and provides a set of specific procedures for generating theory from this data.

Paper Prototype: A paper representation of a system design, able to simulate operation of that system, which is independent of platform and implementation, and can be used for brainstorming, designing, testing and communication of user interface designs and for identifying usability problems at an early stage of the design process.

Paper-Based Mock-Up: A representation of a specific design idea that is built from simple materials such as paper and cardboard, keeping it cheap and understandable, but making it a physical representation of a design idea for a final system, good for envisioning future products in the very early stages of the design process.

Rapid Ethnography: A collection of field methods to provide designers with a reasonable understanding of users and their activities given a limited amount of time spent in the field gathering data.

This work was previously published in Handbook of Research on User Interface Design and Evaluation for Mobile Technology, edited by J. Lumsden, pp. 1-15, copyright 2008 by Information Science Reference, formerly known as Idea Group Reference (an imprint of IGI Global).

Chapter 8.10
Mobile e-Learning for Next Generation Communication Environment

Tin-Yu Wu
I-Shou University, Taiwan

Han-Chieh Chao
National Dong Hwa University, Taiwan

ABSTRACT

This article develops an environment for mobile e-learning that includes an interactive course, virtual online labs, an interactive online test, and lab-exercise training platform on the fourth generation mobile communication system. The Next Generation Learning Environment (NeGL) promotes the term "knowledge economy." Inter-networking has become one of the most popular technologies in mobile e-learning for the next generation communication environment. This system uses a variety of computer embedded devices to ubiquitously access multimedia information, such as smart phones and PDAs. The most important feature is greater available bandwidth. The learning mode in the future will be an international, immediate, virtual, and interactive classroom that enables learners to learn and interact.

INTRODUCTION

The development of new approaches and technologies to support distance learning are undergoing now. In particular Web-based and mobile asynchronous learning environments and virtual classrooms via the Internet have been adopted widely. Static information as an instructional delivery method is the current trend in e-learning. Learners using these kinds of conventional learning methods are only able to browse through the mass static information. This is passive learning by reading online.

In the last decade, technologies enabling e-learning have increased learning location flexibility. Wireless communication technologies further increase the options for learning location. Advances in wireless communication technologies have provided the opportunity for educators to create new educational models. With the aid of wireless communication technology, educational practice can be embedded into mobile life without wired-based communication. With the trend in educational media becoming more mobile, portable, and individualized, the learning form is being modified in spectacular ways (Gang & Zongkai, 2005).

In the third generation cellular system (3G) environment (such as Universal Mobile Telecommunications System, UMTS), the data rate reaches 2Mbps while the user is standing and 384Kbps while the user is moving slowly. Multimedia streaming, video conferencing, and online interactive 3D games are expected to attract increasing numbers of users. Such bandwidth is not sufficient for these increasingly popular applications and would be the major challenge for wireless networks. The 3G bandwidth has great problems with interactive teaching (Bos & Leroy, 2001).

In the future, wireless network traffic is expected to be a mix of real-time traffic such as voice, music, multimedia teleconferencing, online games, and data traffic such as Web page browsing, instant messaging, and file transfers. All of these applications will require widely varying and very diverse quality of service (QoS) guarantees for the different types of offered traffic (Dixit, 2001).

For these reasons, a fourth generation improved mobile communication system is necessary. The 4G system can support more bandwidth than other systems. It has advantages like authentication, mobile management, and quality of service (QoS). How to implement future distance learning environments for the fourth generation mobile communication system is the question. In this article, we distinguish four kinds of interactive courses, virtual online labs, interactive online tests, and lab-exercises training platform to deliver over the fourth generation mobile communication system. The fourth generation mobile communication system can use a variety of computer embedded devices to ubiquitously access multimedia infor-

mation, such as smart phones and PDAs. Most important is that have more bandwidth. Hence, it supply ubiquitous learning environment (Girish & Dennett, 2000).

These new functions can improve the latency and location limits during transmission. Our proposed Next Generation Learning Environment offers learners the opportunities to use all kinds of mobile nodes that can connect to an Internet learning equipment system for access using All-IP communication networks. The Sharable Content Object Reference Model (SCORM) is used to compose information. Hence, as you can imagine, the condition of the learning mode in the future will be an international, immediate, and virtual interactive classroom that enables learners to learn and interact.

The article is organized as follows. We first describe the environments for mobile learning, followed by the virtual online classroom. The 4G testbed system design analyses are dealt with, and then the mobile e-learning results are discussed. The last section concludes the article.

ENVIRONMENTS FOR MOBILE LEARNING

Several investigations have focused on how to support great service for mobile e-learning. How many services will be able to fill the bill? In this session, we are introducing that mobile e-learning environment possesses many unique characteristics as follows (Tony, Sharples, Giasemi, & Lonsdale, 2004).

- Better adaptation to individual needs
- Ubiquitous and responds to urgent learning need
- Flexibility of location and time to learn
- Interactive knowledge acquisition
- Efficiency due both to re-use and feedback
- Situational instructional activities

- Integrated instructional context (Chao, Wu, & Kao, 2004)

The mobile e-learning system includes interactive courses, virtual online labs, interactive online tests, and lab-exercises training platform on the fourth generation mobile communication system. As shown in Figure 1 the following sessions will present each part:

- **Interactive course system**: In learning history learners could experience interactive learning only in the classroom. The e-learning systems support only a single way for learning. These ways cannot support learning anytime and anywhere. We therefore developed an interactive course system to do that. Learners can choose which chapter they want to learn in this system. This learning method is not limited by the environment.
- **Virtual online labs system:** Generally speaking, experiments must be conducted in a laboratory. Learners are thereby limited to a specific learning area. To solve this problem special equipment is required. How can this problem be overcome? We simulated an experiment on laboratory all the time by Flash program. This virtual online lab platform supports step-by-step experimentation. Learners are therefore not restricted in the laboratory.
- **Interactive online test system:** An online interactive testing system is used to examine the teaching effect on students. The instructors can know how many learners were impacted via the testing system. Learners can obtain the learning effect on themselves.
- **Lab-exercises training platform:** The learners have more items for experimentation. NetSmooth Inc. developed a complete solution called NetGuru platform to tackle this issue. The learners can access the lab-exercises training platform via pre-arranged authorization.

A communication system is required to transfer the learning data. The most common communication platform used by students is the third generation cellular system. The data rate reaches

Figure 1. The virtual classroom on 4G system

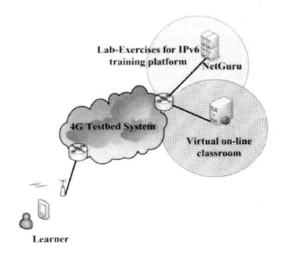

2Mbps while the user is standing and 384Kbps while the user is moving slowly. This kind of system does not have enough bandwidth and no All-IP core network. Therefore, we developed a 4G testbed system that can support high transfer bandwidth.

VIRTUAL ONLINE CLASSROOM

Today there is much work going on in the field of virtual online classrooms around the world. The Web-based virtual classroom via the Internet as an instructional delivery method is a popular trend. Traditional learning methods only allowed the student to browse through mass static information. This is passive learning. In this session, we will introduce an interactive virtual classroom that includes the interactive course, virtual online labs, an interactive online test, and a lab-exercise training platform. For more information, see the virtual online classroom interactive Web site: http://6book.niu.edu.tw/ (6BOOK).

Setting up the Interactive Learning Course Web Site Platform

The Internet has uni-location and unlimited time features. Early online teaching materials included video lessons captured by DV, e-books, poster messages, and so on. These materials were used via the Internet. However, these approaches are single direction learning. These approaches are not good approaches for learning. These ways cannot attain learning anytime and anywhere. Therefore, we developed the interactive course system to do that (see Figure 3). The learners can choose which chapter they want to learn in this system. It can repeat whatever the learners want. The course collocates the interactive online test with interactive capability. The learners can learn anytime and anywhere unlimited by the environment.

Learners can select the chapters that they want to learn or review rapidly. They can study the chapters in order or preview or review any chapters, in any order. They can save all of their previous study processes. During learning, the system supports sliders with hints and oral explanations. Learners can control their learning speed and repeat it at will. Learners can see clearly just like taking the classes live (see Figure 4).

Setting up Virtual Online Lab Exercises

Generally, learner lab exercises must be conducted in a laboratory. They cannot perform experiments without a laboratory. This reduces a lot of opportunity to learn. Therefore, we used FLASH to produce a series of online lab exercises, explaining the lab exercises from the beginning and performing the exercises with detailed background voice and subtitles. There are explanations in great detail for each exercise. These explanations include the experiment goals, steps, and approaches that can help learners understand the background.

Most important, the learners can control the speed at which the lab-exercises proceed by themselves. Relying on online lab exercises, learners can perform lab exercises an unlimited number of times. They can perform experiments anytime from anywhere. The instructors do not have to spent time to prepare lab exercises or setup equipment. If learners have any questions about the exercises, they can use hyperlink to text to the Web site for answers. This teaching platform covers both theory and lab exercises interactively.

Setting up On-Line Exercises

The Virtual online lab exercises and interactive learning Web site platform help learners study efficiently. This system is able to identify the learning effect. We developed online interactive exercises for each chapter. These exercises identify

Figure 2. The interactive virtual online classroom Web site

Figure 3. Interactive learning course Web site platform

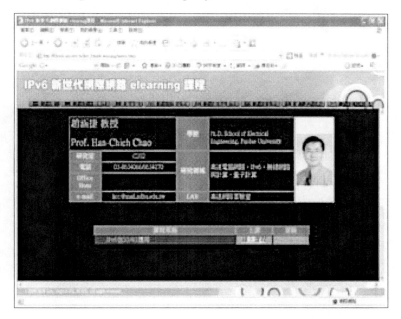

the comprehension of each learner for the instructor that uses these teaching materials. The system tutors learners that do not exhibit complete lesson understanding. Learners can also know clearly what areas should be enhanced and the content of each chapter by practicing the exercises.

Lab-Exercises Training Platform

The lab-exercises training platform is set-up using the NetSmooth Inc. test platform. This platform supports another solution with lab exercises for learners. The proposed NetGuru platform helps instructors to conduct network courses easily with Web-based tutorial courseware. It also assists students to strengthen the concepts of network with hands-on lab experiences (Chiang, Liang, Wu, & Chao, 2005).

The pragmatic lab exercises for the IPv6 training platform use a small-sized personal computer. There are some characters as follows (shown in Figure 7):

- All necessary lab hardware equipment is bundled together. No PC is required.

- Large-scale training labs are supported with multiple Netguru sets.
- The default setting is easily restored to initiate another lab work.
- Built-in 3 hosts and 3 hubs. (Each host has 3 NICs)
- Each set of NetGuru supports 3 groups to do Lab work.
- Simply connect monitor, mouse and keyboard with NetGuru to start Lab work instantly.

NetGuru integrates hardware, lab software, and training media into one complementary training set. We equipped the system with common use software to easily implement network services, such as routing, DNS, VPN, DHCP, NAT, Firewall, and so on. With build-in Ethereal tools for packet analyzing, learners will reinforce their conception about the packet structure. Based on the online commands, the environment will restore and default setting to initiate another lab work easily. In past days, while establishing a network environment, we not only needed computers, but also the heavy and complicated equipment configura-

Figure 4. The teaching slides with voice on the platform

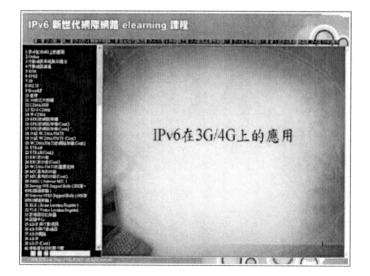

Figure 5. The virtual online lab exercises

Figure 6. The online interactive exercises platform

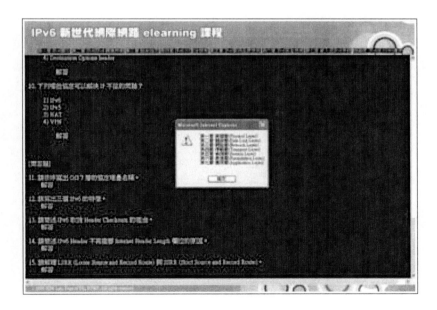

Figure 7. NetGuru platform framework interface

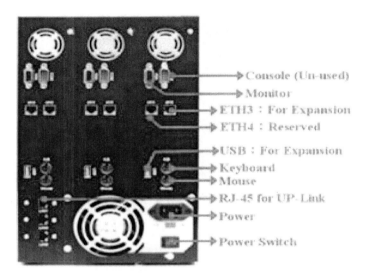

Figure 8. The cross-layer coordination plane

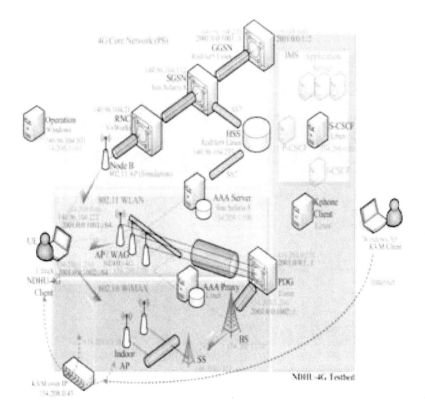

tion. With NetGuru, the TCP/IP lab environment can be easily set-up requiring no PC. We scaled down the size, and the small footprint allows easy relocation. Thus, we can set-up the TCP/IP lab environment anytime and anywhere. As we mentioned before, with multiple sets of NetGuru, large-scale training labs can easily be supported. NetGuru also supports extended network devices. Instructors can design other advanced lab work for use with this system.

4G Testbed System Design Analyses

We propose a fourth generation mobile communication testbed system. The system can support greater bandwidth than other systems. It has advantages like authentication, mobile management, and quality of service (QoS).

This session will introduce our fourth generation communication testbed system. We followed the specification defined in 3GPP to design our system. This system is composed of two main components: RAN (Radio Access Network) and Core-Network. RAN includes RNC and Node B. The Core-Network then includes SGSN (Serving GPRS Support Node), GGSN (Gateway GPRS Support Node), and HSS (Home Subscriber Server), as shown in Figure 8.

At RAN, Node B works like the access point of wireless network, providing the ability for UE (User Equipment) to connect to the core network through radio interface, each RNC can work with single or multiple Node B to form a RNA. RAN is then constituted by these RNS.

At the core network, SGSN is responsible for tasks such as connecting to the core network with single or multiple RAN, access control, location management, routing management etc. GGSN is an interface responsible of connecting core network and outer network, also routing traveling packets. It is also responsible for mobility management (Uskela, 2001).

HSS is a data center responsible for recording the operations of the entire network. HLR is its main component. Its function is to store the user's identity, location, and registered services that are allowed to the user.

Figure 9. The fourth generation mobile communication testbed system

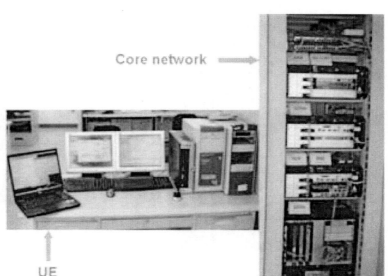

Figure 10. To learn in virtual classroom via PDA

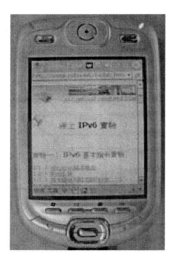

Since the radio frequency used by a 3GPP cell phone is a licensed band, a legal license must be acquired. Therefore we used 802.11g which belongs to the ISM band instead. Through broadcasting UDP packets to simulate the radio network, and because the protocol stack of the

simulation program is executed in UE according to the 3GPP standard, all generated packets are identical to packets generated by an actual 3GPP cell phone. UE enables us to acquire the flow chart of packets generated through the data exchange process between UE and the network. Figure 9 shows the entire system (3GPP, 3GPP TS 23.228, 3GPP TS 23.234).

Measurement Results with Mobile e-Learning

Wireless networks and mobile systems will continue to have explosive growth in the future. The traffic is expected to be a mix of real-time traffic such as voice, music and multimedia, and data traffic such as Web page browsing, instant messaging, and file transfers. All of these applications will require widely varying and very diverse quality of service (QoS) guarantees for the different types of offered traffic. Therefore, the mobile e-learning environment will be replacing traditional e-learning. We proposed a fourth generation mobile communication testbed system with advantages such as high transmission rate,

Figure 11. End-to-end delay

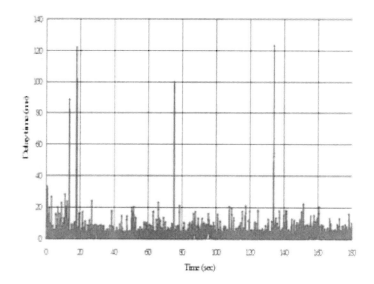

Figure 12. End-to-end bandwidth

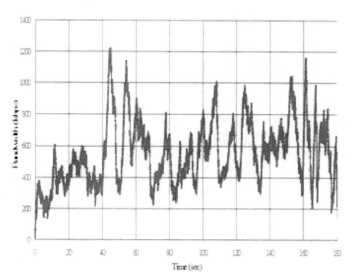

robust wireless QoS control, wide cover area and supply IMS technology. Next generation communication technology can supply a variety of portable devices to ubiquitously access multimedia information, such as smart phones and PDAs. All Learners can use portable devices to log-on to the virtual classroom. Figure 10 shows a portable device surfing the virtual classroom via 4G.

In this session, we measure the mobile e-Learning system results via 4th generation core network. The scenarios are the UEs ability to connect to WLAN. Two scenarios are used for this measurement.

The first scenario is that the UE connects to the core network through WLAN. We measure the end-to-end delay of voice packet delivery. We captured the packets using the Wireshark protocol analyzer. We installed the protocol analyzer at the end of the core network client to capture the packet and decode the voice stream.

End-to-end delay refers to the time cost used for a packet to be transported across a network from the source to destination. For voice packet

transmission, we calculate the end-to-end delay according to RFC 3550. Figure 11 shows the end-to-end delay for voice packet delivery in WLAN.

The second scenario is that the UE connects to core network through WLAN. We measure the throughput of video packet delivery. These results show the transported bandwidth in the 4G testbed system, as shown in Figure 12.

CONCLUSION

The explosive development of the Internet and wireless communications has made personal communication more convenient. Mobile computing uses the Next Generation Learning Environment (NeGL) to set up learning systems. We proposed a mobile e-learning system that includes interactive courses, virtual online labs, interactive online testing, and a lab exercise training platform via the fourth generation mobile communication system. It offers learners opportunities to use all kinds of mobile nodes or anything that can connect to an Internet learning equipment system to be accessed using All-IP communication networks. In order for Content Object Reference Model (SCORM) to compose information, the 4G can use a variety of computer embedded devices to ubiquitously access multimedia information, such as smart phones and PDA. Most important is that more bandwidth is available. As you can imagine, the condition of the learning mode in the future will be an international, immediate and virtual interactive classroom that enables learners to learn and interact.

REFERENCES

3GPP. Third Generation Partnership Project, http://www.3gpp.org

3GPP TS 23.228 V6.10.0 (2005-06). IP multimedia subsystem

3GPP TS 23.234 V6.5.0 (2005-06). 3GPP system to Wireless Local Area Network (WLAN) interworking

6BOOK: http://6book.niu.edu.tw

Bos, L., & Leroy, S. (2001). Toward an all-IP-based UMTS system architecture. *IEEE Network, 15*(1), 36-45.

Chao, H.-C., Wu, T.-Y., & Kao, T. C.M. (2005). Environments for mobile learning: Pervasive and ubiquitous computing using IPv6. Chapter of *Encyclopedia of Online Learning and Technology, Information Science.*

Chiang, F.-Y., Liang, M.-H., Wu, T. Y., & Chao, H.-C. (2005). Pragmatic lab exercises for IPv6 training. *Proceedings of iCEER-2005*, Tainan, Taiwan, March 1-5.

Dixit, S.S. (2001). Evolving to seamless all-IP wireless/mobile networks. *IEEE Communications Magazine, 39*(12), 31-32.

Gang, Z. & Zongkai, Y. (2005). Learning resource adaptation and delivery framework for mobile learning. *Proceedings of Frontiers in Education, 2005 (FIE '05).*

Girish, P. & Dennett, S. (2000). The 3GPP and 3GPP2 movements toward an all-IP mobile network. *IEEE Personal Communications, 7*(4), 62-64.

Tony, C., Sharples, M., Giasemi, V., & Lonsdale, P. (2004). Educational metadata for mobile learning. *Proceedings of the 2nd IEEE International Workshop on Wireless and Mobile Technologies in Education 2004*, pp. 197-198.

Uskela, S. (2001). All IP architectures for cellular networks. *Proceedings of the Second International Conference on 3G Mobile Communication Technologies*, pp.180-185.

This work was previously published in International Journal of Distance Education Technologies, Vol. 6, Issue 4, edited by S. Chang and T. Shih, pp. 1-13, copyright 2008 by IGI Publishing, formerly known as Idea Group Publishing (an imprint of IGI Global).

Chapter 8.11
An Interactive Wireless Morse Code Learning System

Cheng-Huei Yang
National Kaohsiung Marine University, Taiwan

Li-Yeh Chuang
I-Shou University, Taiwan

Cheng-Hong Yang
National Kaohsiung University of Applied Sciences, Taiwan

Jun-Yang Chang
National Kaohsiung University of Applied Sciences, Taiwan

INTRODUCTION

Morse code has been shown to be a valuable tool in assistive technology, augmentative and alternative communication, and rehabilitation for some people with various conditions, such as spinal cord injuries, non-vocal quadriplegics, and visual or hearing impairments. In this article, a mobile phone human-interface system using Morse code input device is designed and implemented for the person with disabilities to send/receive SMS (simple message service) messages or make/respond to a phone call. The proposed system is divided into three parts: input module, control module, and display module. The data format of the signal transmission between the proposed system and the communication devices is the PDU (protocol description unit) mode. Experimental results revealed that three participants with disabilities were able to operate the mobile phone through this human interface after four weeks' practice.

BACKGROUND

A current trend in high technology production is to develop adaptive tools for persons with disabilities to assist them with self-learning and personal development, and lead more independent lives. Among the various technological adaptive tools available, many are based on the adaptation of computer hardware and software. The areas of application for computers and these tools include training, teaching, learning, rehabilitation, communication, and adaptive design (Enders, 1990;

McCormick, 1994; Bower et al., 1998; King, 1999).

Many adapted and alternative input methods now have been developed to allow users with physical disabilities to use a computer. These include modified direct selections (via mouth stick, head stick, splinted hand, etc.), scanning methods (row-column, linear, circular) and other ways of controlling a sequentially stepping selection cursor in an organized information matrix via a single switch (Anson, 1997). However, they were not designed for mobile phone devices. Computer input systems, which use Morse code via special software programs, hardware devices, and switches, are invaluable assets in assistive technology (AT), augmentative-alternative communication (AAC), rehabilitation, and education (Caves, 2000; Leonard et al., 1995; Shannon et al., 1981; Thomas, 1981; French et al., 1986; Russel & Rego, 1998; Wyler & Ray, 1994). To date, more than 30 manufactures/developers of Morse code input hardware or software for use in AAC and AT have been identified (Anson, 1997; http://www.uwec.edu/Academic/Outreach/Mores2000/morse2000.html; Yang, 2000; Yang, 2001; Yang et al., 2002; Yang et al., 2003a; Yang et al., 2003b). In this article, we adopt Morse code to be the communication method and present a human interface for persons with physical disabilities.

The technology employed in assistive devices has often lagged behind mainstream products.

This is partly because the shelf life of an assistive device is considerably longer then mainstream products such as mobile phones. In this study, we designed and implemented an easily operated mobile phone human interface device by using Morse code as a communication adaptive device for users with physical disabilities. Experimental results showed that three participants with disabilities were able to operate the mobile phone through this human interface after four weeks' practice.

SYSTEM DESIGN

Morse code is a simple, fast, and low-cost communication method composed of a series of dots, dashes, and intervals in which each character entered can be translated into a predefined sequence of dots and dashes (the elements of Morse code). A dot is represented as a period ".", while a dash is represented as a hyphen, or minus sign, "-". Each element, dot or dash, is transmitted by sending a signal for a standard length of time. According to the definition of Morse code, the tone ratio for dot to dash must be 1:3. That means that if the duration of a dot is taken to be one unit, then that of a dash must be three units. In addition, the silent ratio for dot-dash space to character-space also has to be 1:3. In other words, the space between the elements of one character is one unit while

Figure 1. System schematics of the mobile phone human-interface

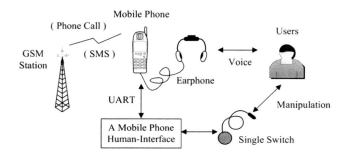

the space between characters is three units (Yang et al., 2002).

In this article, the mobile phone human interface system using Morse code input device is schematically shown in Figure 1. When a user presses the Morse code input device, the signal is transmitted to the key scan circuit, which translates the incoming analog data into digital data. The digital data are then sent into the microprocessor, an 8051 single chip, for further processing. In this study, an ATMEL series 89C51 single chip has been adopted to handle the communication between the press-button processing and the communication devices. Even though the I/O memory capacity of the chip is small compared to a typical PC, it is sufficient to control the device. The 89C51 chip's internal serial communication function is used for data transmission and reception (Mackenzie, 1998). To achieve the data communication at both ends, the two pins, TxD and RxD, are connected to the TxD and RxD pins of a RS-232 connector. Then the two pins are connected to the RxD and TxD of an UART (Universal Asynchronous Receiver Transmitter) controller on the mobile phone device. Then, persons with physical disabilities can use this proposed communication aid system to connect their mobile communication equipment, such as mobile phones or GSM (global system for mobile communications) modems, and receive or send their messages

(SMS, simple message service). If they wear an earphone, they might be able to dial or answer the phone. SMS is a protocol (GSM 03.40 and GSM 03.38), which was established by the ETSI (the European Telecommunications Standards Institute) organization. The transmission model is divided into two models: text and PDU (protocol description unit). In this system, we use the PDU model to transmit and receive SMS information through the AT command of the application program (Pettersson, 2000). Structurally the mobile phone human-interface system is divided into three modules: the input module, the control module, and the display module. The interface framework is graphically shown in Figure 2. A detailed explanation is given below.

INPUT MODULE

A user's input will be digitized first, and then the converted results will be sent to the micro controller. From the signal processing circuit can monitor all input from the input device, the Morse code. The results will be entered into the input data stream. When the user presses the input key, the micro-operating system detects new input data in the data stream, and then sends the corresponding characters to the display module. Some commands and/or keys, such as *OK, Cancel, Answer, Response, Send, Receive, Menu, Exit,*

Figure 2. Interface framework of mobile phone for persons with physical disablities

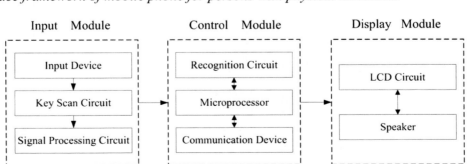

and so forth, have been customized and perform several new functions in order to accommodate the Morse code system. These key modifications facilitate the human interface use for a person with disabilities.

CONTROL MODULE

The proposed recognition method is divided into three modules (see Figure 3): space recognition, adjustment processing, and character translation. Initially, the input data stream is sent individually to separate tone code buffer and space recognition processes, which are based on key-press (Morse code element) or key-release (space element). In the space recognition module, the space element value is recognized as a dot-dash space or a character space. The dot-dash space and character space represent the spaces existing between individual characters and within isolated elements of a character respectively. If a character space is identified, then the value(s) in the code buffer is (are) sent to character translation. To account for varying release speeds, the space element value has to be adjusted. The silent element value is sent into the silent base adjustment process.

Afterwards, the character is identified in the character translation process.

A Morse code character, x_i, is represented as follows:

$$m_1(x_i), b_1(x_i), \ldots, m_j(x_i), b_j(x_i), \ldots, m_n(x_i), b_n(x_i)$$

where

$b_j(x_i)$: jth silent duration in the character x_i.

n: the total number of Morse code elements in the character x_i.

$m_j(x_i)$: the jth Morse code element of the input character x_i.

DISPLAY MODULE

Since users with disabilities have, in order to increase the convenience of user operations, more requirements for system interfaces than a normal person, the developed system shows selected items and system condition information on an electronic circuit platform, which is based on LCD (liquid crystal display). The characteristics

Figure 3. Block diagram of the Morse code recognition system

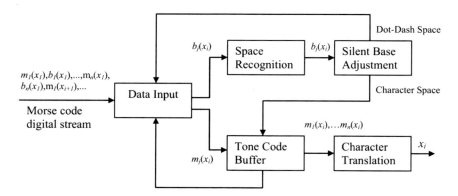

of the proposed system can be summarized as follows: (1) easy operation for users with physical disabilities with Morse code input system, (2) multiple operations due to the selection of different modes, (3) highly tolerant capability from adaptive algorithm recognition, and (4) system extension for customized functions.

RESULTS AND DISCUSSIONS

This system provides two easily operated modes, the phone panel and LCD panel control mode, which allow a user with disabilities easy manipulation. The following shows how the proposed system sends/receives simple message service (SMS) message or make /respond to a phone call.

SMS Receiving Operation

First, when users receive a message notification and want to look at the content, this system will provide "phone panel" and "LCD panel" control modes to choose from. In the phone panel mode, users can directly key-in Morse code "..." (as character 'S'). The interface system will go through the message recognition process, then exchange the message into AT command "AT+CKPD='S', 1", to execute the "confirm" action of the mobile phone. The purpose of this process is the same as users keying-in "yes" on the mobile phone keyboard, then keying-in Morse code ". - - . ." (as key '↓'). The system will recognize the message, then automatically send the "AT+CKPD='↓', 1" instruction. The message cursor of the mobile phone is moved to the next line, or key-in Morse code ". - . . -" (as key '↑') for moving it to the previous data line. Finally, if users want to exit and return to the previous screen, they only need to key-in Morse code ". . - ." (as character 'F'), and start the c key function on the mobile phone keyboard. If LCD panel mode is selected, one can directly follow the selected

items on the LCD crystal, to execute the reception and message reading process.

SMS Transmitting Operation

Message transmission services are provided in two modes: phone panel and LCD panel. In the phone panel mode, continually type two times the Morse code ". - . -." (as key '→'). The system will be converted into AT Command and transferred into mobile phone to show the selection screen of the message functions. Then continuing to key-in three times the Morse code ". . ." (as character 'S'), one can get into the editing screen of message content, and wait for users to input the message text data and receiver's phone number. The phone book function can be used to directly save the receiver's phone number. After the input, press the "yes" key to confirm that the message sending process has been completed. In addition, if the LCD panel mode is selected, one can follow the LCD selection prompt input the service selection of all the action integrated in the LCD panel. Then go through the interface and translate to a series of AT command orders, and batch transfer these into the mobile phone to achieve the control purpose.

The selection command "Answer a phone," displays on the menu of the LCD screen, and can be constructed using Morse code. The participants could press and release the switch, and input the number code ". - - - -" (as character '1') or hot key ". -" (as character 'A'). The mobile phone is then answered automatically. Problems with this training, according to participants, are that the end result is limited typing speed and users must remember all the Morse code set of commands.

Three test participants were chosen to investigate the efficiency of the proposed system after practicing on this system for four weeks. Participant 1 (P1) was a 14-year-old male adolescent who has been diagnosed with cerebral palsy. Participant 2 (P2) was a 14-year-old female adolescent with cerebral palsy, athetoid type, who experiences involuntary movements of all her limbs. Participant 3 (P3) was a 40-year-old male adult, with a spinal cord injury and incomplete quadriparalysis due to an accident. These three test participants with physical impairments were able to make/respond to phone calls or send/receive SMS messages after practice with the proposed system.

FUTURE TRENDS

In the future, Morse code input device could be adapted to several environmental control devices, which would facilitate the use of everyday appliances for people with physical disabilities considerably.

CONCLUSION

To help some persons with disabilities such as amyotrophic lateral sclerosis, multiple sclerosis, muscular dystrophy, and other conditions that worsen with time and cause the user's abilities to write, type, and speak to be progressively lost, it requires an assistive tool for purposes of augmentative and alternative communication in their daily lives. This article presents a human interface for mobile phone devices using Morse code as an adapted access communication tool. This system provides phone panel and LCD panel control modes to help users with a disability with operation. Experimental results revealed that three physically impaired users were able to make/respond to phone calls or send/receive SMS messages after only four weeks' practice with the proposed system.

ACKNOWLEDGMENTS

This research was supported by the National Science Council, R.O.C., under grant NSC 91-2213-E-151-016.

REFERENCES

Anson, D. (1997). *Alternative computer access: A guide to selection.* Philadelphia, PA: F. A. Davis.

Bower, R. et al. (Eds.) (1998). *The Trace resource book: Assistive technology for communication, control, and computer access.* Madison, WI: Trace Research & Development Center, Universities of Wisconsin-Madison, Waisman Center.

Caves, K. (2000). *Morse code on a computer—really?* Keynote presentation at the First Morse 2000 World Conference, Minneapolis, MN.

Enders, A., & Hall, M. (Ed.) (1990). *Assistive technology sourcebook.* Arlington, VA: RESNA Press,.

French, J. J., Silverstein, F., & Siebens, A. A. (1986). An inexpensive computer based Morse code system. In *Proceedings of the RESNA 9th Annual Conference, Minneapolis* (pp. 259-261). Retrieved from http://www.uwec.edu/Academic/Outreach/Mores2000/morse2000.html.

King, T. W. (1999). *Modern Morse code in rehabilitation and education.* MA: Allyn and Bacon.

Lars Pettersson. (n.d.). *Dreamfabric.* Retrieved from http://www.dreamfabric.com/sms

Leonard, S., Romanowski, J., & Carroll, C. (1995). Morse code as a writing method for school students. *Morsels, University of Wisconsin-Eau Claire, 1*(2), 1.

Mackenzie, I. S. (1998). *The 89C51 Microcontroller* (3rd ed.). Prentice Hall.

McCormick, J. A. (1994). Computers and the Americans with disabilities act: A manager's guide. Blue Ridge Summit, PA: Wincrest/McGraw Hill.

Russel, M., & Rego, R. (1998). A Morse code

communication device for the deaf-blind individual. In *Proceedings of the ICAART, Montreal* (pp. 52-53).

Shannon, D. A., Staewen, W. S., Miller, J. T., & Cohen, B. S. (1981). Morse code controlled computer aid for the nonvocal quadriplegic. *Medical Instrumentation, 15*(5), 341-343.

Thomas, A. (1981). Communication devices for the non-vocal disabled. *Computer, 14*, 25-30.

Wyler, A. R., & Ray, M. W. (1994). Aphasia for Morse code. *Brain and Language, 27*(2), 195-198.

Yang, C.-H. (2000), Adaptive Morse code communication system for severely disabled individuals. *Medical Engineering & Physics, 22*(1), 59-66.

Yang, C.-H. (2001). Morse code recognition using learning vector quantization for persons with physical disabilities. *IEICE Transactions on Fundamentals of Electronics, Communication and Computer Sciences, E84-A*(1), 356-362.

Yang, C.-H., Chuang, L.-Y. Yang, C.-H., & Luo, C.-H. (2002). An Internet access device for physically impaired users of Chanjei Morse code. *Journal of Chinese Institute of Engineers, 25*(3), 363-369.

Yang, C.-H. (2003a). An interactive Morse code emulation management system. *Computer & Mathematics with Applications, 46*, 479-492.

Yang, C.-H., Chuang, L.-Y., Yang, C.-H., & Luo, C.-H. (2003b, December). Morse code application for wireless environmental control system for severely disabled individuals. *IEEE Transactions on Neural System and Rehabilitation Engineering, 11*(4), 463-469.

KEY TERMS

Adaptive Signal Processing: Adaptive signal processing is the processing, amplification and interpretation of signals that change over time through a process that adapts to a change in the input signal.

Assistive Technology (AT): A generic term for a device that helps a person accomplishes a task. It includes assistive, adaptive and rehabilitative devices, and grants a greater degree of independence people with disabilities by letting them perform tasks they would otherwise be unable of performing.

Augmentative and Alternative Communication (AAC): Support for and/or replacement of natural speaking, writing, typing, and telecommunications capabilities that do not fully meet communicator's needs. AAC, a subset of AT (see below), is a field of academic study and clinical practice, combining the expertise of many professions. AAC may include unaided and aided approaches.

Global System for Mobile Communications (GSM): GSM is the most popular standard for global mobile phone communication. Both its signal and speech channels are digital and it is therefore considered a 2nd generation mobile phone system.

Morse Code: Morse code is a transmission method, implemented by using just a single switch. The tone ratio (dot to dash) in Morse code has to be 1:3 per definition. This means that the duration of a dash is required to be three times that of a dot. In addition, the silent ratio (dot-space to character-space) also has to be 1:3.

Simple Message Service (SMS): A service available on digital mobile phones, which permits the sending of simple messages between mobile phones.

This work was previously published in Encyclopedia of Mobile Computing and Commerce, edited by D. Taniar, pp. 352-356, copyright 2007 by Information Science Reference, formerly known as Idea Group Reference (an imprint of IGI Global).

Chapter 8.12
A Mobile Computing Framework for Passive RFID Detection System in Health Care

Masoud Mohammadian
University of Canberra, Australia

Ric Jentzsch
Compucat Research Pty Limited, Australia

INTRODUCTION

The cost of health care continues to be a world wide issue. Research continues into ways and how the utilization of evolving technologies can be applied to reduce costs and improve patient care, while maintaining patient's lives. To achieve these needs requires accurate, near real time data acquisition and analysis. At the same time there exists a need to acquire a profile on a patient and update that profile as fast and as possible. All types of confidentiality need to be addressed no matter which technology and application is used. One possible way to achieve this is to use a passive detection system that employs wireless radio frequency identification (RFID) technology. This detection system can integrate wireless networks for fast data acquisition and transmission, while maintaining the privacy issue. Once this data is

obtained, then up to date profiling can be integrated into the patient care system. This article discussed the use and need for a passive RFID system for patient data acquisition in health care facilities such as a hospital. The development of profile data is assisted by a profiling intelligent software agent that is responsible for processing the raw data obtained through RFID and database and invoking the creation and update of the patient profile.

BACKGROUND

Health is on everyone's agenda whether they are old or young. Millions of hours of lost time is recorded each week by employers' whose staff are in need of health care. It is and has been known that more research into applications and innovative architectures is needed. To this end the use of Radio Frequency Identification (RFID), a relatively new technology and is showing itself to be a viable and promising technology as an aid to health care (Finkenzeller, 1999; Glover & Bhatt, 2006; Hedgepeth, 2007; Lahiri, 2005; Schuster, Allen, & Brock, 2007; Shepard, 2005). This technology has the capability to penetrate and add value to nearly every area of health care. It can be used to lower the cost of some services as well as improving service to individuals and the health care provider. Although many organizations are developing and testing the possible use of RFIDs, the real value of RFID is achieved in conjunction with the use of intelligent software agents. Thus the issue becomes the integration of these two great technologies for the benefit of assisting health care services.

To begin with, let us look at data collection. In health care, we can collect data on the patients, doctors, nurses, institution itself, drugs and prescriptions, diagnosis, and many other areas. It would not be feasible to do all of these nor would all of these be able to effectively use RFID. Thus for our perspective we will concentrate on a subset with the understanding that all areas could, directly or indirectly, benefit from the use of RFID and intelligent software agents in a health care and hospital environment.

In this research, we begin to look at the architecture of integrating intelligent software agents technology with RFID technology, in particular in managing patients' health care data in a hospital environment.

An intelligent software agent can continuously profile a patient based on their medical history, current illness, and on going diagnostics. The RFID provides the passive vehicle to obtain the data via its monitoring capabilities. The intelligent software agent provides the active vehicle in the interpretation profiling of the data and reporting capacity. There are certain data that is stored about each patient in a hospital. The investigation of this data provides an analysis

that describes the patient's condition, is able to monitor their status, and cross reflect on why the patient was admitted to the hospital. Using this information an evolving profile of each patient can be constructed and analysed.

Using the data and analysis this will allow us to assist in deciding what kind of care he/she requires, the effects of ongoing care, and how to best care for this patient using available resources (doctors, nurses, beds, etc.) for the patient. The software agent is used to build a profile of each patient as they are admitted to the health care institution. Although not shown in the illustration, an additional profile for each doctor can be developed that practices in the hospital can be developed. If this is done, then the patient and doctor profile can be correlated to obtained the availability of the best doctor to suit the patient. However, this will require an additional data repository, as shown in Figure 1.

The patient profiling is useful in a variety of situations:

- The profile provides a personalized service based on the patient and not on symptoms or illness. to a particular patient. For example, by identifying the services that the patient requires this will allow us to target that which will be directed to speeding up their recovery progress;

- A good profile will assist the medical facilities in trying to prevent the need for the patient to return to the hospital any sooner than necessary;

- Disambiguating patient's diagnostic based on patient profile may help in assisting in matching a doctor's specialization to the right patient;

- When a patient needs to re-enter a hospital, a past profile can make it easier to match the patient's needs to a relevant available doctor;

- Presenting information about the patient on an on-going, continuous basis for the

Figure 1. Data repositories for patient and doctors

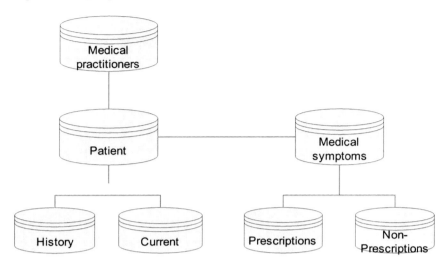

doctors means that current up to date information is available rather than information that needs to be searched for and compiled before it is useful; and

- Providing tailored and appropriate care to reduce health care costs.

Profiling is being done in many business operations today. Often profiling is combined with personalization, and user modeling for many e-commerce applications such as those by IBM, ATG Dynamo, BroadVision, Amazon, and Garden (18). However, there is very little in the way of the use of such systems in hospital and very little in health care in this perspective has been reported. It must be remember that there are different definitions of personalization, user modeling, and profiling. In e-commerce the practice of tracking information about consumers' interests by monitoring their movements online is considered profiling or user modeling. This can be done without using any personal information, but simply by analyzing the content, URL's, and other information about a user's browsing path/ click-stream. Many user models try to predict the user's preference in a narrow and specific domain. This works well as long as that domain remains relatively static and, as such, the results of such work may be limited.

In this research, profiling is a technique whereby a set of characteristics of a particular class of person, patient, is inferred from their past and data-holdings are then searched for individuals with a close fit to symptom characteristics. One of the main aims of profiling and user modeling is to provide information recipients with correct and timely response for their needs. This entails an evolving profile to ensure that as the dynamics of that which is being monitored change, the profile and model reflects these updates as appropriate.

There are several ways in which a patient's visit to a hospital can be recorded. A patient's visit may simply be classified as a regular visit.

This may be for a check up, for tests, or at the request of a doctor. A patient might be at the hospital because of an emergency or an ad hoc appointment due to lack of other facilities being available. Of course there are a whole set of patients that visit the hospital for reasons that are less well defined. In each situation, the needs of the patients are different.

The patient's profile can assist the attending doctor in being aware of the particular patient's situation. This provides the attending doctor with information that is needed without waiting for the patient's regular doctor. The regular doctor may be unavailable and therefore the profile of the patient can be matched with the available doctor suitable to the needs of the patient. The patient to doctor assignment is a type of scheduling issue and is not going to be discussed in this article.

However, in an emergency visit, there is no assigned doctor for such a patient. The doctor in emergency section of the hospital will provide information about a patient after examination and a patient profile then can be created. In this case, the intelligent agent can assist the patient by matching the profile of the patient with the doctors suitable to the needs of the patient. Also the doctors can be contacted in a speedier manner as they are identified and their availability is known.

An appointment visit is very similar to a regular visit but it may happen only once and therefore the advantages mentioned for regular patients applies here.

We will endeavor to describe several of these, but will expand on one particular potential use of RFIDs in managing patient health data. First let us provide some background on RFIDs and present some definitions. We will discuss the environment that RFIDs operate in and their relationship to other available wireless technologies such as the IEEE 802.11b, IEEE 802.11g, IEEE 802.11n, and so forth, in order to fulfill their requirements effectively and efficiently.

This research is divided into four main sections. Section two is based on the patient to doctor profiling and intelligent software agents. The third section is a RFID background; this will provide a good description of RFIDs and their components. This section discusses several practical cases of RFID technology in and around hospitals. It will also list three possible applicable cases assisting in managing patients' medical data. The final section discusses the important issue of maintaining patients' data security and integrity and relates that to RFIDs.

PATIENT TO DOCTOR PROFILING

A profile represents the extent to which something exhibits various characteristics. These characteristics are used to develop a linear model based on the consensus of multiple sets of data, generally over some period of time. A patient or doctor profile is a collection of information about a person based on the characteristics of that person. This information can be used in a decision analyze situation between the doctor, domain environment, and patient. The model can be used to provide meaningful information for useful and strategic actions. The profile can be static or dynamic. The static profile is kept in prefixed data fields where the period between data field updates is long such as months or years. The dynamic profile is constantly updated as per evaluation of the situation. The updates may be performed manually or automated. The automated user profile building is especially important in real time decision-making systems. Real time systems are dynamic. These systems often contain data that is critical to the user's decision making process. Manually updated profiles are at the need and discretion of the relevant decision maker.

The profiling of patient doctor model is base on the patient/doctor information. These are:

- The categories and subcategories of doctor specialization and categorization. These categories will assist in information processing and patient/doctor matching.
- Part of the patients profile based on symptoms (past history problems, dietary restrictions, etc.) can assist in prediction of the patient's needs specifically.
- The patients profile can be matched with the available doctor profiles to provide doctors with information about the arrival of patients as well as presentation of the patients profile to a suitable, available doctor.

A value denoting the degree of association can be created form the above evaluation of the doctor to patient's profile. The intelligent agent based on the denoting degrees and appropriate, available doctors can be identified and allocated to the patient.

In the patient/doctor profiling, the agent will make distinctions in attribute values of the profiles and match the profiles with highest value. It should be noted that the agent creates the patient and doctor profiles based on data obtained from the doctors and patient namely:

- Explicit profiling occurs based on the data entered by hospital staff about a patient.
- Implicit profiling can fill that gap for the missing data by acquiring knowledge about the patient from its past visit or other relevant databases if any and then combining all these data to fill the missing data. Using legacy data for complementing and updating the user profile seems to be a better choice than implicit profiling. This approach capitalizes on user's personal history (previous data from previous visit to doctor or hospital).

The proposed agent architecture allows user profiling and matching in such a time intensive important application. The architecture of the agent profiling systems using RFID is given in Figure 2.

Figure 2. Agent profiling model using RFID

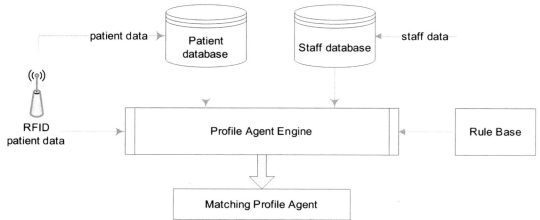

PROFILE MATCHING

Profile matching done is based on a vector of weighted attributes. To get this vector, a rule based systems can be used to match the patient's attributes (stored in patient's profile) against doctor's attributes (stored in doctor's profile). If there is a partial or full match between them, then the doctor will be informed (based on their availability from the hospital doctor database).

INTEGRATION OF INTELLIGENT SOFTWARE AGENTS AND RFID TECHNOLOGIES

Intelligent software agent technology has been used in order to provide the needed transformation of RIFD passive data collection into an active organizational knowledge assistant (Finkenzeller, 1999; Glover & Bhatt, 2006; Hedgepeth, 2007; Lahiri, 2005; Schuster et al., 2007; Shepard, 2005). Intelligent agent should be able to act on new data and already stored profile/knowledge and thereafter to examine its current actions based on certain assumptions, and inferentially plans its activities. Furthermore, intelligent software agents must be able to *interact* with other agents using symbolic language (Bigus & Bigus, 1998; Wooldridge & Jennings, 1995) and able to substitute for a range of human activities in a situated context. (In our case the activities are medical/patient assignment and the context is a hospital environment)

Context driven Intelligent software agents' activities are also dynamic and under continuous development in an historical time related environment (Bigus & Bigus, 1998; Wooldridge & Jennings, 1995).

Medical and hospital patient applied ontology's describing the applied domain are necessary for the semantic communication and data understanding between RFID inputs and knowledge bases inference engines so that profiling of both patients and doctors can be achieved (Gruber, 1993; Guarino, Carrara, & Giaretta, 1994).

The integration of RFID capabilities and intelligent agent techniques provides promising development in the areas of performance improvements in RFID data collection, inference, knowledge acquisition, and profiling operations.

By using mediated activity theories, an RIFD agent architecture could be modeled according to the following characteristics:

- The ability to use patient/doctor profile in natural language, ACL, or symbolic form as communicative tools mediating agents cooperative activities.
- The ability to use subjective and objective properties required by intelligent software agents to perform bidirectional multiple communication activities.
- The ability to internalize representations of medical/patient profile patterns from agents or humans.
- The ability to externalize internally stored representations of medical assignment patterns to other agents or humans.

The Agent Language Mediated Activity Model (ALMA) agent architecture currently under research is based on the mediated activity framework described and is able to provide RFID with the necessary framework to profile a range of internal and external medical/patient profiling communication activities performed by wireless multi-agents.

RFID DESCRIPTION

RFID or Radio Frequency Identification is a progressive technology that has been said to be easy to use and well suited for collaboration with intelligent software agents. Basically an RFID can:

- Be read-only;
- Volatile read/write; or
- Write once/read many times
- RFID are:
  - Noncontact and
  - Non line-of-sight operations.

Being noncontact and non line-of-sight will make RFIDs able to function under a variety of environmental conditions and while still providing a high level of data integrity (Finkenzeller, 1999; Glover & Bhatt, 2006; Hedgepeth, 2007; Lahiri, 2005; Schuster et al., 2007; Shepard, 2005).

MAIN COMPONENTS

A basic RFID system consists of four components:

1. The RFID tag (sometimes referred to as the transponder);
2. A coiled antenna;
3. A radio frequency transceiver; and
4. Some type of reader for the data collection.

Basically there are three components as often components are combined such as the transponder or transceiver or the antenna.

Transponders

The reader emits radio waves in ranges of anywhere from 2.54 centimeters to 33 meters. Depending upon the reader's power output and the radio frequency used and if a booster is added that distance can be somewhat increased. When RFID tags (transponders) pass through a specifically created electromagnetic zone, they detect the reader's activation signal. Transponders can be online or off-line and electronically programmed with unique information for a spe-

cific application or purpose. A reader decodes the data encoded on the tag's integrated circuit and passes the data to a server for data storage or further processing.

Coiled Antenna

The coiled antenna is used to emit radio signals to activate the tag and read or write data to it. Antennas are the conduits between the tag and the transceiver that controls the system's data acquisition and communication. RFID antennas are available in many shapes and sizes. They can be built into a doorframe, book binding, DVD case, mounted on a tollbooth, embedded into a manufactured item such as a shaver or software case (just about anything) so that the receiver tags the data from things passing through its zone (Finkenzeller, 1999; Glover & Bhatt, 2006; Hedgepeth, 2007; Lahiri, 2005; Schuster et al., 2007; Shepard, 2005).

Transceiver

Often the antenna is packaged with the transceiver and decoder to become a reader. The decoder device can be configured either as a handheld or a fixed-mounted device. In large complex, often chaotic environments, portable or handheld transceivers would prove valuable.

TYPES OF RFID TRANSPONDERS

RFID tags can be categorized as active, semi-active, or passive. Each has and is being used in a variety of inventory management and data collection applications today. The condition of the application, place and use determines the required tag type.

Active Tags

Active RFID tags are powered by an internal battery and are typically read / write. Tag data can be rewritten and/or modified as the need dictates. An active tag's memory size varies according to manufacturing specifications and application requirements; some tags operate with up to 5 megabyte of memory. For a typical read/write RFID work-in-process system, a tag might give a machine a set of instructions, and the machine would then report its performance to the tag. This encoded data would then become part of the tagged part's history. The battery-supplied power of an active tag generally gives it a longer read range. The trade off is greater size, greater cost, and a limited operational life that has been estimated to be a maximum of 10 years, depending upon operating temperatures and battery type (Finkenzeller, 1999; Glover & Bhatt, 2006).

Semi-Active Tags

The semi-active tag comes with a battery. The battery is used to power the tags circuitry and not to communicate with the reader. This makes the semi-active tag more independent than the passive tag, and it can operate in more adverse conditions. The semi-active tag also has a longer range and more capabilities than a passive tag (Shepard, 2005). Linear barcodes that reference a database to get product specifications and pricing are also data devices that act is a very similar way. Semi-passive tags are preprogrammed, but can allow for slight modifications of their instructions via the reader/interrogator. However, it is bigger, weighs more, and is more complete than a passive tag. A reader is still needed for data collection.

Passive Tags

Passive RFID tags operate without a separate external power source and obtain operating power generated from the reader. Passive tags,

Figure 3. Semi-passive tag

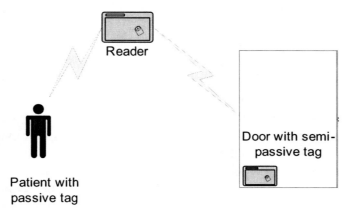

Reader

Patient with passive tag

Door with semi-passive tag

since they have no power source embedded, are consequently much lighter than active tags, less expensive, and offer a virtually unlimited operational lifetime. However, the trade off is that they have shorter read ranges, than active tags, and require a higher-powered reader.

Read-only tags are typically passive and are programmed with a unique set of data (usually 32 to 128 bits) that cannot be modified. Read-only tags most often operate as a data device that utilizes a database for all data storage (Finkenzeller, 1999; Shepard, 2005).

Range

RFID systems can be distinguished by their deployment and frequency range. RFID tags generally operate in two different types of frequencies that make them adaptable for nearly any application. These frequency ranges are:

Low Frequency Range (Short Range)

Low-frequency (30 KHz to 500 KHz) systems have short reading ranges and lower system costs. They are most commonly used in security access, asset tracking, and animal identification applications (Glover & Bhatt, 2006; Hedgepeth, 2007; Lahiri, 2005).

High Frequency Range (Long Range)

High-frequency (850 MHz to 950 MHz and Industry, Science and Medical - 2.4 GHz to 2.5 GHz) systems, offer longer reading ranges (greater than 33 meters) and high reading speeds. These systems are generally used for such applications as railroad car tracking, container dock and transport management, and automated toll collection. However, the higher performance of high-frequency RFID systems incurs higher system operating costs (Glover & Bhatt, 2006; Schuster et al., 2007).

Hospital Environment

In hospitals, systems need to use rules and domain knowledge that is appropriate to the situation. One of the more promising capabilities of intelligent software agents is their ability to coordinate information between the various resources.

In a hospital environment, in order to manage patient medical data we need both types; fixed and handheld transceivers. Also, transceivers can be assembled in ceilings, walls, or doorframes to collect and disseminate data. Hospitals have become large complex environments.

In a hospital, nurses and physicians can retrieve the patient's medical data stored in transponders (RFID tags) before they stand beside a patient's bed or as they are entering a ward.

Given the descriptions of the two types and their potential use in hospital patient data management we suggest that:

- It would be most useful to embed a passive RFID transponder into a patient's hospital wrist band;
- It would be most useful to embed a passive RFID transponder into a patient's medical file (there are several versions and perspectives that we can take no this).

Doctors should have PDAs equipped with RFID or some type of personal area network device. Either would enable them to retrieve some patient's information whenever they are near the patient, instead of waiting until the medical data is pushed to them through the hospital server (there are several versions and perspectives that we can take no this):

- *Active RFID tags* are more appropriate for the continuous collection of the patient's medical data. Since the patient's medical data needs to be continuously recorded to an active RFID tag and an associated reader needs to be employed. Using an active RFID means that the tag will be a bit bulky because of the needed battery for the write process and there is a concern with radio frequency admissions. Thus, it is felt that an active tag would not be a good candidate for the patient wrist band. However, if the patient's condition is to be continuously monitored, the collection of the data at the source is essential. The inclusion of the tag in the wrist band is the only way to recorder the medical data on a real-time base using the RFID technology. As more organizations get into the business of manufacturing RFIDs and the life and size of batteries decrease, the tag size will decrease and this may be a real possible use.

- *Passive RFID tags* can be also used as well. These passive tags can be embedded in the doctors PDA, which is needed for determining their locations whenever the medical staff requires them. Also, passive tags can be used in patients' wrist bands for storage of limited amount of data- on off-line bases, for example, date of hospital admission, medical record number, and so forth.

After examining both ranges, we can suggest the following:

- *Low frequency range tags* are suitable for the patients' band wrist RFID tags. Since we expect that the patients' bed will not be too far from a RFID reader. The reader might be fixed over the patient's bed, in the bed itself, or over the door-frame. The doctor using his/her PDA would be aiming to read the patient's data directly and within a relatively short distance.
- *High frequency range tags* are suitable for the physician's tag implanted in their PDAs. As physicians use to move from one

location to another in the hospital, data on their patients could be continuously being updated.

One final point in regards to the range of RFIDs: until 2002, the permissible radio frequency range was not regulated, that is, it still operated in some low frequency ranges (30- 500 KHz) and in the free 2.45 GHz ISM band of frequency. The IEEE's 802.11b and IEEE's 802.11g (WiFi) wireless networks also operate in the same range (actually there are many other wireless application that operate in that range). This band of frequency is crowded. Where equipment in a hospital is often in the ISM band of frequency, there may be some speed of transmission degradation. The IEEE 802.11n builds upon previous 802.11 standards by adding MIMO (multiple-input multiple-output). MIMO uses multiple transmitter and receiver antennas to allow for increased data throughput via spatial multiplexing and increased range by exploiting the spatial diversity. Note that 802.11n draft 2.0 has been released but the certification of products is still in progress. What this means is that even though 802.11n has greater benefits then previous standards, it is still a draft. The full version is not expected until 2008; thus; products may take several years to be compliant and incorporate that into RFIDs (Hedgepeth, 2007).

Shapes of RFID Tags

RFID tags come in a wide variety of shapes and sizes. Animal tracking tags that are inserted beneath the animal's skin can be as small as a pencil lead in diameter and about one centimeter in length. Tags can be screw-shaped to identify trees or wooden items, or credit card shaped for use in access applications. The antitheft hard plastic tags attached to merchandise in stores are RFID tags (Glover & Bhatt, 2006). Manufacturers can create the shape that is best for the application, including flexible shaped tags that act like and resemble human skin. RFID tags can be flexible and do not have to be rigid.

Transceivers

The transceivers/interrogators can differ quite considerably in complexity, depending upon the type of tags being supported and the application. T\he overall function of the application is to provide the means of communicating with the tags and facilitating data transfer. Functions performed by the reader may include quite sophisticated signal conditioning, parity error checking, and correction. Once the signal from a transponder has been correctly received and decoded, algorithms may be applied to decide whether the signal is a repeat transmission, and may then instruct the transponder to cease transmitting or temporarily cease asking for data from the transponder. This is known as the "Command Response Protocol" and is used to circumvent the problem of reading multiple tags over a short time frame. Using interrogators in this way is sometimes referred to as "Hands Down Polling." An alternative, more secure, but slower tag polling technique is called "Hands Up Polling." This involves the transceiver looking for tags with specific identities, and interrogating them in turn. A further approach may use multiple transceivers, multiplexed into one interrogator, but with attendant increases in costs (Glover & Bhatt, 2006; Hedgepeth, 2007; Lahiri, 2005; Schuster et al., 2007).

Hospital patient data management deals with sensitive and critical information (patient's medical data). *Hands Down polling* techniques in conjunction with multiple transceivers that are multiplexed with each other, form a wireless network. The reason behind this choice is that, we need high speed for transferring medical data from medical equipment to or from the RFID wrist band tag to the nearest RFID reader, and then through a wireless network or a network of RFID transceivers or LANs to the hospital server. From there it is a short distance to be transmitted to the doctor's PDA, a laptop, or desktop through a WLAN IEEE 802.11b, 802.11g, or 802.11n, or wired LAN which operates at the 5.2 GHz band with a maximum data transfer rate exceeding 104 Mbps.

The "Hand Down Polling" techniques, as previously described, provides the ability to detect all detectable RFID tags at once (i.e., in parallel). Preventing any unwanted delay in transmitting medical data corresponding to each RF tagged patient.

RFID TRANSPONDER PROGRAMMERS

Transponder programmers are the means, by which data is delivered to write once, read many (WORM) and read/write tags. Programming can be carried out off-line or online. For some systems re-programming may be carried out online, particularly if it is being used as an interactive portable data file within a production environment, for example. Data may need to be recorded during each process. Removing the transponder at the end of each process to read the previous process data, and to program the new data, would naturally increase process time and would detract substantially from the intended flexibility of the application. By combining the functions of a transceiver and a programmer, data may be appended or altered in the transponder as required, without compromising the production line.

We conclude from this section that RFID systems differ in type, shape, and range; depending on the type of application, the RFID components shall be chosen. Low frequency range tags are suitable for the patients' band wrist RFID tags. Since we expect that a patients' bed is not too far from the RFID reader, which might be fixed on the room ceiling or door-frame. High frequency range tags are suitable for the physician's PDA tag. As physicians use to move from on location to another in the hospital, long read ranges are required. On the other hand, transceivers which deal with sensitive and critical information (patient's medical data) need the Hands Down polling techniques. These multiple transceivers should be multiplexed with each other forming a wireless network.

PRACTICAL CASES USING RFID TECHNOLOGY

This section explains in details three possible applications of the RFID technology in three applicable cases. Each case is discussed step-by-step then represented by a flowchart. Those cases cover issues as acquisition of Patient's Medical Data, locating the nearest available doctor to the patients location, and how doctors stimulate the patient's active RFID tag using their PDAs in order to acquire the medical data stored in it.

Case I: Acquisition of Patient's Medical Data

Case one will represent the method of acquisition and transmission of medical data. This process can be described in the following points as follows:

1. A biomedical device equipped with an embedded RFID transceiver and programmer will detect and measure the biological state of a patient. This medical data can be an ECG, EEG, BP, sugar level, temperature or any other biomedical reading.
   After the acquisition of the required medical data, the biomedical device will write-burn this data to the RFID transceiver's EEPROM using the built in RFID programmer. Then the RFID transceiver with its antenna will be used to transmit the stored medical data in the EEPROM to the EEPROM in the patient's transponder (tag) which is around his/her wrist. The data received will be updated periodically once new fresh

Figure 4. Acquisition of patient data

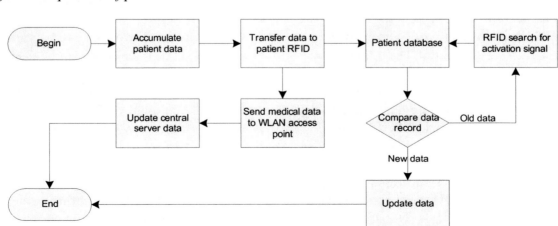

Figure 5. Locating nearest doctor

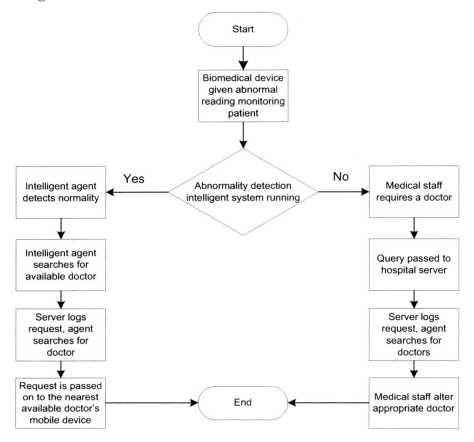

readings are available by the biomedical device. Hence, the newly sent data by the RFID transceiver will be accumulated to the old data in the tag. The purpose of the data stored in the patient's tag is to make it easy for the doctor to obtain medical information regarding the patient directly via the doctor's PDA, tablet PC, or laptop.

2. Similarly, the biomedical device will also transfer the measured medical data wirelessly to the nearest WLAN access point. Since high data rate transfer rate is crucial in transferring medical data, IEEE 802.11b or g is recommended for the transmission purpose.

3. The wirelessly sent data will be routed to the hospitals main server; to be then sent (pushed) to:

    i.   Other doctors available throughout the hospital so they can be notified of any newly received medical data.

    ii. To an online patient monitoring unit or a nurse's workstation within the hospital.

    iii. Or the acquired patients' medical data can be fed into an expert (intelligent) software system running on the hospital server. To be then compared with other previously stored abnormal patterns of medical data, and to raise an alarm if any abnormality is discovered.

4. Another option could be using the in-built-embedded RFID transceiver in the biomedical device to send the acquired medical data wirelessly to the nearest RFID transceiver in the room. Then the data will travel simultaneously in a network of RFID transceivers until reaching the hospital server.

Case II: Locating the Nearest Available Doctor to the Patients Location

This case will explain how to locate the nearest doctor who is needed urgently to attend an emergency medical situation. This case can be explained as follows:

1. If a specific surgeon or physician is needed in a specific hospital department, the medical staff in the monitoring unit (e.g., nurses) can query the hospital server for the nearest available doctor to the patient's location. In our framework an intelligent agent can perform this task.
2. The hospital server traces all doctors' locations in the hospital through detecting the presences of their wireless mobile device; for example, PDA, tablet PC, or laptop in the WLAN range.
3. Another method that the hospital's server can use to locate the physicians is making use of the RFID transceivers built-in the doctor's wireless mobile device. Similarly to the access points used in WLAN, RFID transceivers can assist in serving a similar role of locating doctor's location. This can be described in three steps, which are:

i. The fixed RFID transceivers throughout the hospital will send a stimulation signal to detect other free RFID transceivers—which are in the doctors PDAs, tablets , r laptops, and so forth.
ii. All free RFID transceivers will receive the stimulation signal and reply back with an acknowledgement signal to the nearest fixed RFID transceiver.
iii. Finally, each free RFID transceiver cell position would be determined by locating to which fixed RFID transceiver range it belongs to or currently operating in.

4. After the hospital server located positions of all available doctors, it determines the nearest requested physician (pediatrics, neurologist, and so forth) to the patient's location.
5. Once the required physician is located, an alert message will be sent to his\her PDA, tablet PC or laptop indicating the location to be reached immediately. This alert message could show:

i. The building, floor, and room of the patient (e.g., 3C109).
ii. Patient's case (e.g., heart stroke, arrhythmia, etc.)
iii. A brief description of the patient's case.

6. If the hospital is running an intelligent agent as described in the proposed framework on its server, the process of locating and sending an alert message can be automated. This is done through comparing the collected medical data with previously stored abnormal patterns of medical data, then sending an automated message describing the situation. This system could be used instead of the staff in the patient monitoring unit or the nurse's workstation where nurses observe and then send an alert message manually.

Case III: Doctors Stimulate the Patient's Active RFID Tag Using their PDAs in Order to Acquire the Medical Data Stored in it

This method can be used in order to get rid of medical files and records placed in front of the patient's bed. Additionally, it could help in preventing medical errors- reading the wrong file for the wrong patient and could be considered as an important step towards a paperless hospital.

This case can be described in the following steps:

1. The doctor enters into the patient's room or ward. The doctor wants to check the medical status of a certain patient. So instead of picking up the "hard" paper medical file, the doctor interrogates the patient's RFID wrist tag with his RFID transceiver equipped in his\her PDA, tablet PC, or laptop, and so forth.
2. The patient's RFID wrist tag detects the signal of the doctor's RFID transceiver coming from his\her wireless mobile device and replies back with the patient's information and medical data.
3. If there was more than one patient in the ward possessing RFID wrist tags, all tags can respond in parallel using Hands Down polling techniques back to the doctor's wireless mobile device.
4. Another option could be that the doctor retrieving only the patient's number from the *passive* RFID wrist tag. Then through the WLAN the doctor could access the patient's medical record from the hospital's main server.

RFID technology has many potential important applications in hospitals, and the discussed three cases are a real practical example. Two important issues can be concluded from this section: WLAN is preferred for data transfer;

given that IEEE's wireless networks have much faster speed and coverage area as compared to RFID transceivers\transponders technology. Yet, RFID technology is the best for data storage and locating positions of medical staff and patients as well.

The other point is that we need a RFID transceiver & programmer embedded in a biomedical device for data acquisition and dissemination, and only a RFID transceiver embedded in the doctor's wireless mobile device for obtaining the medical data. With the progress the RFID technology is currently gaining, it could become a standard as other wireless technologies (Bluetooth, for example), and eventually manufacturers building them in electronic devices; biomedical devices for our case.

MAINTAINING PATIENTS' DATA SECURITY AND INTEGRITY

Once data is transmitted wirelessly, security becomes a crucial issue. Unlike wired transmission, wirelessly transmitted data can be easily sniffed out leaving the transmitted data vulnerable to many types of attacks. For example, wireless data could be easily eavesdropped on using any mobile device equipped with a wireless card. In worst cases wirelessly transmitted data could be intercepted and then possibly tampered with, or in best cases, the patient's security and privacy would be compromised. Hence emerges the need for data to be initially encrypted from the source.

In this section, a discussion on how to apply encryption for the designed wireless framework for hospital is considered. Suggesting exactly where data needs to be encrypted and\or decrypted depending on the case that is being examined does this.

First a definition of the type of encryption that would be used in the design of the security (encryption\decryption) framework is discussed, followed by a flowchart demonstrating the framework in a step-by-step process.

Layers of Encryption

Two main layers of encryption are recommended. They are:

Physical (Hardware) Layer Encryption

This means encrypting all collected medical data at the source or hardware level before transmitting it. Thus, we insure that the patient's medical data would not be compromised once exposed to the outer world on its way to its destination. So even if a person with a malicious intent and also possessing a wireless mobile device steps into the coverage range of the hospitals' WLAN, this intruder will gain actually nothing since all medical data is encrypted, making all intercepted data worthless.

Application (Software) Layer Encryption

This means encrypting all collected medical data at the destination or application level once receiving it. Application level encryption runs on the doctor's wireless mobile device (e.g., PDA, tablet PC, or laptop) and on the hospital server. Once the medical data is received, it will be protected by a secret pass-phrase (encryption\decryption key) created by the doctor who possesses this device. This type of encryption would prevent any person from accessing patient's medical data if the doctor's wireless mobile device gets lost, or even if a hacker hacks into the hospital server via the Internet, intranet or some other mean.

Framework of Encrypting Patient's Medical Data

The previous section (Practical Cases using RFID Technology) focused on how to design a wireless framework to reflect how patients' medical data can be managed efficiently and effectively leading to the elimination of errors, delays, and even paperwork. Similarly, this section will focus on the previously discussed framework from a security perspective, attempting to increase security and data integrity.

i.   Acquisition of Patients' Medical Data
ii. Doctors stimulating the patient's active RFID tag using their wireless mobile devices in order to acquire the medical data stored in it.

While the third case which was about locating the nearest available doctor to the patients location, is more concerned about locating doctors than transferring patient's data, so it is not discussed here.

The lower part of Figure 6 represents the physical (hardware) encryption layer. This part is divided into two sides. The left side demonstrates the case of a doctor acquiring patient's medical data via a passive RFID tag located in a band around the patient's wrist. The passive RFID tag contains only a very limited amount of information such as the patients name, date of admission to the hospital and above all his/her medical record number (MRN), which will grant access to the medical record containing the acquired medical data and other information regarding the patient's medical condition. This process is implemented in six steps, and involves two pairs of encryption and decryption. The first encryption occurs after the doctor stimulates the RFID passive tag to acquire the patient's MRN, so the tag will encrypt and reply back the MRN to the doctors PDA for example. Then the doctor will decrypt the MRN and use it to access the patient's medical record from the hospital's server. Finally the hospital server will encrypt and reply back the medical record, which will be decrypted once received by the doctors' PDA.

Figure 6. Functional flow

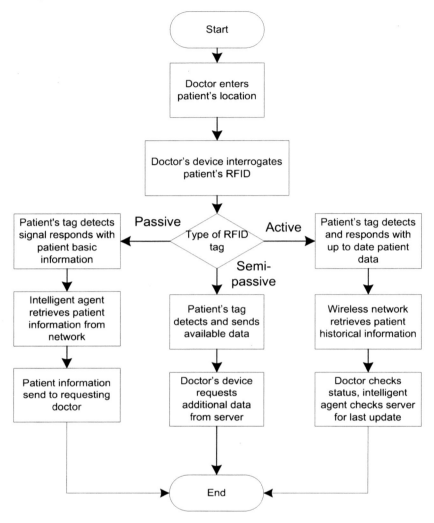

The right side of Figure 6 represents a similar case but this time using an active RF tag. This process involves only one encryption and decryption. The encryption happens after the doctor stimulates the active RFID tag using his PDA which has an in-equipped RFID transceiver, so the tag replies with the medical data encrypted. Then the received data is decrypted through the doctors' PDA.

The upper part of Figure 6 represents the application encryption layer, requiring the doctor to enter a pass-phrase to decrypt and then access the stored medical data. Whenever the doctor wants to access patient's medical data, the doctor simply enters a certain pass-phrase to grant access to either wireless mobile device or a hospital server depend where the medical data actually resides.

CHOOSING LEVEL OF SECURITY FOR THE WIRELESSLY-TRANSMITTED MEDICAL DATA

Securing medial data seems to be uncomplicated, yet the main danger of compromising such data comes from the people managing it, for example, doctors, nurses, and other medical staff. For that, we have seen that even though the transmitted medical data is initially encrypted from the source, doctors have to run application level encryption on their wireless mobile devices in order to protect this important data if the devices gets lost, left behind, robbed, and so forth. Nevertheless, there is a compromise. Increasing security through using multiple layers, and increasing length of encryption keys decreases the encryption\decryption speed and causes unwanted time delays, whether we were using application or hardware level of encryption. As a result, this could delay medical data sent to doctors or online monitoring units.

Figure 6 represents the case of high and low level of security in a flowchart applied to the previously discussed two cases in the last report.

At the end of this section, we conclude that there are two possible levels of encryption, software level (application layer) or hardware level (physical layer), depending on the level of security required. Both physical (hardware) layer and application layer encryption are needed in maintaining collected medical data on hospital servers and doctors wireless mobile devices.

Encrypting medical data makes the process of data transmission slower while sending data unencrypted is faster. We have to have a compromise between speed and security. For our case, medical data has to be sent as fast as possible to medical staff, yet the security issue has the priority.

CONCLUSION

Managing patients' data wirelessly (paperless) can prevent errors, enforce standards, make staff more efficient, simplify record keeping, and improve patient care. In this research report, both passive and active RFID tags were used in acquiring and storage of medical data, and then linked to the hospitals' server via a wireless network Moreover, three practical applicable RFID cases discussed how the RFID technology can be put in use in hospitals, while at the same time maintaining the acquired patients' data security and integrity.

This research in the wireless medical environment introduces some new ideas in conjunction to what is already available in RFID technology and wireless networks. Linking both technologies to achieve the research main goal, delivering patients medical data as fast and secure as possible, to pave the way for future paperless hospitals.

Finally, as reported by Frost and Sullivan, the high cost of radio frequency identification (RFID) technology is a deterrent for health care providers, though RFID has great benefits to hospitals in tracking patients, monitoring patients, assisting in health care administration, and reducing medical costs. With the reduction in cost of radio frequency identification (RFID) technology, increased use of RFID technology in health care in monitoring patients and assisting in health care administration is expected.

REFERENCES

Bigus, J. P., & Bigus, J. (1998). *Constructing intelligent software agents with Java – a programmers guide to smarter applications.* Wiley. ISBN: 0-471-19135-3.

Finkenzeller, K. (1999). *RFID handbook.* John Wiley and Sons Ltd.

Glover, B., & Bhatt, H. (2006). *RFID essentials.* O'Reilly Media, Inc. ISBN: 10-0596009445.

Gruber, T.R. (1993). A translation approach to portable ontology specifications. *Knowledge Acquisition, 5,* 199-220.

Guarino, N., Carrara, M., & Giaretta, P. (1994). An ontology of meta-level categories. Journal of knowledge representation and reasoning. In *Proceedings of the Fourth International Conference (KR94),* Morgan Kaufmann, San Mateo, CA.

Hedgepeth, W. O. (2007). *RFID metrics: Decision making tools for today's supply chains.* Boca Raton, FL: CRC Press. ISBN: 9780849379796.

Lahiri, S. (2005). *RFID sourcebook.* IBM Press. ISBN: 10-0131851373.

Odell, J. (Ed.). (2000, September). *Agent technology.* OMG Document 00-09-01, OMG Agents interest Group.

RFID Australia. (2003). *Why use RFID.* Retrieved February 15, 2008, from http://www.rfid-australia.com/files/htm/rfid%20brochure/page4.html

Schuster, E. W., Allen, S. J., & Brock D. L. (2007). *Global RFID: The value of the EPCglobal network for supply chain management.* Berlin; New York: Springer. ISBN: 9783540356547.

Shepard, S. (2005). *RFID: Radio frequency identification.* New York: McGraw-Hill. ISBN: 0071442995.

Wooldridge, M., & Jennings, N. (1995). Intelligent software agents: Theory and Practice. *The Knowledge Engineering Review,* 10(2), 115-152.

This work was previously published in Encyclopedia of Healthcare Information Systems, edited by N. Wickramasinghe & E. Geisler, pp. 890-905, copyright 2008 by Information Science Reference, formerly known as Idea Group Reference (an imprint of IGI Global).

Chapter 8.13
Widely Usable User Interfaces on Mobile Devices with RFID

Francesco Bellotti
University of Genoa, Italy

Riccardo Berta
University of Genoa, Italy

Alessandro De Gloria
University of Genoa, Italy

Massimiliano Margarone
University of Genoa, Italy

ABSTRACT

Diffusion of radio frequency identification (RFID) promises to boost the added value of assistive technologies for mobile users. Visually impaired people may benefit from RFID-based applications that support users in maintaining "spatial orientation" (Mann, 2004) through provision of information on where they are, and a description of what lies in their surroundings. To investigate this issue, we have integrated our development tool for mobile device, (namely: MADE, Bellotti, Berta, De Gloria, & Margarone, 2003), with a complete support for RFID tag detection, and implemented an RFID-enabled location-aware tour-guide. We have evaluated the guide in an ecological context (fully operational application, real users, real context of use (Abowd & Mynatt, 2000)) during the EuroFlora 2006 international exhibition (EuroFlora). In this chapter, we describe the MADE enhancement to support RFID-based applications, present the main concepts of the interaction modalities we have designed in order to support visually impaired users, and discuss results from our field experience.

INTRODUCTION

Starting from the European Union cofounded E-Tour project, we designed the tourist digital assistant (TDA) concept and developed multimedia tour guides on mobile devices (PocketPC and Smartphone devices) for a number of European tourist sites, such as the Costa Aquarium of Genoa, "Strada Nuova" architectonical area and the city of Genoa, the Castellon region in Spain, and the city of Uddevalla in Sweden (Bellotti, Berta, De Gloria, & Margarone,, 2002).

The tour guide provides multimedia contents, added-value information, and location-based services to the tourists. Added-value services are implemented by integrating the mobile devices with additional hardware and software tools such as GPS, electronic compasses, wireless connectivity, digital cameras, written text input, databases, and so forth.

See Figure 1 for snapshots of tourist guide applications.

Relying on the argument that "play is a powerful mediator for learning throughout a person's life," we developed the "educational territorial-gaming" concept in VeGame (Bellotti, Berta, De Gloria, Ferretti, & Margarone, 2003), a computer-supported educational wireless team-game played along Venice's narrow streets to discover the art and the history of the city (see Figure 2), and in ScienceGame (Bellotti, Berta, De Gloria, Ferretti, & Margarone, 2004), a sort of treasure-hunt game inviting players to discover the mysteries and the marvels of the science (see Figure 3) during the "Festival della Scienza" exhibition held in Genoa every year.

These applications were developed from scratch. From these first experiences, we identified common needs and came up with a system to support design of multimedia applications

Figure 1. Snapshots from the Aquarium and Strada Nuova tour guides on PocketPC device

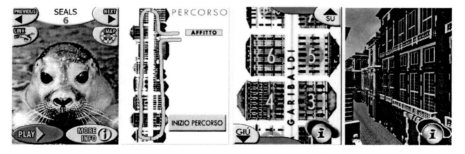

Figure 2. Snapshots from VeGame

Figure 3. Snapshots from ScienceGame

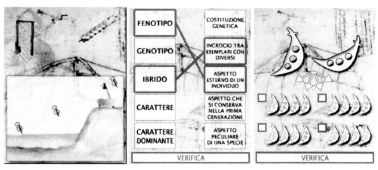

for mobile devices, called Mobile Applications Development Environment (MADE) (Bellotti et al., 2002).

MADE includes M3P (MicroMultiMedia Player), a network-enabled multimedia player easily programmable through the micromultimedia services language (MSL). MSL provides high-level components encapsulating advanced services (e.g., positioning, database query, path search, etc.) that can be easily integrated in multimedia applications. This allows building modular software programs that provide information-rich services to the general public through a coherent and homogeneous HCI that can be learned with low mental workload. On the other hand, MADE hides the low-level aspects of multimedia and service management, allowing designers to focus on the modalities of presentation of information and on user interaction, reducing learning, development, and code maintenance time.

In this chapter, we describe the latest MADE enhancement: we have integrated it with a complete support for RFID detection to allow development of multimedia mobile applications directly connected with the physical world (Want, Fishkin, Gujar, & Harrison, 1999). All low-level aspects of the hardware tag-detection system that are neces-

sary to identify and locate physical objects with attached small RF tags (Want, 2004) are hidden to MSL programmer by the MADE system.

This chapter will also show the use of MADE with the RFID support in a real context such as EuroFlora 2006 international exhibition. This guide differs from others because it has been ad-hoc developed in order to meet strict usability needs. In particular, the novel interface design assists visually impaired people in maintaining "spatial orientation" (Mann, 2004) through provision of information on where they are, hazards that might be in the way, and a description of what lies in their surroundings.

MADE SUPPORT OF RFID TECHNOLOGY

Location-Aware Computing

Recent research has developed several systems, to determinate physical location, that differ by accuracy, cost, and coverage (Boriello, Chalmers, La Marca, & Nixon, 2005). The global positioning system (GPS), which uses signal from satellite to estimate position (Djuknic & Richton, 2001), is the most used system, but only for applications in outdoor areas. In indoor areas and urban areas with poor sky visibility, the system does not work properly. Moreover, it has a long start-up time.

To overcome these limitations, the first indoor positioning system was the active badge system (Want, Hopper, Falcão, & Gibbons, 1992), which is based on sensors that receive infrared ID broadcast from tags worn by people. This system gives a poor (room-grained) localization precision. After the active badge system, typical indoor location systems are based on radio frequency and on the estimation of position computed from the measured signal strength. Various technologies can be used: Wi-Fi (Howard, Siddiqi, & Sukhatme, 2003), Bluetooth (Bruno & Delmastro, 2003) and nowadays RFID (Liu, Corner, & Shenoy, 2006).

The first two solutions can give an accuracy of around some meters, but require expensive fixed base stations. RFID tags, instead, are very inexpensive and have the same performance. The literature reports also of many location estimation algorithms based on cellular radio networks (Xu & Jacobsen, 2005). However, there is not a generally agreed solution today, and each algorithm has pros and cons, depending on environmental issues. Finally, some vision-based algorithms (López de Ipiña, Mendonça, & Hopper, 2002) are promising because they do not require infrastructure (like tags, satellite, or base station). However, it is difficult to set up a system to locate a user with a 1-meter precision. In the selection of the best methodology for our system, we have taken into account three major issues: the possibility to have a system for outdoor/indoor spaces (like the EuroFlora 2006 exhibition area), a technology with a low cost for the deployment of the infrastructure, and a likely pervasive availability of the system in the near future. All these requirements are satisfied by the RFID technology.

RFID Application Fields

Major RFID application domains include monitoring physical parameters, such as temperature or acceleration, during fragile or sensitive products delivery, monitoring product integrity from factory to retail locations (Siegemund & Floerkemeier, 2003), utilities for home and office automation (Langheinrich, Mattern, Romer & Vogt,, 2000). Nowadays we have passive or active inexpensive RFID (approaching 35 cents today, with a goal of 5 cents (Quaadgras, 2005)) that makes these kinds of sensors practical for tourist applications. For example, a museum exposition can place tags attached to each point of interest so that tourists can receive information about exposition in the right moment at the right place; when near to the object. The research community has actively explored this possibility at the Exploratorium, the interactive science museum in San Francisco. The HP Laboratories researchers have implemented a system that uses three types of identification technology: infrared beacon, barcodes, and RFIDs (Fleck, Frid, Kindberg, O'Brian-Strain, Rajani, & Spasojevic, 2002). In Goker et al. (Goker, Watt, Myrhaug Whitehead, Yakici, Bierig, et al., 2004), a special tag that can work with mobile devices to provide ambient information to users on the move is described. In the Cooltown project (Kindberg & Barton, 2001), RFIDs are used to attach pointers from everyday objects to entities in the computational world. A full exploitation of RFID potentials requires study and implementation of human–computer interaction (HCI) modalities able to support usability of the enhanced mobile tool by the general public. This implies the necessity to resort to programming methodologies and tools specifically dedicated to support the RFID technology. Thus, we have extended the MADE toolkit to support a link between applications and physical world through RFID sensors.

MADE Architecture

A typical MADE application consists of a set of pages containing multimedia and service objects. The micromultimedia services language (MSL) script specifies pages' layout and objects' appearance, synchronization, and user-interaction modalities. MSL scripts are interpreted at runtime by the M3P player that manages presentation of contents and user interaction according to the instructions specified in the input MSL script.

M3P player relies on two-layer architecture (see Figure 4) involving a high-level, platform-independent director and a low-level driver. The director is responsible for creating, initializing, and managing the objects that implement the language functionalities. In order to support incremental development of the player, M3P is composed by a set of modules. In particular, the director has been designed to be independent of the components it manages. According to the object-oriented methodology, this has been achieved by encapsulating the functions of the components in the code of their class, and by structuring the hierarchy so that the director can simply keep a reference to the presentation's pages and convey them events.

According to the instructions specified by the MSL developer in the script, events (either from the system or from user interaction) are conveyed to the director that simply redirects them to the components of the page currently on show, which is the higher-priority choice or, with lower priority, to the other pages of the presentation.

Events are implemented as string messages that are to be interpreted by the target objects. This design choice allows the director's code to be independent of the components and the components to be independent of each other. The basic assumption of this schema is that each component exports a well-defined interface (i.e., a set of messages to which it is able to react) and implements this interface (i.e., implements the reaction to such messages).

Thus, components can be seamlessly added and interchanged (in this last case, as long as they comply with the same interface). Adding a new component (i.e., a new functionality) does not involve any change either in the director's code, or in the other components' code.

Figure 4. MADE architecture

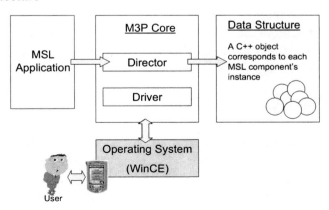

Such a design choice supports easy incremental development, allowing seamless integration of services within a single application framework. This implies that a homogeneous HCI can be applied to an application that hosts several different services that have been developed independently of each other (e.g., intelligent tour planning, interactive maps, positioning, and database access).

MSL relies on a component-based data structure. That is, an MSL file specifies creation of components, attributes of components, and their reaction as a consequence of user interaction. Components are organized in three main libraries: multimedia (e.g., audio, image, video, button), synchronization (utilities like timers that can be used to implement synchronization and scheduling of contents), and services (objects that encapsulate services such as positioning, shortest path search, tour planning, database query, etc).

Every different type of component has its own kind of attributes (fields). The fields record data for specifying the appearance (such as position) and the behaviour (i.e., reactions to events) of the component. In general, components are contained in a special container component, called CARD, that can be thought of as an empty page on which the developer can add components.

The core of M3P involves a platform-independent director and a platform-dependent driver. The director manages the multimedia objects that implement the presentation. Objects are compounded in hierarchical structures. For instance, a CARD (i.e., a multimedia page) may include several images, buttons, and mpeg players. The driver implements the functions to access the hardware, while the director deals with the logic of the multimedia presentation.

Integration of RFID Subsystem

A major feature of MADE consists in the possibility of incrementally adding new hardware and software modules, that are integrated into the HCI framework with no need for modifying the M3P core, since every component's class is responsible for interpreting its receivable messages, independent of the others. MADE can integrate, into a common framework, various hardware modules independently developed to augment the mobile device potentiality. M3P driver's classes, which have to be developed to integrate every new hardware subsystem, manage low-level aspects of the hardware modules, while the MSL interface to the application developer abstracts the services at high level. This implies that a homogeneous HCI can be applied to an application that hosts several different services that have been developed independently of each other (e.g., automatic positioning, intelligent tour planning, and database access can be integrated in an interactive map), and the MSL developer can simply exploit the service modules focusing on the integration of the HCI. Examples of hardware modules already integrated in MADE are a positioning and orientation module that an MSL developer can exploit to get geographical position from a GPS receiver and direction from a digital compass, and the remote communication module able to exploit the hardware available for connection with the external world (e.g., wired/wireless LAN, Bluetooth, GSM/GPRS cellular networks).

In order to enable applications to react to objects in the physical world, our new M3P module, called RFID sensing module (RfidSM), detects presence of RFID tags in the surrounding space and notifies the M3P run-time objects with events implemented as string messages (see Figure 5).

The script interface of the RfidSM is a new MSL component, called RFID, that exposes the fields shown in Table 1.

When the RfidSM component is started, and until it receives a stop event, it scans the surrounding environment to check the presence of tags every "period" of time. The list of detected tags is then sent with the MADE message-exchange modalities to the components specified in the "target" field. In addition, the component has an

Figure 5. Integration (within MADE) of the RFID sensing module (RfidSM)

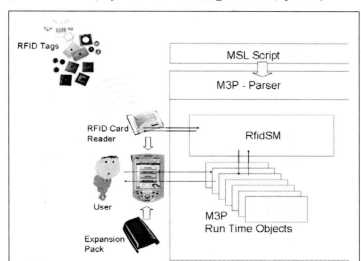

Table 1. RfidSM fields description

Component Field	Description
Target	List of identifiers of the components to which information about identified tags are sent
Period	A time period in milliseconds between two consecutive environmental scans to detect tags
Repetition	A number of tag detection operations executed consecutively on each scanning action
Id	A list of RFID tags that are of interest for the component
Delay	A list of time frames, one for each interesting tag, in which tags are not identified again
dBm	A list of signal strength values, one for each interesting tag, that specify thresholds for tag identifications
onFound	A list of events, one for each interesting tag, that RFID component launch when a tag is identified
Start	If a component launch this event on a RFID component starts the scanning of tags
Stop	If a component launch this event on a RFID component stops the scanning of tags

"id" field to allow programmer expressing interest in a set of tags, and defining (through the field "onFound") the corresponding events list that should be executed. Each interesting tag is also featured with a signal strength threshold (through the field "dBm") that specifies a limit under which the tag is considered in range.

There is the problem of collisions, since the scan results are typically imperfect due to not all tags are detected in every scan. To solve this problem, a tag typically awaits a random number of time slots before it answers the RF pulse sent by the reader. However, the problem still remains and grows as the number of tags in the surrounding environment grows. The MADE RFID sensing module tackles this issue, allowing the programmer to specify, through the field "repetition," a number of times that the reader should repeat the scanning before returning to the founded tags. The list of founded tags is the collection of all tags observed in each scan. A small value of repetition results in a fast scan with high risk of collision, whereas large repetition value results in a slow scan with few collisions. This trade-off should be resolved by the programmer basing his decision on application constrains: long delays can result in human-computer interaction problems if the application allows a user expectation for immediate reaction to tags. This is the case of applications in which user a voluntarily accosts the mobile device to tagged objects to obtain information. Similar problems arise if the application has a short time frame to detect tags, for example, in applications where the user moves at relatively high speed in the environment, like in territorial games. Instead, others type of applications can gain advantage from precise but slow detections. It is the case of a tourist mobile guide for a naturalistic park in which the user moves along a path with some points of interest largely spaced, like tree species or rare flowers.

The other problem affecting the RFID technology is the "tag detection flickering" (Römer, Schoch, & Mattern, & Dubendorfer, 2003): due to the collision problem, some tags can appear and disappear from sequential scanning, generating a fast list of tag identifications. The MADE RFID sensing module allows the programmer to decide how to convert scan results into applications events handling this problem. Programmer can specify, through the "delay" field, a time period (for each interesting tag) starting from the detection. During this time, subsequent detection events of the same tag are discarded; also, the exact definition of this delay is application dependent. Applications with events that occur only one time, like tourist guide for museums with linear path, can have delay values set to infinite. Instead, in ap-

plications with events generated multiple times closer each other, like territorial games, the delay should be short or zero.

Currently, we have implemented the low-level driver support for the iCARD Identec reader in a PCMCIA card format (IDENTEC). This card can be integrated in handheld, portable, or laptop computers to communicate with the iQ and iD active RFID tags at a distance of up to 100 meters. The RF signal is in the UHF radio band (915 MHz or 868 MHz), providing long-range communication and high-speed transmission rates for reliable data exchange.

THE EUROFLORA GUIDE

In order to assess the possibility of using RFID technology to develop widely usable interfaces, we present a real-world application (see Figure 6) developed through the MADE toolkit and deployed in an ecological environment (fully op-

Figure 6. Snapshot of the cover page of EuroFlora Guide application

erational, reliable, and robust application, used by real users and in a real context of use) at EuroFlora 2006 (the international flower exhibition that is held in Genoa every 5 years). With over 500,000 visitors in 10 days, EuroFlora is one of the most important exhibitions of Europe.

The developed application concerns the research area of assistive technologies for visually impaired people. Such assistive applications have the potential to improve the quality of life of a large portion of population (by 2020, there will be approximately 54 million of blind persons over age 60 worldwide (WHO, 1997)).

In this field, maintaining spatial orientation is a major challenge for people with visual impairment. There is the need of systems in providing blind people with information on where they are, hazards that might be in the way, and a description of what lies in their surroundings (Mann, 2004). The notion of "spatial orientation" refers to the ability to establish awareness of space position relative to landmarks in the surrounding environment (Guth & Rieser, 1997). The goal of our application is to support functional independence to visually impaired people, providing support to indoor awareness of elements in the surroundings (Ross, 2004).

The EuroFlora guide is organized in two parts. One part provides general information about the exhibition, the guide, and their services. The other part provides the description of the selected interest points. While first part is directly accessible by the user at any moment, the second one is event driven. More precisely, every interest point description is associated to an RFID tag, and when a user enters that area (i.e., her/his handheld device recognizes the RFID tag), the software asks the user whether to launch the corresponding description.

We placed 99 RFID sensors on an area of 30,000 mq of exhibition, covering 99 points of interest, services, and major areas (see Figure 7). RFID sensors were IP65 compliant in order to resist to water and dust, and self-powered. Power level of sensors could be set in two levels, low and high.

Design Methodology

The necessity for combining the flexibility and multimedia potential of a mobile device with the extreme simplicity of interaction, required for use by a wide audience (also visually impaired people), involves facing three main HCI issues:

Figure 7. a) The packaging of the multimedia guide in a leather case; b) Snapshots from the tests: users visit EuroFlora 2006 supported by the guide and touch some dedicated plants

- **Usability by general users:** The tourist has little time and willingness to learn how to use the new technological tool, since she or he is there to visit the exhibition and not to learn a tool. Most of the tourists use such a tool for the first time and just for a short time (typically, from 30 to 90 minutes). Thus, the complexity of the platform should be hidden from visitors, making the guide immediately usable, with no effort by users. This implies that the interface is to be as simple and intuitive as possible.

- **Usability by visually impaired people:** Visiting an exhibition is a critical task for the blind, mainly for the combination of several reasons: the site is often crowded and unfamiliar to the visitor, it may be noisy, it is difficult to orientate in a highly dynamic place. In this context, the guide should be not intrusive, with few and very recognizable input interface elements (also with tactile feedback), and should give information in a proactive modality when needed by the user.

- **Presentation of information:** Added-value information (e.g., how the various specimens live in their natural environment) should be synergistic with the direct experience of the visitor at the exhibition. Provision of information has to be structured in order to enhance the direct perception of the visitor, leading to a better and more pleasant comprehension of her/his surrounding environment. For example, the guide should make use of environmental sound (e.g., waterfall) and scent (e.g., flower smell) to connect content information and the objects in the space.

We have tackled such issues resorting to the methodologies of the user-centric design (Carroll, 1997), in an iterative development of the guide involving participatory design (Beck, 1993), definition of usability specifications, and contextual design, as shown in the following:

- Participatory design consisted of the participation of botanists at the design decisions, authors skilled in writing for blind people and visually impaired end-users, together with technical developers. The most significant contribution of the first three categories consisted in the definition of the targets and in the concrete perspective they brought into the project.

- Usability specifications provide explicit and measurable targets to verify the suitability of the work done. Examples of such goals are "90% of the users should be able to operate the guide without asking questions to the personnel," "90% of the users should be able to use the interface with no errors," "90% of the users should be able to understand the meaning of all the touchable controls within 120 seconds." All these objectives were verified in early lab and field tests in order to take the appropriate corrective actions.

- Contextual design involved early field tests with experts and users at the exhibition in the preopening days when the infrastructure of EuroFlora was being built. Field tests have been helpful to highlight problems and shortcomings that had been overlooked or ignored in lab.

Structure of the Interface

The interface of the EuroFlora guide has been designed to support immediate use by the general public, also by visually impaired people. To this end, we used general design principles (we already described them in the introduction) such as overall simplicity, low intrusiveness, and support for natural interaction and knowledge acquisition. Moreover, we added further features in order to meet the specific needs of visually impaired people:

- Tactile feedback in the control interface
- Tutorial stage
- Event-driven interface
- Facilities to support orientation

The basic element of the interface is the multimedia card. A multimedia card corresponds to each subject of a presentation (e.g., a flower species). Each multimedia card provides, in an audio format, texts specifically written for visually impaired people (i.e., highlighting olfactive and tactile sensorial information, providing detailed ambient descriptions).

The tactile feedback is necessary to allow impaired people to easily understand the position of the controls and give her/him feedback. Our previous multimedia guides had the interface embedded in the graphic contents, exploiting the touch screen of a pocket-pc device. During the early field tests, visually impaired people pointed out some important shortcomings in these solutions. They felt that the screen was too large and their fingers were lost in a space without roughness. Since most of such users are well acquainted with the common cell phones' relief keyboard, we studied a new solution exclusively based on the hardware buttons (Figure 8).

The hardware buttons of the interface are highlighted. The choice of this area as navigation control allows visually impaired people to have a tactile feedback. The meaning of the button is "up" to accept a content description (which is automatically triggered when the user enters a new cell), "down" to reject it, "right" to exit from a section of the guide, and back to the main menu, "left" to have contextual information about user's current position.

The tutorial stage is an initial guide section in which users could freely experiment with the interface of the tool in order to allow people to use the guide in an independent way. In this stage, users are invited to freely press buttons. A speech description briefly explains the meaning of each pressed button. This tutorial stage prevents the

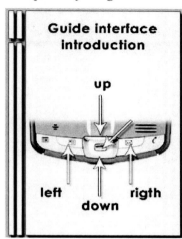

Figure 8. Snapshot of the guide instruction

necessity for providing papers or long explanations when users rent the guide.

The event-driven interface allows a user to get information about points of interest (POIs) and orientation when they are in the proximity of a POI. For example, in Figure 9, a user near the azalea stand is told about the presence of this flower by a pop-up window (the guide is to be usable by everybody) and a corresponding jingle sound. If she/he wants to listen to this content, she/he can press the "up" hardware button. By default, the system skips the presentation. This operational mode has low intrusiveness (users are asked whether to listen to a content), but it also provides a certain degree of proactivity. Information is not only botanical, as in the example of azalea, but also concerns the positioning of the user. Many tags are placed in the proximity of facilities, such as lavatories, cafés, exits, and intersections. This localization system lowers the mental workload necessary for the tourist to synchronize the physical space of the exhibition with the virtual space of the program.

Figure 9. Snapshot of the event-driven interface

This message (accompanied by a jingle) is shown to the user when she/he has just entered a POI area. The combination of audio and graphics is due to the fact that the guide may be used also by not visually impaired people. In the example in this figure, the user is near to the azalea flower, and if she/he is interested in the description she/he can press the "up" hardware button to access the related content.

One of the main tasks of the guide is to assist the visitor in her/his exploration of the exhibition space. A facility to support orientation (not useful for visually impaired people) is a section with the map that helps the tourist to orient herself /himself in the exhibition. The map (see Figure 10) shows the structure of the EuroFlora, including lavatories, café, exits, and so forth, and the location of the points of interests. In order to enhance user's orientation, the map is centered on the position of the user, as determined by the currently perceived RFID tags.

FIELD EVALUATION

Experimental Framework

Real evaluation of advanced mobile device applications and of the impact on their intended population is difficult and costly. Evaluation requires analysis of real users, in a real context of use. In order to adequately evaluate interaction with computation resources, test-people should use a fully operational, reliable, and robust tool, not just a demonstration prototype (Abowd & Mynatt, 2000). Hence, it is important to perform early tests in the authentic context of use in order to verify end-user acceptance and overall usefulness of the system, and to receive feedback to inform future design.

In this chapter, we describe the early stage analysis of acceptance and usefulness of the developed multimedia guide. The tests were performed at EuroFlora 2006, the international flower exhibition that is held in Genoa every 5

Figure 10. Snapshot of the map section of Euro-Flora Guide

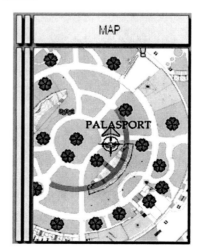

years. With over 500,000 visitors in 10 days, EuroFlora is one of the most important exhibitions of Europe.

The exhibition area (around 90,000 squared metres) was equipped with an infrastructure of 99 RFID tags. The experimentation involved 120 visually impaired tourists who used the tour guide, and were observed and interviewed by expert of disabilities and HCI designers. Subjects were visually impaired (25%) or blind persons (75%) representing a wide range of age (28% age <30; 32% age between 30 and 50; and age >50 40%). Moreover, the tests involve 64 females and 56 males.

The tour guide consisted of a PocketPC equipped with a special leather package with a lace dropping from the neck for a more comfortable use. Headphones were also used in order to isolate the user from the highly noisy surrounding environment (see Figure 1).

Preexhibition Tests

In an early test session-performed 2 days before the official opening of the exhibition, when some stands were already readyenabling a realistic test-we prepared a prototype software version that was used by five selected visually impaired users visiting 30% of the total exhibition area. We followed and interviewed the users in this phase, in order to understand shortcomings, defects and weaknesses, and strong points of the product. In this phase, we understood and solved some problems on user interface and contents, such as the most suited assignment of buttons to presentation control functionalities and the length of the descriptions. Some test-users found the long silence time between a presentation activation and the next one (i.e., the period of time in which the user is walking through areas not covered by RFID tags) frustrating. We partially tackled this issue by periodically providing a message saying that the user is currently in an area not close to a POI.

Ecological Tests

One hundred and twenty blind people used the guide during the exhibition. Sixty of them (aged from 12 to 78 years old) participated in an ecological test conducted by the authors. We interviewed the users at the return of the guide. We evaluated three main performance factors: usability (including effectiveness, efficiency and pleasantness of use), usefulness, and capability to support spatial orientation (in particular the approach to the POIs). We asked users to give a general comment on the guide and a 1-5 grade for each factor (which was carefully explained and defined by the interviewers). An overall survey of results is reported in Table 2; it clearly shows the high acceptance by the users.

Analyzing the variables' correlations based on the chi-square test, we observed that usability is correlated with the perceived support for spatial orientation (χ=25.3, df (degree of freedom) = 16, 90% confidence), and that perceived utility of the tools is strictly correlated with perceived support for spatial orientation (χ=30.2, df=16, 99.9% confidence). This suggests the importance of our design choice to use mobile technology to support orientation of visually impaired people. Moreover, test results also show that the tool is perceived as useful and usable.

Considering the free comments, the guide was judged as an excellent tool for users to orientate themselves inside the exhibition. Several people expressed a similar concept, which we can synthesize with the words of one visitor: "after always having been guided, for the first time I myself have been able to guide my wife and to explain the exhibition!" Such positive comments were also confirmed by the blind assistance experts, who highlighted the significant degree of independence the blind could reach through the guide.

Shortcomings in the interface were reported by some elderly users, while some people asked for more extended descriptions, though each point of interest included at least one. The high

Table 2. Overall survey results

Issue	Average	Standard Deviation
Usability	4.00	0.64
Usefulness	4.25	0.75
Support for spatial orientation	4.20	0.66
Session length time	201 minutes	30 minutes

performance and reliability of hardware, software, and batteries assured long sessions of use with no troubles for the user.

FUTURE TRENDS AND VISION

The research community is envisaging a new model of a "tagged world" as an intelligent environment that allows providing visually impaired people with information about architectonical barriers, safe paths, points of interest, potential danger areas, and other useful information. A sample scenario description may give an idea of this likely future.

Maria is visually impaired. She is in a foreign city on a business trip. Maria owns a mobile device with a mobility-assistance system (MAS: it is similar to the EuroFlora Guide, but with a much larger action range). The MAS accompanies her in her path to her destination office, and signals pedestrian crossings, traffic lights, safe paths in work-in-progress areas, and so forth. All objects in the world send their signals, but Maria's wearable device has an intelligent reasoning algorithm (based on user preferences and interpretation of the user's current activity) and a suitable human-computer interaction (HCI) in order to provide her only with the needed information. This information is extracted from a mass

of data that are continuously received from the close-by RFID tags. Thus, the wearable device notifies Maria about a pedestrian crossing only if it knows that this is useful for her current activity (i.e., going to office). Not useful information will not be provided, in order not to distract Maria. Along her path to her destination, Maria passes by a newsagent. The World Guide scans all the magazines and identifies today's issue of Maria's favourite magazine. It queries Maria's database, which replies that Maria has not purchased this issue yet; so, it notifies her about the opportunity to buy the magazine.

CONCLUSION

The ubiquitous presence of smart tags will offer, in the near future, a critical mass of information, embedded in the world, that will be exploitable to rethink the relationships between people involved in their daily-life activities and the surrounding world.

With MADE we have designed a system that continuously scans the tagged world, interprets the large amount of information coming from the surrounding objects, and provides it to the users through multimedia human-computer interaction. Moreover, the application in the future will filter the raw data coming from the environment (with artificial intelligence behaviour) taking into account the user needs, preferences, and profile.

The field test at EuroFlora 2006 has demonstrated the feasibility of our vision, by deploying the system in a real-world setting (an exhibition area with indoor and outdoor instrumented environments), and performing extensive field tests with real users. In a longer-term view, with such an application, we intend to investigate the future scenarios that will be enabled by a massive presence of RFID tags in our environments. This "early prototyping" has allowed us to understand, as early as possible, costs, limits, strengths, and benefits of the new technology. We have also obtained a significant positive feedback on user acceptance. Usability results show that the guide is perceived as highly usable and useful, in particular because of its ability to support spatial orientation.

The next step towards a "tagged world" will require integration of data and services, and capability of interpreting a variety of sources according to the specific and dynamic user needs. Achieving these goals will involve a huge research effort that will be successful only if it will lead to the deployment of compelling applications that will be perceived as useful by the users. In a user-centered design view, this implies a rapid prototyping of applications and extensive user testing in the real context of use, which was our inspiring principle in the EuroFlora project.

REFERENCES

Abowd, G. D., & Mynatt, E. D. (2000). Charting past, present, and future research in ubiquitous computing. *ACM Transaction in Computer-Human Interaction, 7*(1), 29-58.

Beck, A. (1993). User participation in system design: Results of a field study. In M. J. Smith, *Human-computer interaction: Applications and case studies* (pp. 534-539). Amsterdam: Elsevier.

Bellotti, F., Berta, R., De Gloria, A., Ferretti, E., & Margarone, M. (2003). VeGame: Field exploration of art and history in Venice. *IEEE Computer, 26*(9), 48-55.

Bellotti, F., Berta, R., De Gloria, A., Ferretti, E., & Margarone, M. (2004). Science game: Mobile gaming in a scientific exhibition. eChallenges e2004. *Fourteenth International Conference on eBusiness, eGovernment, eWork, eEurope 2005 and ICT.* Vienna.

Bellotti, F., Berta, R., De Gloria, A., & Margarone, M. (2002). User testing a hypermedia tour guide. *IEEE Pervasive Computing, 1*(2), 33-41.

Bellotti, F., Berta, R., De Gloria, A., & Margarone, M. (2003). MADE: Developing edutainment applications on mobile computers. *Computer and Graphics, 27*(4), 617-634.

Borriello, G., Chalmers, M., La Marca, A., & Nixon, P. (2005). Delivering real-world ubiquitous location systems. *Communications of the ACM, Special Issue on The Disappearing Computer, 48*(3) 36–41.

Bruno, R., & Delmastro F., (2003). Design and analysis of a bluetooth-based indoor localization system. *Personal Wireless Communications, 2775*, 711-725.

Carroll, J. M. (1997). Human-computer interaction: Psychology as a science of design. *International Journal of Human-Computer Studies, 46*(4) 501-522.

Djuknic, G. M., & Richton, R.E. (2001). Geolocation and Assisted GPS. *IEEE Computer, 34*(2), 123-125.

EuroFlora. (s.d.). EuroFlora 2006 Home Page. Retrieved from http://www.fiera.ge.it/euroflora2006/index_eng.asp

Fleck, M., Frid, M., Kindberg, T., O'Brian-Strain, E., Rajani, R., & Spasojevic, M. (2002). From Informing to Remembering: Ubiquitous Systems in Interactive Museums. *IEEE Pervasive Computing, 1*(2), 11-19.

Goker, A., Watt, S., Myrhaug, H. I., Whitehead, N., Yakici, M., & Bierig, R. (2004). An ambient, personalised, and context-sensitive information system for mobile users. *Second European Union Symposium on Ambient Intelligence*. Eindhoven, The Netherlands.

Guth, D. A., & Rieser, J. J. (1997). Perception and the control of locomotion by blind and visually impaired pedestrians. In *Foundation of orientation and mobility* (2nd ed.) (pp. 9-38). AFB Press.

Howard, A., Siddiqi, S., & Sukhatme, G. (2003). *An experimental study of localization using wireless Ethernet*. International Conference on Field and Service Robotics

IDENTEC. IDENTEC Solution Ltd Home Page. Retrieved from http://www.identec.com

Kindberg, T., & Barton, J. (2001). A Web-based nomadic computing system. *Computer Networks, 35*(4), 443-456.

Langheinrich, M., Mattern, F., Romer, K., & Vogt, H. (2000). *First steps towards an event-based infrastructure for smart things*. PACT 2000. Philadelphia.

Liu, X., Corner, M.D., & Shenoy, P. (2006, September). *RFID* Localization for pervasive multimedia. In *Procedings of the 8th International Conference on Ubiquitous Computing (UbiComp '06)*. California, USA.

López de Ipiña, D., Mendonça, P., & Hopper A. (2002). TRIP: A low-cost vision-based location system for ubiquitous computing. *Personal and ubiquitous computing, 6*(3), 206-219

Mann, W. C. (2004). The aging population and its needs. *IEEE Pervasive Computing, 3*(2), 12-14.

Quaadgras, A. (2005). Who joins the platform? The case of the RFID business ecosystem. *38th Hawaii International Conference on Systems Science* (pp. 855-864). Gig Island (HI): IEEE Computing Society Press.

Römer, K., Schoch, T., Mattern, F., & Dubendorfer, C. (2003). T-smart identification frameworked for ubiquitous computing applications. *PerCom 2003*. Fort Worth: IEEE Press.

Ross, D. A. (2004). Cyber crumbs for successful aging with vision loss. *IEEE Pervasive Computing, 3*(2), 30-35.

Siegemund, F., & Floerkemeier, C. (2003). Interaction in pervasive computing settings using Bluetooth-enabled active tags and passive RFID technology together with mobile phones. *PerCom 2003*. Fort Worth: IEEE Press

Want, R. (2004). Enabling ubiquitous sensing with RFID. *IEEE Computer*, 84-86.

Want, R., Fishkin, K., Gujar, A., & Harrison, B. (May 1999). Bridging physical and virtual worlds with electronic tags. *ACM Conference on Human Factors in Computing Systems (CHI 99)*. Pittsburgh, PA.

Want, R., Hopper, A., Falcão, V. & Gibbons, J. (1992). The active badge location system. *ACM Transactions on Information Systems, 10*(1), 91-102.

WHO, W. H. (1997). *Who sounds the alarm: Visual disability to double by 2020*. Retrieved from http://www.who.int/archives/inf-pr-1997/en/pr97-15.html

Xu, Z., & Jacobsen, H. A., (2005). *A framework for location information processing*. 6th International Conference on Mobile Data Management (MDM'05). Ayia Napa, Cyprus.

KEY TERMS

Chi-Square Test: The Chi-square is a test of statistical significance for bivariate tabular analysis (crossbreaks). This test provides the degree of confidence we can have in accepting or rejecting a hypothesis.

Ecological Context: The ecological context is a set of conditions for a user test experiment that gives it a degree of validity. An experiment with real users to possess ecological validity must use methods, materials, and settings that approximate the real-life situation that is under study.

Human-Computer Interaction: Human–computer interaction (HCI), also called man-machine interaction (MMI) or computer–human interaction (CHI), is the research field that is focused on the interaction modalities between users and computers (interface). It is a multidisciplinary subject, relating to computer science and psychology.

Location-Aware Computing: Location-aware computing is a technology that uses the location of people and objects to derive contextual information with which to enhance the application behaviour. There are two ways to acquire information about user context: requiring the user to specify it or by monitoring users and computer activity. Sensor technology, such as RFID, could enable mobile devices to extract information from user position automatically.

Mobile Tourist Guide: A mobile tourist guide is a software application with an intuitive interface, that provides users with multimedia information when and where needed during their visit to museums, city centres, parks, and so forth. Such an application runs on PDA-type terminals or on cellular phones, and could be augmented with GPRS (general packet radio service), GPS (global positioning system), and Bluetooth wireless technology. The guide allows tourists to plan routes according to preferences and ambient conditions (weather, timetables, sites of special interest, etc).

Radio Frequency Identification: Radio frequency identification (RFID) is an automatic identification method based on storing and remotely retrieving data using small and cheap devices called RFID tags or transponders. An RFID tag is an object that can be attached to objects, products, or persons to identification using radio waves. Passive tags (with a few centimeter range of sensitivity) require no internal power source, whereas active tags (with more long range of sensitivity, 100 meters) require a power source.

User-Centric Design: User-centric design is a design process that aims at realizing products that meet users' expectations. The key idea of this design methodology is to start the design strategy taking into account the user's perspective.

This work was previously published in Handbook of Research on User Interface Design and Evaluation for Mobile Technology, edited by J. Lumsden, pp. 657-672, copyright 2008 by Information Science Reference, formerly known as Idea Group Reference (an imprint of IGI Global).

Chapter 8.14
Matching Dynamic Demands of Mobile Users with Dynamic Service Offers

Bernhard Holtkamp
Fraunhofer Institute for Software and Systems Engineering, Germany

Norbert Weißenberg
Fraunhofer Institute for Software and Systems Engineering, Germany

Manfred Wojciechowski
Fraunhofer Institute for Software and Systems Engineering, Germany

Rüdiger Gartmann
University of Münster, Germany

ABSTRACT

This chapter describes the use of ontologies for personalized situation-aware information and service supply of mobile users in different application domains. A modular application ontology, composed of upper-level ontologies such as location and time ontologies and of domain-specific ontologies, acts as a semantic reference model for a compatible description of user demands and service offers in a service-oriented information-logistical platform. The authors point out that the practical deployment of the platform proved the viability of the conceptual approach and exhibited the need for a more performant implementation of inference engines in mobile multi-user scenarios. Furthermore, the authors hope that understanding the underlying concepts and domain-specific application constraints will help researchers and practitioners building more sophisticated applications not only in the domains tackled in this chapter but also transferring the concepts to other domains.

INTRODUCTION

Regarding the trend towards ubiquitous computing and ambient intelligence, modern information systems basically have to support mobile users. As a first step towards fulfilling dynamic demands of mobile users, the concept of context-awareness has been introduced to enable filtering of information based on user-specific context information.

To cope with user acceptance, we abstract from context information and use a situation model. Situations are easy to understand for a user and can be derived from a set of context information, including location and time and even user profile information and other sources. They are named cognitive abstractions of context. When such situations are linked with user goals (e.g., get food when hungry), it is evident that different situations imply the need for different information and services to help a user in achieving his goals. User profiles are used for describing personal data, preferences, and interests of individual users, from which user goals can be derived.

Furthermore, we observe a growing demand to cope with dynamic service offers. Service-oriented architectures mainly integrate Web-based services from different providers. One consequence is the need to cope with unavailability of services, for example, due to broken connections or limited scopes of service validity. To enable an automatic replacement of services, that is, service roaming, service profiles are used that provide for a matching with user profiles and context information.

To enable matching of dynamic user demand and service offers on a semantic level, we use semantic technologies. This includes the development of a description model for service semantics and a semantic registry able to cope with such descriptions. The service ontology is modular, based on other ontology modules covering general concepts, situations, and the application domains. As demands from a large number of users are to be matched dynamically with service descriptions provided by a large number of service providers, the application ontology acts as a semantic reference system.

In the following, we start with the discussion of the conceptual background of our approach, followed by an outline of sample application scenarios. In the main part, we discuss the construction and use of the application ontology as a basis for a semantic matching of demand and offers and give an overview of the system architecture supporting this process. A brief summary of practical experiences gained from the deployment of the system as a mobile tourist guide follows. The chapter closes with a look at future trends.

BACKGROUND

Following Dey (2001, p. 5), "context is any information useful to characterize the situation of an entity. An entity is a person, place, or object considered relevant to the interaction between a user and an application, including the user and application themselves." Context-aware applications are able to adapt their functionality based on existing context information towards the user's environment. This includes filtering and provision of information and services being of interest to the user in his specific context, thus making applications more proactive and reducing the need for explicit user interactions. This property is of value especially for mobile applications due to the restricted interaction capabilities of mobile devices. Mobility always has a location aspect that is an important part of almost any context-aware application. In this way, mobile computing and context-awareness are good supplementations in order to provide users with the right information anywhere and anytime.

Research on context-aware applications started in the beginning of the 1990s. One of the first applications was the Active Badge System (Want, Hopper, Falcao, & Gibbons, 1992) from Olivetti Research Lab. It allowed users to locate people in the office and to redirect incoming calls to the closest phone. This system was later in operation at Olivetti STL, Xerox EuroParc, MIT Media Lab, and Xerox PARC.

The Conference Assistant (Dey, Salber, Abowd, & Futakawa, 1999) was developed at the Georgia Institute of Technology. Its aim was to assist conference attendants. Based on user profiles including a list of research interests, the Conference Assistant displays the timetable with events highlighted that are of interest for the user. When entering a room, the Conference Assistant gives information on the presenter and shows the presentation material. The user can then make notes during the presentation, which are recorded together with additional context information, for example, the time, author, and content information useful for later retrieval.

Another type of popular context-aware applications is location-based tourist guides. There are quite a number of examples available from the mid 1990s. The Cyberguide project (Long et al., 1996) from Georgia Tech was aimed at providing information to a tourist based on his position and orientation. The user could see his position on a map. Selecting points on the map the user could get more information about his environment. A similar guide has been developed by the University of Lancaster and tested between 1996 and 1999 for visitors of the City of Lancaster (Davies, Mitchell, Cheverest, & Blair, 1998). Based on location and user preference, the visitor could get information about points of interest in the region.

Both these tourist guides were restricted to location information. The COMPASS2008 project, which has been realized based on the information-logistical service platform described in this chapter, also aims at assisting tourists in providing suitable information and services dynamically in each situation. In contrast to the previous projects, the COMPASS2008 application is not restricted to the location of the user as a context dimension. Another context dimension is time. Dependent on the current time, different time aspects are

inferred, for example, activity of the user, eating time, opening hours of shops, and so forth. In addition, parts of the user profile and even external sources like event calendars are used as context dimensions. Based on the complex context model, a set of situations is derived to provide the basis for a personalized situation-aware filtering of information and services for a user.

Most of the above described applications are prototypes developed in research labs and the academic world. There are not many complex context-aware commercial solutions. However, there are several location-based services offered by mobile communication providers and service providers. Examples are route planning services, city guides, hotel and shopping guides, and location services for nearby gas stations. Most of the commercial and academic applications only use a few context dimensions, mostly location, time, and identity.

APPLICATION SCENARIOS

In this section we describe and analyze scenarios from different application domains, namely tourism and emergency management, regarding their requirements on dynamic information and service supply, ontology support, and relevant context information and user profile data.

Tourism

One application domain for ontology-based service provision is guidance for tourists. Since the behavior of tourists is not predictable and depends on various influencing factors such as personal moods, personal interests, and so forth, an intelligent system should be able to conclude the user's current needs. Furthermore, information relevant for tourists is provided by many different sources.

To be able to decide what information could be relevant for a tourist, it is crucial to detect in which kind of situation the user currently is in. Context information and user profile information are the basis for that decision. For instance, a user standing in front of a sports stadium in which a sports event is about to start could be there accidentally, could intend to see the event, or could look for tickets. If the user profile indicates no interest in this kind of event, the first option is probably correct, otherwise the user profile could indicate whether the user has a ticket for that event. This information would either lead to provision of, for example, a navigation service to the right entrance and further information about the event (e.g., starting lists), or the system would offer an online booking service.

The COMPASS system (Weißenberg, Voisard, & Gartmann, 2006) being based in the technical infrastructure described in this chapter has recently shown in a field test in Beijing that situation detection is applicable to tourist guide systems and that this is a basis for an intelligent selection of appropriate services, which unburdens the user from searching for desired services among huge offers.

Emergency Response Support

Support for emergency response is a very demanding task. Emergency cases are always different and unpredictable, information needs depend on various parameters, and response times are always critical. A precise efficient demand-specific filtering of information from a huge information offer is needed.

The information needed highly depends on the kind of emergency and a precise recognition of the emergency case is crucial for information selection. Typically, not all relevant parameters are known initially. For instance, fighting a fire in a chemical plant is influenced by the chemical substances stored or processed here. Thus, information about the emergency case is completed gradually, and the system has to refine the provided information accordingly.

An ontology-based service selection, based on situation information such as the type of emergency and context data, is very effective to meet the mentioned requirements. An actual example is the MONA system, the Mobile Emergency Assistant (Holtkamp, Weißenberg, & Speckmann, 2005), developed for the Duisburg fire brigades. This system is fed information about the emergency, such as the location and situation (fire in different levels of escalations, car accident, rescue of jammed persons, and so forth). It has access to all internal information sources of the fire brigades and can additionally access external Web services such as geospatial mapping services to get further information if necessary. That leads to an improved information supply for the officers-in-charge and leads to a more efficient mission processing.

APPLICATION ONTOLOGY

As a basis for semantic matching of dynamic offers with dynamic requests in all scenarios and as a base data model, we use a modular extensible application ontology for the description of both demands and offers. In a first step, the ontology structure is explained. Then dynamic aspects of the ontology are discussed in more detail, such as changes in user profiles, contexts or service sets, and service roaming. Finally, we have a closer look at the implementation side, including performance issues.

Ontology Structure

Following Guarino (1998), an ontology can be structured into different kinds of subontologies as depicted by Figure 1:

- The *upper ontology* is limited to generic and abstract concepts, independent of, and thus addressing a broad range of, application domains. It covers reusable dimensions like

Figure 1. Modular ontology architecture

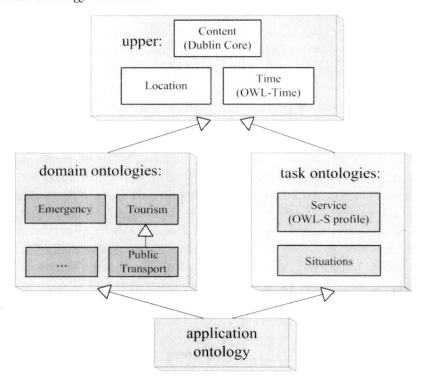

location, time, and content, which may be refined in other ontologies.

- *Domain ontologies* specify concepts of different application domains and scenarios (e.g., tourism, emergency) and may refine concepts from the upper ontologies. For new application scenarios, mainly new domain ontologies are needed.
- *Task ontologies* code knowledge about the usage of domain ontologies, that is, they characterize computational aspects. They make generic use of domain ontologies, that is, they are independent of special domain ontologies.
- The *application ontology* at the lowest level integrates all other ontologies for the application.

Upper Ontologies

Ontology design has to keep in mind for what the ontology is used. In our case, it is intended for dynamic personalized service provision to a huge amount of concurrent users in scenarios as defined above, that is, for information logistics. Existing upper or top-level ontologies like Open-Cyc (Cycorp, 2002) and SUMO (Niles & Pease, 2001) are too large for our scenarios. Hence, we took a more pragmatic approach, concentrating on the main aspects of time, location, and content, which are seen as the main dimensions of information logistics (Deiters, Löffeler, & Pfennigschmidt, 2003).

Location Ontology

For mobile applications, the location aspect is of utmost importance and the use of ontologies for this purpose has been long-praised. Fonseca, Egenhofer, Davis, & Borges (2000) summarize several such approaches. Our location ontology, however, is not a complete geo ontology, but pragmatically provides basic concepts which may be refined in (geo) domain ontologies. There are two layers: the logical or *cognitive* location concepts and their lower-level *geographic extent*, both inheriting from the root concept *Location*. The root concept of the logical layer is *Location-Name*, having subconcepts like *Country, Region,* and *AdministrativeArea,* the latter having subconcepts like *State* and *City*. Multiple inheritance is used to model entities such as *Municipalities,* being a city and a state. A tourism ontology might add concepts like *POI* (point of interest), *Hotel, Shop,* and *Restaurant,* and an emergency ontology might add concepts like *Plant* and its various parts. Instances of the higher-level concepts (i.e., the known locations) are mapped to lower-level concept *GeographicExtent,* having subconcepts like *Point, Box,* and *Polygon.* For example, a *Restaurant* instance is mapped to a *Polygon* instance having some set of points with coordinates (e.g., by using spatial extensions of a database). Using geographic relationships like containment and overlapping at the lower level, corresponding relationship for the higher-level instances can be inferred.

Time Ontology

To define temporal aspects of services and situations, a time ontology is needed. Our time ontology is structured similarly to the location ontology: both have an abstract and a physical layer. The lower physical layer is a subset of OWL-Time (Hobbs & Pustejovsky, 2003), consisting of the *TemporalEntity* subconcepts *Instant* and *Interval,* together with basic relationships *(after, before).*

The additional abstract layer with root concept *PeriodicInterval* is mapped to the lower layer by timestamp patterns, which play the role of coordinates. It has subconcepts like *Yearly* and *Daily.* For example, *Yearly* is instantiated by *January,* representing the month occurring every year periodically, not a concrete month as in the lower layer. Instantiations of *Daily* concepts may even be personalized, depending on a user's context (e.g., *Sunrise*) and preferences (e.g., *Lunchtime, Dinnertime,* and *Morning*), or may be object-dependent (e.g., *TradingHours* of a shop). The personalized time *abstraction* method accesses the user profile and yields a set of known logical time concepts for a user for the current time. While the lower level of our time ontology is based on OWL-Time, the higher level is a simplification of concept *CalendarDescription,* found in some versions of OWL-Time. In the OpenCyc upper ontology it is called *RegularlyRepeatedEvent.*

Content Ontology

For the content dimension, Qualified Dublin Core (Kokkelink & Schwänzl, 2002) is often used, which is mainly a refinement of Dublin Core (DCMI, 2004), providing access to information and services at document metadata level.

Domain and Task Ontologies

The modular application ontology is open for different domain ontologies to be added, to support different scenarios. For example, a tourism ontology has different kinds of POIs, restaurants, hotels, and the like, and may use an ontology of public transport. The domain ontologies are mainly used as value pool for different properties in all other ontologies.

There is no separate *user profile ontology,* but it consists of different domain ontologies covering the interests and preferences of users in the application domain. The profile values stemming from a separate system (e.g., from LDAP) are interpreted using the knowledge of domain ontologies. Additional rules may be meaningful when some profile attributes are to be inferred by others.

Also task ontologies can be added when needed. The main task ontologies in our case are the service ontology and the situation ontology.

Service Ontology

Service (and information) advertisements and demands are described independently by different user groups (i.e., service provider and user), not knowing exactly the needs of each other. The most flexible way to match demands against offers is to use semantic technologies, that is, ontologies and inference. The *ServiceProfile* is a subconcept of concept *Content* having Qualified Dublin Core properties. Thus, services are special content, having content properties and additionally service-specific properties. Registered

services are facts connected by their properties to instances or concepts of other ontologies, which serve as dimensions. The top level ontologies *Location* and *Time* as well as all domain and task ontologies are used as value space for different service properties. This results in a star schema, in which service properties are characterized by subprofiles, which again are characterized by their properties. For example, the *geoRegion* of a specific service may be characterized by a location instance, which itself is characterized by a set of properties and the cost aspect may be characterized by a cost subprofile.

A simplified sample service ontology of this construction is sketched by Figure 2, which is both a relational schema and an ontology, since shadowed boxes indicate the root concepts of subontologies used for a dimension. Only some sample properties are shown here.

Service retrieval is supported by different multivalued classification properties. The values

Figure 2. Modular service ontology schema

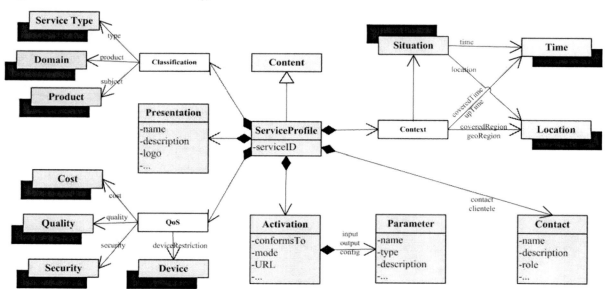

are concepts from different domain or task ontologies. Such rather orthogonal classifications together already cover much of the semantics of a service:

- **General classifications** using a service type taxonomy (property *type*), a product taxonomy (for *products* related to the service), and concepts from other domain ontologies used as service subjects (property *subject*).
- **QoS classifications** summarize nonfunctional quality of service aspects, for example, characterizing of main factors of service cost, quality, security, and possible device restrictions in the case of locally installed services (running on PDAs or home gateways).
- **Context** aspects support restricting a service to a multidimensional context and even to detected situations. This includes location and time properties for service validity (service accessibility, that is, *geoRegion*, *upTime*) and service coverage (for its result, that is, *coveredRegion*, *coveredEpoch*). An example is to find services callable *now* (validity is actual context) but delivering information (coverage) for a restaurant or event to visit this evening.
- **Contacts** and **clientele** summarize relational contact data of different parties involved in the service, like service provider and call center, as well as the clientele (for multiclientele ability).

For *presentation and activation* of retrieved services, the following aspects are specified (not necessarily in an ontology but relational, since these aspects are seldom needed for service retrieval):

- **Presentation** covers all information needed to display retrieved service at the user's front-end, and includes multilingual information such as a service name or description and possibly icons. For use of services by programs, this aspect is not relevant.
- **Activation** provides all information needed to call the service, such as an *URI*, the communication standard used (property *conformsTo*), the *mode* (active, passive, etc.) and the parameters. Since we currently do not use a process model for the service, our grounding is simple.
- **Parameter** describes each input, output, and configuration parameter of the services, for example, its name, type, and a brief description, to be used for GUI generation and parameter marshaling.

The service ontology is influenced by standards like OWL-S (Martin et al., 2004), a Web service ontology submitted to the W3C, but we focus on the service profile. However, OWL-S is not the only approach towards Web service ontologies. The Web Service Modeling Ontology (WSMO) has also been submitted to W3C and a third approach is Semantic Web Services Ontology (SWSO). There is a migration process for these approaches. However, they focus on the process model, while their service profile is only basic. In contrast, the service ontology presented here focuses on the service profile, since it is used for demand-based service retrieval primarily.

Situation Ontology

Situation detection requires a modular ontology with subontologies for all context dimensions, all combined in the situation ontology. Thus, the situation ontology extensively depends on its dimension ontologies. It consists of a hierarchy of situation profile concepts, instantiated to characterize different situations. Situations are described by semantic situation profiles, being named sets of characteristic features of situations. Situation descriptions instantiate these concepts by defining a semantic classification of an aggregate of abstracted user context, user profile, and related information and can be inferred from these. At a given time, a user may be in zero, one, or many situation known by the system.

Ontology Usage

The application ontology is used as follows: Whenever an event occurs that might influence the service set of a user, the set is recalculated by situation detection and service matching (and possibly service roaming). These significant events include:

- **Context changes**: Our application scenarios are mobile, thus location changes occur often. We have developed an algorithm to detect significant location changes based on geographic extents of logical location concepts used in service registrations. This algorithm runs on mobile devices. Any user's GPS locations are only transmitted by his phone or PDA to the context server when a *significant* change has occurred and a new significance specification is returned. The same mechanism can be applied to other context dimensions as well. In this way, frequent context changes of mobile users lead only occasionally to service set recalculations. In a field trial in Beijing discussed in this chapter, only 86 significant context changes were produced by 15 users in approximately 4 hours in total.
- **User profile changes**: Whenever a user entered or modified his user profile, an event is fired, causing the system to react by calculating new situations and an appropriate new service set.
- **Service set changes**: Whenever a new service is provided to the public or whenever a service is changed or removed, an event is fired, causing service set recalculation.
- **Ontology changes:** Our inference engine is RDBMS-based (i.e., inference is directly executed in the relational database management

system), thus ontology changes are controlled by the database and valid for the next semantic query, which is triggered.

Situation Detection

Situation detection occurs when context sensors report *significant* context changes. The abstraction and aggregation mechanisms of all dimensions are used to obtain a set of instances of the higher-level situation concepts. For example, not only the location and time may characterize a situation but also whether an action takes place at that location and time, by consulting for example a social event directory service or weather service. The resulting situation request profile is then semantically matched to all situation profiles known to the system, leading to a (possibly empty) set of situations fulfilling the request profile. A user may be in any of these situations or may be interested in being in this situation. For example, if a user is in a filled stadium, situation *Watching Competition* is detected. If it is personal lunchtime, the additional situation *Eating in Stadium* provides corresponding service offers. Only well-defined situations can be detected. If a user is in a situation not known by the system, he will only get situation-independent support.

Service Matching

The service selection process is a semantic matching of an implicitly dynamically constructed service request profile against the profiles of all known services found in the semantic registry. The request profile uses the matching situations determined previously. User profile and context are also used in the request profile, for example, to select only services matching the user's interests at the current location. Some user preferences are mapped to service types or service subjects, which requires fine-grained taxonomies of these kinds, being related to the preferences hierarchy. Other preferences are used for a personalized instantiation of time ontology concepts like *Morning* and *Lunchtime*, which are used to infer situations. The matching evaluates different types of semantic relationships for all profile properties, like subclass, instance, and containment relationships. Different matching strategies can be realized by defining different semantics when using our *ModelAccess* component described below. For example, for a class-valued property (e.g., property *type* or *subject* in our service ontology), it can be defined whether it matches with subclasses, with superclasses, or with both, and to what semantic distance.

Service Roaming

Mostly, services are defined for a certain scope, which could be a geographical area they cover or certain timeframes or situations for which they are useful. Obviously, a service scope can be described based on restrictions defined on context attributes. Service matching regards the actual user context and adds it to the service request profile in order to select only services which scope covers this context. Based on context-specific service selection, service roaming aims at providing certain service functionality to a user constantly during changing contexts. Whenever the actual user context leaves the scope of the used service, a new service instance with similar functionality but with a scope fitting to the new context has to be found and invoked transparently for the user. An example is a service offering parking information for a certain city. Such a service could, for example, be used in a navigation application. If a user leaves one city and enters another, the navigation application is automatically disconnected from the currently used service and connected to the one covering the area of the new city.

Implementation Aspects

Currently, our extensible ontology comprises about 300 concepts with 1900 properties and 900

instances (among them the registered services and locations), divided into several top-level, domain, and task ontologies. It is completely stored in relational database tables, combined with relational data and accessed from all subsystems by our *ModelAccess* component. Multi-user access is controlled by a sophisticated RDBMS. We have done extensive load testing of the new architecture, which proved to scale well with the number of users (concurrent threads), the size of the ontology, and the size of the answer set. The numbers can be summarized as follows: With 100, 000 registered service profiles and about the same number of related entities as above retrieval times of about a second are achieved on a 3.2 GHz, 2 GB RAM PC, of course depending on the complexity of the query.

SYSTEM ARCHITECTURE

To support scenarios like those described, we have developed an information-logistical semantic service platform. We give a gross outline of the system architecture and the interoperation of its subsystems for semantic matching of user demands and registered offers.

Use of Profiles

All subsystems use profiles for describing entities in their interface methods. A profile is a structured set of properties covering different dimensions and characterizing an entity. Each property has a type (range) and may have several values. Samples are user profiles, service profiles, situation profiles, location profiles, and device profiles. They may be used for characterizing offers and also for describing an actual demand of such entities, and are thus a basis for semantic matching of both.

Profiles may be interpreted either directly or semantically. In a semantic profile, the range and values of the attributes are semantic categories stemming from an ontology, which forms background knowledge for interpreting the syntactic (e.g., relational) data. The ontology can also be used to guide the process of creating or modifying profile properties (e.g., to offer allowed value for properties), and to assure consistency of stored profile properties with the ontology.

Gross Architecture

The information-logistical semantic service platform provides basic functionalities needed for intelligent demand-specific selection and provision of information and services. The key technologies used and combined by the platform are the following:

- **Personalization** is used for the selection of services and information according to a user's profile, preferences, interest, and other user-related information, and for the adaptation of filtered information to the user's needs.
- **Context and situation awareness:** Context information includes any relevant information about the user's state and his environment including the derived situations. It can be used to retrieve the information needed at the location and time or in the situation the user currently is in.
- **Open infrastructure:** The service platform uses and builds on top of existing open and distributed service infrastructures. This enables the dynamic use and selection of already existing information and services.
- **Mobile computing:** A mobile device provides users with information and services everywhere. This allows further integration of the platform in the user's daily life and work processes. The restricted communication and interaction capability of mobile devices, as well as communication costs, reliability, and security aspects have to be considered

when selecting suitable presentation forms and delivery strategies.
- **Information-logistical evaluation:** All described key technologies are combined by application-specific evaluation knowledge. The evaluation component of the platform controls the appropriate selection and presentation of services and information. This may even include business processes, being out of scope for this chapter.

Main Components

The logical architecture defines overall system functionality as a cooperation of different subsystems providing specialized tasks related to the key technologies. The subsystems are application-independent and can also be used stand-alone. They all build on services and models of the core layer. As sketched, the platform developed consists of the following main components:

ModelAccess

Inference engines are not yet as mature as relational database systems. Especially, they are not as fast and only some of them support multithreading, which is a prerequisite for having a large number of concurrent users. Therefore, we developed a *ModelAccess* component with integrated basic and pragmatic inference support. The principle idea of *ModelAccess* is the generation and execution of *closed* structured query language (SQL) queries from semantic profiles based on ontologies that map the original semantics. The generation is based on an extensible set of registered parameterized SQL parts. Predefined parts for standard relationships like *subtype, instanceOf, partOf, geoContains* exist, and rules or characteristics for new kinds of relationships can be stored as user-defined SQL parts. The parts are selected and composed based on stored semantic metadata of table properties. The *closed* queries generated only need simple transactions handled by the RDBMS automatically. The *ModelAccess* component was built with the main design goals to support dynamic online multi-user access to semantic data, to support efficient retrieval on voluminous persistent semantic data, and to combine relational concepts with semantic features by an abstract model access layer and runtime-engine used within all subsystems of the service platform.

Most inference engines and ontology design tools today enable to store ontologies in an RD-BMS. For example, Protégé provides to store ontologies as Protégé database and others even offers to use database tables during inference (which often makes inference slower, and is intended for large ontologies that cannot completely be kept in main memory). However, *ModelAccess* is not the first inference engine using a relational database directly for inference. In Das, Chong, Eadon, and Srinivasan (2004), an approach is

described to implement inference on top of an Oracle RDBMS. Semantic queries are formulated using SQL with additional operators, based on a general schema for storing concepts, properties and relationships. Due to performance reasons they perform an initial materialization of all OWL axioms (e.g., subproperties and transitivity of properties) after loading the ontology, followed by individual inferences for each semantic query. The differences to our approach are: they need initial materialization of, for example, transitivity (computing the transitive closure) to get meaningful performance and directly work on SQL level, while we use transitive discriminates (no transitive closure) and add semantic profiles and SQL generation as an optional abstraction level. In Chong, Das, Eadon, and Srinivasan (2005), the same authors describe a similar approach to realize inference based on resource description framework (RDF). Performance is optimized by

Figure 3. Gross architecture of the semantic service platform

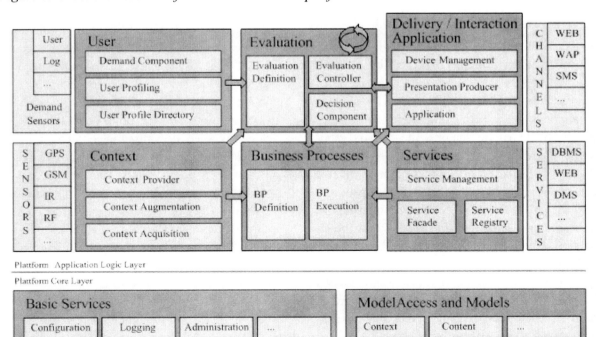

providing indexed materialized views on the two tables of their normalized schema, which *results* in a table design similar to ours. Chong et al. (2005) conclude, "a promising storage representation is *partial* normalization" (2005, p.12).

Service Subsystem

This subsystem is responsible for selecting content and services. It is an open service infrastructure and provides functionality for management and provision of services. This includes the semantic description of services by definable ontology schemas, as described above. The semantic *ServiceRegistry* (implemented by *ModelAccess*) provides dynamic ad hoc integration of services of different kinds from third party providers. It allows for retrieval of registered services and customized service offers. The *ServiceFacade* supports use of services of any kind, provides basic mechanisms for controlling access rights and billing, and enables service roaming. Not only passive services are supported, but also subscribing active services which may fire events.

Context Subsystem

This subsystem provides functionality for definition and provision of application-specific context models, which are a machine readable representation of the part of the world relevant for an application, based on a context meta model. Normally, this model includes the user and other items like locations and relations between these objects. The subsystem provides functionality for detection and provision of context information for any entity. This includes ad hoc integration, management, selection, and use of distributed context sensors, the derivation of related context information and the detection of situations (to enable situation-awareness). The subsystem follows a layered component architecture that separates the different aspects of context detection, integra-

tion, refinement, model management and operation, and context information access.

User Subsystem

This subsystem defines the infrastructure for the personalization of any application, used for centralized management and provision of user information. This includes the provision of user data (relatively static user information like the user's name and gender), user preferences (like preferred language or modality), and user interests (in specific topics). Complex application-specific user model can be defined. Securing privacy of such information is important here. In the current version of the subsystem a lightweight directory access protocol (LDAP) server is used as the basis for management and provision of user information. It also includes a framework for integration of user profile learning components.

Evaluation Subsystem

This subsystem provides information-logistical evaluation logic. The jobs residing in the evaluation subsystem are value-added services defining the main application-specific interoperation patterns between the subsystems. They enable the evaluation of any resources, for example, information and services, its relevance for a specific user, and a delivery strategy. The subsystem executes in cooperation with the other subsystems, thus delegating special evaluation jobs to them, for example, notification of relevant context events or changes of service sets. Reusable scenarios abstract from the implementation of evaluation jobs within the other subsystems. The current implementation of the job model is based on a Boolean ECA-paradigm: events can be subscribed from the other subsystems. The condition is a Boolean expression on events that lead to the action part defining a coordinated execution of functionality using the other subsystems.

Instantiation for Application Scenarios

All application scenarios described above have common requirements on a supporting platform, namely information-logistical support by dynamic information and service supply, based on registered offers, relevant context information, and user profile data. These are the objective of the semantic service platform.

Instantiation of the platform for a new application possibly added to the set of already existing applications (ability to clientele processing) begins with extending the data models (namely ontologies). Each subsystem can be instantiated by configuration and by describing its application-dependent behavior using a domain-specific language. Then the platform component's application programming interfaces (APIs) are used by the new application, and services as well as application-specific jobs have to be registered.

PRACTICAL EXPERIENCES

As the information-logistical semantic service platform is implemented and operational, we have gained first practical experiences regarding ontology integration and performance. Having used the platform as a basis in the COMPASS2008 system that aims at providing visitors of the Olympic Games 2008 in Beijing with personalized situation-aware services, we are also able to include experiences from a recently performed field test in Beijing. During that field test the users were equipped with GPRS- und GPS-enhanced MDA Pro PDAs with the COMPASS front-end.

The field test was conducted July 8-10, 2006, in Beijing. To enable testing of the COMPASS system under real-life conditions, we defined a test scenario for Beijing. This scenario aims at covering the most common situations visitors (especially Western foreigners) experience when visiting Beijing. Regarding the resources avail-able in the project we had to restrict the test to a part of Beijing, for example, to limit the content needed.

The test users represented Beijing Olympic visitors, that is, they acted in the role "tourist". For the field test we had foreign users from the U.S. Korea, Japan, and Italy as well as Chinese, thus representing native and non-native English speakers. Of the 15 users, 12 were male and 3 were female. Their average age was about 26 years. Approximately 40% of the users had experience in the use of PDAs and/or smartphones. The foreign users mostly had only little knowledge of the Chinese language and were to some extent familiar with Beijing. Six foreigners were in Beijing for one month or less.

In the next step, the test users were sent out to perform the test. Each user had to fulfil 16 tasks, some of them repeatedly, for example, find restaurant/coffee shop, order a drink, plan the day, pay, communicate destination to taxi driver, buy an item, and find restrooms. A COMPASS2008 team member accompanied each test user to assure a proper conduction of the different tasks.

Situation-aware service provision was considered useful by most subjects. No test person criticized it, and most people even desired to improve the feature. From the COMPASS system perspective we obtained the following results regarding the quality of the situation awareness feature: recall 95.8% (correct situation identified, only relevant services offered), precision 51.0% (only correct situation identified, redundant services offered). The recall value looks quite satisfying for the first deployment in the field. An analysis of the reason for wrong situation identifications turned out that deviation of the GPS signal led to mismatches of a user's position and the geographical locations of points-of-interest.

During the field test, the semantic service platform was integrated into the Internet infrastructure of a Chinese Internet service provider. It was fully available with no problems in providing its functionality. Even though there was a problem in the context subsystem leading to an unnecessarily high number of context change events, there was no visible delay in providing the user with situation-specific services.

A problem faced was the unreliable and imprecise location detection of a user through GPS. Even when a user did not move, the GPS detector reported a position change of more than 30 meters. Another problem was the unreliability and limited performance of data communication using general packet radio service (GPRS) in China. Beside these problems, the technical performance of our platform during the field test was satisfying.

FUTURE TRENDS

Currently we observe a convergence of communication and information infrastructures towards Internet-based systems. This convergence eases the integration of information flows into applications. This trend is backed by service-oriented architectures where system components communicate via the Internet, residing at arbitrary locations. Consequently, information overflow of users will intensify. Customer satisfaction can only be achieved when an intelligent information supply is provided, taking care of individual user needs.

A broader adoption of semantic registries and situation-aware demand description as standards enables a guided use of offered services and service-specific contents in individual user contexts. This leads to higher acceptance on the user side and at the same time enables the forming of value chains on the business side, as service providers can establish networks where each provider covers a specific service offer that seamlessly integrates with others.

In summary, user profiles, context-awareness, and semantic service descriptions provide the basis for a demand-driven personalized information and service logistics using multistage value chains.

CONCLUSION

In this chapter, we tried to point out that ontologies and their evaluation are well suited to define a semantic reference system accessed by large heterogeneous user groups. In the COMPASS2008 project, an application ontology for Beijing Olympics tourists has been developed. On this basis a dynamic semantic matching of user demands derived from user profiles and context-driven situation detection with semantically described service offers is performed. The COMPASS pilot system proved the applicability of these concepts for situation-aware semantic Web applications in a field test in Beijing.

Although the results from the field test are satisfying, the entire development was not as smooth as it might seem. We had to solve problems on all levels, including nonsynchronized funding on the Chinese and German sides, content procurement, and system integration or technical problems when setting up the field test. Some of these problems are intrinsic to international projects with multiple partners; others are more specific, like the restricted access to digital maps in China or the impreciseness of GPS in a mega city like Beijing. The cooperative atmosphere within the consortium, however, was a major success factor. A more detailed discussion of the problems sketched above is beyond the scope of this contribution. Here we focused on ontology related issues.

The COMPASS system provides for user-individual demand description and situation-aware service filtering in the context of the Olympic Games 2008 in Beijing. The MONA prototype deploys the same technologies for situation-specific information and service provision in emergency cases, supporting emergency response teams on the spot. Here, situation awareness is used for a more precise content selection.

The insights gained from the deployment of semantic Web technologies show that they are very powerful and helpful for the development of adequate models. On the implementation side, however, mass applications are still a critical issue as the performance of inference engines falls short compared with relational database technology. Hence, for larger applications we recommend use of ontology development tools for the conceptual phase and transferring the result in the implementation phase to a database solution.

ACKNOWLEDGMENTS

COMPASS/FLAME2008 was developed in the context of the project "Personalized Web Services on Internet III for the Olympic Games 2008 in Beijing", October, 2002 – September, 2006, supported by the German Ministry of Education and Research (BMBF Grant No. 01AK055) and the Chinese Ministry of Science and Technology (MOST).

REFERENCES

Chong, E.I., Das, S., Eadon, G., & Srinivasan, J. (2005). An efficient SQL-based RDF querying scheme. In *Proc. 31st VLDB Conf* (pp. 1216-1227). Trondheim, Norway.

Cycorp, Inc. (2002). OpenCyc selected vocabulary and upper ontology. Retrieved June 19, 2007, from *http://www.cyc.com/cycdoc/vocab/vocab-toc.html*

Das S., Chong, E.I., Eadon, G., & Srinivasan, J. (2004). Supporting ontology-based semantic matching in RDBMS. In *Proc. 30th VLDB Conference* (pp 1054-1065). San Francisco, CA: Morgan Kaufmann.

Davies, N., Mitchell, K., Cheverest, K., & Blair, G. (1998). Developing a context sensitive tourist guide. In *First Workshop on Human Computer Interaction with Mobile Devices* (GIST Tech. Rep. G98-1) (pp 17-24).

Deiters, W., Löffeler, T., & Pfennigschmidt, S. (2003). *The information logistics approach toward a user demand-driven information supply.* In D. Spinellis (Ed.), *Cross-media service delivery* (pp. 37-48). Boston, MA.

Dey, A. (2001). Understanding and using context. *Personal and Ubiquitous Computing Journal, 5*(1), 4-7.

Dey, A., Salber, D., Abowd, G.D., Futakawa, M. (1999). The conference assistant: Combining context-awareness with wearable computing. In *3rd International Symposium on Wearable Computer,* San Francisco, CA, (pp. 21-28).

Dublin Core Metadata Initiative (DCMI). (2004). Dublin core metadata element set, reference description. Retrieved June 19, 2007, from *http://dublincore.org/documents/dces/*

Fonseca, F., Egenhofer, M., Davis, C., & Borges, K. (2000). Ontologies and knowledge sharing in urban GIS. *Computer, Environment and Urban Systems, 24*(3), 251-272.

Guarino, N. (1998). Formal ontology and information systems. In *Proc. FOIS'98* (pp. 3-15). Trento, Italy: IOS Press.

Hobbs, J., & Pustejovsky, J. (2003). Annotating and reasoning about time and events. In *Proc. AAAI Spring Symposium on Logical Formalization of Commonsense Reasoning* (pp. 74-82). Menlo Park, CA: AAAI Press.

Holtkamp, B., Weißenberg, N., & Speckmann, H. (2005). MONA – A situation-aware decision support system for emergency situations. In *Proc 19th Int. Conf. EnvironInfo - Informatics for Environmental Protection,* Brno, Czech Republic (pp. 186-190).

Kokkelink, S., & Schwänzl R. (2002). Expressing qualified Dublin core in RDF/XML. Retrieved June 19, 2007, from *http://dublincore.org/documents/dcq-rdf-xml/*

Long, S., Kooper, R., Abowd, G. D., & Atkeson, C. G. (1996). Rapid prototyping of mobile context-aware applications: The cyberguide case study. In *2nd ACM International Conference on Mobile Computing and Networking* (pp 97-107).

Martin, D. (Ed.) (2004). OWL-S: Semantic markup for Web services (W3C Member Submission). Retrieved June 19, 2007, from *http://www.w3.org/Submission/OWL-S*

Niles, I., & Pease, A. (2001). Towards a standard upper ontology. In *Proc FOIS'01* (pp 2-9). Ogunquit, ME.

Weißenberg, N., Voisard, A., & Gartmann, R. (2006). An ontology-based approach to personalized situation-aware mobile service supply. *Springer GeoInformatica, 10*(1), 55-90.

Want, R., Hopper, A., Falcao, V., & Gibbons, J. (1992). The active badge location system. *ACM Transactions on Information Systems, 10*(1), 91-102.

Chapter 8.15
A Multi-Agent System Approach to Mobile Negotiation Support Mechanism by Integrating Case-Based Reasoning and Fuzzy Cognitive Map

Kun Chang Lee
Sungkyunkwan University, Korea

Namho Lee
Sungkyunkwan University, Korea

ABSTRACT

This chapter proposes a new type of multi-agent mobile negotiation support system named MAM-NSS in which both buyers and sellers are seeking the best deal given limited resources. Mobile commerce, or m-commerce, is now on the verge of explosion in many countries, triggering the need to develop more effective decision support systems capable of suggesting timely and relevant action strategies for both buyers and sellers. To fulfill a research purpose like this, two artificial intelligence (AI) methods such as CBR (case-based reasoning) and FCM (fuzzy cognitive map) are integrated and named MAM-NSS. The primary advantage of the proposed approach is that those decision makers involved in m-commerce regardless of buyers and sellers can benefit from the negotiation support functions that are derived from referring to past instances via CBR and investigating inter-related factors simultaneously through FCM. To prove the validity of the proposed approach, a hypothetical m-commerce problem is developed in which theaters (sellers) seek to maximize profit by selling their vacant seats to potential customers (buyers) walking around within reasonable distance. For experimental design and implementation, a multi-agent environment Netlogo is adopted. A simulation reveals that the proposed MAM-NSS could produce more robust and promising results that fit the characteristics of m-commerce.

INTRODUCTION

The modern mobile computing world is characterized by one of both ubiquitous connectivity and ubiquitous computational resources (Edwards, Newman, Sedivy, & Smith, 2004). Recent popular forms of mobile computing encompass omnipresent short-range communications (including both infrastructure-based technologies such as WiFi and peer-to-peer technologies such as Bluetooth), and also omnipresent long-range communications (such as cellular telephony networks). This maturing mobile environment justifies conservative estimates based on the 2000 Census report suggesting that by 2006 10% of U.S. workers will be completely mobile, with no permanent office location (Lucas, 2001). This trend will be fueling development of new mobile applications as advances in mobile technology increase coverage, data speeds, and usability (Barbash, 2001; Crowley, Coutaz, & Bérard, 2000; Parusha & Yuviler-Gavishb, 2004; Pham, Schneider, & Goose, 2000; Turisco, 2000).

In this sense, it is no wonder that **mobile commerce** (or **m-commerce**) replaces traditional forms of electronic commerce rapidly. Various types of m-commerce services include mobile shopping, location sensitive information service, traffic updates, and logistic tracking services, all of which utilize the concepts of customization, personalization, location sensitive, context awareness (Lee & Yang, 2003; Schilit, 1995; Schilit, Adams, & Want 1994; Wang & Shao, 2004; Want, Hopper, Falcao, & Gibbons, 1992; Want, Schilit, Adams, Gold, Petersen, Ellis, et al., 1995). M-commerce has been successfully activated in some industries, leading to competitive advantage (Rodgera & Pendharkarb, 2004; Varshney, 1999) and improved workflow as well as reduced costs and risk management (Miah & Bashir, 1997; Porn & Patrick, 2002; Turisco, 2000). However, such a success story is confined to specific applications where the decision support framework is not considered seriously. To reap better results from the users' view, decision makers engaged in a specific type of m-commerce should be supported more intelligently and robustly.

It cannot be overstated that decision makers under a specific m-commerce situation need more timely and robust decision support because they are in several types of contexts. For example, they cannot afford to receive detailed information from a decision support system because of the limited display capability of mobile devices they carry. Besides, they do not have enough time to consider all the related factors before making decisions because they are usually on the move. This kind of environmental limitations require that a **decision support framework** should be developed for enhancing decision making effectiveness for m-commerce users.

For this purpose, this chapter proposes a new kind of decision support framework named **MAM-NSS_**(multi-agent mobile negotiation support system) which can benefit both m-commerce buyers and sellers. MAM-NSS is based on a multi-agent mechanism in which buyers and sellers are respectively represented by agents. Each agent tries to coordinate with each other until reaching a compromised decision. Especially, the proposed MAM-NSS focuses on the fact that decision makers engaged in a specific m-commerce situation are often facing two kinds of needs: (1) to refer to past instances carefully and (2) mull over inter-related factors simultaneously. A literature survey shows that there exist few studies dealing with those research needs. To fill such a research void, this chapter proposes two important mechanisms like **case based reasoning** (CBR) and **fuzzy cognitive map** (FCM).

The proposed MAM-NSS combining CBR and FCM is therefore expected to provide more robust decision support to m-commerce decision makers irrespective of buyers and sellers. To prove the validity of the proposed approach, a hypothetical m-commerce problem is developed in which theaters (sellers) seek to maximize profit by selling their vacant seats to potential customers (buyers) walking around within reasonable distance. For experimental design and implementation, a **multi-agent** environment *Netlogo*[1] is adopted.

BACKGROUND

Recent Trends in M-Commerce

Electronic commerce applications recently provided by mobile communication services include mobile information agents (Cabri, Leonardi, & Zambonelli, 2001, 2002; Mandry, Pernul, & Rohm, 2000-2001), online kiosks (Slack & Rowley, 2002), government applications (e.g., online selling by the postal service, Web-based electronic data interchange, or EDI, in trade applications), and direct online selling systems such as Internet-based (or Web-based) shopping mall systems and Internet-based stock trading systems. In the m-commerce and mobile communication services, their ease of use and multimedia approach to the presentation of information attract potential customers. Some countries and regions have put in tremendous efforts in pushing the development and deployment of m-commerce. These countries include the U.S., Japan, South Korea, Hong Kong, and the Scandinavian countries. There have been many different kinds of m-commerce applications deployed to businesses in these areas. In the U.S., the current rush to wireless communication methods was triggered by the U.S. Federal Communication Commission's auctioning of personal communication-service spectrum space (Senn, 2000). The collaboration of public and private sectors has facilitated the development of m-commerce businesses.

Recently, a large number of organizations have adopted m-commerce for business purposes in order to gain competitive advantages in the electronic market. To cite a few examples, NTT DoCoMo, Vodafone, Verizon, Sprint PCS, and AT&T Wireless have provided "cybermediation" for greater efficiency in supply and marketing channels through m-commerce. M-commerce can benefit business transactions by providing more efficient payment systems, shortening time to markets for new products and services, realizing improved market reach, and customization of products and services (Barnes, 2002; Senn, 2000). Besides, innovative m-commerce applications have been constantly reshaping business practices in terms of enhancing customer service, improving product quality, and lowering cycle time in business processes (Seager, 2003).

As m-commerce supports online purchasing through an electronic channel, that is, the Internet, via electronic catalogs or other innovative formats, customers procure products, services, and information through m-commerce (Bailey & Lawrence, 2001). In m-commerce, potential customers can visit various "virtual malls" and "virtual shops," and browse through their catalogues to examine products in vast detail. New areas of business opportunities for retailers, producers, and consumers can be developed from these virtual markets on m-commerce. Mobile information agents provide an effective method to support the electronic marketplace by reducing the effort involved in conducting transactions (Wang, Tan, & Ren, 2002). Mobile agents can also help search other agents for contracting, service negotiation, auctioning, and bartering (Mandry et al., 2000-2001). Agents roam through Internet sites to locally access and elaborate information and resources (Omicini & Zambonelli, 1998). The introduction of mobile agents into the electronic market scenario reduces the load and the number of necessary connections to suppliers. In this way, the multi-agent approach is a feasible way to model and analyze complex m-commerce applications.

Among the three distinct identifiable classes of electronic commerce applications (i.e., **business-to-customer (B2C), business-to-business (B2B)**, and intra-organization (Applegate, Holsapple, Kalakota, Radermacher, & Whinston, 1996), m-commerce generally falls into the B2C class. M-commerce provides Web presence with information about company products and services and facilities for both online and off-line purchasing. M-commerce also facilitates other business related activities, such as entertainment, real estate, financial investment, and coupon distribution. Usually, m-commerce sellers are required to make competitive offers in order to sell their products or services to the target customers within reasonable distance. In location-based m-commerce applications, sellers should compete with each other to appeal to potential buyers because there could be only a few buyers in a limited area. For sellers, making timely and attractive offers to buyers on the move is very challenging because the buyers continue to receive information and offers from competing sellers.

Intelligent Agents

Fundamentals

The proposed MAM-NSS is basically based on the multi-agents. Both sellers and buyers engaged in a certain m-commerce are represented by specific agents, and each agent is entitled to receiving proper decision support from the MAM-NSS. An intelligent agent (or agent) has various definitions because of the multiple roles it can perform (Applegate et al., 1996; Hogg & Jennings, 2001; Persson, Laaksolahti, & Lonnqvist, 2001; Wooldridge, 1997; Wooldridge & Jennings, 1995). An intelligent agent is simply a software program that simulates the way decision makers think and make decisions. It performs a given task based

on the information gleaned from the environment to act in a suitable manner so as to complete the task successfully. It is able to adjust itself to the changes in the environment and circumstances, so that it can achieve the expected result (Paiva, Machado, & Prada, 2001).

The term "**intelligent agent**" can be disintegrated into two words: intelligence and agency. The degree of autonomy and authority vested in the agent is called its agency. It can be measured at least qualitatively by the nature of the interaction between the agent and other entities in the system in which it operates. An **agent** is an individual and it runs independently. The degree of agency will be enhanced if an agent represents a user in some way. Therefore, collaborative agents represent a higher level of agency because they cooperate with other agents or programs or entities, and so on. The agent intelligence can be interpreted as the degree of reasoning and learned behavior. It is the ability to understand the user's statement of goals and carry out the task delegated to it. Such intelligence can be easily found in the reasoning process of many decision or AI models. Intelligence enables agents to discover new relationships, connections, or concepts independently from the human user, and exploit these in anticipating and satisfying a user's needs (Bonarini & Trianni, 2001; Hu & Weliman, 2001; Schaeffer, Plaat, & Junghanns, 2001).

To retain the characteristics of "intelligence" and "agency." an intelligent agent should possess the abilities of mobility, benevolence, rationality, adaptability, and collaboration (Wooldridge, 1997). Mobility is the ability to move around an electronic network (Bohoris, Pavlou, & Cruickshank, 2000; Lai & Yang, 1998; Lai & Yang, 2000). Benevolence is the assumption that an intelligent agent does not have conflicting goals, and therefore it will always try to complete the assigned tasks (Hogg & Jennings, 2001; Jung & Jo, 2000). Rationality is the assumption that an agent will act in order to achieve its goals and will not act in such a way as to prevent its goals from being achieved, at least insofar as its beliefs permit (Hogg & Jennings, 2001; Persson et al., 2001). Adaptability indicates that an agent should be able to adjust itself to the habits, working methods, and preferences of its user (Jung & Jo, 2000). Collaboration is an ability to cooperate with other agents so that an agent can achieve what a goal decision maker wants to attain (Jung & Jo, 2000; Lee & Lee, 1997; Wu, Yuan, Tseng, & Fuyan, 1999). This chapter places a strong emphasis on the collaboration ability. Although no single agent possesses all these abilities in a real situation, it is certain that these kinds of characteristics are those that distinguish agents from ordinary programs.

Multi-Agent System

To investigate a computational model that actually encodes and uses conflict resolution expertise, a focus can be placed on the **multi-agent framework**, which is adopted from the distributed AI problem (Bird, 1993; Chaib-Draa & Mandiau, 1992; Cooper & Taleb-Bendiab, 1998; Luo, Zhang, & Leung, 2001; Sillince, 1998; Sillince & Saeedi, 1999; Tung & Lee, 1999). Multi-agent systems have offered a new dimension for coordination in an enterprise (Bonarini & Trianni, 2001; Hu & Weliman, 2001; Kwon & Lee, 2002; Sikora & Shaw, 1998; Strader, Lim, & Shaw, 1998; Ulieru, Norrie, Kremer, & Shen, 2000; Wu, 2001). Incorporating autonomous agents into **problem-solving** processes allows improved coordination of different functional units to define tasks independently of both the user and the functional units under control (Cabri et al., 2002). Under a multi-agent system, the problem-solving tasks of each functional unit becomes populated by a number of heterogeneous intelligent agents with diverse goals and capabilities (Lottaz, Smith, Robert-Nicoud, & Faltings, 2000; Luo et al., 2001; McMullen, 2001; Ulieru et al., 2000; Wu, 2001).

The multi-agent system, in which multiple agents work collaboratively to solve specific

problems, provides an effective platform for coordination and cooperation among disputing multiple entities in real world cases. For example, when a conflict occurs between buyers and sellers over a limited resource, it is difficult for a single authority or committee to reconcile it to the full satisfaction of all the entities concerned. Therefore, it is likely that the use of a multi-agent system for coordination will result in a more systematic and organized method in reality without causing unnecessary emotional and behavioral side effects.

Decision Support Mechanisms

MAM-NSS is equipped by two decision support mechanisms such as CBR and FCM. First, **CBR** is a renowned artificial intelligence methodology that provides the technological foundations for intelligent systems (Kolodner, 1993). Given a case base where a number of **past instances** are stored, CBR consists of several phases: indexing cases, retrieving the appropriate candidate cases from the case base, approximating potential solutions from them, testing whether the proposed solutions are successful, and learning to upgrade the decision quality by updating the case base and retrieval mechanism. CBR is most applicable when there is (1) no decision model available; (2) a specific decision model is too hard to acquire; or (3) when past cases are available or easy to generate. With these CBR benefits, the CBR approach is extensively used for negotiation (Kowalezyk & Bui, 1999). Considering the advantages of CBR above, MAM-NSS adopts CBR to allow agents to refer to the past relevant instances that seem to explain a part of current decision making problem before making final decisions.

Second, **FCM** is utilized to provide agents with the capability of analyzing complicated **interrelationships of all the relevant factors** by viewing them simultaneously. FCM was introduced by Kosko (1986, 1987) in which fuzzy causality concept is introduced to represent uncertainty embedded in problem domain. In this way, FCM provides a more flexible and realistic representation of the domain knowledge. For example, Ray and Kim (2002) used it as a tool for understanding and controlling intelligent agents. Liu and Satur (1999) have used FCM as a decision support mechanism for interpreting geographic information as well as designing automatic context awareness function that is one of the important characteristics in m-commerce.

By integrating CBR and FCM, MAM-NSS is designed to provide decision makers on the move with more improved decision support functions. CBR is especially useful for m-commerce users who do not have sufficient time to consider all the constraints before making decisions. By retrieving appropriate past examples and suggesting them as a benchmarking point, CBR can help m-commerce users make fast decisions. There are many factors that are influencing m-commerce decisions either indirectly or directly. However, users cannot afford to consider all the causal relationships among those factors thoroughly in a situation when they need to move and there is not enough time. In that situation, FCM can provide an analytical and systematic way of investigating causal relationships between all the factors related to the m-commerce situation.

MAM-NSS

Basics

Figure 1 depicts a hypothetical m-commerce situation where MAM-NSS is used to provide timely decision support to m-commerce users. Since the term "m-commerce" may cause different interpretations depending on situations, we need to define m-commerce conditions more clearly to make further discussions unambiguous. First, buyers are assumed to carry mobile devices such as PDAs or mobile phones. Second, buyers cannot have access to the telecommunication network

line because they are moving. Third, buyers make reservations with sellers through mobile devices. Fourth, sellers provide information about their services and goods through mobile devices.

The **negotiation process** of MAM-NSS is composed of four steps. Since MAM-NSS runs on a multi-agent framework, a buyer is represented by **B-agent** and a seller **S-agent** from now on. In other words, each agent possesses its own generic knowledge including either buyer's or seller's basic preference that has been predefined.

The first step is to identify buyers' and sellers' location. Such location identification is based on opt-in agreement with mobile telecommunication company.

The second step is for sellers to provide an offer to potential buyers within a fixed distance from where buyers can arrive after a reasonable time. For example, the seller's offer may include an appropriate product/service and its price quote, all of which are assumed to be obtained from CBR inference. For this CBR inference, sellers need various kinds of contextual information such as potential buyers' current location, weather, other events, and so forth.

The third step is for buyers to check the offer from sellers on their mobile devices in which buyers' personal preference is stored. Then the seller's offer is compared with the buyer's predefined preference. If the offer is not appealing, then the buyers modify the offer and send it to the seller. All this process is performed on a multi-agent basis.

The fourth step is for sellers to review the modified offer from buyers. At this time, FCM is used to induce an appropriate price level considering complicated causal relationships among qualitative and strategic factors simultaneously. Depending on marketing strategy, the sellers may change their price offer to lower or higher. Therefore, the sellers' decision can become more strategic and flexible in accordance with changing situations.

Figure 1. M-commerce situation

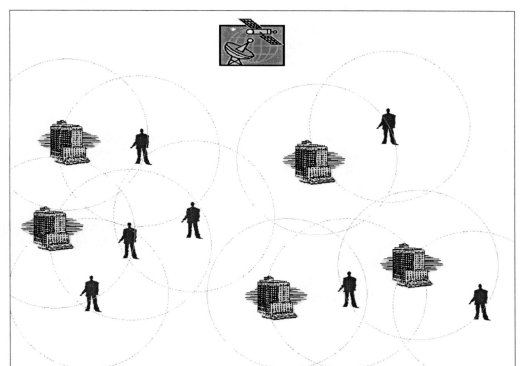

Architecture

MAM-NSS is composed of three entities like **B-agent**, **S-agent**, and **mobile telecommunication company**. B-agent is assumed to be downloaded into buyer's mobile device when she subscribes to the MAM-NSS service. The B-agent becomes personalized according to **buyer's personal preference** about specific products/services, and related prices, quality, brand, and other properties. Especially, B-agent specifies its own utility function following buyer's preference which is compiled from the online questionnaire when the buyer subscribes for the MAM-NSS service. Then the B-agent is stored in the memory of the buyer's carried **mobile device**. The B-agent uses

this information to negotiate prices with sellers. S-agent is basically linked to the seller's back office system and negotiates with B-agent on the price of seller's products/services. S-agent's first price offer is composed referring to CBR inference, and relayed to potential buyers who are moving within a reasonable distance from the seller. When the buyer's modified price offer is entered, S-agent revises its price offer by using FCM and then feeds it back to the buyer. In this process, negotiations are going on until the final deal is struck between buyer and seller.

In the process of negotiations, the mobile telecommunication company acts as an intermediary between S-agents and B-agents. If the **sellers** and **buyers** subscribe to the MAM-NSS service provided by the mobile telecommunication company, then they can share the information needed in negotiation such as the location of sellers and buyers, price offer, and related product/service information.

S-Agent

The ultimate goal of S-agent is to maximize profit. For this purpose, S-agent seeks a potential buyer in the range acceptable to the buyer within a specific time limit. Then it calculates the bid price of the selling product/service based on CBR, and sends the offer including price and product/service to the potential B-agents through the mobile telecommunications company. A wide variety of past selling instances are stored in the case base, and CBR uses the **similarity index** (SI) below to select the candidate case that seems to fit most with the current selling situation. Once such

case is chosen successfully, then the price offer can be made appropriately referring to the price information attached to the selected case.

$$SI_i = \sqrt{\sum_{j=1}^{n}(N_j - S_{ij})^2}$$

where N_j indicates jth attribute value of a new case (j=1,2,…,n), and S_{ij} denotes jth attribute value of ith case in case base of CBR (i=1,2,…, m). Netlogo source code for implementing the CBR mechanism using SI is listed in Table 1.

If the buyer accepts the price offered by S-agent, then the deal between seller and buyer will be completed and the buyer stops negotiating. But if the buyer is not satisfied with the price offered by S-agent, the price level is adjusted and then relayed to S-agent. Finally, S-agent decides whether or not to accept the newly-adjusted price, using the FCM inference. If another price offer

Figure 2. MAM-NSS architecture

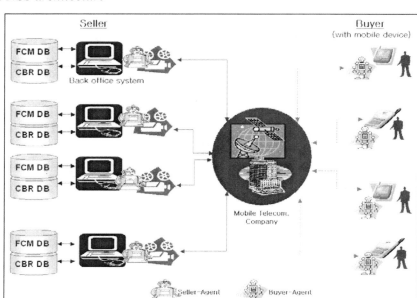

Table 1. S-agent's CBR inference mechanism

```
to change-CBR-price
locals [temp_t temp_i temp_si temp_optimal_si temp_item]
set temp_t(1)
repeat seller_number [
ask seller with [reg_number = temp_t and mobile_service = 1 and
mdss_service = 1 ]
[
   set vacant_percent int (vacant_seat_number / seat_number * 100)
set temp_i (0)
   repeat length CBR_price [
set temp_si sqrt((F1_Current_Value - item (temp_i) CBR_F1_List) ^ 2
                   + ((F2_Current_Value - item (temp_i)
CBR_F2_List) ^ 2
                   + (F3_Current_Value - item (temp_i)
CBR_F3_List) ^ 2
                   + (F4_Current_Value - item (temp_i)
CBR_F4_List) ^ 2
                            )

   if (temp_i = 0)[set temp_optimal_si (temp_si) set temp_item
(temp_i)]
```

Table 2. S-agent's FCM mechanism to adjust price offer

```
to Buyer-decision-for-new-customer-offer
set temp (0)
set temp_i (1)
repeat customer_number [
set inference_list [ ]
set inference_list lput FCM_factor1 inference_list
set inference_list lput FCM_factor2 inference_list
set inference_list lput FCM_factor3 inference_list
set inference_list lput FCM_factor4 inference_list
set inference_list lput FCM_factor5 inference_list
set inference_list lput FCM_factor6 inference_list
set inference_list lput FCM_factor7 inference_list
set inference_list lput FCM_factor8 inference_list
set inference_list lput FCM_factor9 inference_list
set inference_list lput FCM_factor10 inference_list

show inference_list

set FCM_ACCEPT_REULT (FCM_inference inference_list )

ask buyer with [id_number = temp_i ] [
if (reserve != 1 and mdss_service = 1)  [
set temp_utility_adjustment (utility_adjustment)
ask seller with [reg_number = temp2 ] [
  if (available_number_of_product > 0) [
     if (FCM_ACCEPT_REULT = 1 ) [
        show temp_new_price + "<---- accept"
        set vacant_seat_number (vacant_seat_number - 1)
        set temp1 (1) ask customer with [id_number = temp_i ]
                                  [set reserve (1)  set color black]
```

is made, then negotiation proceeds to the next round. This process is repeated until all sellers and buyers find their appropriate partners that meet their respective goals. In Table 2, the FCM mechanism to be used for adjusting the **price offer** is represented in the Netlogo source code.

B-Agent

The buyer represented by B-agent seeks to maximize its own utility in the process of negotiating with the suppliers. Buyers can download B-agents from the subscribed telecommunication company's site and store them into their mobile devices. B-agents incorporate the following **utility functions** where $i=1,2,\ldots,m$ (number of sellers) and $j=1,2,\ldots,n$ (number of utility factors):

$$U_i = \sum_{j=1}^{n} W_{ij} \bullet F_{ij}$$

U_i denotes ith buyer's utility, W_{ij} buyer's preference for jth utility factor, and F_{ij} ith buyer's jth utility factor. It is certain that $\sum_{j=1}^{n} W_{ij} = 1$. Examples of utility factors include not only price, product, and quality, but also **contextual information** such as the buyer's current location and environmental constraints. Table 3 shows the Netlogo source code for calculating the B-agent's utility function.

If B-agent gets the price offer from S-agent and this offer does not meet the buyer's goal utility, then the B-agent suggests a new price using the mechanism shown in Table 4. If the seller accepts the new price offered by the buyer, then the deal is complete. However, if no sellers accept this price, then the B-agent increases the price decreasing its goal utility. In this case, a new round of negotiation resumes.

EXPERIMENTS

Problem Description

Three Groups

The target problem here is that there are a number of movie theaters in an area, and customers want to go to the theater depending on their personal situations. Based on whether customers (i.e., buyers) and theaters (i.e., sellers) are using mobile devices or not, we categorize them into three groups for the sake of the experiment. Group 1, called "**non-mobile group**," is not using mobile devices. Therefore, customers either reserve tickets through non-mobile channels, such as telephone or cable Internet, or buy onsite from the box office. Theaters are assumed to contact customers through the non-mobile channels too. Group 2, called "**passive mobile group**," is using mobile devices but no negotiation functions. Therefore, customers in this group can get information about movies through mobile channels, but they cannot negotiate with theaters through agents. Theaters are also using mobile channels to send movie information to customers. Group 3, called "**active mobile group**," is assumed to use the proposed MAM-NSS for negotiation through mobile channels and agents. Customers and theaters are offering their own preferences such as price and vacant seats utilizing the negotiation mechanism based on MAM-NSS. The three groups will be compared with each other through Netlogo simulation experiments. In fact, group 1 is inappropriate for m-commerce situations because they are not reached by mobile devices. However, group 1 is included so that the other two groups can be compared.

Sellers

- Assumptions about theaters are as follows: they have 200 seats, cost $700 per show, and

Table 3. B-agent's utility calculation

```
to search-buyer
set temp (1)
set temp_id (1)
repeat customer_number [
ask customer with [reserve != 1 and id_number = temp_id] [
set temp_distance (p_distance )
set temp_price (p_price )
set temp_time (p_time )
set temp_boxoffice_ranking (p_boxoffice)
set temp_genre (p_genre )
set temp_customer_x (current_x) set temp_customer_y (current_y)
set utility (0)
set temp_selected_theoter (0)

repeat seller_number [
 ask seller in-radius-nowrap (remaining_time / time_per_patch)
  with [available_product_number > 0 and reg_number = temp1][
set actual_distance (abs (sqrt((temp_customer_x - location_x) ^ 2
+ (temp_customer_y - location_y) ^ 2 ) ))

Convert_factor_point

set temp_util (  temp_P1 * temp_point_F1
          + temp_P2 * temp_point_F2
          + temp_P3 * temp_point_F3
          + temp_P4 * temp_point_F4
          + temp_P5 * temp_point_F5
          )
if (temp_util > utility) [ set utility (temp_util)
          set temp_selected_seller (reg_number)  ]
          ]
          set temp1 (temp1 + 1)] set temp1 (1)
```

Table 4. B-agent's price update process

```
ask buyer with [deal !=1 ] [
 set goal_utility (Current_utility + (utility_adjustment / 100) * Current_utility )
 set temp (selected_buyer)
    ask seller with [reg_number = temp ][
     if (available_number > 0) [
     if (p_temp > 0 ) [
set temp_price_down_request int((goal_utility -
```

start to sell vacant seats an hour before the movie begins. List price for a ticket is $7, and movie genres a theater is showing have four types. All the theaters show the movie with box office ranking from 1 to 10. Every 20 minutes, theaters in group 2 are offering discriminated pricing strategies to buyers through mobile channels, depending on the vacancy rate: $6.5 if vacancy rate < 40%, $6.0 if 40% ≤ vacancy rate ≤ 50%, $5.0 if 50% ≤ vacancy rate ≤ 60%, $4.0 if 60% ≤ vacancy rate ≤ 70%, $3.0 if 70% ≤ vacancy rate ≤ 80%, and $2.0 if 80% ≤ vacancy rate. However, as noted previously, customers cannot negotiate with the theaters in group 2, indicating that they have no choice but to accept the price or not.

- Meanwhile, theaters in group 3 are offering different ranges of price using CBR inference where a case is composed of four input attributes (*current vacancy rate (%), remaining time before the show (minutes), box office ranking of the current show, approximate number of reachable customers*) and one output attribute (*ticket price*). Therefore, the price changes in accordance with the input attribute values theaters are currently facing. Theaters decide whether or not to accept the

newly adjusted price offered by the buyers, using FCM as shown in Figure 3. If the FCM result is less than 1, then the theater rejects the buyer's price. Otherwise, the theater accepts the buyer's price, and the buyer's seat number and show time are specified accordingly. When conducting FCM analysis, input constructs should be transformed into an appropriate value considering the input conditions. Table 5 shows input constructs, its conditions, and transformed values.

Customers

The customer's utility function includes the following five factors: (1) D (distance from customer's current location to theater; for this experiment, it is adjusted between -18 and 18 on the Netlogo platform); (2) R (box office ranking of the movie); (3) G (movie genre); (4) P (newly

Figure 3. Group 3 theaters'

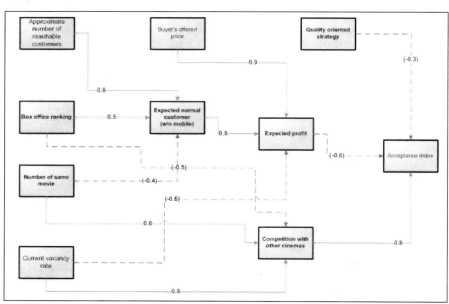

Table 5. Input constructs and conditions for theater's FCM

Input constructs	Condition	Transformed values
Approximate number of reachable customers	Many Normal Few	1 0 -1
Box office ranking	Rank 1, 2 Rank 3,4 Rank 5,6 Rank 7 ~ 10	1 5 −0.5 -1
Number of same movie	4 ~ 2 ~ 3 1 0	1 0.5 -0.5 -1
Current vacancy rate	40% ~ 30% ~ 40% 20% ~ 30% 10% ~ 20% ~ 10%	1 0.7 0.5 -0.5 -1
Quality oriented strategy	Yes No	1 -1
Buyer's offered price	$7 $5 ~ $7 $4 ~ $5 $3 ~ $4 $2 ~ $3 $1 ~ $2 ~ $1	1 0.7 0.5 0 -0.5 -0.7 -1

adjusted ticket price that customers want); and (5) T (timeliness showing whether it is the exact time that customer wants). Using the five factors like this, ith customer's utility function is denoted as follows:

$$U_i = W_{D_i} \cdot D_i + W_{R_i} \cdot R_i + W_{G_i} \cdot G_i + W_{P_i} \cdot P_i + W_{T_i} \cdot T_i$$

- Table 6 addresses the various conditions and their converted values for the five utility factors.

MAM-NSS Simulation

Basics

The MAM-NSS simulation prototype was performed on the Netlogo platform which is a programmable multi-agent modeling environment for simulating natural and social phenomena, and particularly well-suited for modeling com-

plex systems that develop over time. The target m-commerce problem described previously can be well represented by multi-agents composed of B-agents, S-agents, and interactions between them for the effective negotiation. Therefore, MAM-NSS is capable of handling the problem very well.

As shown in Figure 4, MAM-NSS has six types of user interface components as follows:

1. *Behavior space* shows the customer's movement and the location of theaters. The human shape indicates a customer and the house shape represents a theater. Gray color means group 1, green color group 2, and pink color group 3. All customers are designed to move one unit of position over to the random direction at a time. The customers go out of simulation after they buy tickets.

2. *Graph* monitors the change of values such as number of customers, vacant seats, number

Table 6. Customer's utility factors

Utility factor	Condition	Converted value
Distance from the theater (D)	In 20 minutes	50
	In 30 minutes	40
	In 40 minutes	30
	In 50 minutes	20
	More than 60 minutes	10
Box office ranking (R)	1,2	50
	3,4	40
	5,6	30
	7,8	20
	9,10	10
Movie genre (G)	Customer wanted	50
	Customer did not want	0
Ticket price (P)	For any new ticket price adjusted by customers	50 – (new ticket price / list price) * 50
Timeliness (T)	Exact time that customer wants	50
	Otherwise	0

Figure 4. MAM-NSS simulator

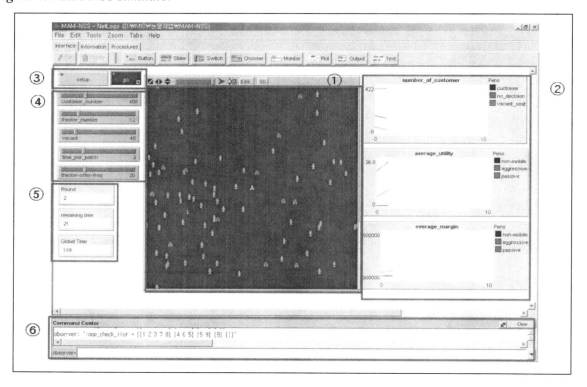

of customers who have not bought a ticket, customers' average utilities, and theaters' average margins.

3. *Control button* prepares and prompts simulation.

4. *Slider* controls the initial conditions of simulation such as number of customers, number of theaters, and maximum number of vacant seats for each theater. Each theater has a number of vacant seats falling between

0 and the "vacant" number that is set by this slide.

5. *Monitor* shows the number such as rounds of simulation, remaining/elapsed before the next show starts, and simulation time.

6. *Command center* shows temporary data generated from the agent activities.

Results and Implications

Twenty six rounds of simulation were done on MAM-NSS with the initial conditions as follows. Total rounds of simulation is 35, number of theaters 12, number of customers ranging between 100 and 600 (evenly assigned to three groups), group 2 theaters sending discriminated price every 20 minutes, and theaters starting to offer discounted price 60 minutes before the show. The simulation results with MAM-NSS are summarized in Table 7 numerically, and in Figure 5 graphically. Under a 95% confidence level, statistical results in Table 8 reveal that in terms of average utilizes and average profits, group 3 can yield the highest value compared with the other two groups. Its implication is as follows:

First, those users belonging to the passive mobile group can benefit from using the mobile devices. However, such mutual benefits increase much more when they use the negotiation support function provided by the proposed MAM-NSS.

Second, multi-agents are very convenient as well as effective for the m-commerce entities to handle them in their decision making process through the use of MAM-NSS. The reason is that agents are basically capable of autonomous operation once the entity's preference is predefined and stored into its memory. In the MAM-NSS environment, users do not have to bother themselves to interact with negotiation partners.

Third, both preference and conditions that users want their own agents to consider in the process of negotiations can be easily incorporated into agents. Since MAM-NSS is installed in the

central server of the telecommunication company, it is very easy for users to use it.

Fourth, since m-commerce users are limited by narrow screen and specified functions of their mobile devices, and agents are capable of replacing users in the real negotiation process in an almost automatic manner, the use of negotiation support mechanism like MAM-NSS would greatly contribute to enhancing users' utilities and profits as well.

CONCLUDING REMARKS

To resolve the negotiation process between buyers and sellers in the context of m-commerce, we proposed a multi-agent mobile negotiation support system called MAM-NSS, in which all the buyers and sellers engaged in a m-commerce situation are represented by multi-agents embedded with each entity's preference and corresponding conditions. Its potentials were proved by the simulation experiments using the theaters' vacant seats negotiation problems. Main contributions of the MAM-NSS are as follows.

First, CBR inference is incorporated to help S-agents decide an appropriate price for a vacant seat. Without using CBR, S-agents will have difficulty finding such appropriate price which is consistent with previous decision making results. Especially, such consistency in setting price for various situations is very important to customers who want be opportunistically exploited by sellers.

Second, FCM finds its great potential in the process of negotiation, due to its generalized inference capability in a presence of a number of inter-related factors. Without FCM, decision makers would feel very stressed to consider all the complicated causal relationships among the relevant factors and expect future inference results. In this chapter, FCM was used to help S-agents accept B-agent's price offer or not.

Third, multi-agent schemes were found very meaningful in being used in the process of m-

Table 7. Simulation result

Round	Average Utility			Average Profit		
	Non-mobile	Passive-mobile	Active-mobile	Non-mobile	Passive-mobile	Active-mobile
1	202	259	458	229	349	472
2	319	388	445	238	291	347
3	361	506	492	161	455	
4	299	365	482	134	295	506
5	311	441	410	66	442	468
6	289	406	587	189	208	496
7	285	431	559	423	253	353
8	309	432	497	178	439	377
9	259	428	477	166	390	355
10	402	439	568	197	220	477
11	326	355	436	332	204	480
12	332	405	498	215	266	410
13	327	485	506	190	356	502
14	252	398	412	152	451	403
15	331	463	533	220	386	473
16	445	393	448	243	400	371
17	305	438	508	101	321	470
18	265	354	534	274	318	362
19	245	370	480	99	395	484
20	387	464	565	52	475	498
21	381	449	488	204	429	401
22	339	444	551	176	347	493
23	245	411	512	143	328	501
24	371	444	562	178	330	471
25	334	431	597	159	344	481
26	225	413	547	103	236	502
27	338	416	492	192	283	498
28	225	392	457	124	288	451
29	319	434	487	169	397	449
30	213	322	401	255	305	457
31	321	491	492	190	409	401
32	257	381	474	220	348	287
33	350	469	509	157	411	483
34	247	426	492	147	431	388
35	349	350	406	264	337	441
Average	**215**	**290**	**347**	**131**	**243**	**308**

commerce negotiation. Such multi-agent approach has been proved useful and effective in a wide variety of problems in literature, but its potentials were not proved yet in m-commerce contexts. Therefore, this study adds meaning to literature in that sense.

This study has several positive implications for future m-commerce research. First, m-commerce is blooming as mobile devices are providing increased convenience in users' daily activities. However, there has been no important negotiation support system to leverage the potentials of m-

commerce. In that meaning, this study will shed a positive light on using the generalized multi-agent framework for designing a mobile negotiation support system. Second, we proposed practical algorithms to be used in upgrading agents' capability in problem solving. Such algorithms would be used in the other business settings with minor adjustments.

But, this study has limitations in the point that (1) all data used in experiment are not real world data; (2) we do not suggest detailed mechanisms for extracting the buyer's preference; and (3) there

Figure 5. Utilities and margins by MAM-NSS simulation

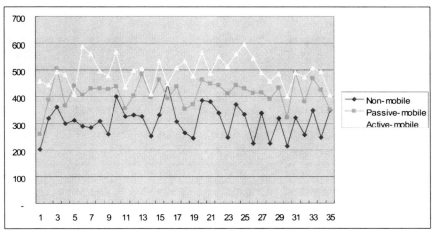

(a) Customers' average utilities

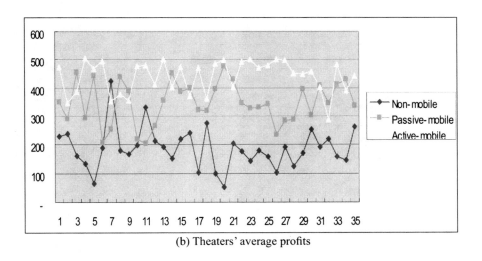

(b) Theaters' average profits

is no comparing our negotiation algorithm with other algorithms. To compare the performance of negotiation algorithms is not simple. Measures need to be developed for comparing negotiation performance before comparing existing algorithms. Additionally, performance measures need to include not only quantitative factors, but also qualitative factors. These three limitations are left as future research topics.

ACKNOWLEDGMENT

This work was supported by grant No. B1210-0502-0037 from the University Fundamental

Table 8. Results of statistical test

Utility

(I) type	(J) type	Mean Difference (I-J)	Std. Error	Sig.	95% Confidence Interval	
					Lower Bound	Upper Bound
non-mobile	passive	-106.366	12.659	0.000	-137.812	-74.921
	active	-188.336	12.659	0.000	-219.782	-156.891
Passive-mobile	non-mobile	106.3665	12.659	0.000	74.921	137.812
	active	-81.9698	12.659	0.000	-113.416	-50.524
Active-mobile	non-mobile	188.3363	12.659	0.000	156.891	219.782
	passive	81.96982	12.659	0.000	50.524	113.416

Profit

(I) type	(J) type	Mean Difference (I-J)	Std. Error	Sig.	95% Confidence Interval	
					Lower Bound	Upper Bound
non-mobile	passive	-159.989	16.403	0.000	-200.735	-119.242
	active	-253.081	16.403	0.000	-293.827	-212.334
Passive-mobile	non-mobile	159.989	16.403	0.000	119.242	200.735
	active	-93.092	16.403	0.000	-133.838	-52.346
Active-mobile	non-mobile	253.081	16.403	0.000	212.334	293.827
	passive	93.092	16.403	0.000	52.346	133.838

Research Program of the Ministry of Information & Communication in the Republic of Korea, 2005.

REFERENCES

Applegate, L. M., Holsapple, C. W., Kalakota, R., Radermacher, F. J., & Whinston, A. B. (1996). Electronic commerce: Building blocks of new business opportunity. *Journal of Organizational Computing & Electronic Commerce, 6*(1), 1-10.

Bailey, M. N., & Lawrence, R. L. (2001). Do we have a new economy? *American Economic Review, 91*(2), 308-312.

Barbash, A. (2001). Mobile computing for ambulatory health care: Points of convergence. *Journal of Ambulatory Care Management, 24*(4), 54-60.

Barnes, S. J. (2002). The mobile commerce value chain: Analysis and future developments. *International Journal of Information Management, 22*(2), 91-108.

Bird, S. D. (1993). Towards a taxonomy of multi-agent systems. *International Journal of Man-Machine Studies, 39*, 689-704.

Bird, S. D., & Kasper, G. M. (1995). Problem formalization techniques for collaborative systems. *IEEE Transactions on Systems, Man, and Cybernetics, 25*(2), 231-242.

Bohoris, C., Pavlou, G., & Cruickshank, H. (2000). Using mobile agents for network performance management. In *Proceedings of Network Operations and Management Symposium "The Networked Planet: Management Beyond 2000"* (pp. 637-652).

Bonarini, A., & Trianni, V. (2001). Learning fuzzy classifier systems for multi-agent coordination. *Information Sciences, 136*(1-4), 215-239.

Cabri, G., Leonardi, L., & Zambonelli, F. (2001). Mobile agent coordination for distributed network management. *Journal of Network & Systems Management, 9*(4), 435-456.

Cabri, G., Leonardi, L., & Zambonelli, F. (2002). Engineering mobile agent applications via context-dependent coordination. *IEEE Transactions on Software Engineering, 28*(11), 1039-1055.

Chaib-Draa, B. (1995). Industrial applications of distributed artificial intelligence. *Communications of the ACM, 38*(11), 49-53.

Chaib-Draa, B., & Mandiau, R. (1992). Distributed artificial intelligence: An annotated bibliography. *SIGART Bulletin, 3*(3), 20-37.

Cooper, S., & Taleb-Bendiab, A. (1998). CONCENSUS: Multi-party negotiation support for conflict resolution in concurrent engineering design. *Journal of Intelligent Manufacturing, 9*(2), 155-159.

Coursaris, C., & Hassanein, K. (2002). Understanding m-commerce. *Quarterly Journal of Electronic Commerce, 3*(3), 247-271.

Crowley, J. L., Coutaz, J., & Bérard, F. (2000). Perceptual user interfaces: Things that see. *Communications of the ACM, 43*(3), 54-64.

Edwards, W. K., Newman, M. W., Sedivy, J. Z., & Smith, T. F. (2004). Supporting serendipitous integration in mobile computing environments. *International Journal of Human-Computer Studies, 60*, 666-700.

Hogg, L. M. I., & Jennings, N. R. (2001). Socially intelligent reasoning for autonomous agents. *IEEE Transactions on Systems, Man, & Cybernetics Part A: Systems & Humans, 31*(5), 381-393.

Hu, J., & Weliman, M. P. (2001). Learning about other agents in a dynamic multiagent system. *Cognitive Systems Research, 2*(1), 67-79.

Jung, J. J., & Jo, G. S. (2000). Brokerage between buyer and seller agents using constraint satisfaction problem models. *Decision Support Systems, 28*(4), 293-304.

Kwon, O. B., & Lee, K. C. (2002). MACE: Multi-agents coordination engine to resolve conflicts among functional units in an enterprise. *Expert Systems with Applications, 23*(1), 9-21.

Lai, H., & Yang, T. C. (1988). A system architecture of intelligent-guided browsing on the Web. In *Proceedings of Thirty-First Hawaii International Conference on System Sciences* (pp. 423-432).

Lai, H., & Yang, T. C. (2000). A system architecture for intelligent browsing on the Web. *Decision Support Systems, 28*(3), 219-239.

Lee, W. J., & Lee, K. C. (1999). PROMISE: A distributed DSS approach to coordinating production and marketing decisions. *Computers and Operations Research, 26*(9), 901-920.

Lee, W. P., & Yang, T. H. (2003). Personalizing information appliances: A multi-agent framework for TV programme recommendations. *Expert Systems with Applications, 25*(3), 331-341.

Lottaz, C., Smith, I. F. C., Robert-Nicoud, Y., & Faltings, B. V. (2000). Constraint-based support for negotiation in collaborative design. *Artificial Intelligence in Engineering, 14*(3), 261-280.

Lucas, J. H. C. (2001). Information technology and physical space. *Communications of the ACM, 44*(11), 89-96.

Luo, X., Zhang, C., & Leung, H. F. (2001). Information sharing between heterogeneous uncertain reasoning models in a multi-agent environment: A case study. *International Journal of Approximate Reasoning, 27*(1), 27-59.

Mandry, T., Pernul, G., & Rohm, A. W. (2000-2001). Mobile agents in electronic markets: Opportunities, risks, agent protection. *International Journal of Electronic Commerce, 5*(2), 47-60.

McMullen, P. R. (2001). An ant colony optimization approach to addressing a JIT sequencing problem with multiple objectives. *Artificial Intelligence in Engineering, 15*(3), 309-317.

Miah, T., & Bashir, O. (1997). Mobile workers: Access to information on the move. *Computing and Control Engineering, 8*, 215-223.

Ngai, E. W. T., & Gunasekaran, A. (2005). A review for mobile commerce research and applications. *Decision Support Systems*. Retrieved August 20, 2007, from http://www.sciencedirect.com

Omicini, A., & Zambonelli, F. (1988). Co-ordination of mobile information agents in TuCSoN. *Internet Research: Electronic Networking Applications and Policy, 8*(5), 400-413.

Paiva, A., Machado, I., & Prada, R. (2001). The child behind the character. *IEEE Transactions on Systems, Man, and Cybernetics - Part A: Systems and Humans, 31*(5), 361-368.

Parusha, A., & Yuviler-Gavishb, N. (2004). Web navigation structures in cellular phones: The depth/beadth trade-off issue. *International Journal of Human-Computer Studies, 60*, 753-770.

Persson, P., Laaksolahti, J., & Lonnqvist, P. (2001). Understanding socially intelligent agents: A multilayered phenomenon. *IEEE Transactions on*

Systems, Man, and Cybernetics - Part A: Systems and Humans, 31*(5), 349-360.

Pham, T., Schneider, G., & Goose, S. (2000). A situated computing framework for mobile and ubiquitous multimedia access using small screen and composite devices. In *Proceedings of the Eighth ACM International Conference on Multimedia* (pp. 323-331).

Porn, L. M., & Patrick, K. (2002). Mobile computing acceptance grows as applications evolve. *Healthcare Financial Management, 56*(1), 66-70.

Rodgera, J. A., & Pendharkarb, P. C. (2004). A field study of the impact of gender and user's technical experience on the performance of voice-activated medical tracking application. *International Journal of Human-Computer Studies, 60*, 529-544.

Schaeffer, J., Plaat, A., & Junghanns, A. (2001). Unifying single-agent and two-player search. *Information Sciences, 135*(3-4), 151-175.

Schilit, W. N. (1995). *System architecture for context aware mobile computing.* Unpublished doctoral thesis, Columbia University.

Schilit, B. N., Adams, N. I., & Want, R. (1994). Context-aware computing applications. In *Proceedings of the First International Workshop on Mobile Computing Systems and Applications* (pp. 85-90).

Seager, A. (2003). M-commerce: An integrated approach. *Telecommunications International, 37*(2), 36.

Senn, J. A. (2000). The emergence of m-commerce. *Computer, 33*(12), 148-150.

Sikora, R., & Shaw, M. J. (1998). A multi-agent framework for the coordination and integration of information systems. *Management Science, 44*(11), 65-78.

Sillince, J. A. A. (1998). Extending electronic coordination mechanisms using argumentation:

The case of task allocation. *Knowledge-Based Systems, 10*(6), 325-336.

Sillince, J. A. A., & Saeddi, M. H. (1999). Computer-mediated communication: Problems and potentials of argumentation support systems. *Decision Support Systems, 26*(4), 287-306.

Slack, F., & Rowley, J. (2002). Online kiosks: The alternative to mobile technologies for mobile users. *Internet Research: Electronic Networking Applications and Policy, 12*(3), 248-257.

Strader, T. J., Lim, F. R., & Shaw, M. J. (1998). Information infrastructure for electronic virtual organization management. *Decision Support Systems, 23*(1), 75-94.

Tung, B., & Lee, J. (1999). An agent-based framework for building decision support systems. *Decision Support Systems, 25*(3), 225-237.

Turisco, F. (2000). Mobile computing is next technology frontier for healthcare providers. *Health Care Financial Management, 54*(11), 78-80.

Ulieru, M., Norrie, D., Kremer, R., & Shen, W. (2000). A multi-resolution collaborative architecture for Web-centric global manufacturing. *Information Sciences, 127*(1-2), 3-21.

Varshney, U. (1999). Networking support for mobile computing. *Communications of AIS, 1*(1), 1-30.

Wang, F. H., & Shao, H. M. (2004). Effective personalized recommendation based on time-framed navigation clustering and association mining. *Expert Systems with Applications, 27*(3), 365-377.

Wang, Y., Tan, K. L., & Ren, J. (2002). A study of building Internet marketplaces on the basis of mobile agents for parallel processing. *World Wide Web, 5*(1), 41-66.

Want, R., Hopper, A., Falcao, V., & Gibbons, J. (1992). The active badge location system. *ACM Transactions on Information Systems, 10*(1), 91-102.

Want, R., Schilit, B., Adams, N., Gold, R., Petersen, K., Ellis, J., et al. (1995). *The PARCTAB ubiquitous computing experiment* (Tech. Rep. No. CSL-95-1). Xerox Palo Alto Research Center.

Wooldridge, M. (1997). Agent based software engineering. *IEEE Proceedings of Software Engineering, 144*(1), 26-37.

Wooldridge, M., & Jennings, N. (1995). Intelligent agents: Theory and practice. *The Knowledge Engineering Review, 10*(2), 115-152.

Wu, D. J. (2001). Software agents for knowledge management: Coordination in multi-agent supply chains and auctions. *Expert Systems with Applications, 20*(1), 51-64.

Wu, G., Yuan, H., Tseng, S. S., & Fuyan, Z. (1999). A knowledge sharing and collaboration system model based on Internet. In *Proceedings of IEEE International Conference on Systems, Man, and Cybernetics* (pp.148-152).

ENDNOTE

[1]   http://ccl.northwestern.edu/netlogo/

This work was previously published in Agent Systems in Electronic Business, edited by E. Li & S. Yuan, pp. 218-238, copyright 2008 by Information Science Reference, formerly known as Idea Group Reference (an imprint of IGI Global).

Chapter 8.16
Intelligent User Interfaces for Mobile Computing

Michael J. O'Grady
University College Dublin, Ireland

Gregory M. P. O'Hare
University College Dublin, Ireland

ABSTRACT

In this chapter, the practical issue of realizing a necessary intelligence quotient for conceiving intelligent user interfaces (IUIs) on mobile devices is considered. Mobile computing scenarios differ radically from the normal fixed workstation environment that most people are familiar with. It is in this dynamicity and complexity that the key motivations for realizing IUIs on mobile devices may be found. Thus, the chapter initially motivates the need for the deployment of IUIs in mobile contexts by reflecting on the archetypical elements that comprise the average mobile user's situation or context. A number of broad issues pertaining to the deployment of AI techniques on mobile devices are considered before a practical realisation of this objective through the intelligent agent paradigm is presented. It is the authors hope that a mature understanding of the mobile computing usage scenario, augmented with key insights into the practical deployment of AI in mobile scenarios, will aid software engineers and HCI professionals alike in the successful utilisation of intelligent techniques for a new generation of mobile services.

INTRODUCTION

Mobile computing is one of the dominant computing usage paradigms at present and encapsulates a number of contrasting visions of how best the paradigm should be realized. Ubiquitous computing (Weiser, 1991) envisages a world populated with artefacts augmented with embedded computational technologies, all linked by transparent high-speed networks, and accessible in a seamless anytime, anywhere basis. Wearable computing (Rhodes, Minar, & Weaver, 1999) advocates a world where people carry the necessary computational artefacts about their actual person. Somewhere in between these two extremes lies the average mobile user, equipped with a PDA or mobile phone, and seeking to access both popular and highly specialized services as they go about their daily routine.

Though the growth of mobile computing usage has been phenomenal, and significant markets exists for providers of innovative services, there still exist a formidable number of obstacles that must be surpassed before software development processes for mobile services becomes as mature as current software development practices. It is often forgotten in the rush to exploit the potential of mobile computing that it is radically different from the classic desktop situation; and that this has serious implications for the design and engineering process. The dynamic nature of the mobile user, together with the variety and complexity of the environments in which they operate, provides unprecedented challenges for software engineers as the principles and methodologies that have been refined over years do not necessarily apply, at least in their totality, in mobile computing scenarios.

How to improve the mobile user's experience remains an open question. One approach concerns the notion of an application autonomously adapting to the prevailing situation or context in which end-users find themselves. A second approach concerns the incorporation of intelligent techniques into the application. In principle, such techniques could be used for diverse purposes, however, intelligent user interfaces (IUIs) represent one practical example where such techniques could be usefully deployed. Thus the objective of this chapter is to consider how the necessary intelligence can be effectively realized such that software designers can realistically consider the deployment of IUIs in mobile applications and services.

BACKGROUND

Research in IUIs has been ongoing for quite some time, and was originally motivated by problems that were arising in standard software application usage. Examples of these problems include information overflow, real-time cognitive overload, and difficulties in aiding end-users to interact with complex systems (Höök, 2000). These problems were perceived as being a by-product of direct-manipulation style interfaces. Thus, the concept of the application or user interface adapting to circumstances as they arose was conceived and the terms "adaptive" or "intelligent" user interfaces are frequently encountered in the literature. How to effectively realize interfaces endowed with such attributes is a crucial question and a number of proposals have been put forward. For example, the use of machine learning techniques has been proposed (Langley, 1997) as has the deployment of mobile agents (Mitrovic, Royo, & Mena, 2005).

In general, incorporating adaptability and intelligence enables applications to make considerable changes for personalization and customization preferences as defined by the user and the content being adapted (O'Connor & Wade, 2006). Though significant benefits can accrue from such an approach, there is a subtle issue that needs to be considered. If an application is functioning according to explicit user defined preferences it is functioning in a manner that is as the user expects and understands. However, should the system autonomously or intelligently adapt its services based on some pertinent aspect of the observed behavior of the user, or indeed, based on some other cue, responsibility for the system behavior moves, albeit partially, from the user to the system. Thus, the potential for a confused user or unsatisfactory user experience increases.

A natural question that must now be addressed concerns the identification of criteria that an application might use as a basis for adapting its behavior. Context-aware computing (Schmidt, Beigl & Gellersen, 1999) provides one intuitive answer to this question. The notion of context first arose in the early 1990s as a result of pioneering experiments in mobile computing systems. Though an agreed definition of context has still not materialized, it concerns the idea that an application should factor in various aspects of the prevailing situation when offering a service. What these aspects might be is highly dependent on the application domain in question. However, commonly held aspects of context include knowledge of the end-user, for example through a user model; knowledge of the surrounding environment, for example through a geographic information system (GIS) model; and knowledge of the mobile device, for example through a suitably populated database. Other useful aspects of an end-user's context include an understanding of the nature of the task or activity currently being engaged in, knowledge of their spatial context, that is, location and orientation, and knowledge of the prevailing social situation. Such models can provide a sound basis for intelligently adapting system behavior. However, capturing the necessary aspects of the end-user's context and interpreting it is frequently a computationally intensive process, and one that may prove intractable in a mobile computing context. Indeed, articulating the various aspects of context and the interrelationships between them may prove impossible, even during system design (Greenberg, 2001). Thus, a design decision may need to be made as to whether it is worth working with partial or incomplete models of a user's context. And the benefit of using intelligent techniques to remedy deficiencies in context models needs to be considered in terms of computational resources required, necessary response time and the ultimate benefit to the end-user and service provider.

SOME REFLECTIONS ON CONTEXT

Mobile computing spans many application domains and within these, it is characterized by a heterogeneous landscape of application domains, individual users, mobile devices, environments and tasks (Figure 1). Thus, developing applications and services that incorporate a contextual component is frequently an inherently complex and potentially time-consuming endeavor, and the benefits that accrue from such an approach should be capable of being measured in some tangible way. Mobile computing applications tend to be quite domain specific and are hence targeted at specific end-users with specialized tasks or objectives in mind. This is in contrast to the one-size-fits-all attitude to general purpose software development that one would encounter in the broad consumer PC arena. For the purposes of this discussion, it is useful to reflect further on the following aspects of the average mobile user's context: end-user profile, devices characteristics, prevailing environment and social situation.

Figure 1. An individual's current activity is a notoriously difficult aspect of an individual's context to ascertain with certainty

User Profile

Personalization and customization techniques assume the availability of sophisticated user models, and currently form an indispensable component of a number of well-known e-commerce related Web sites. Personalizing services for mobile computing users is an attractive proposition in many domains as it offers a promising mechanism for increasing the possibility that the end-users receive content that is of interest to them. Though this objective is likewise shared with owners of e-commerce sites, there are two issues that are of particular importance when considering the mobile user. Firstly, mobile interactions are almost invariably short and to the point. This obligates service providers to strive to filter, prioritize, and deliver content that is pertinent to the user's immediate requirements. The second issue concerns the question of costs. Mobile users have to pay for services, which may be charged on a KB basis, thus giving mobile users a strong incentive to curtail their use of the service in question if dissatisfied.

A wide number of features and characteristics can be incorporated into user models. As a basic requirement, some information concerning the user's personal profile, for example, age, sex, nationality and so on, is required. This basic model may then be augmented with additional sub-models that become increasingly domain-specific. In the case of standard e-commerce services, a record of the previous purchasing history may be maintained and used as a basis for recommending further products. Electronic tourist guides would require the availability of a cultural interest model, which as well as indicating cultural topics of interest to the user, would also provide some metric that facilitated the prioritization of their cultural interests.

Device Characteristics

Announcements of new devices are occurring with increasing frequency. Each generation successively increases the number of features offered, some of which would not be associated with traditional mobile computing devices, embedded cameras and MP3 players being cases in point. Though offering similar features and services, there are subtle differences between different generations, and indeed interim releases within the same generation, that make the life of a service provider and software professional exceedingly difficult and frequently irritating. From an interface perspective, screen size and support for various interaction modalities are two notable ways in which devices differ, and these have particular implications for the end-user experience. This problem is well documented in the literature and a number of proposals have been put forward to address this, the plasticity concept being a notable example (Thevenin & Coutaz, 1999). Other aspects in which mobile devices differ include processor, memory and operating system; all of which place practical limitations on what is computationally feasible on the device.

Prevailing Environment

The notion of environment is fundamental to mobile computing and it is the dynamic nature of prevailing environment in which the mobile user operates that most distinguishes mobile computing from the classic desktop usage paradigm. As an illustration, the case of the physical environment is now considered, though this in no way diminishes the importance of the prevailing electronic infrastructure. Scenarios in which mobile computing usage can occur are multiple and diverse. The same goes for physical environments. Such environments may be hostile in the sense that they do not lend themselves to easily accessing electronic infrastructure such as telecommunications networks. Other environments may experience extreme climatic conditions thus causing equipment to fail.

Developing a service that takes account of or adapts to the local physical environment is an attractive one. Two prerequisites are unavoidable, however. A model of the environment particular to the service domain in question must be available, and the location of the end-user must be attainable. In the former case, the service provider must construct this environmental model, possibly an expensive endeavor in terms of time and finance. In the latter case, an additional technological solution must be engaged—either one based on satellites, for example GPS, or one that harnesses the topology of the local wireless telecommunications networks. Each solution has its respective advantages and disadvantages, and a practical understanding of each is essential. However, by fulfilling these prerequisites, the service provider is in a position to offer services that take the end-users' physical position into account. Indeed, this vision, often termed location-aware computing (Patterson, Muntz & Pancake, 2003), has grasped the imagination of service providers and end-users alike. In essence, it is a practical example of just one single element of an end-user's context being interpreted and used as a basis for customizing services.

Social Situation

Developing a service that adapts to the end-user's prevailing social context is fraught with difficulty, yet is one that many people would find useful. What exactly defines social context is somewhat open to interpretation but in this case, it is considered to refer to the situation in which end-users find themselves relevant to other people. This is an inherently dynamic construct and capturing the prevailing social situation introduces an additional level of complexity not encountered in the contextual elements described previously.

In limited situations, it is possible to infer the prevailing social situation. Assuming that the end-user maintains an electronic calendar, the detection of certain keywords may hint at the prevailing social situation. Examples of such keywords might include lecture, meeting, theatre and so on. Thus, an application might reasonably deduce that the end-user would not welcome interruptions, and, for example, proceed to route incoming calls to voicemail and not alert the end-user to the availability of new email. Outside of this, one has to envisage the deployment of a suite of technologies to infer social context. For example, it may be that a device, equipped with a voice recognition system, may be trained to recognize the end-user's voice, and on recognizing it, infer that a social situation is prevailing. Even then, there may be a significant margin of error; and given the power limitations of the average mobile device, running a computationally intensive voice recognition system continuously may rapidly deplete battery resources.

ARTIFICAL INTELLIGENCE IN MOBILE COMPUTING

Artificial intelligence (AI) has been the subject of much research, and even more speculation, for almost half a century by now. Though failing to radically alter the world in the way that was envisaged, nevertheless, AI techniques have been successfully harnessed in a quite a number of select domains and their incorporation into everyday applications and services continues unobtrusively yet unrelentingly. Not surprising, there is significant interest amongst the academic community in the potential of AI for addressing the myriad of complexity that is encountered in the mobile computing area. From the previous discussion, some sources of this complexity can be easily identified. Resource management, ambiguity resolution, for example, in determining contextual state and resolving user intention in multimodal interfaces, and adaptation, are just some examples. Historically, research in AI has focuses on various issues related to these very topics. Thus, a significant body of research already exists in some of the very areas that can be harnessed to maximum benefit in mobile computing scenarios. A detailed description of these issues may be found elsewhere (Krüger & Malaka, 2004).

One pioneering effort at harnessing the use of intelligent techniques on devices of limited computational capacity is the Ambient intelligence (AmI) (Vasilakos & Pedrycz, 2006) initiative. AmI builds on the broad mobile computing vision as propounded by the ubiquitous computing vision. It is of particular relevance to this discussion as it is essentially concerned with usability and HCI issues. It was conceived in response to the realization that as mobile and embedded artefacts proliferate, demands for user attention would likewise increase, resulting in environments becoming inhabitable, or more likely, people just disabling the technologies in question. In the AmI concept, IUIs are envisaged as playing a key role in mediating between the embedded artefacts and surrounding users. However, AmI does not formally ratify the use of any particular AI technique. Choice of technique is at the discretion of the software designer whose selection will be influenced by a number of factors including the broad nature of the domain in question, the requirements of the user, the capability of the available technology and the implications for system performance and usability.

Having motivated the need for AI technologies in mobile contexts, practical issues pertaining to their deployment can now be examined.

STRATEGIES FOR HARNESSING AI TECHNIQUES IN MOBILE APPLICATIONS

It must be reiterated that AI techniques are computationally intensive. Thus, the practical issue of actually incorporating such techniques into mobile applications needs to be considered carefully. In particular, the implications for

performance must be determined as this could easily have an adverse effect on usability. There are three broad approaches that can be adopted when incorporating AI into a mobile application and each is now considered.

Network-Based Approach

Practically all mobile devices are equipped with wireless modems allowing access to data services. In such circumstances, designers can adopt a kind of client/server architecture where the interface logic is hosted on the mobile devices and the core application logic deployed on a fixed server node. The advantage of such an approach is that the designer can adopt the most appropriate AI technologies for the application in question. However, the effect of network latency must be considered. If network latency is significant, the usability of the application will be adversely affected. Likewise, data rates supported by the network in question must be considered. Indeed, this situation is aggravated when it is considered that a number of networks implement a channel sharing system where the effective data rate at a given time is directly proportional to the number of subscribers currently sharing the channel. It is therefore impossible to guarantee an adequate quality of service (QoS) making the prediction of system performance difficult. Often, the worst case scenario must be assumed. This has particular implications where the AI application on the fixed server node needs either a significant amount of raw data or a stream of data to process.

One key disadvantage of placing the AI component on a fixed server node concerns the issue of cost. There is a surcharge for each KB of data transferred across the wireless network, and though additional revenue is always welcome, the very fact that the subscriber is paying will affect their perception of application in question and make them more demanding in their expectations.

A network–based AI approach is by far the most common and has been used in quite a number of applications. For example, neural networks have been used for profiling mobile users in conversational interfaces (Toney, Feinberg & Richmond, 2004). InCa (Kadous & Sammut, 2004) is a conversational agent that runs on a PDA but uses a fixed network infrastructure for speech recognition.

Distributed Approach

In this approach, the AI component of the service may be split between the mobile device and the fixed network node. The more computationally expensive elements of the service are hosted on the fixed network node while the less expensive elements may be deployed on the device. Performance is a key limitation of this approach as the computational capacity of the devices in question as well as the data-rates supported by the wireless network can all contribute to unsatisfactory performance. From a software engineering perspective, this approach is quite attractive as distributed AI (DAI) is a mature research discipline in its own right; and a practical implementation of DAI is the multi-agent system (MAS) paradigm.

One example of an application that uses a distributed approach is Gulliver's Genie (O'Grady & O'Hare, 2004). This is a tourist information guide for mobile tourists, realized as a suite of intelligent agents encompassing PDAs, wireless networks and fixed network servers. Agents on the mobile device are responsible for manipulating the user interface while a suite of agents on the fixed server collaborate to identify and recommend multimedia content that is appropriate to the tourist's context.

Embedded Approach

As devices grow in processing power, the possibility of embedding an AI based application on the actual physical device becomes ever more feasible. The key limitation is performance, which is a direct result of the available hardware. This effectively compromises the type of AI approach that can be usefully adopted. Overtime, it can be assumed that the capability and variety of AI techniques that can be deployed will increase as developments in mobile hardware continue and the demand for ever-more sophisticated applications increases. From an end-user viewpoint, a key advantage of the embedded approach concerns cost as the number of connections required is minimized.

One example of an application that uses the embedded approach is iDorm (Hagras et al., 2004), a prototype AmI environment. This environment actually demonstrates a variety of embedded agents including fixed motes, mobile robots and PDAs. These agents collaborate to learn and predict user behavior using fuzzy logic principles and, based on these models, the environment is adapted to the inhabitant's needs.

Deployment Considerations

Technically, all three approaches are viable, but the circumstances in which they may be adopted vary. For specialized applications, the networked AI approach is preferable as it offers greater flexibility and maximum performance, albeit at a cost. For general applications, the embedded approach is preferable, primarily due to cost limitations, but the techniques that can be adopted are limited. The distributed approach is essentially a compromise, incorporating the respective advantages and disadvantages of both the networked and embedded approach to various degrees. Ultimately, the nature of the application domain and the target user base will be the major determinants in what approach is adopted. However, in the longer term, it is the embedded approach that has the most potential as it eliminates the negative cumulative effect of network vagrancies, as well as hidden costs.

Thus, for the remainder of this chapter, we focus on the embedded approach and consider how this might be achieved.

So what AI techniques can be adopted, given the inherent limitations of mobile devices? Various techniques have been demonstrated in laboratory conditions but one paradigm has been demonstrated to be computationally tractable on mobile devices: intelligent agents. As well as forming the basis of mobile intelligent information's systems, a number of toolkits have been made available under open source licensing conditions thus allowing software engineers access to mature platforms at minimum cost. Before briefly considering some of these options, it is useful to reflect on the intelligent agent paradigm.

THE INTELLIGENT AGENT PARADIGM

Research in intelligent agents has been ongoing since the 1970s. Unfortunately, the term agent has been interpreted in a number of ways thereby leading to some confusion over what the term actually means. More precisely, the characteristics that an arbitrary piece of software should possess before applying the term agent to it are debatable. In essence, an agent may be regarded as a computational entity that can act on behalf of an end-user, another agent or some other software artefact. Agents possess a number of attributes that distinguish them from other software entities. These include amongst others:

- **Autonomy:** The ability to act independently and without direct intervention from another entity, either human or software-related
- **Proactivity:** The ability to opportunistically initiate activities that further the objectives of the agent
- **Reactivity:** The ability to respond to events perceived in the agent's environment;

- **Mobility:** The ability to migrate to different nodes of a network as the need to fulfill its objectives dictates; and
- **Social ability:** The ability to communicate with other agents using a shared language and ontology leading to shared or collaborative efforts to achieve individual and shared objectives.

To what extent an agent possesses or utilizes each of those attributes is at the discretion of the designer. For clarity purposes, it is useful to consider agents as existing on a scale. At the lower end are so-called reactive agents. Such agents act in a stimulus-response manner, and a typical usage scenario might involve the agent monitoring for user interaction and reacting to it. Such agents are generally classified as weak agents (Wooldridge & Jennings, 1995). At the other end of the scale are so-called strong agents. Such agents maintain a sophisticated model of their environment, a list of goals or objectives, and plans detailing how to achieve these objectives. Such agents support rational reasoning in a collaborative context and are usually realized as multi-agent systems (MAS). This strong notion of agenthood is synonymous with the view maintained by the AI community.

One popular interpretation of the strong notion of agency is that of the belief-desire-intention (BDI) paradigm (Rao & Geogeff, 1995). This is an intuitive and computationally tractable interpretation of the strong agency stance. To summarize: beliefs represent what the agent knows about its environment. Note that the term environment can have diverse meanings here and may not just relate to the physical environment. Desires represent the objectives of the agent, and implicitly the raison d'être for the application. However, at any moment in time, an agent may be only capable of fulfilling some of its desires, if even that. These desires are then formulated as intentions and the agent proceeds to fulfill these intentions. The cycle of

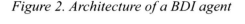

Figure 2. Architecture of a BDI agent

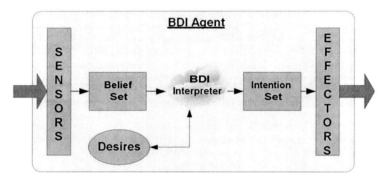

updating its model of the environment, identifying desires that can be fulfilled, and realizing these intentions is then repeated for the duration of the agent's lifecycle (Figure 2).

When should agents be considered for realizing a software solution? Opinion on this is varied. If the solution can be modeled as a series of dynamic interacting components, then agents may well offer a viable solution. However, many see agents as being particular useful in situations that are inherently complex and dynamic as their native capabilities equip them for handling the myriad of situations that may arise. Naturally, there are many situations that fulfill the criteria but, for the purposes of this discussion, it can be easily seen that the mobile computing domain offers significant opportunities for harvesting the characteristics of intelligent agents.

Intelligent Agents for Mobile Computing

As the capability of mobile devices grew, researchers in the intelligent agent community became aware of the feasibility of deploying agents on such devices, and perceived mobile computing as a potentially fertile area for the intelligent agent paradigm. A common approach was to extend the functionality of existing and well-documented MAS environments such that they could operate on mobile devices. It was not necessary to port the entire environment on to the device; it was just necessary to develop an optimized runtime engine for interpreting the agent logic. In this way, the MAS ethos is persevered and such an approach subscribes to the distributed AI approach alluded to previously. A further benefit was that existing agent-oriented software engineering (AOSE) methodologies could be used. In the case of testing, various toolkits have been released by the telecommunications manufacturers that facilitate the testing of mobile applications. A prudent approach is of course to test the application at various stages during its development on actual physical devices, as this will give a more accurate indication of performance, the look and feel (L&F) of the application and so on. For a perspective on deploying agents on mobile devices, the interested reader should consult Carabelea and Boissier (2003).

While a number of environments may be found in the literature for running agents on mobile devices, the following toolkits form a useful basis for initial consideration:

1. **LEAP (Lightweight Extensible Agent Platform)** (Bergenti, Poggi, Burg, et al., 2001) is an extension of the well-documented JADE platform (Bellifemine, Caire, Poggi et al., 2003). It is FIPA (http://www.fipa.org/) compliant and capable of operating on both mobile and fixed devices.

2. **MicroFIPA-OS** (Laukkanen, Tarkoma & Leinonen, 2001) is a minimized footprint of the FIPA-OS agent toolkit (Tarkoma & Laukkanen, 2002). The original FIPA-OS was designed for PCs and incorporated a number of features that did not scale down to mobile devices. Hence, MicroFIPA-OS minimizes object creation, reduces computational overhead and optimizes the use of threads and other resource pools.

3. **AFME (Agent Factory Micro Edition)** (Muldoon, O'Hare, Collier & O'Grady, 2006) is derived from Agent Factory (Collier, O'Hare, Lowen, & Rooney, 2003), a framework for the fabrication and deployment of agents that broadly conform to the BDI agent model. It has been specifically designed for operation on cellular phones and such categories of devices.

4. **JACK** is, in contrast to the three previous frameworks, a commercial product from the Agent Oriented Software Group (http://www.agent-software.com). It comes with a sophisticated development environment, and like AFME, conforms to the BDI agent model.

A detailed description of the each of these systems is beyond the scope of this discussion. However, the interested reader is referred to (O'Hare, O'Grady, Muldoon & Bradley, 2006) for a more advanced treatment of the toolkits and other associated issues.

FUTURE TRENDS

As mobile devices proliferate, and each generation surpasses its predecessor in terms of raw computational capacity and supported features, the potential for incorporating additional AI techniques will increase. In a similar vein, new niche and specialized markets for mobile services will appear. If a more holistic approach is taken towards mobile computing, it can be seen that developments in sensor technologies, fundamental to the ubiquitous and pervasive vision, will follow a similar trajectory. Indeed, the possibility of deploying intelligent agents on sensors is being actively investigated in widespread expectation that the next generation of sensors will incorporate processors of a similar capability to the current range of PDAs. Such a development is essential if the AmI vision to reach fruition.

As the possibility of incorporation of ever more sophisticated AI techniques increases, the potential for extending and refining the adaptability and IUI constructs for the support of mobile users increase. Indeed, adaptability may reach its fulfillment through the incorporation of autonomic computing precepts (Kephart & Chess, 2003). Self-configuring, self-healing, self-optimizing and self-protecting are the key attributes of an autonomic system, and it can be seen that incorporation of AI techniques may make the realization of these characteristics more attainable.

Finally, the practical issues of engineering mobile AI solutions must be considered. Mobile computing poses significant challenges to the traditional software engineering process, and the broad issue of how best to design for mobile services still needs to be resolved. The situation is exacerbated when AI technologies are included. However, it may be envisaged that as experience and knowledge of the mobile computing domain deepens and matures, new methodologies and best practice principles will emerge.

CONCLUSION

Mobile computing scenarios are diverse and numerous, and give rise to numerous challenges that must be overcome if the end-user experience is to be a satisfactory one. IUIs offers one viable approach that software designers can adopt in their efforts to make their systems more usable in what is frequently a hostile environment. However, the pragmatic issue of realizing mobile applications that incorporate intelligent techniques is of critical importance and gives rise to significant technical and design obstacles.

In this chapter, the broad issue of realizing an intelligent solution was examined in some detail. At present, the intelligent agent paradigm offers an increasingly viable proposition for those designers who wish to include intelligent techniques in their designs. To illustrate the issues involved, the intelligent agent paradigm was discussed in some detail.

As mobile developments continue unabated, the demand for increasingly sophisticated applications and services will likewise increase. Meeting this demand will pose new challenges for software and HCI professionals. A prudent and selective adoption of intelligent techniques may well offer a practical approach to the effective realization of a new generation of mobile services.

ACKNOWLEDGMENT

The authors gratefully acknowledge the support of the Science Foundation Ireland (SFI) under Grant No. 03/IN.3/1361.

REFERENCES

Bellifemine, F., Caire, G., Poggi, A., & Rimassa, G. (2003). *JADE — A white paper.* Retrieved January 2007 from http://jade.tilab.com/papers/2003/WhitePaperJADEEXP.pdf

Bergenti, F., Poggi, A., Burg, B., & Caire, G. (2001). Deploying FIPA-compliant systems on handheld devices. *IEEE Internet Computing, 5*(4), 20-25.

Collier, R.W., O'Hare, G.M.P., Lowen, T., & Rooney, C.F.B., (2003). Beyond prototyping in the factory of agents. In J. G. Carbonell & J. Siekmann (Eds.), *Lecture Notes In Computer Science*, 2691, 383-393, Berlin: Springer.

Carabelea, C., & Boissier O. (2003). Multi-agent platforms on smart devices: Dream or reality. Retrieved January, 2007, from http://www.emse.fr/~carabele/papers/carabelea.soc03.pdf.

Greenberg, S. (2001). Context as a dynamic construct. *Human-Computer Interaction*, 16, 257-268.

Hagras, H., Callaghan, V., Colley, M., Clarke, G., Pounds-Cornish, A., & Duman, H. (2004). Creating an ambient-intelligence environment using embedded agents. *IEEE Intelligent Systems, 19*(6) 12-20.

Höök, K. (2000). Steps to take before intelligent user interfaces become real. *Interacting with Computers, 12*, 409-426.

Kadous, M.W., & Sammut, C. (2004). InCA: A mobile conversational agent. *Lecture Notes in Computer Science*, 3153, 644-653. Berlin: Springer.

Kephart, J.O., & Chess, D.M. (2003). The vision of autonomic computing. *IEEE Computer, 36*(1), 41-50.

Kruger, A., & Malaka, R. (2004). Artificial intelligence goes mobile. *Applied Artificial Intelligence, 18*, 469-476.

Langley, P. (1997). Machine learning for adaptive user interfaces. *Lecture Notes in Computer Science*, 1303, 53-62. Berlin:Springer.

Laukkanen, M., Tarkoma, S., & Leinonen, J. (2001). FIPA-OS agent platform for small-footprint devices. *Lecture Notes in Computer Science*, 2333, 447-460. Berlin:Springer.

Mitrovic, N., Royo, J. A., & Mena, E. (2005). Adaptive user interfaces based on mobile agents: Monitoring the behavior of users in a wireless environment. *Proceedings of the Symposium on Ubiquitous Computation and Ambient Intelligence* (pp. 371-378), Madrid: Thomson-Paraninfo.

Muldoon, C., O'Hare, G.M.P., Collier, R.W., & O'Grady, M.J. (2006). Agent factory micro edition: A framework for ambient applications, *Lecture Notes in Computer Science*, 3993, 727-734. Berlin:Springer.

O'Connor, A., & Wade, V., (2006). Informing context to support adaptive services, *Lecture Notes in Computer Science*, 4018, 366-369. Berlin: Springer.

O'Grady, M.J., & O'Hare, G.M.P. (2004). Just-in-time multimedia distribution in a mobile computing environment. *IEEE Multimedia*, 11(4), 62-74.

O'Hare, G.M.P., O'Grady, M.J., Muldoon, C., & Bradley, J.F. (2006). Embedded agents: A paradigm for mobile services. *International Journal of Web and Grid Services, 2*(4), 355-378.

Patterson, C.A., Muntz, R.R., & Pancake, C.M. (2003). Challenges in location-aware computing. *IEEE Pervasive Computing, 2*(2), 80-89.

Rao, A.S., & Georgeff, M.P. (1995). BDI agents: from theory to practice. In V. Lesser and L. Gasser (Eds.), *Proceedings of the First International Conference on Multiagent Systems* (pp. 312-319). California: MIT Press.

Rhodes, B.J., Minar, N. & Weaver, J. (1999). Wearable computing meets ubiquitous computing: Reaping the best of both worlds. *Proceedings of the Third International Symposium on Wearable Computers* (pp. 141-149). California: IEEE Computer Society

Schmidt, A., Beigl, M., & Gellersen, H-W, (1999). There is more to context than location. *Computers and Graphics, 23*(6), 893-901.

Tarkoma, S., & Laukkanen, M. (2002). Supporting software agents on small devices. In *Proceedings of the First International Joint Conference on Autonomous Agents and Multi-Agent Systems (AAMAS)* (pp. 565-566). NewYork: ACM Press.

Thevenin, D., & Coutaz, J. (1999). Plasticity of user interfaces: Framework and research agenda. In (M. A. Sasse & C. Johnson (Eds.), *Proceedings of IFIP TC 13 International Conference on Human-Computer Interaction (INTERACT'99)*, (pp. 110-117). Amsterdam: IOS Press.

Toney, D., Feinberg D., & Richmond, K. (2004). Acoustic features for profiling mobile users of conversational interfaces, *Lecture Notes in Computer Science*, 3160 (pp. 394-398). Berlin: Springer.

Vasilakos, A., & Pedrycz, W. (2006). *Ambient intelligence, wireless networking, ubiquitous Computing.* Norwood:Artec House.

Weiser, M. (1991). The computer for the twenty-first century. *Scientific American, 265*(3), 94-100.

Wooldridge, M., & Jennings, N.R. (1995). Intelligent agents: Theory and practice. *Knowledge Engineering Review, 10*(2), 115-152.

KEY TERMS

Ambient Intelligence: (AmI) was conceived by the Information Society Technologies Advisory Group (ISTAG) as a means of facilitating intuitive interaction between people and ubiquitous computing environments. A key enabler of the AmI concept is the intelligent user interface.

BDI Architecture: The Belief-Desire-Intention (BDI) architecture is an example of a sophisticated reasoning model based on mental constructs that can be used by intelligent agents. It is allows the modeling of agents behaviors in an intuitive manner that complements the human intellect.

Context: Context-aware computing considers various pertinent aspects of the end-user's situation when delivering a service. These aspects, or contextual elements, are determined during invocation of the service and may include user profile, for example language, age, and so on. Spatial contextual elements, namely location and orientation, may also be considered.

Intelligent Agent: Agents are software entities that encapsulate a number of attributes including autonomy, mobility, sociability, reactivity and proactivity amongst others. Agents may be reactive, deliberative or hybrid. Implicit in the agent construct is the requirement for a sophisticated reasoning ability, a classic example being agents modeled on the BDI architecture.

Intelligent User Interface: Harnesses various techniques from artificial intelligence to adapt and configure the interface to an application such that the end-user's experience is more satisfactory.

Mobile Computing: A computer usage paradigm where end-users access applications and services in diverse scenarios, while mobile. Mobile telephony is a popular realization of this paradigm, but wearable computing and telematic applications could also be considered as realistic interpretations of mobile computing.

Multi-Agent System: A suite of intelligent agents, seeking to solve some problem beyond their individual capabilities, come together to form a multi-agent system (MAS). These agents collaborate to fulfill individual and shared objectives.

Ubiquitous Computing: Conceived in the early 1990s, ubiquitous computing envisages a world of embedded devices, where computing artefacts are embedded in the physical environment and accessed in a transparent manner.

Chapter 8.17
mCity:
User Focused Development of Mobile Services Within the City of Stockholm

Anette Hallin
Royal Institute of Technology (KTH), Sweden

Kristina Lundevall
The City of Stockholm, Sweden

ABSTRACT

This chapter presents the mCity Project, a project owned by the City of Stockholm, aiming at creating user-friendly mobile services in collaboration with businesses. Starting from the end-users' perspective, mCity focuses on how to satisfy existing needs in the community, initiating test pilots within a wide range of areas, from health care and education, to tourism and business. The lesson learned is that user focus creates involvement among end users and leads to the development of sustainable systems that are actually used after they have been implemented. This is naturally vital input not only to municipalities and governments but also for the IT/telecom industry at large. Using the knowledge from mCity, the authors suggest a new, broader definition of "m-government" which focuses on mobile people rather than mobile technology.

INTRODUCTION

All over the world, ICT technologies are used to an increasing extent within the public sector. For cities, ICTs not only provide the possibilities of improving the efficiency among its employees and its service towards tourists, citizens, and companies; it is also an important factor in the development of the city and its region, as ICTs today generally are considered to constitute the driving force of economy and social change (Castells, 1997). It is also argued that ICTs can improve efficiency, enhance transparency, control, networking and innovation (Winden, 2003). Thus, several cities are involved in projects concerning the development, testing, and implementation of ICTs. A few examples include Crossroads Copenhagen in Denmark, Testbed Botnia, and TelecomCity from the cities of Luleå and Karlskrona in

Sweden. Within all these projects, triple-helix like organizations are used involving the local municipality or national government, the local university, and the locally-based companies (Jazic & Lundevall, 2003)

Also within the City of Stockholm, there is such a project—the mCity Project. This was launched by the City of Stockholm in January of 2002, with the aim of organizing "the mobile city" through the implementation of relevant ICTs. The mCity Project consists of several small pilot projects, focusing on identifying needs in the community and creating solutions to these. In this chapter, we intend to describe this project, its organization, work processes, and the results. We also discuss the experiences made and how the project can serve as an inspiration towards a broader understanding of "m-government".

BRIEFLY ABOUT THE CITY OF STOCKHOLM

The City of Stockholm is Sweden's largest municipality with about 760,000 inhabitants,[1] but is, compared to other capitals in the world, a small city. Due to the Swedish form of government, Stockholm—as well as all other Swedish cities—has large responsibilities, including child care, primary and secondary education, care of the elderly, fire-fighting, city planning, and maintenance, and so forth. All these responsibilities are financed through income taxes, at levels set by the cities themselves, with no national interference. The operational responsibility lies, in the case of Stockholm, on 18 district councils and on 16 special administrations, depending on the issue. Through 15 different fully-owned or majority-interest, joint-stock and associated companies (hereafter called "municipal companies"), the City of Stockholm also provides water, optical fibre-infrastructure, housing (the City of Stockholm has the largest housing corporation in the country), shipping-facilities (the ports in the

Stockholm area), parking, tourist information, the city theatre, the Globe Arena (for sports, concerts and other events) etc. In total, the city has an organization comprising 50,000 employees, and a yearly turn over of 31.5 billion SEK,[2] which is equivalent to about 5 million USD. For the City of Stockholm, it is only natural to engage in ICT projects of different kinds, as this could be expected to have both financial and pedagogical benefits within this large organization—just as it had for other public organizations in Sweden (Grenblad, 2003).

In fact, ICT projects are encouraged by the City of Stockholm through the Stockholm "E-Strategy". This is a visionary and strategic document, issued by the City Council[3] in the beginning of 2001 which—among other things—firmly states the role of the citizen as the central figure for all activities in the city organization; the development of mobile technologies to enhance flexibility, as well as the importance of the city acting to aid Swedish ICT industry (*The City of Stockholm's E-Strategy, 19th of February 2001*). It is the City Executive Board[4] which is responsible for implementing the resolution of the City Council, but the "E-Strategy" document also points to the responsibility of the management of the different district councils, special administrations, and municipal companies for the strategic development of ICTs within each organization. The document also describes the function of "the IT Council", which is to ensure that the e-strategy is implemented in a good way within the municipal organization, that is, not as a separate strategy, but in close contact with the activities for which the organizations are responsible.

BACKGROUND, ORGANIZATION, AND GOALS

The idea of mCity was born in 2000 when the former EU Commissioner Martin Bangeman suggested a cooperation between European cities in order to stimulate the use of the upcoming 3G network and its services. In January 2001, a workshop was held with representatives from a number of major cities, telecom operators, vendors, and investors. A project proposal was submitted by Bangeman, suggesting that a few other European cities—Stockholm, Bremen, and Berlin among others—should start a holding corporation in order to develop and sell 3G services. However, this collaboration project did not become a reality. Instead, the City of Stockholm decided to proceed with a smaller scale project—mCity.

The following goals have been specified for the mCity Project in Stockholm:

- **To improve the working environment for the employees of the City of Stockholm.** By putting people in the center and letting them lead the development of mobile services, they will help develop services that will ease their own work tasks and their everyday lives.
- **To increase the quality of services for citizens.** The mCity Project strives to improve the service of the city to its citizens and visitors by improving the work environment for employees and by introducing citizen-specific solutions.
- **To stimulate the regional business (IT/Telecom).** By developing new solutions in collaboration with industry, new opportunities for the ICT industry within Stockholm, and throughout Sweden are developed, thereby creating a strong home market for companies in Stockholm.
- **To reinforce Stockholm's profile as an IT capital.** By developing new and useful mobile services, Stockholm's reputation as a leading IT capital will be further reinforced.
- **To spread the good example.** By working with small-scale test environments and small-scale tests, the results can be duplicated if successful. By involving the end users closely in the project, sustainability is ensured. An effect of more deeply involved users is that the users themselves become spokespersons for the services and actually help spread the word.

During its first year, the project was located in one of Stockholm's district councils, which meant close contact with the end users. The project manager felt, however, that in order to keep up with the ICT development in other parts of the city, the project would be better off if it could be located more centrally in the organization. Since then, the project has been moved closer to the central administrative organization in the city.

The project organization of mCity is described in Figure 1. The Steering Committee, organized with representatives from different parts of the city, for example the IT Department and the City of Stockholm Executive Office,[5] make strategic decisions about budget issues, what projects to initiate, and so forth. Different heads have chaired the Steering Committee during the course of the project. There are also members from the Stockholm IT Council in the Steering Committee, to ensure that the mCity Project follows Stockholm's E-Strategy. The different pilot projects are initiated together with district councils, special administrations, or municipal companies which undertake the responsibility of local project management in each case. The mCity Project Manager is in charge of initiating and setting up the local projects in collaboration with the local project management and then keeps track of the day-to-day development of the projects. He/She is also responsible for collecting and spreading information about the projects, and for preparing the meetings with the Steering Committee as well as implementing the decisions of the Steering Committee. In their work, he/she can also use the Think Tank, to which a number of companies within the mobile technology industry belong, to ask for advice concerning technology or market requirements/development. Finally, a researcher

Figure 1. Organization of the mCity Project

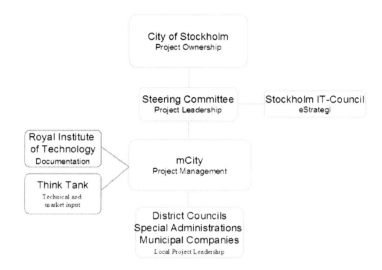

from KTH, the Royal Institute of Technology, has been responsible for documenting the project.

WORKING PROCESS

Within the mCity Project, services for both private and public sectors are tested and thereafter developed in a larger scale if proven relevant. The services are operated and tested in "small islands" because it makes it easier to get close to the users and to change the tested services if something needs to be improved. Using this model, mCity has been able to connect groups with specific needs with companies developing mobile services that can satisfy these needs.

End-user needs, that is, the needs of citizens, visitors and employees within the City of Stockholm, form the starting point of every initiative within mCity—see Figure 2. One way of creating situations where users can make their voices heard

is by initiating hearings, focus groups, interviews, and so forth. In some cases, the mCity Project Manager has been involved in this first part of the process; in other cases, the local management of the different district councils, special administrations, or municipal companies take the initiative of formulating an application, specifying the need. The exact details of the working process have shifted, depending on the organizational setting of the project.

In the next step, the mCity Project management uses their Competence Network to form a group with technical expertise to which the user's need is presented. The group ponders about the possible technical solutions suitable to solve the problems and in this process, the end-users' knowledge of ICTs, their workload, and the financial/technical situation of the user environment are also taken into account. Depending on the situation, mCity can also contribute financially to the pilot project.

Figure 2. Working process within mCity

Through mCity, the hope is to accomplish a better every day life for end users. Therefore, the benefits of the services developed in relation to the concrete needs of users, are of high interest and hopefully, it is also possible to measure the added value. End solutions should be easy to use—it should be almost intuitive to understand how to use the provided service. This is one reason for why simple technology is mostly used in mCity Projects—technology is seldom the problem, the focus is rather on what to introduce and how to introduce it. To summarize, the working process can be described in three keywords:

- user-oriented
- benefit-driven
- simple

It should be pointed out that mCity primarily does small-scale pilot projects; when these have been launched, it is the responsibility of the dis-trict councils, the special administrations, or the municipal companies involved to decide whether to keep running the project, to enlarge it, and also to take the full operational and financial responsibility for the future project.

PILOT PROJECTS

mCity has started and financed several pilot projects since its launch in 2002. Different user groups are in need of different services and the largest segments identified are people who work, live in, and visit the City of Stockholm, as shown earlier in Figure 2. Through the pilot projects, these segments have been further specified, as described in Figure 3: tourists, students, SMEs, commuters, and city employees.

Tourists

The very first project within mCity was carried out in 2002 for tourists, when the official event database owned by Stockholm Visitors' Board[6] was made available via mobile Internet. The city wanted to do this in relation to its 750th anniversary which was to be celebrated that year, and it was decided that something new should be tested, which is why WAP was chosen.

Figure 3. Focus groups of the mCity Project

A few years later in 2004, another service targeting tourists was developed by mCity. This time the development process was conducted by a group of talented students taking a project course at the Royal Institute of Technology. This project, *.tourism*, was initiated by the Art Council at the Cultural Administration in order to find new ways of making information about Stockholm available through new technology. The result, a Web site with information on statues, art objects, and buildings of interest is available via mobile or fixed Internet on the address, www.explore. stockholm.se. The server recognizes if the user is accessing the Web site from a PDA, a laptop, or a mobile phone. By using XML functionality, separate interfaces for the different devices are shown, giving the user the best experience possible depending on the device used.

On the Web site, it is possible to search by the name of an object, a location, or a street. It is also possible to list all attractions within a city district. One can also make a guided tour through the Web site, and making this accessible for others to benefit from. Naturally, the personal tours have to be authorized by an administrator in order to filter non-ethic information.

Students

mStudent is a joint project venture between the Federation of Student Unions in Stockholm (SSCO), the Stockholm Academic Forum, and the City of Stockholm within the framework of mCity. The objective is to develop mobile services which are useful to 80,000 students in the Stockholm region. For example, if students can receive an SMS telling them that a lecture has been cancelled, they might not have to come to the university campus at all that day, saving time to be better used for studies or other activities.

During the spring of 2003, 28 students from eight different universities and university-colleges in the Stockholm region participated in a feasibil-

ity study to identify a number of services interesting to students. This first phase of the project was carried out together with Telia,[7] Ericsson, and Föreningssparbanken.[8] The objective was to identify mobile services that would be useful to students in their everyday life. In order to really use the most of the students' innovative minds, they were all given one of Ericsson's most modern mobile phones and were allowed to use them without limitations. This made them experts on the available services and also good judges on new services.

Today, mStudent initiates and administrates different forms of tests and evaluations of mobile services in cooperation with businesses in Stockholm. The purpose is to encourage companies and universities to develop and use improved mobile services and thereby increase the quality of service to students as a group. The activities carried out are based on the list of mobile services that the students identified as interesting in the first phase; but apart from this, mStudent has also become a testbed which tests and evaluates all types of mobile services that can be useful for students. The "test pilots" are all students from Stockholm's universities and university colleges, and mStudent gathers the students in focus groups for workshops, evaluations, and other activities. Some companies are already working together with student reference groups in order to gain feedback on their planned services.

SMEs

mCity has been involved in one project aiming toward higher use of mobile services among SMEs.[9] In one of the shopping malls in central Stockholm, Söderhallarna, the stores can use the Internet and mobile technology to communicate, both with customers and the mall administration. The choice of Söderhallarna was not a coincidence. The property is actually owned by the City of Stockholm, and it is of importance to the mall administration to keep up with the technological development to be able to attract stores to the premises.

By working closely with the storeowners and the mall administration, mCity managed not only to improve the internal communication, but also to provide new ways of treating customer relations with the aid of mobile services. For instance, stores can now inform their customers of last-minute offers or arrivals of new products with SMS or e-mail. Also, customers can easier interact with some of the companies. One of the lunch providers receives the orders from their customers via SMS. This increases the probability of preparing the food on time when not having to take orders on the phone. The technology is also used by the Head of Marketing for the mall, in order to create VIP offers to customers, and to communicate with SME owners and other mall staff, such as janitors.

Commuters

Up-to-date traffic information, provided by the City of Stockholm and the Swedish Road Administration among others, is today available on the Internet site, www.trafiken.nu. The information can be reached via WAP and Internet, but more ways of accessing the information have been developed. To make traffic information available regardless of place or time is important since it brings the choice to commute at a given time to the commuter. The commuters can improve their itinerary and choice of transportation based on the information about the current traffic situation.

mCity is involved in several pilot projects within the traffic area all initiated with a pre-study to find out what kind of information commuters are interested in and would benefit from. In one project, mCity has financed the development of the use of dynamic voice to present information available on the Internet site. The synthetic voice starts reading the new information when a commuter calls a special telephone number available from both fixed and mobile telephones. In another project, commuters are able to subscribe to information on specific routes. The commuter submits information about specific time spans during which he/she is interested in knowing about traffic disturbances on a Web page. As soon as something happens on the route of interest on the specific time span, an SMS is sent out with this information.

Employees

mCity has initiated several SMS management systems within the municipal organizations of Stockholm. Even though the technology used often is the most basic one, the impact has been extensive. Three examples of SMS solutions developed within mCity are described in the following sub-sections.

Schools: Absence Management

A few compulsory and upper-secondary schools have been provided with an absence management system. By keying in their social security number and a four-digit code, pupils can report themselves absent into an automated solution provided by the school. The information is then automatically sent as an e-mail or an SMS to the teachers, thereby reducing administrative work. The flow of information between the school and the parents is also improved since parents may receive an SMS when the child skips class or when parents should remember to pack extra clothes for special extracurricular activities.

The Care Sector: Scheduling Services

Within the care sector, scheduling is a time-consuming effort. Now, staff can plan and book time slots through the Internet, and changes can be made by management through SMS. Positive effects with the solution is that staff motivation has increased and the Head of Staff can now work with core activities as the administrative workload is reduced. This solution was tested together with the SMS solution described next.

The Care Sector: Substitute Management

Within the care sector, a group SMS service has been implemented to facilitate substitute management. Instead of trying to reach substitutes through regular phone calls, managers can send SMSs to groups of staff, saving several hours every time. This creates better opportunities for planning, resulting in less stress for care staff and great financial benefits for the City of Stockholm. Also, managers have discovered the possibilities of encouraging staff through group SMS; an occasional "Have a nice weekend!", or the like, is very much appreciated by the staff working in mobile care units, not seeing much of their colleagues and managers when spending much time out in the field.

This SMS system has been so successful that it has now been made available to all employees within the City of Stockholm to use and benefit from. An interesting fact is that as more people are getting the opportunity to use the system, new areas of use are discovered every day by the users themselves.

MCITY EXPERIENCES

Looking at the mCity Project, it is clear that by focusing on and involving users who traditionally are considered underdeveloped within the field of ICTs, mCity reduces the digital divide. Areas like education and the care sector present great potential for municipalities and ICT companies as large savings of time and money can be made when administrative tasks are simplified. Also, by focusing on the areas with largest potential,

one can increase average levels of use and knowledge of ICTs in the organization, even if simple technology is used. Thus, even the use of SMS might be an important step toward the use of more advanced mobile services (Williamson & Öst, 2004).

By involving the end user early on, the development process becomes more time consuming. On the other hand, there seems to be a higher chance of successful development and implementation. The involvement of end users in the development of mobile services leads to the appreciation of the users who feel that their experiences are valuable and have real impact. It is important to note that the "end user" is the very person who will use the system in the end, not his or her supervisor or manager. Thus, in small-scale projects, it is often necessary to involve several levels of management, involving the ones who will use the system, the ones who can oversee work processes, as well as the ones who will pay for the system.

It is not always easy to involve people with limited skills and knowledge in technology in projects involving technology. Some people are also more skeptical of changes than others; they may have gone through several organizational changes within a short time span, or might not be interested in revising their working processes at all. This is especially obvious when implementing new technology. Thus, it is important to recognize that technological artefacts are as much social as technological objects, affecting people's way of life as time and space are changing (Brown, 2002; Glimell & Juhlin, 2001; Urry, 2000).

In order to involve the end users, the project must be presented in a way which makes it come across as a project which will lead to obvious changes for the better and not primarily as a technological project. "We're not necessarily positive to technology per se, but we are positive to all new projects and ideas that will improve our work", a manager involved in the SMS project for substitute management stated in an interview (Hallin, 2003).

The information generated through the process also provides the companies involved with valuable input on user behavior and preferences. To engage companies in an m-government project like mCity has been very rewarding for all parties, but even though the pilot projects have been too small to make it necessary to issue invitations to tender, a discussion about the delimitations of working together with the private sector in development projects has taken place within the Steering Committee. This discussion has been similar to the general discussion going on in Sweden, as several public institutions find that the Public Procurement Act makes innovation in the area of public e-services difficult (Grenblad, 2003). In Sweden, there are not many precedents concerning these kinds of simple and quick forms of cooperations between the private and the public sectors. Clear directives as to how and when companies should be involved are needed.

A final lesson from the mCity Project is that simple technology offers great possibilities. mCity has not per se been interested in testing new technology just for the sake of testing new technology; the effects should be real and readily measurable, as described previously. This said, new technological inventions may also be tested and used, as has been the case within the mStudent Project and within the early tourist project. The clue is to always have in mind who is going to use the service. Students are in the forefront when it comes to usage of technology, and tourists also tend to be open minded to use new technology when travelling. Administrators in elderly care or in the school sector might not be as mature in their use of ICTs.

The choice of technology is also often subjected to other types of limitations. When developing new systems based on new technology, you have to be able to answer a lot of questions. One is whether the service should be available for all or just for a small group of people. In the case of mCity, this has been a difficult aspect since all services are tested on a small scale, enlarged when proving relevant. In small-scale environments, technological integration is not really necessary, but when making a service available on a larger scale, it is. In the projects in elderly care and in school administration, this was clearly evident. When making the group SMS project a large-scale implementation, integration to several internal programs was necessary, such as the mail system and the identification portal. This was not impossible, but of course involved more work and thorough consideration.

In a municipality, it is also necessary to consider the cost of implementing new technology. The new services have to deliver lowered cost or some other kind of gain for the city; developing services just for fun or because they are high-tech at the moment is not good enough.

TOWARD A NEW DEFINITION OF M-GOVERNMENT

Is mCity an m-government project? Generally, "m-government" is defined as "a subset of e-government", involving the use of mobile/wireless applications in the public sector, making the public information and services available anytime, anywhere (Lallana, 2004). According to this definition, it could be questioned whether mCity is an m-government project, as there are pilot projects with other goals than the one stated earlier. The mStudent Project, for example, aims at improving the life for students in the Stockholm region by introducing new mobile services from different providers, and in the SME project, small- and middle-sized companies and their customers benefit from the mobile service introduced.

It is clear that the City of Stockholm through the mCity Project takes a broader grip on the task of providing people with the possibility of accessing public information and services, by also taking on a pedagogical role of encouraging people to use ICTs in different areas of city life, and by stimulating the ICT industry to develop new applications as well as rethink old applications. In order to understand this approach we must establish the relationship between the mCity Project and the municipal and national ICT strategies as well as the project's relationship to the vision of Stockholm as an IT capital.

mCity in Relation to Municipal and National Strategy

As described previously, the Stockholm E-Strategy is the policy document according to which the ICT work in the city is done. On its very first page, the document points out that the globalization process inevitably will lead to a new Europe where Stockholm will face tougher competition from other European cities, and that in order to face these challenges, the use of ICTs is an important factor. "IT must help to make Stockholm more attractive by securing the city's long-term goals that Stockholm should continue to be a fine place to live and work in"(*The City of Stockholm's E-Strategy, 19th of February 2001*).

The "E-Strategy" of Stockholm is, on a municipal level, what the "24/7 Agency" is on the national level. The "24/7 Agency" was issued in 2000 by the Swedish government, aiming at extending the public sector's use of ICTs, making services available 24 hours a day, 7 days a week (*The 24/7 Delegation*). The vision entails all parts of the public sector—municipalities, county councils as well as central government—and is the Swedish government's way of trying to cope with expected demographic changes leading to a larger aging population which will demand more of a public administration with fewer employees. At the same time, citizens in general are expected to demand more value for money and a growing internationalization is thought to increase the competitive pressure on public bodies. The development of e-government in Sweden is a way of meeting these challenges (Lund) and the belief of the 24/7 Agency is that the Swedish administrative model, with independently managed central

government agencies, is a factor for the success of rapid development of digital applications and e-services (Lundbergh, 2004).

Swedish authorities primarily call for the most appropriate services, not specific technologies. Thus, the name of "the 24/7 Agency" places focus on the time aspects of service-provision—public services should be provided around the clock—not on specific technologies. The question "how" is subordinated, as, "Accessibility, irrespective of time of day and geographical location, may be achieved through a range of established service channels" (Östberg, 2000). Also, the Stockholm E-Strategy is on purpose called the "E-Strategy", and not the "IT-policy", in order to shift "...focus from IT to activities and show [..] how enhanced integration of *electronic services* ('e-services') can develop the municipality's work" (*The City of Stockholm's E-Strategy, 19th of February 2001*). According to this, the E-Strategy does not prescribe certain technologies, but only points at different areas that the city should work with: Internet, information management, mobile technologies (in general), and so forth.

mCity and the Vision of Stockholm as an IT Capital

The mCity Project not only aims at developing technology which make the city available around the clock. It is also a project used to enhance the image of Stockholm as an IT capital; an image based for example on the fact that Ericsson and other major players within the ICT sector have their development offices within the area. According to the Stockholm E-Strategy, IT can play an important role in making Stockholm an attractive city for people to live and work in, and therefore, the city must take an active part in creating business opportunities for ICT companies. One of the goals stated in the E-Strategy is to, "Be one of the most attractive municipalities for relocation, start-up and running of businesses, in competition with the foremost European cities" (*The City of Stockholm's E-Strategy, 19th of February 2001,* p. 14).

Through the mCity Project, the city has given several ICT companies in the Stockholm area the opportunity to test ideas, develop new applications and market themselves in and outside the country—naturally, in compliance with the Public Procurement Act. This strife to encourage local development conveys an entrepreneurial stance which might be perceived as contrasting with the managerial practices of earlier decades which primarily focused on the local provision of services, facilities, and benefits to the population (Harvey, 1989). However, when cities find themselves competing on a global—not only on a national—arena, a new kind of city management develops, involving proactive management of the images of the city as a management tool. Today, city managers are not only active administrators of the traditional areas of responsibility (Czarniawska, 2000) and the "branding" of the city involves much more than producing colorful brochures (Ward, 1998).

mCity and M-Government

As described earlier, the mCity Project aims at creating "the mobile city", as this is thought to be a good place for people to live, work, and spend their holidays in, since mobility means flexibility. But this does not necessarily mean that the project only deals with the development of mobile technologies, which makes information and services of the City of Stockholm available. "Mobile" here does not refer to the technology, but to the people using it, and "the mobile city" is the city where people have the flexibility to do what they want, where and when they choose. The mobile city can be achieved by the city becoming a role model, using mobile technology for its own activities, for example in schools, in homes for the elderly, or through mobile services which give commuters information about traffic, but also by stimulating the use of mobile technology in general, for ex-

ample by encouraging students in the Stockholm area to ask for and use mobile services.

It is also obvious, that for mCity, the traditional m-government definition is not sufficient, as the city itself is not limited to its municipal organization. As we have showed earlier, the projects within mCity involve cooperation with both national institutions (for example, within the traffic projects), regional institutions (for example, within the mStudent Project) as well as private companies. Thus, rather than focusing on technology or the municipal organization, mCity focuses on people, and to see this project as an m-government project is to broaden the definition of m-goverment from only encompassing the use of mobile/wireless applications in the public sector, making the public information and services available anytime, anywhere. And rather than having the municipal organization as the starting point for its activities, the city, as it is perceived by its citizens, visitors, and employees, is the unit from where the project takes off. Thus, we suggest a new definition of m-government:

A public body which supports the mobility of its people, by providing its services when and where the people need them, and by supporting the development of whatever wireless technologies are needed, and the education of people in these.

THE FUTURE OF M-CITIES

It has been argued that the organizing capacity of a city determines whether the city will be able to develop in a sustainable way, and that the ability to include ICTs is becoming a more important aspect of the organizing capacity of cities (Winden, 2003). This, we believe is true.

Once a small, local initiative, mCity has grown into a project which covers many application areas. Through the project, it has become clear that mobile services can help Stockholm simplify routines, minimize administration, save both time and money, and make life a bit easier for people thus contributing to a better working and living environment by improving the service quality offered by the city. These results further strengthen the notion that the building of m-government is important, probably not only for cities, but for all public bodies. But in order to be successful, a people's perspective has to be adopted and the traditional borders of the public body might have to be challenged. To start with people rather than with technology or with the organization, is an important prerequisite for success.

REFERENCES

The 24/7 Delegation. (No. Dir 2003:81). Retrieved November 19, 2006, from http://www.sou.gov.se/24timmarsdel/PDF/Eng%20version.pdf

Brown, B. (2002). Studying the use of mobile technology. In B. Brown, N. Green, & R. Harper (Eds.), *Wireless world. Social and interactional aspects of the mobile age* (pp. 3-15). London: Springer.

Castells, M. (1997). *The power of identity* (vol. 2). Oxford: Blackwell.

The City of Stockholm's E-Strategy. (2001, February 19). Available through the City of Stockholm +46 (0)8-508 00 000. The Swedish version can be retrieved (last retrieval, November 20, 2006) from http://www.stockholm.se/files/16100-16199/file_16185.pdf

Czarniawska, B. (2000). The European capital of the 2000s: On image construction and modeling. *Corporate Reputation Review, 3,* 202-217.

Glimell, H., & Juhlin, O. (Eds.). (2001). *The social production of technology. On the everyday life with things.* Göteborg: BAS.

Grenblad, D. (2003). *Growth area – E-services in the public sector, analyses of the innovation system in 2003.* Vinnova (The Swedish Agency for Innovation Systems).

Hallin, A. (2003). *Mobile technology and social development – Dialogic spaces in msociety.* EGOS Annual Conference, Copenhagen, July 2-5.

Harvey, D. (1989). From managerialism to entrepreneurialism: The transformation in urban governance in late capitalism. *Geografiska Annaler, 71B*(1), 3-17.

Jazic, A., & Lundevall, K. (2003). *mWatch – A survey on mobile readiness in the Baltic Sea Region.* Presented at the 5th Annual Baltic Development Forum Summit, Riga, Latvia. Retrieved November 20, 2006, from http://www.bdforum.org/download.asp?id=49

Lallana, E. C. (2004). *eGovernment for development, mgovernment definition on and models page.* Retrieved January 13, 2005, from http://www.e-devexchange.org/eGov/mgovdefn.htm

Lund, G. *The Swedish vision of 24-hour public administration and e-government – Speech by Gunnar Lund, Minister for International Economic Affairs and Financial Markets, held December 9th.* Unpublished manuscript.

Lundbergh, A. (2004). *Infra services – A Swedish way to facilitate public e-services development: MEMO.* The Swedish Agency for Public Management.

Urry, J. (2000). *Sociology beyond societies, mobilities for the twenty-first century.* London & New York: Routledge.

Ward, S. V. (1998). *Selling places. The marketing and promotion of towns and cities 1850-2000.* New York: E & Fn Spon.

Williamson, S., & Öst, F. (2004). *The Swedish telecommunications market 2003.* (No. PTS-ER-2004-24), The Swedish National Post and Telecom Agency.

Winden, W. v. (2003). *Essays on Urban ICT Policies.* Rotterdam: Erasmus University Rotterdam.

Östberg, O. (2000). *The 24/7 agency. Criteria for 24/7 agencies in the networked public administration.* Stockholm: The Swedish Agency for Administrative Development.

RELEVANT WEB SITES

www.stockholm.se/mCity
www.stockholm.se/english/
www.mstudent.se
www.telecomcity.org
www.testplats.com
www.24-timmarsmyndigheten.se
www.pts.se
www.trafiken.nu
www.explore.stockholm.se

ENDNOTES

1   All of Sweden has about nine million inhabitants.

2   2004.

3   The City Council is the supreme decision-making body in the City of Stockholm, consisting of 101 members from the six parties represented in the council, and are elected by the Stockholmers every 4th year.

4   The City Executive Board consists of 13 members, who proportionally represent the parties in the City Council.

5   The Office of the City Executive Board.

6   The municipal company in Stockholm providing service to visitors.

7   The largest telecom operator in Sweden today known as TeliaSonera after a merge with the Finish company Sonera.

8   One of the major bank corporations in Sweden.

9   Small- and middle-sized enterprises.

This work was previously published in Mobile Government: An Emerging Direction in E-Government, edited by I. Kushchu, pp. 12-29, copyright 2007 by IGI Publishing, formerly known as Idea Group Publishing (an imprint of IGI Global).

Chapter 8.18
Mobile Speech Recognition

Dirk Schnelle
Technische Universität Darmstadt, Germany

ABSTRACT

This chapter gives an overview of the main architectures for enabling speech recognition on embedded devices. Starting with a short overview of speech recognition, an overview of the main challenges for the use on embedded devices is given. Each of the architectures has its own characteristic problems and features. This chapter gives a solid basis for the selection of an architecture that is most appropriate for the current business case in enterprise applications.

OVERVIEW

Voice-based interaction is a common requirement for ubiquitous computing (UC). However, the idea of having speech recognition on wearable devices is not simply copying the recognizer to such a device and running it. The limitations of the device, especially computational power and memory, pose strong limitations that cannot be handled by desktop size speech recognizers. This chapter gives a brief overview of the different architectures employed to support speech recognition on wearable devices. A background in speech recognition technology is helpful in order to understand them better, but is not required. At some points you will be provided with pointers to the literature to achieve a better understanding. A detailed understanding of the available architectures is needed to select the appropriate architecture for the enterprise, if it wants to support audio-based applications for mobile workers. The selection process has to consider the available resources, such as servers, wireless network, the software that has already been bought in order to save the investment, and to be able to justify the decision to invest more money in required infrastructure.

Most of the figures use UML 2.0 as a means of communicating architectural descriptions. The diagrams are easy to read, even if the reader is not familiar with this modeling language. The UML specification can be obtained from the Object Management Group (OMG, 2006).

A speech recognizer has the task of transcribing spoken language into a text (see Figure 1). The input is the *speech signal,* the human voice that is recorded, for example, with a microphone. The textual output, in this case *"one two three,"* is called an *utterance*.

The architecture of a speech recognizer has not changed over the past decades. It is illustrated in Figure 2 based on Jelinek (2001).

It comprises the main components of recognizers as they are used today, regardless of the technology used. They are available as pure software solutions or implemented in hardware to gain speed. In the following sections we focus

only on the main components involved. Some recognizers may use additional components or components that are slightly different. However, the architectures presented show the main functionalities of each of them and discuss the main challenges that have to be faced when applied to mobile devices.

The *signal processor* generates real valued vectors σ_i from a speech signal, obtained from a microphone. They are also called feature vectors. Currently, most speech recognizers use at least 13

Figure 1. Speech recognition

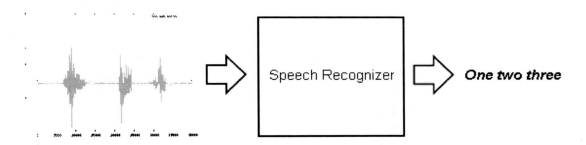

Figure 2. General architecture of a speech recognizer

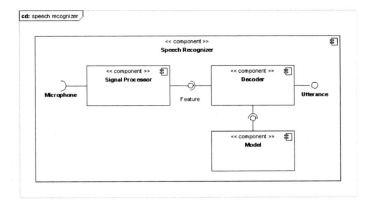

features in each vector. We will have a closer look at them in the section "Evaluation of Sphinx 3.5." Normally computation of the features happens at regular intervals, that is, every 10msec., where the feature vectors are passed to the *decoder* to convert it into the utterance. The *decoder* uses the *model* for decoding. In the simplest case, the *model* contains a set of prototypes ρ_i, which are of the same kind as σ_i. Then, the *decoder* finds the ρ_i closest to σ_i for a given distance function d

$$a_i = \min_{j=1}^{k} d(\sigma_i, \rho_j) \qquad (1)$$

a_i is the acoustic symbol for σ_i, which is emitted to the rest of the recognizer for further processing.

For **word-based speech recognizers** these acoustic symbols are the single words. For the example shown in Figure 1, this would be the concatenation of $\{a_1=one, a_2=two, a_3=three\}$.

A **phoneme-based speech recognizer** would output a concatenation of phonemes for each word. Phonemes are small sound units. The word *this* comprises the following phonemes $\{a_2=TH, a_2=I, a_2=is, a_2=S\}$. Obviously this output requires some post processing to obtain an output comparable to word-based recognizers that can be used by an application.

The benefit of phoneme-based speech recognizers is that they are generally more accurate, since they reduce the decoding problem to small sound units, and that they are more flexible and can handle a larger vocabulary more easily. Remember the first attempts in writing, starting from symbols for each word over symbols for each syllable to the letters that we find today.

This chapter is organized as follows: the section "Speech Recognition on Embedded Devices" gives an overview about the limitations of embedded devices to address speech recognition functionality. Then the two main architectures to work around these limitations are presented, which will be discussed in the two following sections in more detail. The section "Parameters of Speech

Recognizers in UC" names some aspects that are needed to rate the solutions presented in the section "Service Dependent Speech Recognition" and the section "Device Inherent Speech Recognition." The section "Future research directions" concludes this chapter with a summary and an overview of the required computational resources on the device and the server for the architectures discussed.

SPEECH RECOGNITION ON EMBEDDED DEVICES

Speech recognition is computationally expensive. Advances in computing power made speech recognition possible on off-the-shelf desktop PCs beginning in the early 1990s. Mobile devices do not have that computing power and speech recognizers do not run in real time. There are even more limitations, which will be discussed later in this section. Moore's law states that memory size and computational performance increase by a factor of two every 18 months.

Frostad (2003) writes:

"Most of what is written on speech is focused on server based speech processing. But there is another speech technology out there that's powerful enough to sit on a stamp-sized microchip. It's called "embedded speech." Advances in computing power gave server side speech the power boost it needed in the early 90s. Now that same rocket fuel is launching embedded speech into the limelight."

Although computing power is increasing on these smaller computers, making it possible to run a small recognizer, performance is still not efficient enough to enable speech recognizers off-the-shelf on such devices. The attempt to use speech recognition on a mobile device, such as a computer of PDA size or a mobile phone, encounters the same problems that were faced on desktop PCs years ago and which have been solved by the growth of computing power. The following section gives an overview of these limitations.

Limitations of Embedded Devices

The development of all applications, especially speech recognition applications for embedded devices has to tackle several problems, which arise as a result of the computational limitations and hardware resources on the device. These limitations are:

- **Memory:** Storage Capacity on embedded devices, such as a PDA or a cell phone, is very limited. This makes it impossible to have large *models*.
- **Computational Power:** Although the computational power of embedded devices has grown continuously over the last few years, it is still far from that what is available on desktop size PCs. The *signal processor* and the *decoder* perform computationally intense tasks.
- **Power Consumption:** Battery lifetime is a scarce resource on embedded devices. The device will stop working if the battery is empty. Since speech recognition is computationally intensive, processing consumes a lot of energy.
- **Floating Point:** Most processors for PDAs, like the Strong ARM or XScale processor, do not support floating-point arithmetic. It has to be emulated by fixed-point arithmetic, which is much slower than direct support. The value vectors σ_i are real valued and most state-of-the-art recognizers work with statistical methods. Thus, support of floating point arithmetic is essential and emulation results in loss of speed. Moreover, this may lead to a loss of precision. Especially signal processing is a critical task, since the quality of the output has a direct impact on the preserved information. Jelinek (2001) states that "Bad processing means loss of information: There is less of it to extract."

In the following the approaches to work around these limitations will be discussed. A short overview of the technology used is given to understand how they cope with the challenges of embedded devices.

Main Architectures for Speech Recognition on Embedded Devices

Progress in speech recognition has made it possible to have it on embedded devices. Cohen (2004) states that, "Although we did not know in the 1990s all of the tricks we know today, we can use 1990s-like computing resources ... to good advantage to compute a task which would have been difficult in 1990, but is simpler today because of our technical advancements." However, the limitations of mobile devices that were mentioned in the previous section still pose a lot of challenges. There have been several attempts to deal with them and enable speech recognition on embedded devices. An overview of these approaches is given in the following sections. We concentrate on the most common approaches that can be divided into two main categories:

- Service dependent speech recognition, Figure 3(a)
- Device inherent speech recognition, Figure 3(b)

The main difference between these two architectures is the node where the *speech recognizer* component is deployed. Architectures for service dependent speech recognition will be introduced in the section "Service Dependent Speech Recognition" and those for device inherent speech recognition in the section "Device Inherent Speech Recognition."

Figure 3. Deployment of voice enabled service usage with mobile devices

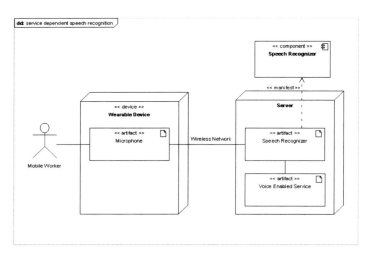

(a) Service dependent speech recognition

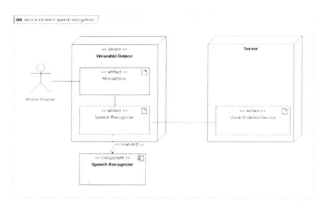

(b) Device inherent speech recognition

Zaykovskiy (2006) proposed another categorization. He distinguishes:

- Client,
- Client-server, and
- Server-based architectures.

The main reason for his differentiation is the location of the *signal Processor* and the *decoder*. In the service-oriented view of ubiquitous computing it makes more sense to emphasize the ability to have speech recognition as a network service or as an independent functionality of the device itself. This is a fundamental fact in smart environments, where services can be inaccessible while the user is on the move. Bailey (2004) requires that "there need to be clear boundaries between the functionality of the device, and the functionality of the network." The technological orientation of these approaches confirms this differentiation. Whereas service dependent speech recognition deal with APIs for remote access to a speech recognizer, device inherent speech recognition uses the techniques of desktop size speech recognition technology to enable speech recognition on the device itself.

Parameters of Speech Recognizers in UC

In order to rate the different architectures, we need an understanding of the core parameters. This section will give a short overview of these parameters.

- **Speaking Mode:** Word boundaries are not easy to detect. The presence of pauses is not enough, since they may not be present. Early speech recognizers forced the user to pause after each word. This is called *isolated word* recognition. If there are no such constraints, the speech recognizer is able to process *continuous speech*.
- **Speaking Style:** This parameter states if a speech recognizer for continuous speech is able to process *read speech*, meaning a very precise and clear pronunciation, or if it is capable of processing *spontaneous speech*, as used when we talk to each other.
- **Enrollment:** Some speech recognizers require an initial training before they can be used. This training is used to adapt to the speaker in order to achieve higher accuracy. These recognizers are called *speaker dependent*. This concept is often used on desktop PCs, but is also possible in UC, where the device is personalized. The opposite case

is *speaker independent* speech recognizers that are trained to work with multiple speakers. Thus they have a lower accuracy. This concept is used, for example, in telephony applications. There are only a few scenarios that really require speaker independence with embedded devices. For these applications, speaker-independent systems do not have an advantage over speaker-dependent systems, but can benefit from a better accuracy.

- **Vocabulary:** The size of the vocabulary is one of the most important factors, since this strongly influences the way in which users can interact with the application. A vocabulary is said to be *small* if it contains up to 20 words. A *large* vocabulary may contain over 20,000 words.
- **Perplexity:** Perplexity defines the number of words that can follow a word. This is an important factor if the recognizer has to decode an utterance consisting of multiple words and tries to find the path with the lowest error rate.
- **SNR:** SNR is the acronym of signal-to-noise-ratio. It is defined as the ratio of a given transmitted signal to the background noise of the transmission medium. This typically happens where the microphone also captures some noise from the background, which does not belong to the signal to decode.
- **Transducer:** A transducer is the device that converts the speech into a digital representation. For speech recognition this may be, for instance, a noise-cancelling headset or telephone. Each of them features different characteristics, such as the available bandwidth of the voice data or the ability to cut background noise as with a noise cancelling headset. In UC environments noise-cancelling headsets are typically used.

In a UC world there are some additional parameters depending on the location, where recognition takes place. These parameters, as presented in Bailey (2004) are:

- **Network Dependency:** One major aspect is the dependency on a network resource. A recognizer located on the device will not need any network to be operated, while a recognizer streaming raw audio data to a server (see the section "Audio Streaming") will not work without a network. Apart from the technical aspect, the user expects the device to work and may not be able to distinguish between a non-functional recognizer and missing network connectivity if the device is "broken."
- **Network Bandwidth:** Available network bandwidth is a scarce resource. Architectures performing recognition on the device have a more compact representation of the data that has to be transmitted than those architectures streaming pure audio data.
- **Transmission Degradation:** With the need to transmit data from the mobile device to a server, the problem of transmission degradation arises. Failures, loss of packets or corrupted packets while transmitting the data means a loss of information. If the raw audio is transmitted to a server, recognition accuracy goes down.
- **Server Load:** In a multi-user scenario it is important that the application scales with an increasing number of users.
- **Integration and Maintenance:** Embedded devices are hard to maintain, especially if parts of the functionality are implemented in hardware. A server, on the other hand, is easy to access and bug fixes are available for all clients at once. This issue goes in a similar direction to the discussion of centralized server architectures versus rich clients.
- **Responsiveness:** A must for speech recognition is that the result is available in real time. This means that the result of the recognition process must be available as fast as possible.

In the following sections the different architectures will be characterized according to these parameters.

SERVICE DEPENDENT SPEECH RECOGNITION

The architectures presented in this section have in common that they require network connectivity to work.

Audio Streaming

An immediate idea to solve the performance bottleneck on embedded devices is not to perform the recognition process on the device itself. A general model of the recognizer, shown in Figure 4, uses the audio recording capabilities of the embedded device as a microphone replacement to record the raw audio as the input for the *signal processor.*

The audio is streamed over the wireless network, for example, Wi-Fi or Bluetooth, to the *signal processor* on a server. This allows the use of a full-featured recognizer with a large vocabulary running on the server. A disadvantage of this solution is that a stable wireless network connection is required. Another disadvantage is a possibly very large amount of data streamed over the network. Since recognition is not performed on the embedded device, we have all the benefits of a desktop-size speech recognizer at the cost of high network traffic.

MRCP

Since server side speech recognition is mainly an immediate idea, developers tend to implement this architecture on their own using a proprietary

Figure 4. Architecture of an audio streaming speech recognizer

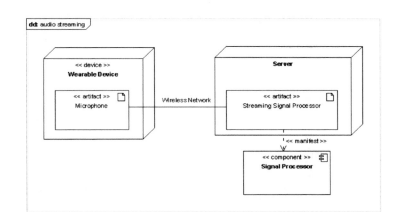

protocol, which makes it unusable with other applications that do not know anything about that proprietary protocol. In addition, real time issues are generally not considered which can result in misrecognition. A standard for server side speech recognition that has been adopted by industry is MRCP. MRCP is an acronym for **m**edia **r**esource **c**ontrol **p**rotocol. It was jointly developed by Cisco Systems, Nuance Communications and Speechworks and was published by the IETF as an RFC (Shanmugham, 2006).

MRCP is designed as an API to enable clients control media processing resources over a network to provide a standard for audio streaming. Media processing resources can be speech recognizers, text-to-speech engines, fax, signal detectors and more. This allows for a use in distributed environments, for example, a small device that accesses a recognizer on the network.

The specification is based on RTSP in Schulzrinne (1998), the **r**eal **t**ime **s**treaming **p**rotocol, as a MIME-type the **M**ultipurpose **I**nternet **M**ail **E**xtension. MIME is used to support, for example, no-text attachments in e-mail messages.

RTSP defines requests, responses, and events needed to control the media processing resources. The protocol itself is text based. Mechanisms for the reliable exchange of binary data are left to protocols like SIP, the **S**ession **I**nitiation **P**rotocol, or RTSP. SIP enables control of sessions such as Internet telephone calls.

A media server that can be accessed by RTSP mechanisms controls all resources, in this case, recognizer and synthesizer.

Figure 5 shows a simplified view on the messages that are exchanged in an **a**utomatic **s**peech **r**ecognition (ASR) request and a **t**ext-**t**o-**s**peech (TTS) request.

In an *ASR request*, the MRCP client initiates the request and delivers the voice data via RTP in parallel. The recognition process is executed on the *MRCP Media Server* and the result of the recognition is delivered to the client as the *ASR Response*.

In a *TTS request*, the MRCP client initiates the request. The *MRCP Media Server* answers with a *TTS response* and delivers the synthesized voice data via RTP in parallel.

Figure 5. Simplified view on MRCP requests for ASR and TTS

(a) MRCP ASR request

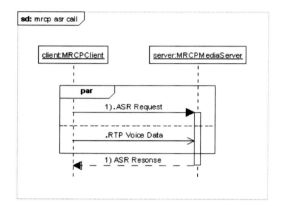

(b) MRCP TTS request

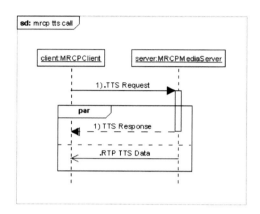

Distributed Speech Recognition

Another possibility to enable speech recognition on mobile devices uses an architectural compromise. Since full-featured recognizers are hard to implement on embedded devices and streaming of raw audio data produces too much network traffic, ETSI, the European Telecommunication Standard Institute, introduced a solution to perform parts of the recognition process on the device and the rest is handled on a server. This architecture is called *Distributed Speech Recognition* (DSR). Pearce (2000) named the component, which is deployed on the device the *DSR Front-end* and the component deployed on the server the *DSR Backend*. This concept is shown in Figure 6.

An obvious point for such splitting is the separation of *signal processor* and *decoder*. Instead of sending all the audio over the network, the feature vectors ρ_i are computed on the embedded device and sent to the *decoder* on a server. In order to reduce the amount of data and to ensure a secure transmission, the data is compressed and a CRC value is added. The architecture of the DSR Front-end is shown in Figure 7.

The DSR Backend, shown in Figure 8, checks the CRC value and decompresses the data before it is passed to the *decoder*.

In this way, the computational capabilities of the device are used for the tasks of the *signal processor* in the *DSR Front-end*, whereas the *decoder* and the *model* reside on the server in the *DSR Backend*. The architecture is a result of discussion between multiple companies, that is, Nokia and Motorola in the Aurora project. The data exchange of DSR Frontend and DSR Backend is standardized by ETSI. This specification includes the features used, CRC check and their compression. Compared to pure audio streaming, the transmitted data is reduced without much loss of information. This also means that the error rates in transmission are reduced. As a positive consequence, DSR also works with lower signal strength, as shown in Figure 9.

Figure 6. Architecture of a distributed speech recognizer

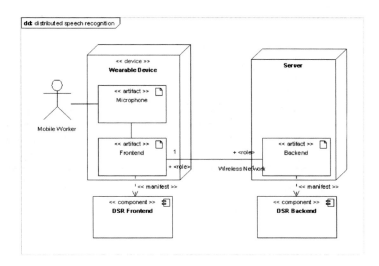

Figure 7. DSR front-end

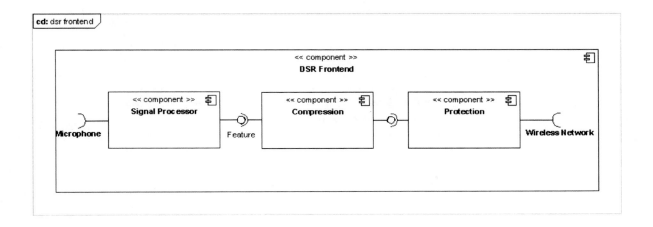

The experiment was conducted in the Aurora project and is described in more detail in Pearce (2000). The figure shows the recognition performance of DSR compared to a mobile speech channel. The measurement proves that recognition still works with lower signal quality. A great advantage of this technology over streaming solutions like audio streaming or MRCP is the reduced network

Figure 8. DSR backend

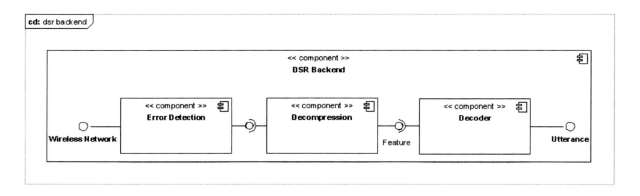

Figure 9. Performance of DSR with channel errors according to Pearce (2000)

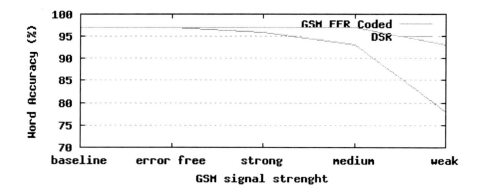

traffic. Like MRCP it defines a standard, but with less acceptance. Speech recognition can be used in various environments, as long as they are compliant to the DSR standard. Unlike MRCP it relies on computation on the device, decreasing its chances of being established in a company's network in contrast to a pure protocol. Again, the recognition has all the features of a desktop size recognizer.

As a negative point, the set of feature vectors is a compromise. This also means that other or additional features used in specific recognizers cannot be transmitted using this technology.

ETSI promises a better use of available resources and better transmission. The following section gives some insight into the computational requirements.

Evaluation of Sphinx 3.5

Sphinx is an open source speech recognizer from Carnegie Mellon University. It was DARPA funded and was used in many research projects in speech recognition.

The anatomy of Sphinx can be divided into three phases:

1. Front-end processing,
2. Gaussian probability estimation, and
3. Hidden Markov evaluation.

The Gaussian phase and the HMM phase are part of the *decoder*. A closer look at it is given in the section "Hidden Markov Models." Mathew (2002) gives an overview of the time that Sphinx 3.5 spends on each phase (see Figure 10).

Obviously, the front-end processing constitutes the smallest part of the computation to be performed. This shows that this is an ideal candidate to be performed by smaller devices, as it is done with DSR. Consequently, Mathew et al. (2000) consider it to be not worthy of further investigation, stopping their analysis at this point. They focus more on the optimization of the latter two phases.

Front-end processing usually comprises the computational steps shown in Figure 11.

The following paragraphs show how these steps are handled in Sphinx. A more general view can be found in the literature, for example, in Schukat-Talamazzini (1995).

Processing starts with a speech signal, as captured, for example, from a microphone. An example of such a speech signal is shown as the input to the speech recognizer in . The transformation into a digital representation, also called *quantization*, means also a loss of information, but this can not be avoided.

Figure 10. Profile information of Sphinx 3.5 phases according to Mathew (2002)

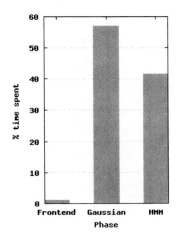

Figure 11. Front-end processing

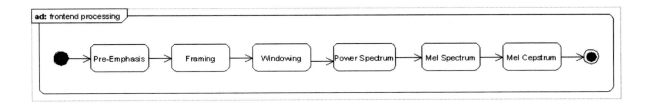

- **Pre-Emphasis:** In this step the quantized signal is filtered. This step becomes necessary from the observation that the signal is weaker in higher frequencies, which can be solved using a digital high-pass filter. Figure 12 shows an example of the speech signal and the effect of this filtering step.

- **Framing:** The input signal is divided into overlapping frames of N samples. The frame shift interval, that is, the difference between the starting points of consecutive frames, is M samples.

- **Windowing:** The Fast Fourier Transformation (FFT) is known from the domain of signal processing to compute the spectrum of a signal. FFT requires a periodical signal, it is assumed that the time segment continues to be periodical. Since speech changes over time, we try to get segments of the signal, where it can be considered to be constant. These time segments last from 5-30 ms. An example for such a windowing function is the *Hamming Window*. The following figure shows four such time segments of the utterance. It is noticeable that the signal is smoothed to the borders of the time segments.

- **Power Spectrum:** For speech recognition, the discrete case of the FFT, the **d**iscrete **f**ourier **t**ransformation (DFT) is used. The output of the DFT usually consists of a power of 2 of complex numbers. The power spectrum is computed by the squared magnitude of these complex numbers. The following figure shows the power spectrum for the word *one* of the utterances.

- **Mel Spectrum:** The next step is a filtering step to filter the input spectrum through individual filters. One of these filters is the Mel filter. An impression of this filter is given in the following figure.

The output is an array of filtered values, typically called Mel-spectrum, each corresponding to the result of filtering the input spectrum through an individual filter. Therefore, the length of the output array is equal to the number of filters created.

Figure 12. Pre-emphasis of the speech signal

(a) Quantized speech signal

(b) Pre-emphasized speech signal

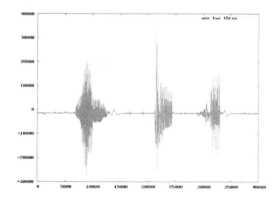

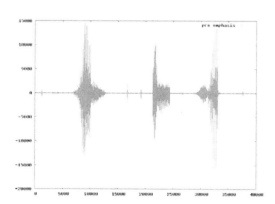

Figure 13. Framing

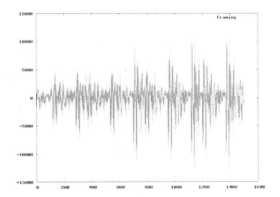

Figure 14. Windowing

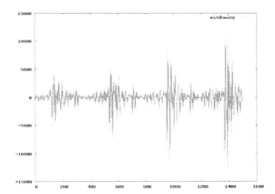

Figure 15. Power spectrum

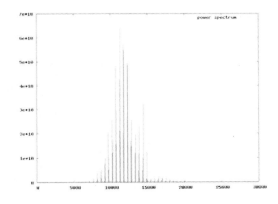

Mel Cepstrum

Davis (1980) showed that Mel-frequency cepstral coefficients present robust characteristics that are good for speech recognition. The artificial word cepstrum is obtained by reversing the letter order in the spectrum to emphasize that this is an inverse transformation. These cepstral coefficients are computed via a discrete cosine transform.

Sphinx uses 16-bit raw audio data as input and produces 13 cepstral parameters as output for each time segment. In order to determine

Figure 16. Mel filter

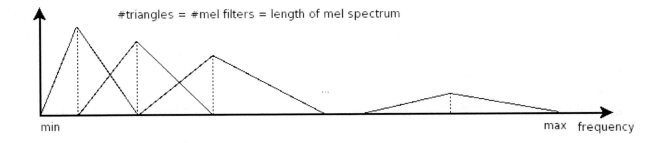

Figure 17. Mel-Spectrum

Figure 18. Mel cepstrum

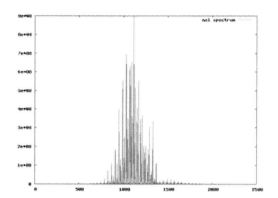

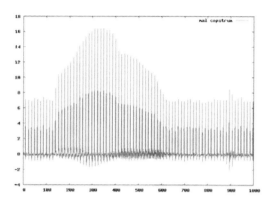

Figure 19. Profile information of sphinx 3.5 front-end

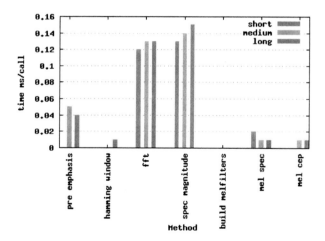

the execution time consumption by individual parts of Sphinx, we used a profiling tool to get detailed information on functions and routines on a Sparc processor-based platform. The profiling was done with three audio files of different lengths as input:

- Short (2.05 sec),
- Medium (6.02 sec), and
- Long (30.04 sec).

The profiling result is shown in Figure 19.

Obviously, the computation of the power spectrum, which comprises the methods fft and spec magnitude, consumes most of the time. Both are part of the power spectrum computation. Tuning this method can speed up the computation a great deal. Alternatively, it can be replaced by a hardware solution, such as a **d**igital **s**ignal **p**rocessor (DSP). This issue will also be addressed in the section "Hardware-Based Speech Recognition."

The process becomes more complicated if the device does not support floating-point operations. Junqua (2001) mentions, "While most automatic speech recognition systems for PC use are based on floating-point algorithms, most of the processors used in embedded systems are fixed-point processors. With fixed-point processors there is only a finite amount of arithmetic precision available, causing an inevitable deviation from the original design." A study by Delaney (2002) showed that for Sphinx 2 a Strong ARM simulator spent over 90% of the time on the floating-point emulation. These results can be transferred to Sphinx 3.5, since they use the same code base for front-end processing.

A way in which to solve these issues is to substitute floating-point arithmetic by fixed-point arithmetic. This is done using scaled integers to perform basic math functions. The scaling factor, that is, the location of the decimal point, must be known in advance and requires careful decision. For adding two numbers, the number n of bits after the decimal point must line up. A multiplication of two numbers yields a number with $2n$ bits after the decimal point.

Unfortunately, this also means a loss of information and the risk of overflowing the register size of 32 bits. This is especially important for the computation of the power spectrum and the Mel-spectrum. Delaney (2002) suggests changing the computation for the Mel-spectrum using a square root to compute the Mel coefficients. It is guaranteed that the square root results in small values, which means that the result of multiplication is small. They also suggest storing the Mel coefficients in a lookup table to avoid the computationally complex calculations of the square root. An experiment conducted in Huggins (2005) showed that feature extraction on a Sharp Zaurus had a 2.7-fold gain in speed using this method. The loss in precision for the result in computing the Mel Cepstrum increased from 9.73% to 10.06%.

DEVICE INHERENT SPEECH RECOGNITION

In contrast to the architectures described above, those described in this section are handled on the device only, without the need for a server or service from the network. These architectures are also often referred to as *software-only* and *embedded* architectures (Eagle, 1999; Frostad, 2003). Embedded architectures require the existence of a dedicated DSP. They reside as hardware-based speech recognition, since the term *embedded* is totally overloaded with the meanings of a DSP, an embedded device or embedded into an application. So this architecture does not deal only with software-based architectures, but also include partial or full support with hardware.

Hardware-Based Speech Recognition

Some manufacturers offer designated chips for mobile devices. An example of such a chip is shown in Figure 20.

The technology that is used in these chips differs. All software-based speech technologies for device inherent speech recognition, as described in the following sections, can be found implemented as a port to a DSP. It is even possible to replace just certain parts of the recognizer, that is, the FFT computation for the feature extraction in DSR, with a hardware solution. The main advantage is that a hardware-based solution does not have the runtime problems of software-based approaches,

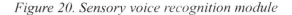

Figure 20. Sensory voice recognition module

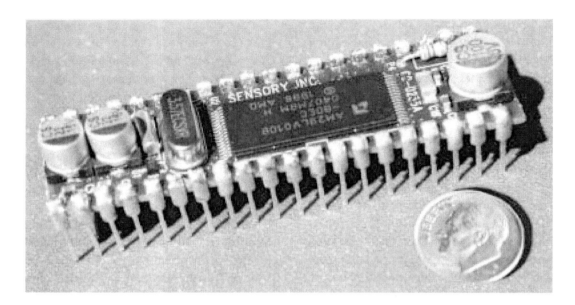

since the hardware is designed to address this specific problem. This is gained at the cost of less flexibility. The range of hardware implementations is as broad as the underlying technology. It starts from a fixed vocabulary used in toys through dynamic time warping, the technology used in most mobile phones, up to programmable DSPs like the sensory chip shown in.

Advantages and drawbacks of these solutions are not discussed in this section, since they are inherited from the technology used. Benefits and drawbacks of the architectures are discussed in the corresponding sections.

Dynamic Type Warping

One of the earliest approaches of enabling speech recognition is the dynamic time warping (DTW). The architecture is shown in Figure 21.

The *signal processor* is responsible for the feature analysis of the raw speech signal. The computational steps are the same as the front-end

Figure 21. Dynamic time warping

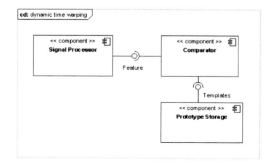

processing of DSR (see). An output of the feature analysis component is a feature vector of a test utterance $\sigma = (\sigma_1,..., \sigma_n)^T$ which is compared in the *comparator*, which replaces the *decoder*, with all reference feature vectors $\rho_i = (\rho_{i,1},..., \rho_{i,m})^T$ stored in the *prototype* storage, replacing the *model* of the utterances ρ_i in the set of trained utterances with the help of a distance function $d(\sigma_i, \rho_j)$ that was already mentioned in the section "Overview." Usually the prototypes are gained in a single recording. The features of this recording are computed, stored in the *prototype storage* and associated with the output. If the distance of the currently spoken word to the template is too big $d(\sigma_i, \rho_j) > \mu$, it is likely that no prototype matches the utterance. In this case, the comparator rejects the input.

The problem of calculating the distance from σ_i to ρ_j with the help of a distance function $d(\sigma_i, \rho_j)$ consists of two parts:

1. Definition of a distance function to calculate the distance of two related feature vectors
2. Definition of a time warping function to define a relationship between the elements of σ_i and ρ_j

Multiple distance functions exist and are used. For a Gaussian distribution, Mahalanobis distance is used. Since this is complex and we do not have many computational resources on the device, Euclidean distance is more common. This requires that the features be normalized to unity variance.

The problem with a pairwise distance calculation is that it is unlikely that the lengths of the template and of the input are the same, that is, the length of the *o* in *word* may vary. DTW uses dynamic programming to find an optimal match between two sequences of feature vectors allowing for stretching and compression of sections [see Sakoe (1990)]. The template word having the least distance is taken as a correct match, if its value is smaller than a predetermined threshold value μ.

The technique of comparison with a template word makes this an ideal candidate for isolated word recognition with a small vocabulary, but unsuitable for continuous speech. Since the templates are generally taken in a single recording, DTW is also speaker dependent with little computational effort. The computational requirements are slightly higher than those for DSR, see the section "Distributed Speech Recognition," but lower than those for hidden Markov models (see next section), or artificial neural networks, see the section "Artificial Neural Networks."

Hidden Markov Models

Most modern speech recognizers are based on hidden Markov models (HMM). An overview of the architecture of a HMM based recognizer is shown in Figure 22, which is in fact a phoneme-based recognizer.

It is also possible to use HMM-based recognition for word-based models. In this case, the architecture is slightly different, as Schukat-Talamazzini (1995) points out. More about the basics of Markov chains and their use can be obtained from the literature, for example, Rabiner (1989). Although this approach is very old, it is still the most successful approach for speech recognition.

Instead of using the computed features as a seed for the states, most recognizers use vector quantization (VQ) to reduce the data rate. Since speech recognition deals with a continuous signal, a certain amount of data arrives periodically. This is called the *data rate*. Since HMM decoding is time consuming, a lower data rate promises real time performance. Furthermore, the storage size is reduced, since only the codebook is stored instead of the cepstral parameters. A *codebook* stores the mapping of the feature vectors as they are computed from the speech signal to a discrete label. Thus the codebook is a discrete representation of the continuous speech data.

Figure 22. Architecture of a HMM-based recognizer

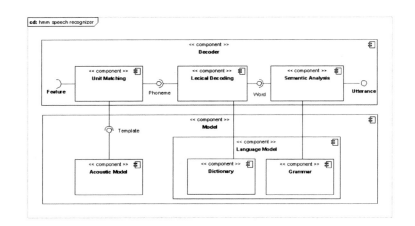

Unit Matching

HMMs are the core of the *unit matching* component. They are described as a tuple $\lambda = (S, A, B, \pi, V)$ with

- $S = \{s_1, ..., s_n\}$ representing a set of states,
- $A = \{a_{i,j}\}$ representing a matrix of transition probabilities, where $a_{i,j}$ denotes the probability $p(s_j, s_i)$ for the transition from state s_i to s_j,
- $B = \{b_1, ..., b_n\}$ representing a set of output probabilities, where $b_i(x)$ denotes the probability $q(x|s_i)$ to observe x in state s_i and
- O as a set of observations, which means the domain of b_i.

A schematic view on a HMM is given in the following figure.

The probability of observing an output sequence $O = O_1 O_2 ... O_r$ is given by

$$P(O = O_1 O_2 ... O_r) = \sum_{\{s_1, s_2, ... s_T\}} \prod_{i=1}^{T} p(s_i \mid s_{i-1}) q(x_i \mid s_{i-1})$$

(2)

Rabiner (1989) raises three basic questions that are to be solved for speech recognition with HMMs.

1. Given the observation sequence $O = O_1 O_2 ... O_r$ and a model λ, how do we efficiently compute $P(O|\lambda)$, the probability of the observation sequence, given the model?

2. For decoding, the question to solve is, given the observation sequence $O = O_1 O_2 ... O_r$ and the model λ how we choose a corresponding state sequence $Q = q_1, q_2, ... q_T$, which is optimal in some meaningful sense (i.e., best "explains" the observations)?

3. How do we adjust the model parameters λ to maximize $P(O|\lambda)$?

The first problem is also known as the *evaluation problem*, but it can also be treated as a *scoring*

Figure 23. Schematic view on a HMM

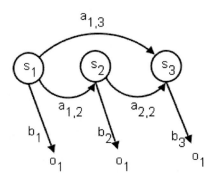

problem. In that case, the solution to this problem allows us to choose the model that best explains the observations.

The third problem tries to optimize the model parameters to describe a given observation sequence as well as possible. This optimization can be used to *train* the model. Training means to adapt the model parameters to observed training data.

The most important one for speech recognition is the second problem, since it tries to find the *correct* state sequence.

A well-known approach to this is the Viterbi algorithm, based on dynamic programming (DP) to find the most likely sequence of hidden states. A more detailed description, related to speech recognition, can be found in the literature, for example, Rabiner (1989) and Jelinek (2001). The Viterbi algorithm tries to find the best score, which means the highest probability, along a single path at time t, also known as *trellis*.

Computational Optimization

The Viterbi algorithm is computationally intensive, especially for larger vocabularies. It requires roughly $|A_u|$ multiplications and additions, where

$|A_u|$ is the number of transitions in the model (Bahl, 1993). In order not to search the entire Viterbi trellis, the number of branch-out search candidates can be limited using beam-search, as Lowerre (1976) points out.

The idea is to eliminate all states from the trellis that have a probability above a certain threshold, which depends on the maximum probability of the states at this stage. This reduces the number of states without affecting the values, if the threshold is appropriately chosen.

Novak et al. (2003) suggest an even more aggressive pruning with their two-pass strategy. Instead of using the probabilities directly, they convert them to probabilities based on their rank. Thus, the probability space is bounded and the values of the best and worst state output probabilities remain the same for each time frame. Instead of computing the output probabilities, they simply take a single value from the tail of the ranked probability distribution. This is based on the approach described in Bahl et al. (1993) where the authors claim a speedup by a factor of 100.

There are many more attempts to simplify the computational effort of Viterbi search. Most of them try to replace multiplications by additions, which are faster to compute (Ming, 2003). Usually these attempts increase speed at the cost of accuracy and/or memory demands.

Lexical Decoding and Semantic Analysis

The result of the unit matching is a scoring for the different recognition hypotheses. The next two steps help to determine the word chain with the highest probability with respect to the constraints imposed by the language model. For word-based recognition with HMMs, the recognition process is finished at this point.

In the *lexical decoding* phase those paths are eliminated that do not have an existing word in the dictionary. In an alternative approach, using a so-called *statistical grammar*, the sequences are reduced a couple of phonemes in a row, for example, trigrams. The output of the latter case is a list of trigrams, ordered according to their probability. This is not suitable for isolated word recognition. The next step is *syntactic analysis,* where those paths are eliminated that do not match an allowed sequence of words from the dictionary.

These steps do not require intensive computation except for fast memory access to the dictionary and the grammar. Again, smaller vocabularies offer a faster result and require less memory.

The word or utterance with the highest probability in the remaining list of possible utterances is taken as the recognition output.

HMM-based recognition is computationally intensive, but shows good results in isolated word recognition as well as continuous speech. If the HMM is trained well, it is also a suitable technology for speaker independent recognition.

Artificial Neural Networks

Artificial neural networks (ANN) is a method in computer science that is derived from the way the human brain works. The goal is to create a system that is able to learn and that can be used for pattern classification. More detailed information about ANN is given in the chapter "Socionics & Bionics: Learning from 'The Born.'" The use of ANN for classification and their use in speech recognition can be found in the literature, for example, Cholet (1999).

Expectations were very high when ANNs were discovered as a means for speech recognition. Modelling of speech recognition by artificial neural networks doesn't require *a priori* knowledge of the speech process and this technique quickly became an attractive alternative to HMM (Amrouche, 2006).

Neural nets tend to be better than HMMs for picking out discrete words, but they require extensive training up front [see Kumagai (2002)].

An output of an artificial neuron (see the chapter "*Socionics & Bionics: Learning from 'The Born'*") in multi-layer perceptron (MLP) networks is computed via

$$f_z = \sum_{i=1}^{n} w_i x_i \tag{3}$$

There is nearly no optimization to reduce the large amount of calculations that have to be done to compute the output of a complex multilayer perceptron. The good point is that there are only additions and multiplications. The bad point is that there are too many of them, which makes it unusable on devices with a lower CPU frequency. A way out of this dilemma is the use of proprietary hardware, as used in hardware-based speech recognition, consult the section "Hardware-Based Speech Recognition".

Nowadays ANNs play a minor role in continuous speech recognition, but are still used in hybrid architectures with HMM-based recognition. In contrast to HMMs, which try to achieve their goal based on statistical and probability models, ANNs deal with classification. They are able to classify a given pattern into phonemes, but are not ideal for the processing of continuous speech. This means that neural networks are used as a replacement for various pieces of a HMM-based recognizer. This is more a philosophical difference with little relevance to use in embedded environments.

As an example of such a network, we look at the multilayer perceptron developed by Bourlard (1992). This network has nine 26-dimensional feature vectors to compute 61 phonemes with 500-4000 neurons in a hidden layer. It allows computing the a posteriori probability $p(q_k|x)$. The Viterbi algorithm requires $p(x_i|q_k)$, which can be guessed using the Bayes theorems via

$$p(x_i \mid q_k) = \frac{p(q_k \mid o_T)p(o_T)}{p(q_k)} \tag{4}$$

where $p(o_T)$ can be treated as a constant for all classes and $p(q_k)$ is the frequency distribution of all phonemes, which is known in advance.

FUTURE RESEARCH DIRECTIONS

This chapter gave an overview of the challenges of implementing speech recognition on mobile devices. None of the architectures is ideal in all aspects. Most researchers in speech recognition hope that embedded devices will become powerful enough to have enough performance running off-the-shelf speech recognizers on embedded devices. However, this attitude does not solve the problems that users have if they want to use speech recognition today.

Currently, there are two main approaches to enabling speech recognition on future mobile devices. The first one is followed by hardware engineers who are trying to improve the performance of embedded devices. The development of better hardware will not be able to solve all the challenges in a short time, but will at least address some of them. One aspect is the lack of support for floating point arithmetic, which is also present for rendering of graphical interfaces. Others, like limited memory capacity, will persist. Evolution in recognition performance currently entails a shorter battery life. This is where research in the domain of electrical engineering is required. An alternative is presented by streaming technologies like MRCP that are increasingly used, for example, on mobile phones. Here, standards are needed that allow the distribution of mass data over a wireless connection, or better reduce the traffic.

The second approach is research in speech recognition, looking for tricks to enable speech recognition on these devices with limited capabilities. Advancements in recognition technology are needed too to overcome the challenges. The current approaches have the drawback that they are accompanied by a loss of precision. Here we need better strategies.

The first steps have been taken, but more work is needed to make the vision of voice input on embedded devices come true.

SUMMARY

There are multiple architectures and technologies for implementing speech recognition on mobile devices. They can be divided into *service dependent speech recognition* and *device inherent speech recognition*. Service dependent architectures require a service running on the network to move the computational burden from the client. These architectures offer the same potential as desktop speech recognition at the cost of environmental dependencies. Speech recognition on the device is independent of services running on the network, but pose high computational effort to the mobile device.

This is also the main reason why the speech recognition parameters of service dependent speech recognition cannot be determined exactly. They depend on the technology used on the server side, resulting in full network dependency and high server load. The values of the additional parameters for UC are generally worse than those for device inherent speech recognition.

The required network bandwidth is better for DSR than for the streaming architectures, since it aims at reducing the transmitted data. As a consequence, transmission degradation and server load is slightly better.

HMM and ANN based recognizers offer the greatest flexibility and have the best scores for the parameters of speech recognition systems. This is the main reason why service dependent speech recognition performs better in that area.

The transducer is in all cases a noise-canceling microphone. Thus SNR is not a crucial factor.

Implemented on the device, these technologies require too many resources to achieve the same performance as their counterparts on the server. This results in smaller vocabularies, smaller

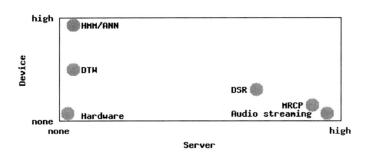

Figure 24. Distribution of computational resources

models and lower perplexity. They have generally a lower recognition rate than server implementations. In addition, implementations may not have real time capabilities, resulting in a low scoring for responsiveness. The decisive factor is the use of computational resources.

Figure 24 gives a graphical representation of how the type of architecture influences the distributed use of computational resources on the device and on the server.

Hardware-based speech recognition seems to be an appropriate candidate to enable speech recognition on mobile devices, but its rigidity makes it impossible to address multiple application scenarios. Thus it has the worst value for integration and maintenance. DTW requires fewer resources on the device than HMM or ANN, but is highly speaker dependent. It requires enrollment, and supports only isolated word-based recognition, which makes it unusable for certain scenarios.

This analysis can serve as a decision criterion for the architecture to implement or to use. None of the architectures is ideal in all contexts. Especially server dependent architectures require a higher invest, hampering their use in enterprise applications.

REFERENCES

Bahl, L.R., Genneraro, S.V., Gopalakrishnan, P.S., & Mercer, R.L. (1993). A fast approximate acoustic match for large vocabulary speech recognition. *IEEE Transactions on Speech and Audio Processing, 1*(1), 59-67.

Bailey, A. (2004). *Challenges and opportunities for interaction on mobile devices* (Tech. Rep.). Canon Research Centre Europe Ltd.

Bourlard, H., Morgan, N., Wooters, C., & Renals, S. (1992). CDNN: A Context Dependent Neural Network for Continuous Speech Recognition. In *Proceedings of IEEE International Conference on Acoustics, Speech and Signal Processing* (Vol. 2, pp. 349-352).

Chollet, G. (Ed.). (1999). *Speech processing, recognition and artificial neural networks*. Berlin: Springer.

Cohen, J. (2004). Is embedded speech recognition disruptive technology? *Information Quarterly, 3*(5), 14–16.

Delaney, B., Jayant, N., Hans, M., Simunic, T., & Acquaviva, A. (2002). A low-power, fixed-point, front-end feature extraction for a distributed speech recognition system. In *Proceedings of the IEEE International Conference on Acoustics, Speech and Signal Processing* (Vol. 1, pp. 793-796).

Eagle, G. (1999, June/July). Software-only vs. embedded: Which architecture is best for you? *Speech Technology Magazine.*

Frostad, K. (2003, April). The state of embedded speech. *Speech Technology Magazine.*

Huggins-Daines, D., Kumar, M., Chan, A., Black, A., Ravishankar, M., & Rudnicky, A. (2005). *Pocketsphinx: A free, real-time continuous speech recognition system for hand-held devices* (Tech. Rep.). Carnegie Mellon University.

Jelinek, F. (2001). *Statistical methods for speech recognition* (3rd ed.). Cambridge, MA: MIT Press.

Junqua, J.-C. (2000). *Robust speech recognition in embedded system and PC applications.* Norwell, MA: Kluwer Academic Publishers.

Kumagai, J. (2002, September 9). Talk to the machine. *IEEE Spectrum Online.*

Lowerre, B. (1976). *The HARPY speech recognition system.* Unpublished doctoral dissertation, Dept. of Computer Science, Carnegie-Mellon University, Pittsburgh, PA, USA.

Mathew, B.K., Davis, A., & Fang, Z. (2002, November 11). *A Gaussian probability accelerator for SHINX 3* (Tech. Rep. No. UUCS-03-02). Salt Lake City, UT: University of Utah.

Ming, L.Y. (2003). *An optimization framework for fixed-point digital signal processing.* Unpublished master's thesis, The Chinese University of Hong Kong.

Novak, M., Hampl, R., Krbec, P., Bergl, V., & Sedivy, J. (2003). Two-pass search strategy for large list recognition on embedded speech recognition platforms. In *Proceedings of the 2003 IEEE International Conference on Acoustics, Speech, and Signal Processing* (Vol. 1, pp. 200–203).

Pearce, D. (2000a, May 5). *Enabling new speech driven series for mobile devices: An overview of the ETSI standard activities for distributed speech recognition front-ends* (Tech. Rep.). Motorola Labs.

Pearce, D. (2000b, May 5). Enabling new speech driven services for mobile devices: An overview of the ETSI standard activities for distributed speech recognition front-ends. *AVIOS 2000: The Speech Applications Conference,* San Jose, CA, USA.

Rabiner, L.R. (1989, February 2). A tutorial on hidden Markov models and selected applications in speech recognition. *Proceedings of the IEEE, 77*(2), 257–286.

Rabiner, L.R. (1997). Applications of speech recognition to the area of telecommunications. In *Proceedings of the IEEE Workshop on Automatic Speech Recognition and Understanding* (pp. 501-510).

Rabiner, L.R., & Juang, B.-H. (1993). *Fundamentals of speech recognition.* Prentice Hall PTR.

Sakoe, H., & Chiba, S. (1990). Dynamic programming algorithm optimization for spoken word recognition. A.Waibel & K.-F. Lee (Eds.), *Readings in speech recognition* (pp. 159–165). Morgan Kaufmann Publishers, Inc.

Schukat-Talamazzini, E.G.(1995). *Automatische spracherkennung.*

Schulzrinne, H., Rao, A., & Lanphier, R. (1998, April 4). *Real time streaming protocol.* Retrieved May 19, 2006, from http://www.rfc-archive.org/getrfc.php?rfc=2326. Shanmugham, S., Monaco, P., & Eberman, B. (2006, April 4). *A media resource control protocol (MRCP).* Retrieved from http://www.rfc-archive.org/getrfc. php?rfc=4463.

Zaykobskiy, D. (2006). Survey of the speech recognition techniques for mobile devices. In *Proceedings of the 11th International Conference on Speech and Computer*, St. Petersburg, Russia.

ADDITIONAL READING

Amrouche, A., & Rouvaen, J. M. (2006). Efficient system for speech recognition using general regression neural network. *International Journal of Intelligent Technology, 1*(2), 183–189.

Burke, D. (2007). *Speech processing for IP networks: Media resource control protocol (MRCP)*. Wiley & Sons.

Chollet, G., DiBenedetto, G., Esposito, A., & Benedetto, G.D. (1999). *Speech processing, recognition and artificial neural networks*. Springer.

Chugh, J., & Jagannathan, V. (2002). Voice-Enabling Enterprise Applications. In *Proceedings of the 11th IEEE International Workshops on Enabling Technologies* (pp. 188–189). Washington, DC: IEEE Computer Society.

Digital speech: Coding for low bit rate communication systems. (1994). John Wiley & Sons, Ltd.

Dynkin, E.B. (2006). *Theory of Markov processes*. Dover Publications.

IEEE (Ed.). (1999). *Speech coding for telecommunications 1999 IEEE workshop*. IEEE Press.

Held, G. (2002). *Voice and data internetworking. Voice over IP gateways*. McGraw-Hill Professional.

Jurafsky, D., & Martin, J. H. (2000). *Speech and language processing: An introduction to natural language processing, computational linguistics and speech recognition*. New Jersey: Prentice Hall.

Jurafsky, D., & Martin, J.H. (2003). *Speech and language processing: An introduction to natural language processing, computational linguistics and speech recognition*. Prentice Hall.

Kahrs, M., & Brandenburg, K. (Eds.). (1998). *Applications of digital signal processing to audio and acoustics*. Springer-Verlag.

Loizou, P.C. (2007). *Speech enhancement: Theory and practice*. Taylor & Francis Ltd.

Manning, C., & Schütze, H. (1999). *Foundations of statistical natural language processing*. Cambridge, MA: MIT Press.

Minker, W., & Bennacef, S. (2004). *Speech and human-machine dialog*. Springer US.

Nakagawa, S., Okada, M., & Kawahara, T. (Eds.). (2005). *Spoken language systems*. IOS Press.

Niemann, H. (1990). *Pattern analysis and understanding*. Springer-Verlag.

Novak, M., Hampl, R., Krbec, P., Bergl, V., & Sedivy, J. (2003). Two-pass search strategy for large list recognition on embedded speech recognition platforms. *Proceedings of the IEEE International Conference on Acoustics, Speech and Signal Processing* (Vol. 1, pp. 200–203).

Oppenheim, A.V., Schafer, R.W., & Buck, J.R. (1999). *Discrete-time signal processing*. Prentice Hall.

Sieworik, D.P. (2001, September 9). *Mobile access to information: Wearable and context aware computers* (Tech. Rep.). Carnegie Mellon University.

Waibel, A., & Lee, K.-F. (Eds.). (1990). *Readings in speech recognition*. Morgan Kaufmann Publishers, Inc.

Wang, Y., Li, J., & Stoica, P. (2005). *Spectral analysis of signals: The missing data case.* Morgan & Claypool Publishers.

William R.G., & Mammen, E.W. (1975). *The art of speaking made simple.* London: Doubleday.

Chapter 8.19
Voice-Enabled User Interfaces for Mobile Devices

Louise E. Moser
University of California, Santa Barbara, USA

P. M. Melliar-Smith
University of California, Santa Barbara, USA

ABSTRACT

The use of a voice interface, along with textual, graphical, video, tactile, and audio interfaces, can improve the experience of the user of a mobile device. Many applications can benefit from voice input and output on a mobile device, including applications that provide travel directions, weather information, restaurant and hotel reservations, appointments and reminders, voice mail, and e-mail. We have developed a prototype system for a mobile device that supports client-side, voice-enabled applications. In fact, the prototype supports multimodal interactions but, here, we focus on voice interaction. The prototype includes six voice-enabled applications and a program manager that manages the applications. In this chapter we describe the prototype, including design issues that we faced, and evaluation methods that we employed in developing a voice-enabled user interface for a mobile device.

INTRODUCTION

Mobile devices, such as cell phones and personal digital assistants (PDAs), are inherently small, and lack an intuitive and natural user interface. The small keyboards and displays of mobile devices make it difficult for the user to use even the simplest of applications. Pen input is available on PDAs, but is difficult to use on handheld devices.

Voice input and output for mobile devices with small screens and keyboards, and for hands- and eyes-free operation, can make the user's interaction with a mobile device more user friendly. Voice input and output can also facilitate the use of Web Services (Booth, Hass, McCabe, Newcomer, Champion, Ferris, & Orchard, 2004) from a mobile device, making it possible to access the Web anytime and anywhere, whether at work, at home, or on the move. Global positioning system (GPS) technology (U.S. Census Bureau, 2006) can provide location information automatically for location-aware services.

Many everyday applications can benefit from voice-enabled user interfaces for a mobile device. Voice input and voice output for a mobile device are particularly useful for:

- Booking theater and sports tickets, making restaurant and hotel reservations, and carrying out banking and other financial transactions
- Accessing airline arrival and departure information, weather and traffic conditions, maps and directions for theaters, restaurants, gas stations, banks, and hotels, and the latest news and sports scores
- Maintaining personal calendars; contact lists with names, addresses, and telephone numbers; to-do lists; and shopping lists
- Communicating with other people via voice mail, e-mail, short message service (SMS), and multimedia message service (MMS).

It is important to provide several modes of interaction, so that the user can use the most appropriate mode, depending on the application and the situation. The prototype system that we have developed supports client-side, voice-enabled applications on a mobile device. Even though the applications support multimodal input, allowing keyboard and pen input, we focus, in this chapter, on voice input and on multimodal output in the form of voice, text, and graphics. The prototype includes a program manager that manages the application programs, and six voice-enabled applications, namely, contacts, location, weather, shopping, stocks, and appointments and reminders.

BACKGROUND

A multimodal interface for a mobile device integrates textual, graphical, video, tactile, speech, and/or other audio interfaces in the mobile device (Hjelm, 2000; Oviatt & Cohen, 2000). With multiple ways for a user to interact with the applications, interactions with the device become more natural and the user experience is improved. Voice is becoming an increasingly important mode of interaction, because it allows eyes- and hands-free operation. It is essential for simplifying and expanding the use of handheld mobile devices. Voice has the ability to enable mobile communication, mobile collaboration, and mobile commerce (Sarker & Wells, 2003), and is becoming an important means of managing mobile devices (Grasso, Ebert, & Finin, 1998; Kondratova, 2005).

The increasing popularity of, and technological advancements in, mobile phones and PDAs, primarily mobile phones, is leading to the development of applications to fulfill expanding user needs. The short message service (SMS) is available on most mobile phones today, and some mobile phones provide support for the multimedia messaging service (MMS) to exchange photos and videos (Le Bodic, 2002). The mobile phone manufacturers are no longer focused on making a mobile phone but, rather, on producing a mobile device that combines phone capabilities with the power of a handheld PC. They recognize that the numeric keypad and the small screen, common to mobile phones of the past, do not carry over well to handheld PCs (Holtzblatt, 2005).

With the emergence of Web Services technology (Booth et al., 2004), the Web now provides services, rather than only data as it did in the past. Of the various Web Services available to mobile users today, the map application seems to be the most popular, with online map services available from Google (2006) and Yahoo! (2006b). Much progress has been made in creating the multimodal Web, which allows not only keyboard and mouse navigation but also voice input and output (Frost, 2005).

GPS technology (U.S. Census Bureau, 2006) already exists on many mobile devices, and can be used to provide location-aware services (Rao

& Minakakis, 2003), without requiring the user to input geographical coordinates, again contributing to user friendliness.

Speech recognition technology (Rabiner & Juang, 1993) has been developed over many years, and is now very good. Other researchers (Kondratova, 2004; Srinivasan & Brown, 2002) have discussed the usability and effectiveness of a combination of speech and mobility. Currently, handheld voice-enabled applications use short commands that are translated into functional or navigational operations. As observed in Deng and Huang (2004), speech recognition technology must be robust and accurate, and close to human ability, to make its widespread use a reality. Noisy environments present a particular challenge for the use of speech recognition technology on mobile devices and, therefore, multimodal interactions are essential. For example, the MiPad system (Deng, Wang, Acero, Hon, Droppo, Boulis, et al., 2002; Huang, Acero, Chelba, Deng, Droppo, Duchene, Goodman, et al., 2001) uses a strategy where the user first taps a "tap & talk" button on the device and then talks to the device.

Distributed speech recognition (Deng, et al., 2002), in which the speech recognition happens at a remote server exploits the power of the server to achieve fast and accurate speech recognition. However, studies (Zhang, He, Chow, Yang, & Su, 2000) have shown that low-bandwidth connections to the server result in significant degradation of speech recognition quality. In contrast, *local speech recognition* (Deligne, Dharanipragada, Gopinath, Maison, Olsen, & Printz, 2002; Varga, Aalburg, Andrassy, Astrov, Bauer, Beaugeant, Geissler, & Hoge, 2002) utilizes speech recognition technology on the mobile device, and eliminates the need for high-speed communication. Local speech recognition limits the kinds of client handsets that are powerful enough to perform complicated speech processing and, thus, that can be used; however, the computing power of mobile handsets is increasing.

THE PROTOTYPE

The prototype that we have developed allows mobile applications to interact with the user without the need for manual interaction on the part of the human. Speech recognition and speech synthesis software are located on the mobile device, and make the interaction with the human more user friendly. The prototype that we have developed processes natural language sentences and provides useful services while interacting with the user in an intuitive and natural manner. A user need not form a request in a particular rigid format in order for the applications to understand what the user means.

For our prototype, we have developed six application programs and a Program Manager. These applications are Contacts, Location, Weather, Shopping, Stocks, and Appointments and Reminders applications. The Program Manager evaluates sentence fragments from the user's request, determines which application should process the request, and forwards the request to the appropriate application.

The prototype is designed to interact with a human, using voice as the primary means of input (keyboard, stylus, and mouse are also available but are less convenient to use) and with voice, text, and graphics as the means of output. The speech recognizer handles the user's voice input, and both the speech synthesizer and the display are used for output. Characteristics of certain applications render a pure voice solution infeasible. For example, it is impossible to convey the detailed contents of a map through voice output. However, voice output is ideal when it is inconvenient or impossible for the user to maintain visual contact with the display of the mobile device, and it is possible to convey information to the user in that mode. Voice output is also appropriate when the device requests confirmation from the user.

Thus, an appropriate choice of speech recognition and speech synthesis technology is vital to the success of our prototype. Our choices were constrained by:

- The processing and memory capabilities of typical mobile devices
- The need for adaptability to different users and to noisy environments

The use of speech recognition and speech synthesis technology on a mobile device is different from its use in call centers, because a mobile device is associated with a single user and can learn to understand that particular user.

The Underlying Speech Technology

The prototype uses SRI's DynaSpeak speech recognition software (SRI, 2006) and AT&T's Natural Voices speech synthesis software (AT&T, 2006). It currently runs on a handheld computer, the OQO device (OQO, 2006). We chose this device, rather than a cell phone, because it provides a better software development environment than a cell phone.

Speech Recognition

The DynaSpeak speech recognition engine (SRI, 2006) is a small-footprint, high-accuracy, speaker-independent speech recognition engine. It is based on a statistical language model that is suitable for natural language dialog applications. It includes speaker adaptation to increase recognition accuracy for individuals with different accents or tone pitches. It can be configured so that it performs speech recognition specific to a particular individual. DynaSpeak is ideal for handheld mobile devices, because of its small footprint (less than 2 MB of memory) and its low computing requirements (66 MHz Intel x86 or 200 MHz Strong Arm processor).

DynaSpeak supports multiple languages, adapts to different accents, and does not require training prior to use. It incorporates a Hidden

Markov Model (HMM) (Rabiner & Juang, 1993). In an HMM, a spoken expression is detected as a sequence of phonemes with a probability associated with each phoneme. A probability is also associated with each pair of phonemes, that is, the probability that the first phoneme of the pair is followed by the second phoneme in natural speech. As a sequence of phonemes is processed, the probability of each successive phoneme is combined with the transition probabilities provided by the HMM. If the probability of a path through the HMM is substantially greater than that of any other path, the speech recognizer recognizes the spoken expression with a high level of confidence. When the response is below an acceptable confidence threshold, the software seeks confirmation from the user or asks the user questions.

The HMM is augmented with grammars for the particular applications that are required for understanding natural language sentences (Knight, Gorrell, Rayner, Milward, Koeling, & Lewin, 2001). When the user says a new word, the word can be added to the vocabulary dynamically. The HMM is also extended by adapting the vocabulary of the speech recognizer to the current and recent past context of interactions of the user with the applications.

Accuracy of the speech recognition system can be increased by training it for the voice of the particular user. There are two kinds of training, explicit and implicit. *Explicit training* requires the user to read a lengthy script to the device, a process that is likely to be unpopular with users. *Implicit training* allows the device to learn to understand better its particular user during normal use. Implicit training can be provided in two modes, confirmation mode and standard mode.

In *confirmation mode*, the system responds to a user's sentence, and the user confirms or corrects the response. If the user corrects the sentence, the learning algorithm tries to match a rejected, lower probability, interpretation of the original sentence with the user's corrected intent. If a match is found, the learning algorithm adjusts the HMM transition probabilities to increase the probability of selecting the user's intent. Initially, a new user of the system will probably prefer confirmation mode.

In *standard mode*, the system does not confirm sentences for which there is one interpretation that has a much higher probability than any other interpretation. If no interpretation has a high probability, or if several interpretations have similar probabilities, the speech recognition system responds as in confirmation mode. More experienced users of the system are likely to use standard mode.

The success of implicit training strategies depends quite heavily on starting with a speech recognizer that is well matched to the individual speaker. It is possible, from relatively few sentences, to classify a speaker and then to download, to the mobile device, an appropriate initial recognizer for subsequent implicit training.

DynaSpeak can be used with either a *finite-state grammar* or a *free-form grammar*. We used the finite-state grammar because it offers greater control over parsed sentences. The tendency for DynaSpeak to accept or reject spoken sentences is heavily influenced by the complexity of the grammar. The *complexity of the grammar* is quantified by the number of paths by which an accepting state can be reached. The greater the complexity of the grammar, the higher is its tendency to accept an invalid spoken request. Conversely, the lower the complexity of the grammar, the higher is its tendency to reject a valid spoken request. To minimize the complexity of the grammar and to improve speech recognition accuracy, each application has its own relatively simple grammar. The program manager determines which applications are involved in a sentence and then reparses the sentence using the appropriate grammars.

Speech Synthesis

Natural Voices (AT&T. 2006) is a speech synthesis engine that provides a simple and efficient way of producing natural (rather than electronic) sounding device-to-human voice interactions. It can accurately and naturally pronounce words and speak in sentences that are clear and easy to understand, without the feeling that it is a computer that is speaking.

Natural Voices supports many languages, male and female voices, and the VoiceXML, SAPI, and JSAPI interface standards. Using Natural Voices, we created text-to-speech software for our prototype that runs in the background and accepts messages in VoiceXML format. Each message contains the name of the voice engine (i.e., "Mike" for a male voice and "Crystal" for a female voice) and the corresponding text to speak.

Managed Applications

For the prototype we developed six multimodal applications (contacts, location, weather, shopping, stocks, appointments, and reminders) that use speech as the main form of input. The stocks, maps, and weather applications exploit existing Web Services on the Internet. Communication with those Web Services uses a local WiFi 802.11 wireless network. The program manager controls the operation of the applications. The graphical user interface for the program manager with the six applications is shown in Figure 1. We now present an explanation of the functionality of each application and its role in the overall system.

Contacts

The contacts application stores personal information regarding friends and acquaintances in a database, including their addresses and phone numbers. The contacts application is a mobile extension of a physical contact list or address book that is controlled by voice input. It retrieves data from Microsoft Office Outlook® to populate the database when in docking mode. After using the mobile device and possibly entering new contact information, the user can synchronize informa-

Figure 1. The GUI of the program manager, showing six applications

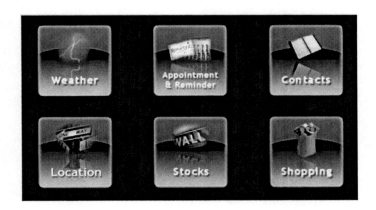

tion on the mobile device with that on a desktop or server computer. The contacts application is configured to interact with other applications that require information about names, addresses, phone numbers, and so forth. The contacts grammar is the least complex of the application grammars that we developed. The contacts vocabulary grows linearly as contacts are added to the user's contact list.

Location

The Location application allows the user to search for restaurants, movie theaters, banks, and so forth, in a given area, using the Yahoo! LocalSearch Web Service (2006b). For example, if the user says to the mobile device "Search for a Mexican restaurant in 95131," the location application on the mobile device sends a Web Service request to Yahoo! LocalSearch, gets back the results, and presents up to 10 results to the user in list form. The user can then view additional information about a single location by indicating the location's number in the presented list. For example, the user can choose to view additional information about

"Chacho's Mexican Restaurant" by speaking, "Get more information about number one." On processing this request, the location application presents the user with detailed information about the restaurant including its phone number, address, and a detailed street map showing its location. Figure 2 shows a screen shot of the graphical user interface for the location application.

The location application is loosely coupled with the contacts application to provide responses related to individuals listed in the user's contact list. For example, the request, "Search for a movie theater around Susan's house" uses the contacts grammar to determine the location of Susan's house and replaces the phrase "Susan's house" with the specific address so that the actual search request looks something like this: "Search for a movie theater around 232 Kings Way, Goleta, CA, 93117." The location application then searches for a movie theater in the vicinity of that address.

The location application is also loosely coupled with a GPS module that is contacted when the user has a question related to the user's current location. For example, if the user says "Look for a pizza place around here.", the word "here" is

Figure 2. An example graphical user interface for the location application

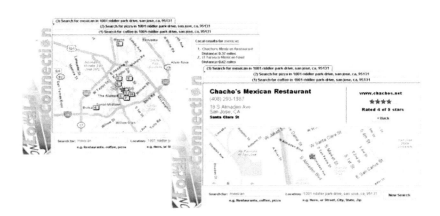

recognized by the application and replaced with the GPS coordinates of the user's current location. The location application then sends a Web Service request to Yahoo! LocalSearch, which returns a map of the user's current location, indicating where the user is, along with the 10 nearest pizza places. The Yahoo! LocalSearch Web Service is ideal to use with GPS because of its ability to locate positions on the map on the basis of longitude and latitude. With GPS, the user is no longer limited to requests involving a particular city or zip code. The user now has the ability to create requests that are truly location-aware.

Compared to the grammars of the other applications, the location grammar is one of the most complex. For information like maps and lists, it is desirable to use a graphical or textual display, as well as speech output, in a multimodal user interface. Thus, the most appropriate kind of output can be chosen, depending on the kind of information, the capabilities of the mobile device, and the context in which the user finds himself or herself.

Weather

The weather application supplies weather forecasts obtained from the Web Service provided by the National Weather Service (NOAA, 2006). It allows the user to query for weekly, daily, and 3-day weather information in major U.S. cities using voice input. It allows the user either to select a city or to use the user's current location, as the location for which the weather forecast is to be retrieved from the National Weather Service. The weather application knows the geographical coordinates of dozens of cities in the continental United States. It references those coordinates when the user requests a weather forecast from the National Weather Service for one of those cities.

A user can say "Tell me the weather forecast in San Jose," which then uses "today" as the starting time of the forecast, and produces the graphical user interface for the weather application shown in Figure 3.

Because the weather application operates on a mobile device, it is necessary to be able to deter-

Figure 3. An example graphical user interface for the weather application

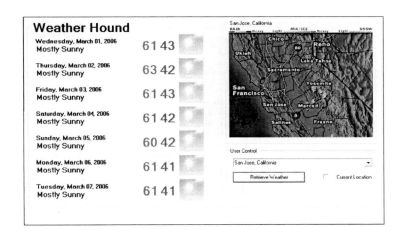

mine the user's location dynamically. If the user asks "What's the weather like here two days from now?", the weather application consults the GPS module to obtain the geographical coordinates of the user, contacts the Web Service, and responds with the high and low predicted temperatures and an indication that there is a change to cloudy in Santa Barbara. Thus, the user does not need to provide his/her current location or to obtain the weather forecast for that location.

Our prototype takes into account the many ways in which a person can convey, semantically, equivalent requests in English. For example, a user can ask for the weather in many ways including "What is the weather in Boston like?" or "Tell me what the forecast is like in Boston." These two requests are semantically equivalent because they both contain the same essential parameter, namely the Boston location.

Shopping

The shopping application provides the user with a service capable of reducing the time that the user

spends on grocery shopping and the associated stress. The shopping application maintains shopping lists, recipes, and floor plans of supermarkets. The multimodal interface includes speech, text, and graphics, which makes the shopping application easy to use. Figure 4 shows a screen shot of the graphical user interface for the shopping application.

The shopping application allows a user to update his/her shopping list and to forward it to another user. When a user issues a command, like "Remind John to go grocery shopping," the contacts application is used to find John's phone number or e-mail address in the user's contact list. A dialog box then appears asking the user if he/she wants to send, to John, not only a reminder to go shopping but also the shopping list. If so, the shopping list, consisting of the product ids and the quantities of the items needed, is formatted in XML, and appended to the message containing the reminder. The message is then sent to John's shopping application.

The shopping application also displays graphically the floor plan of the supermarket and the

Figure 4. An example graphical user interface for the shopping application

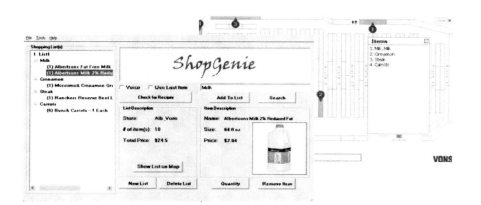

location of items in the store, as shown in Figure 4. This feature provides assistance to the user without the need for the user to contact an employee of the supermarket. The shopping application also allows the user to retrieve recipes while shopping, possibly on impulse, for an item that is on sale. A newly chosen recipe is cross-referenced with the current shopping list, so that needed items can be added automatically. The shopping application has the largest grammar of the applications that we developed, with a vocabulary that depends on the items that the user has purchased recently.

Stocks

The stocks application allows the user to manage his/her stock portfolio using voice input and output. The objective of the stocks application is to monitor stock fluctuations, rather than to trade stocks. The stocks application exploits the Yahoo! Finance Web service (2006a) to store and update stock information in a database. It stores the most recent stock information in the database so that it can reply to the user's requests when connectivity

to the Yahoo! Finance Web Service is limited. Although such stored data can be somewhat stale, it allows the user to obtain information whenever the user requests it. The vocabulary of the stocks application grows to match the user's portfolio each time the user adds a new stock.

Appointments and Reminders

The appointments and reminders application manages the user's calendar and allows the user to send reminders to other people. It supports time-based requests of various forms, for example, "Remind me to go to the dentist on Monday," "Remind me to see the dentist on August 15th," and "Remind me to see the dentist a week from today." It displays an easily readable schedule, so that the user can recall what is planned for the day. The appointments and reminders application interacts with other applications, such as the shopping application. For example, the request "Remind John to go shopping on Monday" sends a reminder to John, along with the current shopping list, if the user wishes to forward that information. It also supports

Figure 5. An example graphical user interface for the stocks application

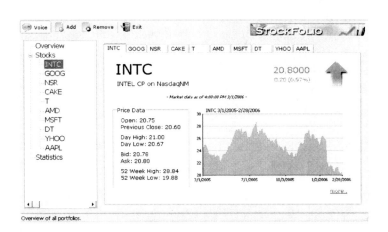

reminders to the user that are location-aware using GPS, for example, if the user is in the vicinity of a supermarket. The appointments and reminders application is an extension of a calendar service. It links to Microsoft Office Outlook®, and updates scheduled appointments and reminders when in the vicinity of the user's desktop.

Program Manager

The program manager evaluates sentence fragments from a user's request, identifies keywords that determine which application or applications should process the request, reparses the sentence using the grammars for those applications, and forwards the parsed request to the appropriate application. If more than one user is involved, the program manager on one user's mobile device sends messages to the program manager on another user's mobile device, which then handles the request.

The program manager leverages DynaSpeak and a weighted keyword recognition algorithm to break down recognized sentences into ap-

plication-specific fragments. Those fragments are then processed by the appropriate applications, and are subsequently merged to form the final sentence meaning. This process allows the program manager to handle requests that involve more than one application, for example, "Search for a gas station around Paul Green's house." The parsing of this sentence, using the location grammar, requests a search centered on a location that the location grammar cannot itself provide. The program manager must recognize a keyword from the contacts grammar, parse the sentence using that grammar, and query the contacts application for the address of Paul Green's house. The response to the query is then sent to the location application to obtain the location of the gas station nearest his house.

Graphical User Interface

The graphical user interface (GUI) of thepProgram manager, shown in Figure 1, displays the current running application programs and allows the user to select an application by using voice or keyboard input. The GUI provides buttons that appear gray when an application has not been started and blue after startup. If the user makes a spoken request that requires an application to display a result, the display for that application is topmost and remains topmost until the user issues another request or a timeout occurs. Whenever the GUI is displayed, the user must provide a keyword in a spoken request to wake up the program manager, or click on one of the application-specific buttons on the display.

EVALUATION

Several experiments were performed to collect qualitative and quantitative data to evaluate the prototype system. Although it is difficult to determine a clear boundary between the user interface and the speech recognizer, it is important to evaluate the user interface and the speech recognizer separately, so that the qualitative and quantitative data gathered from the experiments are not mixed, leading to inconclusive results.

Thus, the experiments were designed as a classical "Don't mind the man behind the curtain" study. In this type of study, the user interacts with a system that is identical to the actual system except that the experiment is being controlled by someone other than the user. The man behind the curtain controls what is spoken as responses to the user's requests and changes the current screen to an appropriate graphical response. This method was used, so that the responses to the qualitative questions would not be biased by the accuracy of the speech recognizer.

To evaluate the system quantitatively, the program manager was instrumented with time segment metrics and data were collected for several performance metrics, including:

- Total time a participant took to complete all tasks
- Overhead of the DynaSpeak speech recognizer during live and batch recognition
- Runtime overhead of the program manager without DynaSpeak
- Spoken length of a request vs. processing time

Figure 6. Processing overhead per task

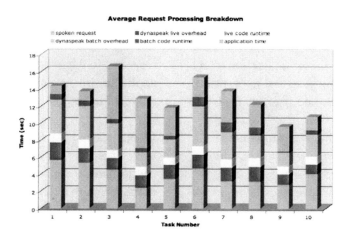

The results are shown in Figure 6. The time segment metrics represent the runtime complexity of the code associated with the speech recognition and processing. The amount of time taken by each segment adds to the delay associated with the user's request. If any of the time segments has a large duration, the user might become irritated. By measuring each segment separately, the bottleneck in the system can be determined.

The speech processing time increases with the size of the grammar. However, by means of a multiphase procedure that uses keywords organized and weighted by application relevance, the grammar size and the speech processing time can be improved. After live recognition, the system provides a keyword-associated request, which it processes for application weights and then reprocesses using an application-specific grammar, possibly more than once with different grammars. This procedure increases both the speed and the accuracy of the speech recognition, by decreasing the size of the grammar size in the initial phase.

An alternative approach (Kondratova, 2004) is to force the user to make repeated requests, possibly from a menu, with responses by which the device asks for the next step or for more information, so that the device arrives at a better understanding of the user's request. Such an approach introduces navigational complexity for the user. Reducing the speech processing time by creating a complex navigational structure is not the best way to improve usability of the system.

The speech recognizer works better for some speakers than for other speakers. The accuracy of the results can be improved by tuning the speech recognition parameters and enabling learning capabilities. However, the developers of DynaSpeak advise against modification of the speech recognition parameters and use of learning until a relatively high success rate is achieved. For appropriately selected users, quite good speech recognition and understanding can be achieved without using learning capabilities. However, speech recognition accuracy can only improve if voice profiling is combined with learning.

Ambient noise and microphone quality also affect speech recognition accuracy. The internal microphone in the OQO device is of rather poor quality. To ameliorate this problem, a Jabra© Bluetooth headset, was used to provide noise cancellation and reduce the distance between the microphone and the user's mouth. In addition, when the confidence score from DynaSpeak falls below an acceptable threshold, the program manager seeks confirmation from the user or asks for clarification. These mechanisms greatly improve the accuracy of the speech recognizer.

The accuracy of speech recognition is degraded when the grammar contains words that are phonetically similar. During preliminary experiments for the shopping application, we had problems recognizing differences between similar sounding requests like "Add lamb to my shopping list" and "Add ham to my shopping list." These problems arise particularly when users are non-native English speakers or when they have accents. Creating more specific requests can reduce the phonetic similarity, for example, by saying "Add a lamb shank to my shopping list" and "Add a ham hock to my shopping list." However, modifying requests in such a way is undesirable because the requests are then less intuitive and natural.

The location, weather, and stocks applications all use Web Services and require communication over the Internet and, thus, have longer application runtimes than the other Web Services. The location application is written in Java, which runs more slowly than C#. Both the weather application and the stocks application cache data associated with previous requests to take advantage of timing locality. Location requests are different because the caching of maps can involve a large usage of the memory, and users are not inclined to perform the same search twice. Memory is a precious commodity on a handheld device and needs to be conserved; thus, the location application is coded so that it does not cache maps resulting from previous queries.

To evaluate the qualitative aspects of the system, we performed a user study with participants from diverse backgrounds of education, ethnicity, and sex. The user study was completed with 10 individuals performing 10 tasks resulting in 100 request results. The participants were given a questionnaire that assessed their general impressions about the prototype, with the results shown in Table 1.

After analyzing the averaged responses of the participants, we found several trends. The participants' scores are not strongly correlated with speech recognition accuracy. Participant G gave the system a high score, but was one of the two participants who encountered the most speech recognition problems. Participant B gave the system a low score despite good speech recognition.

The participants agreed that speaking to a mobile handheld device as if it were a human is not comfortable. It is difficult to get used to interacting with a computer that can understand tasks that would be commonplace for humans. The participants were relatively pleased with the GUI interface design and felt the system is relatively easy to use. However, the ease-of-use metric needs to be taken lightly. Ease of use can be assessed more concretely by measuring the number of times a user must repeat a command.

The scores for response appropriateness and relevance are high, indicating that the spoken responses of the applications were well crafted. The scores related to recommending the service to friends and daily life helpfulness are relatively high, from which one might infer that the participants would purchase a device providing the speech-enabled applications. However, this conclusion is not necessarily justified. The participants were not enthusiastic about having to pay for such a device or for such services. However, most participants in the study were quite pleased with the prototype system and found the user interface helpful and easy to use.

Table 1. Responses to the questionnaire

Questions	A	B	C	D	E	F	G	H	I	J	Mean
Was it comfortable talking to the device as if it were a human?	3	3	4	3	4	3	4	5	3	5	3.7
Was the GUI aesthetically pleasing?	5	4	4	5	5	5	5	5	5	4	4.7
Were the request responses appropriate and easy to understand?	3	3	5	5	5	4	4	5	4	4	4.2
Were the spoken responses relevant to your requests?	5	4	5	5	5	3	4	5	4	5	4.5
Was the system easy to use?	4	5	3	4	4	5	4	5	4	5	4.3
Do you think the services would be helpful in your daily life?	4	4	4	5	4	4	4	4	4	5	4.2
Would you recommend a system like this to your friends?	3	3	4	5	4	4	5	5	4	5	4.2
Would you buy the software if it were available for your phone?	3	2	4	5	3	3	5	5	3	5	3.8

FUTURE TRENDS

Integration of multiple applications, and multiple grammars, is not too difficult for a small number of applications that have been designed and programmed to work together, as in our prototype. However, future systems will need to support tens or hundreds of applications, many of which will be designed and programmed independently. Integration of those applications and their grammars will be a challenge.

Currently, speech-enabled applications typically use short commands from the human that are translated into navigational or functional operations. More appropriate is speech recognition technology that supports a more natural, conversational style similar to what humans use to communicate with each other (McTear, 2002).

A mobile device that listens to its owner continuously can provide additional services, such as populating the user's calendar. For example, when a user agrees to an appointment during a conversation with another person, the mobile device might recognize and automatically record the appointment, possibly confirming the appointment later with its user. Similarly, the mobile device might note that the user habitually goes to lunch with the gang at noon on Mondays, or that the user leaves work promptly at 5pm on Fridays. With existing calendar systems, the user often does not record appointments and other commitments, because it is too much bother using the human interfaces of those systems, greatly reducing the value of the calendar.

A useful capability of speech recognition systems for mobile devices is being able to recognize intonation and emotional overtones. "The bus leaves at 6" is, overtly, a simple declaration, but appropriate intonation might convert that declaration into a question or an expression of disapproval. Existing speech recognition systems do not yet recognize and exploit intonation. Similarly, the ability to recognize emotional overtones of impatience, uncertainty, surprise, pleasure, anger, and so forth, is a valuable capability that existing speech recognition systems do not yet provide.

Speech recognition requires a relatively powerful processor. Typical cell phones contain a powerful digital signal processor (DSP) chip and a much less powerful control processor. The control processor operates continuously to maintain communication with the cellular base stations. The DSP processor uses a lot of power and imposes a significant drain on the battery and, thus, analyzes and encodes speech only during calls. The DSP processor is capable of the processing required for speech recognition, although it might need more memory.

For mobile devices, battery life is a problem, particularly when speech recognition or application software requires a powerful processor. The limit of 2 hours of talk time for a cell phone is caused at least as much by the power drain of the DSP processor as by the power needed for wireless transmission. The DSP processor might be needed for speech processing for more than 2 hours per day. There are several possible solutions to this problem, namely, larger batteries, alcohol fuel cells, and DSP processors with higher speeds, reduced power consumption, and better power management.

Background noise remains a problem for speech recognition systems for mobile devices, particularly in noisy environments. The quality of the microphone, and the use of a headset to decrease the distance between the microphone and the speaker's mouth, can improve speech recognition accuracy.

CONCLUSION

The use of voice input and output, in addition to text and graphics and other kinds of audio, video, and tactile interfaces, provides substantial benefits for the users of mobile devices. Such multimodal interfaces allow individuals to access information, applications, and services from their mobile devices more easily. A user no longer has to put up with the annoyances of a 3-inch keyboard, nested menus, or handwriting recognition, nor does the user need to have a tethered desktop or server computer in order to access information, applications, and services. Providing multiple ways in which the users can interact with the applications on mobile devices brings a new level of convenience to the users of those devices.

REFERENCES

AT&T. (2006). *Natural voices.* Retrieved from http://www.natural voices.att.com/products/

Booth, D., Hass, H., McCabe, F., Newcomer, E., Champion, M., Ferris, C., & Orchard, D. (2004). *Web services architecture.* Retrieved from http://www.w.3.org/Tr/WS-arch

Deligne, S., Dharanipragada, S., Gopinath, R., Maison, B., Olsen, P., & Printz, H. (2002). A robust high accuracy speech recognition system for mobile applications. *IEEE Transactions on Speech and Audio Processing, 10*(8), 551-561.

Deng, L., & Huang, X. (2004). Challenges in adopting speech recognition. *Communications of the ACM, 47*(1), 69-75.

Deng, L., Wang, K., Acero, A., Hon, H., Droppo, J., Boulis, C., Wang, Y., Jacoby, D., Mahajan, M., Chelba, C., & Huang, X. D. (2002). Distributed speech processing in MiPad's multimodal user interface. *IEEE Transactions on Speech and Audio Processing, 10*(8), 605-619.

Frost, R. A. (2005). Call for a public-domain SpeechWeb. *Communications of the ACM, 48*(11), 45-49.

Google. (2006). *Google Maps API.* Retrieved from http://www.google.com/apis/maps

Grasso, M. A., Ebert, D. S., & Finin, T. W. (1998). The integrality of speech in multi-modal interfaces. *ACM Transactions on Computer-Human Interaction, 5*(4), 303-325.

Hjelm, J. (2000). *Research applications in the mobile environment. Wireless information service.* New York, NY: John Wiley & Sons.

Holtzblatt, K. (2005). Designing for the mobile device: Experiences, challenges, and methods. *Communications of the ACM, 48*(7), 33-35.

Huang, X., Acero, A., Chelba, C., Deng, L., Droppo, J., Duchene, D., Goodman, J., Hon, H., Jacoby, D., Jiang, L., Loynd, R., Mahajan, J., Mau, P., Meredith, S., Mughal, S., Neto, S., Plumpe, M., Stery, K., Venolia, G., Wang, K., & Wang, Y. (2001). MiPad: A multimodal interaction prototype. In *Proceedings of the International Conference on Acoustics, Speech and Signal Processing, 1*, 9-12.

Knight, S., Gorrell, G., Rayner, M., Milward, D., Koeling, R., & Lewin, I. (2001). Comparing grammar-based and robust approaches to speech understanding: A case study. In *Proceedings of Eurospeech 2001, Seventh European Conference of Speech Communication and Technology* (pp. 1779-1782). Aalborg, Denmark.

Kondratova, I. (2004, August). Speech-enabled mobile field applications. In *Proceedings of the IASTED International Conference on Internet and Multimedia Systems*, Hawaii.

Kondratova, I. (2005, July). Speech-enabled handheld computing for fieldwork. In *Proceedings of the International Conference on Computing in Civil Engineering*, Cancun, Mexico.

Le Bodic, G. (2002). *Mobile messaging, SMS, EMS and MMS.* John Wiley & Sons.

McTear, M. (2002). Spoken dialogue technology: Enabling the conversational user interface. *ACM Computing Surveys, 34*(1), 90-169.

National Oceanic and Atmospheric Administration (NOAA). (2006). *National Weather Service.* Retrieved from http://www.weather.gov/xml/

OQO. (2006). *The OQO personal computer.* Retrieved from http://www.oqo.com

Oviatt, S., & Cohen, P. (2000). Multi-modal interfaces that process what comes naturally. *Communications of the ACM, 43*(3), 45-53.

Rabiner, L., & Juang, B. H. (1993). *Fundamentals of speech recognition.* Upper Saddle River, NJ: Prentice Hall.

Rao, B., & Minakakis, L. (2003). Evolution of mobile location-based services. *Communications of the ACM, 46*(12), 61-65.

Sarker, S., & Wells, J. D. (2003). Understanding mobile handheld device use and adoption. *Communications of the ACM, 46*(12), 35-40.

SRI (2006). *DynaSpeak.* Retrieved from http://www.speechatsri.com/products/sdk.shtml

Srinivasan, S., & Brown, E. (2002). Is speech recognition becoming mainstream?. *Computer Magazine,* (April), 38-41.

U.S. Census Bureau. (2006). *Precision of GPS.* Retrieved from http://www.census.gov/procur/www /fdca/library/mcd/7-29%20 MCD_WG_hardware_subteam_report.pdf

Varga, I., Aalburg, S., Andrassy, B., Astrov, S., Bauer, J. G., Beaugeant, C., Geissler, C., & Hoge, H. (2002). ASR in mobile phones—An industrial approach. *IEEE Transactions on Speech and Audio Processing, 10*(8), 562-569.

Yahoo! LocalSearch. (2006a). Retrieved from http://www.local.yahooapis.com/LocalSearch-Service/V3/localSearch

Yahoo! Finance. (2006b). Retrieved from http://finance.yahoo.com/rssindex

Zhang, W., He, Y., Chow, R., Yang, R., & Su, Y. (2000, June). The study on distributed speech recognition system. In *Proceedings of the IEEE International Conference on Acoustical Speech and Signal Processing* (pp. 1431–1434), Istanbul, Turkey.

KEY TERMS

Global Positioning System (GPS): A system that is used to obtain geographical coordinates, which includes a GPS satellite and a GPS receiver.

Hidden Markov Model (HMM): A technique, based on a finite state machine that associates probabilities with phonemes, and pairs of phonemes, that is used in speech recognition systems, to determine the likelihood of an expression spoken by a user of that system.

Location Aware: An application that is based on a particular physical location, as given by geographical coordinates, physical address, zip code, and so forth, that determines the output of the application.

Mobile Device: For the purposes of this chapter, a handheld device, such as a cell phone or personal digital assistant (PDA), that has an embedded computer and that the user can carry around.

Multimodal Interface: The integration of textual, graphical, video, tactile, speech, and other audio interfaces through the use of mouse, stylus, fingers, keyboard, display, camera, microphone, and/or GPS.

Speech Recognition: The process of interpreting human speech for transcription or as a method of interacting with a computer or a mobile device, using a source of speech input, such as a microphone.

Speech Synthesis: The artificial production of human speech. Speech synthesis technology is also called text-to-speech technology in reference to its ability to convert text into speech.

Web Service: A software application identified by a Uniform Resource Indicator (URI) that is defined, described, and discovered using the eXtensible Markup Language (XML) and that supports direct interactions with other software applications using XML-based messages via an Internet protocol.

This work was previously published in Handbook of Research on User Interface Design and Evaluation for Mobile Technology, edited by J. Lumsden, pp. 446-460, copyright 2008 by Information Science Reference, formerly known as Idea Group Reference (an imprint of IGI Global).

Chapter 8.20
Voice Driven Emotion Recognizer Mobile Phone:
Proposal and Evaluations

Aishah Abdul Razak
Multimedia University, Malaysia

Mohamad Izani Zainal Abidin
Multimedia University, Malaysia

Ryoichi Komiya
Multimedia University, Malaysia

ABSTRACT

This article proposes an application of emotion recognizer system in telecommunications entitled voice driven emotion recognizer mobile phone (VDERM). The design implements a voice-to-image conversion scheme through a voice-to-image converter that extracts emotion features in the voice, recognizes them, and selects the corresponding facial expression images from image bank. Since it only requires audio transmission, it can support video communication at a much lower bit rate than the conventional videophone. The first prototype of VDERM system has been implemented into a personal computer. The coder, voice-to-image converter, image database, and system interface are preinstalled in the personal computer. In this article, we present and discuss some evaluations that have been conducted in supporting this proposed prototype. The results have shown that both voice and image are important for people to correctly recognize emotion in telecommunications and the proposed solution can provide an alternative to videophone systems. The future works list some modifications that can be done to the proposed prototype in order to make it more practical for mobile applications.

INTRODUCTION AND MOTIVATION

Nonverbal communication plays a very important role in human communications (Komiya, Mohd Arif, Ramliy, Gowri, & Mokhtar, 1999). However, in telephone systems, only audio information can be exchanged. Thus, using telephony, the transmission of nonverbal information such as one's emotion would depend mostly on the user's conversation skills. Although the importance of nonverbal aspects of communication has been recognized, until now most research on nonverbal information concentrated on image transmission such as transmission of facial expression and gesture using video signal. This has contributed to the emergence of a videophone system, which is one of the most preferred ways to exchange more information in communication. Such services, however, require a wide bandwidth in order to provide real time video that is adequate for a natural conversation. This is often either very expensive to provide or difficult to implement. Besides, in a videophone system, the user has to be fixed in front of the camera at the correct position during the conversation, so that the user's image can be captured and transmitted correctly. This limitation does not happen in the normal telephone system.

Another approach is to use model-based coding (Kidani, 1999). In this approach, instead of transmitting video signals containing an image of the user, only the human action data such as the facial expressions, movement of the mouth, and so on acquired using a microphone, a keypad, and other input devices, are transmitted over the network. When these data are received by the receiver, the polygon coordinate data for each facial feature is recalculated in accordance with the displacement rules and the person's expression is synthesized.

Our approach is similar to the second approach in a sense that a synthesize image is used for the facial expression reconstruction at the receiver side. However, the difference is that only voice is transmitted and the emotion data is extracted from the received voice tone at the receiving side. This is based on the idea that, voice, besides for communication, it is also an indicator of the psychological and physiological state of a speaker.

The identification of the pertinent features in the speech signal may therefore allow the evaluation of a person's emotional state. In other words, by extracting the emotion information from the voice of the speaker, it is possible to reconstruct the facial expression of that speaker. Thus, based on this voice-to-image conversion scheme, we propose a new system known as voice driven emotion recognizer mobile phone (VDERM), as seen in Figure 1. This system uses a voice-to-image converter system at the receiver side that identifies the emotional state of the received voice signal and selects the corresponding facial expression of that particular emotion from the image bank to be displayed. Using this approach, only audio transmission is required. Therefore, the existing second generation (2G) mobile phone infrastructures can be used. Another advantage is that the user does not need to be fixed in front of the camera during the conversation because there is no need for image transmission.

VOICE TO IMAGE CONVERSION

Referring to Figure 1, the voice-to-image conversion for this system is done at the receiving side. The conversion scheme can be divided into two parts: the emotion recognition and facial expression reconstructor. These two processes are done by the voice-to-image converter.

Emotion Recognition

Before we come out with the emotion recognizer design, first we have to deal with these three issues:

1. What kind of emotion to be recognized?

How many and what types of emotional states should be recognized by our system is an interesting yet difficult issue. Besides, there is no widely accepted definition and taxonomy of emotion; it

Figure 1. Basic block diagram of VDERM system

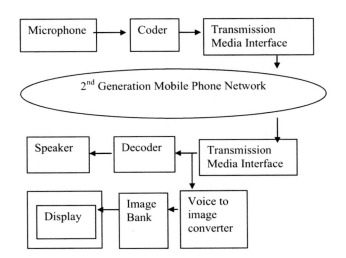

should also be kept in mind that a single emotion can be uttered in different ways. Scherer (1986) distinguishes different categories in a single emotion, for instance, the category "cold anger/ irritation" and the category "hot anger/rage." In our study, we have chosen to consider emotions as discrete categories (Ekman, 1973; Izard & Carroll, 1977; Plutchik, 1980). Six basic emotions defined by Cornelius (1996), that is, happiness, sadness, anger, fear, surprise, and disgust, have been chosen as the emotions to be recognized and reconstructed.

2.   What are the features to represent emotion?

Determining emotion features is a crucial issue in the emotion recognizer design. This is because the recognition result is strongly dependant on the emotional features that have been used to represent the emotion. All the studies in this area point to the pitch (fundamental frequency) as the main emotion feature for emotion recognition. Other acoustic features are vocal energy, frequency, spectral features, formants (usually only one or the first two formants F1 and F2 are considered), and temporal features (speech rate and pausing) (Banse & Scherer, 1996). Another approach to feature extraction is to enrich the set of features by considering some derivative features, such as linear predictive coding cepstrum (LPCC) parameters of signal (Tosa & Nakatsu, 1996). Our study has adopted this approach and uses linear predictive analysis (Rabiner & Schafer, 1978) to extract the emotion features. A detailed analysis has been done on selected emotion parameters (Aishah, Izani, & Komiya, 2003a, 2003b, 2003c). Based on these analyses, a total of 18 features (as in Table 1) have been chosen to represent the emotion features. The 18 features are pitch (f_0), jitter (jt), speech energy (e), speech duration (d), and 14 LPC coefficients (a_1- a_{14}). The LPC coefficients are included because we intended to use LPC analysis for the extraction algorithm. Besides,

Table 1. Speech features and description

No	Feature	Symbol used	Description
1	Energy	e	Average energy of the speech signal
2	LPC Coefficient	$a_1, a_2, a_3, \ldots a_{14}$	The weighting coefficient used in the linear prediction coding analysis.
3	Duration	d	Duration of the speech signal
4	Pitch	f_0	Fundamental frequency (oscillation frequency) of the glottal oscillation (vibration of the vocal folds).
5	Jitter	jt	Perturbation in the pitch

it represents the phonetic features of speech that are often used in speech recognition

3. What technique to be used for recognition?

There are many methods that have been used for emotion recognition/classification. For instance, Mcgilloway, Cowie, Douglas-Cowie, Gielen, Westerdijk, and Stroeve (2000) have compared and tested three classification algorithms, namely linear discriminant, support vector machine (Schölkopf, Burges, & Smola, 1998), and quantization (Westerdijk & Wiegerinck, 2000). Others are using fuzzy model, K-nearest neighbors, and neural networks (Petrushin, 1999). Among all, perhaps the most common and popular method of emotion recognition is neural network. However, the configuration of the networks differs from one researcher to another, as discussed by Morishima and Harashima (1991), Nakatsu, Nicholson, and Tosa (1999), Petrushin (1999), and Tosa and Nakatsu (1996). In this article we applied neural network configuration as described by NETLAB (Nabney, 2001) for the recognition technique. It uses a 2-layer multilayer perceptron

(MLP) architecture with 12-18 elements in the input vector which correspond to the speech features, 25 nodes in the hidden layer, and 6 nodes in the output layer which correspond to the six elements of output vector, the basic emotions. This configuration is illustrated in Figure 2.

Figure 2. The neural network configuration

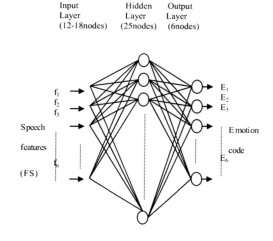

The weights are drawn from a zero mean, unit variance isotropic Gaussian, with variance scaled by the fan-in of the hidden or output units as appropriate. This makes use of the MATLAB function RANDN and so the seed for the random weight initialization can be set using RANDN ("STATE," S) where S is the seed value. The hidden units use the TANH activation job.

During the training, the weights are adjusted iteratively using a scaled conjugate gradient algorithm (Fodslette, 1993) to minimize the error function, which is the cross-entropy function with softmax as the output activation function. In our experiment, 1,000 iterations are found to be sufficient to achieve an acceptable error rate.

Once our network is trained, we test the network using test samples and calculate the recognition rate. The speech features from test samples are fed into the network and forward propagate through the network to generate the output. Then, the resulted classification performance for the predicted output (output which is recognized by the network) is compared to the target output and displayed in the confusion matrix table. A detail discussion on the result of our experiment using neural network approach is presented by Aishah, Azrulhasni, and Komiya (2004). It is found that an emotion recognition rate of 60% is achievable using the neural network method and this result is sufficient based on a human recognition rate done on the same experiment data.

Once we have dealt with the above issues, we come out with an emotion recognition process as shown in Figure 3. Basically this part extracts the emotion content of the speech received from the transmitting user and recognizes it. In addition to emotion, we also identify the voice loudness level of the speech so that it can be used to control the opening of the mouth shape on the facial images later on.

First, the continuous human voice would be chopped into 2 second speech and undergo preprocessing where it is normalized by its maximum amplitude and the d.c. component is removed.

Figure 3. Block diagram of emotion recognition process

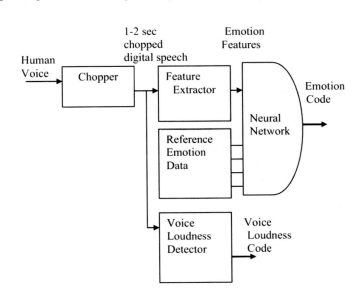

Next, it will go through a feature extractor process where the sample is segmented into 25 msec frames with a 5 msec overlap. LPC analysis is then carried out on these series of frames and the outputs are the 14 LPC coefficients, first reflection coefficient, and energy of the underlying speech segment and energy of the prediction error. Using these outputs, the remaining parameters are determined in the next stage. Speech duration is determined by first classifying the speech frames as voiced or unvoiced using the prediction error signal by simply setting a threshold. The first frame that is classified as voiced will mark the beginning of the speech period. After the beginning of the speech period, if the frame is classified as unvoiced for few consecutive frames, the speech is decided to be ended. The length of the speech period is calculated to get the speech duration. The pitch period for each frame that lies within the speech period is calculated using the cepstrum of the voiced prediction error signal. If an abrupt change in the pitch period is observed, that period is compared to previous pitch periods, and then low-pass filtered (or median filtered) to smooth the abrupt change. With the perturbation in the pitch, jitter is then calculated using pitch perturbation order 1 method, which is obtained by taking the backward and forward differences of perturbation order zero. All the calculation is developed using MATLAB with the use of speech processing and synthesis toolbox (Childers, 1999).

It should be noted that the features extracted so far are based on frame-by-frame basis. As a result, for each sample, it might have many sets of features depending on the number of frames that lie within the speech period of that particular sample. Since we need to standardize the entire sample to have only one feature set, the average of each feature over the frame size is calculated for each sample. The final feature set (FS) for sample n (s_n), consisting of 18 elements is given as

$$\text{FS for } s_n = (e_n, a_{1n}, a_{2n}, a_{3n} \ldots a_{14n}, d_n, f_{0n}, jt_n)$$

$$(1)$$

On the other hand, a copy of the chopped digital speech will be sent to the voice loudness level detector to detect the loudness level. The outputs of this emotion recognition process are emotion code (from the neural network) and voice loudness code (from the voice loudness detector).

Facial Expression Reconstructor

Figure 4 shows the process involved in facial expression reconstructor. First, the code processor will process the emotion code and voice loudness code and convert it to the equivalent image ID used in the database. The code conversion would also depend on which image the user would like to use represented by the model ID.

For the first prototype of this system, we have used Microsoft Access for the image database and Visual Basic is used as its interface. For each images stored in the database, there is a unique ID tagged to it. The ID is generated sequentially by the system automatically whenever an image is uploaded into the system. Before starting the conversation, the user must first choose which image to be used (for example, male or female model) and once the image is selected, the code processor will make necessary conversions on the received emotion code and voice loudness code to match the ID range for that image. Accordingly, the ID number is sent to the image database, and the image with a matching ID retrieved from the database is then displayed. This image database by default consists of 24 images of female models and 24 images of male models. For each model, the images consist of six basic emotions and each emotion has four levels of voice presented by the opening of mouth shape. In addition we also include different eye shapes which are generated randomly among the four levels.

System Interface

Figure 5 shows the main interface of the facial expression reconstructor system. It consists of a

Figure 4. Block diagram of facial expression reconstructor process

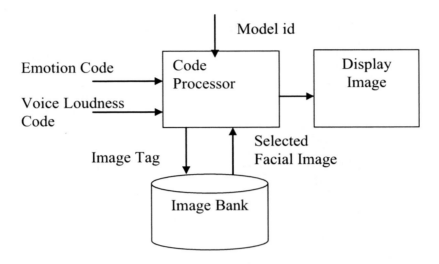

Figure 5. Main interface of facial expression re-constructor

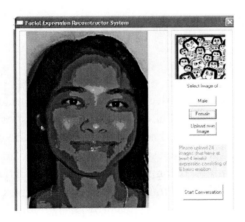

display displaying the facial expression images and buttons for the user to select which model to be used, such as a male or female model. If they click on the "Male" button, the image of male model will be used. Similarly, when they click on the "Female" button, the female image will be displayed, as shown in Figure 5.

In addition to the prestored male and female model, users can also use their own images by using the "Upload own Image" button. When a user clicks on it, a second interface that is shown in Figure 6 will pop up. It has the buttons that show the name of the users that already have their own images uploaded and stored in the system. For new users who want to upload their own image, they can type in their name or any name that will represent them. This will act as the name of the folder which will store all the 24 images of the person. Then users can start to upload their own images which consist of all the six basic emotions which are happiness, sadness, anger, disgust, fear, and surprise with four levels each. The user must have all the 24 images in order to have a complete set of images. At this section, once the user chooses, for example "happy level 1," it will pop up a dialog box and the user will search and upload the appropriate image and save it. Each of the newly uploaded images will

Figure 6. Interface for uploading new image

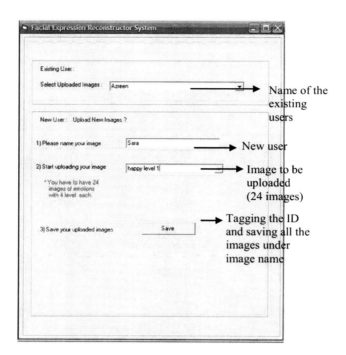

be tagged accordingly with an image ID. After all the 24 images are completely uploaded, users have to click on the "Save as" button for the final step. This is the part where all the images will be put under the folder that has been created and the image ID range for this image name will be recorded and saved for future use. Once this is done, the user can use it by selecting the name from the "uploaded images" box.

EVALUATIONS

Preliminary Evaluations

There are three preliminary evaluations conducted in the process of completing our first prototype. The details of the evaluations are discussed in the next subsections.

PE I

The main objective of this evaluation are to select good quality of emotional voice samples for our voice database. The samples would later be used for training and testing our neural network model for emotion recognition. The second objective is to see how accurate a person can recognize the emotion content in a speech by just listening to the speech/voice. The result of this human recognition rate will be used as a guide for the recognition rate expected to be achieved by our recognition system later on. The evaluation involves two steps:

1. Collecting voice sample

Four short sentences frequently used in everyday communication that could be expressed in all emotional states without semantic contradictions are chosen as the utterance. The sentences are: "Itu kereta saya" (In Malay language), "That is my car" (In English), "Sekarang pukul satu" (In Malay language), and "Now is one o'clock" (In English). Two languages are used for the utterance because we want to compare the emotional parameters for both languages and determine how much difference in language could influence the way emotions are expressed. Then, we asked acting students to utter the same utterance 10 times, each for different emotional states and also in neutral voice as a reference.

2.　Listening test

The emotionally loaded voice samples are then randomized and each sample is repeated three times within short intervals followed by a 30 second pause. The series of stimuli are presented via headphones to 50 naive listeners to evaluate the emotional state within seven categories: happiness, sadness, anger, fear, disgust, surprise, and not recognizable emotional state.

PE II

The main objective of this evaluation is to detect the most appropriate and highly recognizable facial expressions images that can be used to represent the six basic human emotions for our image database. Another objective is to see how accurate humans can detect emotion based on only the facial expression images, without any audio support. The evaluation also involves two steps:

1.　Image collection

For this purpose we have selected three male models and three female models. The facial expressions of the six basic human emotions, which are happy, sad, angry, surprise, disgust, and fear, portrayed by each model are captured, focusing from the neck and above. The background used

is a blank white wall with natural daylight so that the model image is clear and focused. The size of images taken are 1000x1600, using a Sony Cyber shot digital camera. The images are then cropped and resized to 6x4 inches size.

2.　Viewing test

All the images are randomized and presented to 20 assessors consisting of 10 males and 10 females volunteers. The images are displayed for 2 seconds each with a 3 second gap between images. The assessors are asked to identify the emotion of the given images and then the recognition rates for each image and emotion state are calculated.

PE III

The main objective of this experiment is to verify that the combination of voice and image can improve the capability of humans to correctly recognize an emotion and thus justify the importance of a VDERM system.

For the purpose of this evaluation, we have selected three emotional voice samples for each emotion and matched it with the corresponding images. Around 50 assessors have participated in this evaluation and the recognition rate is calculated and analyzed. They are also asked to answer some questions to reflect the importance of voice and facial expressions in effective communications.

System Evaluation

The main objective behind this system evaluation is to evaluate the reliability and feasibility of the idea of a VDERM system using the developed prototype. This evaluation tries to get some feedback from the user on how efficient the system can improve the message conveyed during a conversation, is the displayed image synchronous with the intended emotion of the speech, and how can the interface be further improved according to the user's specification. Responses from the assessors on their perception of the VDERM system are important to determine better research direction for the proposed system. For this initial evaluation, the prototype of the VDERM system has been implemented into a personal computer. The coder, voice-to-image converter, image database, and system interface are preinstalled in the personal computer.

Experimental Set-Up

A subjective assessment technique is chosen due to the practicability and suitability. A total of 20 assessors consisting of experts and nonexperts take part in the evaluation test. Assessors

first went through a demo on the idea behind a VDERM system and followed with a briefing about the evaluation form contents and the way evaluation must be done. The list of evaluation item is given in Table 2. A sample of a 40 second one-way conversation was played, first using a female model and then a male model with a 15 second gap. The facial expression images switched between different emotions and mouth shapes depending on the emotion content and loudness level of the conversation at every two seconds. Assessors were asked to pretend that they were having a conversation with the model and then they were required to rate the quality of each of the evaluation items based on the scale given in Table 3. Then, they were asked to give comments and suggestions on the grade given for each evaluation item.

Table 2. List of evaluation item for preliminary system evaluation

No.	Item
1	Overall
2	Image accuracy in displaying the facial expression
3	Image synchronization with the speech
4	Features and interface
5	Quality of the images
6	Emotion recognition capability

Table 3. Grading scale

Scale	Quality
0	Worse
1	Average
2	Good
3	Best

RESULTS AND ANALYSIS

PE I

From this evaluation, we have achieved an average recognition rate of 62.33%. The average recognition rate is in line with what has been achieved by other studies using different languages (i.e., around 55-65%) (Morishima & Harashima, 1991; Nakatsu et al., 1999; Petrushin, 1999). This result has proven that even a human is not a perfect emotion recognizer. This is because recognition of emotions is a difficult task due to the fact that there are no standard ways of expressing and decoding emotion. Besides, several emotional states may appear in different scale and have very similar physiological correlates, which result the same acoustic correlates. In an actual situation, people solve the ambiguities by using the context and/or other information. This finding indicates that we shall not try to have our machine to achieve a perfect recognition rate. The human recognition rate is used as a guideline towards achieving the satisfactory rate for computer recognition.

Table 4. Confusion matrix table of PE I

Intended emotion	Response from the assessors					
	Happy	Sad	Anger	Disgust		Surprise
Happy	**68**	2	5	8	12	5
Sad	7	**61**	9	3	18	2
Anger	4	21	**46**	11	7	11
Disgust	4	1	5	**77**	7	6
Fear	9	12	5	15	**54**	5
Surprise	8	1	5	8	10	**68**

Table 4 shows the confusion matrix table that is achieved in PE I. The confusion matrix table of PE I suggests how successful the actors were in expressing the intended emotion and which emotions are easy or difficult to realize. We see that the most easily recognizable emotion based on this experiment is disgust (77%) and the least easily recognizable category is anger (46%). A high percentage of confusion occurs in sad-fear (18%) and anger-sad (21%).

A total of 200 samples which have the highest recognition rate are selected for each emotion.

This has resulted in 1,200 samples for the whole voice database.

PE II

From the results in Table 5, it is concluded that among all the facial expression images of emotion, the easiest expressions detected by assessors is happy. This is due to the fact that happiness is the most common emotion shown publicly by humans and it is usually expressed with a smile and bright eyes. Thus it is not difficult to identify

Table 5. Confusion matrix table of PE II

Intended emotion	Response from the assessors					
	Happy	Sad	Anger	Disgust	Fear	Surprise
Happy	**90**	0	0	0	0	10
Sad	0	**80**	0	5	15	0
Anger	0	0	**60**	35	0	5
Disgust	0	0	35	**40**	0	15
Fear	0	5	0	5	**60**	30
Surprise	10	0	0	0	30	**60**

Table 6. Summary of facial gestures according to emotions

EMO-TION	FACIAL GESTURES
Happy	Smile, laughter
Sad	Down turned mouth and eyes, tears
Angry	Eyes bulging, mouth tighten
Disgust	Wrinkled nose, lowered eyelids and eyebrow, raised upper lip
Fear	Eyes squinting
Surprise	Eyes bulging, raised eyebrows, mouth shaped "O"

a happy face even without an audio support. The least recognizable emotion is found to be disgust (40%) and it is often confused with anger (35%). This is because the expressions for both of these emotions are very similar, shown through the "hostile" face; the tight line of the mouth and the squinting eyes. Another thing to note is that based on image, the diversification of confusion in a particular emotion is less compared to recognition based on voice only.

We have also done some analysis on the images which are highly recognizable, and together with the feedback from the assessors, we have identified some main facial gestures which significantly contribute to the recognition of certain emotion. This is summarized in Table 6. Based on the results of Human Evaluation II, we have identified 1 male and 1 female model which have the highest recognizable images to be our model. Then the images of six emotions are recaptured according to the significant facial gestures and each emotion is further developed into four levels of mouth shape, resulting in 24 images for each models.

PE III

From the confusion matrix Table 7, it is illustrated that the recognition rate for all emotions are quite high (70%-87%). According to assessors, fear is difficult to recognize (70%) compared to other emotions as the expression accompanying the voice of fear can be confused or sad. The most easily recognizable emotion is happy (87%), as the cheerful voice is supported by the smiling face.

Figure 7 compares the recognition rate achievable in all the three preliminary evaluations. On average, PE I achieved an average recognition rate of 62.33% with individual recognition rates ranging between 46% and 77%. PE II shows a slightly higher average recognition rate (65%) compared to PE I with a wider range of individual recognition rate (between 40% and 90%). A significant increase in average and individual recognition is clearly seen in PE III with an average recognition of 78.3% and individual recognition concentration between 70% and 87%. The results have clearly illustrated that PE III has the most percentage of correctness in emotion identification by assessors. This shows that combination of both what we hear (voice) and what we see (image) can greatly improve human capability of identifying the emotions. Thus, this result has justified the importance of the proposed system, which is to combine the image and voice to improve the naturalness and efficiency of telecommunication.

Table 7. Confusion matrix table of PE III

Intended emotion	Response from the assessors					
	Happy		Anger	Disgust		Surprise
Happy	**87**	0	0	0	0	13
Sad	0	**78**	0	0	22	0
Anger	0	0	**82**	18	0	0
Disgust	0	6	15	**79**	0	0
Fear	0	16	7	0	**70**	7
Surprise	26	0	0	0	0	**74**

Figure 7. Comparison between recognition rate achieved in PE I, II and III

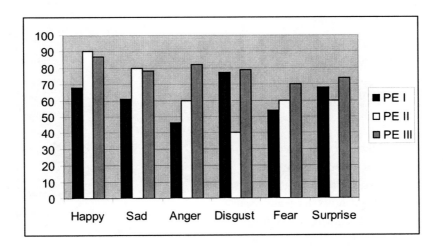

On top of the recognition rate presented above, below we have summarized the findings that were collected from the asessors feedback.

1. Comfortable way to express and detect emotion

For emotion expression (Figure 8), 45% agreed that facial expression is the most comfortable way to express emotion, followed by voice tone (34%), and body gesture (21%).

The pattern is also the same for emotion detection (Figure 9) but the percentage for emotion detection by facial expression is higher at 64%. This is followed by voice tone at 30% and body gesture at 6%.

2.   Medium of communication

The results in Figure 10 show that telephone/ mobile phones are the most popular medium of communication nowadays with 48% as the majority, followed by Internet instant messenger (40%) and short messages service (SMS) (12%). This is because telephones are the most convenient and widely available medium of communication.

3.   Importance of audio (voice tone) and video (facial expression) information for effective communication

The result in Figure 11 show that 98% agreed that both audio and video information are important for effective communication.

4.   Reliability of emotion extraction from voice

The result in Figure 12 show that 64% have agreed that it is reliable to extract emotion from voice.

The result of human emotion recognition based on audio, video, and both highlights two important points. The first one is that emotion recognition is a difficult task and humans can never perfectly recognize emotion. This is because the way people express and interpret emotion might differ from one another, even though some researches have found that it does follow some standard pattern (Cosmides, 1983). The second point is that the ability of humans to correctly recognize emotion is increased to more than 70% when both audio and video information of the speaker are present.

It is also found that facial expression is the most comfortable way for people to express and detect emotion during communication. Thus the presence of facial expressions is very important in communication.

Figure 8. Comfortable way to express emotion

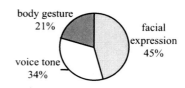

Figure 9. Preferable way to detect emotion

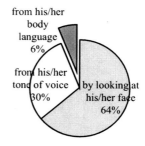

Figure 10. Popular medium of communication

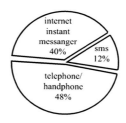

Figure 11. Importance of audio (voice tone) and video (facial expression) information for effective communication

Figure 12. Reliability of emotion extraction from voice

Overall, the results of the preliminery evaluations highlight the importance of facial expressions in providing effective communication, and thus, it is very important to incorporate facial expressions in today's telephone system, as proposed in the VDERM system.

System Evaluation

An average score of each evaluation item was calculated and a bar chart was plotted to represent the results. The preliminary evaluation results are illustrated in Figure 13. From the chart, it is shown that the quality of the images used have the highest scale average with value of 2.85. This shows that the assessors are happy with the quality of the images used, which are clear and focused. This level of quality is not achievable when using a videophone system because the image is transmitted real time and thus subject to transmission quality and the position of the user during the conversation. The next highest scale average is on the emotion recognition capability. This is expected because this system

provides both audio and visual information of the speaker which help the assessors to recognize the emotion more easily compared to just having the audio information, as in the case of normal phone conversation.

The third highest score item goes to features and interface design. Overall the assessors think that the system is user friendly because the system has a straight forward design that does not confuse a user, even if the user is not familiar with a computer system. Another point is that the interface buttons have direct and clear instructions to be followed by the user. Moreover, most of the assessors find that the feature to upload their own image is very interesting because it gives the user customization to make the system personal to them. However, a few are concerned with the image database size as more images are being uploaded, and the difficulty of having a set of 24 images before can use their own image. Some also suggested that the features can be improved by having interactive interface using JAVA and personalized skins for the background.

Figure 13. Result for system evaluation

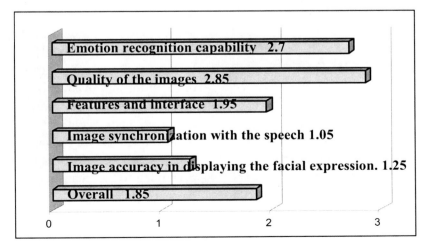

The average score for overall system performance is 1.85. Many of the assessors agreed that this system can improve the efficiency of telecommunication system because the presence of both audio and visual have given them more clues on the emotions being conveyed. Besides they also found that having both elements made the conversation more fun and interesting. In addition, the automatic detection of emotion from voice is also an interesting attempt because most of the currently available chat/Web cam applications require the user to manually select the emotion to be/being conveyed. However, the assessors believed that the system still has a lot of room for improvement, especially in the aspect of image accuracy and image synchronization.

As shown on the chart, image accuracy in displaying the facial expression and image synchronization with the speech has an average score of less than 1.5. The main reason for this is that the level of image for each emotion currently used is only four, which has resulted in switching between images which seems less smooth and the lip movement does not appear to be synchronized with the speech. This is an important issue to address because if the images and voice do not synchronize, the user might not be able to catch the emotion being conveyed. By having more levels for a particular emotion, switching between different emotion states can be smoother, thus the user can have more time to identify the emotion of the images.

FUTURE DESIGN ISSUES

The main improvement in the system is concerned with the accuracy of the images being displayed. Since our intention is to provide real time visual images as in video conferencing, it is very important that the image switching appears to be smooth and synchronized with the speech and emotion content of the speech. One simple modification is to have more levels to represent the voice loudness. However, increasing the level means increasing the number of images needed and consequently can increase the size of our database, which is not desirable.

One possible solution to this is to have the personal images of the user deleted after the call is terminated. However, the problem with this is that the user might need to upload their image every time before the user can start a conversation, which can be time consuming and not practical.

The other advanced alternative for facial expression reconstruction is to use a 3D artificial face model, which can generate facial expressions based on the coded emotion, instead of switching between still pictures. This method is more advanced and complicated but it can provide a more natural facial expressions. For this method, software will be used to convert a person's photo into a face model and a program will be developed to generate the facial expressions on the model based on the emotion code and voice loudness. Using this technique, there is no need for a large image database, which might be more appropriate for application on a mobile phone.

CONCLUSION

In general, based on the results, the system has achieved its main objective, that is, to improve telecommunication by providing voice together with facial expressions and provide an alternative to videophone systems. However it still has a lot of room for improvement in the aspect of interface design and the accuracy of the images being displayed. The evaluation that we have conducted so far was tested on a personal computer. In order to apply the system on a mobile phone, the issues pertaining to the image database size should be thoroughly dealt with.

REFERENCES

Aishah, A. R., Azrulhasni, M. I., & Komiya, R. (2004). A neural network approach for emotion recognition in speech. In *Proceedings of the 2nd International Conference on Artificial Intelligence in Engineering and Technology (ICAIET2004)* (pp. 910-916).

Aishah, A. R., Izani, Z. A., & Komiya, R. (2003a). A preliminary analysis for recognizing emotion in speech. In *Proceedings of IEEE Student Conference On Research and Development (SCOReD 2003)*.

Aishah, A. R., Izani, Z. A., & Komiya, R. (2003b). Emotion pitch variation analysis in Malay and English voice samples. In *Proceedings of the 9th Asia Pacific Conference on Communications (APCC2003)* (Vol. 1, pp. 108-112).

Aishah, A. R., Izani, Z. A., & Komiya, R. (2003c). Towards automatic recognition of emotion in speech. In *Proceedings of the IEEE International Symposium on Signal Processing and Information Technology (ISSPIT2003)*.

Banse, R., & Scherer, K. R. (1996). Acoustic profiles in vocal emotion expression. *Journal of Personality and Social Psychology, 70*, 614-636.

Childers, D. G. (1999). *Speech processing and synthesis toolboxes.* New York: John Wiley & Sons.

Cornelius, R. R. (1996). *The science of emotion: Research and tradition in the psychology of emotion.* Upper Saddle River, NJ: Prentice-Hall.

Cosmides, L. (1983). Invariance in the acoustic expression of emotion during speech. *Journal of Experimental Psychology: Human Perception and Performance, 9*, 864-881.

Ekman, P. (1973). *Darwin and facial expression: A century of research in review.* New York: Academic Press.

Fodslette, M. M. (1993). A scaled conjugate gradient algorithm for fast-supervised learning. *Neural Networks, 6*, 525-533.

Izard, & Carroll, E. (1977). *Human emotions.* New York: Plenum Press.

Kidani, Y. (1999). Video communication system using portrait animation. In *Proceedings of the IEEE Southeastcon '99* (pp. 309-314).

Komiya, R., Mohd Arif, N. A., Ramliy, M. N., Gowri Hari Prasad, T., & Mokhtar, M. R. (1999). A proposal of virtual reality telecommunication system. In *Proceedings of the WEC'99* (pp. 93-98).

Mcgilloway, S., Cowie, R., Douglas-Cowie, E., Gielen, C. C. A. M., Westerdijk, M. J. D., & Stroeve, S. H. (2000). Approaching automatic recognition of emotion from voice: A rough benchmark. In *Proceedings of the ISCA Workshop on Speech and Emotion* (pp. 207-212).

Morishima, S., & Harashima, H. (1991). A media conversion from speech to facial image for intelligent man-machine interface. *IEEE J. on Selected Areas in Comm., 9*(4), 594-600.

Nabney, I. (2001). *Netlab: Algorithms for pattern recognition, advances in pattern recognition.* London: Springer-Verlag.

Nakatsu, R., Nicholson, J., & Tosa, N. (1999). *Emotion recognition and its application to computer agents with spontaneous interactive capabilities.* Paper presented at the International Congress of Phonetic Science (pp. 343-351).

Petrushin, V. A. (1999). Emotion in speech recognition and application to call centers. In *Proceedings of the ANNIE '99.*

Plutchik, R. (1980). *Emotion: A psycho-evolutionary synthesis.* New York: Harper and Row.

Rabiner, L. R., & Schafer, R. W. (1978). *Digital processing of speech signals.* Eaglewood Cliffs, NJ: Prentice-Hall.

Scherer, K. R. (1986). Vocal affect expression: A review and a model for future research. *Psychological Bulletin, 99,* 43-165.

Schölkopf, C. J. C., Burges, A. J., & Smola (1998). *Advances in kernel methods: Support vector learning.* Cambridge, MA: MIT Press.

Tosa, N., & Nakatsu, R. (1996). Life-like communication agent-emotion sensing character MIC and feeling session character MUSE. In *Proceedings of the IEEE Conference on Multimedia* (pp. 12-19).

Westerdijk, M., & Wiegerinck, W. (2000). Classification with multiple latent variable models using maximum entropy discrimination. In *Proceedings of the 17th International Conference on Machine Learning* (pp. 1143-1150).

This work was previously published in the International Journal of Information Technology and Web Engineering, edited by G. Alkhatib, Volume 3, Issue 1, pp. 53-69, copyright 2008 by IGI Publishing, formerly known as Idea Group Publishing (an imprint of IGI Global).

Chapter 8.21
Mobile Multimedia for Speech and Language Therapy

Nina Reeves
University of Gloucestershire, UK

Sally Jo Cunningham
University of Waikato, New Zealand

Laura Jefferies
University of Gloucestershire, UK

Catherine Harris
Gloucestershire Hospitals NHS Foundation Trust, UK

ABSTRACT

Aphasia is a speech disorder usually caused by stroke or head injury (Armstrong, 1993). Related communication difficulties can include word finding, speaking, listening, writing, and using numbers (FAST, 2004). It is most commonly acquired by people at middle age or older, as a result of stroke or other brain injury. Speech and language therapy is "the process of enabling people to communicate to the best of their ability" (RCSLT, 2004). Treatment, advice, and support are provided based on assessment and monitoring activities that conventionally are carried out in face-to-face sessions. This chapter considers issues in providing technology to continue to support aphasic patients between therapy sessions, through multimedia applications for drill-and-practice in vocalizing speech sounds. Existing paper therapy aids are generally designed to be used under the guidance of a therapist. Multimedia applications enable people with aphasia to practise spoken language skills independently between sessions, and mobile multimedia speech and language therapy devices offer still greater promise for blending treatment and support into an aphasic person's daily life.

INTRODUCTION

Current trends in the demography of the developed world suggest that increased longevity will lead to a larger population of patients needing rehabilitation services after a stroke (Andrews & Turner-Stokes, 2005). An essential part of these services is speech and language therapy (SLT) (NHS, 2004) to enable the patient with aphasia to return to the community and live as independently as possible. At present, even in countries where SLT is a well-developed profession, resources in terms of staff and mobile communication devices for loan are limited (Harris, 2004). Therapy generally cannot offer a "cure" for aphasia; instead, the goals of therapy are to support the person in capitalizing on remaining language ability, regaining as much of their prior language skills as possible, and learning to use compensatory methods of communication.

This chapter describes the existing therapy methods based on paper materials and mobile electronic devices commonly called augmentative and alternative communication (AAC) devices and proposes the development of software solutions which could be delivered flexibly via readily available mobile devices such as personal digital assistants (PDA) used in a stand alone mode or via Internet delivered services. These could be designed to suit the needs of not only the patients and their carers, but also those of the professional speech and language therapists (SLTs) who could tailor and monitor the treatment more regularly than presently possible. The process of creating and evaluating prototype applications with SLTs is described and recommendations are made for the direction of future research and development.

CONVENTIONAL SPEECH AND LANGUAGE THERAPY AIDS

Paper-based representations of lip and tongue positions for sounds are a venerable and common speech and language therapy aid. These are generally provided as line drawings, illustrating how specific sounds are made; the aids are intended for use both during therapy and in practice sessions outside of therapy. Figure 1 is typical of this type of therapy material.

While useful, this paper-based material has obvious limitations. The line drawings are static, and fail to accurately represent the movements necessary to make speech sounds (Harris, 2004). No spoken explanation or auditory reinforcement is possible—this would be provided by the speech therapist, during a session or by a carer. The latter would be untrained and may in certain circumstances reinforce errors. Aphasia frequently includes impairments in processing written language. Notice that these sheets include a relatively large amount of text—some of it possibly redundant ("Make the target sound as clear as possible"), some echoing in a less accessible form the line drawings ("Tongue tip raised behind teeth"), some vocabulary that is highly technical and likely to be unintelligible without training in speech therapy ("Quality: Approximant"). These issues can put off users from practising on their own, or can diminish the effectiveness of their practice.

The problem of confining effective therapy to formal, therapist-facilitated sessions is significant. A meta-analysis of evaluations of aphasia therapy (covering 864 individuals) concluded that concentrated therapy over a shorter period of time has a greater positive impact on recovery than less concentrated therapy over a longer period (Bhogal, Teasell, & Speechley, 2003). Clearly, face-to-face therapy with a trained therapist is the ideal, but availability is a bottleneck for aphasia treatment. Even in an economically well-developed country such as the UK, there are only, on average, 0.6 SLTs per 10 beds in rehabilitation units (Andrews & Turner-Stokes, 2005)

Early attempts at software support for SLT have had variable and limited success (Burton, Meeks, & Wright, 1991), in part because of hardware and

Figure 1. Sample paper-based therapy material

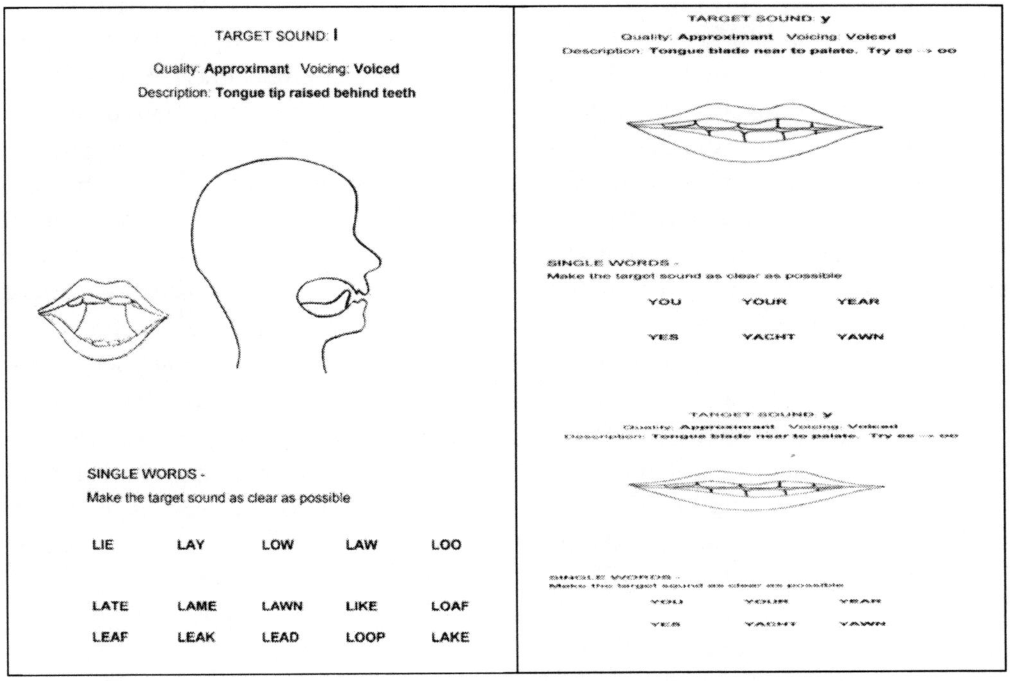

development environment limitations, and in part because there was a limited body of knowledge about the accessibility and usability for aphasic users. As will be discussed next, these barriers are less significant today.

MOBILE DIGITAL COMMUNICATION AND THERAPY TOOLS

Two broad categories of software speech and language therapy applications exist for use by people with aphasia:

- **Drill-and-practice software** that offer instruction and the opportunity to practise language skills. A typical application contains a variety of standard instructional material, and also allows the therapist to record additional words, phrases, or other utterances for playback and practice by the patient.

- **Compensatory software** that provides alternative means for the user to communicate, for example by producing audio, image-based, or written messages for the user. The user selects an appropriate message for playback or display in situations where communication is required—for example, when dealing with commercial organizations or government departments.

Both types of software now commonly include multimedia facilities. Earlier applications were severely limited in scope by tiny (by today's standards) storage available with standard PCs. Larger hard drives, DVD storage, and high-bandwidth Internet connections now support applications that can include video and audio display of large practice sets, audio recording of user practice sessions (for both immediate feedback to the user, and for later evaluation by the therapist), icons for navigating the interface, and speech generation facilities to reduce the need for pre-recording messages used to communicate with others.

Both application categories also have potential to increase their effectiveness by moving to mobile devices. Compensatory communication devices, or AAC devices, would obviously be more useful if they were small and light enough to be easily carried along into conversational situations—so that the user does not have to struggle with a laptop while shopping. Similarly, portable drill-and-practice devices would allow users to practise frequently during the odd breaks that are inevitably sprinkled through the day, and would allow patients to continue therapy when away from home for more extended periods such as vacations (Glykas & Chytas, 2004). However, current commercially-available portable AAC devices are special-purpose pieces of equipment; as such, they are considerably more expensive than standard PDAs and mobiles, even with monochrome screens. As a consequence, portable AAC tools are not widely used at present.

Moving implementations of AAC tools from special-purpose hardware to standard, general purpose devices holds promise for supporting the development of cheaper, more readily available devices. Recent PDA models are now viable platforms for speech and language therapy applications. Screens, while small, now have a high enough resolution to provide a crisp display of images and line drawings. Memory remains relatively small but is sufficient to store a selection of drill exercises and common conversational phrases and sentences. Indeed, there is evidence that including smaller datasets makes these applications more, rather than less, usable. Experience with information display for non-literate (Deo, Nichols, Cunningham, Witten, & Trujillo, 2004) and communication impaired users (Dunlop, Cunningham, & Jones, 2002) emphasizes that these users primarily depend on browsing rather than search to navigate the application. Browsing forces the user to rely on memory to find, and return to, desired documents or exercises, and a too-rich set of options to select from can quickly lead to frustration when the user cannot remember the location of a previously retrieved item or cannot efficiently navigate to a new item. For this type of application, it appears that the limitation is the capacity of the user's memory, rather than the device's storage. Some patients with aphasia have short-term memory problems so the retrieval issue is even more important.

ACCESSIBILITY ISSUES

Funding is one significant accessibility issue for speech and language therapy tools. The cost of a device, software, and training often puts these applications out of reach for many individuals, and local health authorities have extremely limited supplies, if any, for loan (Harris, 2004).

It is clear, however, that the provision of a mobile speech and communication aid is not sufficient in and of itself to ensure that it will be used, and useful, in everyday settings. One study in the UK and the Netherlands demonstrated that, for carefully selected patients, these applications can effectively support therapy—however, 11 of the 28 patients did not choose to use the device in non-clinical settings (van de Sandt-Koenderman, Wiegers, & Hardy, 2005).

Accessibility can also be limited by interface and interaction design. People with aphasia often experience difficulties with reading and understanding text, and may experience a related visual problem that makes reading tiring and error-prone. Investigations into accessibility and usability of software for people with aphasia have produced several recommendations for effective applications (FAST, 2004; Queensland Aphasia Groups, 2001a, 2001b):

- Interfaces should include few, and simple, words, in large print.
- White space should dominate—text should be as widely spaced as possible.
- When possible, include images and icons to explain the words, or to serve as substitutes/reminders of the words.
- Text, images, and functionality should be pertinent to the needs and interests of people with aphasia—not to therapists, caregivers, or members of the medical community. Note that a separate interface may be required for these other potential users of the application (for example, to allow therapists to create new drill exercises).
- Interaction should not be keyboard dependent, and should be designed for ease of use with alternative input/output devices such as screen readers and switches. Aphasia frequently makes construction of text via the keyboard difficult or impossible, and the condition causing the aphasia (for example, a stroke) may also create physical disabilities that hamper keyboarding.
- Applications should be interactive rather than static information displays, and if possible should support the user in expressing his/her own thoughts (rather than literally putting words into the user's mouth with a standard set of utterances).

DEVELOPMENT OF MULTIMEDIA PROTOTYPES

Two prototypes of a speech therapy tool, Sound-Helper, were developed. The tool is intended to support drill and practice in phonetic sounds. In both versions, the user selects a sound for practice, and the sound is represented both through audio and through a demonstration of mouth placement for producing that sound. The design of these prototypes was informed by a speech and language therapist and by an expert in interaction design. On the advice of the therapist the prototypes focus on vowel sounds, as these are the first sounds which are usually addressed in therapy for a person newly aphasic after a stroke or other brain injury.

The SoundHelper interface is organized around the familiar and common "folder" metaphor. The top level of the system presents the folder "containing" all of the exercises (Figure 2a). At the next level, folders are also used to organize and group different classes of sound—for example, exercises pertaining to vowels (Figure 2b).

The two demonstration displays implemented are an animated line drawing (Figure 3a) and a short video clip (Figure 3b). The prototypes were developed using Adobe Premiere to capture the video and Macromedia Flash MX to compress the video clips. Macromedia Flash was then used to rotoscope or motion capture the lip and facial movements, to produce the animated line drawings. The vector graphics produced will automatically rescale to fit a browser window. On a PC monitor, this allows a life-size representation of the animation, creating a "mirror" effect for the user. Automatic scaling also allows the display to be easily ported to a smaller screen such as that of a PDA or other mobile device (Figure 4).

Simplicity and limited use of text are the guiding principles of the interface design, in conformity to interface design principles for users with aphasia. No text or keyboard input is required to use the system. The circular buttons are labelled with speech utterances—in this case, vowel sounds. When the user clicks on a button, an audio recording of the sound is played in synch with the video or animation. If the user cannot read even this limited amount of text, then the

Figure 2a. Top level of SoundHelper

SoundHelper

Please Click the
Folder to Start

Figure 2b. A second-level folder, organizing exercises based on vowel sounds

small number of options helps the user to rely on memory to locate the desired sound. The feedback from selecting a sound is immediate—the audio and visual demonstration—and so this high degree of interactivity supports learning and exploring the application. A black circle around the selected button highlights the current sound, and the appropriate phonetic text is displayed on the folder tab in large font (here, "ay") to provide emphatic feedback. The pause button allows user to develop their understanding and practise the different stages of making the sound.

Note that the video and animation only include the lower part of the face. This further reduces the cognitive load for users by eliminating distracting elements such as the expression of the eyes (Bulthoff, Graf, Scholkopt, Simoncelli, & Wichmann, 2004).

A more complex exercise or interface would require additional support for the user. One possibility is to provide audio "mouseover" help—that is, for mouse pointer contact with screen elements to trigger the playing of an audio file containing spoken help or reading out button labels, rather than the conventional display of help text (Deo

et al., 2004). Textual mouseover displays are unlikely to be useful for users with aphasia—the text is by default displayed in a small font, and users with aphasia frequently find it difficult to interpret text.

The audio in the prototypes was recorded by a female speaker of a similar age to the median age of the intended evaluators of the prototypes (female speech and language therapists). The video prototype is based on a native English speaker of the same gender, race, and median age as the intended evaluators. The importance of matching audio and visual display to the intended user is discussed in the next section.

The prototypes were evaluated in an empirical study with 20 professional speech and language therapists in the southwest region of England. The evaluators rated both prototypes as very easy to use and as potentially more helpful to their patients than conventional paper-based handouts. Eighteen of the evaluators (90%) could identify current patients who might benefit from using this type of application—but only if it were to be made available on a portable device (17 evaluators; 85%). This study was part of an action research

Figure 3a. Prototype line drawing, pronouncing "ay"

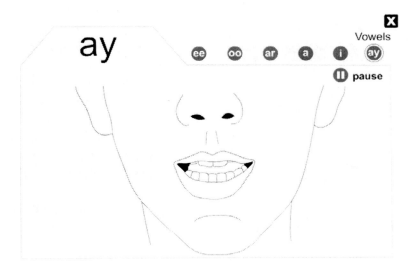

Figure 3b. Prototype video, pronouncing "ay"

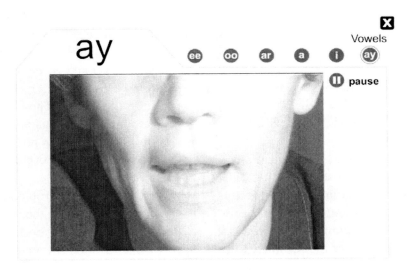

project with the next stage being a refinement of the application to include 3D representations of the formation of sounds made inside the mouth and, provided ethical approval is granted, evaluation with a set of case studies is planned.

Figure 4. Sample display as a PDA application

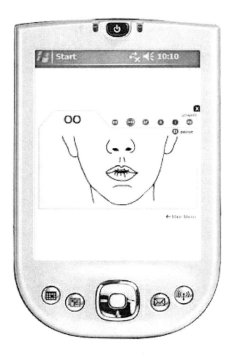

SOCIO-CULTURAL ISSUES IN SPEECH AND LANGUAGE THERAPY APPLICATION DESIGN

Voice characteristics of the speaker featured in speech and language therapy software should ideally match those of the user in significant factors such as age, cultural group, and sex, as it is commonplace for users of communication aids to adopt the intonation and accent of the recorded voice (Harris, 2004). Recording the voice of a family member or friend is therefore usually avoided, as this can cause confusion for the patient.

The user's cultural membership can also have a significant effect on the choice of voice for a speech and language therapy tool of this type—it is important that the user be able to understand and identify with the accent of the audio. The user's

nationality or culture can also affect the example sounds and words to include in the application. New Zealand English provides extreme examples of the accommodations in the exercises that must be possible; for instance, for a New Zealand user the phrase "fish and chips" would be a poor choice for practice in the short i sound as the Kiwi accent usually renders that as "fush and chups", and vowel neutralisation causes word pairs such as "full" and "fill" to be indistinguishable when spoken. Alternative pronunciations are generally seen by individuals as incorrect, with their own pronunciation viewed as the only correct way to speak (Maclagan, 2000). Users are unlikely to accept software that uses pronunciation they regard as "not speaking properly".

The user should also be able to identify with the speaker images, or at the very least should not feel excluded or offended by them. Again, this points to the need to tailor this type of speech and language therapy software to groups of users. A system based on realistic videos, such as the prototype in Figure 3b, obviously would require a greater degree of customisation. The line drawings of Figure 3a are suitable for a broader intended target audience—the animation is less identifiable by gender, race, and age (though not entirely generic). The creation of icons and representations of humans that are completely culturally neutral is not possible, but guidelines exist to reduce the level of cultural bias (del Galdo & Nielsen, 1996).

Note that these problems with providing appropriate matches to the user in voice and appearance exist for face-to-face therapy as well. Again, New Zealand provides an extreme case in point: New Zealand speech is so distinctive that it can be difficult for New Zealand born therapists to work in other English-speaking countries, and conversely New Zealand born clients report difficulties in understanding non-New Zealand therapists (Maclagan, 2000). The creation of multimedia therapy tools offers the chance to provide tailored examples and exercises to an extent rarely possible in conventional therapy, where the number and age/sex/cultural distribution of therapists is rarely large enough to allow a patient to choose a therapist exactly matching his or her own background.

INTERNET-ENABLED THERAPY

The Internet has been suggested for use with speech and language applications in two ways: for delivering therapy and for monitoring therapy. Internet delivery of exercises is highly appealing for the use of the prototypes on mobile devices, as this could address the problem of relatively small memory availability on PDAs and other mobiles: exercises could be streamed in on demand. This solution may be too financially costly for many users, however. Alternatively, selected exercises might be periodically uploaded via a "sync" with a PC or other larger storage device. Remote monitoring possibilities include storing logs or summaries of user sessions in central database, for therapists to later examine (Glykas & Chytas, 2004). This type of monitoring does not provide the capacity for the immediate feedback that is available in a face-to-face session, but does allow the therapist to maintain awareness of the user's progress between sessions. Therapist feedback could be delivered via the Internet, or the monitoring could be used to inform the next face-to-face session.

The potential of Internet-enabled therapy devices for supporting between-session monitoring or care raises several concerns—most notably, that the increased use of technology in therapy could raise barriers between the therapist and patient, and could lead to the dehumanisation of the professional-patient relationship. Issues of legal liability for the efficacy of this more attenuated version of treatment have yet to be fully resolved. There is also a perceived risk that other areas of care could suffer if scarce health funds are diverted to this potentially costly form of telemedicine (including cost of devices, development of mul-

timedia therapy software, tailoring of software to individual patients, Internet transmission costs, therapist time devoted to remote monitoring, and so forth) (Rosenberg, 2004).

A more general anxiety voiced by the therapists evaluating the prototypes of the earlier section, *Development of Multimedia Prototypes*, is that of the ability of therapists to customize therapies as delivered via the Internet, or for that matter through any multimedia application or device. Therapists perceive that therapy as delivered conventionally is tailored to an individual's needs, although it is difficult to see how the current generic paper-based materials are personalized to any great extent. Clearly these new technologies have raised expectations, and any system deployed would have to provide facilities for therapists to inspect, approve, and modify the therapy support being offered.

FURTHER DIRECTIONS FOR RESEARCH AND DEVELOPMENT

The preliminary evaluation with SLTs illustrated that although they were positive about the application, there are clear limitations to the prototypes already developed. In particular, SLTs identified the need for context words and illustrations for each phonetic sound and help with the production of sounds involving movements within the mouth. For example, the plosive sound "t" where the tongue is placed against the front upper palate. There is also a need for an SLT to be able to tailor the learning materials for a particular patient and monitor their progress.

It should be possible to create 3D models of the mouth rather than the vertical sectional drawings currently used. The model could then be rotated by the patient to see different viewpoints. The context words and images could be addressed relatively easily by building up a repository, or digital library, of learning objects which could be chosen by the SLT or added to by them in the same way that current mobile AAC devices can be tailored for a particular patient. A suitable system for this needs to be developed in a cooperative design project with SLT users which will allow the SLT to create drill and practice exercises, capture video and audio together with a further system to allow a patient to upload video of their progress for the SLT to monitor. The technical problems of suitable codecs to compress video need to be addressed although some of this work has already been done in the context of British Sign Language learning (Andrews, 2005). The advent of full 3G services on mobile devices could be utilised to develop a fully mobile therapy service. However, the ergonomics of the devices used will need careful design as it is widely accepted that current mobile phones are unsuitable for use by elderly users due to the small size of their interaction buttons (Goodman, Dickinson, & Syme, 2004).

There are, therefore, a range of future directions in which research in mobile multimedia applications to enable people with aphasia to practise spoken language skills independently between sessions could progress. Blended approaches to therapy are likely to be positively received by SLTs to enable them to support patients with aphasia more flexibly than at present.

REFERENCES

Andrews, J. (2005). Using SignLab for formative and summative assessment. *The University of Bristol Learning Technology Support Service Fifth Annual National Conference, Bristol, June 20. Retrieved April 24, 2006, from* http://www.ltss.bris.ac.uk/vleconf05/Speakers/andrews.doc

Andrews, K., & Turner-Stokes, L. (2005). *Rehabilitation in the 21ˢᵗ century: Report of three surveys.* London: Royal Hospital for Neurodisability.

Armstrong, L. (1993). Assessing the older communication-impaired person. In J. R. Beech, & L. Harding (Eds.), *Assessment in speech and language therapy* (pp. 163-166). London: Routledge.

Bhogal, S. J., Teasell, R. W., & Speechley, M. R. (2003). Intensity of Aphasia therapy, impact on recovery. *Stroke, (34),* 987-993.

Bulthoff, H. H., Graf, A. B. A., Scholkopt, B., Simoncelli, E. P., & Wichmann, F. A. (2004). Machine learning applied to perception: Decision-images for gender classification. *Advances in Neural Information Processing Systems, 17.* Retrieved April 24, 2006, from http://www.cns.nyu.edu/pub/eero/wichmann04a.pdf

Burton, E., Meeks, N., & Wright, K. (1991). Opportunities for using computers in speech and language therapy: A study of one unit. *British Journal of Disorders in Communication, 26*(2), 207-217.

Deo, S., Nichols, D. M., Cunningham, S. J., Witten, I. H., & Trujillo, M. F. (2004). Digital library access for illiterate users. *Proceedings of the 2004 International Research Conference on Innovations in Information Technology,* Dubai (UAE), October (pp. 506-516). United Arab Emirates: UAE University.

Dunlop, H., Cunningham, S. J., & Jones, M. (2002). A digital library of conversational expressions: Helping profoundly disabled users communicate. *Proceedings of the 2ⁿᵈ ACM/IEEE-CS Joint Conference on Digital Libraries* (JCDL), Portland (Oregon, USA), July 14-18 (pp. 273-274). New York: ACM Press.

Foundation for Assistive Technology (FAST). (2004, April). *Reporting on assistive technology in a rapidly changing world* (pp. 11-14). Retrieved April 24, 2006, from http://www.fastuk.org/RAPID.pdf

del Galdo, E. M., & Nielsen, J. (Eds.) (1996). *International user interfaces*. London: John Wiley & Sons.

Glykas, M., & Chytas, P. (2004). Technology assisted speech and language therapy. *International Journal of Medical Informatics, 73*, 529-541.

Goodman, J., Dickinson, A., & Syme, A. (2004). Gathering requirements for mobile devices using focus groups with older people. *Designing a More Inclusive World, Proceedings of the 2nd Cambridge Workshop on Universal Access and Assistive Technology (CWUAAT),* Cambridge, UK, March. Retrieved April 24, 2006, from http://www.computing.dundee.ac.uk/projects/UTOPIA/publications/navigation_workshop.pdf

Harris, C. (2004). Progressing from paper towards technology. *Communication Matters, 18*(2), 33-37.

Maclagan, M. (2000). Where are we going in our language? New Zealand English today. *New Zealand Journal of Speech-Language Therapy, 53-54*, 14-20.

NHS. (2004). *Allied health professionals.* Retrieved April 24, 2006, from http://www.nhscareers.nhs.uk

Queensland Aphasia Groups. (2001a). *Web developer's guidelines.* Retrieved April 24, 2006, from http://www.shrs.uq.edu.au/cdaru/aphasiagroups/Web_Development_Guidelines.html

Queensland Aphasia Groups. (2001b). *What is aphasia-friendly?* Retrieved April 24, 2006, from http://www.shrs.uq.edu.au/cdaru/aphasiagroups/Aphasia_Friendly.html

Rosenberg, R. S. (2004). *The social impact of computers (3rd ed.).* USA: Elsevier Academic Press.

Royal College of Speech and Language Therapists (RCSLT). (2004). *What do speech and language therapists do?* Retrieved January 15, 2006, from http://www.rcslt.org/whatdo.shtml

van de Sandt-Koenderman, M., Wiegers, J., & Hardy, P. (2005, May). A computerised communication aid for people with aphasia. *Disability Rehabilitation, 27*(9), 529-533.

This work was previously published in Mobile Multimedia Communications: Concepts, Applications, and Challenges, edited by G. Karmakar and L. Dooley, pp. 74-84, copyright 2008 by Information Science Reference, formerly known as Idea Group Reference (an imprint of IGI Global).

Chapter 8.22
A Proposed Tool for Mobile Collaborative Reading

Jason T. Black
Florida A&M University, USA

Lois Wright Hawkes
Florida State University, USA

ABSTRACT

This chapter presents a tool for collaborative e-learning using handheld devices that incorporates pair communication via text and speech input. It discusses the current state of e-learning for mobiles and illustrates the lack of such tools in reading comprehension domains. It then describes the tool development as a model for interface design, communication strategies, and data manipulation across mobile platforms. It is argued that such a tool can enhance e-learning among children, due to freedom of movement and variety of input (text and speech). The design is centered on a proven paper-based collaborative learning methodology which should strengthen its effectiveness. A paper prototype test that assisted in determining optimum interface layout and confirming that speech input was preferred among children is described. The system was developed and designed using creative strategies for interface layout and data manipulation. Lessons learned and plans for additional research are discussed.

INTRODUCTION

Collaboration is an important aspect of today's educational learning environment, and the infusion of technology has given rise to various studies in the area of computer-supported collaborative learning (CSCL), computer-supported collaborative work (CSCW), and computer-supported intentional learning environments (CSILE) (Jones, Dircknick-Holmfield, & Lindstrom, 2005; Scardamelia & Bereiter, 1996). The systems developed through these studies have been effectively implemented to produce major gains in comprehension of material in the math and science curriculum, but have yet to explore these benefits when applied to domains which are not math and science. The investigation of how to efficiently apply emerging technology in such environments is resulting in innovations in a wide range of systems and platforms, including handheld computers and other mobile devices.

One of the disciplines that could benefit significantly from such advancements is reading comprehension. At the present, it is apparent that reading comprehension has emerged as a major problem area in American society (Vaughn, Klingner, & Bryant, 2001). It is important to note that there are several reading comprehension tools available for the desktop platform, but the problem becomes enormous when attempting to transfer such applications to the handheld platform. There are many obstacles that must be overcome, such as limited screen real estate, smaller memory capacity, smaller processing power, and limited and often more difficult input mechanisms (such as stylus and virtual keyboard). These obstacles have led developers to steer away from this handheld platform and instead focus on the more common personal computer environment. Yet, research is indicating that the handheld computer is becoming a more viable and attractive platform due to the smaller cost, portability, durability, and increasing advancements in wireless technology (Soloway & Norris, 1999). Additionally, many scientists are investigating more innovative ways to utilize this technology and make it much more readily available to children from diverse backgrounds (MIT Media Lab, 2006).

Question-answer relationships (QAR) is a very successful learning methodology for developing reading comprehension skills (Royer & Richards, 2005; Outz, 1998; Raphael, 1986). QAR has been beneficial to educational research in that QAR not only has demonstrated the ability to improve comprehension skills of student participants, but has also shown effective implementation of peer-assisted learning strategies. There has not been a

significant effort to place QAR in a computerized reading environment, and it is worth investigating whether applying QAR to a handheld learning environment would produce a more efficient reading comprehension software platform.

Thus, this chapter makes the case for collaborative reading comprehension on a mobile platform by illustrating the absence of current research in this area, describes a paper-prototype study for an interface model for collaborative reading comprehension, and then presents a handheld tool supporting collaborative reading using text and speech communication. The tool is designed using QAR as a foundation, and presents a model for development of such systems on mobile platforms. An emphasis is placed on speech input, which can further increase the robustness of user input and collaboration as a result, particularly when implemented for children.

RELATED WORK

Mobile Collaboration in Learning Environments

The explosion of mobile learning (m-learning) in educational environments is largely due to the massive influx of these portable devices in society, and more directly, in the classroom. Mobile learning takes place when users communicate wirelessly via handheld devices (phones, Personal Digital Assistants (PDAs), tablets, etc.) in the process of learning—in other words, learning that takes place with the aid of handhelds (Attewell, 2005). And, since collaboration is a natural and significant extension of a robust learning environment, it is natural to consider ways to facilitate mobile cooperation in learning activities. The mobile environment is rich with a plethora of communication tools (chat, instant messaging, shared workspaces, e-mail, and voice input/output) that make collaborative work a simple and efficient endeavor (Issacs, 2002). It is essential for researchers to explore a wide range of scenarios employing these tools in an effort to improve student learning outcomes. This research takes a look at one such endeavor.

Question-Answer Relationships

Several programs have been implemented that have shown significant development in reading comprehension skills. Among the most successful is Question-Answer Relationships (Royer & Richards, 2005; McIntosh & Draper, 1996; Raphael, 1986), which has been shown to be a particularly effective supplement to a classroom reading program. Question-Answer Relationship teaches students to read by recognizing relationships between questions and possible sources of information, either in the text or in the reader's background. In this technique, readers are asked to read a passage and answer questions about what was read. Then, readers are required to identify the category to which each question belongs: Right There Questions (answer is explicitly in the text), Think-and-Search Questions (answer is implicitly in the text), the Author and You Questions (the answer requires you to use inference to arrive at the answer), and On Your Own Questions (the answer is entirely based on your background knowledge). Several studies have shown that students were capable of generating and answering questions that enhanced their comprehension and led to independent processing and development of knowledge (Royer & Richards, 2005; Outz, 1998). Yet, these approaches have not been incorporated in a desktop or handheld reading comprehension learning environment. It is worth investigating whether doing so will create an electronic comprehension tool which can reinforce through practice, techniques introduced by a human teacher, and hence address these issues (Vaughn, Klingner & Bryant, 2001).

Speech Recognition in Mobile Environments

This increase in the use of mobile devices has created an environment where various types of users are interacting, and as a result, researchers must utilize the full suite of modalities (or modes of input) to facilitate communication (Nanavati, Rajput, Rudnicky, & Siconni, 2006). Almost all mobile devices are equipped for voice input, making speech recognition a viable means of capturing data. In many cases, to compensate for the limited memory and power on these smaller devices, a form of *distributed speech recognition* is implemented (Schmandt, Lee, Kim, & Ackerman, 2004). In such an environment, speech is captured on the mobile device and sent across a wireless network to a server, where processing is done. The translated text is then returned to the device for use. While there are many issues to consider when utilizing this strategy (such as quality of speech, network traffic, noise, etc.), the scope of this work is to present an interface mechanism for facilitating voice input in a mobile collaborative learning session.

OVERVIEW OF SYSTEM DEVELOPMENT

Discussion of Paper Prototype Testing

Paper (also called "low-fidelity" or "lo-fi") prototyping is an interface development strategy that utilizes paper-based designs of the system and interactions with potential users with such system to arrive at an optimum design plan (Snyder, 2003). In paper prototype testing, users are asked to interact with the paper-based interface on a series of popular system tasks, with a designer playing the role of "Computer." The "Computer" mimics the actions and sounds of the system while the user progresses through these tasks, and user choices and behavior are recorded. After the session, the user is questioned in order to learn his or her cognitive processes in making decisions and the results of these answers are used to design and implement the user interface, complete with modifications indicated in the test. The attempt here is to create a "living" prototype—one that is changing to better fit the designs and recommendations of the testers involved—in order to eventually obtain the optimum design methodology for all involved. Researchers have demonstrated the benefits seen in the application of paper prototype testing—preemptive user feedback (changes are suggested before development has begun), rapid iterative development (changes can be incorporated "on the fly"), and enhanced developer/user communication (Snyder, 2003).

Participants in Paper Prototype Test

To obtain a model for interface development, a paper prototype study was conducted (Black, Hawkes, Jean-Pierre, Johnson, & Lee, 2004) involving elementary school students from a local after-school center. Five students were selected based on their background with computers (two had had experience with handhelds, one had moderate experience, and two had no experience), and age (two were in grade 2, two were in grade 3, and one in grade 4). This number of subjects is consistent with Snyder's recommendations of effective numbers of subjects in such tests, which is recommended to be between five and seven (Snyder, 2003; Nielson and Landauer, 1993). Subject #1 was a fourth grader who was a good and constant reader, and was the only subject that had familiarity with a PDA, though not much exposure. Subject #2 was a third grader who had some experience with computers, but was not a strong reader. Subject #3 was the youngest of the group, a second grader with very little computer experience, but was a strong reader. Subject #4

was a third grader who had very little computer experience and was also not a very strong reader. Subject #5 was the oldest of the group, a fourth grader who had computer experience, but was having trouble reading at grade level. All of the students had some exposure to the basic features of a computer application—buttons, passwords, pointers, and so forth—and were eager to participate in the study.

Apparatus

The test was designed using the iPAQ ™ PDA as a model (see Figure 1). A picture of the device was taken, and then scanned and printed, so that the actual size and shape of the PDA could be used in the testing. Then, cut-outs of screens to be presented (as well as buttons, menus, scroll bars, etc.) were designed and used as interchangeable interface components to be presented to subjects during completion of tasks.

Test Design

Screen mock-ups of five basic tasks were created: 1) logging into the system and selecting a partner (for collaboration), 2) reading a story, 3) answering questions, 4) e-mailing the teacher for help, and 5) chatting with their partner. Researchers participated in the test in the roles of the computer (one person transitioned screens as the computer would), and observers (who took notes on user actions and tendencies). Subjects were tested in 30 minute sessions, with two tests conducted on a given day, as recommended by Snyder (2003). During a test session, each subject was introduced to the concept of the test and why it was being conducted. They were then seated at a desk with the "computer" present as well, and the observers looking on.

Each subject was then asked to complete each of the tasks listed, with the question-answer exchanges following each task. After the completion of all five tasks, the subjects were thanked for

Figure 1. Image of mock-up of screen used in Paper Prototype test

their participation and were free to leave. Notes from observers were discussed between tests, and modifications were proposed for future tests.

Test Results

During testing, three of the five subjects preferred writing on the screen for input as opposed to the other presented forms (keypad or speech). This was not surprising, since most of these students had little computer experience, and thus would be more comfortable writing (at least initially) than using the innovative input techniques presented. Of the two subjects that did choose to pick their letters using the keypad, one subject (Subject #4) had trouble navigating the keypad and began pressing buttons on the bottom of the PDA instead of the buttons on the keypad. This action resulted in "beeps" from the "computer" indicating actions that were not allowed by the system, which further confused the subject. But what was gathered from this subject was that he was familiar with the GameBoy™ handheld computer games, which use the directional keypad on the bottom of the device for manipulation of all applications. Research has shown that students' experiences with such gaming devices can be very productive design focuses for scientists developing applications for handhelds. All subjects except Subject #1 had trouble finding the icon during the player selection phase. All subjects had no trouble finding and clicking the "Done" button.

All subjects reported no problem in reading text on the small, handheld-mock up screens, and indicated that the process was enjoyable. Subjects also had no problem transitioning between screens (done by clicking NEXT and BACK buttons presented on the interface). The chat/messaging task perhaps provided the most valuable feedback. All except one subject chose to speak their message instead of the other input features (Subject #4 chose to use the keypad in all writing tasks), indicating that this will likely be a popular feature of the application. The voice input would be very helpful to younger readers, who often do not have the ability to type or write well, and would prefer an alternative to user input. However, two of the subjects were confused when faced with the submenu that appears with the speak feature, which asks them to click on the microphone to begin speaking and to click send to transmit the message. The two subjects were unsure what buttons to press and when to press send. But once this was explained, the subjects were able to complete the task. The reliance on speech for inputting validated an earlier hypothesis which suggested that due to the age of users and simplicity of the action, speech would be chosen more often by younger users (Black, et. al, 2004). The results of this test were then used as blueprints for actual screen development.

System Overview

The interface layout was developed using an application development toolkit that allows for rapid prototyping of applications for mobile devices and provides a series of emulators that can present a simulation of the application running in or on its intended device platform. Upon completion, the finished application can easily be ported to the actual target device, and run as needed. The prototype uses a client-server approach for wireless communication (SEIR-TEC, 2002), which implies that devices are served by a central access point or base station, and communicate with the central access point through the network (see Figure 2). In this configuration, users will send computation-intensive operations to the more powerful server (such as the speech recognition) for remote processing and then download application-specific tasks to the handhelds (Omojokun, 2002). And, when usage has completed, the handhelds synchronize with the server, uploading user session information back to the server for storage in the database.

System Design

The process flow of the application is constructed on the question-answer relationship collaborative reading model mentioned earlier. In implementing this model, students read a passage on the handheld display and then are asked to answer questions which are downloaded from the server about the text just read. Once questions are answered correctly, students must then identify the type of questions that are presented (Right There, Think and Search, Author and You, or On Your Own), based on Raphael's Taxonomy of Questions

Figure 2. High-level system architecture

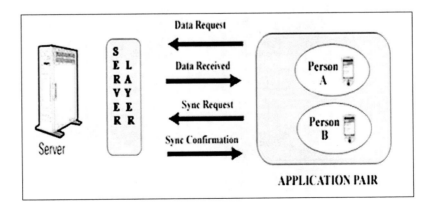

(Raphael, 1982). Students work individually on reading and question-answering tasks, but are allowed to collaborate during periods of reaching a consensus on the correct answer (collaboration is "turned on" when questions are answered incorrectly). Students communicate by chatting with their partner as needed, as well as utilizing a shared workspace for group reflection. Students can also record personal notes in the personal journal as they progress through the lessons, as well as interact with the instructor through e-mail.

All of the activities will be done on the PDA, with lessons downloaded wirelessly from the server to the PDA as requested, and student progression data being stored on the system server.

The application makes use of the standard high-level interface components—forms for user fill-in, canvases for drawing and painting of both text and images, and checkboxes and radio buttons that register user action. The screen is also touch-sensitive, allowing for stylus input at various points on the interface. Textual input is

Figure 3. Introductory screens for user input

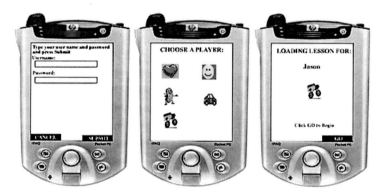

Figure 4. Story and question-answering screens

handled via stylus, keypad, and both the letter recognizer and transcriber (written text using the stylus), and is processed by device standards. The letter recognizer allows users to, after a training period, write letters using the stylus, which are "recognized" by the system and translated to their typed form. The transcriber works similarly, with users writing letters on a text pad, these letters are converted to their typed format. Both have significant learning curves on their usage, but once mastered can serve as very convenient input techniques. Figure 3 shows the initial user login screen (which is essentially a form with text fields and images that behave as buttons), a screen for selecting an icon (which uses images painted on a canvas), and a screen for registering that the user is ready to begin (again, images painted on a canvas).

These screens also make use of the standard mobile menus, which appear at the bottom of the screen just above the device soft buttons. Users can activate these menus either by clicking on them with the stylus or pressing the corresponding soft button.

The story and question screens are similarly done, with images and radio buttons dominating the device display. The user is also presented with icons at the bottom that allow him or her to activate the various system functions (using the *Diary* for personal reflection; sending a message to the instructor, using the *Group Workbook*, etc.). These are illustrated in Figure 4.

Collaboration Components

The collaborative features implemented in the prototype system are shared workspaces, e-mail messaging, personal reflection, and chat services. The shared workspace is implemented as a *group workbook* that is visible to both participants of a team. Each user sees an up-to-the-second image of the workbook and changes made (by entering data in the workbook) are broadcast to each user's device. The system synchronizes access to this feature, locking it while it is being written to so that changes can be implemented before additional writes are allowed. The workbook enables each user to jot down notes that may assist the team in answering questions in later sessions. These notes can be entered either by keypad or writing (textual) or by speaking the text (voice) (see Figure 5).

Figure 5. Workbook and diary screens

The personal journal is used for reflection as the user moves through sessions. Each journal is seen only by that user and is updated upon request. All additional entries into the journal are added to its previous contents, similar to writing in a paper journal. The entries are recorded by being sent to the server for storage upon completion of the session period. Upon the next login, the current contents of the journal are sent to the client should any new entries be desired. As with all other methods of input, the user can provide the journal entry either through textual or voice input (see Figure 5).

The system allows users to send e-mail to the instructor in the event that assistance is needed. The sending of the message is implemented by the client sending a message to the server and the server forwarding that message to the instructor's e-mail address. A record of the transmittal is also stored by the server for reporting purposes. Again, the message can be either in the form of text or voice input (see Figure 6).

Chat Service

The chat service is implemented similar to the standard chat service hosted by any Internet service provider. The system registers that a user wishes to chat and sends a message to the user's partner that he or she wishes to chat. Once a confirmation has been received by the partner, the chat session begins, with users typing in messages (or entering them via voice input) and those messages being displayed on the screen. These messages are also recorded by the server for reporting. When chat is no longer desired, the user indicates this and the session resumes from its previous point. The chat provides the users the opportunity to reach a consensus on certain learning tasks and facilities the peer-tutoring methodology, both techniques present in successful collaborative environments (see Figure 6).

Speech Recognition Strategy

Since the system is designed to be adaptable to a variety of environments, it may be the case that the keypad, recognizer, and transcriber are too complex in a setting of younger users. Thus, the system also allows for Speech Input, where users are allowed to speak their messages into the system, and these messages are converted to text and displayed on the screen (or sent via e-mail if needed). This is done to take into account that

Figure 6. Chat and help screens

younger users may not be good typists or even know how to spell well, but may still wish to enter data.

The ability to provide speech input for users is a major component of the architecture. The current literature does not indicate any use of this feature in studies involving handhelds and collaboration. In the math and science-centered applications, input is often simple, with users asked to select items or to enter numbers as part of equations. This poses a problem in non-science domains, where input may often be sentence-structured and much more verbose. There needs to be an additional method of providing this type of input, and speech or voice input fills this need adequately.

The application environment implements a strategy for dealing with speech input and/or speech output. The system receives the data sent to the server and runs it through a speech recognizer program to produce written text. The written text is then sent back to the application to be displayed on the screen. The server is responsible for handling speech requests sent by the Diary, Help, Journal, Workbook, and Chat applications and funneling them to the appropriate mechanism.

DISCUSSION

It is important to note that while this work demonstrates that this type of interface can indeed be developed for mobile devices, the actual testing of this system in a live classroom will occur in additional studies. The researchers are currently working with school teachers to develop a curriculum model that can incorporate such a system, in an effort to determine if its application would be effective in improving reading skills of younger students. This is a daunting task, but one that holds much promise for both computer scientists and educators as well.

Prior to implementation of a complete system, there are issues to be examined related to data

management, data modeling, logging of system and user operations and functions, and server-side management. There are also issues regarding data security and reliability of data to consider. And, while the screen size is likely appropriate for beginning readers and younger users, there may be an issue regarding displaying of material on the device for more advanced users. The current model only displays one page of data at a time, and pages are turned and not scrolled. More advanced users would likely want to remain on a page and simply scroll down or up to view additional material. This would call for some device other than the PDA, or at the very least, in a revision of the type of screen layout. However, the focus of this project is younger children, and thus the designed system is very appropriate.

CONCLUSION AND FUTURE WORK

The development of this collaborative mobile learning system and its implementation on the actual target handheld devices is an indication that this type of architecture is possible and proved both challenging and rewarding. Each of the desired screen designs was capable of being constructed in the chosen language and the interaction between screens was simple to maintain. The communication between devices and between device and server was easily maintained via a wireless network and access to a server machine. Using a Web server allows for testing and demonstration of the system in any environment where wireless Web access is available.

The implementation of QAR in a collaborative platform was also successful. As mentioned earlier, QAR requires individuals to work in pairs, which is accommodated by the interface in this system. QAR also expects students to not only read, but also answer questions and then identify categories of questions. The multiple screens developed in this system also accomplish this task. And, since QAR is an extremely successful tool (in a paper-based environment) in enhancing reading comprehension skills, it is rewarding to note that the interface presented does not take away from the functionality and robustness of the methodology, but stresses it very well.

Speech input is a very significant feature of any collaborative environment and the tools included in the system provide for that capability. Students are able to speak words of communication with partners, and these words are indeed translated and presented on the screen. This is a major component since mobile devices often have challenging input techniques (using a stylus for large volumes of text can be very cumbersome). This system addresses and solves this issue as well.

The next step is to implement this system in the actual classroom, with the assistance of grade school teachers and administrators, in the effort to study its effect on reading comprehension skills. It is believed that students using this system will become better readers, and that the system's integration into the classroom learning setting will be unobtrusive and seamless. Since most reading comprehension software is developed for the desktop environment, utilization of such a system in this mobile platform could prove very exciting and rewarding, serving to fill a much needed void in the collaborative learning spectrum.

Overall, the system presented in this work provides one possible approach to developing collaborative learning environments on intermittent devices, successfully providing an architecture for modeling interfaces for smaller, more limited machines. This research is just scratching the surface of what is capable for reading comprehension software, showing that tomorrow is promising for addressing the crisis of improving children's reading skills nationally.

REFERENCES

Attewell, J. (2005). Mobile learning: Reaching hard-to-reach learners and bridging the digital device. In G. Chiazzese, M. Allegra, A. Chifari, & S. Ottaviano (Eds.), *Methods and technologies for leaning.* (pp. 361-365). Southampton: WIT Press.

Black, J., Hawkes, L., Jean-Pierre, K., Johnson, I. & Lee, M. (2004, September 13-16). A paper prototype study of the interface for a children's collaborative handheld learning application. In *Proceedings of Mobile HCI 2004,* Glasgow, Scotland.

Isaacs, E., Walendowski, A., & Ranganathan, D. (2002). Mobile instant messaging through Hubbub. *Communications of the ACM, 45* (9), 68-72.

Jones, C., Dirckinck-Holmfeld, L., & Lindström, B. (2005). CSCL The next ten years—A view from Europe. In T. Koschmann, D. Suthers, & T-W. Chan (Eds.), *Computer supported collaborative learning 2005: The next ten years!* Mahwah, NJ: Lawrence Erlbaum Associates.

McIntosh, M.E., & Draper, R. J. (1996). Using the question-answer relationship strategy to improve students reading of mathematics texts. *The Clearing House, 154,* 161.

MIT (2006). *MIT Media Laboratory.* Retrieved from http:// www.media.mit.edu/about/overview. pdf.

Nanavati, A., Rajput, N., Rudnicky, A. I., & Sicconi, R. (2006, September). Workshops: SiMPE: speech in mobile and pervasive environments. In *Proceedings of Mobile HCI 2006.* Helsinki, Finland.

Nielsen, J., & Landauer, T. K. (1993). A mathematical model of the finding of usability problems. In *Proceedings of Conference on Human Factors in Computing Systems INTERCHI '93,* Amsterdam (pp. 206-213). New York: ACM Press.

Ouzts, D. (1998). Enhancing the connection between literature and the social studies using the question-answer relationship. *Social Studies & The Young Learner, 10*(4), 26-28.

Raphael, T. (1982). Question-answering strategies for children. *The Reading Teacher, 36,* 186- 19.

Raphael, T. (1986). Teaching question answer relationships, revisited. *The Reading Teacher, 39,* 516-522.

Royer, R., & Richards, P. (2005). Revisiting the treasure hunt format to improve reading comprehension. Retrieved from http://www.iste.org/Content/NavigationMenu/Research/NECC_Research_Paper_Archives/NECC_2005/Royer-Regina-NECC05.pdf

Scardamalia, M., & Bereiter, C. (1996). Student communities for the advancement of knowledge. *Communications of the ACM, 39*(4), 36-37.

Schmandt, C., Lee, K. H., Kim, J., & Ackerman, M. (2004, June). Impromptu: Managing networked audio applications for mobile users. In *Proceedings of MobiSys 2004* Boston, Massachusetts.

Snyder, C. (2003). *Paper prototyping: The fast and easy way to design and refine user interfaces.* San Francisco: Morgan Kaufmann Publishers.

Soloway, E., & Norris, C. A. (1999). *Schools don't want technology, schools want curriculum.* Retrieved in 2003 from http://www.cisp.org/imp/june_99/06_99soloway-insight.htm

SouthEast Initiatives Regional Technology in Education Consortium (SEIR-TEC) News-Wire. (2002). *Using handheld technologies in schools, 5*(2).

Trifonova, A., & Ronchetti, M. (2005). Prepare for a bilingualism exam with a PDA in your hands. In G. Chiazzese, M. Allegra, A. Chifari, & S. Ottaviano (Eds.), *Methods and technologies for learning* (pp. 343-347). Southampton: WIT Press.

Vaughn, S., Klingner, J. K., & Bryant, D. P. (2001). Collaborative strategic reading as a means to enhance peer-mediated instruction for reading comprehension and content area learning, *Remedial and Special Education, 22*(2), 66-74.

KEY TERMS

Collaborative Learning: An environment where students work alone or in groups to complete a set of tasks, usually lessons, where they assist each other in learning.

Computer-Supported Collaborative Learning (CSCL): The study of users collaborating in a computerized environment on learning tasks.

Computer-Supported Intentional Learning Environments (CSILE): Database software that provides tools for organizing and storing knowledge as a means of sharing information and thoughts with peers, supporting both individual and collaborative learning.

Computer-Supported Collaborative Work (CSCW): The study of how people work with computers and how they can work with each other using them.

Distributed Speech Recognition: The process of capturing speech on a mobile device and transporting it via wireless network to a server to be processed ("recognized") or translated, and subsequently returning the translated speech to the mobile device.

Mobile Learning (M-Learning): Users communicating wirelessly via handheld devices in the process of learning.

Question-Answer Relationships (QAR): An instructional methodology for enhancing reading comprehension skills by teaching students to answer questions and generate their own questions based on text.

This work was previously published in Handbook of Research on User Interface Design and Evaluation for Mobile Technology, edited by J. Lumsden, pp. 1068-1078, copyright 2008 by Information Science Reference, formerly known as Idea Group Reference (an imprint of IGI Global).

Chapter 8.23
Mobile Decision Support for Time-Critical Decision Making

F. Burstein
Monash University, Australia

J. Cowie
University of Stirling, UK

INTRODUCTION

The wide availability of advanced information and communication technology has made it possible for users to expect a much wider access to decision support. Since the context of decision making is not necessarily restricted to the office desktop, decision support facilities have to be provided through access to technology anywhere, anytime, and through a variety of mediums. The spread of e-services and wireless devices has increased accessibility to data, and in turn, influenced the way in which users make decisions while on the move, especially in time-critical situations. For example, on site decision support for fire weather forecasting during bushfires can include real-time evaluation of quality of local fire weather forecast in terms of accuracy and reliability. Such decision support can include simulated scenarios indicating the probability of fire spreading over nearby areas that rely on data collected locally at the scene and broader data from the regional and national offices. Decision Support Systems (DSS) available on mobile devices, which triage nurses can rely on for immediate, expert advice based on available information, can minimise delay in actions and errors in triage at emergency departments (Cowie & Godley, 2006).

Time-critical decision making problems require context-dependent metrics for representing expected cost of delaying an action (Greenwald & Dean, 1995), expected value of revealed information, expected value of displayed information (Horvitz, 1995) or expected quality of service (Krishnaswamy, Loke, & Zaslavsky, 2002). Predicting utility or value of information or services is aimed at efficient use of limited decision making time or processing time and limited resources to allow the system to respond to the time-critical situation within the required time frame. Sensitivity analysis (SA) pertains to analysis of changes in output due to changes in inputs (Churilov et al.,

1996). In the context of decision support, traditionally SA includes the analysis of changes in output when some aspect of one or more of the decision model's attributes change, and how these affect the final DSS recommendations (Triantaphyllou & Sanchez, 1997). In time-critical decision making monitoring, the relationship between the changes in the current input data and how these changes will impact on the expected decision outcome can be an important feature of the decision support (Hodgkin, San Pedro, & Burstein, 2004; San Pedro, Burstein, Zaslavsky, & Hodgkin, 2004). Thus, in a time-critical decision making environment, the decision maker requires information pertaining to both the robustness of the current model and ranking of feasible alternatives, and how sensitivity this information is to time; for example, whether in 2, 5, or 10 minutes, a different ranking of proposed solutions may be more relevant. The use of graphical displays to relay the sensitivity of a decision to changes in parameters and the model's sensitivity to time has been shown to be a useful way of inviting the decision maker to fully investigate their decision model and evaluate the risk associated with making a decision now (whilst connectivity is possible), rather than at a later point in time (when perhaps a connection has been lost) (Cowie & Burstein, 2006).

In this article, we present an overview of the available approaches to mobile decision support and specifically highlight the advantages such systems bring to the user in time-critical decision situations. We also identify the challenges that the developers of such systems have to face and resolve to ensure efficient decision support under uncertainty is provided.

MOBILE DECISION SUPPORT

Recent work on mobile decision support focuses on the implementation of knowledge-based services on hand-held computers. Work on mobile clinical support systems, for example, addresses different forms of intelligent decision support such as knowledge delivery on demand, medication consultant, therapy reminder (Spreckelsen et al., 2000), preliminary clinical assessment for classifying treatment categories (Michalowski, Rubin, Slowinski, & Wilk, 2003; San Pedro, Burstein, Cao, Churilov, Zaslavsky, & Wassertheil, 2004), and providing alerts of potential drugs interactions and active linking to relevant medical conditions (Chan, 2000). These systems also address mobility by providing intelligent assistance on demand, at the patient's bedside or on-site.

Research on location-based mobile support systems uses search, matching, and retrieval algorithms to identify resources that are in proximity to the location of the mobile users and that satisfy multi-attribute preferences of the users and the e-service providers. Examples of such location-based systems are those that recommend best dining options to mobile users (Tewari et al., 2001), locate automatic teller machines nearby (Roto, 2003), and locate nearest speed cameras and intersections using GPS-enabled mobile devices. Most of these mobile decision support systems use intelligent technologies and soft computing methodologies (e.g., rule-based reasoning, rough sets theory, fuzzy sets theory, multi-attribute utility theory) as background frameworks for intelligent decision support. However, none of these systems address the issue of quality of data or quality of decision support while connected or disconnected from the network or consider a comprehensive measure of reliability of data as part of supporting time-critical decision-making.

It should be noted that not all real-time decision situations, which could benefit from mobile DSS, are also constringed by the period of time, in which this decision support should be provided. For example, if a decision problem is more of a strategic, rather than operation nature, the time factor could be less critical, hence, more time can be devoted to improve the quality of data before the final decision has to be accepted by the user. In this article, we mainly address the needs of operational decision making, when time before the final choice is made is limited. In such situations an aggregate measure of quality of data (QoD) is particularly important when aiming to enhance a level of user's confidence and trust.

In recent papers (Hodgkin et al., 2004; San Pedro, Burstein, & Sharp, 2003) the issue of QoD has been addressed. A framework has been proposed for assessing QoD as an indicator of the impact of mobility in decision-making (Burstein, Cowie, Zaslavsky, & San Pedro, 2007; Cowie & Burstein, 2006; Hodgkin et al., 2004; San Pedro et al., 2003). QoD is based on multiple parameters which measure user-specific factors, current technology-related factors, and some factors which can be learned based on past experiences with similar problem situations. By providing a QoD alerting service from the mobile device, the mobile decision maker can be warned against making decisions when QoD falls below a predetermined threshold or when QoD becomes critically low. The assumption made is that a decision maker should feel more confident with a decision when QoD is high, or be alerted when QoD becomes lower than acceptable.

In mobile DSS, QoD can be calculated incrementally at every stage of the decision making process, as the mechanism for alerting the user when more data and/or resources are needed before the best option can be selected. For example, following Simon's classical decision making principal phases (Simon, 1960), when describing a decision situation, QoD can be used to judge how accurate the set of data collected is at the Intelligence phase; when designing alternative actions, QoD can assist in making sure the user is satisfied with the range of possibilities the user is presented with for a choice; when a model is applied for selecting the best alternative, the final output includes a full and explicit representation of the QoD, which is derived as an aggregate of the ones used in the previous stages (Burstein et al., 2007).

Providing the user with a measure of QoD is extremely important in a mobile decision making environment as the focus of decision support moves from strategic long term decision analysis to just-in-time operational decision support (Hodgkin et al., 2004; Malah, 2000). In addition, in a mobile environment, data timeliness, completeness, reliability, and relevance have to be considered as contributing factors of QoD metrics. For example, in the area of contingency management a "good enough" feasible decision achievable "on the spot," anytime, anywhere is often preferable to a perfect solution that may require extensive additional computational resources as well as time.

Further important issues to consider in time-critical DSS are diversity and heterogeneity of data both at the input and output points of the system. For example, in a medical emergency, context DSS needs to meet the varying information and resource needs of the personnel at the site and yet be able to support their physical mobility requirements. The mobile computing approaches seem to provide an ideal environment to reconcile varying data sources while identifying the best form of delivery of time-critical information. For example, aiding ambulance staff involving in the transfer of patients to the most appropriate hospital in the minimal amount of time (Burstein, Zaslavsky, & Arora, 2005; Cowie & Godley, 2006).

APPROACHES TO AND REQUIREMENTS OF TIME-CRITICAL DECISION SUPPORT

Mobile decision support systems can be implemented in a number of ways, depending on user requirements, available technological resources, frequency of data access, urgency of data retrieval, and so forth. Most of these mobile support systems use intelligent technologies and soft computing methodologies, for example, multicriteria decision analysis, rule-based reasoning, rough sets theory (Michalowski et al., 2003; San Pedro et al., 2003), fuzzy sets theory (Zadeh, 1994), and multi-attribute utility theory (Keeney, 1992) as background frameworks for being able to learn about the environment in which the decision is taking place and decide upon appropriate support. Location-based decision support is one of many context-aware applications in which systems "can

discover or take advantage of contextual information (such as user location, time of day, nearby people and devices, and user activity" (Chen & Kotz, 2000, p. 1).

Time-critical decision making problems require establishing system architectures for such systems that allow infrastructure for fault handling and system recovery (Saksena, da Silva, & Agrawala, 1994), for supporting wireless connectivity (Ahlund & Zaslavsky, 2002),

Figure 1. Mobile decision support architectures (Burstein et al., 2008)

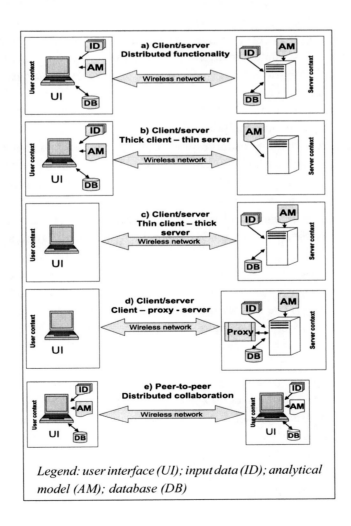

Legend: user interface (UI); input data (ID); analytical model (AM); database (DB)

and provision of network security (Ghosh, 1998; Reis, Hoye, Gilbert, & Ryumae, 2003). Such infrastructures are essential for developing systems that can handle uncertainties due to unreliable communications, possible disconnections from the network, and other technical difficulties that might delay the action or response to a time-critical situation.

As research into such technology is relatively new, optimal architectures for various decision contexts, design configurations, and potential future applications are yet to be investigated. Some generic architectures are proposed and described, for example, by Burstein et al. (2007). They consider how standard DSS component, that is, database (DB), user interface (UI), and analytical model (AM) (Aronson, Liang, & Turban, 2005) can be arranged in mobile decision support architecture. Burstein et al. (2007) describe five possible types of mobile DSS implementation architectures as illustrated in Figure 1.

Portable devices can act as computational platforms for task specific applications, collecting, storing, and providing data for analytical processing. The use of device specific resources or server resources creates a distinction between possible types of DSS that can be provided (Navarro, Schulter, Koch, Assuncao, & Westphall, 2006). Mobile decision support can be client-based, server-oriented, proxy-based, or distributed across an ad hoc network of similar peer devices (Bukhres, Pitoura, & Zaslavsky, 2003). The type of architecture depends on where information is stored and where computations are performed. These varying implementations have associated advantages and disadvantages. The developers can choose between different implementations depending on the user context and technical infrastructure available at the time. A context which requires access to significant amounts of information would be more likely to use a server architecture given the limited processing and information storage capabilities of small portable devices. On the other hand, decision support in

situations where some preliminary information processing could be performed based on some aggregated information can be deployed directly onto a portable device. Mobile and distributed decision support improves a system's fault tolerance and reduced support requirements.

Currently, the most popular implementation is where the functionality is distributed across a client-server environment with a user interface (UI) located on the user's portable device. In this case the data is distributed across both client and server; while user-sensitive data resides on the user device, the bulk of the data, including historical databases, are located on a server (Burstein et al., 2008). In this configuration, the Analytical Model (AM) is also distributed across client and server, with the user device performing elementary computations and delegating more complex and resource-intensive computations to the server.

Thick client-thin server and vice-versa represent more extreme cases and therefore more rare configurations. Given the high likelihood of disconnections in the wireless environment, some systems may use the concept of proxy architecture where a proxy process is located on a server-side representing a client and, if connectivity is good, allowing data and computations to be simply channelled between server and client. However, if a client becomes disconnected (e.g., driving through a tunnel), then the proxy assumes full functionality of the client and caches data and results until the client reconnects. With proliferation of peer-to-peer computing, it is now becoming possible to form ad hoc networks of similar devices, discovered at a time of need, in order to consolidate resources and perform the AM in a distributed computing environment in a cost-efficient manner.

These alternative architectural approaches and set up options enable enough flexibility and scalability for any possible DSS application or scenario. For time-critical DSS, any of these configurations should provide adequate assistance as long as the decision can be reached with a reasonable level of confidence within the required time constraints. Moreover, it is essential to utilize the most current data available while also providing additional information on sensitivity of the selected option to minor variations in context data or more dynamic model characteristics (Cowie & Burstein, 2007)

FUTURE TRENDS

The last decade has seen significant advances in the way humans interact with technology. Users of computers are no longer constrained to the office desktop, but can have much more flexible access to technology almost anywhere, anytime. The spread of e-services and wireless devices has facilitated a new way of using computers, increased accessibility to data, and, in turn, influenced the way in which users make decisions while on the move.

Availability of such an infrastructure coupled with an increase in the demands of users provide new opportunities for developing improved, "just in time" support for decision making. Mobile decision support can be incorporated as an integral component of a mobile commerce infrastructure as a means of an enhanced communication (Carlsson et al., 2006) or as a part of an operational decision support environment for a mobile manager.

Mobile DSS can benefit from storing real-time data and then re-using it at the time of calculating the requested best option (Michalowski et al., 2003). Such systems have been proven to perform well in both stand alone and distributed environments, where they can share historical information to deal with a lack of information when supporting time-critical decisions. Shim, Warkentin, Courtney, Power, Sharda, and Carlsson (2002) suggest that the availability of Web-based and mobile tools within a wireless communication

infrastructure will be a driving force in further development of decision support, facilitating decision support for decision makers "wherever they may be" (p. 112).

Financial decisions present a good example of when real-time decision support could be beneficial (Hartmann & Bretzke 1999). Decision makers, who require getting a real-time update on their financial position in order to make the best use of their money, can be supported by mobile DSS, which will utilise new as well as transaction history data in calculating the options (Burstein et al., 2008).

CONCLUSION

The realities of the changing way in which we make decisions and the advances in mobile technology create multiple challenges and opportunities for decision makers and computer system developers alike. Making decisions on the move under uncertainty requires decision support systems that can adequately provide up-to-date, context specific, complete information in a way that is understandable and useful to the decision maker.

Observing the development of DSS for the future, Shim et al. (2002) envisage that use of mobile devises for providing decision support will lead to greater collaboration and allow the achievement of true ubiquitous access to information in a timely manner. We wholeheartedly concur with this opinion and look forward to developers of DSS embracing current and future technologies that facilitate mobile decision support, building on well-founded methodologies to model decision situations with better precision. In addition, we believe that by accommodating a measure of the quality of the information provided, decisions on the move can be supported just as effectively as those made behind the desk.

REFERENCES

Ahlund, C., & Zaslavsky, A. (2002, October 7-8). Support for wireless connectivity in hot spot areas. In *Proceedings of the International Conference on Decision Support Systems, the First MOST International Conference*, Warsaw-Poland (pp. 152-164). 8-10 June, Atlanta, GA.

Aronson, J., Liang, T., & Turban, E. (2005). *Decision support systems and intelligent systems*. Upper Saddle River, NJ: Pearson Education, Inc.

Bukhres, O., Pitoura, E., & Zaslavsky, A. (2003). Mobile computing. In J. Blazewicz, W. Kubiak, T. Morzy, & M. Rusinkiewicz (Eds.), *Handbook on data management in information systems* (Vol. 3). Springer Verlag.

Burstein, F., Cowie, J., Zaslavsky, A., & San Pedro, J. (2008). Support for real-time decision-making in mobile financial applications. In Burstein & Holsapple (Eds.), *Handbook for decision support systems* (Vol. 2). Springer Verlag.

Burstein, F., Zaslavsky, A., & Arora, N. (2005, July). Context-aware mobile agents for decision-making support in healthcare emergency applications. In *Proceedings of the Workshop on Context Modeling and Decision Support, at the Fifth International Conference on Modelling and Using Context, CONTEXT'05,* Paris, France (pp. 1-16). Retrieved December 14, 2007, from http://ceur-ws.org/Vol-144

Burstein, F., San Pedro, J. C., Zaslavsky, A., Hodgkin, J.(2004, July 12-13). Pay by cash, credit or EFTPOS? Supporting the user with mobile accounts manager. In *Proceedings of the Third International Conference on Mobile Business, m>Business 2004,* (pp. 1-13). Institute of Technology and Enterprise, Polytechnic University, New York.

Carlsson, C., Carlsson, J., & Walden, P. (2006). Mobile travel and tourism services on the Finnish market. In *Proceedings of the 24th Euro CHRIE Congress.*

Chan, A. (2000) WWW+ smart card: Towards a mobile health care management system. *International Journal of Medical Informatics, 57,* 127-137.

Chen, G., & Kotz, D. (2000). *A survey of context-aware mobile computing research* (Tech. Rep. TR2000-381), Darmouth Computer Science. Retrieved December 14, 2007, from http://citeseer.nj.nec.com/chen00survey.html

Churilov L., Sniedovich M., &Byrne A. (1996) On the concept of Hyper Sensitivity Analysis in Decision Making. In the *Proceedings of the First Asian-Pacific Decision Science Institute Conference,* (pp.1157-1160). Hong Kong University of Science and Technology, Hong Kong.

Cowie, J., & Burstein, F. (2007). Quality of data model for supporting mobile decision making. *Decision Support Systems Journal, Decision Support Systems, 43,* 1675-1683.

Cowie, J., & Godley, P. (2006, May). Decision support on the move: Mobile decision making for triage management. In *Proceedings of the 8th International Conference on Enterprise Information Systems: Artificial Intelligence and Decision Support Systems,* Paphos, Cyprus (pp. 296-299). INSTICC Press.

Ghosh, A.K. (1998). E-*commerce security weak links, best defenses* (pp. 21-26). New York: Wiley Computer Publishing.

Greenwald, L., & Dean, T. (1995). Anticipating computational demands when solving time-critical decision-making problems. In K. Goldberg, D. Halperin, J.C. Latombe & R. Wilson (Eds.), *The algorithmic foundations of robotics*. Boston, MA: A. K. Peters. Retrieved December 14, 2007, from http://citeseer.nj.nec.com/greenwald95anticipating.html

Hartmann, J., & Bretzke, S. (1999). *Financial services for the future—mobile, flexible, and agent-based.* Retrieved December 14, 2007, from http://citeseer.ist.psu.edu/correct/287340

Hodgkin, J., San Pedro, J., & Burstein, F. (2004, July 1-3). Quality of data model for supporting real-time decision-making. In *Proceedings of the 2004 IFIP International Conference on Decision Support Systems (DSS2004).* Prato, Italy.

Horvitz, E. (1995, February). *Transmission and display of information for time-critical decisions* (Tech. rep. MSR-TR-9513). Microsoft Research. Retrieved December 14, 2007, from http://citeseer.nj.nec.com/horvitz95transmission.html.

Keeney, R.L. (1992). *Value-focused thinking.* Harvard University Press.

Krishnaswamy, S., Loke, S.W., & Zaslavsky, A. (2002). Application run time estimation: A QoS metric for Web-based data mining service providers. In *Proceedings of ACM SAC.* ACM Press.

Malah, E.G. (2000). *Decision support and data-warehouse systems.* McGraw Hill.

Michalowski, W., Rubin, S., Slowinski, R., & Wilk, S. (2003). Mobile clinical support system for pediatric emergencies. *Decision Support Systems, 36,* 161-176.

Navarro, F., Schulter, A., Koch, F., Assuncao, M., & Westphall, C. (2006). Grid middleware for mobile decision support systems. In *Networking, International Conference on Systems and International Conference on Mobile Communications and Learning Technologies,* (pp. 125-125), *ICN/ICONS/MCL.*

Reis, L., Hoye, D., Gilbert, D., & Ryumae, M. (2000).*Online banking and electronic bill presentment payment are cost effective.* Retrieved December 14, 2007, from citeseer.nj.nec.com/402007.html

Roto, V. (2003). *Search on mobile phones.* Retrieved December 14, 2007, from http://home.earthlink.net/~searchworkshop/docs/Roto-SearchPositionPaper.pdf

Saksena, M.C., da Silva, J., & Agrawala, A.K. (1994). Design and implementation of Maruti-II. In S. Son (Ed.), *Principles of real-time systems.* Englewood Cliffs, NJ: Prentice-Hall. Retrieved December 14, 2007, from http://citeseer.nj.nec.com/saksena94design.html

San Pedro, J. C., Burstein, F., Cao, P. P., Churilov, L., Zaslavsky, A., Wassertheil, J. (2004, July 01-03). Mobile decision support for triage in emergency departments. In *The 2004 IFIP International Conference on Decision Support Systems (DSS2004) Conference Proceedings,* (pp. 714-723). Monash University, Melbourne, Victoria Australia.

San Pedro, J. Burstein, F., & Sharp, A. (2005). Toward case-based fuzzy multicriteria decision support model for tropical cyclone forecasting [Special Issue on Tools for Decision Support Systems]. *European Journal of Operational Research, 160*(2), 308-324.

Shim, J.P., Warkentin, M., Courtney, J.F., Power, D.J., Sharda, R., & Carlsson, C. (2002). Past, present, and future of decision support technology. *Decision Support Systems, 33,* 111–126

Simon, H.A. (1960). *The new science of management decision.* New York: Harper and Row.

Spreckelsen, C. Lethen, C., Heeskens, I., Pfeil, K., and Spitzer, K. (2000) *The roles of an intelligent mobile decision support system in the clinical workflow.* Retrieved January 23, 2008, from citeseer.nj.nec.com/spreckelsen00roles.html

Tewari, G., & Maes, P. (2001). A generalized platform for the specification, valuation, and brokering of heterogeneous resources in electronic markets. In J. Liu & Y. Ye (Eds.), *E-commerce agents* (LNAI 2033, pp. 7-24). Springer-Verlag.

Triantaphyllou, E., & Sanchez, A. (1997). A sensitivity analysis for some deterministic multi-criteria decision making methods. *Decision Sciences, 28*(1), 151-194.

Zadeh, L.A. (1994). Fuzzy logic, neural networks, and soft computing. *Communication of the ACM, 37*(3), 77-78.

KEY TERMS

Mobile Decision Support: Providing support for a decision maker who has access to a mobile device for their decision support, is possibly on the move, and is possibly in a time-critical environment.

Mobile Devices: Mobile devices are portable computers that facilitate access to information in much the same way as a desktop computer. Typically such devices use a small visual display for user output and either some form of keypad, keyboard, or touch screen for user input.

Quality of Data: A measure of the quality of the data being used to assist the decision maker in making a decision. The quality of data measure is an aggregate value which encompasses information about technical factors of the mobile device (such as connectivity) as well as information pertaining to the completeness, accuracy of the data provided, reliability and relevance of the data provided.

Time-Critical Decisions: The idea that the context of a decision, its parameters, options, and best outcomes, are dependent on when the decision is made. A good outcome at one point in time is not necessary a good outcome at a later point in time if the decision is time-critical.

Uncertainty: Decision making under uncertainty occurs when the decision maker has no clear view on how different outcomes of a decision fair in comparison to each other. There is no obvious ranking of outcomes from best to worst.

This work was previously published in Encyclopedia of Decision Making and Decision Support Technologies, edited by F. Adam and P. Humphreys, pp. 638-644, copyright 2008 by Information Science Reference, formerly known as Idea Group Reference (an imprint of IGI Global).

Chapter 8.24
OFDM Transmission Technique:
A Strong Candidate for the Next Generation Mobile Communications

Hermann Rohling
Hamburg University of Technology, Germany

ABSTRACT

The orthogonal frequency division multiplexing (OFDM) transmission technique can efficiently deal with multi-path propagation effects especially in broadband radio channels. It also has a high degree of system flexibility in multiple access schemes by combining the conventional TDMA, FDMA, and CDMA approaches with the OFDM modulation procedure, which is especially important in the uplink of a multi-user system. In OFDM-FDMA schemes carrier synchronization and the resulting sub-carrier orthogonality plays an important role to avoid any multiple access interferences (MAI) in the base station receiver. An additional technical challenge in system design is the required amplifier linearity to avoid any non-linear effects caused by a large peak-to-average ratio (PAR) of an OFDM signal. The OFDM transmission technique is used for the time being in some broadcast applications (DVB-T, DAB, DRM) and wireless local loop (WLL) standards (HIPERLAN/2, IEEE 802.11a) but OFDM has not been used so far in cellular communication networks. The general idea of the OFDM scheme is to split the total bandwidth into many narrowband sub-channels which are equidistantly distributed on the frequency axis. The sub-channel spectra overlap each other but the sub-carriers are still orthogonal in the receiver and can therefore be separated by a Fourier transformation. The system flexibility and use of sub-carrier specific adaptive modulation schemes in frequency selective radio channels are some advantages which make the OFDM transmission technique a strong and technically attractive candidate for the next generation of mobile communications. The objective of this chapter is to describe an OFDM-based system concept for the fourth generation (4G) of mobile communications and to discuss all technical details when establishing a cellular network which requires synchronization in time and frequency domain with sufficient accuracy. In this cellular environment a flexible frequency division multiple access scheme based on OFDM-FDMA is developed and a radio resource management (RRM) employing dynamic channel allocation (DCA) techniques is used. A purely decentralized and self-organized synchronization technique using specific test signals and RRM techniques based on co-channel interference (CCI) measurements has been developed and will be described in this chapter.

INTRODUCTION

In the evolution of mobile communication systems approximately a 10-year periodicity can be observed between consecutive system generations. Research work for the current 2nd generation of mobile communication systems (GSM) started in Europe in the early 1980s, and the complete system was ready for market in 1990. At that time the first research activities had already been started for the 3rd generation (3G) of mobile communication systems (UMTS, IMT-2000) and the transition from the current second generation (GSM) to the new 3G systems will be observed this year. Compared to today's GSM networks, these new UMTS systems will provide much higher data rates, typically in the range of 64 to 384 kbps, while the peak data rate for low mobility or indoor applications will be 2 Mbps.

The current pace, which can be observed in the mobile communications market, already shows that the 3G systems will not be the ultimate system solution. Consequently, general requirements for a 4G system have to be considered which will mainly be derived from the types of service a user will require in future applications. Generally, it is expected that data services instead of pure voice services will play a predominant role, in particular due to a demand for mobile IP applications. Variable and especially high data rates (20 Mbps and more) will be requested, which should also be available at high mobility in general or high vehicle speeds in particular (see Figure 1). Moreover, asymmetrical data services between up- and downlink are assumed and should be supported by 4G systems in such a scenario where the downlink carries most of the traffic and needs the higher data rate compared with the uplink.

To fulfill all these detailed system requirements the OFDM transmission technique applied in a wide-band radio channel is a strong candidate for an air interface in future 4G cellular systems due to its flexibility and adaptivity in the techni-

Figure 1. General requirements for 4G mobile communication systems

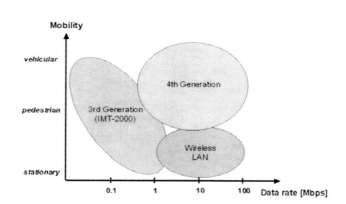

cal system design. From these considerations, it already becomes apparent that a radio transmission system for 4G must provide a great flexibility and adaptivity at different levels, ranging from the highest layer (requirements of the application) to the lowest layer (the transmission medium, the physical layer, that is, the radio channel) in the ISO-OSI stack. Today, the OFDM transmission technique is in a completely matured stage to be applied for wide-band communication systems integrated into a cellular mobile communications environment.

OFDM TRANSMISSION TECHNIQUE

Radio Channel Behaviour

The mobile communication system design is in general always dominated by the radio channel behaviour (Bello, 1963; Pätzold, 2002). In typical radio channel situation, multi-path propagation occurs (Figure 2) due to the reflections of the transmitted signal at several objects and obstacles inside the local environment and inside the observation area. The radio channel is analytically described unambiguously by a linear (quasi) time invariant (LTI) system model and by the related channel impulse response $h(\tau)$ or alternatively by the channel transfer function $H(f)$. An example for these channel characteristics is shown in Figure 3, where $h(\tau)$ and $H(f)$ of a so-called wide-sense stationary, uncorrelated scattering-channel (WS-SUS) are given.

Due to the mobility of the mobile terminals the multi-path propagation situation will be continuously but slowly changed over time which is described analytically by a time variant channel impulse response $h(\tau, t)$ or alternatively by a frequency selective and time dependent radio channel transfer function $H(f, t)$ as it is shown in Figure 5 by an example. All signals on the various propagation paths will be received in a superimposed form and are technically characterized by different delays and individual Doppler frequencies which lead finally to a frequency selective behaviour of the radio channel, see Figure 4. The other two system functions, the Delay Doppler function, $v(\tau, f_D)$ and the Frequency Doppler function, $U(f, f_D)$ can be used as an alternative description

Figure 2. Multi-path propagation scenario

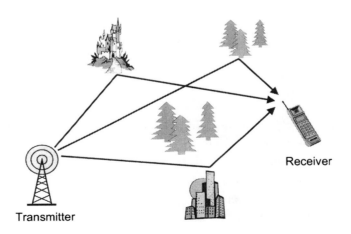

Receiver

Transmitter

Figure 3. Impulse response and channel transfer function of a WS-SUS channel

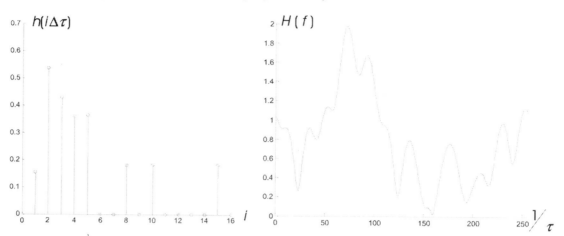

Figure 4. Relationships between different system functions

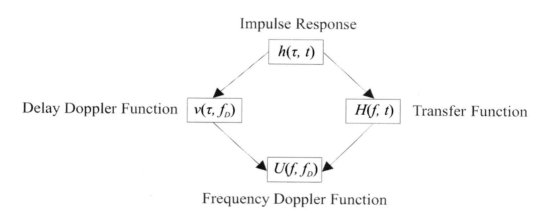

of the radio channel behaviour. The Delay Doppler function $v(\tau, f_D)$ describes the variation of the channel impulse response related to certain values of the Doppler frequency f_D. This means the channel delays change due to alteration of the relative speed between a mobile terminal and the base station. The Frequency Doppler function $U(f, f_D)$ models the same effects for the channel behaviour in the frequency domain.

The radio channel can roughly and briefly be characterised by two important system parameters: the maximum multi-path delay τ_{max} and

Figure 5. Frequency-selective and time-variant radio channel transfer function

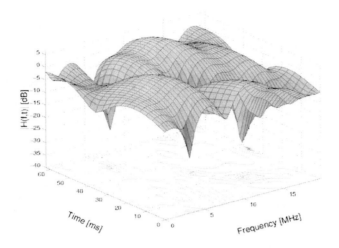

the maximum Doppler frequency $f_{D\max}$ which are transferred into the coherence time T_C and the coherence bandwidth B_C of the radio channel:

$$T_C = \frac{1}{f_{D\max}}, \quad B_C = \frac{1}{t_{\max}} \qquad (1)$$

Over time intervals significantly shorter than T_C, the channel transfer function can be assumed to be nearly stationary. Similarly, for frequency intervals significantly smaller than B_C, the channel transfer function can be considered as nearly constant. Therefore it is assumed in this chapter that the coherence time T_C is much larger compared to a single OFDM symbol duration T_S and the coherence bandwidth B_C is much larger than the distance Δf between two adjacent sub-carriers:

$$B_C \gg \Delta f, \quad \Delta f = \frac{1}{T_S}, \quad T_S \ll T_C \qquad (2)$$

This condition should be always fulfilled in well-dimensioned OFDM systems and in realistic time variant and frequency selective radio channels.

There are always technical alternatives possible in new system design phases. But future mobile communication systems will in any case require extremely large data rates and therefore large system bandwidth. If conventional single carrier (SC) modulation schemes with the resulting very low symbol durations are applied in this system design, it will be observed that very strong inter-symbol interference (ISI) is caused in wide-band applications due to multi-path propagation situations. This means for high data rate applications the symbol duration in a classical SC transmission system is extremely small compared to the typical values of maximum multi-path delay $\tau_{\max}$ in the considered radio channel. In these strong ISI situations a very powerful equalizer is necessary in each receiver, which needs high computation complexity in a wide-band system.

These constraints should be taken into consideration in the system development phase for a new radio transmission scheme and for a new 4G air interface. The computation complexity for the necessary equalizer techniques to overcome all these strong ISI in a SC modulation scheme increases exponentially for a given radio channel with increasing system bandwidth and can be extremely large in wide-band applications. For that reason alternative transmission techniques for broadband applications are of high interest.

Alternatively, the OFDM transmission technique can efficiently deal with all these ISI effects, which occur in multi-path propagation situations and in broadband radio channels. Simultaneously the OFDM transmission technique needs much less computation complexity in the equalization process inside each receiver. The performance figures for an OFDM based new air interface for the next generation of mobile communications are very promising even in frequency selective and time variant radio channel situations.

Advantages of the OFDM Transmission Technique

If a high data rate is transmitted over a frequency selective radio channel with a large maximum multi-path propagation delay τ_{max} compared to the symbol duration, an alternative to the classical SC approach is given by the OFDM transmission technique. The general idea of the OFDM transmission technique is to split the total available bandwidth B into many narrowband sub-channels at equidistant frequencies. The sub-channel spectra overlap each other but the sub-carrier signals are still orthogonal. The single high-rate data stream is subdivided into many low-rate data streams in the several sub-channels. Each sub-channel is modulated individually and will be transmitted simultaneously in a superimposed and parallel form.

An OFDM transmit signal therefore consists of N adjacent and orthogonal sub-carriers spaced by

the frequency distance Δf on the frequency axis. All sub-carrier signals are mutually orthogonal within the symbol duration of length T_S if the sub-carrier distance and the symbol duration are chosen such that $T_S = 1 / \Delta f$. For OFDM-based systems the symbol duration T_S is much larger compared to the maximum multi-path delay τ_{max}. The k-th unmodulated sub-carrier signal is described analytically by a complex valued exponential function with carrier frequency $k\Delta f$, $\tilde{g}_k(t)$, $k = 0, \ldots, N-1$.

$$\tilde{g}_k(t) = \begin{cases} e^{j2\pi k\Delta ft} & \forall t \in [0, T_S] \\ 0 & \forall t \notin [0, T_S] \end{cases} \qquad (3)$$

Since the system bandwidth B is subdivided into N narrowband sub-channels, the OFDM symbol duration T_S is N times larger as in the case of an alternative SC transmission system covering the same bandwidth B. Typically, for a given system bandwidth the number of sub-carriers is chosen in a way that the symbol duration T_S is sufficiently large compared to the maximum multi-path delay τ_{max} of the radio channel. On the other hand, in a time-variant radio channel the Doppler spread imposes restrictions on the sub-carrier spacing Δf. In order to keep the resulting inter-carrier interference (ICI) at a tolerable level, the system parameter of sub-carrier spacing Δf must be large enough compared to the maximum Doppler frequency f_{Dmax}. In Aldinger (1994), the appropriate range for choosing the symbol duration T_S as a rule of thumb in practical systems is given as (compare with Equation (2)):

$$4\tau_{max} \leq T_S \leq 0.03 \frac{1}{f_{D,max}}. \qquad (4)$$

The duration T_S as of the sub-carrier signal $\tilde{g}_k(t)$ is additionally extended by a cyclic prefix (so-called guard interval) of length T_G which is larger than the maximum multi-path delay τ_{max}

in order to avoid any ISI completely which could occur in multi-path channels in the transition interval between two adjacent OFDM symbols (Peled & Ruiz, 1980).

$$g_k(t) = \begin{cases} e^{j2\pi k\Delta ft} & \forall t \in [-T_G, T_S] \\ 0 & \forall t \notin [-T_G, T_S] \end{cases} \quad (5)$$

$$= e^{j2\pi k\Delta ft} rect\left(\frac{2t+(T_G-T_S)}{2T}\right)$$

The guard interval is directly removed in the receiver after the time synchronization procedure. From this point of view the guard interval is a pure system overhead and the total OFDM symbol duration is therefore $T = T_S + T_G$. It is an important advantage of the OFDM transmission technique that ISI can be avoided completely or can be reduced at least considerably by a proper choice of OFDM system parameters.

The orthogonality of all sub-carrier signals is completely preserved in the receiver even in frequency selective radio channels which is an important advantage of the OFDM transmission technique. The radio channel behaves linear and in a short-time interval of a few OFDM symbols even time invariant. Therefore the radio channel behaviour can be described completely by a linear and time invariant (LTI) system model characterized by the impulse response $h(t)$. The LTI system theory gives the reason for this important system behaviour that all sub-carrier signals are orthogonal in the receiver even when transmitting the signal in frequency selective radio channels. All complex valued exponential signals (e.g., all sub-carrier signals) are Eigenfunctions of each LTI system and therefore Eigenfunctions of the considered radio channel which means that only the signal amplitude and phase will be changed if a sub-carrier signal is transmitted in the linear and time invariant radio channel.

The sub-carrier frequency is not affected at all by the radio channel transmission which means

that all sub-carrier signals are even orthogonal in the receiver and at the output of a frequency selective radio channel. The radio channel interferes only amplitudes and phases individually but not the sub-carrier frequency of all received sub-channel signals. Therefore all sub-carrier signals are still mutually orthogonal in the receiver. Due to this important property the received signal which is superimposed by all sub-carrier signals can be split directly into the different sub-channel components by a Fourier transformation and each sub-carrier signal can be demodulated individually by a single tap equalizer in the receiver.

At the transmitter side each sub-carrier signal is modulated independently and individually by the complex valued modulation symbol $S_{n,k}$, where the subscript n refers to the time interval and k to the sub-carrier signal number in the considered OFDM symbol. Thus, within the symbol duration time interval T the time continuous signal of the n-th OFDM symbol is formed by a superposition of all N simultaneously modulated sub-carrier signals.

$$s_n(t) = \sum_{k=0}^{N-1} S_{n,k} g_k(t - nT) \quad (6)$$

The total time continuous transmit signal consisting of all OFDM symbols sequentially transmitted on the time axis is described analytically by the following equation:

$$s(t) = \sum_{n=0}^{\infty} \sum_{k=0}^{N-1} S_{n,k} e^{j2\pi k\Delta f(t-nT)} rect\left(\frac{2(t-nT)+(T_G-T_S)}{2T}\right)$$

$$(7)$$

The analytical transmit signal description shows that a rectangular pulse shaping is applied for each sub-carrier signal and each OFDM symbol. But due to the rectangular pulse shaping, the spectra of all the considered sub-carrier signals are sinc-functions which are equidistantly located on the frequency axis, for example, for the k-th sub-carrier signal the spectrum is described in the following equation:

$$G_k(f) = T \cdot \mathrm{sinc}\left[\mathsf{p}T(f - k\Delta f)\right] \quad \text{where}$$

$$\mathrm{sinc}(x) = \frac{\sin(x)}{x} \tag{8}$$

The typical OFDM-Spectrum shown in Figure 6 consists of N adjacent sinc-functions, which are shifted by Δf in the frequency direction.

The spectra of the considered sub-carrier signals overlap on the frequency axis, but the sub-carrier signals are still mutually orthogonal which means the transmitted modulation symbols $S_{n,k}$ can be recovered by a simple correlation technique in each receiver if the radio channel is assumed to be ideal in a first analytical step:

$$\frac{1}{T_s} \int_0^{T_s} g_k(t)\overline{g_l(t)}dt = \begin{cases} 1 & k=l \\ 0 & k \neq l \end{cases} = \mathsf{d}_{k,l} \tag{9}$$

$$S_{n,k} = \frac{1}{T_S}\int_0^{T_s} s_n(t)\overline{g_k(t)}dt = \frac{1}{T_S}\int_0^{T_s} s_n(t)e^{-j2\mathsf{p}k\Delta f t}dt \tag{10}$$

where $\overline{g_k(t)}$ is the conjugate complex version of the sub-carrier signal $g_k(t)$. The following equations show the correlation process in detail:

$$Corr = \frac{1}{T_S}\int_0^{T_s} s_n(t)\overline{g_k(t)}dt = \frac{1}{T_S}\int_0^{T_s} \sum_{m=0}^{N-1} S_{n,m}g_m(t)\overline{g_k(t)}dt$$

$$= \sum_{m=0}^{N-1} S_{n,m}\frac{1}{T_S}\int_0^{T_s} g_m(t)\overline{g_k(t)}dt = \sum_{m=0}^{N-1} S_{n,m}\mathsf{d}_{m,k} = \underline{\underline{S_{n,k}}} \tag{11}$$

In practical applications the OFDM transmit signal $s_n(t)$ is generated in a first step and in the digital baseband signal processing part of the transmitter as a time discrete signal. Using the

sampling theorem while considering the OFDM transmit signal inside the bandwidth $B = N\Delta f$, the transmit signal must be sampled with the sampling interval $\Delta t = 1/B = 1/N\Delta f$. The individual samples of the transmit signal are denoted by $s_{n,i}$, $i = 0, 1, \ldots, N-1$ and can be calculated as follows (see Equation (7)):

$$s(t) = \sum_{k=0}^{N-1} S_{n,k}e^{j2\mathsf{p}k\Delta f t}$$

$$s(i\Delta t) = \sum_{k=0}^{N-1} S_{n,k}e^{j2\mathsf{p}k\Delta f(i\Delta t)}$$

$$s_{n,i} = \sum_{k=0}^{N-1} S_{n,k}e^{j2\mathsf{p}ik/N} \tag{12}$$

This Equation (12) describes exactly the inverse discrete Fourier transform (IDFT) applied to the complex valued modulation symbols $S_{n,k}$ of all sub-carrier signals inside a single OFDM symbol.

The individually modulated and superimposed sub-carrier signals are transmitted in a parallel way over many narrowband sub-channels. Thus, in each sub-channel the symbol duration is quite large and can be chosen much larger as compared to the maximum multi-path delay of the radio channel. In this case each sub-channel has the property to be frequency non-selective.

Figure 7 shows the general OFDM system structure in a block diagram. The basic principles of the OFDM transmission technique have already been described in several publications like Bingham (1990) and Weinstein and Ebert (1971). In the very early and classical multi-carrier system considerations like Chang (1966) and Saltzberg (1967), narrowband signals have been generated independently, assigned to various frequency bands, transmitted, and separated by analogue filters at the receiver. The new and modern aspect of the OFDM transmission technique is that the various sub-carrier signals are generated digitally and jointly by an IFFT in the transmitter and that

Figure 6. OFDM spectrum which consists of N equidistant sinc-functions

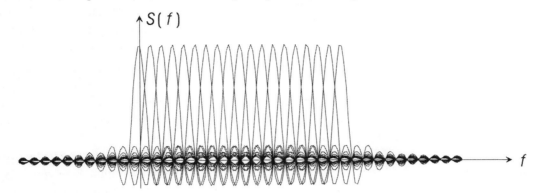

Figure 7. OFDM system structure in a block diagram

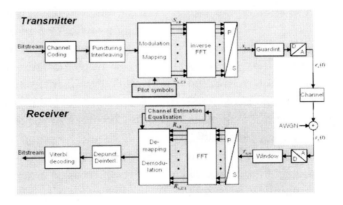

their spectra strongly overlap on the frequency axis. As a result, generating the transmit signal is simplified and the bandwidth efficiency of the system is significantly improved.

The received signal is represented by the convolution of the transmitted time signal with the channel impulse response $h(t)$ and an additive white Gaussian noise term:

$$r_n(t) = s_n(t) * h_n(t) + n_n(t) \qquad (13)$$

Due to the assumption, that the coherence time T_C will be much larger than the symbol duration T_S the received time continuous signal $r_n(t)$ can be separated into the orthogonal sub-carrier signal components even in frequency selective fading situations by applying the correlation technique mentioned in Equation (10):

$$R_{n,k} = \frac{1}{T_S} \int_0^{T_S} r_n(t) e^{-j2\text{p}k\Delta ft} dt \qquad (14)$$

Equivalently, the correlation process at the receiver side can be applied to the time discrete receive signal at the output of an A/D converter and can be implemented as a DFT, which leads to the following equation:

$$R_{n,k} = \frac{1}{N} \sum_{i=0}^{N-1} r_{n,i} e^{-j2\pi iik/N} \qquad (15)$$

In this case $r_{n,i} = r_n(i \cdot \Delta t)$ describes the i-th sample of the received time continuous baseband signal $r_n(t)$ and $R_{n,k}$ is the received complex valued symbol at the DFT output of the k-th sub-carrier.

If the OFDM symbol duration T is chosen much smaller than the coherence time T_C of the radio channel, then the time variant transfer function of the radio channel $H(f, t)$ can be considered constant within the time duration T of each modulation symbol $S_{n,k}$ for all sub-carrier signals. In this case, the effect of the radio channel in multi-path propagation situations can be described analytically by only a single multiplication of each sub-carrier signal $g_k(t)$ with the complex transfer factor $H_{n,k} = H(k\Delta f, nT)$. As a result, the received complex valued symbol $R_{n,k}$ at the DFT output can be described analytically as follows:

$$r_n(t) = s_n(t) * h_n(t) + n_n(t)$$
$$r_{n,i} = s_{n,i} * h_{n,i} + n_{n,i}$$

$$R_{n,k} = S_{n,k} H_{n,k} + N_{n,k} \qquad (16)$$

where $N_{n,k}$ describes an additive noise component for each specific sub-carrier generated in the radio channel. This equation shows the most important

advantage of applying the OFDM transmission technique in practical applications. Equation (16) describes the complete signal transfer situation of the OFDM block diagram including IDFT, guard interval, D/A conversion, up- and down-conversion in the RF part, frequency selective radio channel, A/D conversion and DFT process in the receiver, neglecting non-ideal behaviour of any system components.

The transmitted Symbol $S_{n,k}$ can be recovered, calculating the quotient of the received complex valued symbol and the estimated channel transfer factor $\tilde{H}_{n,k}$:

$$S_{n,k} = \frac{R_{n,k} - N_{n,k}}{H_{n,k}}, \quad \tilde{S}_{n,k} = R_{n,k} \frac{1}{\tilde{H}_{n,k}} \qquad (17)$$

It is obvious that this one tap equalization step of the received signal is much easier compared to a single carrier system for high data rate applications. The necessary IDFT and DFT calculations can be implemented very efficiently using the Fast-Fourier-Transform (FFT) algorithms such as Radix 2^2, which reduces the system and computation complexity even more.

It should be pointed out that especially the frequency synchronization at the receiver must be very precise in order to avoid any inter-carrier interferences (ICI). Algorithms for time and frequency synchronization in OFDM-based systems are described in Classen and Meyr (1994) and Mizoguchi et al. (1998), for example and will be considered in the section, *Self-Organized Cell Synchronization*.

Besides the complexity aspects, another advantage of the OFDM technique lies in its high degree of flexibility and adaptivity. Division of the available bandwidth into many frequency-non-selective sub-bands gives additional advantages for the OFDM transmission technique. It allows a sub-carrier-specific adaptation of transmit parameters, such as modulation scheme (PHY mode) and transmit power (cp. Water Filling) in accordance to the observed and measured radio channel status. In a multi-user environment the OFDM structure offers additionally an increased flexibility for resource allocation procedures as compared to SC systems (Hanzo et al., 2003).

The important system behaviour that all sub-carrier signals are mutually orthogonal in the receiver makes the signal processing and the equalization process realized by a single-tap procedure very simple and leads to a low computation complexity.

OFDM COMBINED WITH MULTIPLE ACCESS SCHEMES

A very high degree of flexibility and adaptivity is required for new mobile communication systems and for the 4G air interface. The combination between multiple access schemes and OFDM transmission technique is an important factor in this respect. In principle, multiple access schemes for the OFDM transmission technique can be categorized according to OFDM-FDMA, OFDM-TDMA, and OFDM-CDMA (Kaiser, 1998; Rohling & Grünheid, 1997). Clearly, hybrid schemes can be applied which are based on a combination of these techniques. The principles of these basic multiple access schemes are summarized in Figure 8, where the time-frequency plane is depicted and the user specific resource allocation is distinguished by different colours.

These access schemes provide a great variety of possibilities for a flexible user specific resource allocation. In the following, one example for OFDM-FDMA is briefly sketched (cf. Galda, Rohling, Costa, Haas, & Schulz, 2002). In the case that the magnitude of the channel transfer function is known for each user the sub-carrier selection for an OFDM-FDMA scheme can be processed in the BS for each user individually which leads to a multi-user diversity (MUD) effect. By allocating a subset of all sub-carriers with the highest SNR to each user the system performance can be improved. This allocation technique based on the knowledge of the channel transfer function shows a large performance advantage and a gain in quality of service (QoS). Nearly the same flexibility in resource allocation is possible in OFDM-CDMA systems. But in

Figure 8. OFDM transmission technique and some multiple access schemes

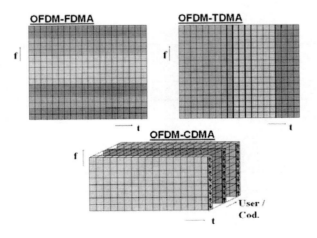

this case the code orthogonality is destroyed by the frequency selective radio channel resulting in multiple access interferences (MAI), which reduces the system performance.

TECHNICAL PROPOSAL AND EXAMPLE FOR A 4G DOWNLINK INTERFACE

Taking all these important results from the previous sections into consideration, a system design example is considered in this section. OFDM system parameters for a 4G air interface are considered and three different multiple access schemes inside a single cell are compared quantitatively. A bandwidth of 20 MHz in the 5.5 GHz domain is assumed. The assumed multi-path radio channel has a maximum delay of $\tau_{max} = 5$ µs (the coherence bandwidth is therefore $B_C = 200$ kHz). Additionally, a maximum speed of $v_{max} = 200$ km/h is assumed, which yields a maximum Doppler frequency of $f_{Dmax} = 1$ kHz and a coherence time of $T_C = 1$ ms. Table 1 shows an example for the system parameters of a 4G air interface.

For the considered OFDM based system three different multiple access concepts have been analysed and compared. The first proposal is based on a pure OFDM-TDMA structure, while the second one considers an OFDM-FDMA technique with an adaptive sub-carrier selection scheme, as described in the section, *OFDM Transmission Technique Combined with Multiple Access Schemes*. The third one is based on OFDM-CDMA where the user data are spread over a subset of adjacent sub-carriers.

In this case MAI occur and an interference cancellation technique implemented in each MT is useful. To compare the different multiple access schemes, Figure 9 shows the bit error rate (BER) for an OFDM system with the system parameters shown in Table 1.

A single cell situation has been considered in this case with a perfect time and carrier synchronization. As can be seen from this figure, the best performance can be achieved by an OFDM-FDMA system which exploits the frequency selective fading of the mobile radio channel by allocating always the best available sub-carrier to each user. Note that a channel adaptive FDMA scheme requires a good prediction of the channel transfer function which has been considered to be perfect in this comparison. If a non-adaptive FDMA technique was used (i.e., fixed or random

Table 1. Proposal of OFDM system parameters

PARAMETER	VALUE
FFT Length	$N_C = 512$
Guard interval length	$N_G = N_C / 8 = 64$
Modulation technique	16-QAM
Code rate	R=1/2, m=6
FDMA	Best available sub-carrier is selected.
TDMA	
CDMA Spreading matrix	Walsh-Hadamard (L=16)
CDMA detection technique	SUD with MMSE, MUD with soft interference cancellation plus MMSE

Figure 9. BER results for a coded OFDM system employing different multiple access techniques

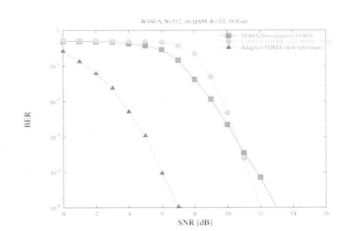

allocation of sub-carriers), the performance would be comparable to the OFDM-TDMA curve.

In the case of an OFDM-TDMA system the frequency selectivity of the radio channel can be exploited by the Viterbi decoder in conjunction with bit interleaving. A pure coded OFDM-CDMA system which utilizes an orthogonal spreading matrix with minimum mean square error (MMSE) equalization and single user detection (SUD) to exploit the diversity of the channel suffers from MAI due to loss of code orthogonality in frequency selective fading. A performance improvement can be achieved for an OFDM-CDMA scheme applying multi-user detection (MUD) techniques. By successively removing inter-code-/-user interference using MUD procedure, a gain of approximately 2 dB can be achieved. But still an OFDM-FDMA system outperforms an optimized OFDM-CDMA system. Additionally, OFDM-CDMA technique has a much higher computational complexity in the MUD scheme.

TECHNICAL PROPOSAL AND EXAMPLE FOR A 4G UPLINK INTERFACE

As shown in the preceding paragraph, there are several system proposals published for an OFDM-based downlink procedure for broadcast and communication systems respectively. But by designing an OFDM uplink transmission scheme some important and additional technical questions will come up. Therefore, OFDM-based uplink systems are still under consideration and research (Rohling, Galda, & Schulz, 2004). As a contribution to this topic, an OFDM-based multi-user uplink system with M different users inside a single cell is considered in this section.

Each user shares the entire bandwidth with all other users inside the cell by allocating exclusively a deterministic subset of all available sub-carriers inside the considered OFDM system. This user specific sub-carrier selection process allows to share the total bandwidth in a very flexible way between all mobile terminals. Hence, as a relevant multiple access scheme an OFDM-FDMA structure is considered in which each user claims the same bandwidth or the same number of sub-carriers inside the total bandwidth respectively. Due to the assumed perfect carrier synchronization and resulting sub-carrier orthogonality in the receiver any multiple access interference (MAI) between different users can be avoided. The sub-carrier allocation process can either be designed to be non-adaptive or adaptive in accordance with the current radio channel state information (CSI).

Since the OFDM transmission signal results from the superposition of a large number of independent data symbols and sub-carrier signals the envelope of the complex valued baseband time signal is in general not constant but has a large peak-to-average ratio (PAR). The largest output power value of the amplifier will therefore limit the maximum amplitude in the transmit signal. Additionally, non-linear distortions due to clipping and amplification effects in the transmit signal will lead to both in-band interferences and out-of-band emissions (Brüninghaus & Rohling, 1997). Therefore, in the downlink case each base station will spend some effort and computation power to control the transmit signal amplitude and to reduce the PAR. The objective is in this case to minimize the resulting non-linear effects or even to avoid any interferences.

But for the uplink case it is especially important to design a transmit signal with low PAR to reduce computation complexity in the mobile terminal and to avoid any interference situation caused by non-linear effects of the amplification process.

It will be shown in this section that an OFDM-FDMA system based on an equidistant sub-carrier selection procedure combined with an additional sub-carrier spreading technique will reduce the resulting PAR significantly (Brüninghaus & Rohling, 1998) for the uplink procedure. Furthermore, this proposal will lead to a modulation technique which becomes technically very simple and where the transmit signal consists of a periodic extension and multiple repetition of all modulation symbols. This is the result of the duality between multi-carrier CDMA and single carrier transmission technique as described in Brüninghaus and Rohling (1998).

Figure 10 shows the general structure of an OFDM uplink signal processing in the mobile terminal, which will be considered in this section. In this block diagram there are two main components in the OFDM-based modulation scheme which will be treated in the design process of a multi-user uplink system: The sub-carrier selection technique, and a user specific spreading scheme applied to the user's selected sub-carrier subset, respectively.

The last two blocks in the block diagram show the characteristic IDFT processing and the guard interval (GI) insertion, that are common in all OFDM-based transmitter schemes.

In the uplink system model of a multi-user, OFDM-FDMA based scheme, an arbitrary num-

Figure 10. Block diagram of a multi-user OFDM-FDMA uplink system

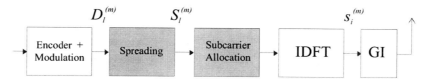

ber of M different users are considered inside a single cell and each user allocates exclusively L different sub-carriers which are considered inside the entire system bandwidth for data transmission. The total number of all considered sub-carriers inside the system bandwidth of the transmission scheme is therefore $N_C = L \cdot M$.

The input data stream for each mobile user terminal m, $m = 0$, ..., $M - 1$, is convolutionally encoded in a first step. Afterwards, the bit sequence is mapped onto a modulation symbol vector $\vec{D}^{(m)} = \left(D_0^{(m)}, D_1^{(m)}, ..., D_{L-1}^{(m)}\right)$ of L complex valued symbols $D_l^{(m)}$ from a given modulation alphabet with 2^Q different modulation symbols inside the constellation diagram. An example for such a modulation alphabet is given in Figure 11 for a 16-QAM.

In this section, a non-differential, higher level modulation scheme is assumed for the uplink case.

Figure 11. 16-QAM as an exemplary alphabet with modulation symbols $D_l^{(m)}$

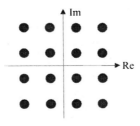

Each user transmits $L \cdot Q$ bits per OFDM symbol. It is assumed in this section without any loss of generality that each user transmits the same data rate or the same number of modulation symbols per OFDM signal respectively.

Sub-Carrier Allocation Process

The first important question in the OFDM-FDMA multi-user uplink system design is the user specific sub-carrier selection scheme. This process is responsible for sharing the bandwidth between M different users, see Figure 12.

There is a large degree of freedom in this system design step to allocate exclusively a subset of L specific sub-carriers to each user. This can either be done by a random or a deterministic allocation scheme. Alternatively there are proposals made for adaptive sub-carrier selection schemes to increase the resulting system capacity (Gross, Karl, Fitzek, & Wolisz, 2003; Shen, Li, & Liu, 2004; Toufik & Knopp, 2004).

In this paragraph a very specific non-adaptive sub-carrier selection procedure is proposed. In this case the allocated sub-carrier subset is equidistantly located on the frequency axis over the entire system bandwidth. This approach is shown in Figure 13 and will be pursued in the following.

In this multi-user uplink system each user m allocates exclusively in total L sub-carriers which are in each case placed in an equidistant way on the frequency axis. The selected L sub-carriers are modulated with L complex valued transmit sym-

Figure 12. Block diagram for an OFDM-FDMA based system with sub-carrier selection process

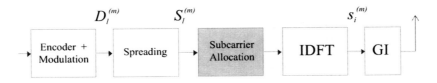

bols $S_l^{(m)}$, described and denoted by the transmit symbol vector $\vec{S}^{(m)}$. The proposed non-adaptive sub-carrier selection and modulation process does not need any radio channel state information (CSI) at the transmitter side.

Due to this specific sub-carrier selection process based on equidistantly located sub-carriers on the frequency axis the resulting OFDM uplink transmit time signal $s_i^{(m)}$ of any user has a periodic structure with period length L and consists in any case of an M-times repetition time signal, see Figure 14.

Equation (18) describes the relation between the sub-carrier transmit symbols $S_l^{(0)}$ and a single period of the resulting OFDM transmit time signal $s_i^{(0)}$ for user 0 analytically.

$$s_i^{(0)} = \frac{1}{\sqrt{L}} \sum_{l=0}^{L-1} S_l^{(0)} e^{j2\pi il/L} \quad \text{for } i = 0,1,\ldots,L-1$$

(18)

This relation in equation is simply an IDFT applied to the transmit symbols $S_l^{(0)}$, as shown in Equation (19).

$$\begin{pmatrix} s_0^{(0)} \\ s_1^{(0)} \\ \cdots \\ s_{L-1}^{(0)} \end{pmatrix} = \text{IDFT} \begin{pmatrix} S_0^{(0)} \\ S_1^{(0)} \\ \cdots \\ S_{L-1}^{(0)} \end{pmatrix}$$

(19)

Because the sub-carrier subset of a single user is assumed to be allocated equidistantly over all N_C sub-carriers inside the entire bandwidth (Figure 13), it can be shown that an N_C-IDFT processing of the sub-carrier transmit symbols $S_l^{(0)}$ inside the OFDM transmitter leads to the same M-times repetition of the user time signal $s_i^{(0)}$ as shown in Figure 14. The periodicity of the transmit signal is directly related to the selection process of equidistantly located sub-carrier on the frequency axis.

Sub-Carrier Spreading Technique

This paragraph addresses the second design element of an OFDM-FDMA based system: a spreading technique applied to the user's selected sub-carriers, see Figure 15. There are several well-known spreading techniques, which can be integrated into an OFDM-based transmission technique (Kaiser, 2002; Linnartz, 2000). Analo-

Figure 13. Equidistantly allocated subset of L sub-carriers for a single user in a multi-user environment

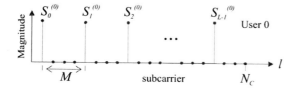

Figure 14. OFDM-FDMA based periodic transmit time signal with period length L and M-times repetition

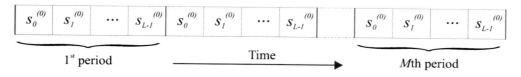

gous to other MC-CDMA systems, described in Kaiser (2002) and Linnartz (2000), the vector $\vec{D}^{(m)}$ of L modulation symbols (see Figure 11) is spread in this case over L sub-carriers which are exclusively allocated to user m applying an unitary spreading matrix $[C]$.

This results in a transmit sub-carrier symbol vector $\vec{S}^{(m)} = \left(S_0^{(m)}, S_1^{(m)}, \ldots, S_{L-1}^{(m)} \right)$ consisting of L complex valued transmit symbols $S_l^{(m)}, l = 0, \ldots, L - 1$. The spreading operation can be denoted mathematically by the following matrix multiplication where each complex valued transmit symbol $S_l^{(m)}$ is calculated by the sum of L user specific modulation symbols $D_l^{(m)}$ weighted by L orthogonal code vectors $\vec{C}_l = \left(C_{l,0}, C_{l,1}, \ldots, C_{l,L-1} \right)$ with $l = 0, \ldots, L - 1$:

$$
\begin{pmatrix} S_0^{(m)} \\ S_1^{(m)} \\ \vdots \\ S_{L-1}^{(m)} \end{pmatrix} = \begin{bmatrix} C_{0,0} & C_{0,1} & \cdots & C_{0,L-1} \\ C_{1,0} & \ddots & & C_{1,L-1} \\ \vdots & & & \vdots \\ C_{L-1,0} & \cdots & \cdots & C_{L-1,L-1} \end{bmatrix} \cdot \begin{pmatrix} D_0^{(m)} \\ D_1^{(m)} \\ \vdots \\ D_{L-1}^{(m)} \end{pmatrix}
$$

(20)

The spreading Matrix $[C]$ consists of L orthogonal spreading codes. It can be designed, for example, by a Walsh-Hadamard matrix like in Kaiser (2002) and Linnartz (2000) or by a DFT matrix as described in Brüninghaus and Rohling (1997, 1998). Both matrix types fulfill the requirements for unity and orthogonality.

Examples for these matrices are shown in Figure 16. In the considered multi-user uplink system, only a DFT matrix based spreading technique will be used, because of the resulting benefits in combination with an equidistant sub-carrier allocation scheme.

After the spreading process, the sub-carrier specific transmit symbols $S_l^{(m)}$ are mapped onto L sub-carrier signals which are exclusively allocated to user m. In principle, the user specific sub-carrier subset can be composed of any L out of N_C sub-carriers that have not been assigned to another user.

Combination of Spreading and Sub-Carrier Allocation

As explained in the previous paragraph, the spreading technique applied to the modulation symbols

Figure 16. Examples for Walsh-Hadamard (left) and DFT spreading matrix

$$
\begin{bmatrix} 1 & 1 & 1 & 1 \\ 1 & -1 & 1 & -1 \\ 1 & 1 & -1 & -1 \\ 1 & -1 & -1 & 1 \end{bmatrix} \quad \begin{bmatrix} 1 & 1 & 1 & 1 \\ 1 & e^{-j\text{p}/2} & e^{-j\text{p}} & e^{-j\frac{3}{2}\text{p}} \\ 1 & e^{-j\text{p}} & e^{-j2\text{p}} & e^{-j3\text{p}} \\ 1 & e^{-j\frac{3}{2}\text{p}} & e^{-j3\text{p}} & e^{-j\frac{9}{2}\text{p}} \end{bmatrix}
$$

Figure 15. Block diagram of a multi-user OFDM-FDMA uplink system with additional spreading technique

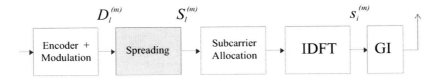

$D_l^{(m)}$ is considered in a way, that a DFT-Matrix can be used as spreading matrix $[C]$. Therefore, the relation between modulation symbols $D_l^{(0)}$ and sub-carrier transmit symbols $S_l^{(0)}$ are described analytically by Equation (21):

$$
\begin{pmatrix} S_0^{(0)} \\ S_1^{(0)} \\ \cdots \\ S_{L-1}^{(0)} \end{pmatrix} = \begin{bmatrix} & & \\ & [C] & \\ & & \end{bmatrix} \cdot \begin{pmatrix} D_0^{(0)} \\ D_1^{(0)} \\ \cdots \\ D_{L-1}^{(0)} \end{pmatrix} = \mathrm{DFT} \begin{pmatrix} D_0^{(0)} \\ D_1^{(0)} \\ \cdots \\ D_{L-1}^{(0)} \end{pmatrix}
$$

(21)

If this DFT-based spreading technique is combined with the earlier explained, equidistant sub-carrier selection process the transmit time signal $s_i^{(0)}$ can be calculated directly by the M-times repetition of modulation symbol vector $\vec{D}^{(0)}$ which consists of L complex valued modulation symbols, see Figure 17. Therefore, it is needless to process the DFT spreading matrix and the IFFT in the OFDM system structure explicitly, which reduces the computation complexity in the mobile terminal, see Equation (22). Hence, a single period

of the resulting time signal $s_i^{(0)}$ is directly given by the calculated modulation symbols $D_l^{(0)}$.

$$
\begin{pmatrix} s_0^{(0)} \\ s_1^{(0)} \\ \vdots \\ s_{L-1}^{(0)} \end{pmatrix} = \mathrm{IDFT} \begin{pmatrix} S_0^{(0)} \\ S_1^{(0)} \\ \vdots \\ S_{L-1}^{(0)} \end{pmatrix} = \mathrm{IDFT} \left(\mathrm{DFT} \begin{pmatrix} D_0^{(0)} \\ D_1^{(0)} \\ \vdots \\ D_{L-1}^{(0)} \end{pmatrix} \right) = \begin{pmatrix} D_0^{(0)} \\ D_1^{(0)} \\ \vdots \\ D_{L-1}^{(0)} \end{pmatrix}
$$

(22)

In almost all OFDM systems, a cyclic prefix of length N_G will be added to the transmit time signal $s_i^{(0)}$ to avoid any ISI. Therefore, the so-called guard interval is also an integral part of the multi-user uplink system described in this paragraph. Thus, the structure of the OFDM-FDMA multi-user uplink system depicted in Figure 18 can be simplified. Figure 18 shows the functionality of the overall system in detail. It becomes clear that because of the cancellation of DFT spreading and IDFT calculation these components can be completely removed in the technical realization. They are replaced by a simple repetition process of the considered user specific modulation symbols $D_l^{(0)}$.

Figure 17. Periodic transmit signal for the multi-user uplink system: Symbols $s_i^{(0)}$ and modulation symbols $D_l^{(0)}$

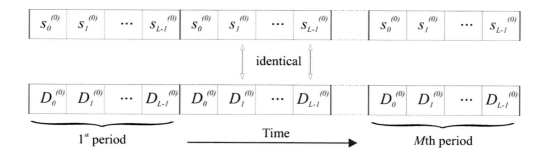

Figure 18. OFDM-FDMA based uplink system including a DFT spreading matrix applied to a set of equidistant sub-carriers

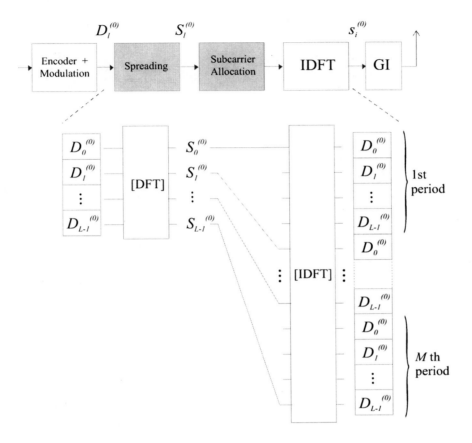

Multi-User Case

The extension from a single to an arbitrary user m is straight forward and will be described in the following. Another user m also allocates an equidistantly spaced subset of all sub-carriers which is shifted in the frequency space by m sub-carriers, see Figure 19.

Any frequency shift results in a multiplication of the transmit time signal $s_i^{(m)}$ with a complex valued signal $e^{j2\pi im/N_C}$, see Equation (23).

Figure 19. Shifting the total sub-carrier subset in a multi-user environment

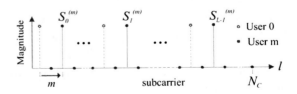

Figure 20. OFDM-FDMA uplink transmit signal for an arbitrary user m

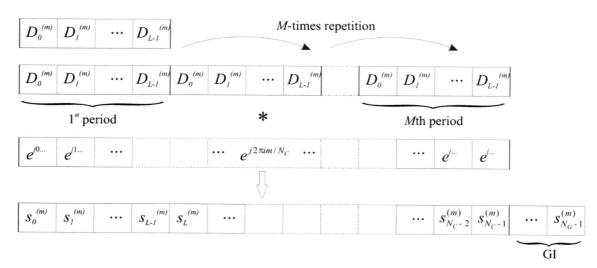

$$S_l^{(m)} \cdot d(l-m) \quad \bullet\!-\!\circ \quad s_i^{(m)} \cdot e^{j2\rho im/N_C} \qquad (23)$$

This yields a phase rotation of the transmit time symbols $s_i^{(m)}$ with the constant frequency $f_0 = m/N_C$. But this has no significant impact on the complexity of the transmitter structure. Also, the signal envelope of a single OFDM symbol is still constant. The simplified synthesis of the transmit time signal for the multi-user case is depicted in Figure 20. First, the vector of L modulation symbols $\vec{D}^{(m)}$ is calculated and repeated M-times on the time axis. Then, the time sequence is elementwise multiplied by the user-specific, phase rotating sequence $e^{j2\pi im/N_C}$. In the last step, the guard interval is added. Figure 20 describes the simple transmit signal processing and the low computation complexity at the transmitter side and in the mobile terminal for the uplink case.

Figure 19 and Figure 20 show that the time signal of the OFDM-FDMA based uplink scheme with DFT spreading can be considered as a blockwise single carrier periodic transmission system where a cyclic prefix is integrated into a single block as a guard interval. Therefore, the signal envelope is nearly constant and additional techniques like $\pi/4 - $ QPSK can be employed to even reduce the resulting small PAR for this single carrier system. An additional advantage of this OFDM-FDMA based uplink system is the flexible use of sub-carrier allocation process and data rate adaptation for a certain user.

OFDM-BASED AND SYNCHRONIZED CELLULAR NETWORK

In the preceding sections, several uplink- and downlink-schemes for the connection between mobile terminals and base stations were discussed. In this section, the focus will be broadened from individual links to the overall cellular network. In this context, resource allocation and synchronization of the network play an important role.

As before, the OFDM receiver in a cell has to deal with ISI effects, which occur in multi-path propagation situations in broadband radio channels. In a sufficiently designed OFDM system, these effects can be completely avoided.

Consequently, the OFDM receiver can also deal with superimposed signals which have been transmitted by several distinct and adjacent base stations (BS) in a cellular environment, if the cellular network is synchronized in time and carrier frequency. All adjacent BS operate simultaneously in the same frequency band which leads to a reuse factor of 1.

In current cellular radio networks each base station assigns resources independently and exclusively to its users. To be able to use a TDMA or FDMA multiple access scheme in a cellular environment, an off-line radio resource planning is required to avoid co-channel interference situations between adjacent cells. As a consequence only a small fraction of the available resource determined by the spatial reuse is assigned to each cell which can dynamically be accessed by its us-

ers (Zander & Kim, 2001). However, due to this fixed resource distribution among adjacent cells, a dynamic and flexible shift of resources between cells is technically difficult. Such a conventional cellular network with a fixed frequency planning is shown in Figure 21 for a time division duplex (TDD) system as an example.

By introducing the OFDM transmission technique in such a cellular environment, the limitations of fixed resource allocation can be overcome. Since the OFDM transmission technique is robust in multi-path propagation situations, a synchronized network can be established. All BS and MT are synchronized in this case and the signals from adjacent BS will be received with a mutual relative delay no longer than the guard interval. Under these synchronized network conditions each BS can use all available resources simultaneously. With this technique at hand it is possible to add an additional "macro" diversity to a cellular environment by transmitting the same signal from synchronized BS.

Synchronized networks have been intensively studied, for example, for DVB-T broadcast systems as a single frequency network (SFN). In this case the same information signal is transmitted

Figure 21. Conventional cellular network with fixed resource allocation

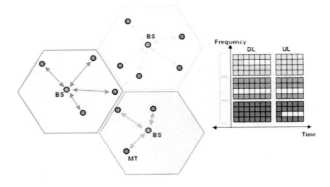

on the same resources from different BS. In the communication case and in a synchronized network different information signals are transmitted by the adjacent BS but all received signals can be considered as co-sub-carrier interferer which allows in general the allocation of all available resources for each BS.

A synchronized network will also be considered to implement a dynamic resource allocation scheme by assigning different sub-carriers of an OFDM-FDMA multiple access scheme to users in adjacent cells. Since the OFDM sub-carriers remain orthogonal in a synchronized network, no MAI between different user in adjacent cells will occur as long as the sub-carriers have been allocated in an exclusive way.

All resources can be accessed in this case by the MT inside a cellular network. Synchronized networks can be used to provide the needed flexibility inside a cellular environment to allocate system resources in those cells where this bandwidth is needed. Especially for non-uniformly distributed users inside a cellular environment or for hot spot situations the system capacity can be largely increased in synchronized networks. The synchronization concept is shown in Figure

22 for an OFDM-FDMA and TDD system as an example. In this case the resource management could be based on co-channel interference (CCI) measurements processed in each BS.

Self-Organized Cell Synchronization

The dynamic sharing of all available resources between adjacent cells requires a tight time and frequency synchronization of all BS and all MT inside the cellular environment. All MTs are synchronized to a single BS using a specific test signal which is transmitted in a downlink preamble. It is assumed in this paragraph that the required network synchronization is achieved without any assistance of a central controller but in a totally decentralized and self-organized way. Furthermore a TDD system is assumed. Synchronization between adjacent BS can be achieved not in a direct way but indirectly if all MT inside a single cell transmit a specific test signal at the end of each frame (or super frame) in an uplink postamble. These different test signals transmitted from all MT in adjacent cells will be received in all BS inside a local environment. Each BS can process this information to synchronize

Figure 22. Flexible radio resource management by making all resources available to all BS in a synchronized OFDM-based cellular environment

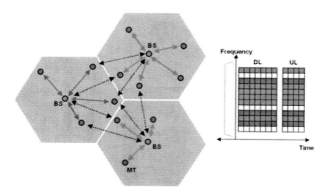

clock and carrier simultaneously to establish a synchronized network.

Test signals will therefore be used in the down- and uplink to synchronize all BS in a local environment and all MT inside a single cell, see Figure 23. The test signal itself is designed to allow an almost interference-free time and frequency offset estimation.

To generate the test signal structure, each BS selects a single pair of two adjacent sub-carriers for each frame inside the preamble as it is shown in Figure 24. The sub-carriers inside the test signal are chosen randomly and independently by each BS from a set of allowed sub-carrier pairs placed equidistantly in the frequency band and separated by a guard band of unused sub-carriers to reduce interference in a non-synchronized situation. During the downlink preamble each BS transmits the specific test signal on the individually selected pair of sub-carriers.

In the uplink all MT inside a single cell transmit a test signal which is identical to that one they have received in the preamble at the beginning of the data frame. Each BS receives these test signals in

Figure 23. Test signal structure which is used for the synchronization of MT to a single BS during down-link and between all BS during the uplink phase

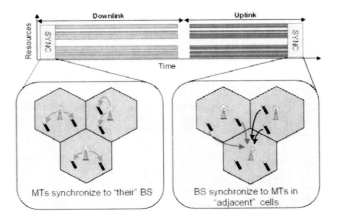

Figure 24. Sub-carrier allocation of test signals

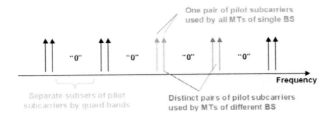

a superimposed form from all MT inside the cell on the same sub-carrier pair. Test signals from MT in adjacent cells will be observed by the BS on distinct pairs of sub-carriers and can therefore be distinguished and processed separately. Each BS selects randomly the sub-carrier pair for the test signal in the preamble of each data frame. Therefore data collisions between test signals of adjacent BS will only occur rarely but do not influence the synchronization process at all. All received test signals are evaluated in the frequency domain as shown in Figure 25.

The signal processing and test signal evaluation is identical in the downlink and uplink. To avoid ISI and ICI during the fine synchronization procedure the test signals are designed to be phase continuous for the duration of N_p consecutive OFDM symbols as it is shown in Figure 25.

In the downlink case and in the MT synchronization phase a single FFT output signal already contains the time offset information between BS and MT in a certain phase rotation between the two considered adjacent sub-carriers. The carrier frequency offset between BS and MT

is given by the phase rotation between the FFT output signals of the same sub-carrier but the two consecutive FFT.

Using this synchronization technique in each BS and MT which is based on phase difference measurements the time and frequency offset estimates are obtained simultaneously for each possible received sub-carrier pair. But only those measurements which exceed a certain amplitude threshold will be used for the subsequent adjustment of the BS time and frequency offsets.

Self-Organized Resource Management

One additional important design aspect for a 4G system is the capability to serve the time-varying data rate demands of all MT efficiently, incorporating high traffic peaks at isolated BS. Therefore dynamic channel allocation (DCA) is considered as an important feature for future networks. Centralized resource management schemes in which a central unit has the complete knowledge about the resource allocation in all cells have been

Figure 25. Time interval free of ISI and ICI between different test signals is used for the estimation of fine time and frequency offsets

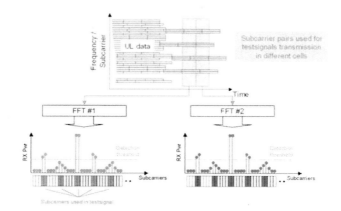

investigated with respect to OFDM systems in Wahlqvist et al. (1997) and Wang et al. (2003), for example.

In the following, however, it is assumed that each BS decides in the radio resource management (RRM) procedure and in the sub-carrier allocation process in a self-organizing (SO) way without any cooperation and communication between adjacent cells and without a central management unit. Therefore, the proposed system concept is termed SO-DCA.

The assumed OFDM-FDMA and TDD scheme shown in Figure 22 is only one possible way of arranging the resource management. The SO-DCA concept can be applied for any orthogonal multiple access scheme with a TDMA and/or an

Figure 26. Each BS determines the resource allocation process by measuring the signal power on all sub-carriers inside the available bandwidth

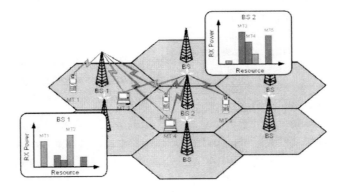

Figure 27. Resource allocation and PHY Mode selection based on the interference measurements at the MT and BS

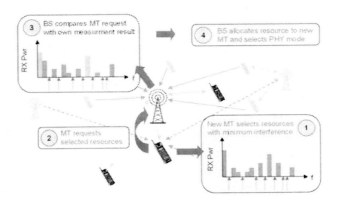

FDMA component. A MAC frame consists of one down link (DL) and one uplink (UL) period and has a total duration of $T_F = T_{UL} + T_{DL}$.

This paragraph introduces a suitable DCA algorithm which strongly benefits from the tight synchronization between all BS and MT inside the cellular environment. The RRM process is mainly based on continuous CCI measurements in each frame. Based on the available CCI measurements (see Figure 26), each BS decides independently of other BS which resources will be covered for a new MT.

In order to increase the system throughput, a link adaptation (LA) procedure is further introduced. Each BS makes decisions about the modulation scheme and channel code rate (PHY mode) which can be used currently on the individual link. The choice of the applied PHY mode is derived from the radio channel measurement. The main task for the DCA algorithm is to assign a sufficient number of sub-carrier resources to a specific user (MT) to satisfy the current quality of service (QoS) demand. The sub-carrier selection process in the DCA procedure is important to allocate those sub-carriers which are less attenuated by the radio channel. This selection process is mainly based on CCI measurements in the MT and BS. The resource allocation process is summarized in Figure 27.

CONCLUSION

Some aspects for future mobile communication networks have been considered in this chapter. The OFDM transmission technique itself has a large potential due to the robust behaviour in wideband frequency selective and time variant radio channels. The combination with multiple access schemes showed good performance under realistic channel assumptions. A system proposal for an air interface structure for downlink and uplink has been discussed. Future cellular networks require high flexibility for data sources with different and

time variant data rate in multi-path propagation environments. Therefore a synchronized cellular network has been proposed and the completely decentralized and self-organized time and carrier synchronization aspects have been discussed. Finally, a self-organized RRM has been proposed to establish a totally decentralized organization inside each BS. All these different techniques and technical concepts can be combined in a way to establish a future powerful and flexible mobile communications network for the 4G.

REFERENCES

Aldinger, M. (1994). Multicarrier COFDM scheme in high bitrate radio local area networks. *Proc. of Wireless Computer Networks 94*, Den Haag, Netherlands (pp. 969-973). New York: IEEE.

Bello, P. A. (1963). Characterization of randomly time-variant linear channels. *IEEE Transactions on Communications, 11*, 360-393.

Bingham, J. (1990, May). Multicarrier modulation for data transmission: An idea whose time has come. *IEEE Communications Magazine, 28*, 5-14.

Brüninghaus, K., & Rohling, H. (1997). On the duality of multi-carrier spread spectrum and single-carrier transmission. *Zweites OFDM-Fachgespräch*, Braunschweig, Germany (pp. 210-215). Braunschweig: TU Braunschweig.

Brüninghaus, K., & Rohling, H. (1998). Multicarrier spread spectrum and its relationship to single carrier transmission. *Proc. of the IEEE VTC'98*, Ottawa, Canada (pp. 2329-2332). New York: IEEE.

Chang, R. W. (1966). Synthesis of band-limited orthogonal signals for multichannel data transmission. *Bell Syst. Tech. J., 45*, 1775-1796.

Classen, F., & Meyr, H. (1994). Frequency synchronization algorithms for OFDM systems suitable for communication over frequency selective fading channels. *Proc. IEEE VTC 94*, Stockholm, Sweden (pp. 1655-1659). New York: IEEE.

Galda, D., Rohling, H., Costa, E., Haas, H., & Schulz, E. (2002). A low complexity transmitter structure for the OFDM-FDMA uplink. *Proc. IEEE VTC'02 Spring*, Birmingham, Alabama, May (pp. 1024-1028). New York: IEEE.

Gross, J., Karl, H., Fitzek, F., & Wolisz, A. (2003). Comparison of heuristic and optimal subcarrier assignment algorithms. *Proc. of Intl. Conf. on Wireless Networks (ICWN)*, Las Vegas, Nevada (pp. 249-255). Las Vegas: CSREA Press.

Hanzo, L. et al. (2003). *OFDM and MC-CDMA for broadband multi-user communications, WLANs and broadcasting*. New York: Wiley.

Kaiser, S. (1998). *Multi-carrier CDMA mobile radio systems: Analysis and optimization of detection, decoding and channel estimation*. Fortschritt-Berichte VDI, Reihe 10, Nr. 531, VDI-Verlag, Düsseldorf, Germany.

Kaiser, S. (2002). OFDM code-division multiplexing in fading channels. *IEEE Trans. on Communications*, *50*, 1266-1273.

Linnartz, J. P. (2000). Synchronous MC-CDMA in dispersive, mobile rayleigh channels. *Proc. of 2nd IEEE Benelux Signal Processing Symposium (SPS-2000)*, Hilvarenbeek, The Netherlands (pp. 1-4). New York: IEEE.

Mizoguchi, M. et al. (1998). A fast burst synchronization scheme for OFDM. *Proc ICUPC 98*, Florence, Italy (pp. 125-129). New York: IEEE.

Pätzold, M. (2002). *Mobile fading channels*. New York: Wiley.

Peled, A., & Ruiz, A. (1980). Frequency domain data transmission using reduced computational complexity algorithms. *Proc. IEEE ICASSP*, Denver, Colorado (pp. 964-967). New York: IEEE.

Rohling, H., Galda, D., & Schulz, E. (2004). An OFDM based cellular single frequency communication network. *Proc. of the Wireless World Research Forum '04*, Beijing, China (pp. 254-258). Zurich: WWRF.

Rohling, H., & Grünheid, R. (1997). Performance comparison of different multiple access schemes for the downlink of an OFDM communication system. *Proc. IEEE VTC'97*, Phoenix, Arizona (pp. 1365-1369). New York: IEEE.

Saltzberg, B. R. (1967). Performance of an efficient parallel data transmission system. *IEEE Trans. on Communications*, *15*, 805-811.

Shen, M., Li, G., & Liu, H. (2004). Design tradeoffs in OFDMA traffic channels. *Proc. of IEEE ICASSP '04*, Montreal, Canada (pp. 757-760). New York: IEEE.

Toufik, I., & Knopp, R. (2004). Channel allocation algorithms for multi-carrier systems. *Proc. of the IEEE VTC '04*, Los Angeles, CA, September (pp. 1129-1133). New York: IEEE.

Wahlqvist, M. et al. (1997). Capacity comparison of an OFDM based multiple access system using different dynamic resource allocation. *Proc. IEEE VTC'97*, Phoenix, Arizona (pp. 1664-1668). New York: IEEE.

Wang, W. et al. (2003). Impact of multiuser diversity and channel variability on adaptive OFDM. *Proc. IEEE VTC 2003 Fall*, Orlando, Florida, October (pp. 547-551). New York: IEEE.

Weinstein, S. B., & Ebert, P. M. (1971). Data transmission by frequency-division multiplexing using the discrete fourier transform. *IEEE Transactions on Communication Technology*, *19*, 628-634.

Zander, J., & Kim, S. L. (2001). *Radio resource management for wireless networks*. London: Artech House Publishers, Mobile Communications Series.

This work was previously published in Mobile Multimedia Communications: Concepts, Applications, and Challenges, edited by G. Karmakar and L. Dooley, pp. 151-177, copyright 2008 by Information Science Reference, formerly known as Idea Group Reference (an imprint of IGI Global).

Chapter 8.25
Malicious Software in Mobile Devices

Thomas M. Chen
Southern Methodist University, USA

Cyrus Peikari
Airscanner Mobile Security Corporation, USA

ABSTRACT

This chapter examines the scope of malicious software (malware) threats to mobile devices. The stakes for the wireless industry are high. While malware is rampant among 1 billion PCs, approximately twice as many mobile users currently enjoy a malware-free experience. However, since the appearance of the Cabir worm in 2004, malware for mobile devices has evolved relatively quickly, targeted mostly at the popular Symbian smartphone platform. Significant highlights in malware evolution are pointed out that suggest that mobile devices are attracting more sophisticated malware attacks. Fortunately, a range of host-based and network-based defenses have been developed from decades of experience with PC malware. Activities are underway to improve protection of mobile devices before the malware problem becomes catastrophic, but developers are limited by the capabilities of handheld devices.

INTRODUCTION

Most people are aware that malicious software (malware) is an ongoing widespread problem with Internet-connected PCs. Statistics about the prevalence of malware, as well as personal anecdotes from affected PC users, are easy to find. PC malware can be traced back to at least the Brain virus in 1986 and the Robert Morris Jr. worm in 1988. Many variants of malware have evolved over 20 years. The October 2006 WildList (www.wildlist.org) contained 780 viruses and worms found to be spreading "in the wild" (on real users' PCs), but this list is known to comprise a small subset of the total number of existing viruses. The prevalence of malware was evident in a 2006 CSI/FBI survey where 65% of the organizations reported being hit by malware, the single most common type of attack.

A taxonomy to introduce definitions of malware is shown in Figure 1, but classification is

Figure 1. A taxonomy of malicious software

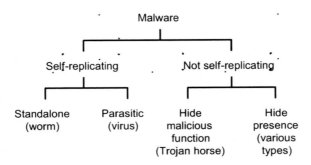

sometimes difficult because a piece of malware often combines multiple characteristics. Viruses and worms are characterized by the capability to self-replicate, but they differ in their methods (Nazario, 2004; Szor, 2005). A virus is a piece of software code (set of instructions but not a complete program) attached to a normal program or file. The virus depends on the execution of the host program. At some point in the execution, the virus code hijacks control of the program execution to make copies of itself and attach these copies to more programs or files. In contrast, a worm is a stand-alone automated program that seeks vulnerable computers through a network and copies itself to compromised victims.

Non-replicating malware typically hide their presence on a computer or at least hide their malicious function. Malware that hides a malicious function but not necessarily its presence is called a Trojan horse (Skoudis, 2004). Typically, Trojan horses pose as a legitimate program (such as a game or device driver) and generally rely on social engineering (deception) because they are not able to self-replicate. Trojan horses are used for various purposes, often theft of confidential data, destruction, backdoor for remote access, or installation of other malware. Besides Trojan

horses, many types of non-replicating malware hide their presence in order to carry out a malicious function on a victim host without detection and removal by the user. Common examples include bots and spyware. Bots are covertly installed software that secretly listen for remote commands, usually sent through Internet relay chat (IRC) channels, and execute them on compromised computers. A group of compromised computers under remote control of a single "bot herder" constitute a bot net. Bot nets are often used for spam, data theft, and distributed denial of service attacks. Spyware collects personal user information from a victim computer and transmits the data across the network, often for advertising purposes but possibly for data theft. Spyware is often bundled with shareware or installed covertly through social engineering.

Since 2004, malware has been observed to spread among smartphones and other mobile devices through wireless networks. According to F-Secure, the number of malware known to target smartphones is approximately 100 (Hypponen, 2006). However, some believe that malware will inevitably grow into a serious problem (Dagon, Martin, & Starner, 2004). There have already been complex, blended malware threats on mobile devices. Within a few years, mobile viruses have grown in sophistication in a way reminiscent of 20 years of PC malware evolution. Unfortunately, mobile devices were not designed for security, and they have limited defenses against continually evolving attacks.

If the current trend continues, malware spreading through wireless networks could consume valuable radio resources and substantially degrade the experience of wireless subscribers. In the worst case, malware could become as commonplace in wireless networks as in the Internet with all its attendant risks of data loss, identity theft, and worse. The wireless market is growing quickly, but negative experiences with malware on mobile devices could discourage subscribers and inhibit market growth. The concern is serious because wireless services are currently bound to accounting and charging mechanisms; usage of wireless services, whether for legitimate purposes or malware, will result in subscriber charges. Thus, a victimized subscriber will not only suffer the experience of malware but may also get billed extra service charges. This usage-based charging arrangement contrasts with PCs which typically have flat charges for Internet communications.

This chapter examines historical examples of malware and the current environment for mobile devices. Potential infection vectors are explored. Finally, existing defenses are identified and described.

BACKGROUND

Mobile devices are attractive targets for several reasons (Hypponen, 2006). First, mobile devices have clearly progressed far in terms of hardware and communications. PDAs have grown from simple organizers to miniature computers with their own operating systems (such as Palm or Windows Pocket PC/Windows Mobile) that can download and install a variety of applications. Smartphones combine the communications capabilities of cell phones with PDA functions. According to Gartner, almost 1 billion cell phones will be sold in 2006. Currently, smartphones are a small fraction of the overall cell phone market. According to the *Computer Industry Almanac,* 69 million smartphones will be sold in 2006. However, their shipments are growing rapidly, and IDC predicts smartphones will become 15% of all mobile phones by 2009. Approximately 70% of all smartphones run the Symbian operating system, made by various manufacturers, according to Canalys. Symbian is jointly owned by Sony Ericsson, Nokia, Panasonic, Samsung, and Siemens AG. Symbian is prevalent in Europe and Southeast Asia but less common in North America, Japan, and South Korea. The Japanese and Korean markets have been dominated by Linux-based phones. The North American market has a diversity of cellular platforms.

Nearly all of the malware for smartphones has targeted the Symbian operating system. Descended from Psion Software's EPOC, it is structured similar to desktop operating systems. Traditional cell phones have proprietary embedded operating systems which generally accept only Java applications. In contrast, Symbian application programming interfaces (APIs) are publicly documented so that anyone can develop applications. Applications packaged in SIS file format can be installed at any time, which makes Symbian devices more attractive to both consumers and malware writers.

Mobile devices are attractive targets because they are well connected, often incorporating various means of wireless communications. They are typically capable of Internet access for Web browsing, e-mail, instant messaging, and applications similar to those on PCs. They may also communicate by cellular, IEEE 802.11 wireless LAN, short range Bluetooth, and short/multimedia messaging service (SMS/MMS).

Another reason for their appeal to malware writers is the size of the target population. There were more than 900 million PCs in use worldwide in 2005 and will climb past 1 billion PCs in 2007, according to the *Computer Industry Almanac*. In comparison, there were around 2 billion cellular subscribers in 2005. Such a large target population is attractive for malware writers who want to maximize their impact.

Malware is relatively unknown for mobile devices today. At this time, only a small number of families of malware have been seen for wireless devices, and malware is not a prominent threat in wireless networks. Because of the low threat risk, mobile devices have minimal security defenses. Another reason is the limited processing capacity of mobile devices. Whereas desktop PCs have fast processors and plug into virtually unlimited power, mobile devices have less computing power and limited battery power. Protection such as antivirus software and host-based intrusion detection would incur a relatively high cost in processing and energy consumption. In addition, mobile devices were never designed for security. For example, they lack an encrypting file system, Kerberos authentication, and so on. In short, they are missing all the components required to secure a modern, network-connected computing device.

There is a risk that mobile users may have a false sense of security. Physically, mobile devices feel more personal because they are carried everywhere. Users have complete physical control of them, and hence they feel less accessible to intruders. This sense of security may lead users to trust the devices with more personal data, increasing the risk of loss and appeal to attackers. Also, the sense of security may lead users to neglect security precautions such as changing default security configurations.

Although mobile devices might be appealing targets, there are certain drawbacks to malware for mobile devices. First, mobile devices usually have intermittent connectivity to the network or other devices, in order to save power. This fact limits the ability of malware to spread quickly. Second, if malware is intended to spread by

Bluetooth, Bluetooth connections are short range. Moreover, Bluetooth devices can be turned off or put into hidden mode. Third, there is a diversity of mobile device platforms, in contrast to PCs that are dominated by Windows. Some have argued that the Windows monoculture in PCs has made PCs more vulnerable to malware. To reach a majority of mobile devices, malware writers must create separate pieces of malware code for different platforms (Leavitt, 2005).

EVOLUTION OF MALWARE

Malware has already appeared on mobile devices over the past few years (Peikari & Fogie, 2003). While the number is still small compared to the malware families known for PCs, an examination of prominent examples shows that malware is evolving steadily. The intention here is not to exhaustively list all examples of known malware but to highlight how malware has been developing.

Palm Pilots and Windows Pocket PCs were common before smartphones, and malware appeared first for the Palm operating system. Liberty Crack was a Trojan horse related to Liberty, a program emulating the Nintendo Game Boy on the Palm, reported in August 2000 (Foley & Dumigan, 2001). As a Trojan, it did not spread by self-replication but depended on being installed from a PC that had the "liberty_1_1_crack.prc" file. Once installed on a Palm, it appears on the display as an application, Crack. When executed, it deletes all applications from the Palm (www. f-secure.com/v-descs/lib_palm.shtml).

Discovered in September 2000, Phage was the first virus to target Palm PDAs (Peikari & Fogie, 2003). When executed, the virus infects all third-party applications by overwriting them (http://www.f-secure.com/v-descs/phage.shtml). When a program's icon is selected, the display turns gray and the selected program exits. The virus can spread directly to other Palms by infrared beaming or indirectly through PC synchronization.

Another Trojan horse discovered around the same time, Vapor is installed on a Palm as the application "vapor.prc" (www.f-secure.com/v-descs/vapor.shtml). When executed, it changes the file attributes of other applications, making them invisible (but not actually deleting them). It does not self-replicate.

In July 2004, Duts was a proof-of-concept virus, the first to target Windows Pocket PCs. It asks the user for permission to install. If installed, it attempts to infect all EXE files larger than 4096 bytes in the current directory.

Later in 2004, Brador was a backdoor for Pocket PCs (www.f-secure.com/v-descs/brador.shtml). It installs the file "svchost.exe" in the Startup directory so that it will automatically start during the device bootup. Then it will read the local host IP address and e-mail that to the author. After e-mailing its IP address, the backdoor opens a TCP port and starts listening for commands. The backdoor is capable of uploading and downloading files, executing arbitrary commands, and displaying messages to the PDA user.

The Cabir worm discovered in June 2004 was a milestone marking the trend away from PDAs and towards smartphones running the Symbian operating system. Cabir was a proof-of-concept worm, the first for Symbian, written by a member of a virus writing group 29A (www.f-secure.com/v-descs/cabir.shtml). The worm is carried in a file "caribe.sis" (Caribe is Spanish for the Caribbean). The SIS file contains autostart settings that will automatically execute the worm after the SIS file is installed. When the Cabir worm is activated, it will start looking for other (discoverable) Bluetooth devices within range. Upon finding another device, it will try to send the caribe.sis file. Reception and installation of the file requires user approval after a notification message is displayed. It does not cause any damage.

Cabir was not only one of the first malware for Symbian, but it was also one of the first to use Bluetooth (Gostev, 2006). Malware is more commonly spread by e-mail. The choice of Bluetooth

meant that Cabir would spread slowly in the wild. An infected smartphone would have to discover another smartphone within Bluetooth range and the target's user would have to willingly accept the transmission of the worm file while the devices are within range of each other.

In August 2004, the first Trojan horse for smartphones was discovered. It appeared to be a cracked version of a Symbian game Mosquitos. The Trojan made infected phones send SMS text messages to phone numbers resulting in charges to the phones' owners.

In November 2004, the Trojan horse—Skuller—was found to infect Symbian Series 60 smartphones (www.f-secure.com/v-descs/skulls.shtml). The Trojan is a file named "Extended theme.SIS," a theme manager for Nokia 7610 smartphones. If executed, it disables all applications on the phone and replaces their icons with a skull and crossbones. The phone can be used to make calls and answer calls. However, all system applications such as SMS, MMS, Web browsing, and camera do not work.

In December 2004, Skuller and Cabir were merged to form Metal Gear, a Trojan horse that masquerades as the game of the same name. Metal Gear uses Skulls to deactivate a device's antivirus. This was the first malware to attack antivirus on Symbian smartphones. The malware also drops a file "SEXXXY.SIS," an installer that adds code to disable the handset menu button. It then uses Cabir to send itself to other devices.

Locknut was a Trojan horse discovered in February 2005 that pretended to be a patch for Symbian Series 60 phones. When installed, it drops a program that will crash a critical system service component, preventing any application from launching.

In March 2005, ComWar or CommWarrior was the first worm to spread by MMS among Symbian Series 60 smartphones. Like Cabir, it was also capable of spreading by Bluetooth. Infected phones will search for discoverable Bluetooth devices within range; if found, the infected phone will try to send the worm in a randomly named SIS file. But Bluetooth is limited to devices within 10 meters or so. MMS messages can be sent to anywhere in the world. The worm tries to spread by MMS messaging to other phone owners found in the victim's address book. MMS has the unfortunate side effect of incurring charges for the phone owner.

Drever was a Trojan horse that attacked anti-virus software on Symbian smartphones. It drops non-functional copies of the bootloaders used by Simworks Antivirus and Kaspersky Symbian Antivirus, preventing these programs from loading automatically during the phone bootup.

In April 2005, the Mabir worm was similar to Cabir in its ability to spread by Bluetooth. It had the additional capability to spread by MMS messaging. It listens for any arriving MMS or SMS message and will respond with a copy of itself in a file named "info.sis."

Found in September 2005, the Cardtrap Trojan horse targeted Symbian 60 smartphones and was one of the first examples of smartphone malware capable of infecting a PC (www.f-secure.com/v-descs/cardtrap_a.shtml). When it is installed on the smartphone, it disables several applications by overwriting their main executable files. More interestingly, it also installs two Windows worms, Padobot.Z and Rays, to the phone's memory card. An autorun file is copied with the Padobot.Z worm, so that if the memory card is inserted into a PC, the autorun file will attempt to execute the Padobot worm. The Rays worm is a file named "system. exe" which has the same icon as the system folder in the memory card. The evident intention was to trick a user reading the contents of the card on a PC into executing the Rays worm.

Crossover was a proof-of-concept Trojan horse found in February 2006. It was reportedly the first malware capable of spreading from a PC to a Windows Mobile Pocket PC by means of Active-Sync. On the PC, the Trojan checks the version of the host operating system. If it is not Windows CE or Windows Mobile, the virus makes a copy of itself on the PC and adds a registry entry to execute the virus during PC rebooting. A new virus copy is made with a random file name at each reboot. When executed, the Trojan waits for an ActiveSync connection, when it copies itself to the handheld, documents on the handheld will be deleted.

In August 2006, the Mobler worm for Windows PCs was discovered (www.f-secure.com/v-descs/mobler.shtml). It is not a real threat but is suggestive of how future malware might evolve. When a PC is infected, the worm copies itself to different folders on local hard drives and writable media (such as a memory card). Among its various actions, the worm creates a SIS archiver program "makesis.exe" and a copy of itself named "system.exe" in the Windows system folder. It also creates a Symbian installation package named "Black_Symbian.SIS." It is believed to be capable of spreading from a PC to smartphone, another example of cross-platform malware.

At the current time, it is unknown whether Crossover and Mobler signal the start of a new trend towards cross-platform malware that spread equally well among PCs and mobile devices. The combined potential target population would be nearly 3 billion. The trend is not obvious yet but Crossover and Mobler suggest that cross-platform malware could become possible in the near future.

INFECTION VECTORS

Infection vectors for PC malware have changed over the years as PC technology evolved. Viruses initially spread by floppy disks. After floppy disks disappeared and Internet connectivity became ubiquitous, worms spread by mass e-mailing. Similarly, infection vectors used by malware for mobile devices have changed over the past few years.

Synchronization: Palm and Windows PDAs were popular before smartphones. PDAs install software by synchronization with PCs (Foley & Dumigan, 2001). For example, Palm applications are packaged as Palm resource (PRC) files installed from PCs. As seen earlier, Palm malware usually relied on social engineering to get installed. This is a slow infection vector for malware to spread between PDAs because it requires synchronization with a PC and then contact with another PC that synchronizes with another PDA. Much faster infection vectors became possible when PDAs and then smartphones started to feature communications directly between mobile devices without having to go through PCs.

E-mail and Web: Internet access from mobile devices allows users away from their desktops to use the most common Internet applications, e-mail and the World Wide Web. Most mobile devices can send and receive e-mail with attachments. In addition, many can access the Web through a microbrowser designed to render Web content on the small displays of mobile devices. Current microbrowsers are similar in features to regular Web browsers, capable of HTML, WML, CSS, Ajax, and plug-ins. Although e-mail and the Web are common vectors for PC malware, they have not been used as vectors to infect mobile devices thus far.

SMS/MMS messaging: Commonly called text messaging, SMS is available on most mobile phones and Pocket PCs. It is most popular in Europe, Asia (excluding Japan), Australia, and New Zealand, but has not been as popular in the U.S. as other types of messaging. Text messaging is often used to interact with automated systems, for example to order products or services or participate in contests. Short messages are limited to 140 bytes of data, but longer content can be segmented and sent in multiple messages. The receiving phone is responsible for reassembling the complete message. Short messages can also be used to send binary content such as ringtones or logos. While SMS is largely limited to text, MMS is a more advanced messaging service allowing transmission of multimedia objects—video, im-

ages, audio, and rich text. The ComWar worm was the first to spread by MMS (among Symbian Series 60 smartphones). MMS has the potential to spread quickly. ComWar increased its chances by targeting other phone owners found in the victim's address book. By appearing to come from an acquaintance, an incoming message is more likely to be accepted by a recipient. MMS will likely continue to be an infection vector in the future.

Bluetooth: Bluetooth is a short-range radio communication protocol that allows Bluetooth-enabled devices (which could be mobile or stationary) within 10-100 meters to discover and talk with each other. Up to eight devices can communicate with each other in a piconet, where one device works in the role of "master" and the others in the role of "slaves." The master takes turns to communicate with each slave by round robin. The roles of master and slaves can be changed at any time.

Each Bluetooth device has a unique and permanent 48-bit address as well as a user-chosen Bluetooth name. Any device can search for other nearby devices, and devices configured to respond will give their name, class, list of services, and technical details (e.g., manufacturer, device features). If a device inquires directly at a device's address, it will always respond with the requested information.

In May 2006, F-Secure and Secure Networks conducted a survey of discoverable Bluetooth devices in a variety of places in Italy. They found on average 29 to 154 Bluetooth devices per hour in discoverable mode in the different places. In discoverable mode, the devices are potentially open to attacks. About 24% were found to have visible OBEX push service. This service is normally used for transfer of electronic business cards or similar information, but is known to be vulnerable to a BlueSnarf attack. This attack allows connections to a cellular phone and access to the phone book and agenda without authorization. Another vulnerability is BlueBug, discovered in March 2004, allowing access to the ASCII Terminal (AT) commands of a cell phone. These set of commands are common for configuration and control of telecommunications devices, and give high-level control over call control and SMS messaging. In effect, these can allow an attacker to use the phone services without the victim's knowledge. This includes incoming and outgoing phone calls and SMS messages.

The Cabir worm was the first to use Bluetooth as a vector. Bluetooth is expected to be a slow infection vector. An infected smartphone would have to discover another smartphone within a 10-meter range, and the target's user would have to willingly accept the transmission of the worm file while the devices are within range of each other. Moreover, although phones are usually shipped with Bluetooth in discoverable mode, it is simple to change devices to invisible mode. This simple precaution would make it much more difficult for malware.

MALWARE DEFENSES

Practical security depends on multiple layers of protection instead of a single (hopefully perfect) defense (Skoudis, 2004). Fortunately, various defenses against malware have been developed from decades of experience with PC malware. A taxonomy of malware defenses is shown in Figure 2. Defenses can be first categorized as preventive

Figure 2. A taxonomy of malware defenses

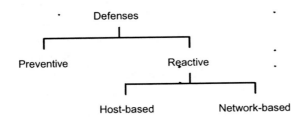

or reactive (defensive). Preventive techniques help avoid malware infections through identification and remediation of vulnerabilities, strengthening security policies, patching operating systems and applications, updating antivirus signatures, and even educating users about best practices (in this case, for example, turning off Bluetooth except when needed, rejecting installation of unknown software, and blocking SMS/MMS messages from untrusted parties). At this time, simple preventive techniques are likely to be very effective because there are relatively few threats that really spread in the wild. In particular, education to raise user awareness would be effective against social engineering, one of the main infection vectors used by malware for mobile devices so far.

Host-Based Defenses

Even with the best practices to avoid infections, reactive defenses are still needed to protect mobile devices from actual malware threats. Reactive defenses can operate in hosts (mobile devices) or within the network. Host-based defenses make sense because protection will be close to the targets. However, host-based processes (e.g., antivirus programs) consume processing and power resources that are more critical on mobile devices than desktop PCs. Also, the approach is difficult to scale to large populations if software must be installed, managed, and maintained on every mobile device. Network-based defenses are more scalable in the sense that one router or firewall may protect a group of hosts. Another reason for network-based defenses is the possibility that the network might be able to block malware before it actually reaches a targeted device, which is not possible with host-based defenses. Host-based defenses take effect after contact with the host. In practice, host-based and network-based defenses are both used in combination to realize their complementary benefits.

The most obvious host-based defense is antivirus software (Szor, 2005). Antivirus does auto-

Malicious Software in Mobile Devices

matic analysis of files, communicated messages, and system activities. All commercial antivirus programs depend mainly on malware signatures which are sets of unique characteristics associated with each known piece of malware. The main advantage of signature-based detection is its accuracy in malware identification. If a signature is matched, then the malware is identified exactly and perhaps sufficiently for disinfection. Unfortunately, signature-based detection has two drawbacks. First, antivirus signatures must be regularly updated. Second, there will always be the possibility that new malware could escape detection if it does not have a matching signature. For that case, antivirus programs often include heuristic anomaly detection which detects unusual behavior or activities. Anomaly detection does not usually identify malware exactly, only the suspicion of the presence of malware and the need for further investigation. For that reason, signatures will continue to be the preferred antivirus method for the foreseeable future.

Several antivirus products are available for smartphones and PDAs. In October 2005, Nokia and Symantec arranged for Nokia to offer the option of preloading Symbian Series 60 smartphones with Symantec Mobile Security Antivirus. Other commercial antivirus packages can be installed on Symbian or Windows Mobile smartphones and PDAs.

In recognition that nearly all smartphone malware has targeted Symbian devices, a great amount of attention has focused on the vulnerabilities of that operating system. It might be argued that the system has a low level of application security. For example, Symbian allows any system application to be rewritten without requiring user consent. Also, after an application is installed, it has total control over all functions. In short, applications are totally trusted.

Although Windows CE has not been as popular a target, it has similar vulnerabilities. There are no restrictions on applications; once launched, an application has full access to any system function including sending/receiving files, phone functions, multimedia functions, and so forth. Moreover, Windows CE is an open platform and application development is relatively easy.

Symbian OS version 9 added the feature of code signing. Currently all software must be manually installed. The installation process warns the user if an application has not been signed. Digital signing makes software traceable to the developer and verifies that an application has not been changed since it left the developer. Developers can apply to have their software signed via the Symbian Signed program (www.symbiansigned.com). Developers also have the option of self-signing their programs. Any signed application will install on a Symbian OS phone without showing a security warning. An unsigned application can be installed with user consent, but the operating system will prevent it from doing potentially damaging things by denying access to key system functions and data storage of other applications.

Network-Based Defenses

Network-based defenses depend on network operators monitoring, analyzing, and filtering the traffic going through their networks. Security equipment include firewalls, intrusion detection systems, routers with access control lists (ACLs), and antivirus running in e-mail servers and SMS/MMS messaging service centers. Traffic analysis is typically done by signature-based detection, similar in concept to signature-based antivirus, augmented with heuristic anomaly based detection. Traffic filtering is done by configuring firewall and ACL policies.

An example is Sprint's Mobile Security service announced in September 2006. This is a set of managed security services for mobile devices from handhelds to laptops. The service includes protection against malware attacks. The service can scan mobile devices and remove detected malware automatically without requiring user action.

In the longer term, mobile device security may be driven by one or more vendor groups working to improve the security of wireless systems. For instance, the Trusted Computing Group (TCG) (www.trustedcomputinggroup.org) is an organization of more than 100 component manufacturers, software developers, networking companies, and service providers formed in 2003. One subgroup is working on a set of specifications for mobile phone security (TCG, 2006a). Their approach is to develop a Mobile Trusted Module (MTM) specification for hardware to support features similar to those of the Trusted Platform Module (TPM) chip used in computers but with additional functions specifically for mobile devices. The TPM is a tamper-proof chip embedded at the PC board level, serving as the "root of trust" for all system activities. The MTM specification will integrate security into smartphones' core operations instead of adding as applications.

Another subgroup is working on specifications for Trusted Network Connect (TCG, 2006b). All hosts including mobile devices run TNC client software, which collects information about that host's current state of security such as antivirus signature updates, software patching level, results of last security scan, firewall configuration, and any other active security processes. The security state information is sent to a TNC server to check against policies set by network administrators. The server makes a decision to grant or deny access to the network. This ensures that hosts are properly configured and protected before connecting to the network. It is important to verify that hosts are not vulnerable to threats from the network and do not pose a threat to other hosts. Otherwise, they will be effectively quarantined from the network until their security state is remedied. Remedies can include software patching, updating antivirus, or any other changes to bring the host into compliance with security policies.

FUTURE TRENDS

It is easy to see that mobile phones are increasingly attractive as malware targets. The number of smartphones and their percentage of overall mobile devices is growing quickly. Smartphones will continue to increase in functionalities and complexity. Symbian has been the primary target, a trend that will continue as long as it is the predominant smartphone platform. If another platform arises, that will attract the attention of malware writers who want to make the biggest impact.

The review of malware evolution suggests a worrisome trend. Since the first worm, Cabir, only three years ago, malware has advanced steadily to more infection vectors, first Bluetooth and then MMS. Recently malware has shown signs of becoming cross-platform, moving easily between mobile devices and PCs.

Fortunately, mobile security has already drawn the activities of the TCG and other industry organizations. Unlike the malware situation with PCs, the telecommunications industry has decades of experience to apply to wireless networks, and there is time to fortify defenses before malware multiplies into a global epidemic.

CONCLUSION

Malware is a low risk threat for mobile devices today, but the situation is unlikely to stay that way for long. It is evident from this review that mobile phones are starting to attract the attention of malware writers, a trend that will only get worse. At this point, most defenses are common sense practices. The wireless industry realizes that the stakes are high. Two billion mobile users currently enjoy a malware-free experience, but negative experiences with new malware could have a disastrous effect. Fortunately, a range of host-based and network-based defenses have been developed from experience with PC malware. Activities are underway in the industry to improve protection of mobile devices before the malware problem becomes catastrophic.

REFERENCES

Dagon, D., Martin, T., & Starner, T. (2004). Mobile phones as computing devices: The viruses are coming! *IEEE Pervasive Computing, 3*(4), 11-15.

Foley, S., & Dumigan, R. (2001). Are handheld viruses a significant threat? *Communications of the ACM, 44*(1), 105-107.

Gostev, A. (2006). *Mobile malware evolution: An overview.* Retrieved from http://www.viruslist.com/en/analysis?pubid=200119916

Hypponen, M. (2006). Malware goes mobile. *Scientific American, 295*(5), 70-77.

Leavitt, N. (2005). Mobile phones: The next frontier for hackers? *Computer, 38*(4), 20-23.

Nazario, J. (2004). *Defense and detection strategies against Internet worms.* Norwood, MA: Artech House.

Peikari, C., & Fogie, S. (2003). *Maximum wireless security.* Indianapolis, IN: Sams Publishing.

Skoudis, E. (2004). *Malware: Fighting malicious code.* Upper Saddle River, NJ: Prentice Hall.

Szor, P. (2005). *The art of computer virus research and defense.* Reading, MA: Addison-Wesley.

Trusted Computing Group (TCG). (2006a). *Mobile trusted module specification.* Retrieved from https://www.trustedcomputinggroup.org/specs/mobilephone/

Trusted Computing Group (TCG). (2006b). *TCG trusted network connect TNC architecture for interoperability.* Retrieved from https://www.trustedcomputinggroup.org/groups/network/

KEY TERMS

Antivirus Software: Antivirus software is designed to detect and remove computer viruses and worms and prevent their reoccurrence.

Exploit Software: Exploit software is written to attack and take advantage of a specific vulnerability.

Malware Software: Malware software is any type of software with malicious function, including for example, viruses, worms, Trojan horses, and spyware.

Smartphone: Smartphones are devices with the combined functions of cell phones and PDAs, typically running an operating system such as Symbian OS.

Social Engineering: Social engineering is an attack method taking advantage of human nature.

Trojan Horse: A Trojan horse is any software program containing a covert malicious function.

Virus: A virus is a piece of a software program that attaches to a normal program or file and depends on execution of the host program to self-replicate and infect more programs or files.

Vulnerability: Vulnerability is a security flaw in operating systems or applications that could be exploited to attack the host.

Worm: A worm is a stand-alone malicious program that is capable of automated self-replication.

This work was previously published in Handbook of Research on Wireless Security, edited by Y. Zhang, J. Zheng, and M. Ma, pp. 1-10, copyright 2008 by Information Science Reference, formerly known as Idea Group Reference (an imprint of IGI Global).

Index